Station S

ASSESSMENT OF MEN
Selection of Personnel for the
OFFICE OF STRATEGIC SERVICES

ASSESSMENT of MEN

SELECTION OF PERSONNEL FOR
THE OFFICE OF STRATEGIC SERVICES

THE OSS ASSESSMENT STAFF

RINEHART & COMPANY · INC.

Publishers · New York

FOURTH PRINTING, NOVEMBER 1958

COPYRIGHT, 1948, BY RINEHART & COMPANY, INC.
PRINTED IN THE UNITED STATES OF AMERICA

STAFF MEMBERS

The following is a list of the men and women who, for one period or another, served on the various assessment staffs. Most of them contributed something to the contents of this book, at least in its initial stages.

† A single dagger signifies that the person participated in the final five-month period of research and composition (September, 1945, to January, 1946) and/or wrote the first draft of a small section of the book.

‡ A double dagger signifies that the person is one of the five—all participants in the final five-month period of research and composition—who not only wrote the longest sections but assumed responsibility for the final over-all revision of the book during the succeeding year (February, 1946 to April, 1947).

The educational or medical institution with which each individual was officially connected before his or her enrollment in the government service is printed in parentheses. The rank of personnel who were in the armed services is the highest attained while the individual worked for the OSS, Schools and Training Branch.

The assessment station at which the person worked is indicated by a letter, as follows:

C—Ceylon
F—Potomac, Maryland
H—Hsian, China
I—Calcutta, India

K—Kunming, China
S—Fairfax, Virginia
W—Washington, D.C.
WS—Doheny Park, California

Donald K. Adams, Ph.D. (Duke University) S, W
Egerton L. Ballachey, Ph.D. (Michigan State College) S, W, C, F
† Urie Bronfenbrenner, Ph.D., *S/Sgt.* (Harvard University) S
G. Colket Caner, M.D. (Harvard University) F, S
† Dwight W. Chapman, Ph.D. (Bennington College) S, W
Robert Chin, Ph.D., *2nd Lt.* S, K
Mabel B. Cohen, M.D., Ph.D. (Chestnut Lodge Sanitarium, Rockville, Md.) W
† Robert A. Cohen, M.D., Ph.D., *Comdr.* (*USNR*) (Sheppard-Pratt Hospital, Towson, Md.) W, F
Bingham Dai, Ph.D. (Duke University) S, K
Alfred P. Daignault, B.S., *Cpl.* W, C, I, K, H

v

† Charles C. Davis, B.S., *S/Sgt.* S, WS

† John M. Fearing, M.D., *Capt.* (Duke University) S, F

† Kenneth A. Fisher, M.A., *Sgt.* S

‡ Donald W. Fiske, A.M., *Lt. (USNR)* S

Bertram R. Forer, Ph.D., *T/Sgt.* S

John W. Gardner, Ph.D., *1st Lt. (USMCR)* (Mt. Holyoke College) S, WS

Joseph A. Gengerelli, Ph.D. (University of California at Los Angeles) S

† Jacob W. Getzels, M.A., *T/3* S, WS

† Jacob V. Golder, M.A., *T/3* (Boston University) S, W, F

James A. Hamilton, Ph.D., M.D., *Capt.* (University of California) S, W, C

Edward S. Handy, Ph.D. S

‡ Eugenia Hanfmann, Ph.D. (Mt. Holyoke College) S, W

Lucien M. Hanks, Ph.D. (Bennington College) S, C

John S. Harding, Ph.D., *Sgt.* (Princeton University) S

Sidney L. Harrow, LL.B., *S/Sgt.* S

† Ralph W. Heine, M.S., *1st Lt.* (Northwestern University) F

† Bradford B. Hudson, A.B. (Tufts College) S, W, C, I, K, H

† J. E. Hulett, Jr., Ph.D. (University of Illinois) S

† Robert E. Jones, A.B., *S/Sgt.* S, WS

Fred Kerpen, A.B., *T/4* S

Robert H. Knapp, A.B. S

John A. Kneipp, M.D., *Capt.* (Duke University) S, WS, F

† David Krech, Ph.D., *M/Sgt.* (Swarthmore College) S, W, WS

David M. Levy, M.D. W

† Richard S. Lyman, M.D. (Duke University) S, C, K

‡ Donald W. MacKinnon, Ph.D. (Bryn Mawr College) S

Harold M. March, Ph.D. (Swarthmore College) S

‡ James G. Miller, M.D., Ph.D., *Capt.* (Harvard University) S, F, W

† O. H. Mowrer, Ph.D. (Harvard University) S, W

‡ Henry A. Murray, M.D., Ph.D., *Lt. Col.* (Harvard University) S, F, K

Theodore M. Newcomb, Ph.D. (University of Michigan) S

Orleans A. Pitre, B.S., *Maj.* S

Janet Rioch, M.D. S, W

† Harvey A. Robinson, A.M., *1st Lt.* (Harvard University) S, F, W

† R. Nevitt Sanford, Ph.D. (University of California) S

Bert D. Schwartz, B.S., *T/4* S

† Bernard R. Schweid, A.B., *M/Sgt.* S, W

W. Douglas Spencer, Ph.D. (Queens College, N. Y.) S

Alfred H. Stanton, M.D. (Chestnut Lodge Sanitarium, Rockville, Md.) W

† Eliot Stellar, M.S., *S/Sgt.* (Brown University) S

† Morris I. Stein, A.M., *Sgt.* (Harvard University) S

Percival M. Symonds, Ph.D. (Columbia University) S

† Milton Theaman, M.S., *2nd Lt.* S

Edward C. Tolman, Ph.D. (University of California) S, W
Ruth S. Tolman, Ph.D. W, S
† Frieda B. Tryon (University of North Carolina) W
Robert C. Tryon, Ph.D. (University of California)

Consultants

Ryong C. Hahn, Ph.D. (Harvard University)
Clyde Kluckhohn, Ph.D. (Harvard University)
Alexander H. Leighton, M.D., *Comdr.* (Office of War Information, War Department)
Kurt Lewin, Ph.D. (University of Iowa)
Joseph G. Yoshioka, Ph.D. (Oriental Science Literature Service)

Executive Officers

Capt. Ray Davis   *Capt.* Stanley H. Lyson
Capt. Perry Lethgo   *Maj.* Orleans A. Pitre
               Maj. Ezra Shine

Executive and Secretarial Staff

Mrs. Donald W. Fiske   *S/Sgt.* Myron Solomon
Mrs. Marjorie C. Ingalls   *T/5* Charles A. Thurstone
Mrs. Henry B. LeBourgeois   Miss Jeannette Wicks
               Sgt. Leopold Zippin

CONTENTS

CONTENTS

ILLUSTRATIONS

TABLES

Tables

ASSESSMENT OF MEN
Selection of Personnel for the
OFFICE OF STRATEGIC SERVICES

INTRODUCTION

This volume is the account of how a number of psychologists and psychiatrists attempted to assess the merits of men and women recruited for the Office of Strategic Services. The undertaking is reported because it represents the first attempt in America to design and carry out selection procedures in conformity with so-called *organismic* (Gestalt) principles. As a novel experiment it might interest a wide range of readers, but more specifically we hope it will invite the attention of those who are concerned with the problem of predicting human behavior, especially if they are engaged in practicing and developing clinical psychology and psychiatry and in improving present methods of diagnosis, assessment, and selection.

All told, 5,391 recruits were studied intensively over a three-day period at one station or over a one-day period at another. These were the two areas in the United States where the bulk of assessment was done. Of these the performances of 1,187 who went overseas were described and rated by their superior officers and associates in the theater.

Some standard procedures, elementalistic in design, were included in our program, because the best of these instruments are especially efficient in picking out disqualifying defects of function and so in eliminating men who are definitely inferior. Organismic methods, on the other hand, are to be recommended in addition whenever it is necessary to discriminate unusual talent, to measure ability in the range running from low average to high superior.

The plan described in this book was devised to fit the special needs of the Office of Strategic Services, but it would not take much ingenuity to modify some of the techniques and to invent others of the same type to meet the requirements of other institutions.

These methods were first used on a large scale by Simoneit, as described in *Wehrpsychologie,* and the German military psychologists, and after them by the British. Our particular debt is to the band of imaginative and progressive psychiatrists and psychologists who devised and conducted the War Office Selection Board (WOSB) program for testing officer candidates for the British Army. From them we gained the valuable idea of having staff and candidates live together in the country during the testing period, and the conception of leaderless group situations.

Several months of statistical calculation on the part of more than a dozen psychologists and psychiatrists, working with the International Business

3

Machines, went into the making of this book, but at the end the time available for reflection and critical analysis was not enough to permit the fruits of our exertions to ripen fully. Since we did not intend to write a textbook, no attempt has been made to cover the literature or to refer to the numerous researches which contributed to the construction of our program of procedures. The layman will not find the language of this book difficult. In all but a few sections, technical terminology was avoidable.

How did this program of assessment come about? As the following pages will reveal, it embodied many conceptions. It was the work directly and indirectly of many hands and brains. The formal opening of the program came about as a result of a genuine need. By late 1943, OSS, then hardly a year old, was busily and somewhat hazardously recruiting personnel without benefit of any professional or uniform screening process. Then came the exciting stimulus: the suggestion by an official from OSS in London who had recently visited a WOSB unit in Britain that a psychological-psychiatric assessment unit be established in the United States. This idea was presented in October, 1943, at one of the morning executive staff meetings of General William J. Donovan, head of OSS. It was well received by those of the recruiting branch who were present and especially by Cols. John A. Hoag and Henson L. Robinson of the Schools and Training Branch, whose training programs had carried the brunt of too many cases of bad recruitment. Impressed also was the only psychologist present, Dr. Robert C. Tryon, Deputy Chief, Planning Staff, who saw at once a real opportunity for his fellow psychologists to contribute. He recommended that the Schools and Training Branch and the Planning Staff collaborate in setting up an assessment program.

During the following month of November Colonel Robinson and his staff set to work to procure the facilities which would be required. In the Planning Staff, Dr. (later Capt.) James A. Hamilton, Dr. (later 1st Lt.) John W. Gardner, and Dr. Joseph A. Gengerelli rapidly sketched out in a general way the principles and methods that were to characterize the new program.

These hurried preparations culminated in a final two-day conference of all these men from the two branches and also Dr. (later Lt. Col.) Henry A. Murray and Dr. Donald K. Adams who had been invited as consultants in working out the details of the program. This was a stimulating session, held at "The Farm," a secluded intelligence briefing area. Shortly thereafter the director of OSS issued the order authorizing the establishment of the assessment unit and within fifteen days a task force of six psychologists and psychiatrists greeted the first group of bewildered assessees. Three of the task force—Dr. John W. Gardner, Dr. Joseph A. Gengerelli, and Dr. James A. Hamilton—were old OSS hands by this time; three were newcomers—Dr. Donald K. Adams, Lt. Donald W. Fiske (USNR), and Dr. Henry A. Murray.

The affair got under way very rapidly in a gale of resourceful activity and good will, largely due to the contagious zest of our administrator, Dr. Hamilton.

The locus of the undertaking was a country estate forty minutes outside Washington, a farm with rolling meadowland and self-respecting shade trees, massive barn and satellite sheds and kennels, which provided ample space for setting up all sorts of stressful situations, indoors and outdoors, to test the intelligence and stamina of the candidates. This was known as "Station S," or "S School" (since it belonged to the Schools and Training Branch), or simply "S." "S" was synonymous with Secret.

The candidates, it was arranged, would come in groups, or "classes," each group numbering about eighteen men. The duration of each testing period was three days.

Within a month the staff was strengthened by the arrival of Dr. Egerton L. Ballachey, Dr. Richard S. Lyman, and Dr. Donald W. MacKinnon, and later by a host of others, for longer or shorter periods, many of them specialists of one sort or another, such as Dr. Janet Rioch, Dr. Edward C. Tolman, Dr. Theodore M. Newcomb, and Dr. David M. Levy.

During the late winter of 1944 the torrent of candidates at Station S became so great that it was decided to set up Station W in Washington in order to take care of the overflow, with a staff composed of Captain Hamilton, Dr. Adams, Dr. Ballachey, M/Sgt. David Krech, and Dr. Rioch. Theirs was a one-day program of assessment. Two months afterwards, Station WS, located on a Pacific beach, was assessing candidates recruited in the West. And then, in the midst of these developments, a request arrived from the Far East for specialists to screen native agents. In answer to this call, Dr. Lyman, Dr. Lucien M. Hanks, and Captain Hamilton set out for Ceylon, to be succeeded six months later by Dr. Ballachey and Mr. Bradford B. Hudson. Finally, in the spring of 1945, Dr. Bingham Dai, Mr. Hudson, Dr. Lyman, and Colonel Murray, with the assistance of six able Chinese psychologists, assessed some 800 Chinese recruits for the paratroop-commando units that were in training at Kunming, Yunnan Province. A fortnight before V-J day, Mr. Hudson, who had previously directed a short-lived assessment unit near Calcutta, went far north to Hsian to assess a special group of Korean agents.

To take care of the unassessed personnel who in the fall of 1944 were being rapidly transferred from France via Washington to the Far East, a reassessment unit was inaugurated by Colonel Murray, Dr. G. Colket Caner, and Capt. James G. Miller at Area F. The direction of this undertaking eventually became the responsibility of Captain John A. Kneipp, who had administered Station WS after the departure of Lieutenant John W. Gardner.

For the last year of its history the director of Station S was Dr. MacKinnon.

The comparable position at W during this period was held successively by Dr. Adams, Dr. Ballachey, Dr. Dwight W. Chapman, and Commander Robert A. Cohen.

For most of those engaged in this undertaking the whole experience was an exceedingly happy and rewarding one. Besides the essential feeling that we were forwarding the success of OSS activities and in this way contributing to the defeat of Fascism, there were countless satisfactions to be derived from working as members of a congenial, stimulating, dedicated group.

Particularly gratifying was the proof that psychiatrists and psychologists (men of science drawn from universities) could work harmoniously and fruitfully with businessmen and professional soldiers (men of action drawn from the world of affairs). No college president or faculty, we suppose, ever gave any psychological endeavor the backing and encouragement that was given our assessment units by the administrators of OSS, by such men as General William J. Donovan, Col. G. Edward Buxton, Mr. Charles S. Cheston, Mr. John O'Gara, Mr. Whitney H. Shepardson, Dr. William L. Langer, Col. J. Russell Forgan, Mr. James R. Murphy, and Col. Richard P. Heppner. Dr. James L. McConaughy and Colonel Robinson and the staff of the Schools and Training Branch were especially staunch in our support. Dr. Edward L. Barnhart, psychologist in the Presentation Branch, was of great assistance in the planning and production of tests and other materials. To them, as well as to many others, we are grateful for making possible a high degree of coordination between the activities of the assessment staff and those of other branches. Our experience encourages the hope that collaborations of a similar sort between social and medical scientists and government officials will, with mutual benefit, be even more effective in peacetime.

Last to be mentioned but first in the magnitude of their contribution to our project were the thousands of candidates, most of whom, to our astonishment, were able unresentfully to tolerate the indignities and ordeals that we invented for them. We wish to thank them once more not only for participating fully in the whole program but especially for bringing to our homestead at Station S so great a diversity of interests and talents. To this diversity may be attributed the extraordinary fact that in twenty months not a single member of the staff complained of boredom. It was as if we were the recluse who had invented the new mousetrap. For the whole world, men and women of all nationalities and temperaments, seemed to be intent on beating a path to our retreats.

We hope that we shall meet and recognize many of these three-day friends of ours in years to come. In any event, we shall be ever on the lookout for news of them, especially of those for whom we predicted notable successes— this man to become Senator from Arizona, this one to edit a newspaper which would make Centreville more famous than Emporia, that tall young man to penetrate the mystery of mysteries of enzyme action, this fellow to complete his authoritative treatise on Chinese philosophy, that other one to play an important role in attaining the final acceptance of a world government, and the stocky one with red hair to find the summit of contentment with his wife and children on a dairy farm in Maryland, to mention but a few. We trust that these will not fail to make paths for their potentialities so that our predictions will be verified and there will be triumphs in which we can partake vicariously as we say to ourselves: "Ah! years ago this was foreseen."

April 30, 1947

Chapter I

THE NATURE OF THE TASK

The task confronting the OSS assessment staff was that of developing a system of procedures which would reveal the personalities of OSS recruits to the extent of providing ground for sufficiently reliable predictions of their usefulness to the organization during the remaining years of the war. In this sentence everything hangs on the meaning of "sufficiently reliable predictions."

It is easy to predict precisely the outcome of the meeting of one known chemical with another known chemical in an immaculate test tube. But where is the chemist who can predict what will happen to a known chemical if it meets an unknown chemical in an unknown vessel? And even if all the properties of all the chemicals resident in a given laboratory are exactly defined, is there a chemist who can predict every chemical engagement that will take place if Chance, the blind technician, is in charge of the proceedings? Can a physician, steeped though he may be in the science of his profession, say for certain whether or not the body he has just examined will contract contagious jaundice next summer in Algiers? How, then, can a psychologist foretell with any degree of accuracy the outcomes of future meetings of one barely known personality with hundreds of other undesignated personalities in distant undesignated cities, villages, fields, and jungles that are seething with one knows not what potential harms and benefits? Fortune—call the old hag or beauty what you will—can never be eliminated from the universe of human interactions. And this being forever true, prophetic infallibility is beyond the reach of social scientists.

Furthermore, we would guess that no matter how substantial are the advances of scientific psychology, the best series of predictions of *individual* careers—apperception operating as it does—will involve the play of experienced intuitions, the clinical hunch, products of unconsciously perceived and integrated symptomatic signs. The assessment of men—we trust that Samuel Butler would agree—is the scientific art of arriving at sufficient conclusions from insufficient data.

Within reach of those who are trained in assessment, we hope, are "sufficiently reliable predictions," or "sufficient conclusions," that is to say, predictions or conclusions which will serve, by the elimination of some and the

8

better placement of others, to decrease the ultimate failures or unsatisfactory performers, by such a number that (i) the *amount saved* plus (ii) the *amount of harm prevented* plus (iii) the *amount gained* is greater than the cost of the assessment program. The *amount saved* can be roughly computed in terms of the average expenditure of money and time (spent by other members of the organization) in training, transporting, housing, and dealing with an individual who in the end proves to be incapable of discharging his duties properly. The most important item, the *amount of harm prevented,* is scarcely calculable. It consists of the friction, the impairment of efficiency and morale, the injury to the reputation of an organization that results from the actions of a man who is stupid, apathetic, sullen, resentful, arrogant, or insulting in his dealings with members of his own unit or of allied units, or with customers or citizens of foreign countries. To this must be added the irreparable damage that can be done by one who blabs. Diminution in the number of men of this stamp—sloths, irritants, bad actors, and free talkers—was one of the prime objects of the assessment program. The *amount gained* is equally hard to estimate. It consists of the average difference between the positive accomplishments of a failure and of a success. An unsatisfactory man, by filling an assignment, deprives the organization of the services of a man who might be capable of a substantial contribution. Some OSS schemes, in fact, were entirely abandoned because in each case the man who arrived in the theater to undertake the project was found to be unsuitable. Thus every pronounced failure costs the organization a good deal of time and money, lowers the efficiency and reputation of one of its units, and, by taking the place of a competent man, prevents the attainment of certain goals.

Needless to say, no OSS official was urged to weigh these subtleties and come out with an answer in dollars and cents. For even if it had been possible to make such an estimate, no use could have been made of it, since the one figure that was needed for an evaluation of the assessment program was not obtainable: the percentage of failures among the thousands of unassessed men and women who had been recruited prior to December, 1943. The available records were not accurate or complete enough to give the staff at Station S this level against which to measure its results, and so at the outset we had to face the fact that we would never know certainly whether we had been an asset or a liability to the OSS.

The chief over-all purpose of the OSS assessment staff—to eliminate the unfit—was similar to that of the conventional screening board, but in certain other respects the task of the former was unique: the number and nature of the billets to be filled by "bodies," the adequacy of the information about the different assignments, the types of men who came to be assessed, the conditions under which the work was done, the kinds of reports that were required, and so forth. A full description of these differences should constitute the best possible definition of the task undertaken by the psychologists and the psychiatrists of the OSS.

The Office of Strategic Services was a wartime agency set up by the President and Congress to meet special conditions of World War II. It was the first of its kind in the history of the United States. Its functions were varied. On the one hand its purpose was to set up research units in the United States and overseas as well as an elaborate network of agents to gather strategic information concerning the activities and vulnerabilities of the nation's enemies, to analyze and evaluate this information, and to report it to those concerned. On the other hand, its object was to conduct a multiplicity of destructive operations behind enemy lines, to aid and train resistance groups, and, by radio, pamphlets, and other means, to disintegrate the morale of enemy troops and encourage the forces of the underground.

To carry out these functions it was necessary that hundreds of special skills outside the sphere of civilian experience be learned rapidly by thousands of Americans, many of whom did not feel like fighting. And these novel skills, taught by men who had mastered them but recently, had to be put into practice in some of the most inaccessible, least known, and outlandish parts of this broad earth. And here is where General Donovan came in.

General Donovan himself was a mobile unit of the first magnitude. Space was no barrier to him—the Sahara Desert was a little stretch of sand, the Himalayas were a bank of snow, the Pacific was a mere ditch. And, what is more, Time was no problem. Circling the globe, according to good evidence, he would catch up with Time and pass it. No one was at all surprised if he left one morning and returned the previous afternoon.

The General's triumph over the two fundamental dimensions of our universe is certainly the leading reason why OSS men, seen or unseen, were operating on most of the strategic surfaces of the earth.

But more elementary than this—for one has to explain why he was inclined to fly about the way he did—was General Donovan's power to visualize an oak when he saw an acorn. For him the day was never sufficient unto itself: it was always teeming with the seeds of a boundless future. Like Nature, he was prodigal, uncontainable, forelooking, and every completed project bred a host of new ones. His imagination shot ahead, outflying days and distances, and where his imagination went, there would his body go soon afterward, and at every stop, brief as it might be, he would leave a litter of young schemes to be reared and fashioned by his lieutenants and transmuted finally into deeds of daring. This is the key to the problem. It explains why OSS undertook and carried out more different types of enterprises calling for more varied skills than any other single organization *of its size* in the history of our country.

Now it is not for us to say to what extent these far-flung undertakings were successful. Our purpose here is merely to call attention to the situation that deserves first place on the list of conditions which differentiated our endeavor from those of most other selections and placement agencies:

Variety and Novelty of OSS Functions; Variety and Remoteness of the Situations.—Among the various consequences of this combination of factors, the following deserve mention:

i) It was many months before our conceptions of the different jobs were more than half accurate. We were given the briefest possible time in which to prepare. No one arranged a preliminary world tour for the staff so that the conditions at each base and the operations in progress could be observed at first hand. The information that came in from the theaters was scanty; and even if it had been ample and adapted to our purpose, there would have been too much to learn in the time available, too much to remember. Not until much later did some of us who visited installations in the field come to realize the magnitude of the discrepancy between even the better job descriptions—those received in the later months—and the various dispositions and skills that were actually required in the field.

ii) It was not possible to arrange a unified three-day program, much less a one-day program, which would test so great a variety of functions. It would have been a comparable situation, for example, if a dozen educators were asked to set up a school with a six-month term for the training of farmers, machine workers, salesmen, stockholders, explorers, chemists, diplomats, physicians, philosophers, congressmen, and theologians.

iii) Many of the jobs proposed for candidates were different from anything they had ever done before, and so the staff could not rely on the work histories of these men as evidence of ability or aptitude.

iv) Many foreigners and first-generation Americans were recruited because they were familiar with the language, people, and territory of their respective lands of origin. It was difficult for a staff of Americans to judge men from cultures so diverse and to predict how well they would succeed in dealing with their own countrymen.

Let us now consider these points in more detail, and subsequently a few other points.

Lack of Adequate Job Descriptions.—The task assigned to us was to decide in each case whether the candidate was fit or could be made fit for the job designated on the Student Information Sheet which accompanied him. Here and elsewhere the term *job* (or *assignment, mission, task*) is used to designate (i) a certain *set of functions* constituting a *role* fulfilled in (ii) an *environment* composed of a certain *set of situations* that prevail in a given theater. Thus *job* includes both the *role* (with its functions) and the *en-*

vironment (with its situations). Therefore the first thing that the members of the staff should have done was to familiarize themselves with the situations that were likely to be encountered in all the theaters of operation as well as with all the functions that men would be expected to perform there. But since this, as we have said, was not possible at the start, it was necessary to compare the candidate with an abstract idea, or with images that were indefinite or incorrect. The knowledge that many of the candidates were to play parts in unbelievable dramas thousands of miles away served to cast a veil of enchanting irreality over the whole endeavor.

No member of the assessment staff possessed intimate knowledge of more than a small fraction of OSS activities. All of us had a fairly clear idea of the functions of a secretary, an office clerk, an administrator, a medical technician, a historian engaged in analyzing the economic, political, and social structure of this or that country. But less definite certainly was our knowledge of the qualifications for the job of script writer, base station operator, demolitions instructor, field representative, section leader. And hazier still were our notions of the typical operations of a paratrooper, resistance group leader, saboteur, undercover agent, liaison pilot, pigeoneer.

One member of the staff, Dr. Lyman, had lived in China, and several had traveled extensively in prewar Europe, but none had worked in London during the blitz or had been under shellfire in Italy. Specific information about present conditions was lacking. What was the strength of the resistance groups in France? Was it necessary for an agent to look and speak like a native? What special problems confronted an operator in Yugoslavia or Greece? Was a tendency to alcoholism facilitated in Calcutta? How potent were the demoralizing effects of malaria in Burma? Were the Kachins difficult to work with? What were the living conditions in Kandy? Could we assume that most of the Chinese would be cooperative? No doubt the answers to some of these questions might have been found in books which none of us had time to read. But where could we have learned about the very special activities of OSS men in the field? Many of the operations were still in the planning phase; others were being carried out behind enemy lines outside the range of witnesses, and even at the most advanced bases the officer in charge was often for long periods uncertain as to what his men were doing out there in the unknown. It was sometimes months before enough knowledge was accumulated to form the basis of a report that could be hurried back through channels to the United States. Rarely were the details in any series of reports sufficient to give the officers in Washington vivid concrete pictures of the real circumstances in this or that OSS installation overseas. We realized, for example, that the performances of many men would vary according to the personalities of their associates, the temperaments of their immediate superiors. But such factors were unpredictable. The personnel had a way of changing from month to month. At one time it would be rumored that a certain overseas branch was very badly managed: anyone who could not tolerate a good deal of snafu would become a nervous wreck in no time. A little later we would learn that things were moving very smoothly there under a new chief. And so it went.

Most of our information was obtained from the branch chiefs and their administrative officers in Washington. But much of what has just been said about us is also to some extent applicable to them. Few, if any, had ever operated in the field. Most of them had been drawn from civilian life and were doing their level best to learn a new game, the rules of which were changing from season to season, or even from week to week. To be sure, a few of the administrators had visited OSS headquarters in distant theaters, but the knowledge they acquired there was out of date a few months after they returned; and much of what they could remember they were too busy to impart or unable to communicate in terms that were usable by us. They did more than could reasonably have been expected of them, but it was nevertheless a long time before the assessment staff was able to piece together bits of information from various sources and arrive at adequate conceptions of the jobs that needed filling. The following excerpt is fairly typical of the form in which our information was received. We would class it neither among the least nor among the most helpful communications that were sent in from the theaters. It is about average.

The organization has been recruiting too many men, civilian or military, who have intelligence and sometimes the necessary mechanical training but who lack common sense, know nothing about working with men or how to look after the welfare and the morale of men under them. We simply must have men who can shoulder responsibility and use initiative with common sense. Simply because a man has intelligence does not qualify him for this type of work. In some instances we also have had men who fall into the class of the high-strung or emotional type. We simply cannot use men of that type in the field when they have to live with Chinese, eat Chinese food, and be under pressure at times. In most cases these men have suffered nervous breakdowns and other nervous ailments. Whether men are recruited in the States or here in the field they must be checked by a doctor and a psychiatrist before being pronounced fit for the field. The check by a psychiatrist is especially desirable. If for the Army and Navy there have been provisions made for psychiatric checks, then for us it is more important since our men spend from three to six months in the field without seeing American installations. We have had at least eight men, who for various quirks in their make-up, have had to be pulled from the field. Some of them could have been used at headquarters and should never have been sent to the field, and others simply wouldn't fit anywhere. One was definitely a psychiatric case.[1]

---

[1] It should be said that the breakdowns mentioned in this message occurred in men who had not been previously assessed.

Many of the projects were planned at theater headquarters, in London, Algiers, Cairo, Kandy, or Kunming, and it was there that the personnel requirements for each project were determined. The Washington office was merely informed that so many men of this and of that type were needed. It takes an expert to write a job description, and no experts in the theaters were free for such tedious employments. Consequently, in no instance was the information received in Washington as precise as it might have been. Furthermore, by the time the recruiting officers of the OSS Personnel Procurement Branch had engaged the interest of the required number of prospects, the specifications that had been sent by the administrative officer overseas were lost in the files of the corresponding officer in Washington. In any event, when a candidate arrived at the assessment station there was usually but one term (language expert, news analyst, team member, cartographer, or the like) on his Student Information Sheet to designate the nature of the assignment. It was months before these brief designations were successful in evoking in our minds images of definite duties that the candidate would be expected to perform.

In the beginning, the judgments of many of us were confused by the influence of an enduring lodger in our minds, the figure of the Sleuth, acquired from Somerset Maugham's *The British Agent,* from Helen MacInnes' *Assignment in Brittany*, from the thrillers of E. Phillips Oppenheim, and from who-can-say-what motion pictures and detective stories. Even the legendary cloak-and-dagger hero may have come into it. But that was natural enough. In those days our heads were empty billets waiting to be filled, and in the absence of the figures we had invited—images of operators in the field—a number of theatrical deceivers moved in and made themselves conspicuous. These intruders were driven out one by one and replaced by the proper personages eventually—(1) when the branch administrative officers finally received job specifications that were more precise; (2) when, many months later, some of the men who had served in the field returned to Washington and devoted hours of their time to answering our questions; (3) after several of the assessors had taken the course at one or another OSS school and learned most of the tricks that were taught agents; and (4) after a few other members of the staff had crossed the ocean and come home with firsthand observations.

Heterogeneity of the Jobs Proposed for Members of Each Group of Candidates.—Each British selection board was limited to the task of deciding suitability for *one type* of job, and so, at each station, a unified program could be set up with an interrelated variety of procedures to test the different functions that comprised a single role. These functions could be kept in mind by the assessors as they witnessed the performance of the candidates. In contrast to the British boards, the assessment stations in the

United States were expected to estimate suitability for a *great variety* of jobs. This expectation would not have been nearly so embarrassing if the members of each group that came to be examined had been recruited for jobs of the same general class: one group, say, composed of prospective administrators—branch chiefs, branch administrative officers, finance officers, supply officers, and so on; another group made up of prospective field operators: including parachutists, instructors and leaders of guerilla units, mortar experts, saboteurs; and a third consisting of propagandists: idea men, script writers, radio speakers, actors, artists, and the like. If this practice could have been instituted, it would have been possible to construct a number of different programs, each restricted to testing the qualities most necessary for a single class of jobs.

But homogeneity was out of the question. The candidates had to be taken pretty much as they arrived, regardless of the jobs proposed for them. They could not be kept waiting. It was always hard to find rooms for them in the city. No one was tolerant of delays. Either a candidate would be accepted, in which case the branch administrative officer was bent on having him start his course of training as soon as possible, or he would not be accepted, in which case he was usually anxious to return to the work that he had dropped abruptly on being summoned by OSS. As a result, a "class" of "students" at one of the assessment stations was apt to contain men selected for at least six or seven different kinds of jobs.

Since what we had available in the way of staff, facilities, and time did not permit the carrying out of six or seven different programs simultaneously, a more or less uniform schedule was established, parts of which were necessarily irrelevant to the question of the suitability of one or another class of recruits. Thus unavoidably a few of the hours of each man were wasted by us instead of being used gainfully by having him engage in activities that were pertinent to the duties he was slated to perform.

Also, the heterogeneity of the jobs to be considered eliminated the possibility of a unified orientation on the part of the assessors. Each focus of attention (candidate) called for a special frame of reference (job description—when we had it). For example, observing candidate Bud at meals, or during an interview or outdoor group test, one had to ask oneself: Will this man survive the rigorous training in Scotland? Will he get along with the British? Will he be able to govern his anxiety up there in the plane as the moment for the drop approaches on that fateful night? Will he favorably impress the members of the resistance group into whose territory he will jump? Is his French fluent? Will he make a good instructor? Will he play safe, or will he manifest initiative and daring in setting up road blocks and harassing the Germans generally? Will he find isolation in a lonely farmhouse tolerable when he hears that the Gestapo are searching for him in the neighborhood? Can he hold his liquor? At one of those dinners the French will give in his honor will he rant and boast of the prowess of America? Will he get mixed up in politics? Will he succeed in persuading the rival French factions in his locality to cooperate or are his actions likely to increase antagonisms?

Sitting next to candidate Bud at breakfast, or entering as he left the interview room or working alongside him in the group test, was candidate Roy who was slated for another job operationally defined by other images. Here one had to ask oneself: Will this man tolerate with equanimity the monsoon season in Calcutta? Will his mind provide a barrier to irritability when his body breaks out with prickly heat and athlete's foot? Has he a good head for business? How much does he know about the transportation of supplies? Will he increase or lower the morale of those about him? Will he spend so many of his evenings in nightclubs with OSS girls that his working efficiency will be impaired? By perpetual kidding and gossiping will he create in his office a frivolous playboy atmosphere? Will he treat the Hindus with patronizing condescension or contempt? Will he do anything to discredit the organization in the eyes of the British? Is he so rank-centric that he will whine and grouse when his promotion is postponed? If he is transferred to less desirable quarters or shifted to another job involving less interesting or important duties, will he feel slighted and humiliated to the point of losing zest?

Next to be considered, let us say, was a man who had been selected as a liaison pilot for the Mediterranean theater, a job which was represented by another set of images; and then after him, a candidate with still different qualifications, and so on down the line to the last man.

Now, human minds are hardly capable of regimenting so many images, hardly capable of calling forth the catalogue of a single cluster at the proper moment and holding back all others. Therefore, the heterogeneity of the jobs which had to be considered during each period of testing was a condition that interfered with clear thinking and so, no doubt, decreased the reliability of our predictive judgments.

Impossibility of Testing Special Skills.—The great diversity of particular skills called for by OSS projects presented a problem with which the assessment staff found itself incapable of dealing satisfactorily. It devised tests of a number of special aptitudes: ability to observe, remember, and report, ability to analyze news, ability to improvise subversive propaganda, ability to instruct, ability to recruit, and so forth. It also used certain standardized tests, such as one for aptitude in using the Morse code and one for mechanical comprehension. But for many other skills there were no already accredited tests on the market and it would not have been possible for the assessment staff, fully occupied as it was, to develop and standardize thirty or forty tests to cover such activities as policy making, calculating enemy vulnerabilities, editing an Austrian newspaper, practicing tropical medicine, nursing, parachuting, underwater swimming, training homing pigeons, running a linotype machine, drawing Japanese posters, and so forth. And then there was the great problem of language. We had no one on the staff who was fluent in Rumanian, Albanian, modern Greek, Danish, Malay, and so forth. It would, in truth, have required a staff of twenty or thirty experts to pass judgment on the degrees of special talent possessed by the totality of our candidates.

Consequently, estimations of rare proficiencies were left to the branch administrative officers and to the recruiters of the Personnel Procurement Branch, who had to come to their conclusions on the basis of work history, reports of others, personal acquaintance, and the candidate's estimate of his own qualifications.

Thus, in many cases, special aptitude, the most important variable in determining success or failure in the theater, was all but excluded from our deliberations. The men who failed in the theater because of insufficient technical skill were nevertheless counted among the errors of assessment.

Degrees to Which Jobs Differed from Anything Candidates Had Done Before.—Democracies are congregations of peace-minded citizens. War coming up as quickly as a cyclone catches them unprepared. Everyone must hurriedly learn new tricks. This time, because of the total multiplex character of World War II, there was an unusually large number of new tricks to be learned. Jumping from a plane, for example, which is a triumph of the will over one of our least manageable instinctive fears, is not a common civilian pursuit. (OSS, however, did recruit a man who claimed to have jumped over 2,300 times.)

The novelty of so many of the assignments is included among the special conditions which distinguished our task from that of so many other selection boards, because the greater the novelty of the job the more unreliable is the work history as a guide for inference. Since the work history is the granite on which vocational judgments depend most for their support, it is worth noting that in many instances we could build no argument on this since it bore no relation to the proposed assignment. Even when the transition from past to future involved a shift so slight as that between research at a university and research in Washington, adjustability to new conditions was often the decisive variable. Judgment as to the suitability of an eminent political scientist recruited for research and analysis, for example, would always rest, to some extent, on evidence that was pertinent to this question: Will this man be able to shift gears and work under pressure, turning out memoranda, well ahead of military action, which are accurate, terse, organized for quick comprehension and pointed toward strategic decisions? The degree of transformation of old habits that was required of most candidates was far greater than this, and it was our job to determine whether or not they would be equal to it.

Heterogeneity of the Recruits: Strangeness (to Us) of Many of Them. —To fill the great diversity of positions mentioned earlier, individuals of a wide variety of backgrounds were recruited, and this made assessment difficult for American psychologists, most of whom were unfamiliar with the conventional assumptions, patterns of behavior, and modes of speech of Spaniards, Greeks, Albanians, Yugoslavs, Rumanians, Hungarians, Austrians, Germans, Poles, French, Hollanders, Chinese, and Koreans. There was not only the language impediment—many of these foreigners and first-generation Americans were embarrassed by their halting and stumbling use of English, and allowances had to be made in rating their written work —but there was our own uncertainty in trying to interpret properly some of their actions, gestures, and insinuations. Furthermore, it was not always easy for them—aliens in a group of hearty Americans—to adjust to the assessment situation, or easy for us to guess how they would act in other environments. Take that stubborn lantern-jawed fellow over there who is so irritating to his fellow candidates; is it not possible that he is the very man to appeal to a band of guerillas in the mountain passes of Albania? And observe that Frenchman gesturing so excitedly to that slightly scornful circle of Americans; how effective would his relations be with the lower, middle, and upper classes in his native country? It was hard to find solid ground for deciding questions like these.

Occasionally when we had a class composed entirely of Japanese, one or two cultural anthropologists, acquainted with the patterns of conduct prevalent among these Orientals, would help us by joining the staff for the duration of the testing period. But, for the most part, we had to feel our way through the complexities of cultural differences as best we could, blindly and without aid. Several of the errors we made can be attributed to our inclination to give foreigners the benefit of every doubt.

The difficulties of cross-cultural assessment become apparent when one listens closely to appraisals of his own countrymen by foreigners. For example, although numerous American groups were very successfully assessed by British boards, striking misinterpretations of the behavior of these men were not infrequent.

Difference between Jobs Assigned Men in the Theater and Those for Which They Had Been Assessed.—This difference was inevitable. During the two, four, six, or even eight months that elapsed between the day that personnel for a certain project were requested in the theater and the day that the men arrived there, the situation in the area had usually changed considerably. Perhaps the original plan had been abandoned for one reason or another, and new and more urgent undertakings were being launched. Incompetent men here and there had been released; illness had claimed others. Branch heads were clamoring for substitutes. As a result, a new arrival might very well be given a task for which he had been neither recruited, assessed, nor trained.

During most of their existence, Stations S and W were expected to judge the suitability of each recruit for a selected assignment, nothing more. Sometimes the writer of the evaluation note would state that the candidate was recommended for the designated job provided he would not be expected to perform this or that function, but the assessor would have been overstepping the bounds of his function if he had suggested an entirely different mission for which the candidate appeared to be better fitted. It is hard to account for the fact that this policy was maintained long after it was discovered that there was no certainty as to the job the candidate would be given in the theater. Anyhow, adjustability to a variety of assignments came to be regarded at the assessment stations as an asset that might very well be critical.

About three months before the war was won a new form of report sheet was belatedly adopted. This called for a fitness rating not only for the job selected for the recruit, but also for each of several other classes or types of jobs. The purpose here was, first, to give the branch chief in the theater some assistance in placing a man in a position other than that for which he had been chosen in the United States, and second, to give the staff the opportunity to record their impressions of each man's fitness or unfitness for other kinds of work, so that, whatever role was eventually assigned to him, there would be an assessment rating with which the final rating of performance in the field could be compared. However, since none of the men so rated had time to get into action before the cessation of hostilities, all of our follow-ups and our evaluations of assessment procedures were done on men whose suitability was rated for one job only, a job which not infrequently was different, as we have stated, from the one which became his eventually. Such considerations notwithstanding, in our calculations all failures in the field were counted as errors of assessment.

To summarize the chief factors so far discussed, it should be stated that (i) it was not possible—because of the nature of OSS activities—to obtain adequate job descriptions, the first requirement for an assessment program; (ii) it was not possible for any one staff at any one station to test suitability for such a great variety of novel assignments; and, even if it had been possible, (iii) the job that the candidate was assigned in the theater was in a large proportion of cases different from the one which had been selected for him in Washington.

This being the situation, it was decided at the start that we would judge each candidate not primarily in relation to our conception, such as it was, of the designated mission, but in relation to a set of general qualifications (dispositions, qualities, abilities) which were applicable to the great majority of assignments of OSS personnel overseas. How this was done will be explained in the next chapter.

Now let us turn to some other conditions—further hindrances encountered in attempting to arrive at clear conceptions of the personalities and at valid estimates of the capacities of the candidates examined.

Variations among Recruits in Temporary State of Health, Physical Training, Mood.—Some men were in the pink of condition when they came to assessment, others were in the clutches of a severe cold, or depleted, or otherwise out of sorts. Some who had been confined to sedentary occupations for years, and had not recently engaged in physical exercise, appeared at a great disadvantage alongside young men fresh from basic training, or from officers' candidate school. Some recruits, who had spent a restless, wakeful night on the sleeper hurrying to the city where they were to report, were forced to whip their brains to keep them pulling for four hours during the first evening of written exercises. One candidate had just come from the bedside of a sick child, several were in the midst of divorce proceedings, some had suffered recent reverses in business. The wife of one candidate had shot herself in the abdomen accidentally and was undergoing a surgical operation at the very time her disquieted husband was doing his best to participate in the to-him-empty assessment situations.

These temporary factors, and their name is Legion, were so diverse, so subtle, and so varying in their effects that it was not possible to be certain what correction should be made for them. Thus we must list this uncontrollable variable among the conditions that increased the difficulties of assessment.

Variations in the Amount of Previous Information Recruits Had Acquired Concerning Assessment Procedures.—Some men were given no clarifying information about the OSS and its activities by the officer who recruited them, and on arriving in Washington were sent to Station S or W without any explanation· of what was afoot. They arrived at the assessment center in a state compounded of amusement, curiosity, mystification, confusion, defensiveness, and resentment, the proportion of these feelings varying with their temperaments and the type of treatment they had received along the way. The degree of error that is possible when a man first enters one of these hush-hush agencies is illustrated by the candidate'who started the testing program under the impression that he was being considered for a position in the State Department. At the other extreme were those who, having worked for a year or more in the OSS in Washington, had been able, from stories indiscreetly passed on to them by former "graduates" of assessment, to piece together fragmentary conceptions of the proceedings which served to prepare them for the shocks to come.

Although at the end of each testing period the recruits were enjoined not to tell anyone until the war was over what happened at S or at W, it was not easy for them to comply with this regulation. For most of those who went to Station S, the three days in the country was a novel, stimulating, and stressful experience, sometimes humiliating or annoying, but almost always memorable for one reason or another. They were full of it all when they returned to town and when they came together with other graduates this was an almost irresistible topic of conversation. Their reminiscences were occasionally overheard by men who were destined to go to one of these stations at some later date. In any event, the few men who arrived at S or at W with some preparation had an appreciable advantage over the innocent and unsuspecting raw recruits. Here again was an uncontrollable variable which undoubtedly influenced the emotional and intellectual set with which the candidates faced their tasks at the assessment center.

Anonymity of Candidates.—Since the administration had decided that it would be better for security reasons to keep the personal identity—name, family and vocational background, rank, and so on—of each recruit unknown to his fellows, it was arranged to have all the candidates leave their own clothes in town and come out to Station S dressed in Army fatigues, each with an invented pseudonym to distinguish him during the period of testing. Although this practice opened the way for some otherwise unworkable procedures and facilitated the creation of a convivial atmosphere, in other ways it augmented the difficulties of assessment.

In the first place, it deprived the staff of some of the cues that are commonly utilized in judging character—the material, cut, and condition of a man's clothing, the color-pattern of his tie, the folds and creases of his hat and the angle at which he wears it, how he carries his handkerchief, with or without a monogram, and so forth. In those instances in which the candidate wore his own socks and shoes, these, as sole indicators of taste and social status, received an unusual amount of attention.

The advantage of being able to observe the candidates in the garb of the Common Man, dispossessed of all symbols of authority and station, was further offset by the fact that under these conditions some men act in a manner that differs from their manner in real life. Take the buoyant, successful journalist, for example, who, caught in the draft at the age of thirty-four years, had been somewhat shamefacedly wearing the stripes of a T/5. At the assessment station, this man, rid of the uniform that suppressed his spontaneity, came into his own again. The somewhat tense young man of twenty-eight, on the other hand, who had enlisted before Pearl Harbor and risen rapidly to the rank of major, lost, when stripped of his leaves, some of the support upon which his mounting confidence had been relying. As a result, the older and more sophisticated writer conveyed an impression of greater self-assurance at assessment than did the young officer. But transplanted back within the framework of the Army hierarchy, it was not unlikely that the journalist, deprived of certain privileges, or pushed around, would find alcohol an inviting refuge from a humiliating position; whereas the young major, heartened by evidences of respect, might very well outdo himself in striving to live up to his official role.

Thus the wearing of fatigues at the assessment stations served to conceal if not to obliterate the often powerful effects of rank differences. As a result, predictions of the subsequent effectiveness of enlisted men were apt to be too high; those of field grade officers, too low. (Another factor tending in the same direction was the operation among our staff members of sentiments favorable to the less appreciated man, the underdog.)

Length of Time That Elapsed before Securing Evaluation of Assessment Ratings.—After being passed at one of the assessment stations in the United States, a man would usually spend from one to three months in attending OSS schools and awaiting transportation out of the country. It might be two months more before he was well started on a definite assignment overseas. And then not until another month or two had passed would his superior officers and associates feel that they had enough evidence on which to rest a judgment of his efficiency. Thus one had to wait anywhere from four to eight months to evaluate an assessment rating; and to do it even as quickly as this it was necessary for a member of the assessment staff to go overseas himself and collect appraisals in the theater. By the time he had returned to Washington and written up his report, six to ten months had elapsed. The first evaluation reports on 137 cases appraised in the ETO were finished in late October, 1944, ten months after Station S was started. Thus, for this long period the assessors had to proceed without knowing what proportion of their shots was missing the target. Furthermore, the early reports from overseas did not include the information that was required to appraise the efficacy of the different procedures. And no one on the staff was free to make the necessary statistical correlations, to determine the degrees of conformity that existed between the S or W ratings on each variable on each test and the ratings given in the theater. Validating correlations of this sort constitute the best ground for deciding which tests should be retained without modification, which revised, and which eliminated. The OSS psychologists and psychiatrists, fully occupied with the routine of assessment, were unable to obtain these figures until after the war was over.

This will suffice as a list of the chief complications which confronted the OSS assessment staff. The description of these conditions has served, we hope, to define the nature of our task as distinguished from that of the average selection board. Two other important differences deserve brief mention.

High Quality of the Majority of OSS Candidates.—The OSS board had to appraise the relative usefulness of men and women who fell, for the most part, in the middle and upper ranges of the distribution curve of general effectiveness or of one or more special abilities, people who had already been selected because of demonstrated skill in some field of activity. OSS standards, in other words, were somewhat higher than those of the majority of institutions which make use of screening devices. Consequently, some of the tests which are successful in distinguishing people who, because of some defect or handicap, are incapable of functioning effectively, were not suitable for our program.

Necessity of Judging Social Relations.—As was mentioned above, the OSS psychologists and psychiatrists were expected to estimate a candidate's ability to cooperate and to get along well with others, and also, in the majority of cases, his ability to lead, to organize the activities of others, and to evoke respect. Since there are no standardized procedures for measuring these qualities and abilities, new methods had to be improvised.

The difficulties listed above, by challenging the imagination, acted as stimulants to the members of the staff rather than as depressants; furthermore, they were balanced by certain rather *unusual advantages* which greatly facilitated the process of assessment.

Excellent Locations for Assessment.—Except for its roominess there was nothing noteworthy about the drab brownstone building in Washington, D. C., in which the W staff carried on its operations; but the country house and farm in Fairfax County, Virginia, where Station S was located, and the beach club facing the Pacific, which was known as Station WS, were both peculiarly suited to the requirements of a comprehensive assessment program. Sleeping, messing, and recreation facilities were adequate for candidates and staff at both places. There were small rooms for interviews and large rooms for the administration of group procedures; and, outdoors, particularly at S, the terrain had plenty of features which lent themselves to the construction of tasks to test physical and mechanical competence, cooperativeness, and leadership.

Although it might have been better to select or prepare locations which would strain the candidates' tolerance of ugliness, dirt, disorder, and discomfort, the beauty of the landscape and the agreeableness of the architecture at S and at WS were sources of great satisfaction to the staff members who worked at one or the other station month after month. Furthermore, the candidates' delight in finding on arrival that they were to live amid such attractive surroundings was an important determinant of their enjoyment of the three-and-a-half day period; it lifted their morale and increased their capacity to endure the ordeals and humiliations which they experienced along the way. Thus periodically stressful tasks were imbedded in a satisfying setting, the result being that, in the end, the over-all impression of the majority of assessees was pleasant rather than unpleasant. We were assured that several other factors—the friendly atmosphere, the informality and zest of the staff members, the novelty of the test situations, the orderly manner in which the program was administered—entered into the creation of the candidates' largely favorable judgment, a judgment which in numerous cases was generalized to include the entire organization. For instance, several S "graduates" informed us that the assessment program engendered the belief that, since the OSS took such pains in the selection of its personnel, it must be a pretty fine outfit. Anyhow, in many cases, the process of assessment served as a morale-raising force, and the point that we are stressing here is that one of the components of this force was the agreeable environment in which the program was carried out.

Moderate Flow of Candidates.—Although the assessment staffs operated under full steam most of the time—not often did the work at Station S end before midnight—the pressure was due to the fullness of the schedule rather than to the number of candidates that had to be assessed. It would have been simple enough, by omitting a few procedures, to make time for the examination of more candidates—or, possibly, for a spot or two of leisure. But none of the staffs saw fit to do this.

In the beginning (January, 1944), Station S assessed candidates at the rate of 120 per month, but before the winter was over this number had risen to almost 250, which was judged to be too heavy a load for the system that had been adopted. Another assessment unit, Station W, with a one-day schedule of procedures, was therefore set up in Washington. This change decreased the flow at S and so permitted a slight reorganization of the program, which lengthened the testing period by half a day and allowed for a short period of relaxation between the departure of one group and the arrival of another. This new schedule provided for the screening of 6 groups ("classes") of about 18 men each (a total of 108 candidates) per month. Station W assessed candidates at the rate of about 200 a month. In June, 1944, Station WS on the Pacific coast was opened. These three units—S, W, and WS—were able to handle all the personnel recruited for OSS during the height of its procurement season. When six months later the flow of candidates in

more especially of Americans. It seems to be an acquired habit, a resultant of our democratic way of life, of the intermingling and necessary collaborations, in the United States, of persons of irreconcilable cultures, of years of religious tolerance, if not indifference, ending in the assumption that beliefs in themselves are of negligible import, of our short-range materialistic outlook, of the widespread belittlement of theory and the excessive preoccupation with facts, acts, and gadgets.

That there had been some suppression of theoretical convictions at Station S was indicated by the outbursts of divergent views that occurred as soon as the practical work had been completed, when those of us who remained turned to the task of evaluating our policies and practices.

Still, the fact that we had been able to work together so harmoniously seemed to justify the belief that we enjoyed a broad, though perhaps unconscious, basis of agreement, that most of us had been acting on similar assumptions despite differences in our preferred ways of drafting them. It was this supposition that encouraged us to plan to devote this chapter to an exposition of the rationale of our program, of the principles which were implicit in everything that we did in common.

We thought, in addition, that it would be possible to carry the logical process back one step further and arrive at the psychological postulates which conformed to the stated principles of assessment. These postulates could then be compared to all the facts and theories of personality with which we were familiar. If it was found that the postulates were in accord with current knowledge then we would be in possession of the best possible theoretical foundation for our technical practices. If not, adjustments would have to be made. Either the principles and methods of assessment or some of our contemporary theories, or both, would have to be modified.

In presenting a conceptual framework for the OSS system of assessment we did not suppose that it would be possible to include the whole range of theories and hypotheses entertained by the men and women who, at one time or another, had taken part in the undertaking. As we have said, their views were never expressed except incidentally and "off the cuff" in a fragmentary manner. But we did expect that we could arrive at a number of generalizations to which most members of the staff would give assent. Together we had garnered an abundant harvest of experiences; would it be right to leave the sheaves standing, the grain unthreshed? Preferable to this, in our judgment, was to allow three or four members of the staff, unrepresentative as they might be, to work the material and extract what scientific nourishment they could from it.

This decision gave rise to several months' labor on the conceptual level which resulted in a brood of theoretical propositions. But when these were finally examined with a cool, impartial eye, the impression was inescapable that they were not of the sort that would be accepted readily by a majority of the staff members. Regretfully we concluded that any serious attempt to define basic concepts and postulates underlying assessment practices would lead almost inevitably to new conceptions, very possibly requiring new terminology, which, at best, could scarcely invite immediate and unanimous approval.

There was no possibility of testing this suspicion by assembling our collaborators, most of whom, at that date, were scattered far and wide, some in the Far East. A symposium was out of the question. And so it was decided that, rather than run the risk of publishing theories to which many of the staff could not subscribe, it would be better to curb ambition, scrap our speculations, and resign ourselves to the more modest task of explaining the OSS system of assessment on a relatively concrete level and then, possibly, of setting down a few of the assumptions about personality on the basis of which our procedures could be rationalized. This chapter is our attempt to do just this and no more.

The scheme employed by us might be called the multiform organismic system of assessment: "multiform" because it consists of a rather large number of procedures based on different principles, and "organismic" (or "Gestalt," or "holistic") because it utilized the data obtained through these procedures for attempting to arrive at a picture of personality as a whole; i.e., at the organization of the essential dynamic features of the individual. The knowledge of this organization serves as a basis both for understanding and for predicting the subject's specific behavior.

The system may be set forth most simply as a series of steps each of which is based on one or more psychological principles.

Every step described below is either one which was taken by us or one which would have been taken by us if conditions had permitted it.

At the end of the undertaking, a rigorous analysis of our results disclosed errors which could be attributed to methodological defects, for each of which reflection yielded remedies. These remedies are described in the last section (Recommendations) of Chapter X. Consequently, the reader must combine pertinent parts of this chapter and of the final chapter to obtain a full account of the guiding principles which we would advocate today.

Step 1.—*Make a preparatory analysis of all the jobs for which candidates are to be assessed.* This step, of course, is fundamental, since it is impossible to predict whether a given person, no matter how accurately his skills are estimated, is suitable for a job of an unknown nature. To state this more generally, it is impossible to predict whether one thing, A, which is present and open to measurement, will fit another thing, B, which is absent, if the dimensions of B are not known.

As explained in Chapter I, this most important first step in an assessment program could not be achieved, except to a slight extent, in setting up the OSS screening process. Furthermore, we were unable to recruit, as members of the assessment staff, men who had had military experience overseas of such a nature as would equip them to judge, without the benefit of job analyses, the suitability of candidates for OSS assignments. Therefore, as already described, our conceptions of the various jobs were products of our imaginations working with the few facts that were supplied by branch chiefs, their administrative officers, and other administrators in Washington.

Inasmuch as the duties of the OSS assessment staff did not include the measurement of a hundred and one highly technical skills, analyses of the latter were not required. Hence, in this respect, our task was less inclusive and exacting than that of other selection agencies.

At the time of the initiation of the program the members of the staff did not realize how thoroughly this first step, or principle, should be applied in order to justify a scientific system of assessment. They did not realize that besides obtaining (1) a functional analysis of each role and (2) an analysis of each of the physical and social environments in which these roles would have to be performed, it was necessary to design, at the very start, a satisfactory system of appraisal (validation), which would include (3) a scale for theater ratings of effectiveness in the performance of each function. The members of the staff, at this early date, did not distinctly see that the actual target of their undertaking, the standard against which their efforts would eventually be evaluated, was the worth of each man as rated, not by an ideal omniscient judge, but by his all too human associates. For scientific assessments it is necessary to determine, first of all, the range of functional effectiveness and of general conduct that is acceptable to the administrators of the organization to be served, and, also, an account of all the factors which may operate to put a man outside the range of acceptability. Since the OSS staff did not take these steps, the description of them will be postponed until Chapter X (Recommendation 2).

The psychological principle underlying Step 1 may be stated as follows: a large proportion of the determinants of the direction and efficiency of a person's behavior consists of components of the environmental situation; therefore, the more precise and complete the definition of the environment, the more accurate will be the predictions of behavior. Among the chief components of the environment are the institutional expectations in respect to the role-functions which the individual has had assigned to him.

Step 2.—*On the basis of the preparatory analysis of jobs, list all the personality determinants of success or failure in the performance of each job; and from this list select the variables to be measured by the assessment process.* As explained earlier, the OSS staff was unable to follow this directive in any thoroughgoing fashion. In the first place it was agreed that it was not possible for the assessment staff at any one station to test suitability for the great variety of highly technical functions embraced by the OSS (e.g. piloting an airplane, parachuting, translating Albanian, drawing posters to influence Germans, setting Japanese type, and so on); hence the measurement of such very specific factors was not included among the responsibilities of our staff. In the second place, we did not obtain sufficient information about the less special functions and about the conditions in the different theaters to enable us to discover most of the nontechnical determinants of success or failure. Finally, even if we had secured the required information, passing judgment on a candidate according to his apparent suitability for a specific assignment turned out, in a large proportion of cases, to be more or less irrelevant, since the job that was assigned to him in the theater was different from the one proposed for him in Washington.

For these and other reasons it was decided at the start that we should assess each man not primarily in relation to our conception, such as it was, of a special designated assignment, but in relation to a cluster of general qualifications (dispositions, abilities, traits) which were essential to the effective performance of almost every OSS job overseas. Before Station S was opened, in fact, one of the members of the staff (Lieutenant Gardner), by interviewing various branch chiefs and their administrative officers, obtained what seemed the next best thing to job descriptions—a list of abilities and qualities which these officers considered necessary for the accomplishment of the projects planned by their section. At the end of this inquiry we had a sizable array of requirements which could be abbreviated without much distortion by resolving differences in terminology and by combining related factors under a single term. For the first five months we worked with a list of about twenty variables, some of which, as time passed, had their hair trimmed, their beards shaved, and their names changed. At the end of this period we succeeded in combining these into the following seven major variables (basic to the needs of OSS):

1) *Motivation for Assignment:* war morale, interest in proposed job.

2) *Energy and Initiative:* activity level, zest, effort, initiative.

3) *Effective Intelligence:* ability to select strategic goals and the most efficient means of attaining them; quick practical thought—resourcefulness, originality, good judgment—in dealing with things, people, or ideas.

4) *Emotional Stability:* ability to govern disturbing emotions, steadiness and endurance under pressure, snafu tolerance, freedom from neurotic tendencies.

5) *Social Relations:* ability to get along well with other people, good will, team play, tact, freedom from disturbing prejudices, freedom from annoying traits.

6) *Leadership:* social initiative, ability to evoke cooperation, organizing and administering ability, acceptance of responsibility.

7) *Security:* ability to keep secrets; caution, discretion, ability to bluff and to mislead.

Such were the *general qualifications* for all OSS men and women (leadership excepted in some cases). Distinguished from these were the *special qualifications* applicable for the most part to the undertakings of one or two branches only. Of these, three were added to the list of general qualifications printed on the formal report sheet:

8) *Physical Ability:* agility, daring, ruggedness, stamina.

9) *Observing and Reporting:* ability to observe and to remember accurately significant facts and their relations, to evaluate information, to report succinctly.

10) *Propaganda Skills:* ability to apperceive the psychological vulnerabilities of the enemy; to devise subversive techniques of one sort or another; to speak, write, or draw persuasively.

Besides these there were a few abilities (Teaching Ability, Recruiting Ability, for instance) which were measured in special cases and an indefinite number of variables used in writing sketches of the candidates' personalities, which were not included in the formal list, either because they were too specific (pertinent to a few jobs only), or because they were not readily measurable in all candidates under the conditions set up at S and at W.

For the last three months of its twenty months' service, the assessment staff, besides rating the seven general variables mentioned above, assessed the suitability of every candidate for each of three locations in the theater (relative to the front), for each of three levels of authority, and for each of ten job categories. This seemed to be the only way of partially solving two of our most vexing problems: how to record (for later evaluation) our estimates of a candidate's fitness for jobs other than the one proposed for him in Washington, and how to transmit judgments that would help in the reassignment of a candidate in the theater.

One might almost say, exaggerating a little, that in the OSS the conventional role of the administrator and the role of the technical expert were reversed. Commonly it is an administrator who passes on the general suitability of a candidate in respect to personal appearance, energy, temperament, interest in the job, likability, tact, cooperativeness, leadership qualities, and so forth; and it is the personnel psychologist who classifies him according to his special talents. In the OSS, on the other hand, it was the recruiting officers and the administrative officers who decided (on the basis of work history and other data) whether a candidate had the required technical proficiency and it was the professional assessment staff that passed on his general social qualifications, his mental health, and his power to abstain from actions which might bring discredit to the organization.

Step 3.—*Define (in words that are intelligible to the personnel officers and administrators of the organization) a rating scale for each of the personality variables on the selected list as well as for the one over-all variable Job Fitness.* The members of the OSS staff found a six-point rating scale well suited to their purpose:

0	1	2	3	4	5
Very Inferior	Inferior	Low Average	High Average	Superior	Very Superior
7%	18%	25%	25%	18%	7%

The percentages indicate the proportion of men that would fall in each category if the variable in question happened to be normally distributed in the candidate population. One of the advantages of this scale is that it can easily be converted into a two-point, three-point, or four-point scale, or, by using pluses and minuses in marking, into an eighteen-point scale (in practice a sixteen-point scale, since the extreme ratings 0— and 5+ are rarely used). By combining the lower two categories and the upper two categories, the six-point scale becomes a four-point scale, which, according to our experience, is the most useful one in obtaining ratings from nonprofessionals (other members of the organization):

1	2	3	4
Inferior Unsatisfactory	Low Average Satisfactory	High Average Very Satisfactory	Superior Outstanding

All this is explained at greater length in Chapter X (Recommendation 2.4 and Recommendation 3).

Rating variables is an exceedingly crude and abstract mode of representing certain realities of personality; but it is a useful and defensible procedure notwithstanding. It serves to focus the attention of the assessors on the most crucial components and to force them to make repeated attempts to justify their ratings by recalling concrete samples of behavior. It provides a rough summary of a large number of judgments which assists the staff in arriving at a final assessment. It transmutes clinical observations into the only form which can be handled statistically. Finally, it constitutes a brief and intelligible mode of communicating estimates and predictions to the officers of the institution. The errors to which abstract symbols of this sort are liable to give rise may be corrected to some extent by combining them with a more concrete personality sketch which describes the interactions of the rated variables and their characteristic manifestations under varying conditions.

The unsatisfactoriness of variables that are as general and ambiguous as those used by OSS assessment units can be reduced to some extent by listing under each heading, as we did, several more specific modes of behavior which may be regarded either as components or as criteria of the variable. Thus under Emotional Stability we included adaptability, maturity, steadiness under pressure, snafu tolerance, freedom from neurotic symptoms. We made a practice of underlining on the final report sheet the subvariables which were considered strong and crossing out those which were considered weak.

The rating techniques employed by the OSS staff are described in Chapter V.

Step 4.—*Design a program of assessment procedures which will reveal the strength of the selected variables.*

Substep 4.1.—*Plant the assessment procedures within a social matrix composed of staff and candidates.* Our experience shows that it is not difficult to create an informal, sincerely genial atmosphere at the assessment station and that under these conditions most of the assessees will enjoy themselves and be more inclined to tolerate an exacting and stressful schedule of procedures than they would be in a less agreeable social climate; and also under these conditions they will be disposed to relax during the times when they are not engaged in assigned tasks and conduct themselves somewhat as they would in everyday life. Further, our experience shows that the staff can acquire invaluable impressions of the candidates during these hours of relaxation: from a wisecrack overheard in the hall, from a heated conversation at dinner, from the way a clique forms in the living room, from the gesture with which a man reacts to defeat in a game of bridge, from a breakfast-table report of the sleeping behavior of one of the candidates, from frank comments on the testing procedures elicited during a casual conversation after supper, from sentiments privately expressed while taking a snack in the kitchen before going to bed, and so forth. When the candidates live and eat with the staff members for two or three days, the situation has some of the flavor of a house party, and consequently the offering of liquor on the last evening comes within the range of habitual expectations and is not often interpreted as a stratagem to entangle the unwary.

It is hard to get to know a man merely by observing him behave in a controlled situation. Impressions obtained at such times require complementation and reinforcement by others gained from numerous casual contacts at moments when the candidate is less guardedly aware that his actions are under scrutiny. Also, in the process of developing a conception of the man's character it is advantageous to have him under the same roof so that he will be repeatedly seen in the ordinary course of events, and can, when necessary, be engaged, as if off-handedly, in conversation.

Furthermore, if the candidates live for several days together and suffer the same trials and frustrations, and together laugh at the same humorous incidents, the majority become welded, even in this short space of time, into a mutually sympathetic whole, and on leaving, each man—with some exceptions, naturally—carries with him a favorable opinion of the assessment process which has become solidified in his mind by the consensus of the group. It was found, for example, that the "graduates" of the three-day system at S were decidedly more enthusiastic about the merits of assessment than were the "graduates" of the one-day system at W, who had little chance to develop mutuality of feeling. Thus if it happens to be necessary to convince the members of an organization of the value of assessment procedures, the living-together system as practiced at Station S can be highly recommended. Finally, under "house party" conditions the candidates have numerous opportunities to size each other up, and, therefore, more reliance can be placed on the returns of a sociometric test which may advisedly be scheduled as the last procedure on the program.

Substep 4.2.—*Select several different types of procedures and several procedures of the same type for estimating the strength of each variable.* In the *ideal* assessment program there will be *numerous* procedures for predicting the strength of *each* variable, since experience has shown that no single test has a very high degree of validity. These procedures will be of different types (e.g., interview method, questionnaire method, situational method) because each type (method) has certain specific advantages as well as specific disadvantages. Some subjects are better revealed by one method, others by another. Finally, each method will be represented by several different procedures (varieties of the same method), since no one operation of personality can be taken as a valid index of what an individual will or can do in dealing with situations of a certain type. It is necessary to know the degree of consistency of a personality.

At Station S, for example, the variable Social Relations (disposition and ability to get along with others) was revealed by six different methods:

1) Interview.

2) Informal observations through three-day period.

3) Individual task situations, where the single candidate was faced by the necessity of dealing with one or more persons (sometimes stooges) in achieving his end.

4) Group task situations, where a team of candidates was instructed to cooperate in performing a prescribed task.

5) Projection tests which revealed some of the inhibited or unconscious social tendencies of the candidates.

6) Sociometric questionnaire in which the candidate's acceptance or rejection by his fellow candidates was estimated.

Furthermore, several of these methods were represented by two or three different procedures. For instance, there were three individual task situations:

3a) *Construction Test*, in which the candidate had to direct two recalcitrant "assistants" (stooges) in helping him to erect a wooden structure within a given length of time.

3b) *Recruiting Test*, in which the candidate had to interview a person (stooge) applying for a position in a secret organization.

3c) *Improvisations*, where two candidates had to deal with each other in a face-to-face situation of a prescribed character.

The multiform method of examination does not require ten or twelve times as many procedures as there are variables, because many procedures yield ratings on several different factors. Almost every factor, for instance, can be roughly estimated on the basis of an interview. Or, to take another example, one questionnaire can be constructed which lists every condition that is likely to be encountered in the field and which asks the subject to estimate the positive or negative appeal of each of these for him.

Underlying our recommendation for the inclusion of *many varied* procedures is the well-accepted fact that in order to formulate a personality one must know many of its components, and therefore, since in a single event only a relatively few components are exhibited, the more events of which we have accurate reports the better. Also, since a man reacts differently to different situations, we need reports of a wide variety of events in which the subject has participated. As a rule, the more varied the situations, the more varied will be the components of personality which are evoked. The conclusion is obvious: to arrive at a conception of the different systems and different resources of a man's personality, one must discover his emotional responses to, and his effectiveness in dealing with, *different kinds* of situations.

Finally, it is necessary to ascertain how the subject reacts to various situations of the *same kind*, since no man is entirely consistent. As a rule, each need or system of a personality is characterized by an area of generality (a large number of situations which evoke similar patterns of response) and a few foci of specificity (a small number of situations which evoke contrasting patterns). There are some people, for example, who are generally timid —that is, they have a high degree of sensitivity to most of the different varieties of danger—and yet they are fearless in certain situations which frighten many of their associates. Contrariwise, there are other people who are not sensitive to most dangers but suffer from a single intense phobia. Thus we require several procedures to discover the consistencies and inconsistencies of each reaction system of the personality. The same applies in the sphere of abilities.

In an ideal assessment program the candidate's ability to perform (or to learn to perform) each of the several functions of a given role would be estimated separately, since it cannot be assumed that excellence in one function is highly correlated, in a given individual, with excellence in another. Furthermore, since no function (disposition and ability) can be accurately measured by a single test, a battery of tests is required to provide a sound basis for predictions.

In obtaining records of *many varied* proceedings of a personality, members of an assessment staff have three sources available: (1) the subject himself, who can be encouraged to talk or to write about his past experiences; (2) acquaintances of the subject; (3) the assessors, who create many varied situations the responses to which can be observed directly. No explanation of all this is required; it is clear that the more one knows about a man the more comprehensive will be one's understanding of his unique nature.

If it is discovered that an increase in the number of procedures (length of the assessment period) is not accompanied by an increase in the amount of pertinent data obtained, or that an increase in the amount of pertinent data is not accompanied by greater accuracy and completeness of the personality formulations, then one should suspect the intrusion of errors in theory or in practice. This point will be discussed in Chapter X.

We are recommending a variety of methods, not only because each method, by confronting the subject with a somewhat different situation, is likely to evoke different components of personality, but because each method which merits consideration has certain unique advantages and disadvantages, and the disadvantages of one method may be overcome by the advantages of another. For instance, a method may be very economical—it can be administered by one man to a large group of subjects at once—but the whole situation may be artificial, unlike anything which the subjects are apt to meet in everyday life, and their actions may be artificially constrained to a few preselected categories which allow no place for typical individual patterns of response. Other contrasting methods present the subject with a lifelike situation permissive of spontaneity, but are very expensive in man-hours—subjects must be taken one at a time or in small groups requiring two or three observers. Some methods yield objective, mechanically obtained quantitative scores, but the relation between the segmental processes so measured and the functioning of the total personality is dubious, if not definitely insignificant. Other methods bring important components of personality into operation, but estimates of the intensity of these components are matters of unreliable subjective judgments. And so it goes.

A brief list of some of the ways in which techniques may vary should be helpful at this point:

1) *The kinds of components of personality that are revealed,* such as energy level, temperament, sentiments, knowledge, theories, needs, con-

crete goals, degree of integration, ability to deal with things, with people, with ideas, and so forth.

2) *The components and structure of the situation confronting the subject.*

a) *Physical setting:* outdoor or indoor; open or confined space; degree of temperature and light; and so on.

b) *Nature of objects to which subject must relate his efforts:* physical obstacles to be overcome; physical objects (materials, tools, gadgets) to be manipulated; human objects (interviewer, stooges, co-actors) to govern or adjust to; symbols (oral or written words or concepts, pictures, ink blots, or other representations) and areas of symbolic reference (topics of discourse and knowledge) to be dealt with.

c) *Social structure:* number, roles, types, and attitudes of persons engaged in the situation.

i) *Number, roles, types, and attitudes of assessors:* physical presence or absence of official observer (if absent, whether a recording device or system of mirrors which permits overhearing or overseeing is suspected); number of assessors (e.g., interpersonal interview or board of judges); physique, age, sex, rank, race, type of assessor(s) (e.g., conspicuous or inconspicuous, detached or participating, formal or informal, strict or lenient, friendly or unfriendly).

ii) *Number, roles, types, and attitudes of other subjects:* presence or absence of other subjects; an interpersonal or group situation; a mere aggregate (e.g., sitting at separate desks) or a reciprocating or collaborating group; physique, age, sex, rank, race, type of other subjects; attitude of others (e.g., friendly or not, helpful or not, critical or not).

d) *Expectations of assessor(s) as understood by subject:* number of directions (rules) or no directions; degree of constraint of directions (e.g., formal or informal, strict or lenient, definite or ambiguous). The assessor says or seems to say (according as subject interprets his aim) one, two, or all of three things: "Show me how much you know or how well you can do this" (performance test), or "Let me see how you react (emotionally or directionally) to this situation" (reaction study), or "Tell me all (or all I want to know) about yourself" (self-communicative situation).

e) *Degree of situational control exercised by assessor(s):* extent to which the situation is made to conform to an inflexible, uniform, prearranged pattern (e.g., an entirely uncontrolled natural situation at one extreme and, at the other, a situation in which all variables are kept constant).

3) *The method of recording subject's behavior.* Reliance may be placed on the assessor's unaided observation and memory, or recording aids (e.g., motion-picture camera with sound track) may be employed. In a great many procedures the subject records his responses on a paper form; in others his responses are recorded mechanically (e.g., psychogalvanometer).

Clinical psychology and psychiatry have yet to reach their full growth. No methods are entirely satisfactory. There must be constant experimentation. Since it is too early to limit a program of assessment to a fixed number of procedures, space should be left open for new techniques.

For a short over-all assessment the interview is probably the best and only indispensable method we have, but many others are very useful: intelligence tests (Bellevue-Wechsler, Mechanical Comprehension, and others), projective tests (Rorschach, TAT, Sentence Completion, for example), questionnaires (e.g., psychosomatic inventory, attitude scales, Study of Values, Minnesota Multiphasic), autobiography (or filling out a personal history form), informal observations of behavior, and situational tests. Since the last are not well known and need to have attention called to them, we are making a separate recommendation in their behalf.

Substep 4.3.—*Include in the program a number of situational tests in which the candidate is required to function at the same level of integration and under somewhat similar conditions as he will be expected to function under in the field.* This is based on the principle of consistency (the most fundamental of scientific assumptions), which states that the interactions that occur in two identical situations will be identical, or more specifically, that a given subject will respond to similar environmental situations in a similar manner. Of course we know that the personality of one man at two different times is never the same, and that one can rarely say that two situations are identical, and finally that there seems to be a force (which might be called the need for novelty) in some people that prompts them to act differently from the way they did before "just for a change." And then, as far as assessment is concerned, it is not possible to predict the forms of the scores of situations a candidate will encounter in the future; consequently strict conformity to the scientific ideal is out of the question. The best that can be done—and this is a good deal—is to expose a man to a *variety of situations of the same type as those he will meet in the field* and, allowing for certain expected developments in his personality during the coming months, predict future performance level on the assumption of consistency.

All we are affirming here is that the "real" test of a football player is playing in a real football game, or, if you choose, in a season of football games; and therefore the best way to assess a football player is to confront him with the necessity of playing in a simulated football game which includes as many components of a real game as possible. This assumption, a commonplace to laymen, is not without novelty in the field of psychological testing. It is fundamental, however, to the organismic method as distinguished from the widely accepted elementalistic method of assessment—a statement which calls for an explanation.

The organismic method of assessment is based on the fact that behavior of the highest order of effectiveness depends on (1) the individual's ability to perceive and interpret properly the whole situation that confronts him (e.g., to distinguish the major and minor determinants, to omit nothing that is critically important, to predict the probable course of events if he does not intervene) and (2) his ability to coordinate his acts and direct them in proper sequence toward the proper objects (to visualize the end that will appease his needs, to see the shortest pathways to this end and the agencies that are available to him, and to order the spatio-temporal sequence of his actions, and so on) in such a way that a satisfying effect will be produced. Ordinarily the majority of these processes occur automatically, many of them unconsciously, but, in any event, they all require *organization*: the organization of successive perceptions into a rough schema of the developing event; the organization of images, words, and concepts in relation to this schema to constitute its diagnosis and prognosis; the organization of this prognosis in relation to a visualized purpose (images of a desired modification); the organization of actones (muscles and words) and of agencies (instruments and fellow workers); the organization of these means in relation to the environmental objects that must be adjusted to, interested, or controlled; and then, finally, the organization of these partial or subordinate aims in relation to the visualized purpose. The effectiveness of the whole action depends on the integration (internal coherence) of the constituent operations in the brain and on the adjustment (congruent application) of these operations to successive parts of the environment. Consequently, in devising tests of effectiveness the organismic psychologist will choose tasks and situations which cannot be properly solved without organization, since it is the power to organize, as much as any other power, that he wishes to measure.

The elementalistic approach, on the other hand, calls for an analysis of a proposed function into its component operations and then the invention and standardization of one or more tests for each operation. Some of these tests can be administered to many subjects at once, others must be administered individually.

The elementalistic method is abstract and unrealistic, since no attempt is made to reproduce the conditions under which the man will eventually perform. It is scientific, however, in the sense that each test measures the goodness and speed of a well-defined process in objective quantitative terms, thus eliminating from the scoring the all too frequent errors inherent in subjective judgments. In adopting this method, however, the psychologist makes a radical subjective judgment at the very start by electing to abstract from a complex configurated process a few elementary constituent processes, testing for these separately, and then *adding* the scores to arrive at a final rating. He does this even though he knows that in actual life the mind does not *add* sequences of elementary processes to produce results, but *organizes* them into effective forms.

The organismic method depends for its success upon the ability of the psychologist to observe the pattern and effectiveness of the candidate's behavior and to identify the factors which promote and the factors which impede the forward course of the action. And so it could be said that this method calls for the improvement of the psychologist as observer and interpreter rather than the improvement of mechanical instruments and test materials. Because of the well-known unreliability of individual judgments, the organismic method as it stands today requires two or three competent observers for each event. Thus it is much more expensive in respect to time and personnel than elementalistic tests, many of which are suitable for large groups.

Leaving aside the great factor of motivation and considering only the nature of good thinking—the over-all importance of organization and of imagination—and the conditions under which it must ordinarily proceed, in contact with men and under stress, it must be clear that an elementalistic intelligence test could not possibly be an adequate measure of effective intellection, even of abstract intellection, in an adult member of society. What the intelligence test certainly can do is to distinguish those who lack the pieces with which to build the whole, who are incapable of the partial comprehensions that are necessary for a total act of comprehension. In doing this efficiently, the classic intelligence test has proved itself a useful instrument and deserves to be retained. But it is necessary to recognize its limitations since great injustice can be done to individuals if the test is used as a criterion of thinking capacity among those whose scores range above a certain level.

The striking and impressive feature of all elementalistic methods is that they provide quantitative objective measures of relatively simple processes, and thus seem to conform to the great tradition of science. An elementalistic testing program can be made into a series of almost mechanical procedures which can be conducted for the most part by technicians pure and simple, and the psychologist as observer, interpreter, diagnostician, and valuator is all but eliminated. Everyone who scores the tests gets precisely the same result and this gives rise to a general feeling of satisfaction, a feeling of "truth," since consensus among experts is the nearest we can ever get to justified certainty. But suppose a biologist comes along and says: "Gentlemen, I am impressed by the unanimity of your judgments. I can see no evidence of subjective bias in your readings, scorings, and computations. But on the other hand, it seems to me that subjective bias figured prominently in your decision to separate out one fraction of the concrete complex event and accept the measurement of this as a proper index of the total process. There, at the very start, is where the personal element—the feeling and the sentiment—entered into your procedure. As I see it, this focalization is an example of what Whitehead calls 'misplaced concreteness.' Actually the score that you have obtained on this test is not a representation of reality —any more than the measurement of one muscle contraction is an adequate representation of the form and effectiveness of a complete bodily movement, the act, let us say, of driving a golf ball." This judgment, it seems to us, cannot be gainsaid. The subjectivity of the elementalist comes in at the beginning when he plans his procedure, and at the very end when, despite protestations to the contrary, he is inclined to rely on his test as a valid measure of over-all ability.

The elementalistic approach calls for accurate quantitative measurements of partial, isolated processes, whereas the organismic approach comes down to inaccurate estimations of total integrated processes. From a practical standpoint the question is, Which method has a higher predictive validity? At the moment this question cannot be answered, no adequate researches bearing on this point having been reported. The result of an investigation along these lines will depend in large measure on which areas of personality are chosen for study, on the suitability of the elementalistic tests that are selected, and on the ability of the organismic psychologists who act as observers. At present the great advantages of elementalistic methods are (1) that they can be administered by almost anyone after a short training period; (2) that many of them can be presented to a large group at one time or to individuals in rapid succession, and hence are suitable for mass testing; (3) that they are generally successful in picking out those who are entirely unqualified for a certain task, or those who have some definite defect; and (4) that subjective bias does not enter into the scoring of the results. Furthermore, elementalists can point to positive correlations in a large number of studies to prove the effectiveness of their methods, whereas organicists have as yet nothing definite to show for their theories.

The differences between elementalistic and organismic methodology have been magnified in this section in order to clarify the theoretical ground on which situational tests are founded. The OSS assessment staffs were faced by the problem of discriminating between candidates who fell, for the most part, in the upper half of the distribution curve of general competence or of some special skill, men who had been recruited because of demonstrated ability in some particular field of endeavor. Consequently, elementalistic tests which had proved valid in testing children and in distinguishing adults at the lower end of the distribution curve, but not in accurately predicting different degrees of excellence among adults in the upper brackets, could not be counted on to carry the whole burden of answering the questions that were asked of us. Therefore we added procedures of a different kind, tasks which required mental operations on a higher integrative level; and since there is a difference between "know-how" and "can-do"—the two are not always correlated—we made the candidates actually attempt the tasks with their muscles or spoken words, rather than merely indicate on paper how the tasks could be done. We were prompted to introduce realistic tests of ability by such findings as this: that men who earn a high score in Mechanical Comprehension, a paper-and-pencil test, may be below average when it comes to solving mechanical problems with their hands. Furthermore, because a great deal of the work of the world must be accomplished in a social context and also because the OSS staff was expected to estimate every candidate's disposition and aptitude for harmonious social relations, a good many of the tasks which we devised for the candidates had to be accomplished in collaboration with others. Finally, since most of the critical situations which were confronting the majority of OSS men in the field were both novel and stressful, we made our testing situations novel and stressful. Thus it may be said that the situational tests used at OSS assessment stations were as lifelike as circumstances permitted, incorporating some of the major components of situations that would naturally arise in the course of operations in the field. In other words, we tried to design assessment situations that would be somewhat similar to the situations in the management of which candidates would be judged by their superior officers and associates in the theater.

In retrospect it seems a little peculiar that for thirty years we psychologists should have devoted so much time to improving the reliability of our tests and so little time to improving their validity. Even more peculiar is the almost exclusive attention to paper-and-pencil tests when the results of studies of the reliability of these tests were all pointing to the importance of the principle of similarity—similar situation, similar response. Time and time again test constructors have found that to obtain a high correlation between two tests of the same function, the forms of the tests must be very similar. For some reason, however, the principle of similarity has rarely been applied to the primary task of test invention. Few people seem to have been at all disquieted by the fact that taking a conventional paper-and-pencil test is very different from solving a problem in everyday life. Finally, as previously stated, all of us have been lax in bringing our critical reflections and techniques to bear on the crucial task of validation. Surely, the essential criterion of a good test is its congruence with reality; its coherence with other tests is a matter of secondary concern. At this stage, in fact, the problem of validity is so important that we would suggest a reversal of the usual procedure: that tests which are being developed should be administered only to persons who have been thoroughly studied, persons about whose activities sufficient data have already been collected.

Situational tests have a long and honorable pedigree that reaches back into Biblical times, and if American psychologists were as pious as the early settlers of their country they would undoubtedly have come upon the records of these ancient experiments and recast them into modern forms. It was none other than Jehovah who improvised the first large-scale

situational test, the object being to provide Gideon with a reliable basis
for picking the best warriors from among ten thousand volunteers.

And the Lord said unto Gideon, The people are yet too many; bring them
down unto the water, and I will try them for thee there: and it shall be, that
of whom I say unto thee, This shall go with thee, the same shall go with thee;
and of whomsoever I say unto thee, This shall not go with thee, the same shall
not go. So he brought down the people unto the water: and the Lord said
unto Gideon, Everyone that lappeth of the water with his tongue, as a dog
lappeth, him shalt thou set by himself; likewise every one that boweth down
upon his knees to drink. And the number of them that lapped, putting their
hand to their mouth, were three hundred men; but all the rest of the people
bowed down upon their knees to drink water. And the Lord said unto Gideon,
By the three hundred men that lapped will I save you, and deliver the Midianites
into thine hand: and let all the other people go every man unto his place.
(Judges 7: 4-7)

As proof of the efficacy of this test is the recorded fact that the three hundred put to rout the host of Midian, drove them across the Jordan and out
of the land of Israel. There was no mention of cowards among the three
hundred, who even while drinking had remained alertly aware of the possibility of being attacked by the enemy.

Step 5.—*Construct a sufficient formulation of the personality of each
assessee before making specific ratings, predictions, and recommendations.* This is the second of the two major technical principles of the
organismic system of assessment. Like the first major principle (Substep
4.3), it is derived from the general proposition that the whole and its parts
are mutually dependent. If this is true—and, today, who doubts it?—it follows that to explain or to predict the manifested parts of a personality
in a specified situation one must discover the nature of the personality
as a whole. Although the expression "personality as a whole" has become
fashionable in certain professional circles, it has never been precisely defined
and the best we can do, as we proceed, is to explain what we mean by it in
the context of this section.

Let us start by placing personality in space. Where is it? The processes
and integrations of processes which constitute personality *occur in the brain.*
This is the seat of the government of the organism, since it is the only
place where sensory processes from the entire body terminate and motor
processes to the entire body originate. It is the locus of the feelings which
evaluate events as they occur and discriminate goals for action. It is the
seat of consciousness, of thought, of conflict, and of decision. It is also the
repository of all traces of past experiences, of percepts, symbols, concepts,
values, emotional attachments, commitments, plans, resolutions, and anticipa-

tions. Thus the enduring latent establishments as well as the kinetic processes of personality are in the head.

Next, let us place personality in time. What is the duration of personality? Personality is a developing "institution" which functions from birth to death. During sleep, unconscious anabolic processes regenerate the sources of the energies that are expended in the ceaseless activities which constitute its waking life. The history of a personality might be represented as a long sequence of *proceedings*. Some of these are *internal proceedings* during which the personality, abstracted from its environment, is daydreaming, or attempting to understand and evaluate past events, or to predict the future, or to assess its own capacities, or to settle some conflict, or to solve some intellectual problem, or to lay out a course of action, or to decide what to say on an anticipated occasion. Others are *external proceedings* during which the personality is overtly engaged in dealing with its environment, in observing, enjoying, manipulating, complying with, defending itself against, or avoiding, other personalities or physical objects. Every proceeding leaves behind it some traces of its occurrence, traces of its novel elements especially. In this manner the more or less enduring *establishments* of personality—its supplies of facts, concepts, values, action-patterns—are extended and modified from day to day by the results of its functional operations. Most personalities are developing along certain lines—by assimilations, differentiations, and integrations—throughout life, although in other respects they may be merely conserving what they have acquired, or perhaps losing it regressively. Anyhow, the establishments of personality, cross-sectionally considered at different points in its life history, are different.

Since we cannot observe the establishments of personality in the brain, and we have no instruments capable of directly recording its functional processes, and, since it has been shown that not all these processes have the property of consciousness, it is evident that the components and structures of personality *must be inferred* from their manifestations in the stream of consciousness and from their manifestations in the flow of overt speech and action. The data consist of *subjective facts* reported by the individual and of *objective facts* observed by the psychologist or by others. With these in mind the psychologist attempts to arrive at a conception of the forms of the determining variables. Thus the personality is not a series of perceptible facts, but, in actual practice, a *hypothetical formulation,* the aim of which is to *explain* and to *predict* the perceptible facts.

Another point which must be held firmly in mind is that in analyzing and reconstructing each of the significant external proceedings of personality, it is as necessary to define the structure of the environmental situation, the attitudes and actions of the object, as it is to define the attitudes and actions of the subject. One must not represent a personality as if it existed in a vacuum. Its establishments must be connected with the objects and situations

which evoke them. This is particularly true in formulating the developing series of proceedings, or the *serial*, which constitutes the history of an
interpersonal relationship, a friendship, or marriage: the representation of
the personality of the object is essential to an understanding of the subject.
In other words, although the processes of personality occur in the brain,
they cannot be described or explained without reference to external objects
and settings. Consequently, *the environment is included in every adequate
formulation of personality.*

Now, perhaps, we are in a position to consider the meaning of "whole"
as applied to personality. Some people use "whole personality" comprehensively to denote the total or entire personality. Here there are two
possibilities: the whole longitudinal, or temporal, personality, and the whole
cross-sectional personality. The former is relatively concrete and referential:
personality is the entire sequence of organized psychological processes in
the brain from birth to death. The cross-sectional definition, on the other
hand, is very abstract and hypothetical: personality is the entire constitution of *potential* psychological processes and structures in the brain at a
given moment. This latter definition depends on a morphological supposition inasmuch as it assumes the existence or some more or less enduring
physicochemical structures, or establishments of personality, which remain
dormant except when activated by certain stimuli. The establishments, however, are never described in morphological terms, but rather as they are
objectified in temporal patterns of activity. These two conceptions of the
"whole personality" might be combined into an all-inclusive notion which
embraces not only the history of the proceedings of personality (longitudinal view), but the history of its developing establishments as portrayed
by a series of cross-sectional formulations.

The next point to be noted is that a *complete* formulation of the *whole*
personality, longitudinal or cross-sectional, is not only far beyond the powers
of any group of psychologists today, but, if achievable, would be much too
long and complicated for ordinary use. Consequently, we speak of a *sufficient* formulation, meaning sufficient for a designated purpose, which, in
the present case, is the assessment of men and women. Inasmuch as a complete formulation is both impossible and undesirable, the term "formulation" can be used to denote a "sufficient formulation." Since a formulation
that is sufficient for one purpose—say, assessment—will not usually be sufficient for another—say, psychotherapy—there may be several different formulations of the same personality, all of which are correct. But, as we see it,
every formulation should give an outline, not of the "whole personality,"
but of the "personality as a whole."

"Personality as a whole" does not mean the whole, entire personality; it
means the over-all unity and organization of parts that is attained during
a designated period of the subject's life. It refers to the degree of unity

and coordination (wholeness) that the personality exhibits during one short functional operation, or in a long series of progressions, day after day, toward a distal goal, or in the establishment, over a lifetime, of a harmonious way of life which allows for the successive satisfaction of its major needs. Whatever the degree of unity that is achieved, it comes out of conflicts and resolutions of conflicts; and these should be included in the formulation. This conception of the "personality as a whole" points to a goal-directed force, or conation, as the chief unifying and integrating factor in personality. Psychologists are not yet agreed as to the proper representation of the basic determinants of effective action, but universal human experience teaches us that it is emotional, intellectual, and conative energy directed toward a defined *purpose* which organizes the psychological processes into a temporal whole. This is the outstanding *conscious* fact, regardless of the number and nature of the underlying needs or drives which will be appeased by the action. An extreme case of wholeness would be a personality that is completely controlled by one persisting, superordinate, long-range purpose. The definition of this purpose would be enough to explain most of the functional operations. Since in actual life one never finds a personality so unified, the representation of "wholeness" is more complicated. It usually comes down to a formulation of the relations between the major dynamic systems, each of which consists of a combination of needs directed toward a combination of goals, and, integrated with these, one or more valued goal objects and goal places, and a large number of action patterns and agencies. The degree of effectiveness of each dynamic system should be included in the account.

Beside vectorial forces there are a number of other variables which have a broadly determining, and so, in a sense, unifying, influence on the personality. Among these are energy level, temperament, subjectivity-objectivity, introversion-extraversion, egocentricity-sociocentricity, conformity-nonconformity, and so forth. But we are not going to discuss the problem of what variables are required for a sufficient formulation of personality, first, because there is no possibility of doing justice to the subject in the space allotted, and, second, because we abandoned the plan of attempting to set forth the products of our theoretical reflections, fearing, as explained in the first part of this chapter, that no statement would conform to the views of the majority of the members of our staff.

Up to now no proposed definition of personality has proved satisfactory to all schools of psychology, and there has been no unanimity as to how one should go about formulating the events of a person's life for purposes of explanation, prediction, and control. There are no available holistic conceptions for representing *normal* personalities. But the psychologist is not without instruments of thought. He possesses, in fact, a large number of fairly well-defined concepts which stand for (1) certain hypothetical structures of the personality (e.g., ego, superego, ideal ego); (2) certain hypothetical components (e.g., inferiority complex, sentiment *pro* underprivileged, agoraphobia, need for support, political orientation); (3) certain modes of feeling, thought and action (e.g., cycloid temperament, objectivity, flight of ideas, impulsivity); (4) certain kinds of effectiveness (e.g., general intelligence, mechanical ability); and also (5) certain disease entities (e.g., compulsion neurosis, schizophrenia). The latter might be considered holistic formulations in so far as each of them defines a rather large number of intercorrelated variables and (for each disease) the general structure of their interactions. But the compound concept of each disease reconstructs a certain variety of disturbance (conflict, dissociation, and so on) which occurs *within* a total personality. The effective health-producing processes of the personality, which vary from case to case, are not included in the formulation.

Besides concepts of this sort, there are excellent descriptions in the literature of rudimentary typologies based on a few variables, usually a dichotomy (e.g., subjective-objective, introversive-extratensive) or a trichotomy (e.g., narcistic, obsessive, and erotic). But all of these require further analysis in conjunction with studies of other variables. To identify a man as an introvert, for example, gives us no information as to his energy level, his fluctuations of mood, his enduring emotional attachments, his membership systems, his political ideology, the pattern of his erotic fantasies, the strength of his conscience, his major dilemmas, his intelligence, his initiative and resourcefulness, the degree of his self-confidence, his dominant aims, the level of his aspiration, his chief abilities, and a great many other important components. Psychiatrists and psychologists are just now in the process of identifying and defining these separable variables. They have not reached the point of attempting to combine a sufficient number of them into tentative formulations susceptible of verification by detailed personality studies. It is worthy of note that very many of the concepts which are commonly used today in formulating personalities have been contributed by psychoanalysts and psychiatrists who are inclined, partly by the demands of their profession, to an organismic frame of reference.

We shall make no attempt to list the notions which were most commonly employed in attempting to represent the personalities of the candidates at assessment. Since there was no time to construct a common conceptual scheme, each senior staff member whose duty it was to write personality sketches used the concepts which he considered most adequate in portraying to himself and to his fellow workers the underlying dynamics. Since the sketches were composed for laymen (the administrative officers of the OSS), they were not written in abstract terms, but on the level of ordinary discourse. These sketches were the only records that were made of the results of holistic reflections, and so it is not possible now to state how far toward "wholeness" the staff members carried their conceptualizations of the different personalities. The process which took place in their heads is not on paper. Certainly most of us never approximated the ideal: a formulation of the "personality as a whole." This expression, consequently, must be understood as a somewhat pretentious overstatement. But current usage provides no other term to distinguish our *attempt* from the elementalistic mode of procedure.

Here it is perhaps worth pointing out that the task of a present-day clinical student of psychology is that of an explorer and experimenter rather than that of a diagnostician. To make this plain we might consider a greatly oversimplified statement of the problem in the form of an analogy. Take the case of the organic chemist whose function is to predict the behavior of a sample of any compound that is handed to him. What will he do? He will note its physical properties and then observe its reactions to a number of known substances. The results of a few tests of this sort will usually enable him to name the substance and then to predict immediately the processes which will ensue when it is confronted by this and that compound under specified conditions. Now, one reason, among several, why the predictions of the chemist are highly valid is the fact that the properties of most of the objects with which he deals have been thoroughly studied, and so his routine task is that of distinguishing (naming) an entity about which there is a mass of ordered knowledge summarized in manuals and textbooks, rather than that of discovering the nature of an entity about which little or nothing is known. (The latter is the task of an experimental chemist.) Here it should be noted that knowledge about a compound is mostly contained in statements as to its chemical properties, that is, in representations of the nature and effect of its reactions with other *known* compounds under *known* conditions. In other words, to know (understand, formulate) a compound in "functional" terms, one must possess an equal amount of knowledge about (1) each of the different entities with which it reacts, (2) the product of each reaction, and (3) the setting in which the reaction occurs. One thing is defined in relation to each of a number of other things. Since about three hundred thousand compounds have been defined, the population of entities within the modern chemist's empire includes a great many "knowns"; and as soon as he has identified (named) one of them, he is prepared, with the manual at his side, to predict its behavior in the presence of each of a large number of others. The naturalist, with his definitions of thousands of different species, and the physician, with his integrated mental representations of scores of different ailments, are in a similar position, in so far as each is able to make a number of reasonably valid predictions (prognoses) as soon as he has correctly discriminated the entity before him. He can do this because, like the chemist, he has at his disposal a mass of scientific information—collected, sifted, correlated, and ordered by generations of workers—about most of the entities which belong within his province.

Now, for the moment, let us imagine a state of affairs which would enable a psychologist to function as does the chemist, the naturalist, and the physician. Let us suppose that the most fundamental and most crucial variables of personality have already been discovered, and, for simplicity's sake, say that these variables are dynamic systems, each of which involves a pattern of specified actions in relation to a pattern of specified situations. Let us suppose that millions of people have been thoroughly studied and it has been found that they fall into one thousand types, each of which has been properly defined and named. Let "definition of a type" be equivalent to "formulation of the personality as a whole." Since in the process of arriving at the different types (the thousand different conceptions), minor variables (slight differences in form and numerous insignificant elements) were necessarily disregarded, a formulation will not represent the "whole" (entire, complete) personality of a man, but his personality "as a whole"; that is, the organization of the dominant action systems. Let us further suppose that the lives of one hundred individuals corresponding to each of the thousand types have been exhaustively studied and there is now available a great deal of ordered knowledge about the behavioral variations within each type. According to this fantasy the psychologist is now in the position of a chemist, naturalist, or physician. His task is to make a diagnosis, to identify the type, to recognize an entity about which much is known. Since to accomplish this, a few tests will often be sufficient, it could be said that this fictitious professional, by discovering a little about a man, can suddenly know a lot—everything that has been written about the given type. With this knowledge he is able to predict with a reasonable degree of accuracy how he is likely to react and with what effect in this and that situation.

All this, of course, is a wish-fulfilling fairy tale. For no satisfactory formulation of a personality as a whole has ever been published. None of us knows exactly what elements should be included, or how the various inter-relationships, or patterns, of these elements should be represented. At present the psychologist is more in the position of a chemist who encounters an entirely new and different compound, except that he is not acquainted with all the elements that could possibly exist in the object of his interest, and he is not familiar with the consequences of different possible combinations of the elements with which he *is* acquainted. His task is not one of recognizing an old acquaintance (apperception), but of discovering the nature of a stranger (conceptualization).

We have violently oversimplified the contrasting situations of chemist and psychologist in the hope of clarifying the latter's job and of indicating a strategic course for research and reflection, namely, the development of a typology which incorporates a sufficient number of variables. Since the formulation of a type must be based on an understanding of the mode of *organization* of variables, the undertaking calls for an organismic, or holistic, approach. This is another reason why we are not enthusiastic about the elementalistic method of testing when dissociated from the study of each person functioning as a unit. The elementalistic statistical mode of advance may succeed in telling us what variables are commonly combined in one person, but, as yet, it cannot reveal the form in which they are combined.

At this stage in the development of our science, each conception of a personality is a compound of inferences, a product of the imagination, which must be verified by observations of behavior in the future. It is a conception which might be compared to a model of an extinct type of man constructed by a paleontologist, except that the paleontologist, having learned a good deal about the evolution of the human skeleton, is probably justified in making his rough reconstruction of the never observed whole body of a primitive man on the basis of one or two fragments—an unearthed jaw-bone, or even a single tooth. But if no entire human skeleton had ever been studied, the discovery of a few pieces of bone could hardly lead to a valid inference as to the total structure. One could not even "understand" the pieces. It would be necessary to collect a great many more fragments in order to build a rough model of the whole, and only then would it be possible to perceive the relations, and hence the meaning and significance, of the initially discovered parts.

This illustrates in a crude way one of the chief purposes of a conception of the whole: it provides ground for a reinterpretation and re-evaluation of the manifested parts, the very parts which led to the conception. Another analogy, though static, might serve to clarify this point. Suppose you were given only twenty (out of a total of two hundred) pieces of a jigsaw picture puzzle. If you tried to guess the meaning of each of these pieces isolated from the others, you might conclude that a particular light blue piece, for example, was a fragment of sky because 80 per cent of all light blue pieces in one thousand puzzles studied represented sky. But, on the other hand, if you examined all twenty pieces in relation to each other, it might become apparent that the light blue piece was probably not sky at all, but part of a woman's dress, since there was another piece which showed a light blue sleeve reaching to the wrist of a delicate bejeweled hand. Furthermore, several other pieces might clearly indicate that you were dealing with an indoor rather than an outdoor scene. Finally, if the twenty selected pieces came from critical areas of the picture, it might be possible for you to draw a rough hypothetical sketch of the whole design, many details being necessarily omitted. This hypothetical picture-as-a-whole would be analogous to one of the several meanings of the term "personality-as-a-whole."

The method we are supporting here is that of predicting the future by
thinking inductively from an observed set of facts to a conception (a
hypothetical formulation of the personality), and then by thinking de-
ductively from this conception to the facts which should be expected. In
contrast to this is the practice, common among those using testing techniques
today, of predicting the future by proceeding mechanically from the observed facts to the expected facts. To make this clear we shall once more call
to mind the elementalist, the fictional character portrayed in the previous
section, and exaggerate the differences between his methodology and that
of the organicist.

Let us assume that the task is to predict the rating of over-all effectiveness
which will be given a man after one year of vocational performances in a
specified environment. If the members of the assessment staff are elementalists, they will perform this task by administering a number of specific
tests which can be scored objectively and mechanically, and then, by combining in a formula the scores obtained by the candidate on the different
tests, calculate a quotient which will rigidly determine the prediction of
the future rating. Thus from relatively precise measures of a few performances the elementalist will directly and mechanically arrive at his
estimate, without the embarrassment of any intermediate process of thought.
The advantages of this method are considerable: (1) it is relatively quick,
because it eliminates interviewing as well as all reflection and discussion
as to the character and merits of each candidate; (2) because it is quick,
it permits the assessment of a relatively large number of candidates in a
given unit of time; (3) it is relatively cheap, because it is quick and because
suitable staff members can be engaged at a relatively low salary, since,
once the separate tests have been constructed, they can be administered
and scored by anyone capable of learning the simple technical rules; (4) it
can be employed on a large scale, because it is quick and cheap, and because it is possible to find a relatively large number of technicians with
sufficient ability to practice it; and, finally, (5) it eliminates the errors inherent in subjective judgments. If the elementalist is scrupulous about
validating each test against adequate criteria, he will discover, by trying
one test after another, which battery has the highest predictive value.

The organicist does, or should do, everything that the elementalist does;
but he does something in addition which takes time and thought: he carries
out a number of supplementary procedures (interviews, situational tests,
and so on), makes tentative interpretations of the facts so gained, and
attempts to arrive at a plausible representation of the personality as a whole.
The efficacy of this process in sizing up some kinds of cases, such as
neuropsychiatric disorders, is generally acknowledged, but its efficacy in
assessing the run of normal persons is still to be determined.

Organismic assessment is based on the hypothesis that a trained psychologist
or psychiatrist, with a fund of additional facts at his disposal, is, today,

capable of improving to a significant degree the accuracy of mechanical predictions derived from test scores alone. The truth of this hypothesis depends on the definition of "significant degree" as well as on (1) the competence of the psychiatrist or psychologist, (2) the number and kinds of procedures used for obtaining additional facts, (3) the time allowed for diagnosis and prognosis (the length of the assessment period), (4) the kinds of jobs which assessees will be expected to perform, (5) the adequacy of the psychologist's or psychiatrist's knowledge of these jobs; and so forth.

The second hypothesis made by the advocates of organismic assessment is that, whether the first hypothesis be true or false, the repeated practice of this system will result in developments of techniques and of the abilities involved in making dependable observations and judgments which together will eventually lead to a decided increase in the validity of predictions.

Finally, there is the supremely important point that the organismic system is an admirable way of studying personality and, if systematically pursued, should greatly advance the science of man, which, in turn will lead to practical knowledge, useful not only in the field of selection and placement, but in many other fields.

The organismic system is founded on several well-accepted facts, one of which is that the action patterns observed or the performances measured during the assessment period are not always representative of the candidate's usual behavior, because of the operation of transient factors or because some commonly recurrent variables of personality are either intentionally inhibited or not excited by any of the tests or situations constituting the program.

Among the transient factors which were often found to be operating at Station S are the following: (1) poor athletic condition (being out of training) as the result of months without exercise; (2) state of mental exhaustion when taking the tests on the first night as the result of a sleepless night on the train; (3) excessively high motivation because of the candidate's disposition to exert himself to the limit when competing in the presence of others (supervisors, critics, judges); (4) low motivation because of a candidate's transient underestimation of the proposed assignment or because of a doubt as to the suitableness of the job proposed for him. In addition to these are the disturbing preoccupations (overlapping situations) which the candidates bring with them—temporary worries about family and business affairs, and so forth.

Every assessee, on the other hand, will possess numerous established dispositions which will not be manifested during the assessment period, either because he is able to inhibit them over a period of a few days (e.g., neurotic tendencies, unacceptable sentiments, inclination to indolence, moodiness, or irritability), or because no situation excites them (e.g., fear of horseback riding, dislike of colored people, stubborn aversion to domineering leaders), or because there are no free time and no favorable conditions for their operation (e.g., alcoholism, pursuit of distracting and wholly personal aims).

These considerations have led organicists to the conclusion that additional procedures (e.g., autobiography, interviews, situational tests, psychodrama, projection tests) should be included in the assessment program in order to obtain the information necessary (1) for estimating the strength of other determining variables (besides those which are directly involved in vocational activities), and (2) for arriving at a sufficient formulation of the personality as a whole. These two aims are complementary, since the exposition and preliminary estimation of the additional variables (energy, motivation, emotional stability, social relations, and so on) are steps along the path to a formulation, and a formulation provides the framework for a final re-evaluation of these variables.

It was one of the noteworthy features of the OSS assessment system that it recognized explicitly the necessity of relating all observations to each other, not in a mechanical way, but by an interpretive process aiming at the discovery of general patterns and action systems, and made this the guiding principle of all its operations. At times a thoroughgoing application of this policy was blocked by the pressure of work which reduced to a minimum the time available for discussions and reflections. The discontent of the staff members with the results of their work at such times indicates that this phase of assessment was felt to be indispensable.

Not less noteworthy is the way in which this basic principle was implemented and at the same time guarded against subjective distortion, through group participation in all phases of the work. The policy of group discussion and group decision as distinct from a mere mechanical process of averaging scores or counting votes, presupposes the possibility of arriving, in a favorable case, at a common conception. Whenever this common conception succeeds in encompassing and integrating all the aspects of a personality noted by the different staff members it comes as near to the status of an objective judgment as it is possible to come under the given conditions.

Step 6.—*Write, in nontechnical language, a personality sketch of each assessee, which predictively describes him as a functioning member of the organization.* A list of ratings is an exceedingly abstract mode of representing a personality. It conveys no impression of the man in action. It does not show how the different variables are integrated into a purposive whole. It obliterates subtle characteristics which may be crucially important. Therefore, a personality sketch which incorporates the information that is not conveyable through ratings is an essential supplement to the latter. It is our conclusion, indeed, after canvassing the opinions of

OSS administrative officers, that the personality sketch is capable of communicating the more useful findings.

The personality sketch is a translation of the abstract formulation into everyday speech with the elimination of everything that is not relevant to the administrator's task of placement and management of personnel.

For the first few months the sketches written at Station S were very short—one or two paragraphs—but they increased in length as time went on, and for the last year of assessment averaged about eight hundred words each. Although the writers of these sketches were not bound to follow a rigid form, it became customary to start each sketch with an outline of the candidate's past history and record of achievement; to follow this with an account of his performances during the three-day period at Station S; and to end the sketch with a discussion of the interpretations and conclusions which led to the final recommendation.

A survey of these sketches has revealed two outstanding defects: space devoted to an array of uninterpreted facts and space devoted to the diagnosis of variables the relevance of which is not explained. In both cases the administrative officer is left to make up his own mind as to the meaning and significance of the findings.

To turn in a personality sketch composed entirely of accounts of the subject's behavior in a variety of situations is scientifically useless, if not harmful, unless it goes to an officer who is more talented and experienced than the assessor who made the observations. A fact is a fact, and as such provides no ground for a predictive judgment. In order to predict one must at least infer, implicitly or explicitly, that a persisting disposition or attribute of the personality lies behind the fact. It is the professional function of the psychologist to make inferences of this sort as well as to report the observations which justify them. In writing sketches for laymen, facts which do not justify inferences should be omitted, because the layman will certainly make his own inferences, automatically if not deliberately, and if these are unjustified, the decisions that flow from them may be unfortunate.

Most of the members of the staff were psychiatrists or clinical psychologists who had been trained to explore the minds of their subjects for memories of childhood events and to report their formulations of family structure, infantile dispositions and fantasies, unconscious complexes, and so forth. Naturally, they were inclined to proceed along the same lines in interviewing candidates at S and in writing their personality sketches. But in most instances we ourselves did not know to what extent, if any, these childhood situations and events were relevant to the administrator's task of placing and managing his men, and certainly the administrator himself could not be expected to make the legitimate deductions. Consequently, the inclusion of diagnoses of this order represented so much wasted time and space; and, by confusing the administrator, might occasionally have resulted in unwarranted decisions.

The ideal personality sketch is one which pictures the candidate in action, performing work similar to that which he will be expected to do in the future. It is, of course, the product of the assessor's subjective processes, of intuition and reason, but this is unavoidable at the present stage of psychology. So long as a subjective factor must operate in every decision that is made, it is better to bring it out into the open by making explicit predictions, each one of which is virtually a hypothesis which will be proved or disproved in the course of events.

At Station S the subjective factor was held in check by the collective effort of the staff. The sketch itself was the work of two assessors, who, though covering different phases of the personality, were obliged to arrive at conceptions acceptable to both. Then, the reading of the report in the staff conference, as we shall see, brought further checks. Each generalization had to be supported by sufficient evidence to make it plausible, and no generalization that seemed unwarranted or disregarded contradictory data was permitted to go unchallenged. Thus each personality sketch corresponded to the conclusions of several different minds.

Step 7.—*At the end of the assessment period hold a staff conference for the purpose of reviewing and correcting the personality sketch and of deciding on the ratings and recommendations of each assessee.* Our experience has shown that it is better to have the personality sketch written *before* the conference, so that it can be read at that time to the entire staff. One advantage of this practice is that the discussion of a case, instead of being random and diffuse, is focused on certain crucial points which have been high lighted, after some reflection, by the only assessor who is in possession of the intimate facts of the candidate's past history. Another and still greater advantage is that no personality sketch is incorporated in the official report and sent to the administrative officers which has not been approved by all the assessors.

According to this scheme, then, the personality sketch provides structure for the discussion, the purpose of which is to change or eliminate statements unjustified by the evidence, and, if necessary, to add other statements to cover manifestations of the personality which escaped the notice of the writer.

Our hypothesis is that individual judgments made *before* listening to a group discussion are generally less valid than individual judgments made *after* listening to a group discussion. The chief reason for this would seem to be that group discussion brings into each man's sphere of reflection more facts and more interpretations than were there before. Thus the errors that come from ignorance of all the available evidence and the errors that come from an inability to conceive of all plausible interpretations will be reduced. As a rule, those who abandon the decision they reached before discussion in favor of one proposed by another member of the group do so because the latter seems more valid to them. Certainly they are influenced, but they are influenced in the right direction more often than in the wrong direction, because, in general, those who are most competent in analyzing and reconstructing events, in distinguishing the chief determinants, are those whose presentations and arguments are most convincing.

There are a number of other factors, of course, besides sheer diagnostic ability, which play a part in determining to what extent a given assessor's judgments will be accepted or rejected: energy, desire to persuade, verbal facility, egocentricity, valuation of his own ideas, attitude toward the ideas of others, general social attitudes, reputation, role (in line of authority), popularity, and so forth. Also, a number of factors besides intelligence determine the extent to which a given assessor will accept the opinions of others: need for affiliation, dislike of controversy, suggestibility, negativism, obstinacy. Variables of this class may operate powerfully in some cases, as when a modest, able man is overshadowed by an aggressive one with less ability; but in a group of five or more, which is controlled in a democratic fashion, these factors become less significant as time goes on. The insightfulness of the unobtrusive man becomes recognized, and the force of the more assertive person is corrected for. Anyhow, there is a tendency for these determinants to balance out, leaving diagnostic ability as the chief factor in deciding the course of group opinion.

The other hypothesis on which the staff conference is founded is that the judgments of the majority are, in the long run, more valid than the judgments of any one member of a group, assuming that the disparity in ability among the members is not great. One can, of course, imagine a group composed of one incomparable genius and several bumptious ignoramuses who do not recognize his superiority, in which the judgment of the majority would be regularly less valid than the judgment of the talented individual, but a group of this order is confined, as far as we know, to the world of fantasy. Under certain circumstances, however, it may be advisable to leave final decisions to a diagnostic council composed of the more talented and experienced members of the staff.

Step 8.—*Construct experimental designs as frames for assessment procedures so that all the data necessary for the solution of strategic problems will be systematically obtained and recorded.* At this early stage in the development of psychology the evaluation of each technique, of the final ratings, and of the over-all conclusions should be considered an essential part of every assessment program. The efficacy of no psychological test is so well established that one can afford to continue using it without periodic checks. This means that a satisfactory *appraisal* system[1] must be devised for estimating the effectiveness of every accepted assessee after he has worked for a number of months as a member of the organization. The appraisal system must be devised and tested at the very start, because it defines the target at which all assessment procedures should be directed. If the target is not precisely discriminated, there will be no definite criteria for deciding which tests should be included in the original schedule. Since this important principle was not put into practice in inaugurating the assessment program, we shall postpone discussion of it until the last chapter.

Besides the evaluation of the different technical procedures there are many important psychological problems which can be illumined, if not solved, by a multiform organismic assessment program. But to accomplish this in a scientific manner it is necessary to set up an experimental design suitable to each problem. Consequently, before selecting the techniques and arranging the schedule, the members of the staff should decide which problems they will attack first. Here again it is a matter of delineating goals, so that means can be improvised for obtaining the necessary data and provisions made for tabulating them in an orderly manner. Since the solution of many of the problems will involve hundreds of statistical computations, and since it is desirable to know as soon as possible which tests are of little value in predicting appraisals of job performances, the practice of transferring the data onto punch cards at regular intervals can be highly recommended.

These are the chief points, or principles, of the OSS system of assessment. A few of them will be discussed at greater length in the last chapter, together with some further recommendations which we are submitting as remedies for obvious defects in the original system. The next chapters will describe in detail how the principles outlined in this chapter were applied in the three-day program at Station S, in the one-day program at Station W, and at the other assessment stations.

---

[1] Throughout this volume the term "appraisal" is used to denote the process of arriving at ratings and other judgments of a man's effectiveness *after* he has been working at his job for some time. In contrast to "appraisal" is the term "assessment," which we have been using to denote the process of arriving at *predictive* ratings and other judgments of a man's effectiveness *before* he has begun working. The term "validation" or "evaluation" refers to the process of comparing assessments with appraisals.

Chapter III

ASSESSMENT AT S: PROCEDURES

The present chapter describes the program at Station S during the last phase of its career, at which time, we should like to think, S was at its highest level of effectiveness, although there is certainly no member of the staff who would not claim that at least one test which had been used earlier fulfilled its purpose better than the procedure which replaced it. Had assessment continued for another six months the picture to be presented here would undoubtedly have been different in certain respects, though it is unlikely that its basic structure would have been radically altered, for the latter had remained unchanged since the summer of 1944. No account of a single session of S can do full justice to its ever changing program, to the variety of constellations of tests and procedures which characterized its history, or to the interesting theoretical and practical considerations which led to each of the changes. To ignore these aspects of the program is to lose much of its unique quality. It can only be hoped that other sections of this book will succeed in conveying to the reader something of the ferment and onward surge of S.

In the present account, the procedures of the program will be presented in the order in which they were experienced by the candidates, thus in effect taking the reader, as the candidates were taken, through all steps of assessment. But whereas the success of the assessment program required that the purposes of the various tests and the meanings of the situations should be hidden from the candidates, the exposition of the program requires that the reader be taken behind the scenes and into the staff room where he may become acquainted with the aim and rationale of each procedure. In other words, the reader will have an opportunity to view each part of the program, first, as it was experienced by the candidates, and second, as it was conceived and utilized by the staff.

RECRUITMENT OF CANDIDATES

It was not the function of S or of any of the assessment units to recruit OSS personnel, but merely to assess them as persons and as candidates for the particular OSS overseas assignments for which they had been recruited through one of three channels.

Within the organization a Personnel Procurement Branch (PPB) was charged with the responsibility of recruiting personnel from the various armed services. It was the practice of the other branches of the organization to supply PPB with their own job descriptions and to requisition through it the number of "bodies" which would be required to fill these assignments. With these job descriptions in hand and with authority granted by the Joint Chiefs of Staff to recruit military personnel, recruiting officers of the OSS visited various Army camps and naval stations to interview likely candidates.

The secrecy of OSS operations and the restrictions placed by considerations of security upon what recruiters might say when interviewing men lessened considerably the precision of their descriptions of the jobs for which they sought volunteers. Consequently many men had only the haziest idea of the kind of organization they were joining or the kind of work for which they were volunteering when they expressed a willingness to be assigned to OSS. Thus though the very purpose of PPB was to select men best suited for OSS assignments, the restrictions placed upon its officers inevitably introduced into their recruitment a selective factor of special appeal to a particular type of person. Indeed, there is reason to believe that this method of recruiting brought to the OSS as volunteers a disproportionately large number of men attracted by the mystery of secret missions and by the adventure of what appeared to be unusually hazardous duty, and there is good reason to doubt that this type of person was always best suited for the kind of work for which he volunteered. Of course, among the men who did volunteer for service, a request for transfer to OSS was made only for those who, in the recruiter's judgment, were especially qualified.

It is clear that every recruiting officer had a picture of the requirements for successful performance in the various jobs, but unfortunately it is not so clear that the pictures were identical with each other or with those in the minds of the members of the assessment staff. Indeed, so convinced did we become of their discrepancy that steps were taken to bring them together by arranging that recruiting officers go through the one-day assessment at W as students and then visit S as observers.

Whatever the agreement or disagreement between the concepts of job fitness held by procurement officers and by the assessment staff, recruiting constituted a first rough screening through which volunteers for OSS had to pass. There was no guarantee, however, that those whom the recruiters were willing to let through the screen would ever reach OSS. Requests for their transfer were made through channels, but channels sometimes became blocked. Anyway, for a variety of reasons only a portion of the military personnel requested was ever transferred to OSS.

The second channel through which individuals came to OSS, and eventually to assessment (provided they were slated for overseas assignment), was the Civilian Personnel Branch. This branch recruited, for the most part, though not entirely, civilian men and women, for secretarial and stenographic positions in the various branches of the organization and consequently the majority of its recruits were women. Many persons who knew of the existence of OSS sought employment in it through this channel, but they were by no means numerous enough to meet the large need for civilian personnel. For this reason the branch employed the usual and recognized techniques for attracting applicants for the positions which it had to fill—vaguely worded newspaper and magazine advertising, and so on.

The various branches at all times did a certain amount of their own recruiting. This was the third channel of entry into OSS. Persons already within the organization and aware of its needs for personnel understandably enough often recommended friends, acquaintances, and sometimes relatives for positions known to be vacant. This sort of individual recruitment can be very effective provided the sponsor is a good judge of others, primarily interested in the welfare of the organization, and impersonal in the recommendations, which he makes, but it is also subject to various forms of abuse, only one of which is nepotism. One of the important contributions, not to be overlooked, which an assessment staff can make to any large organization is the check which it places upon such abuses, unwittingly since it knows the names and family connections of none of the candidates whom it assesses. In OSS, however, this check was placed only upon those who were being considered for assignment overseas; assessment units were not asked, except in rare cases, to pass upon the fitness of candidates for jobs in Washington or within the continental limits of the United States.

Regardless of the channel through which a new recruit came to OSS, he was told little about the nature of the organization he was joining or of the specific assignment for which he was being considered. This was especially true in the case of candidates for overseas assignments, who, if not recommended by the assessment staff for their projected billets, were seldom retained in the organization. If military personnel, they were usually transferred back to the unit from which they had been recruited; if civilians, they were simply not employed, but in neither case were they told that their failure to be retained in OSS had anything to do with their performance in assessment. It was important that persons who might not be retained in OSS should not know too much about the organization. For this reason candidates came to Washington with little idea of what they were getting into and by the time they had been briefed for their sojourn at S they knew little more.

Men who had been interviewed at military installations, who had volunteered for the kind of work so sketchily outlined to them, who had passed the recruiting officer's screening, and whose transfer to OSS, requested by PPB, had been granted by the proper authorities, received, though sometimes not until weeks or even months after the recruiting interview, orders to report to Washington. These, following their arrival, were kept in holding areas or given leave until such time as they could be sent to assessment school. This meant a further delay of usually not more than a day or two, but seldom more than a week. This whole period of waiting on the part of men eager for a new assignment was not unimportant in creating some of the tension which candidates frequently showed upon arrival at the assessment area.

Civilians who had expressed interest in an overseas assignment with OSS were asked if they would be willing to come to Washington for a few days, and in most cases were told frankly that they would spend this time at an assessment school where an attempt would be made to determine where they could best be fitted into the organization. If they agreed to this they were entered in an assessment class and asked to report in Washington either on the day they would go to the assessment station or, in some cases, on the preceding day.

Whether he knew it or not, and regardless of whether he had been recruited from one of the armed services or from civilian life, every person slated for an assignment with OSS was checked thoroughly by the Security Branch of the organization. In many cases the security check of candidates had been completed before they entered assessment as students.

BRIEFING CANDIDATES FOR S

After his arrival in Washington and prior to being sent to S, each candidate was interviewed by a representative of the branch for which he had been recruited. This was usually the officer who would supervise the candidate throughout his training in the OSS schools, provided he received a recommendation from the assessment board. This interview, at least upon occasion, served as a second screening of candidates, for there were instances in which an administrative officer was so certain that a candidate was not up to the work for which he had been recruited that he canceled his registration in the S class and requested his transfer out of OSS at once.

Practice varied widely among the branches as to what was told candidates about their projected assignments and in any one branch the amount of information given candidates was far from constant. It was sometimes our impression that there was a high correlation between what a candidate knew about his projected assignment and the impression which he had made upon the branch administrative officer at the time of his interview. Information possessed by students had varied from detailed knowledge of the specific jobs for which they were slated to no knowledge at all about their proposed

assignments and even complete misunderstanding about the nature of the
organization which they had volunteered to join.

At the time of his briefing the candidate furnished the data required for
his Student Information Sheet, provided this had not already been obtained
from the very complete form which he had earlier filled out for use by the
Security Branch. The Student Information Sheet was an important paper,
for it accompanied the candidate to S and provided the staff with all the
information they would have about him at the beginning of his assessment.
But of this, he, of course, knew nothing.

Then he was told that he was being sent to the country to attend an
assessment school for three days where he would be asked many questions
and given a number of tests by a group of psychologists and psychiatrists.
It was important that he do his best, and lest he feel apprehensive about such
a program of analysis he was assured that those who had preceded him had
almost invariably enjoyed it; it was likely that he would too. And then he
learned for the first time that during his stay at the assessment school he
would not be known by his own name. He was going incognito. He was
not to talk about himself or say or do anything that would reveal his true
identity. Letters, photographs, and anything marked with his initials would
have to be left behind. All this, he was told, was for his own protection, and
for the security of the organization. And now he would have to choose
a name, a student name by which he would be known during assessment.

To those who had heard of OSS as a cloak-and-dagger society this seemed
like the real thing at last, but to those who thought of OSS as a straight
military outfit, or to those who had no idea of what OSS was, this was a
little puzzling. But to all alike the loss of name and identity, suddenly announced to them, must have created at least some measure of insecurity and
tension. To be bereft of one's *persona*, at least such tangible parts of it as
name, address, profession, and present status, whether military or civilian,
was to have the ground cut from under one's feet. But there was no turning
back now. For some, what lay ahead must have appeared as an exciting adventure, for others a frightening experience, for others nothing but foolish-
ness, and for still others merely an interesting challenge of their resourcefulness in playing their part without a slip. For each it had a special meaning. The pity is that we had no way of fathoming these meanings at the
time. Had we been able to discover them we should already have known
something significant about our candidates.

The student was then given a mimeographed copy of his instructions.
These were a reminder to him of all he had been told, of his student name
and class number, which he would do well to learn at once. They also indicated clearly the exact time when, later in the day, he was to report to
Schools and Training Headquarters in the old red brick schoolhouse at the
corner of 24th and F Streets. He was warned not to lose this copy of his

instructions, which was to be his pass for transportation and admission to S. Prior to his reporting at headquarters, he was to go at a specified time for a routine physical checkup at the Medical Dispensary.

If the candidate was an enlisted man he discovered that he was to report at headquarters at 3:30, if a civilian at 4:00, if an officer at 4:30. The purpose of this staggered reporting was to keep students from learning about the military or civilian status of their classmates. Ideally each student would have reported at a different time, but this was not practicable. The arrangement actually employed served at least to keep the students in any one group ignorant of the status of those in the other two groups, and this was an advantage.

Having reported at headquarters, students were led to the basement of the building and there asked to remove all their outer clothing and to destroy all identification marks on their underwear. Each man was then issued two pairs of Army fatigues, one of which he donned at once, a pair of heavy Army boots if he had none, and in winter an Army coat and cap. Now he knew that for the next three days he would be without his clothes as well as without his name and true identity. And with his clothes went his eagles if he were a colonel, or his stripes, three up and three down, if he were a master sergeant, or the comfortable cut and reassuring feeling of his tweeds if he were that kind of civilian. All that he had experienced in the day when he was told that he would have to hide his name and true identity was increased when he found himself now deprived of the even more tangible signs of his rank and station.

Having accustomed himself as well as he could to his fatigues, he was led with others into a room, there to wait until five o'clock. When others joined him later he had no knowledge of their rank; he could only guess and they could only guess about him. This was not precisely an atmosphere in which one felt at ease, and when one spoke it was usually humorously in an attempt to ease the tension. After all, one could not talk about the things it would have been so natural to discuss at such a time.

At last a sergeant came to call the roll of student names, and if one watched carefully one could observe those who already felt at home in their new roles and those who, on the other hand, failed to recognize their names when called. All present and accounted for, they were led outside to a canvas-covered Army truck. In this they were transported over the eighteen winding miles to S.

ARRIVAL AT S

Upon arrival at S, usually between 5:30 and 6:00 in the evening, the students were welcomed by the director and one or two other members of the staff, dressed, as members of the staff always were, in civilian clothes with name tags on their shirts. It was our desire that the candidates should feel genuinely welcomed, and we hoped that this informal greeting would help to allay whatever feelings of uncertainty, insecurity, or resentment they might be experiencing at this moment. But even a simple, civil greeting was enough to disturb the equilibrium of some students. One of them, rigidly GI in his attitudes, complained upon his return to Washington about his reception at S: he thought the candidates should have been addressed in military fashion.

It was usually a fairly solemn and somewhat uncomfortable group of men who climbed out of the truck, a group quite different in mood from the one that would leave the area four days hence. Often they had ridden to the area in silence, intent upon sizing up each other or upon trying to observe road signs indicating where they were being taken. Their day in Washington had done much to create in them a mood of tension, and now most unexpectedly, instead of finding themselves in an Army camp, they were deposited at the front entrance of a fine country estate. What sort of organization was this OSS?

And now having been greeted they were invited into the main house. There, settled in the room which they would come to know well as the classroom in which all group written tests would be given them, they were asked for their admission passes to the area. (These were then checked against the Student Information Sheets which the driver of their truck had brought to S, and from them the class list was made up and a name tag for each student prepared.) After their passes had been collected, they were addressed by the director somewhat as follows:

Please make yourselves at home. Once more, on behalf of the staff, I want to welcome you to Station S and to express the hope that your stay here will be a pleasant one.

I believe most of you have been told that this is an assessment school. Our job is to seek to discover your special skills, unique abilities, and individual talents in order that they may be put to the fullest use in this organization. As a matter of fact, I know of no agency or institution or organization that takes more pains in the selection and placement of its personnel than does the one with which we are all connected. It is our job here to see that square pegs are not put into round holes.

Although this is our function, it is important that this fact as well as the fact of our connection with the organization should be kept secret from the community in which we are located. And so to hide the nature of our work here we gave out for local consumption a "cover story" designed to conceal our true activity. That story was that this is an Army Rehabilitation and Reallocation Center for men returned from overseas. The residents in the near-by village accepted this fiction, but in the richness of their imaginations they proceeded to embroider the story until today they are firmly convinced that you are all serious mental cases. We hope you do not mind that those in the community think you are peculiar; we know that you are not.

The security regulations of the area were then explained to the students: they were to remain within the limits of the farm during their stay at S; they were not to speak to the two farmhands; they were not to go to the kitchen during the day but were invited to do so in the evening if they wished to raid the icebox; finally, during their stay at S they would have no communication with the outside world except, of course, in case of emergency.

Now a word about your own security at S. Each of you has come here under the cover of a student name. That name may be your first name, or middle name, or nickname, or a name that has been arbitrarily assigned to you. We don't know which it is, and we don't care. The important thing is that during your stay here you will be known to your associates and to the staff alike only by your student name. There are many things which we on the staff will want to know about you, but we do not need to know and do not want to know your real name or true identity.

Since, for reasons of your own security later in this organization you have to be under cover during your stay here, we have sought to make the most of this fact and so have created something of a game and very definitely a test out of this requirement of cover. Just as we, as an area, have a cover story, so each of you will be asked to develop, to spread, and to maintain as consistently as possible a cover story designed to hide your true identity during your stay here.

In creating your cover story there are certain facts about yourself which each of you must change. With your associates as well as with us on the staff, you must claim to have been born some place other than the place where you were born; you must claim to have been educated in institutions other than those where you were educated; you must claim to have engaged in and today to be engaged in work other than your true one; and you must claim to live in a place other than the one in which you really reside.

These are the minimum requirements for your cover story; obviously the more elaborate you can make it, yet still succeed in maintaining it, the more interesting your story will be for all of us. Let me warn you, however, that before leaving this area your ability to defend your cover story under grilling will be tested. Accordingly, it will be well for you not to make your cover story entirely out of the blue. For example, it might be unwise for you to claim to be a medical doctor if you know nothing about medicine, for there just might be a doctor in this group who by questioning you could soon demonstrate that you know nothing about medicine. Similarly, it might be very unwise for you to claim Chicago as your place of residence if you have never been there and know nothing about it. On the other hand, if you have visited there or lived there as a boy you might well claim it now as your residence. In the same way, a hobby or interest of yours might well serve as the basis for the job or profession which you will claim as yours. In other words, you will do well to draw upon your experience—in fact you have to—but you should do it in such a way as to hide your true identity and to meet the conditions which have been outlined to you.

With the exception of certain conditions which we call X conditions and which I shall explain to you in a moment, you are at all times during your stay here to give your cover story both to your associates and to members of the staff. But let me warn you now that members of the staff from time to time will try to trap you into breaking cover; for example, by asking you casual questions about yourself when you are off guard. Don't be caught.

In order to do our job here we have to learn a good deal about you and about your training and experience, and to get that information we will establish from time to time between you and ourselves what are known as X conditions. Under X conditions you will be at liberty to speak and to write freely and frankly about yourself, with this exception, that you will never reveal your true name here.

You will all be under X conditions for the first time this evening in this room when you will be asked to fill out a personal history form. In filling out this questionnaire you will be writing under X conditions, which means that you are to answer the questions fully and truthfully. No questions will be asked which will break your security. Remember, however, to sign this paper, as you will sign all papers here, with your student name only. I want to emphasize this, for upon occasion there has been misunderstanding on this point; and a student in answering the personal history questions has given us his cover story rather than the true facts of his life. That makes interesting, if fantastic reading; but it is not what we want or need.

During your stay here each of you will be interviewed by a member of the staff. This interview, marked by an X on the individual schedule of appointments which will be given you, will be held under X conditions, and during it you will be allowed and indeed expected to speak quite fully and frankly about yourself. But here again you will not give your true name.

It sometimes happens that in the period scheduled for an interview there is not time to discuss with you all the things we should like to discuss. In that case, your interviewer may arrange to meet with you another time, and if he does so, stating that the second interview is to be held under X conditions, then again you will be free to speak quite freely and frankly about yourself.

If at any time a member of the staff takes you away out of earshot of others and asks to speak with you under X conditions, then again, with X conditions established, you may speak freely.

Finally, if you, for any reason, feel you must speak truthfully about yourself to a staff member, ask for X conditions and if they are explicitly agreed to, then again you are at liberty to speak quite frankly and honestly about yourself.

So much about your individual security and your cover story; now a word about the program here.

During your stay you will be given many tests, put into many situations, asked to take part in many procedures. I think you will find all of them interesting; you will probably find some amusing; you may find some upsetting. It is important that you do your very best in every situation; but having done your best, don't worry about your performance. You may feel that you have done badly, but if you inquire of your associates about their feelings, I'm sure you will discover that their reactions will be much the same as yours.

With a few exceptions, the same tests will be given to all of you, though we know that they are not equally relevant for all of you. We expect you to do well in some of the tests, but not so well in others. Different ones of you will naturally excel in different fields. So just do your best and don't worry. If you can adopt this attitude you will do a better job and you will be much happier during your stay here than if you worry about your performance.

You will certainly want to talk about the various procedures with each other, but we have to ask you not to do so until you have all been through them. I am sure you will understand the reason for this request, for if those of you who first take a test tell others about it before they have taken it, the test will not be comparable for all of you. It is important that you all be equally uninformed about the situations in which you will find yourself. We do not wish, however, to impose any unnecessary silence upon you, so when all of you have had the same test you may talk about it. You will know that time has come when staff members are willing to discuss the test or situation with you.

The welcoming talk ended with an explanation of the conditions under which students would live at S. They were informed that they would sleep in the main house with the senior staff, that they would be awakened by an alarm clock at 7:00, that breakfast would be served at 7:30, lunch at 12:30, and dinner at 5:30. They were asked at mealtimes to distribute themselves at the small tables in the dining room so that members of the staff might eat with them. They were informed that the Post Exchange Supply Store would be open only for about ten or fifteen minutes after each meal and were urged to buy at such times what they would need until the next time the supply store would be open. Finally, they were urged to make themselves at home and assured that whatever they were thinking or feeling at the moment about the program that lay ahead, we were sure they would enjoy their stay at S.

Then they were taken to their sleeping quarters on the second floor, where they chose beds in the three student rooms. Here they were given student name tags to wear on their fatigues and a few minutes later were summoned by bell to dinner.

FIRST EVENING

The work of assessment started at the moment the students climbed out of the truck at S. The way a candidate greeted the staff members, the ease with which he used his student name in introducing himself, the position he took spontaneously with respect to the others, whether leading the group into the house or slowly bringing up the rear, were only the first of the many observations that would contribute to the final picture of each man.

There were those, both old and young, who jumped agilely out of the truck, others who climbed down haltingly, awkwardly, or even timidly. There were those who walked briskly toward the staff members, those who indeed had more the manner of greeting than of being greeted, those who hung back, obviously shy and embarrassed. There were those who spoke their names as though they were their own, loudly and confidently, those who spoke them softly and with guilt as though telling a lie, those who became blocked, unable to speak any name, in their confusion remembering only that they were not to use their own names yet unable to recall the new name given to them so short a while ago, and those who, having spoken their true names, suddenly realized what they had done, and, much embarrassed, tried to correct their mistakes. Each man shook hands in his own way, and each, in so doing, told us something about himself.

As they sat in the classroom listening to the director explain the rules by which they would live for the next few days they could not help revealing more of themselves. There was Karl, middle-aged, obviously a foreigner from his manner, possibly a German refugee—one would have to check on that later—who leaned forward on the edge of his chair eagerly trying to follow everything and who, in the tenseness of his manner, revealed the intensity of both his mood and his motivation. There was Bob, alert in mind and body, delighted by the instructions about the cover story, clearly impatient to match his wits with us on that score. There to the left was Andy, sprawling in his chair and slouched against the wall, evidently taking delight in acting hard-boiled and doing his best to show us we could not intimidate him. There was Matthew, probably a keen fellow in his day, but now certainly tired and confused, and we wondered for what possible job in OSS he could have been recruited. Then there was the young fellow who looked hardly seventeen who had chosen a seat in the front row and who, when the group was asked if there were any questions, raised his hand and stood up to ask his, like a little boy in school. And on the back row was the fellow who insisted that he could not make up a cover story because he had known a member of the class at a previous station. Of course, we did not know any of their student names at this time, but we would learn them later and remember how they had behaved during the welcoming talk.

Even the way in which they behaved when shown their sleeping quarters was often significant. Most of them took their assignments without question, but there were those who asked for special consideration, to move to a larger bedroom, because it was more airy or because there they could sleep in a lower rather than an upper bunk. A sense of humor or a dead seriousness about the situation was sometimes revealed by a lack of concern or fussy meticulousness.

The first meal was extremely important in the program of assessment, for here most members of the staff got their initial impressions of the candidates. For the most part, conversation tended to be reserved if not inhibited. After all, most of the things which would have been the natural topics for conversation—the places from which the candidates had come, the things they had done, what they hoped to do in the immediate future, the places and persons they might have known in common—all these were excluded from conversation, and rarely did a candidate so early in the program feel safe enough in his cover story to talk about his fictitious self or risk being asked questions by others.

Usually what conversation there was focused upon such innocuous topics as the weather, the trip to S, the food, and the like. We sometimes found it interesting to ask the candidates what sort of place they imagined they were being taken to when put into the truck, and thought at times that we noted a congruence of their answers—Army tents, an Army camp, a country estate, a country club—with other characteristic attitudes and expectations which they later revealed. Of course, there was the latest news to discuss, had anyone known it, but the students had usually been so busy all day being briefed and made ready for their trip to S that they had had no time to read a paper or listen to the radio. For this reason, those who were able to speak of the latest developments of the war, especially if they could also discuss the background of the more recent events, revealed themselves as the more highly motivated of the group. Something of the social and political sentiments, the racial and sectional prejudices of the students could be sensed not only at meals but also at other moments of informal gathering and conversation.

If the first meal had done nothing more than to reveal clearly those students with sufficient self-assurance to be immediately at ease in a novel and uncertain situation and those who, unlike them, were full of uneasiness and apprehension, it would have been a valuable part of the program. Actually it revealed much more. Every conversation in which a student took part, especially those which he initiated, revealed attitudes and sentiments, biases and prejudices, ideologies and faiths, purposes and hopes, more richly and with more subtle nuances than any standardized paper-and-pencil tests which we might have employed for the purpose.

Even the half hour after dinner yielded data for our assessments. Whether the students adjourned to the living room to read, to listen to the radio, to play darts, to engage in conversation among themselves or with staff members, or to withdraw by themselves—all this was grist for the assessment mill.

The work of the first evening began at seven o'clock when students were called into the classroom. There they were given a number of paper-and-pencil tests of intelligence and of personality and were asked to fill out a rather detailed personal history questionnaire. The schedule of procedures chosen for this first evening had one central purpose—gathering material which would prepare the staff members for their interviews with the candidates. From first to last the clinical interview with the student was the nucleus of the assessment program, but our experience soon taught us that the amount of profit derived from an interview was greatly increased if the interviewer was well prepared before meeting the subject.

There are many historical facts which the average person does not hesitate to reveal, and these it seemed might as well be written down by the subject in advance; especially so since the limited time of the Interview would probably be taken up with matters which were not easily set down in black and white. Moreover, if the interviewer could be oriented with respect to the manner of man he was to deal with and have at hand a broad outline of the life history he was to explore, he started with a definite advantage. Accordingly, on the first evening of his stay at S the student was asked to fill out a Personal History Form, and the interviewer made it his business to study this product before seeing his subject the following day, or on the day after that.

More important, it seemed that the interviewer would make the best use of his time if he knew in advance what were the "problem areas" in the subject's personality. If the interviewer could know in a general way what were the subject's major preoccupations, sentiments, and attitudes, he could decide what things ought to be explored in more detail; and if he knew what general type of personality he was to face and had some idea as to the unconscious trends that were at work, so much the better. Accordingly, the students were given certain projective procedures early enough in the program so that the interviewer could make use of the results.

It seemed important also for the interviewer to have an approximate idea of the general intellectual ability of the candidate before interviewing him, and for this reason two tests of intelligence were included in the battery of group procedures administered on the first evening.

And then, to aid the interviewer in questioning his subjects, especially in attempting to determine the degree of their emotional stability and the extent to which they suffered from nervous tension and anxiety or tended to convert such tensions into physical symptoms, each candidate was asked to fill out a psychosomatic inventory and a health questionnaire.

To get some indication of their attitudes toward widely different conditions of work and their willingness and ability to adjust to them, the candidates were also given a work conditions questionnaire.

Those group procedures which involved the more conscious, overt, and public layers of the personality were given first, while those which were designed to tap the deeper dispositions of the person were not offered until the novelty of the situation had disappeared and with it some of the candidate's self-esteem defenses.

It seemed wise to begin the evening program with a type of procedure which would be well known to the majority of candidates. For this reason a standard intelligence test such as most of them had taken in the past was the first given. During the last months at S, this was the Otis Self-Administering Test of Mental Ability (Higher Examination) with a twenty-minute time limit. The instructions were easy to give and the scoring was rapid. It was adopted near the end of the program because the change in the assessment population had removed the reasons for using the nonverbal tests previously employed. Earlier there had been many Europeans recently arrived in the United States who were characterized by varying degrees of language handicap. Also the use of a standardized, well-known test permitted a direct comparison between the assessed population and other populations.

Sentence Completion Test.—The second test of the evening was Sentence Completion which, though not included in the original program at S, was increasingly valued by the staff. One of a number of projective techniques tried out in the program, it was the only one in use at the end.

The purpose of this test, like that of all projective procedures, is to entice the subject into revealing himself without his becoming aware of the fact that he is doing so.

In all projective procedures the object is to stimulate imaginative processes and to facilitate their expression in word or in action. This is accomplished by asking the subject to respond—to complete, or explain, or interpret, or give associations—to more or less ambiguous stimulus material. The subject attempts to give responses which are reasonable or logically related to the stimuli, but a personal factor usually introduces itself into his constructions, and it is possible to derive from them knowledge of his wishes, fears, sentiments, and attitudes.

In the sentence completion procedure employed at S, the ambiguous material consisted of the beginnings of a hundred sentences, and the subjects were given the task of completing the sentences as rapidly as possible.

This was essentially an association test. Since the instructions emphasized speed of response, students tended to finish the sentences with the first thoughts which came to mind. Responding under the pressure of time, they expressed much which they would ordinarily have inhibited. The peculiar advantage of the Sentence Completion Test over a simple word-association test lay in the fact that the dynamic relationship between the structured stimulus and the response was more easily discerned in a completed sentence than in a pair of words. Thus instead of "driving force—failure," the stimulus and response might be, indeed in one case was, "The main driving force in my life is—my fear of failure."

In developing the test an attempt was made to include phrases whose completions would shed light on at least twelve areas of personality. These were the areas of (1) Family: attitudes toward parents, siblings, and the family as a unit; (2) The Past: childhood and early events that may have resulted in lasting impressions; (3) Drives: the major motivating forces that spur the subject on to action; (4) Inner States: the subject's feelings and attitudes toward himself; (5) Goals: the ends toward which the subject strives; (6) Cathexes: the objects which the subject likes, the activities in which he participates, and the ideas which interest him; (7) Energy: the productivity of the subject; (8) Reaction to Frustration and Failure; (9) Time-perspective: orientation to the past or to the future; (10) Optimism-Pessimism: expectations of success and failure; (11) Reaction to Others: inferiors, equals, and superiors; (12) Reactions of Others: what, according to the subject, his friends think of him.

The items in the test underwent many revisions. Those retained at the end were the ones which were discovered to have low indices of stereotypy or, conversely, high indices of uniqueness. This index depends, in part, upon the item itself. Those words or phrases which, in the Gestaltists' terminology, "demand" a single word or phrase for satisfactory closure are bad items for a sentence completion test. For example, "At the end of a long job, Joe usually . . ." invariably had a high index of stereotypy since it demanded "was tired" for its completion. Widespread social and cultural factors also produce high indices of stereotypy. "When he heard the news of Pearl Harbor, Paul . . ." required the completion "enlisted" as often from civilians and draftees as from volunteers. Stereotyped completions are dead wood; they add nothing to the understanding of the single case, and it was the individual case with which we were constantly concerned in assessment.

All of the items in the test were relatively unstructured. Obviously there was no right or wrong response, and no single word or group of words was better than any other except in so far as it might reveal more of the person who had written it.

All sentence beginnings referred either to the subject (e.g., "I admire . . .") or to another person (e.g., "Charlie was happiest when . . ."). This made for variety in construction of items and helped to disguise the true purpose of the test. The chief reason, however, for using sentences which referred to another person was the assumption which underlies all projective procedures: that in his interpretations of the behavior of others, a man is very likely to reveal some of his own motivations.

The test was divided into two parts, each consisting of fifty incomplete sentences, with approximately half an hour of other activity interposed between the giving of the two sections. Early experience with the test given as a unit had shown that it was too long. Such factors as fatigue and boredom tended to reduce the amount of material that could be obtained when students were asked to complete one hundred sentences without any interruption; many sentences were left blank, or single words rather than phrases were used for completions. The splitting of the test into two halves with a break between them obviated these difficulties and, in addition, provided an opportunity for the subject to change his mental set toward the task. This was not often necessary, but there were instances in which a student who had adopted a flippant attitude toward the first half of the test became serious when the second half was presented and completed the sentences in a straightforward manner in accordance with the directions.

In splitting the test, care was taken to make the two halves as nearly comparable as possible, distributing between them items which were designed to elicit the same or similar attitudes and sentiments or which described the same or similar situations. Several items were introduced into both halves in exactly the same form; others were presented in the first person in one half and with reference to another person in the other half, thus providing internal checks on the reliability of the test as a whole.

The oral instructions for the Sentence Completion Test were as follows:

Please do not turn these papers over until I tell you to do so.

The first thing you are to do when you turn your paper over is to write your name and class in the spaces provided at the top of the page.

Beneath that you will find some words which are the beginnings of sentences. Your task is to complete these sentences as quickly as possible, bearing two things in mind: first, when you are through with the sentence it must be a complete sentence; and second, it must make sense.

For example, suppose you should see on the page, "Today is . . ." You might add, "a sunny day," or "Friday," or "the day after yesterday." It does not matter whether you use two dozen words or just one word, so long as it is a complete sentence and makes sense.

You are to do this task as quickly as possible. Therefore, when you are finished, raise your hand and I shall collect your paper and mark the time on it.

There are three sheets containing fifty sentences, so be sure you have not skipped any pages before you hand in your paper.

Are there any questions?

Remember, first write your name and class at the top of the page and then proceed immediately to completing the sentences.

Ready? Begin!

Approximately half an hour later the second half of the Sentence Completion Test was presented with the following instructions.

Did any of you notice that it said "Part I" at the top of the Sentence Completion Test you took earlier this evening? Well, it did.

Here is Part II.

The instructions are exactly the same as they were for Part I. Please do not begin until I give the signal.

Remember, first you write your name at the top of the page and then proceed immediately to completing the sentences. When you finish, raise your hand and I shall mark the time on your paper.

Ready? Begin!

The Sentence Completion Test was not scored; it was interpreted. There was little standardization of the interpretations; they were largely individual affairs and staff members learned how to interpret by interpreting, although it was clear that the goodness of their interpretations depended upon the degree of their psychological insight and the amount of experience which they had had with this test or with other projective procedures. Certainly skill was acquired by experience in examining many papers, but each member of the junior staff, whose responsibility it was to score the Sentence Completion Test, had his own approach to its content and his own method of interpreting it. Although no general principles were ever formally established, informal discussions of the problems of interpretation led to a certain uniformity of technique.

The task which confronted the interpreter was that of constructing a picture of a student solely on the basis of his sentence completions. He may have seen the candidate for a few minutes at dinner that evening and without doubt he had read the meager facts about him as given on his Student Information Sheet, but with the exception of this, which was not much, the candidate whose sentence completions he interpreted was a stranger to him. At least this was the case for the majority of candidates whose sentence completions were interpreted the first evening while they were still in the classroom and before they were observed in any of the group situations.

The usual procedure was for the staff member to read through both parts of the test, underlining all responses that were unusual or which seemed likely to be significant. A number of criteria of significance were held tentatively in mind during the reading: the uniqueness of the response, the amount of material included in the completion, the repetition of any one response, and the psychological relatedness of different responses. Here, as in all such material, we looked for the novel and for the repetitious. Two fundamental assumptions were constantly borne in mind even though they were held only as tentative hypotheses: (1) the rarer the response of a subject, in comparison with the responses given by other subjects to the same item, the more significant it is; and (2) the more frequently a response is given by any one subject to different items, the more significant it is, presuming that the repetition is not the result of perseveration. During the first reading the aim was to note the significant completions and to detect consistent patterns among them, the interpreter thereby gaining a general impression of the major trends in the subject's personality.

When the underlinings were completed it was a common practice to reread the responses and to record them in their appropriate categories on a score sheet prepared for this purpose. The score sheet was, in practice, an organized note sheet on which the interpreter could record his impressions. It was divided into sections, in the left-hand margins of which were printed the numbers of the sentences whose completions were expected to shed light on a single aspect of personality. In any actual case, of course, the meaning of a completion might make it fall into some category other than the expected one, and if so it would be recorded there. Some completions did not yield material for any of the designated areas of personality indicated on the recording sheet, but that did not necessarily prevent them from contributing significantly to the picture of the candidate. Often a single response had meaning for more than one of the rather arbitrary categories. Wherever they fitted, the completions were recorded on the score sheet and then the data for each category were considered separately, e.g., one might seek to guess, on the basis of sentence completions alone, what the goals of the student were, quite apart from any consideration of his family or past history. When these brief summaries had been written it was the task of the interpreter to organize them into a fuller picture in the form of a tentative personality sketch of the candidate.

For most members of the staff the task of interpreting a sentence completion test and writing the personality sketch took no more than half an hour, a remarkably short time compared to that required for scoring the Rorschach or the Thematic Apperception Test.

The personality sketch of the candidate drawn on the basis of his sentence completions was never treated as anything more than a very tentative conception which the interviewer might seek to check in his clinical interview with the candidate. The test was used solely as an aid to the Interview, and no attempt was made to obtain scores on the variables upon which it was designed to shed light.

The prestige of the instrument grew steadily as the interpreters and interviewers gained experience and skill in its use. The interviewer read the interpretations carefully and noted the suggested significant traits or problems to be checked in the Interview. He also examined the individual responses to make his own interpretations of the case and to sense for himself the unique flavor of the personality. Fortified with a preview of the student gained through a study of his responses, the interviewer was able to make more efficient use of the limited time at his disposal and not infrequently to confirm significant aspects of a candidate's personality which well might never have been uncovered without a prior study of his sentence completions.

Health Questionnaire.—Although all students were examined medically before coming to S it seemed wise to investigate the state of health, physical as well as mental, of each candidate as a part of the assessment program. The reasons for this decision were many. The physical examination of students in Washington tended to be routine and rather superficial, and subsequent questioning of candidates at S not infrequently suggested the presence of a physical or health problem which was later confirmed by a second medical examination. To many candidates the physical checkup in town appeared as just another Army examination. Since it had to be made

Student Name_____ Class S-_____

Please read the following list and mark with an X the answer that, in your judgment, is GENERALLY TRUE ABOUT YOU. DO NOT SKIP. Do not fuss too much about the exact reply. They are only approximations.

Do you have any particular physical or health problem?   Yes   Undecided   No

What is your problem?_____

Have you any physical disabilities that prevent or limit your participation in any type of physical activity?   Yes   No

If your answer is "yes," what are these disabilities?_____
_____

Have you ever had

Asthma or hay fever?	Yes	No	Stomach ulcers?	Yes	No
Persistent tiredness?	Yes	No	Hemorrhoids?	Yes	No
Allergies?	Yes	No	Marked weight fluctuations?	Yes	No
Fits or convulsions?	Yes	No	Nervous breakdown?	Yes	No

You have plain headaches.....	Never	Once in several months	2 or 3 times a month	4 or more times a month
You have headaches with nausea or vomiting.........	Never	Once in several months	2 or 3 times a month	4 or more times a month
Fainting spells—(spells in which you have passed out).	Never	Once in your life	2 or 3 times	4 or more times
Almost fainted—(you did not pass out, but felt near it)....	Never	Once in your life	2 or 3 times	4 or more times
Unconscious but not a faint, through a blow to the head, or for any other reason.....	Never	Once in your life	2 or 3 times	4 or more times
Before you fall asleep, it usually takes	Less than ½ hour	½ hour to 1 hour	1 to 2 hours	2 or more hours
After falling asleep, and before you are ready to get up and dress, you awake..........	Not once	Once	Twice	Three times
You take sleeping medicine or any kind of sedative.......	Never	Once a month or less	Once a week	2 or 3 times a week or oftener
Your sleep may be described as........................	Very deep	Deep	Light	Very light
You have scary or frightening dreams....................	Never	1 or 2 times a year	Once in 1 or several months	Once in 1 or several weeks
Your eating habits may be described as...............	You can eat almost anything	1 or 2 things do not agree	You have to be careful	There are many things you cannot eat
You take bicarbonate of soda or an alkali or any other medicine for a stomach ailment.....................	Never	Once in 1 or several months	Once in 1 or several weeks	Every day or two
You have had attacks of diarrhea — (running of the bowels)	Never	Once or several times a year	Once in 1 or several months	Once in 1 or several weeks
You take medicine for constipation...................	Never	Once in 1 or several months	Once in 1 or several weeks	Every day or two

You have been drunk........	Never	Once or several times in your life	Once or twice a year	Once in 1 or several months
You have dizzy spells in which objects in the room seem to be moving..............	Never	Several times in your life	Once or twice a year	Once in 1 or several months
You have trouble speaking, so that you stutter or stammer	Never	On rare occasions	Occasionally	Often
You have attacks in which you get cold sweats, your heart beats so hard you can hear it	Never	Once or twice a year	Once in 1 or several months	Once in 1 or several weeks
You have attacks in which you suddenly get anxious or frightened................	Never	Once or twice a year	Once in 1 or several months	Once in 1 or several weeks
You have had smothering sensations, or shortness of breath not immediately following physical exercise....	Never	Once or twice	Once or twice a year	More than twice a year
Your friends think of you as..	Always cool and collected	Calm most of the time	Nervous temperament	Very tense and high strung
Your emotional state may be described as..............	Steady	Somewhat moody	Ups and downs	Either very high or low
You get so discouraged that it interferes with your work...	Never	Once or twice a year	Once in 1 or several months	Once in 1 or several weeks
In relation to people you meet for the first time, you are...	Friendly	Shy until you get to know them	Rather withdrawn	On guard
Of the people you do know, you have................	Many friends intimate and otherwise	Many friends— few intimates	Some or many friends, few intimates	One or two intimates, no others
You have gone to a doctor....	Never	Only when very ill	Once or twice a year	3 or more times a year
You have gone to a doctor for "nervousness," nervous symptom, personality difficulty, or personal problem..	Never	Once or twice	Three times	More than 3 times
Your associates consider you..	Unduly attentive to details	Very careful about details	A little careless about details	Very careless about details
In the face of sudden physical danger you are.............	Generally calm and well controlled	Anxious but well controlled	Frightened and poorly controlled	Panicky
In regard to social activity and solitude	You can't stand being alone	You prefer social activity but like to be alone sometimes	It's about fifty-fifty	You much prefer to be alone

rather hurriedly, there was little opportunity for a relationship of real rapport to develop between the examining physician and the candidates. This,
combined with the fact that the vast majority of candidates had volunteered
for the OSS and most of them were eager for an overseas assignment with
the organization, made them sometimes less than completely frank in answering questions about their medical history and present physical condition.
In the more intimate atmosphere at S and in the privacy of an hour-and-a
half interview with a member of the staff, many medical problems hidden,
or at least not mentioned, at the time of the medical examination were
frankly and fully discussed.

Another reason for considering questions of health was that many conditions which disqualify men for duty overseas may not be recognized by them
as physical symptoms and are consequently more often and more easily discussed with a psychologist or a psychiatrist than with an internist. Perhaps
the most important reason was that candidates seemed willing to reveal
themselves fully only when they felt that all aspects of their personalities
were being considered, and they recognized that health and disease were
among the most important of these aspects.

It was only in the intimacy of the Interview that anything like an adequate
picture of the candidate's health could be expected, but just as it was possible
to obtain a preliminary sketch of his personality through paper-and-pencil
tests, projective techniques, and personal history questionnaires, so also was
it possible to get some idea of his physical and mental health by asking him
to answer two health questionnaires.

From the very beginning of S, health questionnaires were given to the
candidates early in the program as an aid to the subsequent interview. We
tried many forms of inventory; some were of our own making, others were
standardized questionnaires. In the last months of S two forms were used.

The first of these sought primarily to uncover the more frank physical or
somatic symptoms, though some questions touching upon the more psychological and behavioral manifestations of tension and anxiety were also included. This was not greatly different from many other health questionnaires, but it seemed to us to have two advantages. Its range of questions
was more adequate than most for the topics which, we believed, needed to
be surveyed in considering the fitness of a candidate for an overseas appointment. Its second advantage was the greater specificity in the alternative
frequencies of symptoms and experiences which subjects were asked to
check. Instead of presenting a candidate with such alternatives as

    "Never"   "Seldom"   "At times"   "Often"

it offered him, for example,

    "Never"   "Once in several   "2 or 3 times   "4 or more times
                   months"   a month"   a month"

This questionnaire was not scored. Standardized norms were never worked out; the assessment school came to an end before there had been a sufficiently large number of cases or time in which to do so. It is doubtful whether, even with these conditions fulfilled, we would have worked out scoring norms, for the main purpose in giving the questionnaire was to provide the interviewer with suggestive hints and leads for his meeting with the candidate. It was our strong conviction that indices of health based upon such questionnaires would have told us little, and more often than not would have been misleading. It was our common experience that a discussion of a candidate's check marks with him frequently changed their meanings, and it was the meanings of the checks (answers) that were especially important for assessment.

In the last months of our program, the second health questionnaire given to candidates was Part II of the McFarland-Seitz *P-S Inventory*. Since this form duplicated, with only slight changes in wording, a few of the questions in the other questionnaire, the two were not given in succession. Interposed between them was the questionnaire on preferences for various conditions of work.

At an earlier date in the program both parts of the Psycho-somatic Inventory had been used. At first it was scored in the usual manner, the two part-scores and the total score being converted into percentiles according to tables supplied with the test. When scores for a sufficiently large population had been acquired, the three raw scores of the test were converted into ratings on the six-point scale used at S and throughout the assessment program. But soon in practice we found ourselves not paying much attention to either percentile scores or ratings. Instead, the actual answers to the specific questions seemed much more significant. Many of them were in such a form as to make unnecessary the asking of certain routine questions in the Interview. But even more valuable were the leads for questioning suggested by an examination of those responses which were shown by the scoring weights to be atypical. They often revealed definitely abnormal trends. Occasionally the actual response of a candidate could be brought up for discussion in the Interview. If, for example, in answer to a question in the Interview a candidate denied the frequent occurrence of a certain type of experience, he might be asked what he had in mind when, in checking the Psycho-somatic Inventory, he had indicated that he "often" had such an experience. Frequently significant material was uncovered in this way, and if not, then usually a misunderstanding was clarified.

Eventually all scoring of the P-S Inventory was dropped since the labor of scoring was incommensurate with the contribution made by scores to our needs and to the use, as preparation for the Interview, to which we came increasingly to put the inventory.

In our experience Part I (Psychosomatic) was less satisfactory than Part

II (Psychoneurotic), and accordingly the health questionnaire already described was developed and substituted for Part I. Part II, however, seemed effective in evaluating the more psychological and behavioral indices of emotional instability and so was retained.

Work Conditions Survey.—The great variety of jobs for which candidates were assessed, and the heterogeneity of the conditions under which they would work if given their projected assignments, made it necessary to ascertain as accurately as possible the conditions of living and of work to which candidates could adjust and in which they could function effectively. This was a topic which could be discussed in an interview but it was also one which there was reason to believe could be explored in a preliminary manner in a questionnaire. Of course, here, as in all questionnaires, there was the possibility of falsification of answers; a candidate can always give those answers which he believes will get him the job he wants if he wishes to do so. Against such misrepresentation there is no perfect defense. Even with the best intentions to report honestly and accurately, a person may misjudge or not know at all his capabilities of adjusting to new and difficult conditions of work. The best defense against both witting misrepresentation and unwitting misjudgment of psychological fact is the true insight of the skillful clinician. It was, then, the task of the staff member in his interview with a candidate to assess the validity of the candidate's answers to all questionnaires. The answers given by a candidate to questionnaires were never taken as statements of fact, but only as crude indications of the kind of person one *might* meet in the Interview. The hypotheses yielded by the techniques of the first evening were subject to later checking, however, not only by the interviewer in his meeting with the candidate but also by every member of the assessment staff in every observation of the man made throughout his stay at S. Statements made by the candidate in the Interview might contradict his checks on the Work Conditions Survey, and his adjustment, good or bad, to the conditions of living and working at S might belie them even more clearly; yet to have from each candidate early in the program an indication of the conditions of work which at one extreme he would welcome and at the other extreme he would emphatically reject was decidedly helpful.

The Work Conditions Survey listed forty-three different conditions that do exist (or can exist) in any job. The candidates were asked to rate their own reactions to each condition on the basis of the following rating scale:

1. Highly desirable—exactly what you want.
2. Desirable.
3. Acceptable—it doesn't make any difference one way or the other.
4. Difficult to accept, though something to be put up with if necessary.
5. So difficult you doubt if you could manage it.
6. It would make a job impossible—you would refuse it.

WORK CONDITIONS SURVEY

Student Name:_____ Class S—

1. Monotonous work............................1 2 3 4 5 6
2. Months of idleness.........................1 2 3 4 5 6
3. Irregular hours.............................1 2 3 4 5 6
4. A strict harsh boss.........................1 2 3 4 5 6
5. Very routine work..........................1 2 3 4 5 6
6. Periods in which you have to work all night...1 2 3 4 5 6
7. Stuck away somewhere with little or no social contact 1 2 3 4 5 6
8. Desk work exclusively......................1 2 3 4 5 6
9. Always under supervision 1 2 3 4 5 6
10. No one to talk to...........................1 2 3 4 5 6
11. A lot of paper work.........................1 2 3 4 5 6
12. Great physical danger.......................1 2 3 4 5 6
13. Full of excitement..........................1 2 3 4 5 6
14. A large office, many people, desks close together.1 2 3 4 5 6
15. Nothing routine, you never know what they'll ask you to do next...........................1 2 3 4 5 6
16. Work requires a lot of social activity...........1 2 3 4 5 6
17. Climate monotonously hot and humid.........1 2 3 4 5 6
18. Climate in which there is prevailing zero weather and bleak landscape...................1 2 3 4 5 6
19. Work requires a great deal of responsibility.....1 2 3 4 5 6
20. Work requires much initiative 1 2 3 4 5 6
21. A job in which everything depends on your decisions....................................1 2 3 4 5 6
22. Poor food...................................1 2 3 4 5 6
23. Office job, regular hours, well-defined clerical job...1 2 3 4 5 6
24. Job requires great physical endurance...........1 2 3 4 5 6
25. Climate with constant rain....................1 2 3 4 5 6
26. Working in close relations with Negroes.......1 2 3 4 5 6
27. Working in close relations with Orientals......1 2 3 4 5 6
28. Job requires intimate personal interviews with every variety of individual....................1 2 3 4 5 6
29. Working exclusively with women.............1 2 3 4 5 6
30. See only men for long periods of time..........1 2 3 4 5 6
31. Dirty surroundings..........................1 2 3 4 5 6
32. An area in which syphilis is common..........1 2 3 4 5 6
33. An area in which malaria is common...........1 2 3 4 5 6
34. An area in which tuberculosis is common.......1 2 3 4 5 6
35. An area in which a large majority of people tend to become alcoholic...........................1 2 3 4 5 6
36. Advising people about their personal difficulties.1 2 3 4 5 6
37. Work requiring the highest degree of accuracy and fine detail...............................1 2 3 4 5 6
38. Work which often requires the meeting of deadlines.......................................1 2 3 4 5 6
39. Selection of personnel.......................1 2 3 4 5 6
40. Work involving abstract and theoretical formulations—the kind of thinking done by philosophers.....................................1 2 3 4 5 6
41. Work requires practical intelligence and quick decisions....................................1 2 3 4 5 6
42. Work requiring slow deliberate, cautious, leisurely thinking...............................1 2 3 4 5 6
43. Frequent "snafu" 1 2 3 4 5 6

After candidates had checked this survey—there was no time limit, but candidates seldom took more than ten minutes to complete it—they were given the second health questionnaire (Part II of the P-S Inventory) and then presented with the second part of the Sentence Completion Test. By the time the candidates had completed these it was usually nine o'clock, and since they had been working without a break for two hours, they were given a fifteen-minute intermission. Reminded of the invitation to raid the icebox in the evening, most of them proceeded forthwith to do so.

After the break, the candidates were given three forms to fill out, but since none of them was timed, they were presented in a group to the men, who were then left free to work at them at their own pace. The only requirement was that they all complete the procedures in the same order, first taking a Vocabulary Test, then filling out a Personal History Form, and finally answering a Projective Questionnaire.

Vocabulary Test.—Many candidates were handicapped in the assessment program, especially in tests of intelligence, by their foreign background and by their poor mastery of the English language. To estimate the degree of this handicap a vocabulary test was given to all recruits the first evening, but there were other reasons also for including such a test in the program. Provided an individual is tested in his native tongue, his score on a vocabulary test is known to be a good indication of his general intelligence. Tests of vocabulary are especially useful in appraising the level of intelligence of older men who may be handicapped by such speed tests as the Otis. Finally, they can give some indication of a subject's verbal facility, a factor of the greatest importance in propaganda activities, the ability for which we had to test in many candidates.

The vocabulary test used in the assessment program was composed of fifty items borrowed from the American Council on Education Psychological Examination (ACE), the Institute of Educational Research Intelligence Scale CAVD, and the Atwell-Wells Wide-Range Vocabulary Test. It was. a multiple-choice test with four alternatives for each item.

Personal History Form.—Of all the material gathered from the candidates in the first evening, none was more important than their personal histories, the salient facts of which they were asked to record under X conditions, in a booklet especially prepared for this purpose.

The Personal History booklet was designed in such a way as to make it convenient for the interviewer to record in appropriate places therein the material he obtained from the Interview. When the booklet was opened, the questions put to the subject always appeared on the left-hand page only, together with plenty of space for writing his answers. When a subject had filled out his Personal History booklet the interviewer could study it, make notes on the margin, take it to the Interview with him, and then use the right-hand blank pages for recording data gained there.

Several considerations entered into the selection of questions for inclusion in the Personal History blank. Since the candidates would be working on it during the evening of their arrival, after they had taken a number of paper-and-pencil tests, it was thought wise to make the blank as short and simple as possible. Yet to meet the requirements outlined above, some attention had to be given to various aspects of the man's background, history, and present situation. The task, then, was to make every question count for the most, and a great deal of experimentation went on—during which questions were put in and taken out and reworded and reinserted—before a form was hammered out that all the staff could regard as reasonably satisfactory.

There had to be good reasons for finally including a question. And the reasons were always the same: in the first place, the question included was one which on one theory or another promised to yield material that was significant for personality and, in the second place, there had to be evidence from experience to show that the question actually did, reasonably well, what it was supposed to do.

A glance at the Personal History blank, given on pages 84 to 89 without attention to the spacing that held for the original, will show that most of the old "stand-bys"—that is, topics and questions which have turned up time and again in application blanks and personal data sheets—are very much in evidence. There is a great deal of agreement among psychologists today as to what are the major determinants of personality development. Though they would differ in what they regarded as most important, few psychologists would want to leave out any of the following: national or racial background, socioeconomic status, personalities and interests of the parents, interpersonal relations within the family, traumatic events and fixations of early childhood, educational influences and experiences at school, vocational history, military record, marital history, present interests, sentiments and preferences, and health past and present.

None of the questions was very difficult or profound, and an effort was made to leave out everything that seemed likely to embarrass, frighten, or annoy the candidate. These more personal or emotionally loaded matters could be taken up in the Interview.

Candidates were allowed as much time as they liked to complete the Personal History form. Some finished in an hour; others had to be asked to bring it to a close after working three hours; the average time was approximately one and a half hours. These differences in amount of time spent on the Personal History corresponded rather closely to differences in the amount of material obtained—and these differences, as it turned out, were significant intimations of the subject's conscientiousness and motivation. But the differences were most largely due, as it seemed to us, to variations in the degree of the subject's intraception, that is, his capacity and

PERSONAL HISTORY

The personal questions which you are asked in this form (under "X" conditions) should be answered candidly and completely. All information which you may give us is confidential, and will be so treated. Other than for your true name, security regulations for this area are suspended.

———————————

STUDENT NAME: Age: Sex:

Class: Date of Birth:

Marital Status (check):   Single   Married   Widowed   Divorced   Separated

Place of birth: Date of immigration:

Present citizenship: Date of naturalization:

Religion: Politics:

I am of the 1st 2nd 3rd or later generation of my family to be born in America. (Encircle the appropriate number.)

ABOUT YOUR FATHER: Age if living: Age at death: Your age at his death:

Place of birth: Citizenship:

National origin of his family:

Education:

Occupation (s):

Interests and Recreations:

Politics:

Religion:

What sort of person is (or was) your father?

ABOUT YOUR MOTHER: Age if living: Age at death: Your age at her death:

Place of birth: Citizenship:

National origin of her family:

Education:

Occupation (s):

Interests and Recreations:

Politics:

Religion:

What sort of person is (or was) your mother?

Have your parents ever been divorced or separated? If so: What was your age at the time? With which parent did you live afterwards?

Give other details.

ABOUT ANY STEP-PARENTS, FOSTER PARENTS OR ANYONE ELSE WHO TOOK THE PLACE OF A PARENT FOR YOU. (If more than one, give same information on opposite page.):

                                                                                        her

Age if living: Age at death: Your age at his death:

Place of birth: Citizenship:

                 her

National origin of his family:

Education:

Occupation (s):

Interests and Recreations:

Politics:

Religion:

What sort of person is (or was) he (or she)?

Which parent do you think had more to do with your becoming the kind of person you are?

To which parent did you feel closer at the ages of

6   10   16   25   now?

Which parent exercised the discipline in your family?

Give the ages of all brothers and sisters in relation to your own: Thus, if you have or had a brother 5 years older and a sister 2 years younger than you, write B+5, S−2; if any have died, indicate by inclosing in parentheses:

B   B   B   B   B   B   B

S   S   S   S   S   S   S

What major satisfactions did you derive from your relationship with your brothers and sisters?

What kinds of frictions existed in the family? Has any member of your family ever brought embarrassment or unpleasant notoriety upon the rest of you?

What other people (relatives, guardians, friends, etc.) influenced your development? In what way?

At what age, approximately, did you stop wetting the bed?

Did you ever:

suck your thumb?   bite nails?
have temper tantrums?   have nightmares?
walk in your sleep?   stammer?
talk in your sleep?

Were you considered a nervous child?

In what part of the United States did you spend the major part of your childhood?

Did you live in a city?   Small town?   Farm?

Adult life?

What foreign travel have you had?

ABOUT YOUR WIFE (OR HUSBAND): Age if living: Age at death: Your age at his death: (her)

Place of birth: Citizenship: Date of marriage:

National origin of his (her) family:

Education:

Occupation (s):

Interests and Recreations:

Politics:

Religion:

What sort of a person is (or was) he (or she)?

Write a brief marital history, including date of marriage, ages and sex of children, also separations, divorces, remarriages.

How is your health?

List in chronological order, with approximate ages, all illnesses, operations, and accidents.

How often and under what circumstances do you drink alcoholic beverages?

As a result of drinking have you ever   (1) been arrested?   (2) lost your job?

(3) publicly disgraced yourself?   (4) damaged your health?   (5) embarrassed or hurt your family?

List *every time* you have been arrested for any cause.

Date   *Charge*   *Outcome*

Have you ever brought suit or been sued at law?   (Give details)

List kinds of schools, names of colleges and universities, dates of attendance, major fields of study.

INSTITUTION   *DATE OF ATTENDANCE*   *MAJOR STUDIES*

Was your school record   Poor Average Good   Excellent? (encircle)

Was your college record   Poor Average Good   Excellent? (encircle)

What were your best subjects?

What were your worst subjects?

Any fellowships, honors, scholarships?

Extra-curricular activities and achievements?

What sports have you participated in? What teams have you played on? Have you ever been captain of a team?

Comparing yourself with others of the same age and sex, rate yourself on the qualities listed below, using the following scale: Very inferior, Inferior, Average, Superior, Very Superior.

    1. Agility   1. _____

    2. Endurance   2. _____

    3. Speed   3. _____

    4. Physical strength   4. _____

    5. Physical courage   5. _____
       (Daring)

What recreations and hobbies other than sports have you engaged in?

Were you ever suspended or dropped from a school or college for academic or other reasons? Describe in detail.

What public speaking have you done?

List in chronological order each of the jobs you have held since you started to work full time, giving for each dates of beginning and ending, kind of work, how you liked it, salary and reason for leaving. (Do no include military service.)

EMPLOYER	KIND OF WORK	DATE BEGAN	DATE ENDED	HOW YOU LIKED IT AT START	HOW YOU LIKED IT AT FINISH	SALARY (PER YEAR) BEGAN	SALARY (PER YEAR) ENDED	REASON FOR LEAVING

What books have you read and liked best?

What magazines do you ordinarily read most regularly?

What kinds of clubs or organizations do you belong to (vocational, social, political, religious, etc.)?

What offices have you held in the clubs or organizations of which you have been a member?

Did you hold any jobs in school or college? Describe in detail.

What do you plan to do after the war?

Draft status (if male civilian) and reasons:

If you are a member of the armed services

    Which one?

    Date of induction:

List of ranks or grades, special duties, and responsibilities in your military duties' and dates for each.

Station	Rank or grade	Duties	Dates

If you have ever been discharged from any branch of the armed forces, state the type and circumstances of the discharge.

inclination for paying attention to his own thoughts, feelings, and attitudes, and for being inquisitive about their sources. Some told us much, others very little. At one extreme there were the constricted personalities who answered with single words or pinched and barren phrases at most, and at the other extreme the exuberant and expansive individuals who repeatedly overflowed in their writing onto the blank pages reserved for the interviewer's notes. In the tone of one man's answers there was no mistaking his depression, while in another's the hypomanic temper was equally manifest. The awkwardness of style, the beautiful phrasing, the dull reporting, the bright and witty answers—all these gave a picture of the candidate long before he was seen in situations or in the privacy of the Interview. To have read a man's Personal History with care was to know a lot about him. There was no better way to prepare oneself for an interview with him.

Projective Questionnaire.—A separate unit, inserted into the Personal History form, was a sheet on which twelve projective questions were asked of the candidate. These questions ranged widely:

1. It seems that no matter how careful we are, we all sometimes have embarrassing moments. What experience makes you feel like sinking through the floor?
2. What things or situations are you most afraid of?
3. What kinds of things do you most dislike to see people do?
4. If you had a large fortune and few responsibilities, how would you spend your life?
5. If you were (are) a parent, what things would you try most to teach your children?
6. What might push a person into a nervous breakdown?
7. What would you most like people to say of you after you have lived your life?
8. What moods or feelings are the most unpleasant or disturbing to you? How often do you have them?
9. Everyone has bad dreams or nightmares at some time or another, such as after overeating; what would be the worst dreams to have?
10. If you were (are) a parent, what things would you try to guard your children against most carefully?
11. What great people, living or dead, do you admire most?
12. What was the greatest lack in your childhood?

These questions might well have been asked in the Interview, but to have the answers to the questions ahead of time was in many cases to know something about the candidate's emotional life, something of his most impressive experiences, something of his attitudes and sentiments, and, knowing these, to be better prepared to interview him.

The term "projective" is used, for want of a better term, to describe the fact that the subject, unless he was psychologically sophisticated, rarely saw the implications of these questions, and the fact that the answers to them usually were not to be taken at their face value but regarded rather as responses which could be interpreted—interpreted in the light of the total setting in which they appeared or in the light of other facts about the subject's personality. There was a great deal of theory behind each question—theory which determined its selection and guided the interpretation of the response. For example, the question, "What kinds of things do you most dislike to see people do?" was based on the notion that the tendencies which a person dislikes to see another express are sometimes the very ones which he has tried to suppress in himself. But not necessarily. The responses have to be interpreted.

It would be difficult to say which question was most revealing; that varied from candidate to candidate and possibly, too, from interviewer to interviewer, depending upon what he saw in each answer. A projective test for a subject is always to some extent a projective test for the psychologist who interprets it. The value of such tests lies not in the quantitative data which they yield but in what they reveal to a sensitively and critically perceptive examiner. One must always count on the possibility of projection in interpreting the results of any projective test; yet not to use them for that reason is to deny oneself insights which can hardly be gained so easily or so quickly with any other procedure. This is not to claim that every finished projective questionnaire was revealing; many of them were drab and banal, indicating little or nothing about their authors. They stirred nothing in our minds, supplied us with no hypotheses which could be tested in the Interview.

To consider but one question, "What moods or feelings are the most unpleasant or disturbing to you?" the frequency with which replies to it provided a key to the candidate's personality, for example, his frustrations, his feelings of inadequacy, his loneliness, or his homesickness, was striking. It was common to find such frank answers as, "Loneliness for my parents," "Thinking perhaps there's something I have missed in life or failed to do," "Feeling sorry for myself," or "Having someone dislike me." But, of course, there were other answers that told us nothing.

Reading the candidate's answers frequently gave us some impression of the manner of man with whom we had to deal. But more than this, the projective questionnaire gave a picture of the man which could be integrated with the factual material in his Personal History and with material from his other written products into a set of impressions and hypotheses regarding his personality which made it possible to use the time devoted to interviewing to maximum advantage.

During the latter part of the evening, while writing their Personal Histories, candidates were twice called from the classroom, first, singly, to have their pictures taken, and later, in groups of two or three, to be given a test of observation and inference which was known as the Belongings Test.[1]

[1] In content, this test overlapped the Brief Case (at first given on the morning of the first full day, but later dropped from the program), and the Murder Mystery which the candidates were asked to solve on the last day. Together these three tests created a world of fantasy into which the candidates were introduced at S. This fantasy was built around a mythical psychologist-consultant to Station S who had hurriedly departed from the area, leaving behind him a number of personal effects which it was the candidate's task to examine in the Belongings Test. As the candidates discovered later, this notorious psychologist was involved in an extramarital affair and had become the dupe of a group of spies who lived in the neighborhood of the area and were trying to penetrate it. As will be described below, this climate of fantasy, laid over S, into which the candidates became drawn, played a most important role in the development of their morale in the assessment program. The scheduling of the Belongings Test in the first evening was important since it was clear that the sooner the candidates were introduced into this fantasy world the more effective that fantasy would be as a morale-builder.

Belongings Test.—For this problem, the candidates were conducted to a room in the basement where, before entering the room, they were given the following instructions:

This is a test of your ability to observe and draw correct conclusions from your observation. This room was occupied several months ago by a man who was a guest here for several days. On his departure he left a number of his things, a number of belongings behind him in the room, planning at the time to return. We have collected these and laid them out so that they are all in plain sight. Your task is to examine them to try to size up the man, to learn all you can about him, what he was like, in any respect. You will have four minutes for the examination, and then you will be asked to answer some questions about this man. You will go in as a group, but you will work individually. Please do not talk to one another during the examination or make any comments on your observations. You may pick up things to examine them if you wish, but please replace everything exactly as you found it for the other persons in the group. Any questions?

The room into which the candidates went was set up as a bedroom. Twenty-six items, among them articles of clothing, written materials, newspaper clippings, time table and ticket receipt, and so on, were placed openly on the bed, chairs, and tables.

The candidates were allowed to remain in the room for the allotted four minutes, while the staff member who was also present noted in as much detail as possible the manner in which they examined the objects.

They were then taken to another room where they were asked to answer thirty-six questions about the man whose belongings they had just examined. These were questions of inference about the mythical figure—for example, questions concerning his age, marital status, weight, occupation, color of hair and eyes, residence, for some of which there was clear evidence, for others doubtful evidence, and for still others no evidence at all. The task of the subject was twofold: (1) to answer the question, i.e., to draw inferences from what he had seen, and (2) to indicate the clue or clues which led him to each conclusion. He was explicitly directed not to answer any question for which he had found no evidence. The raw score, computed by adding the number of correct inferences and the number of correct clues, was converted into a rating on the S basic six-point scale and recorded as one measure—others would be obtained later—of the candidate's ability to observe and draw correct inferences.

This was the program of the first evening at S. It was a full one. It kept the candidates busy from seven o'clock until nearly midnight. In rare cases, where a man for one reason or another had not finished by 12:30, he was interrupted, and it was left to his interviewer to obtain the material which the man had not had time to record.

There is no doubt that this was a difficult and tiring evening. It was, however, extremely valuable from our standpoint for it yielded a great deal of badly needed information about the candidates at the very beginning of the program. And, tiring though it was for the candidates, it served for them, too, a most important function. Its value as a builder of morale for the organization and as a first experience determining the attitude of the candidates toward the assessment program was crucial. Repeatedly subjects reported being very much impressed by the intensive scheduling of the first evening. Their reaction was to feel that any organization that took such pains in the selection of its personnel must be an unusual one, and if they were accepted by it after such testing, then they too must be good.

FIRST DAY

The first full day at S, like those that were to follow, began with breakfast at 7:30, but even before this, while the candidates were waiting in the living room, each had been given a schedule of his appointments for the day.

Breakfast on this day was usually a livelier meal than dinner the night before. Much of the initial tenseness had worn off. By now each man was talking about himself in terms of his cover story, and most of them appeared to be enjoying the experience. There were always some who were not yet at ease in their new roles.

Many wanted to know about Mr. Weeks, whose belongings they had examined the night before, and they were given answers, for we made it a point to discuss with recruits any test they had taken, once it was all over. We did not tell them how they had done, but where there was no reason to believe that discussing tests with them would influence their performance on later tests, we talked about them freely. It seemed to us important to do this after all tests, but especially so after situations which were decidedly unpleasant or in which the candidates were made to endure extreme frustration. It was essential in the assessment of men for overseas assignments in time of war that we see them in stressful and upsetting situations. Yet it was clear that the success of the program depended on our ability to ensure their cooperation and their best efforts in all test situations. A special effort was therefore made to dispel the disturbing effects of certain procedures. We made it a principle, after each upsetting test, to provide an opportunity for catharsis by having the candidate talk the situation over with a member of the staff, who tried to help him get over his feelings of failure and restore his self-confidence. Furthermore, a discussion of each procedure among the men themselves, once they all had passed through it, was permitted and encouraged; and these discussions, often participated in by staff members, had a greatly relieving effect. A playful expression of aggressions against the staff and the procedures was encouraged by staff members, who entered into the game with frank enjoyment. Through this process of socialization and release the disquieting episode soon became a good joke to be enjoyed in retrospect, and the attitude of apprehension with regard to what was coming next was replaced by one of pleasant anticipation. But more than any special devices for dispelling the after effects of upsetting procedures, the cheerfulness and good humor of the staff members, their obvious enthusiasm in their work, their enjoyment of the company of each other and of the candidates, and above all their constant interest in the candidates themselves, were the important factors in inducing the same spirit in the candidates and in making most of them feel, not like psychologists' guinea pigs, but like full-fledged members of the assessment program.

And so this first morning candidates talked about Mr. Weeks and the things they had written about him. They argued as to whether his eyes were blue or brown, whether he was married, whether the whiskey he had left behind in the glass on his bedside table was an indication that he had had a cold or a sign that he was an alcoholic. And so in good-spirited disagreement and interest in the program, the candidates began their first full day.

Breakfast over, the recruits assembled at 8:20 in the classroom. The individual schedules which had been given each man were explained, and the importance of meeting all appointments on time was stressed.

Instructions for Terrain Test.—Candidates were told that at noon of the following day their abilities to observe the terrain of S and its buildings and, from their observations, to infer what the history of the farm had been, would be tested. To aid in this task, a map of S was given each candidate. These they could carry with them as they explored the grounds, and they were free to make whatever notes they wished; but at the time of the examination they would have neither their notes nor their maps. They were specifically instructed to discover what every lettered object on the map represented and to orient the farm and its buildings to the points of the compass. The assignment was to be carried out in their free time and to be treated as an individual problem, each man exploring the grounds by himself.

Immediately after the instructions for the terrain test had been given, the candidates scattered, some with maps in hand to explore the terrain, others to the third floor of the main house for their clinical interviews, a group of them to the main hallway where they gathered before being taken by their staff team to engage in two outdoor situational tests, the Brook and the Wall.

The Brook.—In the execution of this problem the candidates, in a group of four to seven members, were taken to the brook which ran through the

The Brook Situation

The Wall Situation

The Rings

THE OBSTACLE COURSE

The High Wall

The Catwalk

estate.[2] This was a shallow, narrow, quiet stream, the banks of which were about eight feet apart. On one bank was a heavy rock, on the other a log. There were trees on both sides of the brook and scattered around on the side where the group stood were a number of boards, none long enough to reach from bank to bank, three lengths of rope, a pulley, and a barrel with both ends knocked out.

Having come to the brook, the candidates were instructed as follows:

In this problem you have to use your imagination. Before you, you see a raging torrent so deep and so fast that it is quite impossible to rest anything upon the bottom of the stream. The banks are sheer, so it will be impossible for you to work except from the top of them.

You are on a mission in the field, and having come to this brook you are faced with the task of transporting this delicate range-finder, skillfully camouflaged

[2] It was our custom to divide classes of candidates into subgroups in order the more easily to observe individual behavior and the more adequately to perform our task of assessment. It was too much to expect that all members of the staff could get to know every candidate equally well when the usual number of men in a class was eighteen. To have tried to observe the behavior of all eighteen recruits in various group tests would have led only to a chaos of impressions. For these reasons we divided S classes into subgroups: three subgroups of six for a class of eighteen; three subgroups of five for a class of fifteen, and so forth. To each subgroup was assigned a team of three staff members who were primarily responsible for the assessment of the candidates in their group.

In assigning candidates to a subgroup, primary attention was paid to the proposed assignment, the age, and the educational status of the men, since it was our desire to have each group as homogeneous as possible with respect to these factors. With larger classes we were usually able to form three rather distinct groups: (1) men recruited for sabotage operations behind enemy lines—young, athletic men, as a rule, many of whom had not gone to college; (2) men recruited for secret intelligence work—in early middle age, generally, with a better education and less athletic ability than those in the first group; (3) men recruited for propaganda activities—in the early days of S, many of these were émigrés from Europe, artistically inclined, and belonging to the "verbal type." This group was likely to be more heterogeneous than the other two. To it would also be assigned men who had been selected as administrators and those who were to work in the field of social research and analysis.

There would have been some advantages in adopting the opposite policy, in making each subgroup as heterogeneous as possible, but it seemed, on the whole, better to bring together the kind of men who would work together overseas. Then, too, with homogeneous groups the danger that a man would be overrated or underrated by the staff because he stood out in either a positive or negative way from his teammates was minimized.

The team of three assigned to each subgroup of candidates was composed of one junior and two senior staff members (each of whom acted as interviewer of half of the men in the group). Those who were primarily responsible for recording the behavior of candidates in the various situational tests were designated as "situationists," in contrast to the "interviewers." This distinction in names, however, did not mean that the interviewers saw candidates only in the interview or that only the situationists saw them operating as a group. All staff members observed all the members of their subgroup in all situational tests. This meant that each candidate was rated independently by at least three members of the staff on every situation, and in some situations where all candidates and all staff members were brought together, every candidate was rated by every staff member.

The independent ratings given by members of any one staff team were always subsequently discussed in conference and converted to a final rating agreed to by all. (The details of staff work and the procedures by which final ratings as well as the final reports on candidates were prepared are described at length in Chapter IV.)

as a log, to the far bank, and of bringing that box of percussion caps, camouflaged as a rock, to this side. In carrying out this assignment, you may make
use of any materials you find around here. When the job is done, all of you,
as well as any material you have used, are to be back on this side.

The limits within which you are to work are marked by the two white stakes
on each bank [the stakes were approximately fifteen feet apart], and you are not
permitted to jump across the stream.

This is a group problem. We would suggest that you first discuss your method
of procedure. When you have decided upon your plan and are ready to go to
work, let us know so that we may time you, for in the actual execution of this
problem you will be working against time. Do not start any work until you have
decided upon your plan and until we have given you the signal to start.

Whenever the candidates indicated that they had agreed upon a plan, or
at the end of ten minutes if they were still undecided about their course
of action, they were given the signal to start.

The fancied elaboration of the physical situation, as well as the restriction
upon jumping, was introduced in order to prevent too easy solutions of
the problem. Actually, all solutions involved getting one or more men to the
other side of the brook by building a bridge with the boards and rope, by
roping a branch of a tree on the far bank and rigging an overhead cable,
or by swinging out and across on a rope tied to a high branch of a tree
on the near bank. The transfer of the objects across the brook was then
achieved by utilizing the bridge or the overhead cable, with or without the
use of the pulley, and by tying ropes around the objects and manipulating
them from both sides of the brook.

The instructions were worded so as to place all candidates on an equal
footing in approaching their task. Since no one was designated to take
charge of the proceedings, the situation provided an opportunity for those
who were eager for leadership to assert it and to maintain it if they could.
In fact, an attempt was made in the Brook, as in all similar tests, to structure
the situation as little as possible, beyond outlining the rules and physical
boundaries of the task, and saying that it was one for them to solve as a
group.

Each situational test in the program was designed to reveal certain variables of personality. Those that could be rated at the Brook were Energy and
Initiative, Effective Intelligence, Social Relations, Leadership, and Physical
Ability. It would be difficult if not impossible to list all the varieties of behavior which were subsumed under these categories, but some of the more
recurrent forms may be noted as illustrative of what we had in mind when
we rated these variables.

Energy and Initiative, as a single variable of personality, was conceived
to be the amount of overt physical and verbal activity which the candidate
directed toward the solution of the problem and the degree of his interest

and persistence in applying himself to the task. During the discussion of possible plans, Energy and Initiative could be seen in a recruit's offering various suggestions, showing an interest in the ideas of others, and working actively with the group for a final plan of action. Once the work got under way, it was manifest in a candidate's contributing energetically to the physical work, volunteering for the more difficult or more unpleasant tasks and actually doing them, suggesting solutions as new problems arose, and maintaining a high level of interest in carrying the project through to the end. The candidate with high energy and initiative was the man to cross the stream, to climb the tree, to rig the rope, to fasten the log with rope whether it was soft and pliable or frozen stiff or covered with mud; he was ready to propose new ideas when they were needed and to direct others in their execution. On the other hand, the recruit with low initiative and energy said little or nothing in the period of discussing plans, took little or no part in the actual doing of the work, made slight effort to cooperate with his associates, and evinced little interest in their efforts to solve the problem.

Effective Intelligence, it seemed to us, was displayed in many forms at the Brook: the insight of the candidate into the general requirements of the problem; his speed and resourcefulness in meeting these demands; the relevance and usefulness of his ideas and suggestions; his evaluation of the proposals of others; his ability to see certain physical relationships (the fact, for example, that while no single board was long enough to bridge the stream, two tied together would serve this purpose); his ability to solve the mechanical problems involved in the situation (rigging the ropes and pulley, tying knots, securing the boards of the bridge); and so forth. The recruit of low intelligence showed none of these characteristics. Instead, he made inappropriate or inadequate suggestions, persisted in ideas that were not feasible, and was incapable of implementing the plans of others with the available materials.

The variable of personality designated by us as Social Relations was to be observed in all that a candidate did in relation to his fellows. Typical positive manifestations of good social relations at the Brook were seen in the willingness of a recruit to work with his group for a common end, tactfulness in criticizing or opposing the ideas of others, the disposition to take criticism or rejection of his own ideas good-naturedly, a reliable sense of humor, warmth, friendliness, and insight into others. A candidate with good social relations was usually an active participant in the group, eager to cooperate, and obviously liked and respected by his associates. Among the indices of good social relations was included a ready and warm response of his teammates to him. There were fully as many ways in which a candidate could manifest poor social relations: he could withdraw from the group and work by himself, or not work at all; he could be hostile or annoying, irritable or caustic, surly or tactless in his dealing with his teammates.

Of all the variables of personality rated at the Brook none was more interesting to observe or more varied in its appearance than Leadership. Indices of this trait were taken to be a man's initiative and forcefulness in guiding others in the solution of the problem; in his organizing of the group into an effective working team; in his diplomatic planning of the solution, judiciously combining ideas from several sources; and in his skillful directing of the proceedings in the final execution of the plan. The good leader was the one who commanded the respect and following of others, who had the ability to organize their ideas into a plan, and who was forceful enough to guide his colleagues to the completion of their task with a minimum of friction and a maximum of coöperation. On the other hand, a poor leader might be a man who was simply content to take orders from others, a man without interest in leading, or a man without forcefulness or initiative. But leadership was not always so simple as this.

Sometimes the group formally elected a leader at the start and retained him to the end despite his demonstrated lack of competence. More often some man would assert himself by proposing a plan of action or by asking each man for his ideas and thus taking charge of the discussion. If he succeeded in gaining the lead in either of these ways, he might continue to guide his teammates from then on, even though his ideas were faulty and his plans poorly conceived. But a man who took the lead at the beginning was not always directing things at the end, and it was just these cases in which the leadership role changed that were particularly interesting. Sometimes a man who started by guiding the discussion lost his place when the work began to one who was more adept in manipulating physical objects. On another occasion a man would lose his leadership when a teammate proposed a new idea that was adopted by the others, who then turned to this second man for direction in its execution. If it worked, the group was apt to regard him as the leader from that point on. Not infrequently two or more men competed for leadership throughout the task, acknowledgment shifting from one to the other as they varied momentarily in resourcefulness or power. But it was not always the most assertive individual who dominated the enterprise. He might try for leadership and even hold it for a time, but the group might reject him eventually in favor of a quieter member who had made suggestions that had really worked. It was clear that leadership assertion and leadership efficiency were two different things, though, to be sure, a single individual could manifest both qualities in high degree.

The quality of leadership at the Brook was almost infinitely varied. There were those who pitched into the work and did much of it themselves, setting the pace and the direction of the solution by their own actions, encouraging the rest to work with them. Others directed from a distance, giving orders without soiling their hands. Usually, however, the leader was close to the work; rarely did a man who stood aside succeed in maintaining his authority. Still others shared the responsibility, selecting one or two "lieutenants" and collaborating with them in directing the affair. In some groups the division of role was such that it was difficult to designate any one person as leader.

While Physical Ability was a variable to be rated at the Brook, there was seldom a good opportunity to measure it with certainty. Only a few indications of it could be seen: a man's strength in lifting and manipulating the boards, log, or rock, or in pulling on a rope; his skill in crossing hand-over-hand on the overhead cable, or balancing on a precarious bridge.

Not only were there individual differences to be observed but also marked group differences. Some groups worked like busy beavers, moving so fast and skillfully and harmoniously that there was little need for verbal communication or even direction from a leader. When the problem was solved —usually quickly—it was difficult to know who had done what. Other groups were disrupted by argument and disagreement, everyone competing for the lead and none willing to do the dirty work. There were verbal groups who talked and talked with little result; there were sluggish groups and energetic groups.

In the program at S one hour was allotted for the two outdoor tasks, the Brook and the Wall. Something of the range of ability among groups in dealing with such problems is shown in the fact that, though the fastest time for the Brook was four minutes, there were groups who after an hour had not yet succeeded in transporting the rock and the log over the stream.

The Wall.—Immediately following their completion of the Brook problem, the group was taken across a field to a wooden wall, ten feet high and fifteen feet long. As the candidates stood before it, they were told to imagine themselves at the foot of a barrier that extended, like the wall of China, for thousands of miles. For this reason it would be impossible for them to go around it (nor would they be permitted to look around it). Actually, they were facing two parallel walls of equal height and width, eight feet apart, only the first of which, however, could be seen by them. In front of them was a heavy log, and near by on the ground were an old board a few inches longer than the log, and a couple of two-by-fours, one two feet and the other three feet in length.

The men were informed (fancy being mixed with fact as in other situational tests) that although they could not see it, the barrier before them actually consisted of two walls (fact) separated by a two-hundred-foot canyon (fancy). They were escaping from some Japanese soldiers, and in order to save themselves they would have to get to the other side of the far wall, and to fulfill their mission they would have to take their king-size bazooka (the log) with them. They might get across the wall in any way they wished, but they must not walk around the ends of the wall, and, of course, whoever or whatever fell into the canyon would be counted lost. With no time allowed for preparation of a plan of action, they were told at once that they were being timed.

The solution of this problem proceeded somewhat as follows. Two men would climb to the top of the first wall, pushed up by their companions or by using the short two-by-fours braced against the wall. Having reached the top, they would see that the problem was to build a bridge between the two walls and that the log might be used for this purpose—if it were long enough. Sooner or later someone would see that the long, light board could be used to measure both the length of the log and the distance between the two walls. By comparing measurements they would discover that the log was long enough to reach from one wall to the other. But how to get it across? Soon someone would see that if the board were supported on the far wall and held by someone on the near wall, the log could be pushed across it. Once the log was in place the men would straddle it and work themselves across to the other side, and, then, using the board again as a support, they would pull the log over to them, drop it to the ground and finally jump down themselves. On rare occasions a candidate would stand on the narrow shelf on top of the first wall and jump to the second. Then, by reaching out to support the log as it was pushed toward him, he would succeed in getting it onto the second wall without the aid of the board. Although the men would sometimes stand the log up on one wall and drop it down neatly onto the top of the other wall, such attempts to solve the problem without using the board were seldom successful.

The same variables that were rated at the Brook were also rated at the Wall, and since the two situations were so similar and since they followed so immediately upon each other, it was our practice to treat them as a unit, the final rating of each variable being based upon a man's performance in the two situations. The Wall served to amplify our recently gained impression of how the candidates would handle a physical problem. We were anxious to know what changes a fresh start in a new but similar problem would reveal in the behavior of individual members and in the structure of the group.

Since the Wall, like the Brook, was a leaderless situation, it was interesting to see whether the same man would take charge of both undertakings, or whether a new man would seize the opportunity offered by the change to exert authority. Frequently the same man directed both tasks, but often, too, a new man would take over, particularly if the leader at the Brook had been old and heavy-set and thus unable to get quickly to the vantage point on top of the wall. The original leader in this situation was often the man who got to the top of the wall first. If this was his only qualification, he soon lost his authority when others got up beside him, but a man with some aptitude for leadership could gain a decided advantage simply by getting to the top first. The good leader would see that too many men did not crowd the top of the wall while the log was being passed up, he would have the stronger men remain below to pass up the log but yet avoid the predicament of having the last man a heavy, awkward person who could not reach the top without help from below. Similarly, he would direct traffic across the log to the other side, sending a lithe, confident man first to help the more timid and awkward ones who would come in the middle while he or some other brought up the rear. The man with good physical ability would be quick and agile in climbing the wall; he would show strength in handling the log, and be without fear or awkwardness in crossing it. In physical ability, the man who jumped from one wall to the other without falling (fortunately none who attempted this feat ever failed) was clearly very superior.

The occurrence of these two outdoor situations on the first morning usually served to engender a state of high morale among the candidates. The contrast between a group before and after the Brook and the Wall was striking. On the way down conversation was usually scanty and somewhat strained; on the way back it was characteristically lively and good-humored. The awkwardness that had led to slips such as dropping the rock or a teammate into the brook was recalled with laughter, and those who had been responsible had to tolerate the ribbing of their teammates. Comments and compliments about the special feats of certain men made for good feeling, and discussions, encouraged by the staff, of how the group would go about these tasks were they to do them again provided an opportunity for making new suggestions or criticizing those of others. Such talk revealed something more of the practical intelligence as well as the social relations of the candidates. Frequently a group in which *esprit de corps* was beginning to develop would start planning how they would coordinate their efforts if and when they worked again as a group. In general the amount of interest shown in discussing situations and in planning for future ones varied with the degree of previous success. Groups which had failed to solve the Brook problem in the allotted hour had few ideas as to how they would do it again and little zest for similar undertakings in the future. But they, like others, though perhaps for different reasons, wanted to know how other groups had solved the problem; and if there were some who had shown their resentment in any way, these were data to be observed, remembered, and interpreted, if possible, in the light of other information that would be subsequently obtained about these candidates.

Construction.—Sometime during the morning of the first day each candidate had an appointment behind the barn. If hearing of the location of this appointment made the men recall, sometimes with amusement, events in their boyhood when they had kept similar appointments with their fathers, it is safe to assume that even such recollections failed to prepare them for what they would experience on this occasion.

Ostensibly this was a test of the candidate's ability to direct two helpers in building with him a frame structure out of simple wooden materials. Actually the situation was not so benign as it first appeared. To be sure, it was a test of Leadership, but more truly it was a test of Emotional Stability and frustration tolerance. Energy and Initiative in carrying out the work and the Social Relations of the candidate in relation to his helpers were also rated.

The building materials for this test were wooden poles of two lengths (5 and 7 feet), wooden blocks with sockets into which the poles could be fitted, and small pegs to hold the poles and blocks together. The blocks were of two sorts, full blocks and half blocks. The full blocks were of octagonal shape with sockets cut into each of the eight sides. Running through the center of each block was a circular hole of the same diameter as that of the poles. The half blocks had sockets in only three sides but attached to and protruding from the opposite long side was a dowel the thickness of a pole which could be inserted through the center hole of a full block. This equipment was a great magnification of the "tinker toy" sets of childhood. With this, each candidate was directed to build a 5-foot cube with 7-foot diagonals on the four sides.

When the candidate came to the area where the test was to be conducted the staff member said to him:

We have a construction problem for you now. We want you to build a structure using the equipment lying around here. Let's see. (*The staff member appears to ponder which of two or three models of different design to use.*) I guess we'll give you this model to copy. (*Staff member picks up the model which is always used from among the others and shows it to the student.*) You see there are short 5-foot and long 7-foot poles lying on the ground. (*Staff member points out one of each size.*) The sides of the frame which you are to build are made of 5-foot poles, and the diagonals of 7-foot poles. (*Staff member demonstrates this on the model.*) Do you understand?

Now the corners where the poles come together are made like this. You take a half block and put it through a full block. Then you cinch it with a peg, like this. (*Staff member demonstrates all this.*) Then when you put the corner down on the ground, you can put 5-foot poles in here, here, and here, and the 7-foot diagonals here and here. Do you understand?

Now (*staff member picks up the corner and points to the peg*) you will notice there are holes for pegs like this at each socket, and similar holes in the end of each pole. Be sure, whenever you put a pole into a socket, to cinch it with a peg, because unless that is done all over the structure it will not be stable. (*Staff member then throws the sample corner to the ground.*) Is this all clear?

This is a construction problem, but even more important than that, it is a test of leadership. I say that because it is impossible for one man working alone to complete this task in the ten minutes allotted to do it. Therefore we are going to give you two helpers who work here on the estate. You are to be the supervisor, their boss. You are to guide them in their work, but as foreman, you will follow more or less of a hands-off policy. Let them do the manual labor. You can assume that they have never done such work before and know nothing about it. Any questions? (*Final pause to amplify any details not understood by the candidate.*)

All right. It is now ten o'clock. You have just ten minutes in which to do the job. I'll call your two helpers.

At this the two assistants, who had been working in the barn, were asked to come out and help the candidate. They complied, but waited for him to take the initiative. These two members of the junior staff traditionally assumed the pseudonyms of Kippy and Buster. Whoever played the part of Kippy acted in a passive, sluggish manner. He did nothing at all unless specifically ordered to, but stood around, often getting in the way, either idling with his hands in his pockets or concerned with some insignificant project of his own, such as a minute examination of the small-scale model. Buster, on the other hand, played a different role. He was aggressive, forward in offering impractical suggestions, ready to express dissatisfaction, and quick to criticize what he suspected were the candidate's weakest points.

The two assistants were not permitted, by their secret instructions, to disobey orders, and they were supposed to carry out whatever directions were given to them explicitly. Within the bounds of this ruling, though, it was their function to present the candidate with as many obstructions and annoyances as possible in ten minutes. As it turned out, they succeeded in frustrating the candidates so thoroughly that the construction was never, in the history of S, completed in the allotted time.

At first the assistants appeared cooperative, but if the candidate did not introduce himself and ask their names, Buster would observe that a boss interested in getting along with his men would at least find out their names. If the candidate did not explain in detail what they were to do, referring to the model, Buster would complain that they were receiving inadequate directions and remark that the candidate must be inexperienced. If he were either peremptory or passive, he would be criticized for this. Buster might say that that was a poor trait in a leader, and add that he found it hard to understand how anyone could ever have thought the candidate was worthy of holding an important position in the organization. If the candidate became so incensed at their unmanageableness that he laid a hand on them with the intention of getting them to work faster, the helper who was touched would take great offense. After the work had begun, Buster, or occasionally Kippy, might criticize the candidate's plan of operation and suggest other, often incorrect, ways to proceed in order to test the forcefulness of the man's leadership. Kippy, for instance, might attempt to involve the boss in a debate about the relative advantages of the two plans. Or he might get into an argument with the other assistant over alternative methods of building a corner. Again, he might say that the octagonal edges of the corner blocks were the "rolling edges," and that they would not rest firmly enough on the ground to hold the structure. (Actually they would and that was the correct way to build the cube.) The assistants might try to get the leader to lay the blocks down flat, which was incorrect. They might even point to four holes in the ground, suggesting that those must be the places where previous workers had laid the corners flat. Or, in another attempt to divert the candidate from his plan, they might point out to him that the model was mounted on cardboard, and suggest that he search the area for cardboard with which to make a base for the structure so that it would be exactly like the model. If the candidate acceded to their suggestion, he wasted time, because he was not directed to build such a base.

Frequently the candidate began to construct the cube incorrectly. When this happened the assistants would follow his orders for a while and then point out the errors, at the same time tearing down the structure if the leader did not stop them. From time to time, if Buster discovered a pole that was not pegged into its socket, he would kick the two pieces apart, saying sharply that no sensible person would expect such a framework to hold together unless it was pegged. It was discouraging to any man to see his cube collapsing before his eyes, but the reactions differed. Some candidates became bitter; others gave up and refused to continue. On the other hand, good leaders would patiently begin again or direct the helpers to stop tearing the pieces apart until they had decided whether the mistakes could be more easily rectified.

Another stratagem used by the two assistants when the work was well under way was to distract the candidate's attention from the job. They asked questions about him—where he came from, what his real name was, how long he had been in the Army, where he got his accent, and so on. They made an effort to break through his cover story if he answered these questions, and often their attempts were successful. If he refused to reply to their queries because of concentration on the job, they accused him of being unsociable. If they noticed anything particularly distinctive about him—for example, a peculiar accent, baldness, a reserved attitude—they burlesqued this trait in order to irritate him further. If he mentioned any special interest, they encouraged him to discuss it. If he became distracted, they continued on that line for a while, and then Buster might suddenly tell the candidate he was neglecting the job. He might accuse him of being "the poorest leader I ever saw around here," and suggest, since he was so obviously inept, that he give up the assignment entirely. If, after a few minutes of such frustrations, the candidate stopped directing the others and began to do the work by himself, or showed any evidence of emotion, Buster would immediately note this reaction and make some caustic comment designed to heighten it.

While Buster was needling the candidate in this way, Kippy was moping about, doing little. If he was given a direction, he complied slowly and clumsily, showing no initiative, stopping as soon as he had completed the specific task. He sometimes went up to the candidate to request permission to leave for a minute "to go get a drink." In general he followed the policy of passive resistance, doing everything possible to sabotage the construction by his inertia.

To illustrate how the helpers turned the conversation in Construction into banter which could be exploited for purposes of personality assessment, a typical protocol is reproduced here.

STAFF MEMBER (*calling toward the barn*): Can you come out here and help this man for a few minutes?

BUSTER AND KIPPY: Sure, we'll be right out.

STAFF MEMBER: O.K., Slim, these are your men. They will be your helpers. You have ten minutes.

SLIM: Do you men know anything about building this thing?

BUSTER: Well, I dunno, I've seen people working here. What is it you want done?

SLIM: Well, we have got to build a cube like this and we only have a short time in which to do it, so I'll ask you men to pay attention to what I have to say. I'll tell you what to do and you will do it. O.K.?

BUSTER: Sure, sure, anything you say, Boss.

SLIM: Fine. Now we are going to build a cube like this with 5-foot poles for the uprights and 7-foot poles for the diagonals, and use the blocks for the corners. So first we must build the corners by putting a half block and a whole block together like this and cinching them with a peg. Do you see how it is done?

BUSTER: Sure, sure.

SLIM: Well, let's get going.

BUSTER: Well, what is it you want done, exactly? What do I do first?

SLIM: Well, first put some corners together—let's see, we need four on the bottom and four topside—yes, we need eight corners. You make eight of these corners and be sure that you pin them like this one.

BUSTER: You mean we both make eight corners or just one of us?

SLIM: You each make four of them.

BUSTER: Well, if we do that, we will have more than eight because you already have one made there. Do you want eight altogether or nine altogether?

SLIM: Well, it doesn't matter. You each make four of these, and hurry.

BUSTER: O.K., O.K.

KIPPY: What cha in, the Navy? You look like one of them curly-headed Navy boys all the girls are after. What cha in, the Navy?

SLIM: Er—no. I am not in the Navy. I'm not in anything.

KIPPY: Well, you were just talking about "topside" so I thought maybe you were in the Navy. What's the matter with you—you look healthy enough. Are you a draft dodger?

SLIM: No, I was deferred for essential work—but that makes no difference. Let's get the work done. Now we have the corners done, let's put them together with the poles.

KIPPY: The more I think of it, the more I think you are in the Army. You run this job just like the Army—you know, the right way, the wrong way, and the Army way. I'll bet you are some second lieutenant from Fort Benning.

SLIM: That has nothing to do with this job. Let's have less talk and more work.

KIPPY: Well, I just thought we could talk while we work—it's more pleasant.

SLIM: Well, we can work first and talk afterward. Now connect those two corners with a 5-foot pole.

BUSTER: Don't you think we ought to clear a place where we can work?

SLIM: That's a good idea. Sure, go ahead.

BUSTER: What kind of work did you do before you came here? Never did any building, I bet. Jeez, I've seen a lot of guys, but no one as dumb as you.

SLIM: Well, that may be, but you don't seem to be doing much to help me.

BUSTER: What—what's that? Who are you talking to, me? Me not being helpful —why, I've done everything you have asked me, haven't I? Now, haven't I? Everything you asked me. Why, I've been about as helpful as anyone could be around here.

SLIM: Well, you haven't killed yourself working and we haven't much time, so let's get going.

BUSTER: Well, I like that. I come out here and do everything you ask me to do. You don't give very good directions. I don't think you know what you are doing anyway. No one else ever complained about me not working. Now I want an apology for what you said about me.

SLIM: O.K., O.K., let's forget it. I'll apologize. Let's get going. We haven't much time. You build a square here and you build one over there.

BUSTER: Who you talking to—him or me?

KIPPY: That's right—how do you expect us to know which one you mean? Why don't you give us a number or something—call one of us "number one" and the other "number two"?

SLIM: O.K. You are "one" and he is "two."

BUSTER: Now, wait a minute—just a minute. How do you expect to get along with people if you treat them like that? First we come out here and you don't ask us our names—you call us "you." Then we tell you about it, you give us numbers. How would you like that? How would you like to be called a number? You treat us just like another 5-foot pole and then you expect us to break our necks working for you. I can see you never worked much with people.

SLIM: I'm sorry, but we do not have much time and I thought—

KIPPY: Yes, you thought. Jeez, it doesn't seem to me that you ever did much thinking about anything. First you don't ask our names as any stupid guy would who was courteous. Then you don't know what you did before you came here or whether you are in the Army, Navy, or not, and it's darn sure you don't know anything about building this thing or directing workers. Cripes, man, you stand around here like a ninny arguing when we should be working. What the hell is the matter with you, anyway?

SLIM: I'm sorry—what are your names?

BUSTER: I'm Buster.

KIPPY: Mine's Kippy. What is yours?

SLIM: You can call me Slim.

BUSTER: Well, is that your name or isn't it?

SLIM: Yes, that is my name.

KIPPY: It's not a very good name—Dumbhead would be better.

BUSTER: Where do you come from, Slim?

SLIM: Cincinnati.

BUSTER: That's out in Ohio, isn't it?

SLIM: Yes.

BUSTER: What's the river it's on?

SLIM: Uh—why the Ohio.

BUSTER: You don't sound very sure. I almost wonder if you do come from there. I'd think any Cincinnatian would remember the name of the river.

SLIM: I'm from Cincinnati, all right. I lived there for eight years.

BUSTER: Down by the river? In the tenement district?

SLIM: No, in a residential region up to the north.

BUSTER: What street?

SLIM: Why, 1490 Kingsbury Street. What does that have to do with the present problem?

BUSTER: The reason I asked was you don't seem to be very well dressed, and I thought probably you hadn't made much of a success of your business and couldn't live in a nice part of town.

SLIM: Be that as it may—we've got to get back to work. You aren't doing anything except talking and the time is passing rapidly.

BUSTER: Well, what kind of a boss are you anyway? You haven't told me anything to do. You stand there and say "get to work, get to work," but you don't say what I should do. Another thing, Kippy's just sitting over there trying to make that pole stick into the dirt and you don't make him work. You might at least treat us both the same. Why don't you act like a boss? Why don't you say, "Come here, Kippy, you good-for-nothing, and justify your existence. Get some work done!"

SLIM: Come on over, Kippy; he's right. We all have to work together. You haven't been doing your part. Don't you want to help?

KIPPY: Sure I do, but you haven't told me anything to do.

SLIM: I certainly did. I said to make some corners and you just went over there and sat down.

KIPPY: If that's the way you're going to talk to me—yelling and hollering and losing your temper—just because you can't give orders a fellow can understand, I don't have to work for you. You've got to be decent.

SLIM: Well, O.K., I'll show you exactly. I want you to help me make four corners for the bottom of this using a whole block and a half block pegged together with a peg like this.

KIPPY: Well, why didn't you say so long ago? You sure wasted a lot of time.

BUSTER: We've got to work faster.

SLIM: That's right, Buster.

BUSTER: I suppose you know you're not very observant.

SLIM: What do you mean?

BUSTER: See those four holes in the ground? They're just 5 feet apart in a square, aren't they? What does that bring to your mind? Could it be the place to lay the corners down on the ground to make them firm? You have your corners standing up on the rolling edges and that isn't very stable.

SLIM: It looks all right to me, if the four poles were put into the corners.

BUSTER: O.K., if you want to sacrifice stability for mobility, it's up to you. But you might at least accept a suggestion in the spirit in which it's given. "I'm the boss," you say. "I'm better than those other guys. If I'm in charge I'm not going to listen to them. Even if they are right, I won't admit it, because I'm going to show them who's in control around here."

SLIM: Well, we'll try your way, but I don't think it's necessary.

BUSTER: Slim isn't your real nickname, is it? It couldn't be with that shining head of yours. What do they call you, Baldy or Curly? Did you ever think of wearing a toupee? It would keep you from getting your scalp sunburned.

SLIM: I don't see what difference that makes! Come on, both of you, and put an upright in each corner.

KIPPY: He's sensitive about being bald.

BUSTER: Yeah. . . . Well, Captain, we don't seem to be getting much done here, do we?

SLIM: Well, if you guys would get to work we would.

BUSTER: Well, it seems to me it's sorta late now. Why don't you be a man and admit that you can't do this job? After all, it's only a toy and sort of foolish for a grown man. It's nothing to be ashamed of that you can't build it. It's just not in your line.

SLIM: Well, I'd like to do as much of this as possible. Will you help me?

BUSTER: Sure, sure, we'll help you, but it doesn't seem to be much use. What do you want us to do now?

SLIM: Well, one of you build a square over there just like this one while the other one puts in the uprights and diagonals on this one.

KIPPY: May I ask a question?

SLIM: Sure, go ahead.

KIPPY: Why build one over there? What are you going to do with it then?

SLIM: Well, we'll put it on top—the top of this cube is like the bottom.

KIPPY: Well, if that isn't the most stupid thing I ever heard of. Since when do you build the roof of a house and lift it to the top? Why not build it right on the top? Listen, when you build a house you build the foundation, then the walls, and then the roof. Isn't that right?

SLIM: Well, that is usually the way it's done, but I think we can do this job this way. In fact, I don't think it matters much which way we do it. Either way is O.K., I guess.

BUSTER: You guess, you guess. What kind of a man are you anyway? Why in hell don't you make up your mind and stick to it? Be decisive—didn't they tell you that in OCS?—be decisive—even if you are wrong, be decisive, give an order. What are you—man or mouse?

KIPPY: Oh, it's no use talking, Buster, when he doesn't have a bar on his shoulder he doesn't know what to do. Listen, Mac, you're not on Company Street now. You haven't a sergeant to do your work for you. You're all alone and you look pretty silly. Why, you can't even put together a child's toy.

SLIM: Now listen to me, you guys, are you going to work for me or aren't you?

BUSTER: Sure, we want to work for you. We really don't care. We'd as soon work for you as for anyone else. We get paid all the same. The trouble is we can't find out what you want done. What exactly do you want?

SLIM: Just let's get this thing finished. We haven't much more time. Hey there, you, be careful, you knocked that pole out deliberately.

KIPPY: Who, me? Now listen to me, you good-for-nothing young squirt. If this darned thing had been built right from the beginning the poles wouldn't come out. Weren't you told that you had to pin these things? Why, none of it is pinned; look at that, and that, and that! (*Kicks the poles which were not pinned out of position and part of the structure collapses.*)

SLIM: Hey—you don't have to knock it all down!

BUSTER: Well, it wasn't built right. What good was it without pins?

SLIM: I told you guys to pin it.

KIPPY: I pinned every one you told me about. How did I know you wanted the others pinned? Jeez, they send a boy out here to do a man's job and when he can't do it he starts blaming his helpers. Who is responsible for this—you or me? Cripes, they must really be scraping the bottom of the barrel now.

STAFF MEMBER (*Walking in from the sidelines*): All right, Slim. That is all the time we have. The men will take this down.

BUSTER: Take what down? There's nothing to take down. Never saw anyone get so little done.

It is difficult to say what is the most desirable behavior for a candidate under such trying circumstances. Certainly disparate sorts of solutions were attempted. Some candidates, after they had seen that they were being hindered rather than helped by the assistants, either neglected them or actually discharged them, trying to do as much as they could by themselves. However, this certainly was not the correct procedure according to the directions, because one man could not complete the task in the allotted time, and moreover he had been told he must act as a leader. Others became authoritative or military, attempting to discipline the assistants, but this tended to anger such "sensitive workers" and made them work even more poorly. Still others simply relinquished their authority and followed the directions of the assistants. Some lost their tempers or became frustrated easily, and more than one candidate struck an assistant with his fist out of anger.

The best solution, presumably, was one in which the leader first explained what he wished to have done, then delegated specific tasks to each assistant, keeping his eye on both of them, directing them, and keeping them working. At the same time he had to maintain good social relations, treating his helpers like equals, answering their suggestions, justifying his decisions to them, and taking their criticisms lightheartedly. He did well to reply to them with responses calculated not to offend overmuch their delicate sensibilities. It was, of course, hard for the candidate to decide whether he could get more done in the ten-minute period by acting entirely alone or by relying on the dubious cooperation of the helpers. At any rate, the problem was never completed in the allotted time, and usually it was scarcely begun.

Just what was measured in this situation is difficult to state exactly. One criticism leveled at it has been that many of the candidates looked on it merely as an artificial test instead of as a real-life problem, and so it was not indicative of anything significant. This criticism applies to every situational test. But the truth is that, while some candidates afterward said they did not take the problem seriously because they knew it was a test, a larger number admitted that they forgot themselves in it as they would in a real situation. The cases where the candidates lost their tempers, hit their assistants, or showed other marked evidences of emotion bear this out.

Starting for the candidate as an opportunity to demonstrate leadership, Construction would gradually become for him a test of his capacity to work toward completion of the task in the face of increasing pressures furnished by the stooges. His helpers were cooperative at the beginning but each candidate inevitably did or said something which furnished an excuse for criticism, vilification, and active interference. The stooges made a strong effort to incite anger, impulsiveness, and the suspension of the normal controls of behavior. Except for attacking the candidate physically, practically every other technique for making him feel foolish and miserable was employed. The presence and behavior of these helpers represented the provoking stress in the situation.

Another force in the environment operating upon the candidate was the presence of the staff members observing on the side lines. Their presence had the effect of impressing upon the candidate the need for controlled and sensible action. He was partly aware that he was on the spot and that any untoward behavior on his part would be counted against him. There is some basis for arguing that if the staff observers had not been there his behavior might have been more unstable, or at least less restrained and hence easier to assess. On the other hand, the presence of the staff was an additional strain which tended to magnify conflicts and tensions within the recruit. Undoubtedly this Construction test represented a unique kind of stress which in intensity would probably never be matched by many field situations. Certainly it did evoke emotion and was a constant challenge to the student to keep himself under control and to continue at the task. And it was more than a "snafu" tolerance test, for it afforded insight into the candidate's range of affective behavior as well as the security measures which he took against anxiety. For various candidates it had different degrees of artificiality, some guessing immediately that the "helpers" were really staff members bent on upsetting their control, while others, having accepted the test as a real situation, remained naïve to the very end. Even though an occasional candidate had quick insight about what was going on, the situation was generally stressful. Obviously the degree of insight possessed by a candidate was always taken into account in interpreting his observed behavior, even though our best measure of his insight was not obtained until the Post-Construction Interview was held.

Emotional responses revealed at Construction seemed to provide a good gauge of tolerance for frustration and "snafu," particularly in the field of interpersonal relationships. At times it exceeded a candidate's limit. There were men so shaken by their experience behind the barn that they begged to be released from the assessment program and from OSS, if work in the organization required that one remain calm and in control of himself in such circumstances.

This situation was also a test of leadership, at least of a sort. How good a leader a man was was gauged by the way he dominated the situation; how he outlined the task to his subordinates and explained why they should follow the course he set; how he took suggestions from subordinates; how much consideration he showed them; how pleasant his relationships with them were despite their criticisms; and how much respect and work he could elicit from them. Leadership was hard to measure because the golden mean between authoritarianism and laxness was scarcely achievable in this situation.

It is obvious that a man's ability to maintain agreeable social relationships could be well tested in such a difficult situation, and it was usually found that this trait was easier to evaluate satisfactorily than either Emotional Stability or Leadership. It was also possible to rate the candidate's interest in the problem and his zest and energy in attempting to get it done.

To provide candidates with an opportunity for emotional catharsis after this situational test, as well as to employ another technique for assessing them, a Post-Construction Interview was introduced into the program.

Post-Construction Interview.—After a candidate was told that his time was up in Construction, the staff member who had given him the instructions accompanied him as he walked away from the scene. Establishing a friendly rapport with the candidate, the staff man asked what he had thought of the whole thing. There were those who very early had sensed that the helpers were only stooges; they had perceived the situation as a test and were able to refrain from emotional involvement throughout the situation regardless of the pressure which the stooges applied. On the other hand, there were those who never gained any insight into the situation, who at the end were still complaining about the caliber of our hired help, and who solicitously inquired if we could not find better workmen. Sometimes a man who had kept an unruffled exterior during the situation admitted in the interview that he had been extremely disturbed or had only with great effort refrained from hitting his assistants. Quite different were those who, with quivering upper lips and trembling hands, nevertheless insisted that they had not been the least upset by the insults and lack of cooperation of their helpers. This interview provided candidates with an opportunity to evaluate their performance and to indicate how they would seek to handle the helpers if they were to find themselves in this situation again. It gave them a chance to speak modestly or boastfully about their past experiences in charge of men, and thus, if they were not on their guard, they might be tricked into breaking cover, for X conditions were not established at this time.

In keeping with the philosophy of assessment, the Post-Construction Interview was intended to be therapeutic, to help the candidate adjust to his unpleasant experiences as quickly as possible. It was also immensely valuable in revealing how the student viewed the situation, how much insight he had, into himself and others, how objectively he viewed himself, and how he rationalized his performance. Here, too, it was possible to make some estimate of how quickly the man could recover from disturbing experiences.

After the termination of the Post-Construction Interview, the staff member returned to his colleagues, to whom he reported briefly the gist of what the candidate had said, and the new meaning which, as he saw it, the candidate's remarks gave to his performance in Construction. Here, as in all procedures at S, the aim was to evaluate every bit of behavior in the context of all the information that could be gathered about a candidate. Neither Construction nor the Post-Construction Interview was construed as giving independent measures of Emotional Stability or of any other trait. Instead, they were thought of as rather unusual conditions created to elicit fragments of behavior which, when considered in relation to fragments of behavior evoked in other situations, might yield a picture of the personalities of the candidates.

The Interview.—Immediately after the instructions for the Terrain Test had been given, some students went to the third floor for their Personal History Interviews under X conditions. Others were seen for this purpose later in the morning, and still others were interviewed that afternoon or the next day. Usually all first interviews with candidates were completed by noon of the second day, leaving that afternoon and the following day for any follow-up interviews which might be required in difficult cases. These interviews were, without doubt, the most important single procedure in the program at S, though they were not its most original feature.

No procedure yet devised by psychologists for the study of the person can take the place of the clinical interview. At S it contributed more heavily than any other procedure to the final rating of all personality variables. It provided the frame of reference in which all other observations were evaluated. From it came a large measure of the understanding of the person which made it possible either to recommend him or not to recommend him for his proposed assignment.

Though at S projective techniques and situations were used to find out some of the things about a man that he could not or would not tell, this did not diminish the importance of what a man could and would tell freely. Nor was there any reason why we should have sought a substitute for the Interview, for there was certainly no technique that yielded more that was relevant and significant than the hour and a half spent in listening to a candidate talk about himself.

The contributions of other procedures to the Interview have already been indicated. Chiefly they provided data descriptive of the personality at any instant of time; that is, data which were more or less static. It is obvious that the conclusions drawn from the candidate's performance in the test situations did not necessarily offer reliable evidence for predicting the future. It was, of course, important to know how he reacted in a strange environment and under the simulated field conditions which obtained at the assessment school. But in the last analysis, the test performance was a response to a peculiar, possibly even a unique, set of circumstances. The number of such situations which could be employed even in a three-day test period was comparatively small, and could never approach the great variety of reality problems met in everyday life. Further, it was necessary to know whether these reactions were indeed typical of his responses to various life situations, whether they fitted into his general behavior pattern, or whether they were atypical and had not previously been manifested. Still another factor of considerable importance which could best be estimated by scrutiny of the life history was the matter of adaptability. Had the candidate been able to accept increasing responsibilities, or had he become rigid, anxious, and insecure when faced with the necessity of acting on his own initiative and without the support offered by competent authority or by expressions of approval from his associates? These and many other significant facts could not be derived from observation of the test situations alone.

Before he saw the candidate, the interviewer had available to him much important information. He knew how the candidate had reacted on entering S and how he had comported himself since. The subtle nuances and undertones in the candidate's approach to new and unfamiliar tasks had provided hypotheses which would be tested. The interviewer had the Personal History record, the Health Inventories, the Projective Questionnaire, the Sentence Completions, and the Work Conditions Survey, which had been filled out by the candidate. These provided not only facts with which to work, but also a source for inferences which might be drawn from the amount and type of material produced in response to the various questions. Were these remarks stereotyped? Were they superficial? Or did they reveal a richness of emotional life and a degree of understanding of self and others which might prove invaluable in certain missions? The interviewer knew the job for which the man was a candidate, and the special personality attributes considered important for achieving success in that position. There would also be made available to him any significant items which might have been uncovered by the Security Branch in its investigation of the candidate's record. All these observations, as well as those made in the Interview, were utilized for further investigation of the candidate's reactions, and for the integration of the final picture of his personality.

What did we obtain from the Interview? We learned, of course, what the candidate said about himself, his past, his wishes and fears, his hopes and aspirations. An important distinction was made between what he said that was factual, and what he said that belonged to the realm of fantasy, opinion, and sentiment.

The factual material was that which could be checked by independent observation or investigation. The subject told us at what school he had been educated, when he obtained his first job, what the members of his family were doing, how much he earned, and so on. Facts of this order could be obtained from other sources, but it was convenient to ask the subject directly for them, and since in most instances the subject had no reason to conceal the truth and little reason to be biased, what he said could be taken at its face value, that is, as a statement of what actually happened or was happening. Much indispensable material of this kind was obtained in the Interview.

Most of the interview material, however, was made up of the subject's interpretations of and reactions to what had happened in his past, and to his situation of the moment—avowals of opinions, sentiments, attitudes, wishes. Statements of this kind were not to be regarded from the point of view of their truth or falsity; they were simply expressions of how the subject thought or felt, and when they were considered in relation to other findings they were of the greatest importance for understanding the personality. For example, what a subject said about his father may or may not have been true in an objective sense, but it was a good indication of his attitudes or of what he thought his attitudes ought to be. These statements, when interpreted in the light of the total context in which they appeared, comprised the most revealing interview material. When one had explored in this fashion the major areas in which one might expect to find the determinants of personality—family relations, childhood events, socioeconomic status, national or cultural background, school and religious influences—and interpreted the material according to a dynamic theory of personality, he had a fairly good conception both of the subject's actual situation past and present and of the dispositions which had been set going in him.

Another kind of material was obtained by watching the subject's behavior in the interview situation, by noting what a candidate was most inclined to talk about, what he spoke of with the most satisfaction or with the most distress, what were the topics which, when mentioned, caused him the most embarrassment or inhibition. In other words, it often happened that *how* a thing was said seemed just as important as *what* was said, and it was only in the Interview that this aspect of the candidate's revelations could properly be appraised.

The technique of the Interview was very flexible. It was felt that any effort to force the inquiry into previously determined channels would inevitably result in loss of spontaneity and make for an artificiality of atmosphere in which no real understanding of the person could be attained. The Interview was regarded not only as a source of important historical data, but also as an exceptionally revealing test situation. It was not always what the candidate produced in the way of factual information which was important in studying his reaction patterns; in many instances his behavior during the Interview constituted the most significant datum. How did he handle the natural discomfort of being scrutinized and called upon to explain his life record? Was he frank, open, and sure of himself? Was he timorous, uncertain, and lacking in self-esteem? Was he friendly or withdrawn? Was he surly or did he display a degree of equanimity? Did he manifest an interest in learning about himself or was he evasive, rigid, and inclined to rationalize his personality liabilities?

There was no attempt to establish a standard method for dealing with these attitudes. Some interviewers uniformly welcomed the candidate in a friendly manner, setting him at ease by offering a cigarette, by defining the purpose of the Interview, and by directing the discussion first to some more or less innocuous topic such as the subject's work history, his military record, or the manner in which he had first learned about the OSS. Others deliberately made the candidate uncomfortable by asking direct questions, or commenting upon obvious emotional reactions, of apprehension, resentment, undue levity, and the like. Still others adapted themselves to each new situation without following a preconceived plan; they were pleasant and reassuring or they deliberately permitted tensions to arise, whichever course seemed most likely to produce significant material.

It is likely that each of these aproaches was most productive with some subjects, and less so with others; yet it would be difficult to state a relationship between the subject's personality type and the most adequate approach, since which method got results was a function of the interviewer's personality as much as of the candidate's. An attempt to stir up tension was made in many instances, particularly in the cases of the overly obliging, obsequious, or blandly indifferent students. This because it was felt that the candidate could discuss those tensions he actually experienced during the

Interview much more easily than he could recall specific emotional conflicts when the topic was mentioned in the course of conversation. Needless to say, this investigation was not carried on in a destructive manner: in fact, not infrequently it served a therapeutic purpose. The objective ever in mind was that the candidate should leave with a feeling that a sincere effort had been made to understand and evaluate his assets, and that the recommendation made by the assessment staff would take these into account.

It is apparent then that, to a degree proportional to the experience and skill of the interviewer, the Interview might be, and indeed was, almost completely flexible. In the space of one and a half hours the candidate could be closely observed in a variety of interpersonal relationships. One could study his behavior when he felt comfortable, friendly, and fully at ease; when he was tense and apprehensive; when he was puzzled and uncertain what might happen or what was expected of him.

As the foregoing remarks imply, the interviewer was free to cover the whole range of human behavior in his effort to form a trustworthy estimate of the candidate's potentialities. But in practice, there was usually a certain uniformity in the material discussed. There are determinants of behavior which are commonly experienced by every individual in the normal course of his development. The Personal History Form as finally evolved covered these major determinants, and the candidate was called upon to amplify his written responses whenever need for amplification was indicated. Consideration of the family record, the history of past illnesses, and the scholastic achievement contributed to some impression of the candidate's constitutional endowment. The description of the parents and siblings, and of the family home and interests afforded a picture of the environment which shaped his early behavior patterns. The discussion of the neuropathic traits of childhood (night terrors, temper tantrums, enuresis, nail biting, and the like) showed the extent of early emotional conflicts; further questioning would bring out the very important information of how the candidate eventually learned to handle the anxiety of which these traits are manifestations. A consideration of the school record not only supplied evidence as to his effectiveness in using his native talents but also delineated his reaction to an increasing range of social opportunities and responsibilities. The investigation of his sexual development enlarged upon the picture of his social adjustment, and gave further information as to his emotional maturity by defining his attitudes toward the most complex and demanding of all interpersonal relationships, marriage. It also gave a picture which might possibly serve as an archetype of his reactions to other disturbing problems when instinctual drives and group sanctions were in conflict. A consideration of his record, hobbies, interests, and social activities afforded evidence of how effectively and productively he had been able to utilize his talents and training, of his ability to learn from experience, of his stability and steadfastness, as well as of numerous other attributes of personality.

It was, of course, in the Interview, too, that the clearest picture of a man's attitude toward his proposed assignment was obtained. His motives for overseas duty, and specifically for an assignment in the OSS, were investigated both as to their number and strength and as to their soundness and durability. The history and present state of the candidate's war morale, as well as his personal and ideological involvement in the war, were considered significant factors in the assessment of his fitness for overseas duty, and it was clear that these factors could be nowhere so effectively and so thoroughly studied as in a clinical interview.

It was not always easy to get a true picture of a candidate in the Interview at S. Many of them had good reason to be less than completely frank in talking about themselves. It was understandable that a candidate might try to put his best foot forward, to minimize, if not actually to conceal, those personality attributes which might prevent his selection for an assignment he very much desired. Further, it must be remembered that these candidates were, for the most part, essentially normal persons. They could point to impressive records of achievement as evidence of their ability to meet the requirements of the OSS field assignments. In the ordinary situations of everyday life, they had their emotional conflicts under such effective control that they had little insight into the circumstances which might engender feelings of insecurity. Consequently, they were only imperfectly aware of emotionally toned judgments and reactions; the relatively unconscious determinants of their behavior were numerous. Yet despite these difficulties, it was our hope not only to evaluate their records, but also to gain so thorough an understanding of their personality dynamics (conscious and unconscious) that we could predict reliably how they would perform under the rigorous conditions to which they would be exposed.

The question of the relation of the Interview to the rest of the assessment program is an interesting and important one. The issue can be readily put by asking what happened when the interviewer's findings and impressions were in conflict with the results of observation in the test situations. Though this was not a regular occurrence, it is something that happened fairly often. There were instances in which a man who earned high marks in the test situations taken as a whole was "dinged"[3] solely on the basis of material from the Interview. Sometimes this was because the Interview offered the candidate his only opportunity to reveal that, though he was personally ambitious and had good war morale, his motivation for his particular assignment was impossibly low; but more often the Interview uncovered a character defect or serious neurotic trend which did not express itself in the objective ratings of the situational behavior. Sometimes it was simply a view

[3] Assessment program slang for "not recommended."

of the man's whole history that allowed one to see the negative trend in the personality; though he was a man who could make a good impression in many situations, even difficult ones, he had a "weakness" or "instability" which upon occasion came to light. Also there were cases in which the interviewer gained insight into the subject's character so that one could interpret the high scores he was making in assessment tests as an instance of his ability to put up a good front. In such instances, however, by looking again and more closely at the subject's behavior one could usually note that, although he continued to earn high ratings by objective standards, there were indeed behavioral signs of the underlying defect. In these instances the Interview served as a guide for further observation; and the further observation came to support the conclusion which was reached in the Interview.

Why, one might ask, if the Interview was sufficiently revealing and dependable to be given this crucial role, did we not rely entirely on it instead of going on with a long and expensive testing program? Of course the answer is obvious: we were interested not so much in what a subject had done or what he said he could do, as in what he could actually do, and the direct way to discover this was to test him. There remains an interesting possibility for the future: that one could in time develop interviewing to give such high correlations with test and situation performances that ultimately the former could largely replace the latter. Yet there is a definite, though poorly understood, limitation here. Not infrequently in our experience a curious discrepancy occurred between the over-all picture of a man, obtained from the Interview, and his performance in situations resembling those in the field. Of two men who had the same basic personality structure —even the same basic unconscious complex—investigation at times showed that one was hopelessly inadequate in most life situations, while the other had transformed his neurotic drives in such a way that they led to real accomplishment. It was sometimes impossible to tell which was which—one had to put them in real situations to see. Then when the behavior was taken in conjunction with the Interview a meaningful total picture usually emerged. It is the assessment philosophy that it is this total picture, a formulation of what is relatively central and enduring in the person, that offers the soundest basis for prediction. We could best predict behavior when we understood as many of its aspects as possible. Without the observations of behavior, on the one hand, our predictions would have been highly abstract, generalized, and hence impractical; without the Interview we would have been reduced to predicting future behavior wholly from present behavior, without thorough knowledge of antecedent determinants; and since the same manifest behavior may have different determinants, we should have been wide of the mark much more often than we were.

The luncheon period on the first day, like all meal hours, was a time for staff members and candidates to discuss the tests and situations which had recently occurred. Since no places were assigned at the tables this period was an opportunity for staff members to become acquainted with candidates other than those whom it was their primary responsibility to assess, and it also provided an opportunity for candidates to get to know men who were not members of their own subgroups. In a spirit of identification with their own subgroup and of friendly rivalry with others, candidates asked how other teams had fared at the Brook and at the Wall. What method had they used? How long had it taken them to transport the log and rock across the brook? Had anyone fallen into the water, and if so, how had it happened? Here was a time to recall their clever solutions and their foolish mistakes as if to learn from their errors and successes how they should tackle such a problem again. It was also a time to laugh as they recalled how one group had tied a rope to a high branch of the tree on the near side of the brook and had insisted that little Joe hold onto the rope, and then, grabbing him by the seat of the pants, they had pulled him back and swung him out—but instead of letting go and jumping as he approached the other bank, Joe had held on and, completing a 180° arc, had landed back in the brush on the near side from which he had started; and how the men who had cast Joe off in this manner had paid no more attention to him once he had missed the far bank, so busy were they in trying a new solution, and Joe had been left to scramble back through the brush as best he could. It was a time to recall how Bill, the aggressive and rigid leader of another group, had sent three of his men to a "watery grave," each in exactly the same way, so insistent was he that his plan was going to work. It was amusing to recall how Dick had teetered and balanced on the rickety bridge until finally he had fallen into the creek; but it was not so much fun for the members of one group to have to admit that they had dropped both log and rock and had had to retrieve them from the near-freezing water. Nor was it easy for others to admit that they had not solved the problem at all. There were almost always unusual feats of skill to remember: Karl's lassoing of the branch of the tree on the far side on his first try; Pete's jumping from the top of the first wall and landing squarely on the top of the second wall. In addition there were the serious errors in planning and judgment to be remembered.

Luncheon on this first day also provided an opportunity to release in a social setting the tension that had been provoked by the Construction Test. The entrance of the stooges into the dining room usually evoked from the candidates a chorus of epithets and boos. By this time most of them had recovered from the initial shock caused by the treatment they had received behind the barn; and the realization that everyone else had been in the same "impossible" situation, and had probably done no better than they, was sufficient to replace the first feelings of wounded vanity with a feeling of having shared with others an experience which, while harassing at the time, had, in retrospect, its amusing aspects. Of course, there were those who griped throughout the meal about the test, insisting that it had been unfair, that the instructions had not been clear, that they had been deceived, or that no one could be expected to tolerate such insults as had been heaped upon them. Others were silent but clearly as resentful, if not more so. For the most part the experience behind the barn was taken in good humor, though the continuing preoccupation of candidates with this experience long after they had left S showed that it had touched most of them deeply and, like several other situations in the assessment program, had taught them something about themselves.

Even a casual observer could see that a central part of the whole assessment program was the fact that everyone lived and ate together, staff members and recruits alike. In such casual contacts the perseveration or nonperseveration of disturbing emotions could be seen. The ease with which a candidate was able to tolerate disquieting feelings and to admit experiences of failure and inadequacy without anxiety or resentment revealed something of his basic social and emotional security or lack of it. The sense of humor and objectivity with which he could observe himself and his relation to others and then make his observations public even when they were not such as to inflate or even to support his self-esteem were significant facts to know about him. The ease with which a candidate developed rapport with his associates, especially when he was the object of their ribbing, or, on the other hand, the extent to which he withheld himself from others out of diffidence, or opposed them with irritation or even hostility, revealed to the staff facets of social relations and emotional stability which, rightly or wrongly, contributed to our final conceptualization of his personality.

If the half hour for lunch provided the staff with an opportunity for an intuitive grasp of the nature of some candidates, the half hour of recreation after lunch was no less rewarding. This was especially true in summer and fall, when games of baseball or volley ball with candidates *vs.* staff were likely to exhibit not only the degree of team spirit and good will of a man, but also something of his athletic ability. The fact that some men never entered into such games but preferred to remain alone, whether reading or listening to the radio or walking around the estate or taking a short nap in their rooms, made the half hour no less profitable so far as the attempt to assess them was concerned. The truth is that every minute of the day can be rewarding when assessors and subjects live together away from all external distractions. Under such conditions the chief restrictions placed upon assessment are those imposed by the limitations in the energy, initiative, intelligence, psychological intuition, and insight of the assessors.

At 1:30 P.M. this first day of the assessment, after the hour for lunch and recreation, all candidates gathered again in the classroom to be given a test of propaganda skills, a test of observation and memory, and a test of mechanical comprehension, and to be assigned the task of preparing in their free time during this and the next day some materials which would be used as another test of their abilities as propagandists.

OWI Test.—This was administered to discover how "culture-sensitive" the candidate was, how aware of the many elements in a society different from his own which ought to be considered in devising propaganda for such a people. The assumption was that if a candidate was not sensitive to cultural differences, he would have little success as a propagandist no matter how great his writing skill, his proficiency in the graphic arts, or his administrative ability.

Administered to the group as a whole, the test lasted twenty minutes. Each candidate was given a single sheet of paper at the top of which was typed the following hypothetical assignment and question:

Suppose you have been placed in charge of propaganda activities for OWI in Korea, to work out a program designed to win the Koreans over to our side, *what information would you want to have?* (Assume that you know nothing about the country. Omit administrative questions of staff, finances, and OWI policy. Use outline form if you prefer.)

No further instructions were given other than that they would have twenty minutes and that both sides of the paper could be used.

The results were scored with the aid of the chart reproduced on page 123. A tally mark was made for each candidate in the rectangle opposite the phrase which best described each of his requests for information. From these tallies two scores were derived. The first score was simply the total number of tallies or, in other words, the total number of requests for information. The second, and more significant, score was the total of the weights of all the categories mentioned by a candidate. Different weights had been rather arbitrarily assigned to three groups of categories differentiated on the basis of an analysis in which final total scores were compared to the frequencies with which items in the various categories were mentioned. The categories which were mentioned more often by candidates receiving high scores on the test were given higher values. A weight of 3 was assigned to each of the first eight categories, a weight of 2 to categories nine through seventeen, and a weight of 1 to categories eighteen through twenty-seven.

In the course of time, distribution curves for each of the raw scores based on a large number of cases were obtained and, on the basis of these curves, the two scores were converted into ratings on the standard six-point scale and combined into a single final rating, which was raised or lowered slightly

CHART FOR SCORING OWI TEST

	Name											
Class S- —— O.W.I. Test	Grade											
	Score											
1. Attitudes toward Korea												
2. No. of radio sets												
3. Literacy												
4. Racial groups												
5. Internal conflicts												
6. Communications (words)												
7. Changes with time												
8. Other dynamic ideas												
9. Economics												
10. History of Korea												
11. Leadership												
12. Social classes												
13. Religion												
14. Taboos												
15. Language, dialects												
16. Outside propaganda												
17. Others												
18. Transportation												
19. Education												
20. Governments												
21. National goals												
22. National movements												
23. Living conditions												
24. Enemy influences on Korea												
25. Attitudes toward Japs, Allies												
26. Customs, habits												
27. Other												

according to whether the amount of dynamic content in the candidate's paper (e.g., references to *changes* in attitude, leadership, or other conditions) was great or slight.

The reasons for emphasizing the weighted category score were two. In the first place, the candidates, writing under the pressure of speed, were very apt to repeat themselves in almost the same or in very similar words. It was obvious that such repetitions were not additional ideas and hence should not be given extra credit. Second, the aim of the test as conceived at S was to assess the breadth and sensitivity of the candidate's approach to a whole culture rather than the fineness of his discriminations within some categories —such, for example, as economic conditions or means of communication (favorite categories with many candidates). The individual who asked for all sorts of detailed information within a few categories but completely ignored other important areas such as racial and class conditions, living conditions, food supply, and the like, deserved, we felt, a lower score than an individual who requested information in many different categories.

Map Memory Test.—When the papers for the OWI Test had been collected, each candidate was given a map with the request that it be placed face down on the desk. The examiner then proceeded to give the instructions for the Map Memory Test.

In this test, you are all to assume that you are agents operating in the field. You have just made a secret rendezvous with a courier who has for you a map of the territory you will be covering. But time is short and he can stay with you for only a few minutes while you study the map. He must then leave and take the map with him. As a matter of fact, it turns out that you have only eight minutes to look at the map. Since it would be unsafe to have papers with you, you cannot take notes or make sketches while studying the map. Instead, you must look it over as thoroughly as possible; every part of the map is likely to be important, so commit as many as possible of its details to memory before he takes it away. Do you have any questions? All right, turn the map over and take eight minutes to study it. Go ahead.

After the students had been allowed eight minutes to examine the map (see page 125), they were asked to pass it in without looking at it any more. Sets of multiple-choice statements (see pages 126-127) and standard IBM answer sheets were then distributed to the candidates, who were told:

You have a number of incomplete statements about the map which you must finish. In each case an incomplete statement is made and five possible completions of it are listed, labeled a, b, c, d, e. Your task is to pick out the correct conclusion for each statement and then blacken the space under the appropriate letter on the separate answer sheet. Any questions? All right, go ahead. You have twelve minutes.

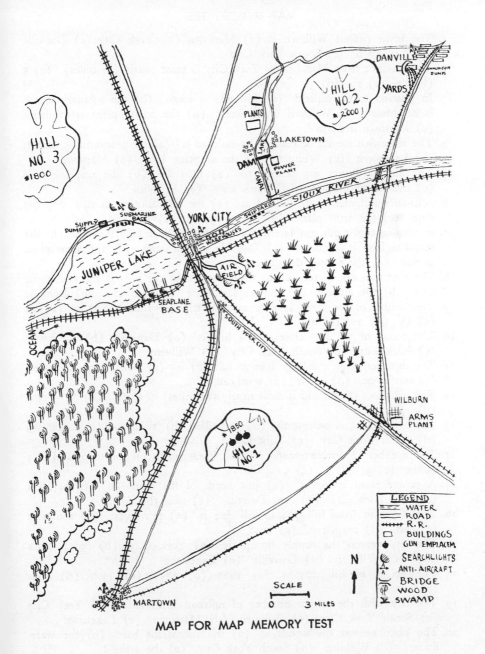

MAP FOR MAP MEMORY TEST

DANVILLE

YARDS

AMMUNITION DUMPS

HILL NO. 2
*2000

PLANTS

LAKETOWN

LAKE

DAM

CANAL

POWER PLANT

HILL NO. 3
*1800

SHIPYARDS

SIOUX RIVER

SUPPLY DUMPS

SUBMARINE BASE

YORK CITY

WAREHOUSES

JUNIPER LAKE

AIR FIELD

AA

OCEAN

SEAPLANE BASE

SOUTH YORK CITY

WILBURN

ARMS PLANT

*850

HILL NO. 1

LEGEND

═══ WATER
───── ROAD
+++++ R.R.
▢ BUILDINGS
● GUN EMPLACEM.
SEARCHLIGHTS
ANTI-AIRCRAFT
BRIDGE
WOOD
SWAMP

SCALE
0   3 MILES

N

MARTOWN

125

MAP MEMORY TEST

1. The town nearest Wilburn is (a) Martown (b) York City (c) Danville (d) Laketown (e) South York City
2. The distance from Martown to York City is most nearly (in miles) (a) 5 (b) 12 (c) 19 (d) 30 (e) 46
3. In relation to the airfield (a) hill #2 is south (b) the submarine base is northwest (c) Wilburn is northeast (d) the power plant is southeast (e) Martown is north
4. The place that cannot be reached by railroad is (a) the ammunition dumps (b) Laketown (c) Wilburn (d) the seaplane base (e) Martown
5. The supply dumps are nearest to (a) Danville (b) the seaplane base (c) the submarine base (d) York City (e) Wilburn
6. Anti-aircraft batteries are located at (a) the ammunition dumps (b) the dam (c) the arms plant (d) the shipyards (e) hill #1
7. In relation to the gun emplacements (a) South York City is south (b) the seaplane base is southeast (c) Danville is southwest (d) the arms plant is east (e) the supply dumps are northeast
8. The area that can be reached by train but not by car is (a) the submarine base (b) the airfield (c) the seaplane base (d) hill #1 (e) Danville
9. The length of the large lake is most nearly (in miles) (a) 5 (b) 10 (c) 15 (d) 20 (e) 25
10. The name of the city closest to a hill is (a) Danville (b) Laketown (c) York City (d) South York City (e) Wilburn
11. The direction from the large lake to hill #1 is (a) north (b) northwest (c) southwest (d) south (e) southeast
12. The length of the airfield is most nearly (in miles) (a) ¼ (b) ½ (c) 1 (d) 1½ (e) 2
13. The arms plant is nearest to (a) Danville (b) Wilburn (c) Laketown (d) South York City (e) York City
14. The number of double-tracked railroad lines shown on the map is (a) 1 (b) 2 (c) 3 (d) 4 (e) 5
15. A power plant is located (a) just north of the dam (b) on the river (c) near York City (d) near Danville (e) near the canal
16. The direction from hill #3 to hill #2 is (a) northwest (b) southeast (c) east (d) southwest (e) west
17. The city nearest the supply dumps is (a) York City (b) South York City (c) Wilburn (d) Danville (e) Laketown
18. The height of hill #1 is (a) 1800 (b) 1850 (c) 1900 (d) 1950 (e) 2000
19. The city with the largest number of railroad facilities is (a) York City (b) South York City (c) Wilburn (d) Martown (e) Laketown
20. The place nearest the woods is (a) the submarine base (b) the warehouses (c) Wilburn (d) South York City (e) the airfield
21. The number of bridges across the river is (a) 1 (b) 2 (c) 3 (d) 4 (e) 5
22. The dam is nearest to (a) hill #2 (b) York City (c) the shipyards (d) Laketown (e) the warehouses

Map Memory Test (*Continued*)

23. The facility that is least protected by anti-aircraft or searchlight defenses is (a) the supply dump (b) the railroad yards (c) the power plant (d) Martown factories (e) the warehouses
24. The smallest city in the area is (a) Martown (b) York City (c) Danville (d) South York City (e) Laketown
25. The ammunition dumps are nearest (a) York City (b) Wilburn (c) Laketown (d) Martown (e) Danville
26. In relation to the seaplane base (a) the warehouses are southeast (b) hill #1 is northeast (c) the supply dumps are northwest (d) the swamp is southwest (e) Laketown is south
27. The distance by railroad from Martown to Wilburn is most nearly (in miles) (a) 12 (b) 18 (c) 24 (d) 30 (e) 36
28. The town nearest Laketown is (a) Danville (b) Wilburn (c) South York City (d) Martown (e) York City
29. In relation to Wilburn (a) hill #3 is northwest (b) Martown is north (c) the river is south (d) the airfield is northeast (e) the gun emplacements are south
30. Searchlights without anti-aircraft batteries are located at (a) the submarine base (b) the arms plant (c) the shipyards (d) the ammunition dumps (e) the seaplane base

The candidates were allowed at least twelve minutes to indicate the correct completions on their answer sheets. If a candidate had not finished at the end of twelve minutes, he was allowed more time unless it was felt that for some special reason, such as a language handicap, he would hold up the group too long. For such a candidate, the group norms were of course inappropriate.

In this test, as for all paper-and-pencil tests used at S, a distribution curve of raw scores based on a sufficiently large number of cases was plotted and periodically revised, on the basis of which raw scores were converted into ratings on our standard six-point scale. These ratings furnished another measure of the ability of candidates to observe and to report.

Mechanical Comprehension Test.—As another measure of intelligence, especially as a measure of innate ability to understand physical principles in everyday situations, the Bennett Mechanical Comprehension Test was given to the candidates immediately after the completion of the Map Memory Test.

The need for a test of mechanical comprehension in the battery of intelligence tests employed at S was obvious, for many of the candidates were being considered for field assignments in which a knowledge of physical and mechanical principles would be absolutely essential. Since each item in the test consists of a plainly and clearly labeled pictorial illustration and a short, simply worded question, even candidates with moderate language handicap had little difficulty with it. Experience with the test soon indicated that for the population at S, the first eight items could be omitted as nondiscriminating and the remaining sixty-eight administered with a fifteen-minute time limit. Ideally, it would have been preferable to use it as an untimed ability test. However, even with the time limit necessitated by the limitations of the schedule, it yielded a very wide range of scores, and its low correlation with other paper-and-pencil tests indicated that scores on it were little influenced by any verbal factor.

Manchuria Test.—The chief measure of the propaganda skills of candidates was derived from an examination of two pieces of propaganda which they were directed to devise for the purpose of disturbing and lowering the morale of the Japanese railway workers and guards on the South Manchuria Railway. This assignment, given to candidates at the end of the testing hour on their first afternoon at S (about an hour after they had taken the OWI Test), was to be executed by them individually and to be completed by 6:30 P.M. of the following day. In order to standardize the problem as much as possible, each candidate was given a printed outline containing background facts about the country and people of Manchuria and a list of ideas which might be incorporated into his propaganda, though he was also explicitly directed to include other, more effective ideas if he could think of them. Actually most of the papers produced by the candidates differed only in effectiveness of writing, since only the most able propagandists conceived additional disturbing ideas.

Two kinds of propaganda were to be prepared by the candidates:

1) A leaflet to be distributed by agents to employees and guards of the South Manchuria Railway.

2) A two-minute (the equivalent of 200 English words) spot radio broadcast script, directed at the same group and their families in Manchuria.

Candidates were encouraged, in the preparation of their leaflets, to use whatever graphic skills they might possess. While the average candidate spent about two hours actually writing his propaganda, some highly motivated and perhaps pedestrian candidates spent much more time than this on the assignment, working at it far beyond midnight.

All papers were read regularly by the same member of the staff so that, although the marking (on the usual six-point scale) was subjective, there was a relatively constant frame of reference. To guide himself in marking these papers the staff member set up and referred constantly to a check list of criteria. An experiment in the rescoring of papers yielded a reliability coefficient of .66. In several cases, however, the grade was changed as much as two steps on the second scoring. In view of this fact, in crucial instances where the ability to write or to evaluate propaganda was an essential part of the candidate's proposed assignment, his papers were also read and evaluated by the other members of the staff who were responsible for the final report on the candidate.

With the hour of testing over, candidates scattered, some to their interviews, others to explore the terrain, others to work on the Manchuria problem, and still others in a group to an indoor situational test known as Discussion, in which, before the afternoon was over, all subgroups of candidates would have participated.

Discussion.—This was a panel discussion set up to observe candidates in a situation which called for verbal resourcefulness. In many ways, Discussion was the indoor, verbal counterpart of the Brook. Here again the candidates were called upon to work together toward a common end, as a group, with no leader designated, but this time with different tools. Having grouped themselves around a table, and facing the staff team that sat at the other end of the room, they were instructed as follows:

For the next forty minutes, we should like you to discuss the following question: What are the major postwar problems facing the United States and (if you have time) along what lines do you think they should be solved? This is to be a group discussion. The object should be to allow each man a chance to express his opinion, to discuss these opinions, and to arrive at some conclusions with which most of you agree. Just before the end of the period, we should like one of you to give us the conclusions of the group.

During the discussion most of the candidates would make some contribution affording a basis for rating their Effective Intelligence as reflected by their factual knowledge and understanding of current events, contemporary national issues, and international problems. Their teamwork and tact in discussing conflicting views allowed a rating on Social Relations, while their efforts to guide the group toward the goal provided a basis for rating Leadership. As in all situations, the Energy and Initiative variable was also observed and rated.

At the close of the allotted time, the summary was presented to the staff, whose members noted how the speaker obtained the role and how well he organized the available material. Then the candidates were asked to vote on a secret ballot for the man or men they considered most persuasive and the man or men they would wish to have as their chairman in an assumed future discussion.

There were many ways in which a group might begin in this situation. Often a member of the group would suggest that a chairman, and perhaps also a secretary, be appointed; sometimes these roles would be assumed by individuals without awaiting nominations or election. Some groups were concerned with outlining topics for discussion and with organizing their work as efficiently as possible at the very beginning, while others broke at once into the discussion of a single postwar problem, such as the racial question, with no concern for what might follow. Often the discussion would be undertaken by two or three of the group and only considerably later would others join in. Some groups would devote themselves to one topic throughout the period, whereas others would range far and wide in their discussions.

Regardless of the approach of the groups to the problem, individual members assumed certain obvious roles: leaders and followers; active speakers and passive listeners. Clear-cut differences would frequently be observed: some were intelligent and well informed, others obviously naïve and inexperienced; some were pleasant and friendly, others hostile, dogmatic, or pedantic.

In estimating the Energy and Initiative of candidates in Discussion there were a number of signs to watch: the point at which a man came actively into the Discussion; the total amount of talking that he did; the forcefulness and intensity with which he spoke; the degree of personal involvement in what he said as well as in what was said by others. These were some of the more obvious signs. Less obvious but nonetheless significant indicators of Energy and Initiative had to be looked for in those who were less bright or more socially inhibited. Such persons had little to offer or were afraid to offer whatever they had, but within the narrower limits of their abilities they could reveal interest in the situation by attentive posture and attitude, by remaining alert to and interested in what others were saying, or by taking notes.

Of all variables, perhaps Intelligence was the most difficult to rate at Discussion, not because of a lack of behavior to be observed—there was plenty of that—but because of an inability to be sure of the meaning of what we heard or saw. After all, it was the content of what men said that had to be rated as indicative of intelligence. But when discussion is in the area of social, economic, and political problems, who can assert what is intelligent and at the same time be sure that his own biases are not influencing his judgment? If our disagreements in rating Intelligence in this situation meant anything, it was probably that to some members of the staff a stupid liberal seemed more intelligent than a smart reactionary. But fortunately more than the content of economic, social, and political agreements was to be rated in this situation, and upon the meaning of these other signs of intelligence there was more unanimity, and consequently more agreement, in our ratings. The vocabulary that a man used, the fund of information at his disposal, the manner in which he organized his points, the internal consistency of his arguments, the level of abstraction and generalization at which he spoke, the pertinence of his remarks to the topic under discussion, the speed with which he grasped the implications of what others were saying, the originality of his ideas, the degree to which his comments at any moment answered the needs of the group in their handling of a problem, the use to which he was able to put, for group aims, the contributions of others, his resourcefulness in supporting his own ideas and in refuting arguments brought against them—these were but a few of the many signs of intelligence upon the varying degrees of which we found it not too hard to come to agreement in our ratings.

In this situation, as in many others, there was bound to be a high correlation between Leadership and Effective Intelligence, but the ways in which a man might demonstrate qualities of leadership were indeed various. Although it was characteristic of the leader that in some sense he organized and guided the group in its discussion, he could do this by acting as a moderator who simply coordinated the ideas of others and summarized them for the group, or by actively initiating ideas for discussion and leading the group by the very forcefulness with which he handled topics. Whereas one leader immediately suggested a way of organizing the discussion, got everyone to express his ideas, and then outlined a method of procedure for handling these contributions, another took charge only after the discussion had proceeded for some time without a leader and sometimes only when the discussion was in danger of disintegrating completely. Of course, at times a man was elected leader by formal vote of his colleagues, though this was no assurance that he would exercise that leadership effectively or be able to maintain it for forty minutes. Certainly the mere choice of a man as leader was no sign that he possessed the necessary ability. Often the choice was determined by some unique characteristic of the individual, such as his greater age or white hair, which made him stand out as a personage.

To summarize the more frequently observed manifestations of effective leadership in this situation, we might say that the good leader commanded the respect of his colleagues by his confident and convincing discussion of topics, and by skillful means he encouraged their participation and cooperation, making certain that each man had a chance to speak; he coordinated the various opinions of others and from time to time summarized them succinctly for approval by the group before moving on to new topics; he presented his own ideas in such a way as to excite others to a greater degree of involvement in the discussion; he saw to it that the discussion was completed within the limits of time set by the instructions and in doing so was ever watchful for digressions from the central points of the discussion, keeping both himself and the group oriented to the task at hand, and though capable of being both assertive and forceful in leading the group, he knew when to defer to the wishes of others and was not afraid to do so.

One more variable was rated in this situation, namely, Social Relations. Cooperation and good will marked the man with superior Social Relations. He was tolerant of the expression of opinions with which he did not agree, and no matter how forcefully he might attack them he never did so with meanness or malice, and never with *ad hominem* arguments. Just as he was fair in his criticism of the views of others, so he accepted willingly and pleasantly criticism of his own opinions. He was patient in hearing others out, courteous and considerate of his colleagues in their attempts to present views even though they clashed with his. More reliable than any other sign perhaps was a good sense of humor and an ability to laugh at himself. In contrast to this type, the man with poor social relations often took himself too seriously; he was inclined to be too argumentative, dogmatic in express-ing his views, unwilling to listen to others or to yield on a minor point for the sake of unanimity. There were also many whose relations with others were neither strikingly good nor obviously bad. For the most part, they were quiet, somewhat diffident individuals who said little and annoyed no one. It was clear that discussion was not their forte.

When this situation was over, it was interesting to compare the behavior of the candidates and the roles they had played in the outdoor morning tasks as compared to this indoor afternoon discussion. There were some who excelled or led in both types of problem; others who, though outstand-ing in one sort of situation, were completely at a loss in the other; and still others who were ineffectual in both. Something of the generality or speci-ficity of a man's skills and abilities and his traits of personality was thus revealed.

This was the program of the afternoon of the first day at S, but if candi-dates thought that, after supper and a half hour of relaxation listening to the radio, reading, or playing some game, their day was done, they were mis-taken. All of them that evening were to experience a Stress Interview, de-signed to test their ability to tolerate severe emotional and intellectual strain, and a Post-Stress Interview, calculated to provide both a catharsis for the emotion experienced in the Stress Interview and an opportunity for the can-didate to be trapped, if he were not on his guard, into breaking his cover. Those who had been recruited for intelligence work would be given written instructions for the Interrogation Test which would be held on the follow-ing day as a measure of their ability to elicit information from an "escaped prisoner of war" in the course of a twelve-minute interview with him. Later in the evening these same men would be given the SIX-2 Test, designed as a measure of the ability to evaluate and abstract intelligence material. Those who had been recruited for a teaching assignment in OSS would be asked to prepare a fifteen-minute instructional talk which they would give on the following day to members of the staff. When they were not busy with any of these tests or procedures they had their Manchuria assignment to occupy them. If they then had any spare time left this evening, they could, of course, enjoy themselves in the living room—reading, listening to the radio, playing games, or talking among themselves or to members of the staff.

Instructions for the Interrogation Test (Escaped Prisoner).—Throughout the history of the assessment program, various procedures were developed to measure the skill of eliciting information in an interview and the ability to make use of the information so gained. During the last months of S, we employed a test of this nature, appropriate to the current military situation and having as its imaginary locale Central China. Since this procedure required the attention of two staff members for each candidate observed, it was given only to those men who had been selected for intelligence work. These selected men were called together at 6:15 P.M. and given a map[4] and the following instructions:

A tail gunner, one of ten members of a B-29 crew which had made a crash landing, escaped from a Jap prison camp where he had been held for three months. Damage done by an air raid and the subsequent confusion enabled him to escape. In nearly two days he covered fifty miles or so before he was picked up, near Ankong, by a scouting party of the Chinese Nationalist 60th Army, which was returning from the Nantze River sector nearest Kiantang. The scouting party has brought him to the combined U.S.-Chinese Military Intelligence Office in Chaofu.

You are to question the tail gunner T/Sgt. Smith, for the purpose of finding out and reporting to intelligence headquarters:
  (1) the location of the camp where Smith was held,
  (2) information regarding treatment of prisoners,
  (3) information regarding size of camp,
  (4) any other intelligence deserving of report.

The candidates were told that each of them would have twelve minutes to interview T/Sgt. Smith on the afternoon of the following day. As they were told, the purpose of forewarning them was to give them time in which to prepare for the interview.

Stress Interview.—This procedure was designed primarily to test the candidate's capacity to tolerate severe emotional and intellectual strain. The strain was created by rapid and merciless cross-questioning under disagreeable conditions with the aim of detecting flaws in a cover story which the candidate had been given only a few minutes to invent.

The method of conducting the test was as follows. At exactly 6:25 P.M. the whole group was assembled in the classroom and to them one of the members of the staff made the following statements:

This evening we are going to conduct one of the most important tests of the whole program. What you are to do is simple, but it is necessary for the success of the procedure that you carry out every detail precisely. It is particularly essential that you be completely punctual in following the schedule set for you. Beginning at 6:30 you will go one by one into the small room labeled

4 The map was the same as that used in the SIX-2 Test (see page 143).

A-13. Each of you in your individual schedules will find the time of your own appointment recorded. In the room will be a clock and a set of directions on the table. You will remain there alone for exactly twelve minutes, reading and carrying out the directions. Are there any questions?

By the time these instructions had been given it was about 6:30 P.M., and at that hour the first candidate went to the little room, where, on entering, he found the clock on the table together with a paper on which the following was written:

INSTRUCTIONS FOR RESOURCEFULNESS TEST

Read these instructions carefully.

The examination you are to undergo is designed to test your resourcefulness, agility of mind, and ability to think quickly, effectively, and convincingly. This is an important test and it is important that you do well. *In twelve (12) minutes report to the basement room at the foot of the stairs.*

The test will measure your ability to establish and maintain a cover story for the situation outlined below. Your cover story must be told convincingly, intelligently, and clearly. The examiners will try to trip you up on your story, to lead you into inconsistencies, and in general to confuse you.

Several students in the past have failed in this test because they forgot or did not understand the directions and requirements. We are listing below the important "rules" of this examination. If you do not remember these rules you will fail.

1. YOUR COVER STORY MUST GIVE A PLAUSIBLE *AND INNOCENT* REASON FOR YOUR ACTIONS.
2. *YOU MUST ANSWER EVERY QUESTION ASKED.* ANSWERS LIKE, "I DON'T REMEMBER," "I DON'T KNOW," "I AM NOT PERMITTED TO DISCLOSE THAT INFORMATION," ETC. ARE NOT PERMISSIBLE AND WILL COUNT AGAINST YOU IN THE FINAL RATING.
3. YOU MUST AVOID BREAKING EITHER PERSONAL OR ORGANIZATIONAL SECURITY IN YOUR ANSWERS. NONE OF YOUR REPLIES SHOULD DISCLOSE YOUR FORMER OCCUPATION, PLACE OF RESIDENCE, ETC.

Here is the situation for which you are to construct a cover story:

A night watchman at 9:00 P.M. found you going through some papers in a file marked "SECRET" in a Government office in Washington. You are *NOT* an employee of the agency occupying the building in which this office is located. You had no identification papers whatsoever with you. The night watchman has brought you here for questioning.

In developing your cover story you may assume that you are clothed in any manner you wish.

At the expiration of the twelve minutes granted him to construct his story, the candidate immediately went downstairs to the basement room. A voice

from within commanded him to enter, and on complying he found himself
facing a spotlight strong enough to blind him for a moment. The room was
otherwise dark. Behind the spotlight sat a scarcely discernible board of in-
quisitors, several members of the staff. The interrogator gruffly ordered the
candidate to sit down. When he did so, he discovered that the chair in which
he sat was so arranged that the full strength of the beam was focused directly
on his face. The questioner then addressed him as follows:

If you had an innocent reason for being in the building where you were
caught, we expect you to be able to give it to us without any hesitation. We
warn you, however, that any statement you may make will be subjected to a
searching examination, so you would do well to be very careful in what you
tell us, and also very accurate. Our first question is, "Why were you in that
building?"

In reply the candidate then began to tell his story as he had devised it.
Perhaps he made use of the cover identity which he had been developing
for himself ever since the security talk given on his arrival at S. Or perhaps
he fabricated a whole new tale which he thought would explain more satisfactorily why he was discovered investigating a secret file. Whatever his
story was, it was searchingly examined as soon as he had told it.

At first the questions were asked in a quiet, sympathetic, conciliatory manner, to invite confidence. Frequently this led the candidate to let down his
guard and expand his story, adding unplanned details on the spur of the
moment. After a few minutes, however, the examiner worked up to a
crescendo in a dramatic fashion. Any error, slip of the tongue, forgetting, or
even halting response was likely to be seized on by the examiner as a suspicious sign. When an inconsistency appeared, he raised his voice and lashed
out at the candidate, often with sharp sarcasm. He might even roar, "You're
a liar," or some such phrase, if a falsehood in the cover story became apparent. Sometimes, after such an outburst, the questioner might lapse back into
his soothing tone and suggest that it was understandable that such a false
statement might be made if the suspect wished to cover up in order to pro-
tect his family. Occasionally the candidate would bite at this bait, and agree,
whereupon the examiner would burst out accusingly, yelling, "Now we have
the truth—you admit that you lied."

At the beginning of the grilling the questions were put slowly and
smoothly, but as the end neared they were hurled in rapid-fire, staccato
fashion. The questioning was shifted quickly from one topic to another
and then back again in a very confusing manner. Beginning with generalities, the question soon forced the accused to give particular, specific information. The accused was asked about exact dates, hours, addresses, telephone
numbers, and proper names of people involved in his story. Later he was
questioned on the wider field of his past life, his profession, his place of resi-

dence, and so forth. Many of these items he had not, of course, had time to work out in the twelve minutes immediately preceding the questioning, so he was forced to improvise answers on the spot.

Another stratagem, often employed by the interrogator in an effort to confuse the victim, was to repeat, after a lapse of a minute or two, details of his testimony incorrectly; for instance, rearranging the numerals in a telephone number or Army serial number, in order to see if the candidate recognized the change and also to fill his mind with a bewildering mass of figures. Sometimes, too, the questioner could make a suggestible candidate contradict himself by asking him a number of leading questions, to each of which he agreed, until the questioner could at last jump on an inconsistency. For example, by this technique, a candidate could often be made to agree that he had no dependents, that he was healthy, that he was a citizen, and that he was not in an essential industry or the Armed Services. If he were then asked, "What is your draft classification?" there was almost no reply he could make without involving himself in a contradiction. Or by a similar procedure it was sometimes possible to get a candidate to admit that he had arrived in Washington some days or weeks before with little money, and to lead him to deny any sources of income while he was in the city, and then suddenly to ask how he had supported himself while in Washington.

An effort was also made to keep the suspect tense by not allowing him to relax. He was made to sit upright in a hard chair. If he was smoking he was told to stop. If he crossed his legs, he was told to uncross them. If he lowered his head to avoid the light, he was commanded to look up. If he wore glasses, he was directed to take them off. All this served to keep him from attaining a comfortable position, so adding to his stress.

After ten minutes of such grilling the examiner broke off the questioning abruptly with a dissatisfied air, saying, "We now have abundant evidence that you have not been telling the truth. That is all." Then the board of staff members whispered together for a few seconds as if arriving at a verdict. Finally the examiner asked solemnly, "Your name is Buck, isn't it?" When the candidate assented, the interrogator announced, "It is our decision, Buck, that you have failed this test." There were then about five seconds of silence while the candidate's reaction was observed. Occasionally he would burst out at this pronouncement and protest, but more often he accepted it silently with some slight show of emotion. Then the examiner directed the candidate to go immediately up to a room on the third floor to see one of the members of the senior staff. Thereupon the subject left, to go to the Post-Stress Interview. After he had gone, and before the next subject was admitted, the staff observers rated the man who had just left the room on the personality variables of Emotional Stability and Security.

As usual, Emotional Stability was judged by the degree of control and poise exhibited by the subject, as well as by the extent to which he seemed to remain free of neurotic traits when placed under stress. Searching for evidences of tension, the staff members noted whether the candidate sat rigidly in his chair, whether he moved about restlessly, whether he smoked nervously, whether he played with objects in his hands or with his fingers or fingernails, whether he paid much attention to the bright light, and how he reacted to the sudden shouting of the examiner. The candidate was also watched for signs of autonomic disturbance, such as sweating, flushing, swallowing, or moistening of the lips. Other common signs of emotion were stuttering; blocking of speech, sometimes for many seconds; explosions of anger; weeping or lacrimation; and characteristic changes of facial expression, particularly when the candidate was told he had failed.

Positive indications of good Emotional Stability were judged to be an air of calm and dignity, little reaction to shouting or an insistence that it was not called for, quick responses, an aggressive effort to control the interview and prevent the questioner from talking down all opposition, and laughing or joking. Sometimes suspects would obviously appear to enter the spirit of the grilling and act a role, even on occasion pretending to appear frightened, as they would admit when the examination was over. Such behavior was, of course, a sign of emotional control rather than the contrary.

The rating of the candidate's ability to maintain Security was based on an estimate of his cautiousness, inconspicuousness, skills in misleading and bluffing, and resourcefulness. Also taken into consideration was whether his story was plausible, ingenious, and original, as well as whether it followed the directions given him.

In conclusion, it should be pointed out that the Stress Interview was designed primarily to measure emotional stability under strain, which is a factor to be evaluated in selecting personnel or making a diagnosis of personality. The situation lent itself admirably to our specific project of testing men who were being selected to do intelligence work, however, and this fact determined the specific characteristics of the procedure. Many of the candidates might some day have to live under cover, or their work might possibly involve them in a situation in which they would be either interrogator or suspect in a grilling of this sort.

Mild as this situation may seem from our description, it was nevertheless sufficiently stressful to arouse in some of our subjects crippling and incapacitating attacks of anxiety, and sometimes in just those candidates who by background and experience might have seemed most admirably qualified for undercover work. One refugee from Europe, who had had a brush with the Gestapo and had so skillfully come through the questioning to which they had subjected him that he was allowed to go free, became very much disturbed in the Stress Interview. In Post-Stress he asked to be released from S and from any commitments to the OSS. Attempts to quiet him were of no avail. The emotion stirred in him by Stress kept him awake that night;

and the next morning his anxiety had reached the point where, in another situational test, he fainted. It was clear that it would be unwise to force him to finish the assessment program since he was completely unfit to operate in Europe under cover.

Another candidate, who as a boy had endured many hardships in Russia during World War I and during the Revolution, could not tolerate the emotions reactivated in him by the Stress Interview. Before his assessment was completed he, too, had to be returned to Washington and his home.

The mere instructions for the Stress Interview could serve as a most revealing projective test, as indeed they did strikingly on one occasion when a man, after reading the instructions, insisted that he could not go through with the test. A little later the director of S found the candidate in his bedroom, sitting on the edge of his cot, sobbing. Upon reading the instructions he had imagined that on reporting to the basement he would be beaten by the staff, and he was overcome with fear that under this provocation he might commit some extreme act of violence. As he talked with the director about some of his early experiences, a few of the factors responsible for his unusual reaction became clear, but the anxiety aroused by his fantasy continued to increase until, in his case, too, it seemed wisest to excuse him from the rest of the program.

Post-Stress Interview.—It is a maxim of secret agents and investigators that security breaks occur most frequently when a man is enjoying a moment of relaxation after a period of tension, for under such circumstances his inhibitory mechanisms are momentarily in abeyance, and he is off guard. It was our belief, therefore, that a candidate's ability to keep cover would not be adequately tested unless an effort were made to get him to reveal true facts about himself at a time of relaxation after tension. Consequently, immediately following his Stress Interview and the shock of hearing that he had failed, each candidate was told to report to a member of the staff on the third floor. There he was cordially greeted and made to feel at ease in the company of a sympathetic listener who, despite his innocent manner, would actually do his best to induce the candidate to break his cover. Though the chief purpose of this situation was to test the candidate's security, it served two other ends: it provided an opportunity to estimate the strength of the candidate's motivation for his proposed assignment, and his emotional stability. The Post-Stress Interview also allowed for catharsis of emotion and for reassurance of the candidate about his performance in Stress and Post-Stress.

The schedule was so arranged that there was no waiting between Stress and Post-Stress Interviews. Each candidate went immediately from the basement to the third floor, where he was greeted by an interviewer, who talked with him for ten minutes and then sent him on his way before the next man arrived.

The room in which the Post-Stress conversation took place was one of those on the third floor in which candidates knew that Personal History Interviews were held under X conditions. As a consequence, although all candidates had been specifically directed not to mention any facts about themselves except under specifically designated X conditions, they drifted easily, in this setting, into a discussion of past events. Afterward they often admitted, sometimes in an attempt to excuse their security breaks, that it was the room, as much as the manner of the staff member, that led them to fall naturally into a feeling of intimacy and a mood for confession in the Post-Stress Interview.

From the moment the candidate arrived upstairs, the interviewer did everything possible to encourage ease and relaxation after his stressful experience in the basement. He pointed to an easy chair and said hospitably, "Sit down and make yourself comfortable." He offered him a cigarette and himself lolled back informally in his chair. Then he asked in an off-hand manner, "Well, how have things been going?" The question was phrased in this vague way in order to get the strategic advantage of having the candidate make the first reference to the Stress Interview. Two things were gained by this maneuver: first, it served to dissociate the Post-Stress and Stress situations, so helping to beguile the candidate into letting down the guard he had developed in the earlier test; and second, it enabled the interviewer to gauge, from the rapidity and vigor with which the candidate referred to the former test, the degree of his emotional involvement in it.

Almost always the candidate reported at once that things were going very badly, that he had just failed a very important test. The way in which a candidate said this—whether he interpreted it as failure in a single test or as failure in the whole assessment program—revealed much about his motivation for work in the OSS and his ability to tolerate failure and frustration. The emotion or lack of it with which he spoke, as well as his willingness or reluctance to discuss his experience, was noted. In any case, the interviewer, on being told of the failure, sympathized with the candidate, but not unduly.

The candidate was then asked how it had happened that he had failed. Some, by their replies, would indicate a subservient attitude to authority; others, an outspoken skepticism that they had failed; while still others revealed the kinds of alibis and rationalizations they were inclined to use to explain their failures. Whatever the reply, the interviewer pursued this topic further by asking the candidate how well he had felt he was doing while being grilled. Replies to this question frequently revealed not only a candidate's ability to make a dispassionate judgment at such a moment, but also how eager he had been to succeed in the Stress situation. From this, some indication of his motivation could be obtained.

Usually the interviewer sought next to investigate the kinds of errors which the candidate had made in Stress—this to trap the unsuspecting candidate into breaking cover. He might ask, "What details did they manage to trip you up on?" or "At what points did you find yourself treading on thin ice?" In reply, the candidate usually gave concrete examples of confusion or near confusion in his story, although occasionally one claimed, truthfully or not, that he knew of no flaws that were discovered in his story. What he replied was of little importance, for in either case the questioner's purpose had been achieved: the topic now concerned details of the cover story. Taking advantage of this transition, the interviewer said, employing some flattery if he believed it would be effective in the given case, "Of course, it's really impossible to think out all the aspects of a cover story in twelve minutes. If it could be done, I'm sure you would have done it. Undoubtedly you used the device of employing experiences from your real life in constructing your fictional story, though of course so jumbled that no one could identify you." Almost invariably the candidate agreed that he had, whereupon the questioner asked in a matter-of-fact tone, "Just what events did you use from your real life and how did you alter them? I'm interested in the technique you used." At this point many a candidate broke cover.

The interviewer was always on the lookout for any slight evidence in the candidate's expression, actions, or manner of speech of his becoming suspicious that an effort was being made to break his cover. If no such signs appeared, the interviewer forged ahead in his efforts to get facts about the candidate's real life. If signs of uncertainty did appear, he immediately took steps to allay the candidate's suspicion by changing the topic. He wished to forestall any queries about X conditions at this time so that he could return to the attack later with more hope of success. If the subject actually began to ask whether X conditions prevailed, the interviewer interrupted the sentence if he could, or if this was not possible, he would give some vague answer such as, "Things are just as they were downstairs," and hurry on to another topic. A determined and alert candidate would, of course, not be trapped by this, but would insist upon a definite answer to his question. In such a case, the interviewer would admit that X conditions did not prevail.

The topic to which the interviewer turned the conversation whenever the candidate's suspicion forced him to change it was an explanation of the purpose of the interview. "The test downstairs is a fairly new test," he would say, "and we hope it is a good one. However, we need the comments of men who have experienced it and who know something about it, and therefore I have asked to have you sent up here. I should greatly appreciate any criticisms you may have of it or any suggestions as to how it can be improved." This maneuver changed the line of the candidates' thought so radically that, in an effort to think of criticism, he often forgot about the perplexing problem of X conditions.

After the candidate had made some comments on the test, the examiner inquired, "Have we succeeded in creating a stressful situation downstairs? How did you feel during it? Did the grilling upset you?" In his replies to these queries the candidate revealed much about his emotional stability, and this topic was pursued as long as it appeared to be fruitful.

Then came another transition, again for the purpose of going to a field in which it was easy to lure the unsuspecting into breaking cover, "Have you ever been in such a situation before?" the interviewer would ask. "For instance, were you ever cross-examined, as in court, or interviewed for a job? Perhaps you have done some such interviewing yourself?" Treading gingerly, the questioner might try in this way to get information about the candidate's vocation. If this failed the examiner might ask, "Well, in college weren't you ever grilled like this in a fraternity initiation?" and, caught off his guard, the candidate might reply that he never went to college or, conversely, state the name of his college or even of his fraternity.

Another fruitful issue to raise at this juncture was that of childhood events. The interviewer might say, "As a psychologist I've been wondering whether there weren't times in your childhood somewhat similar to this—times when you concealed petty things from your parents by telling fibs when they questioned you." Most students would agree that there had been such episodes, whereupon the interviewer would ask, "Did your family make a great point of complete truthfulness and honesty? Perhaps you are like some candidates we have had at S who have found it difficult to make up a cover story because their early training in honesty made it hard for them to tell lies." Often this approach led quite naturally into a discussion of the candidate's childhood, his parents, and often his religion.

If a further line of attack on the candidate's cover was desired, an effort could be made to get him to reveal the branch of the OSS for which he worked. One way to do this was to ask, "Do you think this really is a good test?" After the candidate had replied, the interviewer might ask, "Do you think it is a good test for members of your branch? By the way, which branch do you belong to?"

Usually when these questions had been answered, the allotted time for Post-Stress was nearly over, so the interviewer asked if X conditions had existed during the conversation. Candidates responded to this in different ways, which gave excellent insight into their security consciousness as well as into their intellectual resourcefulness and emotional stability. Some looked stunned and guilty, admitting immediately that they had been caught. Frequently they were ashamed and distressed to realize that by breaking cover they had failed another test. Others bluffed at this point, or perhaps said correctly that all the facts they had related about their "real life" were false. (This could be confirmed from the Personal History Forms they had filled out the first night; indeed, all "facts" told by candidates in Post-

Stress had to be checked in this way, for a really clever candidate might "confess" to have broken cover in Post-Stress only to have a check of his story reveal that all that he had said was a cover which he had kept intact. Sometimes, it must be confessed, we did not know who was deceiving whom in the Post-Stress Interview.) Still others insisted that they had assumed all along that they were under X conditions, and gave a variety of reasons and rationalizations for making this assumption.

The interviewer then told them, if they had broken cover, that they had erred in doing so and instructed them to be more careful in the future, a lesson which most candidates thought had been well learned and which they took in good spirit. Those, on the other hand, who had gone through the Post-Stress Interview without breaking cover were complimented and told to continue the good work.

From this point on in the interview everything was done to help the candidate regain his equanimity and to prevent his becoming embittered toward the assessment program by the evening's events. First he was asked how he had felt when he had been told downstairs that he had failed. Then he was questioned about how much he had wished to succeed in the test. After that he was told that it was very likely that he had not failed, and that as a matter of fact he probably had done very well. It was explained to him that all the candidates were told at the end of the Stress-Interview that they had failed, even if in reality their performances had been good. It was explained that such an announcement had been made to test their emotional reactions. Then the candidate was reassured and asked to pardon the staff for appearing to have been so inconsiderate. He was told that it was thought essential to see how well he could withstand such strain, and he was complimented on his control under these difficult circumstances. Finally, he was requested not to tell the other candidates what had occurred until all had been through both sessions. With this the interview was concluded. After the candidate had left the room, the Post-Stress interviewer rated him on the six-point scale on Security, Emotional Stability, and Motivation for his Assignment in OSS.

All told, more than half the candidates broke cover at one point or another in this casual relaxing interview which followed the high-tension grilling downstairs.

The Stress and Post-Stress interviews of candidates were so scheduled that those men who had been recruited for work as intelligence agents and were being assessed for such assignments were free in the early part of the evening to be given, as a group, a test designed to measure the ability to evaluate and to abstract "intelligence" material.

SIX-2 Test.—The materials of this test consisted of four documents which purported to be (1) a report on the interrogation of Chinese refugees sent by a Chinese colonel in Military Intelligence in Chungking to an American major in G-2 stationed in the same city; (2) the translation into English of a captured report from a Japanese captain, en route, to Major Shojiro Kobayashi, Propaganda Dissemination Unit, Shanghai; (3) a report on conditions in occupied territory by an American lieutenant in Nausha, China, to a major in G-2 at Chungking; and (4) a translation of a Chinese military document sent from Kanchow to Chungking reporting on recent enemy activity in that sector; a map of the Central China front; a sheet of instructions; and an answer sheet.

The instructions to the candidates read as follows:

You are an aide in the Military Intelligence Division at a Headquarters establishment in China. A staff meeting is scheduled to start within a short time and one of the subjects to be discussed is the possible future action of the Japanese in the direction of Lingsien and Kanchow indicated on the map provided. You are operating under conditions of emergency where the available facts must be reported in the absence of time enough to wait for the whole story. The available facts in this case are contained in the four documents and the map attached.

For the purposes of this test the date of today is 15 December 1944.

The test was composed of two parts. Part I, for which thirty-five minutes were allowed, had two requirements. From the documents provided, candidates were instructed:

1. To make a numbered list of *all* items of information bearing on future enemy action in the direction of Lingsien and Kanchow.
2. Considering the source of the information and also considering how well or how poorly it agrees with other information in these documents, to make an evaluation of the truth, credibility, or probability of each item of information according to the following classification:
   A. PROBABLY TRUE (reliable source and consistent with independent information from another source).
   B. POSSIBLY TRUE (reliable source and neither confirmed nor contradicted by information from another source).
   C. RUMOR (known to be rumor, or from unreliable source, or contradicted by other items of information).

Part II required that the candidates prepare a fifty-word dispatch transmitting the most significant information to headquarters. In this part of the test, candidates were specifically instructed not to draw any conclusions regarding possible enemy action, but simply to transmit the information they had gathered from the documents. For Part II ten minutes were allowed.

Although these documents and map were fictitious, an attempt was made to render the test as realistic as possible by making Central China the locale of the problem and by writing the four basic documents as nearly as possible in the style of the organizations whose personnel was supposed to have written them.[5]

Raw scores on Part I were obtained by allowing two points for each item and one point for its correct classification. On Part II the raw scores were obtained by allowing two points each for the seven most significant items in the dispatch. Norms were provided for converting raw scores into ratings on the standard six-point scale. If the assumptions upon which the test was based were correct, the candidate should have earned a score that was more or less directly related to his ability to perform at least some of the operations involved in processing intelligence material.

Successful performance on the SIX-2 Test required more than a simple listing of items copied from the documents and a guess as to the credibility of each. Because of the time limit, the candidate penalized himself if he failed to stick closely to the specific instructions given and instead wasted his time giving information not called for. Moreover, he could not decide that certain obscure items were relevant unless, to take one example, he perceived the difference in content of two short items of propaganda. He could not properly classify several of the items until he had read all four documents and compared those portions that referred to the same fact. The correct inference regarding the time of the expected enemy action could be made only through close attention to the dates of the documents and to two ostensibly unrelated numerical data regarding the production of one or two series of propaganda leaflets by the enemy.

Preparation for Teaching Test.—Sometimes during the course of the evening those candidates who had been recruited to serve as instructors were taken aside individually and told that on the following day they would be asked to give a short demonstrational lecture as a test of their teaching ability. In most cases the candidate was given the task of explaining the construction and use of the time-pencil, a simple device which is essentially a delayed-reaction fuse used in demolition work. On this evening the candidate was given a supply of time-pencils; some were assembled and others had been taken apart to reveal their construction. In addition each man was given a typed 400-word description of the construction, function, and uses of the time-pencil, and an enlarged cross-sectional view of the device. The candidate was allowed unlimited time to study this material and prepare whatever notes he might wish to make in anticipation of his talk on the following day. He was told to prepare a talk that would not last more than fifteen minutes and which would make clear to a group of

---

[5] Some of the content of the documents was based upon authentic models secured from a number of sources; the rest was based on suggestions made by persons familiar with this type of material.

men who were going to instruct natives in the field in the use of the time-pencil all they would need to know about the device. A half hour to an hour was sufficient time for most candidates to prepare themselves for this assignment.

A lecture on the time-pencil was requested only from those candidates who had been recruited to instruct in demolitions, firearms, or some other weapon or instrument. Instruction in OSS schools was extremely varied, including such disparate subjects as cultural background, meteorology, intelligence reporting, fieldcraft, mapping, and so on. It seemed best merely to ask instructors in such topics to be prepared on the following day to give a fifteen-minute talk on some aspect of their specialty.

The program at S, up and through the evening of the first full day, was designed to keep the candidate under fairly constant tension. After this, an atmosphere of increasing relaxation and sociability was encouraged, even though the tempo at which candidates were confronted with new tests and situations did not slacken. As has been stated before, it was our intention in designing the S program to arrange that every period of unpleasant stress be followed by an opportunity for the candidate to release his emotion in the company of the staff member responsible for his situationally induced frustration or failure. It was in keeping with this principle that the member of the staff who had interrogated the candidates so unmercifully in the Stress Interview made it a point at the end of the evening to join the candidates in the living room.

As the interrogator entered the room with characteristic exuberance he congratulated the group on its performance in the dungeon. Recognizing his identity, they would respond to his greeting in a manner that reflected their reactions to the test itself. Some of them would make critical or derogatory comments, others would reply quietly, smilingly, indifferently, and still others would rise to meet him with eager inquiries as to the quality of their performance. A few would remain aloof.

There was usually at least one member of each class who spontaneously inquired whether the staff member really thought that their group had done well. It was such a question which evoked a discussion about the test that lasted for, perhaps, a half hour. The answer ordinarily was that on a comparative basis the cover stories of the present group equaled those that had been considered best in previous groups. The interrogator would then single out a candidate in the group and laughingly point out, to the amusement of the other candidates, how he, the examiner, had been worsted by him. Then other cover stories would be reviewed, in the course of which weaknesses in them would be glossed over or joked about pleasantly.

The interrogator would then tell the class some amusing incidents that had occurred during previous Stress Interviews, some of them fictitious and some exaggerated, but all having for their purpose the amusement of the group. In each of these cases the examiner placed himself in the subordinate position. A story always received with satisfaction was that of a strapping Texan who was ordered to uncross his legs by the examiner, a much less powerfully built individual. That command was hurled sharply at the Texan several times, but was always ignored. Finally, the Texan looked in the direction of the voice and threateningly said: "Come and make me!"

To enliven the proceedings further, the staff member might parody a candidate's actions during the interview with exaggerated humor. Following these reminiscences the candidates would usually ask further questions about the test. Almost all became involved in attempts to learn what constituted acceptable cover stories, suitable ways of meeting unexpected questions, and appropriate behavior in such circumstances. The answers were general enough to encompass the performances of the evening and couched in terms that made it appear that the candidates had performed better than they had thought.

And so, except for those who would continue to play cards or darts, or read, or listen to the radio, or engage in further conversation in the living room or in the kitchen while raiding the icebox, or work on some assignment for the next day, or sit alone in thoughtful meditation, the second evening at S came to an end.

Chapter IV

ASSESSMENT AT S: PROCEDURES (*Continued*)

SECOND DAY

At 8:30 on the morning of the second full day at S, candidates gathered in the classroom to be asked by a member of the staff to record on slips of paper before them two things, each in a sentence or two: (1) the basic facts of the cover story which the candidate had developed at S; and (2) a statement of his postwar plans. This latter report on what he would most like to do in the postwar world was to be given truthfully if it could be told without seriously breaking his cover; otherwise he was to record the activity which was most similar to that in which he intended to engage after the war.

These two bits of information were gathered to aid the staff in preparing situations, tailor-made to fit each candidate, known as Improvisations, which would be held in the early evening of this day.

Aside from the Personal History Interviews scheduled for some candidates, the major procedure of this morning was a series of situational tests in which each man in turn would be assigned the leadership of his group in the solution of an operational problem.

Assigned Leadership.—It was recognized early at S that situations like Brook and Discussion afforded only a limited view of the ability of candidates to lead their fellow men. What was observed in these procedures was largely initiative and assertiveness, for it was inevitable that in situations in which no leader was appointed a premium would be placed upon just these attributes. Furthermore, a large number of candidates who sought to gain authority never attained it, at least to the extent which would allow them to demonstrate what they could do if placed in full charge of a project. Moreover, those who did succeed in directing operations were not always free to exercise their planning, organizing, and executive abilities to the full, since often right up to the very end the rivalry of others meant that they had to devote a good deal of attention to the very maintenance of their status. While this type of leaderless situation was useful in identifying assertive men with a strong drive for dominance, and while it did yield a measure of leadership in many cases, there was clearly a need for procedures which offered each man a chance to reveal his true ability when a position of authority was definitely assigned to him.

In view of these considerations five assigned leadership problems were devised, each of which demanded a somewhat different type of command.[1] Since there were usually more than five candidates in a group, one or two candidates, whose proposed mission did not demand leadership ability, were not assigned a problem. Each of the others was given the problem which seemed particularly suitable to him.

The preliminary instructions for the Assigned Leadership situations were as follows:

You are now going to participate in a number of field problems. In each of these you will work together as a team with one member assigned the role of leader. In each problem, we will tell you what the situation is. From then on you are on your own. If you happen to go beyond what we consider the necessary limits of the problem, we'll let you know; so you can proceed as you wish unless we tell you otherwise. We will let you know when each problem is over. All right, let's go to the first one, and let's try to make each situation as realistic as possible.

MINED ROAD.—The group was then taken to a road where one candidate, in the presence of the whole group, was addressed in the following manner:

JOE, you're the leader in this situation. You're leading this group back from a mission in enemy-occupied territory. You and your men have blown up a bridge about a mile away in this direction (*points behind them*). According to prearranged plans, you must meet a guerrilla truck about a mile away from here in this direction at a time which leaves you only ten minutes to spend getting across this road. You have discovered that this road has been mined with a new type of sensitive Jap mine which you won't be able to neutralize or dig up. The limits of the problem are this: the road is assumed to be between these white lines, and you can work up and down the road as far as the white lines extend. The explosion at the bridge has aroused the enemy, but so far they don't know in which direction you have gone. Your problem is obvious: to get across and leave as little trace of your escape route as possible. O.K., go ahead.

The distance between the white lines was approximately twelve feet. Bordering the road were trees and bushes, and scattered about near by were a twelve-foot and a fourteen-foot log, some stones, a few two-by-fours about four feet in length, and two lengths of rope.

The problem which faced the leader in this situation was that of organizing his men for action under pressure of time, and leading them across the road without setting off any of the mines. In accomplishing this, the material

[1] Several of these situations were adapted from procedures used by the British War Office Selection Boards.

at hand could be used in any one of a number of ways: catching a stick, tied into the end of the rope, on the crotch of a tree on the far side of the road and constructing an overhead cable; tying or looping the rope over a branch of a tree above the road and using this to swing over the road; lowering a log against the trunk of a tree on the far side of the road in such a way that the base of the log was held securely on the near side, thus making an inclined bridge on which the group could cross; laying a log as a bridge on rocks on the far and near sides of the road, and so forth.

The way in which the leader conducted the discussion of the various possible solutions gave the staff insight into his ability to organize ideas as well as to spur the group to the quick action that the situation demanded. Furthermore, since the authority for directing the project was given to one man, it was possible to get some idea of how well he could bear the responsibility of leadership, that is, how much and in what ways he leaned upon his men for advice; whether he retained his position or gave up a good deal of his authority to more assertive and more imaginative followers.

The situation was also one in which the ability of men to work as willing and cooperative subordinates could be noted. Certainly it was fully as important to know how our candidates took orders as it was to know how effectively they gave them, since all who were passed by S would have to fit into a military, or at least a quasi-military, chain of command. At the Mined Road one could observe whether a man placed in a subordinate position was cooperative and obedient, or lazy and refractory, whether he acted as a willing and effective lieutenant or hampered the leader's direction and the group's effectiveness by his unwillingness to suppress his own ideas, or by his importunate desire to take over and direct the problem.

When the assignment had been completed, with the group safely across the road, or when fifteen minutes had passed without a successful solution, the staff member in charge called the group together for a critique of the execution. He first inquired of the leader what he thought of his solution and in what ways, if any, he would change it if he had to do it again. The leader's response gave some measure of his confidence in handling the project and his ability to learn quickly from the mistakes he had made. It seemed only fair to offer the leader a chance to review his own performance before calling for a critique from his subordinates. In turn they were asked their opinions of the leader's handling of the problem. By their comments they revealed not only their assessment of the leader, their respect for him and confidence in him if they felt he merited such trust, but also their own intelligence, or lack of it, in the proposals they now made for other ways of performing the task.

By the time the problem and the critique of it had been completed, the staff members were ready to rate the subordinates in the group on the variables of Energy and Initiative, Effective Intelligence, and Social Relations, and, in addition to these traits, to rate the leader on the variable of Leadership.

SENTRY.—The group was then led to a hedge of boxwood on the side of an open field where another member of the group was instructed as follows:

AL, you're the leader in this situation. You have all just gathered at this rendezvous point after completing an intelligence mission to an enemy airfield, and you are still in enemy-occupied territory. Unfortunately, Gus has just broken both legs in a fall down a ravine and from this point on will have to be carried on this stretcher (*points to one on the ground*). A plane will make a point contact with you at a secret airfield in that direction (*points across road*), so that you have only 10 minutes to get across. It is going to land and take off right away. In getting there, you must pass this road, which is patrolled by the enemy. You can see a sentry from here. The boundaries of the problem are about 10 yards beyond that bush and 10 yards beyond that fence (*points*). So far you have been able to operate in this territory without the enemy suspecting your presence and that's important for future operations. One more thing—as long as you are standing behind this path [40 feet from the road], you may consider yourself under complete cover. From here on the terrain is as you see it. O.K., go ahead.

The role of the sentry in this problem was played by a member of the junior staff carrying a rifle. His beat was laid out in such a way that he was actually unable to see a part of the road for about 45 seconds of each of his tours, and he was instructed not to detect the candidates unless it was unavoidable, but to act as if he were suspicious from time to time.

As soon as the instructions had been given, the members of the staff observing the proceedings made themselves as inconspicuous as possible so that the verisimilitude of the situation would not be lessened by their obvious presence in front of the sentry. The leader would then discuss the situation with his men, calling for their plans or outlining his own, and sending out scouts or reconnoitering himself. If the group were an alert and intelligent one, someone would note the orderly character of the sentry's beat and call attention to the fact that at regular intervals the road could be crossed without detection. Often this fact was not noted and even at times when it was observed no use was made of it. Instead, the leader might order one of his men to distract the sentry while the group, at another point, attempted to cross the road unobserved; or he might direct that the sentry be killed.

The discussion of the proposed methods of solution provided a good opportunity to observe the leader's organization of ideas into a final plan, and in his execution of it the staff could observe his forcefulness, his skill in evoking cooperation and in directing the actions of his men. This problem usually afforded insight into certain aspects of leadership not brought out in the first situation, for while the Mined Road problem required close direction of a group of men in a relatively simple construction task, the Sentry problem made more demands upon the leader's ability to handle a fairly complex operation where the men were spread out in space and where some of them had to work relatively independently. Here the leader was expected to select his men carefully and to brief them adequately for the different jobs, such as reconnoitering, carrying the stretcher, attacking the sentry. He had to devise some system of communication with his men by messengers or signals and in such a manner that they would not give away their presence to the sentry. The good leader had to be open-minded enough to listen to the counterplans of his subordinates, yet confident enough of his own judgment not to be led astray by the impulsiveness which this situation seemed to bring out. He had to be firm in his adherence to his directive, which demanded crossing the road by all of the men at the opportune moment without being discovered by the enemy, and without leaving traces behind (such as the body of the sentry or a missing sentry).

In a similar way, the problem enabled the staff to observe the subordinates faced with a type of situation different from the first one. Here the followers had greater freedom of action and more individual responsibility. Since they were not always directly under the supervision of the leader, the success of the operation depended more upon their ability to remember their instructions and yet to act in accordance with the spirit of them on their own initiative, as the situation changed. Some displayed a healthy capacity for sound individual action; others were content to do nothing until specifically directed.

Many of the points were brought to light in the critique that followed the completion of the task. Here the leader could explain to the staff that he had not intended that his men should kill the sentry, or that his decision not to kill him had come at the last minute. Likewise the candidates in their criticism of the leader would reveal to the staff which of them felt impelled to kill the sentry in disobedience of the leader, which ones could obey the leader even though they were convinced he was wrong, which ones thought the situation would have been better if they had had closer supervision, and which ones, on the other hand, preferred more individual action.

Here, as in all situations of Assigned Leadership, candidates were rated on Energy and Initiative, Effective Intelligence, and Social Relations, either as subordinates carrying out the orders of a superior or as a leader directing a group of men in meeting an emergency situation. In addition, the leader was rated on Leadership.

AGENT'S ROOM.—The instructions for this situation were given at the entrance of a large, unused carriage house on the second floor of which was a crude living room.

HARRY, you're the leader here. This problem takes place in German-occupied France before D day in Europe. You have just received a radio message from headquarters saying that a friendly agent who was living in this room made a hurried getaway and was forced to leave some important papers behind; it is up to you and your men to recover these papers, if possible. You and your men have been passing as natives, for you have forged credentials, you are dressed in native costume, and speak the native tongue. Headquarters wants a report by radio within ten minutes.

With nothing more than this to guide him the leader had to make his plans, scout the terrain, and organize a warning system against surprise by the Germans. Some leaders were extremely cautious in their approach to the room, fearing a trap. Others, heedless of possible enemy intrusion, led all of their men upstairs in a concerted effort to search the room. Usually, however, the leader and one or two men would make their way to the room in a circumspect manner while the others took inconspicuous positions as lookouts, prepared with a system of signals to warn of enemy approach. In any case, shortly after the candidates began to search the room, a junior staff member, armed with a rifle and identified as a German guard, approached the carriage house, and if not delayed by the lookouts, proceeded upstairs and belligerently demanded an explanation of the men's presence there.

In addition to gaining, as usual, an impression of the leader's ability to plan and carry out a critical task and the subordinates' capacity to cooperate and follow their leader effectively, the staff had the opportunity to observe how the leader and his men reacted to sudden threat, and how ingenious and resourceful they could be in meeting it. Observing the leader's method of approach, the staff could learn how impulsive or how cautious he was; how well he could distribute his men in a situation that demanded, on the one hand, speed and thoroughness in searching the room, and, on the other, caution and completeness in guarding against detection by the enemy. Here again was a situation which did not permit the leader to supervise each man directly from beginning to end. Special note was taken of the leader's reaction when he discovered that an enemy soldier was approaching, whether he was calm or upset in the face of the emergency, and how effectively he could cope with the intruder and still accomplish his prime mission of gaining possession of the important papers. Some leaders forgot the aim of the undertaking and sought only to effect the escape of their men; others sought personal safety or led a retreat in rout; some tried to overpower the guard and continue the search; still others attempted to depend on their cover and talk their way out of the predicament on the strength of their forged credentials and native dress.

Of course much of what the leader did in this situation was often the result of the ideas and behavior of his men, for the subordinates had considerable opportunity for independence of action. For example, when the German soldier appeared, some lookouts would give the warning signals immediately while others would wait until the soldier was on the stairs. Some would attempt to kill the guard, others would try to delay him by making conversation, asking advice, or inventing some emergency. Still others would simply do nothing and avoid the guard and even hide from him. Light was shed upon the Energy and Initiative, and Effective Intelligence of the subordinates, and on the men's capacities for calm individual action in keeping with the spirit of the leader's orders.

In the critique the leader again had an opportunity to evaluate his own performance first and say how he might have handled the situation differently or why he would do it the same way again if he had another chance. The followers could then explain their behavior and offer alternative solutions, as well as criticize how the leader had handled the problem.

BLOWN BRIDGE.—This situation had some resemblance to the Mined Road since it, too, was a problem of construction. For this test there had been erected, in an open field, two abutments three feet high and, in the intervening twenty-five feet, five posts were set up which formed an X pattern (as on the five of spades) which rose vertically five feet out of the ground. On the side where the group stood a number of boards were strewn around. One might think that these could be used to make a bridge from one abutment to the other over the pilings, but actually there were not enough boards of sufficient length to permit the building of a single, continuous bridge. The instructions for this situation were:

BIM, you're the leader in this one. You and your men are returning from a mission of sabotage. You arrive at this bridge, which you had planned to use in crossing this stream, and find that it is demolished. The stream is a raging torrent at the bottom of a rocky gorge and is impassable except by bridge. (*Points to limits of stream.*) It flows between the abutments, running this way. There is nothing left of the bridge but the abutments and pilings as you see them and this debris. There are no other bridges you can use in getting across. Enemy patrols come through here along the stream roughly every seven minutes. We'll give you a minute or two to talk this over and when you are ready to go, you can assume that a patrol has just passed. O.K., go ahead.

As in other assignments, the brief period of discussion provided the staff members with a chance to see whether the leader could size up the whole situation and to what extent he was capable of organizing the ideas of his men into an effective plan of action. Similarly once the work began, they could observe the leader's ability to direct his men without relinquishing the lead to a more energetic or intelligent teammate and his competence in coordinating the efforts of his men toward the common goal.

The problem of the Blown Bridge made certain special demands upon the leader's ability to maintain control, since the first man to get out on the pilings was in an excellent position to take over the direction of the work. This man could see the chief problems involved in arranging the boards properly. according to size in spanning the pilings. He, better than anyone else, could discover the fact that only one board would bridge both the span from the near abutment to the first piling and the span from the last piling to the far abutment. If the candidate who happened to be first out on the pilings was a man of initiative, as he very often was, he might be inclined to take charge of things from then on. The reactions of leaders to this threat varied; some immediately accepted the role of subordinate and followed orders just as if they had not been appointed leaders; others realized the other man's vantage point and allowed him to play the role of the good lieutenant, without relinquishing control of the group; others tried to put through their own ideas, ignoring much of the valuable information coming from out front. In some cases, of course, the leader was the first one out on the pilings and consequently this conflict never arose for him.

At about the time the seven minutes were up, or just before the men had worked their way across the pilings, a staff member would inform them that the enemy patrol could be heard approaching not far off. Shortly thereafter, on a prearranged signal, a stooge concealed behind a near-by wall would open fire on the group with blank cartridges. The reaction of most leaders to the first warning was merely to urge their men to hurry, but many ignored it. When the actual firing began, some leaders would call feverishly for greater haste in pursuing the initial plan; others would change their plan to the extent of having the men jump from the last piling to the bank, a difficult feat; some would order their men to take cover behind the pilings and sit tight; others would tell them to jump into the river and swim for it, despite the fact that it was a "raging torrent"; and still others, immobilized by the shock, would momentarily lose control, or, preoccupied with their own personal safety, would leave the rest to shift for themselves. In cases where the group succeeded in reaching the shore, some leaders would order their men to take cover in the near-by bushes, but most of them would rush for cover themselves, expecting their men to do likewise.

The information gained about the subordinates at the Blown Bridge was much the same as that learned in the preceding assignments up to the point where the enemy patrol approached and opened fire. Here, if the leader gave specific orders, some men would obey blindly even if it meant jumping into the torrent, whereas others would choose to ignore his authority and seek safety in their own way. Still others were too confused to decide on any consistent course of action.

Here the staff gained a more or less definite impression of the effectiveness of the leader, particularly the extent to which he could evoke immediate respect and obedience in a crisis, and knowledge of the degree to which other members of the group were able to function as intelligent, energetic, agreeable, and resourceful subordinates. Given the opportunity to discuss their performance, some leaders sought to explain away their shortcomings by saying that the man first out on the pilings had assumed too much authority, or that it was every man for himself in this emergency, or that their predicament was hopeless once the patrol had spotted them.

KILLING THE MAYOR.—As soon as the fourth outdoor situation was over, the candidates were assembled in the classroom around a large sand-table model of a town and its surroundings. Pointing to a clearing in the woods in the extreme northwest ·corner of the sand table, the examiner told the assigned leader that he and his men had just jumped in on a special mission to German-occupied France. Their orders were simply to kill the mayor of the town who lived in a house on the outskirts of the village about three miles as the crow flies from where they had landed. They were told that they had parachuted from the plane at twelve midnight and that the plane would land at the same place twenty-four hours later, at twelve midnight of the next evening, to make a spot contact and pick them up. The staff member then informed them that they could all speak the native tongue, wore native clothes, and had forged credentials so that they could readily pass for natives of the region; furthermore, they could assume that they had all the light equipment necessary for this mission, such as knives, ropes, sidearms, small quantities of demolitions. The sand table could be used as a map in planning the mission, but once the work got under way, they were to behave just as though they were walking through the actual terrain.

Then the candidates were informed that they had just hit the ground and the mission had begun; the examiner would at intervals announce the passage of time. After the discussion had continued for a few minutes the staff member would interrupt to say that it had taken them some time to gather up their equipment and find cover after landing, and that it was now 12:30. If the talk went on, in another minute or so the examiner would say that it was 12:45. Ordinarily, the discussion would consist of talking over plans for getting into town undetected, arranging signals and rendezvous points, planning reconnaissance of the area around the mayor's house, deciding on the best way to kill him, and so forth. Some leaders failed to adjust to the pressure of time and carried on the discussion until three or four o'clock was announced, even though they had originally planned to kill the mayor before dawn. Others decided to wait out the night in the woods, reconnoiter the town the next day, and carry out the mission the following evening.

Just before the group was ready to leave its landing place the staff member would announce the first emergency problem: the leader had suddenly become aware of a stranger, ten feet away, looking at them all intently; he was dressed in hunting clothes and carrying a gun. The examiner would say that he would play the part of the hunter, and then he would ask, "What are you doing here?" Some leaders impulsively decided to kill the man on the spot; others to knock him down, bind, and gag him; others attempted to talk their way out of the situation by using the advantages of their cover; still others started to interrogate him on points pertinent to their undertaking. When questioned, the hunter would be vague about his loyalties and his knowledge of conditions in town; if pressed, he would reveal that there was a garrison of Germans in the town but he did not know how many troops there were. Eventually· the leader would have to decide what to do with the hunter; either kill him, tie him up, place him under guard, or let him go, hoping that he would not report them.

At the agreed-upon time, the men would set out for town, singly, in small groups, or in a body, describing their routes at the request of the staff member. By means of introducing incidents such as arrests, hearing important information from the residents, or being questioned by guards, the staff member could test the candidates' reactions to emergencies and, by controlling the passage of time, he could regulate their movements according to the way he wanted the problem to develop. Usually, however, the main emergency situations were presented to the leader. For example, if the men were attempting to cross the river by means of the highway bridge, the staff member could tell them that, as they approached, they noticed that the guards were questioning everyone and turning back some, letting others through, and detaining still others. The leader might decide to attempt to get by the guards anyway, in which case he might be turned back or let through. Or the leader might decide to try to cross the railroad bridge, or to ford or to swim the stream. In any case the staff would gain some indication of the candidate's resourcefulness and judgment, his tendency to be impulsive or cautious in an emergency, and his ability to control men who offer unwise suggestions.

Some leaders developed the simple plan of going directly to the mayor's house, expecting to find him in. If it suited the staff member, the mayor would be at home; otherwise, he would be out. In the latter case, the staff member might have the men overhear someone say that the mayor was spending the night at the German officers' club, but would be home the next night. Other leaders developed more comprehensive plans which involved reconnoitering the whole region, collecting information or even, at times, setting incendiaries with a time fuse in a barn at the opposite end of town in order to distract the population at the hour set for the murder. Others seriously complicated their main plan by seeking to accomplish other purposes: they might send out men to blow up the railroad tunnel or the bridges. Thus, in most cases, the situation permitted assessment of the leader's purposefulness, of his ability to plan simply and effectively, and of his foresight and sense of responsibility for his mission and his men.

By the simple expedient of having the leader arrested as the group was leaving the vicinity of the mayor's house, it could be arranged to have another man take the group back to the rendezvous with the plane. The candidates were merely told that while escaping they noticed that some German soldiers stopped the leader and then immediately led him off under guard; the remainder of the men were unnoticed and, shortly after the incident, got together and elected the now-designated man as their new leader.

The situation at the time of this change presented the new leader with a question that required an immediate answer: should the group attempt to rescue the original leader? Some men passed over this problem and proceeded to the rendezvous point. Others debated the point with their men and abandoned the idea. Still others felt impelled to attempt the rescue, ignoring for the moment the necessity of getting back to meet the plane. The way in which this dilemma was resolved gave the staff some insight into the judgment of the new leader, his discretion, his loyalty to his men, his sense of responsibility for the mission.

When the time came for the return of the group to the rendezvous the leader had to plan this maneuver and execute it in the face of incidents and accidents created by the staff member in such a manner as to interfere with the carrying out of the initial plan. As the men were finally making their way through the woods to the rendezvous at 11:30 P.M., the examiner would inform them that they had almost walked into a large German patrol which was feverishly searching the area and, overhearing the talk of the soldiers, they had learned that the hunter whom they had encountered the first night was the instigator of the search. The hunter had been a collaborationist; if they had killed or detained him, the fact that he was missing in that area had led to the search; if they had released him, he had reported to the Gestapo. Anyhow, the patrol was covering the area between the candidates and their rendezvous point and time was passing; it was now 11:40. In meeting this predicament, some leaders urged that they retreat and attempt a more circuitous route; others decided to wait and see what would develop; others attempted to infiltrate the area under cover; others decided to fight their way through. By 11:55 it was conceded by the staff member that the group had made its way to the rendezvous point successfully but that the patrol was still searching the area only a short distance away. The leader was told that they could now hear the motors of the plane that was coming to pick them up; and, if he did not realize it himself, he was told that it was certain that the Germans could hear the plane

too. At this point some proposed that they seek to warn the plane away
by flares or gunfire, and then if possible hide from the patrol; others would
let the plane land and take the chance of boarding it successfully despite
the proximity of the Germans; others decided they would fight the enemy
off until the plane landed and try to make a getaway; still others thought
of some ruse such as dispatching one man several hundred yards away
to set off an explosive or incendiary charge to distract the Germans; others
thought only of escaping from the patrol without even warning the pilot
of the plane.

Usually the problem ended with the candidates discussing whether or
not they actually could have made their getaway. Using this as a point of
departure, the examiner would start the critique, with other members of
the staff joining in from time to time. The original leader might be asked
why he had treated the hunter as he had, and the others encouraged to say
how they would have handled this problem. Often it was impossible to say
whether one decision was better than another; what revealed both the intelligence and the planning ability of a leader were the reasons he offered for
each decision he had made.

For the success of this assignment, the skill with which the examiner
conducted it was crucial. It was he who kept it alive and exciting or let
it become flat through lack of imagination in creating emergencies and
unexpected incidents. Yet his role could not be too dominant, for if it were,
the distinctive traits of personality of the candidates would be obscured. His
job primarily was to make the candidates face the more-or-less standard
emergency situations that were designed to arise in the course of carrying
out the problem: for the first leader, handling the hunter, killing the mayor,
and perhaps getting by the sentries; for the second leader, taking over the
responsibility of a mission without warning, deciding about rescuing the first
leader, getting past the patrol, and deciding what to do about the landing
of the plane. In addition, the examiner had to keep the problem going by
putting the leaders under pressure, by announcing the passage of time
every so often, and by delaying the men with minor incidents in case they
went too fast. Despite the fact that the mission was always the same in this
problem, every time it was run the proceedings developed somewhat differently. No matter what special turn a group of candidates gave to the assignment, it always worked out as a test of planning ability and skill in meeting
new emergencies. It gave the staff insight into how a man went about planning and handling such an operation: the freedom he allowed his men, the
methods he designed to maintain control, his capacity for detail, his
foresight, his adaptability, the rigidity with which he adhered to his original
plan in the face of emergencies and changed conditions, the extent to which
he discussed problems with his subordinates, his capacity for quick and
independent decision, his sense of responsibility to his men and the mission,

his decisiveness. In respect to the subordinates, the staff could rate their energy and Initiative, Effective Intelligence, and Social Relations, and gain insight into their ability to cooperate in the planning and execution of a mission. The situation also permitted appraisal of their reaction to emergencies, their capacity to help make decisions, their judgment, responsibility, and resourcefulness.

Teaching Test.—During the course of the morning the teaching abilities of candidates slated for assignment in the OSS schools were tested. These men had been forewarned and given an opportunity to prepare themselves for this on the previous evening. The procedure was conducted in the classroom, where the candidate had the use of a blackboard and any other materials which he requested, provided we were able to furnish them. His awareness of and desire for such teaching aids, as well as his use of them, were noted in our estimation of his teaching ability.

The candidate had as students a group of three to six staff members who supposedly knew nothing of the subject of his talk, but who were later to teach it to others. He was allowed fifteen minutes, which was ample time in which to present his material if he had planned it well.

Whenever possible, observers who were not familiar with the subject of the candidate's talk were included in the "class" to report on the efficacy of the instruction. Each candidate's performance was evaluated in terms of the specific teaching assignment for which he was being considered. Neither his over-all performance nor any aspects of it were rated on our six-point scale. The appraisal was qualitative, taking into account the candidate's understanding of his material, his organization of it, his efforts and success in maintaining the interest of the class, and the effectiveness of his presentation. The ease with which the candidate spoke, as well as any signs of nervous tension in this difficult situation, was considered in relation to the man's previous teaching experience or lack of it.

Terrain Test.—The last forty-five minutes of the morning, after all subgroups had participated in the Assigned Leadership problems, were devoted to the Terrain Test which required candidates (1) to answer thirty multiple-choice questions concerning the physical aspects of the farm on which S was located, and (2) to write as fully as possible concerning the activities which in the past had been carried on there, the people who at one time or another had been connected with it, the interests of its owners, and any other significant facts relating to its past history. Scores on this test were converted into ratings to yield another measure of the ability of candidates to observe, infer, and report.

Names and Identifications.—The first test of the afternoon, a conventional test of memory, was given in a most unconventional manner. It was designed to test the ability to associate names and identifications with faces, and to remember them upon subsequent presentation of the faces alone. This ability is important in many types of work, but it takes on special significance in the gathering of intelligence.

Two sets of twelve slides were prepared for this test. Each slide of the first (or learning) set had on it the photograph of a man, his name (pseudonym), age, occupation, and city and state of residence. The second (or testing) set had only the photographs. The first set of slides was shown in groups of four, each slide being exposed for twenty seconds. After each group of four had been presented, the corresponding slides of the second set were shown for thirty seconds each, in random order. The task of the candidates was to record during the exposure of a slide of the second set all of the data that had been printed on the corresponding slide of the first set. In the scoring of this test credit was given for each item recalled.

The member of the staff who had acted as interrogator in the Stress Interview presented the instructions for this test in his own unpremeditated, nonsensical, witty fashion. This performance of his, unique in the history of testing in America, provoked much laughter among the candidates, and in this way served to dispel whatever resentment against him might have been hanging over from the preceding evening. It would have run against the grain of this particular staff member—who contributed so much to the high morale of the candidates at S—to administer any test in accordance with orthodox scientific principles. We shall make no vain attempt to reproduce here the verve and torrent of his inimitable discourse.

Lest our professional colleagues be shocked that instructions embellished by a barrage of farcical comments should have been allowed to precede a test of memory, it should be here recorded that the odd-even reliability of this test, computed for 100 cases in Classes S-124 through S-133, was .78, corrected by the Spearman-Brown formula to .88.

Movie Observation Test.—For this test of observing and reporting, the candidates were shown two motion-picture sequences, each of which ran for about two and one half minutes. They were instructed to assume that they were agents in the field who had been assigned the task of trailing two men who would be identified for them when they first appeared on the screen. They were told to be prepared, following the observation of the film, to report everything they had seen these men do.

After each sequence the candidates were presented with printed statements about the action depicted in the film, supposedly written by a companion who had seen everything they had seen. Their task was to indicate which of the reported observations were correct and which incorrect, and if unable to answer definitely, to indicate their uncertainty.

Candidates were allowed ten minutes for checking each set of statements.

The scoring formula for the test was the number right minus one half the number wrong.

These two tests, Names and Identifications and Movie Observation, which yielded ratings of the ability to observe and to report, were given to all recruits. After completing them, the candidates who had been recruited for intelligence work in the field were given a test of aptitude to learn Morse code.

Code Aptitude Test.—The test employed for this purpose was the Signal Corps Code Aptitude Test (standard in 1943), which is automatically administered by phonograph records giving the instructions, sample problems, and seventy-eight pairs of patterns of code sounds for each of which it is the task of the subject to decide whether the patterns of sound are the same or different. Army norms were used in interpreting the scores obtained by the subjects.

Interrogation Test (Escaped Prisoner).—After he had completed the group written tests of this afternoon and before he reported to run the Obstacle Course, each man who had received instructions for the Interrogation Test on the previous evening went individually, each at an appointed time, to the third floor. There he was taken into a moderately large room and introduced to "T/Sgt Smith" (a member of the junior staff). While Smith and the candidate seated themselves at opposite sides of a desk, the staff member conducting the test withdrew into the background, slightly behind the candidate, to observe the interview and to make a record of its content by checking the topics covered on a check list.

T/Sgt Smith had a fixed story, which is indicated by the information on the check list reproduced on pages 162-163. He played a definite role, answering questions with relevant information, but volunteering no additional data. Once or twice during the interrogation, he would drop a hint of other facts in order that the alertness of the interviewer might be observed.

At the end of twelve minutes the candidate was conducted to another room and instructed to write a report of his findings. Immediately after the interview the staff member who had acted as observer and the one who had played the role of T/Sgt Smith made independent ratings of the candidate's skills in developing rapport, in asking productive questions, and in following up leads and hints. From these two scores, together with a rating on the completeness and the organization of the candidate's written report and a rating on his performance based on the check list, a single, final grade was derived. Although this rating procedure was not fully standardized before V-J day, the score and the qualitative observations made during Interrogation were used in determining the final rating of the variable known as Observing and Reporting.

CHECK LIST FOR INTERROGATION TEST

Students' Names

SMITH'S UNIT.

LOCATION OF THE CAMP WHERE SMITH WAS INCARCERATED (10 mi. S. of Wuchang).
Don't know location of the camp.
Bomber was headed from Kweisien airfield to bomb Jap-held airbase at Hangchow to east.
In air only 20–30 minutes when pilot said elevators weren't working at all. Brace selves for crash landing. Couldn't climb above bad weather.
Unconscious. Regained consciousness on being loaded into back of truck.
Rode about two hours before arrival at prison camp.
Could hear trains to west or north of prison camp.
Think I traveled in southwesterly direction on escape from camp. May have been south, may have been west. Escaped at night. Traveled 2 days through woods.
Crossed no railroad.
Crossed no river until, with party, the Wuking near Chaofu was reached.
Came through no cities.
Crossed no main highways.
Fairly level ground, wooded.
Airfield under construction—level, wooded.
(Also credit suggestion to check Kweisien airbase to find what area had been bombed on day of rescue.)

TREATMENT OF PRISONERS.
FOOD: Most of prisoners very poorly fed.
(In response to request for more clarification.) About 600 of healthiest men fed a little better. More bread.
(On further questioning, gives evidence of airfield preparation—steamrollers, etc., seen.)
2 "meals" per day. Usually just a little rice in morning, with tea sometimes. Thin soup and bread at evening. Sometimes horsemeat once a week. Just a bite. Soup thick when Red Cross visited.
Lost 15 pounds.

CLOTHING: Some articles provided in March when Red Cross worker appeared.

SHELTER: Two huge flimsy shelter houses, 300′ × 200′. No heat. Lice-infested straw and thin blankets.

WORK: About 10 hours a day for those not too weakened by malnutrition to stand up long. Digging postholes, cleaning latrines, making long clearing in adjacent ground, digging graves.

PUNISHMENT: Many rules. Violations often brought flogging to individuals, further restricted diet to whole group.

(See any prisoners killed outright?) Saw one resting worker bayoneted.

MEDICAL CARE: If couldn't walk.

INTERROGATION: Interrogated but no force used.

MAIL: Some got mail.

SIZE OF CAMP.

SIZE AND SHAPE: 10 acres—400 × 1000 ft.

PERSONNEL: Four shifts at meals—500 at my shift.

EXPANDING: (1) 500 moved into adjacent shelter house just after ·arrival.

(2) Lieutenant Colonel, an engineer, replaced a captain in charge.

NUMBER OF GUARDS: About 100. Second-rate troops.

COMPOSITION: Chinese in one house and Americans in other.

Americans—100 14th Air Force personnel. Rest—49th division. Officers and men thrown together.

OTHER INTELLIGENCE ASKED FOR.

1. Cause of crash landing.
   Probably elevator blocks not removed.
2. What happened to rest of crew?
   Told that 4 died in crash, 4 shot resisting capture.
3. What did you see on way back from camp?
   Saw small party of Japs a couple of hours before the Chinese picked me up.
4. Damage by air raid.
   Only a couple of bombs were dropped. Many injured, however.
5. Number escaping at same time as Smith.
   A few, but they took separate routes.
6. Morale of guards.
   Officers strict.
   Men somewhat indifferent.

Obstacle Course.—The latter half of this afternoon was given over to running an obstacle course designed to test the candidate's physical agility and daring. Although the course yielded some indication of physical condition, it could not be regarded as a measure of capacity for endurance. That could have been tested adequately only after the candidates had undergone a period of physical conditioning. However, the willingness of a man to make an effort, that is to say, his motivation, could be rated fairly accurately. It was too much to expect that all candidates whom we had passed at S would be in top condition in the field when (possibly after months of relative inactivity) they might be called upon to exert themselves to the limit in carrying out a mission, or in escaping the enemy. It seemed to us important, then, to estimate how much effort a man was willing to make in an obstacle course even though he was not in the pink of condition. At the same time we had to be on the alert for those exhibitionistic candidates who might willingly "knock themselves out" before the audience at S but who might fail to expend themselves in an emergency in the field.

Several obstacle courses were built and used during the history of S. An early course which traversed a large part of the farm and which required quick resourcefulness in emergencies, in addition to agility, daring, and endurance, was eventually abandoned because it was too time-consuming both for the staff and for the candidates. In its place the staff developed a more efficient course which measured only physical agility and daring, no attempt being made here to test resourcefulness and fitness for emergencies. During the last months of S, the Obstacle Course which was used combined parts of two separate courses. Any man under forty-five or fifty who had not allowed himself to become soft and who had taken reasonable care of his weight was allowed to run the course. It was our practice, however, to set forty years as the upper limit unless a candidate over that age expressed a strong desire to participate. None of the obstacles was either extremely difficult or extremely dangerous, though some appeared to be. Further, they did not test any special skills; they were constructed on the assumption that every man has had some experience as a boy, swinging on rings, climbing walls, fences, and ropes.

The first part of the course was so constructed that a candidate could select obstacles of greater or lesser difficulty. A man's score on a given obstacle was, therefore, a function of the difficulty of the obstacle he selected and the skill with which he overcame it. The course was set out so that each member of the staff could observe the performances of all the candidates for whom he was particularly responsible. He was thus in a position to obtain impressions of subtle, unscorable components of behavior which have special significances for one who has already arrived at a partial conception of a personality. For example, does the candidate give up easily on a difficult obstacle to select an easier one? Does his interest lag with failure? Does he meet each obstacle with a determination and a persisting drive to overcome it? Is he quick to evaluate and size up a situation? If he refuses one of the tests of daring, how does he rationalize his decision? The bits of behavior which shed light on these questions could not be given a score and by themselves could not serve as bases for generalizations about traits of personality. If they had already been observed in other test situations, however, they now acquired significance in the diagnosis of the man's personality. Since each of the several obstacles had characteristics devised to sample slightly different aspects of performance, each is described briefly and in the order that the candidate encountered it on the course. The candidates were given a written description of the course, and started on their way at five-minute intervals.

The first obstacle presented two alternatives, one requiring daring and considerable agility, the other demanding little of either. The former consisted of a set of four rings attached to separate ropes which in turn were suspended from a rope stretched between two large maple trees that were about 50 feet apart. The rings were about 12 feet from the ground when hanging freely, but sagged with the weight of a man to approximately 9 feet. The candidate's task was to climb to a platform nailed to a branch of the first tree, about 15 feet above the ground, and, with the first ring in hand, to swing off, and, on the upward arc of the swing, to grab the second ring, and then by swinging from ring to ring, to bring himself up finally into a large crotch of the second tree. The task was a difficult one to complete; only about 5 per cent of candidates were able to cross all the way from one tree to the other. The ease with which a candidate executed his swings was a good measure of his agility. The way in which he approached the problem was an even better measure of his daring. The obstacle was not very dangerous, though it appeared so. Many men, to be sure, lost their grip on the rings but, because of the sag in the rope, fell no more than two or three feet. But the platform looked very high as seen from the ground and once a man had reached it the apparent distance to the ground was such as to make the initial swing a real test of daring. Some paratroopers reported to us that it was fully as difficult for them to swing off the platform in this test as to step out of the door of a plane.

A man who was unwilling to attempt the rings could choose the alternative obstacle: a rope stretched horizontally between two trees 20 feet apart on which a man could cross hand over hand. The rope was about 10 feet off the ground. Once across the candidate could lower himself on a rope which hung vertically from the second tree.

The second obstacle presented the candidate with three alternatives and was primarily a measure of agility, although it provided in addition a measure of a man's confidence in his own ability. The task was to get over a hedge by going up a wide board inclined at a 60° angle from the ground and down the other side on a board placed at a corresponding angle, the two wooden planes forming a sort of pup tent bridging the hedge. There were three such structures of different degrees of difficulty whose sides measured 6, 8, and 9 feet, respectively. Here, as also in the next part of the course, a candidate who failed an obstacle was permitted to try an easier one if he so desired; and he was allowed as many attempts as he wished to get over any chosen obstacle.

The third obstacle was a smooth wall 24 feet long built in three sections, 8, 10, and 12 feet high. On the face of it were cleats providing few and uncertain footholds. The candidate was judged by the height of the wall which he attempted to climb and the strength, agility, and persistence of his efforts.

Having scaled the top, or failing that, having been allowed to climb to the top by means of steps provided for this purpose, the candidate found himself facing the fourth obstacle: two catwalks, one 10 feet and the other 8 feet above the ground, leading off at right angles from the wall. These catwalks extended for 20 feet over a sawdust pit. On the far end of each walk a narrow ramp led down to the ground. The instructions to the candidate were to cross on either walk he chose in any manner he wished—walking, crawling, sliding, but not running. He would receive more credits if he chose the higher one and more credits for walking than for crawling or sliding. Both walks were 3½ inches wide. They looked firm, but actually, since they were not supported in the middle, they oscillated sideways to an alarming extent as soon as anyone stepped out on them. It required rare balance and skill to get across either catwalk without falling off. This was a test of both daring and agility.

When all candidates had finished these obstacles, they were taken as a group to the second part of the test, which was an adaptation for our purposes of the Army's Running Time Course. The course, which was laid out around the sides of a large square field, consisted of twelve identical pairs of obstacles, three pairs on each side of the field, thus making a two-lane course. The obstacles were placed about 15 feet apart except at the corners, where there were stakes instead of obstacles. From the starting line, which was on slightly higher ground than the rest of the course, the staff could observe the candidates on every obstacle.

In order to heighten motivation two candidates ran the course in competition. Each man's score was based upon his total time and his success in negotiating the obstacles. If a man failed an obstacle he was made to try it a second time. After that, regardless of the outcome, the rules were that he was to go on to the next obstacle. Each man was also rated on motivation, agility, and stamina.

The obstacles of the Running Time Course, in the order in which they were encountered, were as follows:

1) Three low hurdles of increasing height, spaced about 4 feet apart.

2) Three firmly braced high hurdles, all about 5 feet high, which had to be vaulted with the use of hands and legs.

3) Parallel bars about 5 feet long.

4) A cobweb obstacle which was a 10-foot stretch of irregular wire entanglement 18 inches off the ground. To get through the obstacle the candidate had to step high over the wires and find spaces between them through which his feet could reach the ground.

5) An overhead horizontal bar, 12 feet long, 7 feet above the ground at the start and 8 feet above the ground at the end, which was to be traversed by the candidates hand over hand.

6) A double row of twenty open boxes, each a foot square and 6 inches deep. The problem here was to run through the obstacle stepping in every box.

7) Two parallel fences 10 feet long and about 2 and a half feet apart, from which, alternately on the right and on the left, partitions extending two thirds of the way to the other parallel fence were built, thus forcing the candidate to zigzag his way through the area between the fences.

8) A catwalk about 3 inches wide and 3 feet off the ground which made four 145° turns from beginning to end, alternating from left to right.

9) Wire mesh 2 feet wide and 25 feet long stretched 18 inches above the ground and forming a passage through which the candidate had to crawl.

10) A pit only 2 feet deep but 6 feet wide and filled with water to be jumped after the candidate had run up an incline.

11) An 8-foot wall to be scaled. This was difficult because it came toward the end of the course when candidates were tired and was so placed that they had to run up a hill to do it. On the face of the wall were no cleats or grips.

12) A pit, 2 feet deep and 8 feet wide, in crossing which the candidate had the use of a rope suspended from a beam over the center of the pit. The rope, which was just long enough to enable a man to swing safely to the far side of the pit, hung motionless as a candidate approached. The technique for executing this obstacle was to run and jump for the rope, swing on it and then let go the moment one's feet touched the far bank, at the same moment throwing one's body forward so as not to fall back.

To complete the course, candidates ran to the finish line.

The exercise taxed even those who were in the best of condition. One distinct advantage it had over earlier courses used at S was that it required the use of all parts of the body, rather than placing a great premium upon strong arms.

Improvisations.—After supper on the second full day, one of the most revealing of our assessment procedures was conducted. By this time, all candidates had been interviewed. They had been observed both casually and in many planned situations; and their performances on a variety of paper-and-pencil examinations—standard tests, tests of our own making, projective techniques, and special assignments—had been read, scored, analyzed, and interpreted. By now we had a pretty good idea of the kind of men with whom we were dealing. Despite the shortness of our acquaintance, some of us were beginning to feel that we understood the candidates better than we understood some of our old friends. Yet again and again it was our experience that just at this point, a question as to the presence of some suspected tendency would arise, the answer to which was necessary before our conceptions of their personalities could become clarified. We needed some procedure which could be used to prove or disprove these critical hunches. Ultimately we came to what we wanted by adjusting Moreno's psychodrama to the purposes of assessment. The trick was to invent for each candidate appropriate dramatic situations to which he had to respond realistically. These we called Improvisations.

Two sessions of Improvisations were run simultaneously from 6:30 to 9:00. Half of the group met in the living room, the other half in the classroom. The props were simple: a table and two chairs at the front of the room; around the room other chairs for the audience.

The staff member's opening remarks, which described the procedure of Improvisations to the candidates, will serve also to explain it to the reader.

Tonight we are going to have you do something a little different from the other things you have done here. We think you will enjoy it. Most other classes have in the past, as soon as they got the idea of what we were doing.

You are going out to fill a variety of jobs in this war. In most of them it will be very important for you to deal effectively with other people. It will be necessary for you in many cases to size up others quickly and make quick decisions on the basis of your judgments. We have seen you in a number of tests and more or less artificial situations here, but we have never had an opportunity to see you in action in real-life situations, that is to say, in your day-to-day social and business dealings. We have therefore taken the liberty of making up some situations dealing with real life, and we are going to ask you to take part in them. So that you won't be in an entirely strange situation and at a loss for words, we will base these roles on your cover stories and on the postwar plans we collected from you this morning. You will be dealing therefore with things with which you are familiar, about which you at least know the lingo. We are going to ask you to come up here two at a time to sit in these chairs and work out the problems we will give you, to the best of your ability.

Approach the problem in any way you like. If you find that you can settle the situation to your own satisfaction in one minute, you are free to do so. Usually, however, you will talk for about five minutes and then I will warn you that you have about one or two minutes to come to some sort of decision and bring the situation to a close. We are not interested in your ability as an actor. As a matter of fact, acting usually shows up very badly here. What we are interested in is how effective you can be in the role in which you are placed. For instance, if you are given the part of a farmer, we don't want to see a portrayal of the typical hayseed, but just yourself as you would be if you should happen to own a farm. We would like you to approach each situation seriously and try to do your best. I think you will find that there will be plenty of laughs without any clowning on your part and that you will be much more effective if you make a serious effort.

During your stay here you have attempted to break each other's cover. Tonight we are not interested in breaking cover, at least not in that sense. None of you believes these stories anyway by now, but we would like to get some idea of your ability to judge character, to break through and tell what kind of men you are actually dealing with here. We are going to ask you, therefore, after each of these short situations is over, to comment upon two things: one, the effectiveness of the individual in his part, not as an actor, but in his actual handling of the situation; and two, how much he was like or unlike himself as you have come to know him in the past few days.

Remember that the most important things are to be as effective as possible in the situation you are given, and to handle it as you actually would in real life. I think further description will only confuse you and that you will understand exactly what we are doing after you have seen the first situation.

The first pair of participants was then called and the outline of the problem to be worked out before the group was explained to them in the hearing of all. One member of the staff conducted the session. Upon him in large measure the success of the improvisations depended. He made the opening remarks, instructed each pair of students in the parts they were to take, kept time on the situations, and handled the discussion. Three or more staff members sat toward the back of the room as observers, taking part in the group discussion and acting as sounding boards for comments from the candidates. As a rule, there were as many situations as there were candidates, each man participating in two. Eight was considered the maximum number of situations which could be handled in one session, however, and if there were more than eight candidates, some of them took part in only one situation.

Because of the unique function which Improvisations came to serve in the assessment process, and because of our belief that it can be one of the most valuable procedures for personality diagnosis, it has seemed worth while to describe its development. Originally it was employed for the purpose of revealing leadership potentialities, with the hope that incidentally other components of personality, especially social skills, would be exhibited as well. The first situations, therefore, were set up with the two roles in each scene clearly defined, one as "superior," the other as "inferior," and with some point of conflict between the two characters. Each staff member prepared a number of scripts, and from them, nine were chosen. Two are given as illustrations.

1) Mr. F. of this organization has been working as an administrative assistant for about two months. He feels he has been doing a good job. His superior, Mr. G., however, is so dissatisfied with the work of his assistant that he decides to call him into his office. The scene to be enacted is the conversation between Mr. F. and Mr. G.

2) E., the leader of a guerrilla band, must order F., one of his men, to undertake what is likely to be a suicide mission. He does not feel that he can go himself because he will be needed to command the rest of his men. F. feels that the proposed mission is not likely to succeed and that he should be saved for something for which he is better qualified. He goes to E. to protest. The scene is this meeting between E. and F.

A mimeographed copy of the nine scripts was given to each candidate, who was asked to mark his preferences of roles. It was thought that this procedure would give some indication of whether a given candidate had a leaning toward leadership or toward dependency. After the men had made their choices, they were paired off and allowed to act out their roles in front of the group. Discussion and comments followed.

It soon became apparent that little could be ascertained in this way about leadership as an isolated trait, but that the procedure was nonetheless rewarding: the men were revealing a good deal about their modes of conducting interpersonal relationships. The test was then developed along much broader lines than had been originally intended.

Experience proved that the original situations were inadequate in many ways. In some of them the conflict centered around a factual argument and there was little room for a clash of personalities; in others there was no opportunity for the free expression of moods and attitudes. For instance, in the second script the pattern of F.'s response is already defined: "He goes to E. to *protest*." Also, in situation 1: "He *feels* that he has been doing a good job." The directions tended to block rather than to facilitate individual modes of reaction. Other scenes gave too much leeway for imaginative rambling or "play-acting"; the conflict was not specific enough.

In order to elucidate these points we will discuss one scene which we came to use repeatedly and which we felt fulfilled our criteria:

A. moved to a small city about three months ago and opened a business there. He has been doing quite well and one month ago sent in an application for membership in a club in the town. He has heard nothing in response to this application and goes to the home of B., a prominent member of the club, with whom he is pleasantly acquainted. (A. is then sent out of the room and B. is told that A. has received several blackballs.) A. is then called back into the room.

Here no mood is set. The neutral tone of "pleasantly acquainted" leaves the participants free to express any variety of emotional response. There is a minimum of factual argument and a maximum of personal interaction, yet there is a definite point at issue. Both men are put on the spot, one with the task of informing the other of his failure, the other of accepting that failure. In addition, this situation and others on which we came to rely had the advantage of a certain amount of specificity. They could be used for free expression, but they were also of value as tests of certain attitudes. This one, for instance, proved effective in revealing in the case of A. his reaction to rejection, and in the case of B. his tact and diplomacy. Success depended on the exact structuring of the situation and careful casting of each candidate so that weaknesses would appear if present.

There were good reasons for abandoning the original practice of having candidates choose their roles, one being that free choice allowed the man to adopt the role in which he would appear in the best light, instead of compelling him to play an unfamiliar or uncongenial part which might expose some specific defect of character. But, since the role selected for a candidate could not be placed entirely outside his sphere of interest and competence without running the risk of checking his motivation, a special role was invented for each man based on his cover story and his postwar plans as written out for us that morning. It was comparatively easy to pair the candidates in appropriate situations. Each situation[2] put each man into a position in which he would have to reveal the faults he was suspected of having, if such faults were present. As time went on, a number of standard situations were developed which satisfied our criteria and which could be used repeatedly, although there were always some candidates who required specially created situations.

When Improvisations was first adopted an attempt was made to use the rating system, but this was soon abandoned as incongruent with the subtle and unpredictable forms of behavior exhibited under these conditions. It was striking, however, that although no formal score could be made, there was usually good agreement among the staff members as to the nature and significance of the observed behavior. This opportunity to observe the elusive and unique qualities of each candidate's behavior without the necessity of rating it turned out to be the most valuable aspect of this technique, which, it was felt, justified the time devoted to it. The procedure brought out personality characteristics which had not appeared or had been barely discerned in other tests. Immediately after the session the staff members would meet for thirty or forty minutes to discuss the behavior of each participant and its meaning for his over-all assessment.

---

[2] These tailor-made situations were created by the staff in sessions which they called Brainstorms and which were held on the afternoon of the day of Improvisations while the candidates were occupied with the group memory tests.

Some of the functions of the staff member who conducted Improvisations have already been mentioned. It was his responsibility to make the idea of Improvisations inviting to at least a few of the group within the first few minutes, and then to overcome the resistance of the others during the course of the performances. He had to present each situation clearly and succinctly so that the participants could understand it exactly as it was designed. On a few occasions gross misinterpretations occurred which were extremely revealing.

The most important as well as the most difficult task was to lead the discussion of each performance in such a way as to gain the optimal emotional response from the spectators without increasing their reluctance to participate themselves. Maintenance of this delicate balance—in which a man is goaded to give himself away as completely as possible while maintaining his prestige within the group—was the crux of Improvisations, the responsibility for which fell very largely upon the administrator of the test.

First, the administrator had to set the proper tone, by his own enthusiasm and air of confidence. He had to be good-humored and yet establish the idea that the Improvisations were a serious part of the testing program. There was some doubt about the amount of humor which should be introduced. A certain amount of levity was clearly helpful in loosening up the audience at the beginning and there always was and should have been considerable laughter during some of the performances. Most of the Improvisations, however, and surely the more important ones, were serious affairs. During the critique some humor was interjected at times to relieve tension or embarrassment, but here again most of the significant comments were made seriously.

The administrator was also required to stimulate each man's interest in the role assigned to him; and here a simple measure which seemed to work well was to change a candidate's story in such a way as to flatter him before the group. For instance, an enlisted man who wanted an army career after the war was made an officer. The audience never knew the man's real status, but he felt temporarily elevated in their eyes. It was often necessary to appeal to a candidate to be himself rather than a "character" and to keep this as an objective constantly before the others. The individual's absorption in his part was considered of paramount importance because it was felt that the more completely this occurred the more likely he was to reveal his characteristic patterns of behavior.

The presiding staff member decided on the duration of each scene. Ordinarily, he allowed a pair of improvisers to talk for four or five minutes and then warned them that they had a minute or two to bring the affair to a close. In the cases of complete failure of a scene, of embarrassing awkwardness, or of loss of interest on the part of the audience, the action was terminated as quickly and as gracefully as possible. When the argument came down to a matter of technical fact, for instance, nothing could be gained by allowing it to continue. When, however, a spirited discussion developed which entertained the spectators, the scene might last as long as fifteen minutes. As a rule it was stopped as soon as the trends of the two improvisers became obvious.

As soon as an improvisation was brought to a close, criticisms were invited by such questions as: "Was Joe like himself in the part?" "How unnatural was he?" "Was he acting?" "Is that how he usually behaves?" "What would you have done in the same fix?" The men who took the parts were asked to comment on their own feelings in their roles: "Were you uncomfortable or at home in the part?" "Did you really behave as you would have under the circumstances given?" A common tendency was to discuss the factual issue involved; and the presiding officer had to be constantly alert to turn attention back to the personalities and behavior of the participants. The comments and the countercomments aroused were often very revealing.

When comments by the candidates were not forthcoming, questions were directed at particular members of the audience. Sometimes it became necessary for the staff members to enter the discussion. Their comments might be expressed in such a way as to split the group into conflicting sides and thus to provoke an argument. At times a deliberately unjust criticism by a staff member was necessary to arouse the candidates to a performer's defense. In the same way two staff members sometimes argued a point in order to draw the spectators into the discussion. It is clear, of course, that such arguments should take place only as "part of the act" with complete mutual understanding on the part of the staff members engaged. Otherwise, the staff will be putting on an improvisation for the benefit of the candidates.

Occasionally anger threatened to wreck the whole undertaking, and it was necessary to re-create an atmosphere of good feeling before going on to the next improvisation. In any event, as soon as the administrator felt that the critique had served its purpose he would begin to work the group into shape for the next round. A few joking remarks about the participants in the last scene were usually enough to effect this transition. Sometimes if a man had shown himself in a bad light, it was necessary to point out that he had been placed in a tough spot, thus excusing his behavior.

It was found that an unbroken two or two and a half hours of improvisations resulted in fatigue, no matter how interesting the scenes, and that there was marked lessening of attention and interest as time passed. To remedy this, Improvisations was scheduled just before the Debate at which, from the very beginning of S, it had been our custom to entertain our guests with hard liquor. Now, instead of waiting until the Debate for our drinks, we had them brought in at a break that was introduced after three or four of the scenes had been enacted. An intermission of five or ten minutes allowed time for everyone, candidate or staff member, to pour himself a drink. During the rest of Improvisations (and indeed through the whole evening) candidates were encouraged, by example and invitation, to help themselves whenever they desired.

The effect of alcohol on Improvisations is difficult to estimate. It sometimes changed the behavior of a candidate. As might be expected, the timid, self-conscious person gained confidence, and since we had learned little from his previous silence, we considered this a gain. As a rule, inhibitions were weakened and criticisms became freer. If the drinking went on too long, the men passed this stage, however, and grew inattentive and uninterested, or noisy and difficult to control. Consequently, the practice of offering alcohol only during the last hour of the session proved most effective. At this point it came as a welcome diversion and helped to revive interest and energy for the second half of the session.

What were the psychological factors at work in Improvisations? To this question we have no scientific answers; no intensive studies were made, no controlled experiments were conducted. But there was general agreement, nevertheless, among the intuitive judgments of the staff.

First, as in all the tests, there was the drive to give a satisfactory performance, if not to excel, to make a favorable impression on the staff, and so to "pass" the examination and be accepted for a position in the OSS. The vast majority of the candidates were volunteers; they wanted jobs. This drive was heightened by the presence of competitors and the presence of an audience. The men wanted to make a favorable impression on their teammates. We might call this the need for recognition, for prestige, for the maintenance, if not the elevation, of self-esteem. In many candidates the complementary negative drive to prevent rejection (by the organization), to prevent ridicule and depreciation (by the audience), to prevent a fall of self-esteem, may have acted more powerfully than the incentive of success, the image of themselves as masters of the situation. Some individuals with an exhibitionistic tendency outdo themselves in public, despite a good deal of internal perturbation; for them spectators are a facilitating stimulant. For others, however, a large or formal audience is a deterrent; their natural tendency is to avoid conspicuous participation. For these, Improvisations was more or less of an ordeal which they could not avoid without abandoning their proximal goal—to be accepted by the OSS. Thus the social pressure in the situation was considerable, enough to force everyone to say something—whatever it might be—and so to generate in many a good deal of tension, anxiety, and embarrassment. Another important factor was the pressure of time; there was no opportunity to reflect, to decide on a course of action, to select the most telling words. A candidate was compelled to give vent to most of the trends and words which were evoked by the situation; there was little time to choose among a variety of possible tactics. Each man was thrown back upon more or less involuntary action patterns, habitual or emotional.

As a rule, candidates were given roles which we felt they could not fulfill successfully. Many of them sensed this; they realized they were on the spot. Also, their difficulties were augmented by the element of surprise which was introduced into most of the scenes. The stable candidate who felt more or less at ease in the situation usually handled it satisfactorily in his accustomed way. The obtuse individual, unaware of his faults, also carried on as usual. But then there was another type, the man who realized that the pattern which was natural to him would convey a bad impression and that he had to substitute some other mode of behavior which we came to distinguish as the made-up-on-the-spur-of-the-moment reaction. Insightful candidates in the audience were often quick to recognize these suddenly invented, unnatural patterns of behavior.

When a candidate had the thought that his first spontaneous idea for action would prove inadequate or reveal too much of his deeper feelings, he might respond in any one of several ways: the most common was immobilization, momentary speechlessness. In some extreme cases there was complete inability to carry on. As a rule, after this initial blocking, the man would continue but diverge from the original script. At times this reaction appeared to be due to the loss of the original instructions amid the turmoil of his emotion. At other times the man seemed to be working deliberately away from the original argument, substituting a plot of his own which was more manageable.

Frequently a candidate would resort to "ham acting" to avoid revealing himself, even though the whole group had been repeatedly warned against this course. "Ham acting" almost invariably drew laughter from the candidates, which relieved tension for the moment. The deep emotional involvement of such an actor would often be displayed in the discussion which followed, when he responded heatedly to criticism of his mode of dealing with the problem. Sometimes a person would display a hostile or resistant attitude to the proceedings when first presented with a role and would refuse to take part on the grounds that the whole affair was pointless. One case which illustrates several of these points is worth citing.

A young man, very able in his field, was suspected of having a very low tolerance for adverse criticism, the suspicion being based largely on reports we had received on him from outside sources. Very little of this came out in the interview or in his general behavior at S. He was put into an improvisation in which he, as an actor, had been severely "panned" by a drama critic. He was deliberately put up against a very cool, smooth-talking fellow.

In this situation the candidate displayed a great deal of genuine anger, stormed at the "critic," and finally pretended to shoot him. When his colleagues criticized this "solution of the problem," he defended himself by saying that of course he put on the shooting simply as a gag.

Later in the evening, he was put into a somewhat similar situation. This time he put on a very "hammy" act, tried to be funny, and, although the two scenes were really unrelated, he managed to worm in an apology for the previous "murder." After this scene, the candidates were reluctant to criticize him. A staff observer, however, asked him flatly why he had put on such an act after being told to behave as naturally as possible. He became very bitter in defending himself, criticized the way his scene had been set up, condemned Improvisations in general, and showed a marked lack of insight into the difficulties of personality which at the moment he was manifesting in his behavior. In this case, as in many others, the improvisation was useful as confirmation of an hypothesis.

Improvisations is a technique by means of which a person is led unwittingly to reveal his typical social attitudes. It is used best as a supplement to other methods, to prove or disprove the presence of specific traits or trends which are suspected on the basis of previous findings.

We have come to feel that the emotional involvement of the improviser both in the situation and in the succeeding critique is the *sine qua non* of a significant expression in Improvisations. Creating this involvement should be the aim of the staff's efforts. We are inclined to feel that under these conditions the individual gives a more accurate impression of his methods of dealing with others than can be obtained in any other way.

After the last improvisation the staff members withdrew to the conference room to discuss the meaning of the behavior they had just seen. The meeting lasted from a half to three quarters of an hour, during which time the candidates were free to do whatever they wished. Most of them remained downstairs, continuing to drink and discussing animatedly their performances in Improvisations. It might have been rewarding to have had members of the staff mingle with the candidates at this time to hear what they had to say about each other. But, on the whole, it seemed wiser to leave them to drink as freely as they wished, in order to lessen any suspicion which may have arisen that liquor was being offered as a test of their discretion and control. Of course, in large measure, it was just this, but we did not wish to underscore the fact. First, by drinking with the candidates we sought to emphasize the social nature of the occasion, then by withdrawing we hoped to make them feel that in no sense were they being subjected to unrelenting scrutiny. After all, we would join them later and have plenty of time in which to note their drinking habits.

It was our hope to make this evening a pleasant time of relaxation for the candidates and if incidentally we discovered that some of them drank to excess, or could not hold their liquor, or talked too much under its influence, this was so much grist for the assessment mill. Of course it was not the amount of liquor that a man drank as such which concerned us, but how he behaved after drinking that amount. The fact that a person drank to excess was not by itself sufficient cause to "ding" him, nor, on the other hand, could we ever be sure that a man who drank nothing was not an alcoholic. But when a man, knowing full well, of course, that he was being assessed for an assignment overseas, drank to the point where he broke cover seriously, or revealed difficult and unpleasant traits of personality, or became sick, or showed, in any other way, a marked deficiency of control, this was ground, certainly, for questioning his suitability; and such lack of control was exhibited often enough to justify many times over the expense of the never-mentioned, never-named liquor test.

Debate.—When, upon completion of their conference, the staff members returned to the living room, it was to attend a group situation in which all candidates would participate. This was the Debate, though actually it was not so much a debate as it was an informal panel discussion. The topic chosen for discussion was a timely one. In the early days of 1944 it was "What are we fighting for?" and the candidates were arbitrarily divided into two groups which were sent to separate rooms to prepare their arguments before being called back to the living room for the debate. Later the procedure was changed so as to ensure more opposition between the sides, by having the candidates set down their opinions on an attitude scale and then dividing them into two groups on this basis. For example, with such a topic as "What shall we do with Germany after the war?" each man was asked to place himself on a scale of opinion running from (1)—"A lenient peace with restoration of Germany to the family of nations as rapidly as possible"—to (10)—"The destruction of the German state as we now know it." Thus one team was composed of those who favored more lenient measures and the other of those who advocated harshness. Other topics for discussion included, among others, "What shall we do with Japan after the war?" "Can we trust Russia in the postwar world?"

A member of the staff acted as chairman for the Debate. After announcing the topic and the composition of the opposing teams he directed them to retire to separate rooms where they would have twenty minutes for a discussion and formulation of their views and policies. He suggested that each team select a chairman to organize the discussion as well as the presentation of its position, but he also stressed the fact that although agreement was desirable, minority opinion should not be disregarded.

When the men separated, it was customary for a few staff members to join each group and sit to one side observing events as inconspicuously as possible. Usually the candidates would start by airing their individual views without deciding on a plan of procedure, but before very long the need for organization would become apparent and often at this point a chairman would be selected. Sometimes he was self-appointed; sometimes he was appointed by a dominant and assertive member of the team; sometimes he was elected. Other groups, however, merely chose a secretary or a temporary chairman, postponing the election of their real leader until just before the debate. At times this policy was adopted by the men to ensure their having the best leader when they faced the opposition, but in other cases it was a matter of the last-minute ditching of a chairman who had proved to be unfair or ineffectual in conducting the group meeting. Some teams obviously chose the man who had most impressed them with his knowledge, but others with less foresight chose a man who had been a leader in some earlier situation or simply an older man whose appearance and manner commanded respect. Once the group became organized, each man would have an opportunity to express his views and to suggest strategy for meeting the opposition.

These meetings of the teams in preparation for the Debate were often most revealing. Though the staff members made it a rule never to make written notes during the evening lest they inhibit the candidates in the free expression of their opinions, they were constantly alert to all forms of behavior which might serve as a basis for the ratings which they would make either before going to bed that evening or early the next morning. The traits to be rated when possible were Energy and Initiative, Effective Intelligence, Social Relations, and Leadership. It was hardly possible to rate all these variables in all candidates because of the large number of men involved, and the length of time that inevitably elapsed between the making of the observations and the recording of the ratings.

When, after twenty minutes, the two teams were called together in the living room, they were seldom as well prepared as they had hoped to be, but the intellectual resourcefulness of the candidates could be better estimated, so it seemed to us, when they were forced to organize and express their thoughts under the pressure of time.

In opening the Debate, the staff member acting as presiding officer made it clear that the affair was to be informal, that the men could dispense with the customary "Mr. Chairman" or "my honorable opponent," and finally, that there was a rule that glasses be kept filled. Everyone, he said, was to feel free to fill his glass at any time; formality was out for the evening. At this point the staff members interrupted the speaker by walking up and filling their glasses, an example followed by a majority of the candidates.

Depending on the amount of responsibility spontaneously assumed by a chairman, the presiding officer either kept in the background or took over his functions by calling on the members of his team, keeping time, and encouraging participation by everyone. His aim was to create and maintain a free and easy atmosphere, to entice· the reluctant candidates to speak, and to partition the time fairly among those who requested it.

In order not to influence the expression of opinions, neither the moderator nor the other staff members took any part in the argument. The usual procedure was to start by having each chairman address the entire assembly, presenting the major points agreed upon by his team, offering a few salient arguments himself, and then calling upon his colleagues one by one to speak briefly on the special aspects of the subject about which they presumably knew most or about which they felt most strongly. It sometimes happened, though, that a chairman, either at the request of his group or on his own initiative, spoke for the entire time allotted to his side. In any event, after both groups had presented their views, they were allowed a few minutes in which to prepare rebuttals and then about five minutes in which to present them to the assembly. When the rebuttals were finished, it was customary for the moderator to suggest that the men elect one of their own number to preside over the general discussion that would follow and to stress the fact that they were free to pursue the topic in any manner they saw fit; moreover, anyone who was tired or uninterested could go to bed (by now it was likely to be well after eleven o'clock).

Though the Debate was in some ways similar to the round table Discussion of five or six participants, in other ways it was quite different. In both cases there was a timely topic to be discussed and in both the same variables of personality were rated. However, the larger audience, the division of the group into two teams, the use of debating techniques with the speaker standing before the whole group, and, perhaps most of all, the liquor, made the Debate qualitatively quite different from Discussion. The Debate presented a better opportunity than did Discussion for a display of eloquence in formal speeches, for objective or emotional argument in rebuttal and counterrebuttal, as well as for organization and leadership on a larger scale. In addition, by the end of the second full day, when the Debate took place, the candidates were better acquainted with each other and better adjusted to their environment than they had been at the time of the Discussion. This resulted in greater freedom of social interaction. Because of these many differences between the Discussion and the Debate, the value of the latter was not confined to what it supplied in the way of confirmatory evidence of previous conclusions. Very often the Debate revealed new aspects of a candidate's personality which led to a rounding out or to a modification of the conception held at that time.

The quality of the candidates' contributions to the Debate varied greatly, depending on their knowledge, intelligence, and facility of expression. The speeches of many were merely repetitions of glittering generalities and hackneyed phrases, delivered in a stumbling awkward fashion; other men presented forceful and fervent appeals; still others contributed competent, well-organized, and informative discussions of the complex problems at issue. The Debate provided an excellent opportunity for candidates to display whatever special knowledge or propaganda talent they possessed. It also served to evoke assertions of emotional and ideological sentiments and attitudes such as vengefulness, a passion for justice, for democracy, abhorrence of aggression, humanitarian sentiments, and so forth. Confirmed political attitudes were often revealed, especially by foreign-born candidates who had programs of reform for their own countries. Information of this sort was often valuable in deciding a candidate's fitness or unfitness for a particular job. Expressions of feelings of national superiority or racial intolerance, for example, were indications that a man was not well suited for a job that required sympathetic understanding and tactful handling of native peoples.

As in other procedures, there were always some candidates who did not actively participate. A few in each class never spoke unless called upon and then only briefly; they were usually the ones who became bored as the evening wore on and were among the first to go to bed. Nondrinkers were also apt to retire early, especially if it happened to be one of those occasions which developed into a real party. Some candidates sat back quietly and drank, giving no more than half an ear to the arguments; others, getting drunk, boisterously interrupted the speakers with more or less humorous comments; others went further and tried to transform the meeting into an out-and-out drinking party. Unruly behavior, however, was exceptional.

Candidates who became intoxicated revealed things that would never have been so apparent had they remained sober. Some made serious breaches of cover; others exposed deep prejudices or extreme political leanings which they had more or less successfully concealed up to that time. One man who in earlier tests had given hints of rather bizarre fantasies exhibited a well-developed persecution complex in a speech loaded with warnings against a preposterous trap that was about to be laid in the government. Another spoke in tones frankly sympathetic with the Nazis when earlier he had claimed that he was a German refugee and an anti-Nazi. Another candidate who had maintained a resolute calm and detachment for two days showed how inveterate was this mechanism of defense by making every effort for an hour or more to appear sober and poised, when actually, having drunk to excess, he was on the verge of becoming violently ill. One middle-aged man, who had boasted of his drinking prowess to a staff member, drank a quart of brandy in about fifteen minutes and promptly passed out cold.

After the Debate was over most of the candidates and some of the staff members were apt to remain downstairs drinking and talking, often into the early morning hours and, as one might expect, significant trends of behavior occurred at this time. Sometimes a long and serious discussion of world affairs developed; more often it was an occasion for reminiscing (with or without breaking cover) and storytelling; sometimes the meeting turned into a song fest, or broke up into little groups filling the air with barbershop harmony.

For the candidates this was a long-to-be-remembered evening of pleasant relaxation, especially welcome to those who had been in service for a long time, and appreciated the more by all, coming, as it did, immediately after the exhausting obstacle course, at the end of two days of unrelenting effort. It provided a better opportunity than they had yet had to get to know their fellow candidates and members of the staff. Much that they learned this evening would influence their ratings and their personality sketches of each other which they would be asked to give the next morning.

THIRD DAY

Sociometric Questionnaire and Judgment of Others.—By the morning of the third day of assessment the candidates had become pretty well acquainted. They had been engaged in numerous undertakings with the members of their own subgroup. They had come to know the others, too, through living in close quarters with them. In Improvisations they had had a rare opportunity to watch at least half of their class perform under pressure, and in the relaxed and convivial atmosphere of the Debate they had heard every man speak at least once and had observed some in a new light. This, then, was the appropriate moment to get from each man his opinions of the other members of his class. From 8:30 until noon they were kept busy writing their judgments or, let us say, assessments, of each other. The procedures used for this purpose were answering a sociometric questionnaire about their associates and writing personality sketches of those whom they had come to know best.

The results of these techniques can be immensely valuable or completely worthless, depending upon the degree to which the subjects can be induced to take the assignment seriously and to execute it with complete honesty and candor. In preparation for it, candidates had been told upon their arrival at S that before leaving the area their ability to size up others would be tested. But advance notice was not enough; it was important that the instructions for the Sociometric Questionnaire and the Judgment of Others be given to the candidates so as to make them feel that in writing fully and honestly they were serving the best interests of themselves, their associates, and the OSS.

The instructions for both tests, given by the director of S, were as follows:

Since arriving the other day you have been asked to do many things. This morning we have something else for you to do, something which some of you may find difficult, but something which we on the staff consider very important. When you arrived you were asked to get to know one another and told that before you left your ability to judge each other would be tested. Now the time has come, and this morning we would like to ask you to come on the staff as psychologists and give us the benefit of the insights into your associates which you have gained during your stay here. There are two reasons why we will ask you to indicate to us what you think about your fellow men in this class. First, we know that you can help us. You have been living with each other in a more intimate manner than any of us on the staff have been able to live with you and it would be strange indeed if you have not seen aspects of one another which we have missed. We know from the aid which past classes have given us that you can help us very much in our attempt to understand you. The second reason why we ask you to write about each other this morning is, frankly, to test your ability to size up other people. We have given you a number of tests and observed you in many situations and we have a pretty good idea of the kind of people you are. Now we want to discover what is the correspondence, or lack of correspondence, between the judgments which we have formed of you and the opinions which you have formed of each other. We give you this test because we believe that the success of whatever mission or job you will carry out in this organization will depend in large measure upon your ability to judge others accurately.

Now the assignment this morning consists of two parts. First, I shall give each of you a sheet of paper with a number of questions typed on it and attached to that sheet, a slip of paper with the names of the members of the class with a number assigned to each man's name. We would like you to answer the questions by writing after them the numbers corresponding to the names of the men who, in your opinion, have the traits or characteristics indicated in the various questions. For example, one question reads: "Whom would you recommend as supervisor of a group dealing with problems of planning and organization?" After that question write down the numbers which correspond to the names of the men who, in your opinion would be good at supervising groups dealing with problems of planning and organization. Write down the numbers of as few or as many men as in your opinion would be good supervisors. Another question reads: "If you were a member of a group on a dangerous mission, whom would you prefer to have as your leader?" After this question write down the numbers assigned to the men whom you would like to have lead you on a dangerous mission. Again put down the numbers of as few or as many men who in your opinion would be good leaders of a dangerous mission. And so on with the other questions—eleven in all. There is no time limit to this first part of the assignment. It will probably take you one half to three quarters of an hour to finish. When you do so, will you please take your answer sheet upstairs and place it, face down, in the basket on the table outside the staff room.

Now for the second part of the assignment, I shall give each of you five blank sheets of paper and ask you to write on the sheets personality or character sketches of those five men in the class whom you have come to know best. Write one description on each sheet—five descriptions in all. At the top of the page write your own name and then under that the name of the man you are about to describe. We would like you first to describe his traits of personality, of character, of mood and temperament, his special skills, his unique abilities, his traits which you feel would be pleasant and agreeable as well as those which would be irritating and disturbing. It is important to give the full and complete description of the man. You may hesitate to write down those things which would seem critical or unfavorable, and your hesitation to write them is certainly understandable; but I would like to point out that it does no service to the man or to the organization if we blind ourselves to what may seem to be a man's negative traits or the less favorable aspects of his nature. If such traits are recognized there is without doubt a place for the man where those traits will not interfere with his performance or his relations with others, but if they are not recognized the man may be put in a position where he will fail and where others will be hurt. Then, too, remember that this is a test of your ability to judge others and that you will be scored upon the keenness of your psychological insight in the descriptions which you write this morning. If you see only half of the man, whether it be the good half or the less favorable half, you are not so good a judge as though you see the man in his entirety. It is the full and complete picture we want, and if you are a good judge of your fellow men you will be able to give that full picture. So make your descriptions just as full and just as detailed as you can. Having written the personality or character sketches, please draw a line, either at the foot of the page or on the back of the sheet, and under that line put down those things which you think are reasonable guesses about the man's past experience and background. Having written these, draw another line, and under it please indicate whether or not you saw the man before getting into the truck with him in Washington. If, having seen him, you know his military or civilian status, or his rank if he is in the service, please so indicate.

Finally, if you have known the man about whom you write for a longer period than the time of your acquaintanceship here at S, will you indicate at the top of the page the approximate length of time that you have known him. If you have known a man before coming to S there is no reason why you should not write about him. As a matter of fact, we wish you would write about those you have known for a longer time. Your descriptions in such cases will probably be more detailed, more accurate, and accordingly more valuable for us, but since we are scoring you on these write-ups for your ability to judge others, it would be unfair to score descriptions based upon a longer acquaintanceship on the same basis as descriptions based on short acquaintanceships. So if you have known the man before coming to S, please indicate that fact, stating the approximate length of time of your acquaintanceship—two weeks, six months, a year, or whatever the time may be. The man about whom you will write will probably return the compliment and write about you and indicate similarly that he has known you for a longer period of time than your short stay at S.

Are there any questions about this assignment? If not, I shall give you these papers. You will have until twelve o'clock to finish your writing of the five personality sketches. We give you ample time in which to do this, for we consider this an important assignment. When you have finished the descriptions, will you take them upstairs and leave them, face down, in the basket on the table outside the staff room door.

Now this is the kind of job which, if it is to be done well, must be done with a feeling of psychological free space. Accordingly, I would like you to feel free to move these chairs around any way you wish or even to take these papers into the living room and write there, or up to the bedrooms, or outdoors. And if you feel you know a man well but have forgotten his name, do not hesitate to go up to him and read his name tag or ask him what his name is.

All right, you have, then, until twelve o'clock to finish your writing. Please be back here at that time.

SOCIOMETRIC QUESTIONNAIRE.—For this part of the morning's assignment each candidate was given a copy of the following questionnaire with instructions as indicated.

Instructions. Here are a few questions for you to answer about the members of your group. Think about the men carefully before you answer the questions. Then answer each question by putting down the *numbers* of the men whom you choose. You may mention as many men as you wish in answering each question. *Do not hold back* any honest opinion.

1) With whom would you enjoy continuing your acquaintance?
2) Which men expressed the most realistic and convincing opinions in the debate last night?
3) If you were given the responsibility of picking men who would have to live together and work together on a group project, which men would you hesitate about because of their difficulty in getting along with others *over a long period of time?*
4) Whom would you recommend as supervisor of a group dealing with problems of planning and organization?
5) Whom would you be inclined to avoid socially?
6) Which men were the most inconspicuous; i.e., least noticeable?
7) Which men seemed to get along most easily with the other members of the group?
8) If you were a member of a group on a dangerous mission, whom would you prefer to have as your leader?
9) Which men seemed to antagonize other members of the group?
10) With whom do you feel you could work most harmoniously?
11) What men, if any, *annoyed* you by talking too much or being too dogmatic in their statements?

No limit was placed on the number of choices permitted in response to any of the questions, nor was a candidate compelled to list anyone in response to any question for which he felt he could make no honest choice.

Originally the candidates were requested to rank their choices if more than one choice was made for any question. During the experimental stages the number of choices allowed was sometimes limited, sometimes unlimited. The ranked data were analyzed by various statistical procedures which weighted the choices in accordance with the rank. The same data were then analyzed by assigning equal weight to each choice, no matter what the rank. This last method correlated at least .90 with any other analysis of the data. It was therefore adopted as regular procedure since it had the advantage of being simple and timesaving.

Questions 1, 7, and 10 indicated the extent to which a man was *accepted* by the other members of his group. There was some relation among the answers to the three questions. Usually more candidates were listed in answer to Question 1 than to Questions 7 or 10. Those who were only mildly accepted were generally listed under Question 1, while the candidates who were accepted more wholeheartedly were listed under one or both of the other questions as well. For each man an acceptance raw score was computed by adding up the total number of times his name was mentioned by the other members of his class in answer to Questions 1, 7, and 10.

In the same way, Questions 3, 9, and 11 indicated the extent to which a man was *rejected* by his classmates; the answers to Questions 4 and 8 were combined to give a *leadership* raw score exactly analogous to the other two.

Until late in the program, when Propaganda Skills was changed to refer specifically to written propaganda ability, Question 2 was considered by the staff before assigning the final score on this variable. Question 11 revealed which of the outstanding participants in the debate of the previous evening had antagonized their classmates by their forwardness. It sometimes occurred that a man who dominated the debate in a self-assertive manner was not listed in response to this question, although he had seemed presumptuous and overbearing to the staff. Without the questionnaire it would have been difficult to realize his actual success and his true (or potential) ability as a leader.

The statistical treatment of Questions 2, 6, and 11 consisted merely of ranking the members of a given class according to the frequency with which they were mentioned in response to each question. Only the extreme ranks were regarded as significant. The scores on leadership, acceptance, and rejection, however, were thought to be somewhat more important and so were converted to fit the standard six-point scale.

There was a great deal of variation in the different classes which were assessed at S, not only in size but also in composition. It was desired, however, that the sociometric scores be as nearly as possible independent of these variations so that they would be comparable from class to class, as well as within a given class. To this end statistical tables were drawn up which corrected not only for differences in size of class but also for differences in the general readiness of the members of a class to accept each other, reject each other, or choose each other for positions of leadership.[3]

In addition to this standardized information, the Sociometric Questionnaire yielded other data of a more qualitative sort. It was easy to determine not only how frequently an individual was accepted by his classmates, but also to what extent he accepted others. For each class charts were prepared showing whom each person accepted and by whom he, in turn, was accepted, whom he rejected and by whom he was rejected, which men he picked as leaders and which men picked him. Some individuals seemed to be more acceptable to the men in their subgroup, who presumably knew them best; whereas others were more acceptable to the men who knew them least.

Diagrams were also drawn showing the relative standing of the members of the class on acceptance, rejection, and leadership. An indication of the cohesiveness of the group could be obtained, first, by noting the average

---

[3] Briefly, the statistical theory and method employed was this: All the members of a class could be arranged on a linear scale according to the degree to which they were, for example, *accepted* by their classmates. The reference point was taken as the average number of acceptances received by the members of that class. The measure of a man's deviation from the average (i.e., the measure of the degree of his acceptance) was taken as the probability of his obtaining "by chance" (i.e., by random sampling) a number of acceptances as large as the number which he actually received. The smaller this probability, the greater the deviation was from the average and hence the higher the acceptance (if above average) or the lower (if below average).

The chance probability of obtaining a given number of acceptances was determined from tables of the binomial distribution. In any specific group the probability of a given number of acceptances depended both on the number of individuals in the group and on the average number of acceptances which the group gave. If these acceptances were given strictly at random, that is, if there were no correlation between the fact of a man's being accepted by individual A and his being accepted or not accepted by B, C, and D, then the actual distribution of acceptances would follow the theoretical binomial distribution. However, because of the frequency with which a man who was accepted by one person was also accepted by others, there was a great excess of individuals with very high or very low acceptance scores. In converting to our six-point scale it was necessary to make some assumption about the extent of this correlation between acceptances in order to determine the proper standard rating for each probability level on the binomial distribution.

The first working assumption was that a standard rating of 5 would correspond to a number of acceptances so *great* that it would be obtained only once in 10,000 times by random sampling, and a standard rating of 4 would correspond to a number so great that it would occur only once in 100 times by random sampling. A standard rating of 0 would correspond to a number of acceptances so *small* that it would be obtained only once in 10,000 times by random sampling, and a standard rating of 1 to a number so small that it would occur only once in 100 times. A rating of 3 would represent a number of acceptances that was above the mean but not sufficiently improbable to justify a 4, and a rating of 2 would represent a number that was below the mean but not low enough for a 1.

The same method of analysis was used to convert the rejection scores and the leadership scores to standard ratings on the six-point scale. Experience with a larger number of classes showed that, while the probability levels we originally set up as equivalent to standard ratings were satisfactory in the case of the rejection scores, they did not allow enough 1's and 4's on acceptance and leadership. For this reason the boundary line between a rating of 3 and a rating of 4 on these two variables was changed to a number of acceptances so great that it would occur twice (instead of once) in 100 times by random sampling; and the same change was made in the boundary line between 1 and 2.

number of choices made by the candidates in response to the acceptance and the rejection questions; and, second, by drawing lines on these two diagrams between those members of the subgroups who accepted each other (mutual acceptances) and those who rejected each other (mutual rejections). A closely knit group showed many of these lines on the acceptance diagram but few on the diagram of rejection. Other types of relationship stood out prominently on these diagrams. An isolate was outstanding when mutual acceptance lines connected all the members of a subgroup except this one. Similarly conspicuous were small "mutual admiration societies" composed of men who accepted each other wholeheartedly, but rejected and were rejected by the remaining members of the class.

Considerable weight was given to the sociometric findings in deciding the final rating on Social Relations, since it was felt that the ultimate test was the man's cathexis (valuation) in the minds of his associates. In some cases, however, the staff overruled the verdict presented by the sociometric scores; in the case of an individual, for example, who revealed defects in character which, it was felt, would be unbearable over a long period but which had been overlooked by his fellows during the three-day assessment period because of compensating qualities. A more common illustration would be that of a man of great sincerity and good will who was too quiet to impress others with his worth in so short a time, and so was both accepted and rejected by very few. For the most part, however, there was a fairly high correlation between the final rating on Social Relations and the sociometric scores (see Table 62, Appendix C).

Judgment of Others.[4]—For this test each candidate was given five sheets of paper, one for each of the personality sketches he would write.

The finished sketches were analyzed with three objects in mind:

1) To determine the psychological insight of the writer. The ability to size up others correctly, to estimate their merits, to sense their thoughts and feelings, seemed to us an important factor in the establishment of good social relations and in the conception and execution of any program of propaganda. Incidentally, the assignment to write five personality sketches proved to be a fairly good test of projection: to attribute one's faults to others is a common tendency.

2) To obtain in detail, as was not possible in the Sociometric Questionnaire, information as to why candidates were accepted or rejected or picked as leaders by their associates. Also a few other facts of significance were often to be culled from these sketches.

3) To determine the extent to which candidates had broken cover among themselves. If several men in writing about the same candidate reported

[4] The instructions for this test were given along with those for the Sociometric. For a detailed account of both instructions, see pages 182-183.

similar correct facts about his past, it was safe to assume that the man in question had been indiscreet. Naturally the obverse did not hold: there was no proof that a man about whose past the candidates wrote nothing had not talked about himself. Perhaps his friends did not wish to give him away. The personality sketches, however, did call attention to several serious breaks in security.

The collection of sketches written about each candidate was submitted to the staff member who had interviewed the candidate, and each sketch was rated on our six-point scale on the goodness of the psychological insight which it revealed. Later the grades received by each candidate for each of the five sketches he wrote were totaled. Final ratings of the candidates' ability to judge others were then assigned in terms of the distribution of these totals. The interviewer also assigned a cover rating for each of his interviewees based on the amount and importance of the information the writers of the sketches had obtained about him.

This method of scoring did not prove satisfactory. The character sketches were, of necessity, very hastily read by the interviewers. They received the write-ups a few hours before staff meeting on the final day. At that time they were engrossed in the all-important task of writing their final reports, and the job of scoring the candidates' sketches could be regarded only as an interruption. As a result, the interviewers' ratings on this test were far from reliable. Furthermore, some interviewers were found to rate these descriptions consistently high, while other interviewers were more severe in their scoring. (Mean scores from different interviewers ranged from 2.0 to 3.1.) This meant that a candidate's rating on Judgment of Others depended not only upon the quality of the sketches he wrote, but also upon which interviewer happened to rate them.

Yet, despite the impressionistic nature of the ratings of these personality sketches, the fact remains that the sketches themselves were often of considerable value in forming our final judgments of candidates. Indeed, not infrequently a candidate succeeded in describing an associate so aptly that we felt we could do no better than to quote his comments in writing up the personality sketch for the branch administrative officer.

During the whole of the third day, most of the staff members were occupied scoring tests, meeting in team conferences to decide on the contents of their reports, writing them, and, finally, from three-thirty until ten in the evening, with an hour's break for supper, meeting in staff conference to discuss each case and arrive at a recommendation as to suitability. With the exception of one final score on the athletic events of that afternoon, the collection of data involved in the assessment of the candidates was completed by noon, when the last of the personality sketches for the Judgment of Others Test had been written.

Since the candidates could not be received in Washington until the next morning, after the reports on them had been delivered, something had to be invented to keep them busy and contented during the afternoon and evening of this last day. For this purpose one final problem was presented to them with the same seriousness as all other tests and projects had been presented. This problem, the Murder Mystery, was described as a test of investigative ability as well as of the ability to make correct inferences. Its execution was pursued energetically, but usually with increasing awareness of the mock nature of the whole endeavor, until ten o'clock in the evening, when the several candidate-teams announced their solutions at the final evening session, over which a member of the staff presided as chairman or "judge."

Murder Mystery.—At noon the candidates were assembled and given copies of the mythical *Fairfield Chronicle*, announcing in some detail the discovery of the dead body of a woman on a road not far from S. They were told that it was up to them to investigate this occurrence and decide whether the presumption of suicide subscribed to by the local district attorney in the newspaper was correct, or, if they found evidence of foul play, to discover who committed the murder. Inasmuch as the candidates were not permitted to leave the area, they were invited to question certain designated members of the junior staff who were supposed to have been to the village recently and picked up a little information. The candidates were cautioned that these staff members had heard a great deal of gossip and it might be difficult to extract the specific items required for the solution of the case. Anyhow, the staff members would have to be approached in the right way and the questions they were asked would have to be properly phrased and based upon correct hypotheses.

In investigating this tragedy the candidates worked in three competing groups of six. The composition of these groups was the same as it had been throughout the program. Thus, the carrying out of this assignment became something of a game in which each team tried to keep from the other two whatever facts it had been able to discover and the promising hypotheses it had reached.

A familiar element of fantasy was discovered by the candidates as soon as their investigations of this crime disclosed that the deceased was intimately associated with a number of fictitious personages with whom they had become acquainted in several previous tests, namely Belongings, Brief Case,[5] and, indirectly, the Terrain Test; and furthermore, that these connections established the possibility of the existence of further criminal activity in the vicinity. Challenged by this tie-up to recall the details of previous tests, and irritated or amused by the suddenly assumed reticence and bucolic naïveté

---

[5] Given for a long period at S, but not during the last months.

of the informants, the investigating teams developed their solutions by methods that varied widely, depending on the ingenuity and perspicacity of the participants.

Three of the junior staff members designated as possible informants possessed certain items of evidence, both direct and hearsay, that gave clues to the solution; in addition they, like all members questioned, frequently encouraged false leads when the candidates asked irrelevant questions. Before the investigation had proceeded an hour, the candidates usually found themselves possessed of a large number of unconnected clues and irrelevant data which produced a distinct sense of frustration, combined with amusement, irritation, discouragement, or increased determination to solve the problem.

Two typical scenes between Sid, a member of the staff, and a group of interrogating candidates are recorded below as illustrative of the frustrating, yet good-humored, situations which developed in the course of the Murder Mystery investigation.

The Demise of Mrs. J. W. Weeks

Scene I

The living room, immediately after lunch

CHORUS: Hey, Sid, can we talk to you a minute?

SID: Certainly, fellows. I've got a stop watch here and can time you.

ABLO: Do you mind sitting down?

SID: Not at all. I'd rather sit than stand. And, of course, I'd rather stand than kneel, and rather . . .

ABLO: We'd like to ask you a few questions.

SID: Oh, of course. You probably have a hangover from that little interview in the dungeon. Sure, fire away, but don't aim at me.

ABLO: We represent the *Fairfield Chronicle.*

SID: How do you do? I represent fair play, and furthermore if I am elected . . .

BILL: Keep quiet. Ablo wants to ask you a few questions.

SID: Sorry, old boy. I thought he was introducing himself, and for the sake of politeness I wanted him to know . . .

CARL: Can't you keep quiet?

SID: I certainly can. Why, back where I come from I was known as Silent Sid, the Slobbering Stool Pigeon.

ABLO: I'd like to ask you just a few questions. Do you know Weeks?

SID: Do I know Weeks? Excuse me. You wanted to ask me the question. You bet I do. Fifty-two of them and each one has seven days.

ABLO: No, no. J. W. Weeks.

SID: Oh, him. Hmm.

ABLO: (EAGERLY) Do you?

SID: (SHAKING HEAD NEGATIVELY) Yes.

ABLO: That's what we wanted to find out.

SID: In that case I guess I can go now.

CARL: Just a minute.

SID: And then I have to come back?

CARL: Sit down. We're not finished with you.

SID: Y—y—y—yes sir.

ABLO: What do you know about Weeks?

SID: I—I—I—

DAVID: (THREATENINGLY) Come on!

SID: Well, if I told you, you wouldn't believe me, and then you'd think I'm lying, and even if I lied you wouldn't believe me.

CARL: How would you like to go down to the dungeon?

SID: Oh no, no! Not that! Please! Anything but that! Take me to the movies, take me out to the ball game, but don't fence me in.
(PAUSE)

ABLO: Let me handle him, fellows. You were going to tell us something you knew about Weeks.

SID: Oh, yes, I almost forgot. I do know something about him.

ABLO: All right, is Weeks married, for instance?

SID: I—I—I—

DAVID: Come on!

SID: Well, I—I—

CARL: What are we wasting time with him for? Let's take him down to the cellar.

SID: Oh no, no! I can't stand that! It's so—so—how do you say—dark down there!

ABLO: If you answer our questions we won't take you down there.

SID: Sure, sure. Anything you want. Just ask me. I'm not the kind of fellow who refuses anything. Why, I remember years ago. . . .

CARL: Shut up.

SID: Yes, sir.

ABLO: Was Weeks married?

SID: Er . . . this is strictly ontrez noose?

ABLO: Of course.

SID: Also between us?

ABLO: Sure.

SID: You won't tell the other fellows?

ABLO: You can trust me.

SID: And you can trust me.

DAVID: Well?

SID: Oh yes. I almost forgot. Weeks. Hmm. I don't know.

CARL: What?

SID: N—n—n—now, please. Leave us not get excited.

BILL: We're wasting time with him. He doesn't know anything.

ABLO: Wait a minute. I've got another question to ask him.

SID: May I go now?

DAVID: Didn't you hear Ablo say he has another question to ask you?

SID: Yes, but sometimes my memory is bad. Take that memory test I gave you yesterday afternoon as an example. I don't even remember the name of Darius Horn.

ABLO: Just take it easy, Sid. Tell me, were you in town today?

SID: Wh—wh—why d—d—do you ask?

DAVID: Answer him!

BILL: Uncross your legs!

ABLO: If you answer me you won't be hurt.

SID: Oh, I'll answer you. What do you want to know?

ABLO: Were you in town today?

SID: (SHAKING HEAD NEGATIVELY) Yes.

ABLO: What did you see?

SID: A horse.

BILL: No, no. Anything interesting?

SID: Yes, I did.

CARL: Oh, oh. I'm afraid of what's coming.

DAVID: What was it?

SID: The horse was hoarse . . . Do you want me to go to the third floor and report to a staff member?

CARL: You stay right here. We're not through with you yet.

SID: No, sir.

ABLO: While you were in town, did you hear anything about a . . . murder?

SID: A m-u-r-d-e-r?

ABLO: Just take it easy, Sid. We're not accusing you of anything.

SID: Y—you must excuse my emotion. M-u-r-d-e-r. Sometimes it comes as a shock.

ABLO: Yes, we know.

CARL: How would you like to be murdered?

SID: No, no! Not that. You can be killed that way.

ABLO: Now think, Sid. Did you hear anything?

SID: Well, now that you mention it, I believe I did.

CHORUS: What did you hear?

SID: Draw up chairs, fellows, and I'll tell you a story that's positively guaranteed to grow hair on a billiard ball. Well, I usually go into town for black and white ice-cream sodas which they make very well there except for the fact that sometimes they make them a leetle bit too sweet. When I got my soda today I discovered that . . .

CHORUS: Yes, yes.

SID: It was a leetle bit too sweet.

SOUND: (GROANS)

SID: Well, there I was sipping the soda through two straws (SOUND OF SIPPING) when suddenly . . .

CHORUS: Yes, yes.

SID: The door opened and they walked in. Now at that time . . .

ABLO: Who is "they"?

SID: Oh, you wouldn't know them. So at first I . . .

BILL: Who were they?

SID: All right, if you insist. Both of them were prunes.

ABLO: What do you mean, "prunes"?

SID: They were old and wrinkled.

DAVID: How were they dressed?

SID: Both wore long black dresses down at and to the heels. The dresses were tight around the waist and had collars around the neck. Each had a watch pinned on the left side . . . right above the . . . er . . . ventricle.

ABLO: Do you mind telling us what you heard?

SID: A favor? Any time. Unfortunately, though, we've got to stop here because another test is coming up. You'll like this one.

CHORUS: What is it this time?

SID: First we're going to have some field events and then a softball game. Okay, fellows, everybody out.

SOUND: (RUNNING FOOTSTEPS)

Scene II

The living room, immediately after dinner

SID: Hello, fel—say, what's happened? There's a group in this corner, one over there, and another there. Aren't you fellows talking to each other any more?

ABLO: We have to work that way.

SID: That's too bad. I suppose the other two groups are too difficult to get along with . . . Well, if you fellows will excuse me, I think I'll take a walk to town.

BILL: If you don't mind, we'd like to continue that discussion.

SID: You mean about what to do with Germany after the war?

BILL: No. About that murder.

SID: Oh, that. Wasn't that terrible? Why should anyone want to be murdered?

CARL: That's what we want to find out.

SID: Let's ask the fellows in the group over there if they know anything about it.

BILL: Just a minute. We're going to ask you.

SID: Why, certainly. (RAISING VOICE) You can ask me anything you wish about the murder. Go ahead. Ask. This is ridiculous. Murder!

ABLO: Can't you keep your voice down?

SID: (SHOUTING) Down? And why should I keep my voice down? I was once a coloratura.

XENO: (FROM THE OTHER SIDE OF THE ROOM) Hey, Sid. Can you come over here? We'd like to ask you something.

SID: Sure. I'll be right over.

CARL: Oh, no, you won't. We got you first.

SID: But . . .

ABLO: Here, sit down. Don't worry about the other fellows.

SID: But I can't help feeling sorry for them. They look so lonesome. Only six of them together.

ABLO: Remember what we were talking about this afternoon?

SID: Let's call the other fellows over here, and then we can all be together. One big, happy family. (CALLING) Hey, fellows, come on over.

CARL: Stay over there, you guys. We got him first.

JOHN: You had him this afternoon, didn't you? We want a chance too.

SID: Who are they talking about? You, Carl?

CARL: No, you!

SID: Me?

CARL: Yes, you.

SID: B—b—b—but I don't know anything about murder. I've never practiced it. Why should they want me?

ABLO: If you keep your voice down and answer our questions we won't let them get you. They're a pretty tough bunch.

SID: (CALLING) H-e-l-p! Doctor MacKinnon!!

BILL: Keep quiet. What are you calling him for?

SID: Protection. He's the leader of the mob at S.

ABLO: Fellows, I think we'll have to take him downstairs. Maybe he'll answer our questions down there.

CARL: We should have done that before.

SID: Why?

CARL: You'll find out soon enough. Come on, fellers.

ABLO: Let's give him another chance . . . Now, look, Sid. All we want you to do is think.

SID: Trying to make it tough for me, eh?

ABLO: This afternoon you started to tell us about something you heard in town today. We'd like to hear the rest of that story.

SID: That's easy. But . . .

ABLO: But, what?

SID: I think it would be better if you asked me questions. I'm not sure I know what you want to know.

BILL: Did you ever hear of a man by the name of Kirsch?

SID: Who?

BILL: Kirsch.

SID: Isn't that what you said before?

CARL: Answer the question.

SID: You mean Irsch, Hirsch, Smirsch, Birsch, Kirsch?

ABLO: Who?

SID: Irsch, Hirsch, Smirsch, Birsch, Kirsch.

ABLO: Who are they?

SID: All those people are one person.

BILL: Then why do you call him Stirsch, Firsch, Nursch . . . whatever it is?

SID: That's the way it sounded to me when I first heard them speaking. One of those names was mentioned. Which one, I don't know, so I give you all of them secure in the knowledge that one must be correct. It's much better than feeling insecure. I should like to develop this point . . .

ABLO: You said you heard "them" speaking. Who are they?

SID: Why, the prunes, of course.

ABLO: What did they say?

SID: Do you want to know exactly or approximately?

ABLO: Approximately will do.

SID: I can tell you exactly. Why do you want to know approximately?

ABLO: Okay. Exactly.

SID: Fine. Do you mind if I cross my legs. Well, there I was sipping my black and white ice-cream soda (SOUND OF SIPPING) when my left antenna picked up something. At this point I'd like you to know that I am not, definitely not, an eavesdripper. Can I help it if the reception was very good that day and I could hear every drip of conversation?

BILL: Stop dripping and go on with the story.

SID: Certainly. Well, one of the old prunes said to the other old prune: "Did you hear about the foreign-looking man who just bought a farm in Fairfield?" And the other old prune said to the other old prune: "No. I didn't hear about the foreign-looking man who just bought a farm in Fairfield. Tell me about the foreign-looking man who just bought a farm in Fairfield."

ABLO: Why did you stop? Is that·all there was to the conversation?

SID: Gracious, no! I had to refuel. Just came up for some air.

BILL: What did the other prune say?

SID: Oh, yes . . . And the other prune said: "That's it. A foreign-looking man just bought a farm in Fairfield."

ABLO: Wasn't anything else said?

SID: De seguro que si. English translation—"of course."

CARL: Well, go ahead. What are you waiting for?

SID: Bill's eyes just flashed red. I thought I'd wait until the light changed.

BILL: You'd better start talking.

SID: Right. And then prune number 2 said to prune number 1: "Do you know his name?" And 1 said to 2: "Yes. His name is . . ." And just at that crucial moment there was some disturbance in the ether which made the reception bad, and I couldn't make out the answer. It sounded like Irsch, or Hirsch, or Smirsch, or Birsch, or Kirsch. So, in the interests of accuracy, I say IrschHirsch-SmirschBirschKirsch, knowing that one of them must be correct. (DRAMATICALLY) And then . . . suddenly the door opened, and one of the prunes dropped her voice. Quickly, I stooped, picked it up, and handed it back to her, and I heard her say: "Sh . . . Here he comes now." Quick like a bunny I turned around . . . like that. Wasn't that fast?

ABLO: Pretty fast.

SID: I was faster then . . . I turned around and there he was.

CARL: Who?

SID: IrschHirschSmirschBirschKirsch.

ABLO: What did he look like?

SID: Exactly or approximately?

ABLO: Exactly.

SID: I don't remember.

ABLO: All right. Approximately.

SID: That I can tell you. That I can tell you. He had close-cropped hair
           . . . a long cigar on his right cheek . . .

CARL: You mean scar.

SID: That's what I said . . . cigar.

BILL: How tall was he?

SID: Exactly or approximately?

ABLO: Approximately.

SID: I can tell you exactly. Why do you want to know approximately?

BILL: All right, exactly.

SID: Well, he was about (INDICATING SIX FEET WITH HAND) . . . five feet tall.

ABLO: Did he have an accent?

SID: I don't know. He didn't look as if he had been hurt.

ABLO: Accent. Not accident.

SID: Oh, yes. Come to think of it, he did.

BILL: What kind?

SID: Foreign.

BILL: What kind of foreign accent would you say it was?

SID: Well, not Polish. No . . . not Polish. Not Russian. No . . . not Russian.

ABLO: Would you say German?

SID: Yes, I would. That's it! German! Say, I'll bet you were there and
           heard the same conversation. Did you have a black and white
           ice-cream soda, too?

ABLO: I think we ought to turn him over to the other groups. We'll get him
           again later. Okay, Sid. You can go now, but we'll want to see
           you again later.

SID: Thanks, fellows. It was nice of you to let me listen to you. We ought
           to get together more often. See you later.

In this crazy, frustrating, yet good-natured vein, the investigation of the
Murder Mystery continued through the day. Most of the candidates entered
into the spirit of the task with obvious good will. There were those, however, who, overly serious or short of temper, could not tolerate the continued frustration to which they were subjected in trying to gather clues
for the solution of the mystery. They reacted with ill will, and in rare instances resorted to definitely sadistic treatment of junior staff members.
These reactions, reported to the staff members during their deliberations,
were frequently useful in rounding out the picture of a candidate or in
confirming a hunch which up to this point had not been substantiated by a
definite clinical observation. The skill and patience with which candidates
queried staff members were also noted. On more than one occasion a man

recruited from some investigative agency to do intelligence work for the organization showed himself to be dull and inept at this kind of work. So the Murder Mystery, designed in the first instance to maintain the morale and good spirits of the candidates during their last day at S, contributed not infrequently to a better understanding of them and often shed light in interesting ways upon their fitness for their projected assignments.

Athletic Events.—At two o'clock of this afternoon the candidates gathered at the athletic field where there was to be another test of the physical ability of the men under forty who had run in the Obstacle Course. Three events were scheduled: broad jump, high jump, and shot-put. The intention was to conduct the affair in the spirit of a game rather than as a serious test. Each man had two tries at each event, and after his scores in all three had been converted into a rating on our standard scale, the average rating was recorded on the board in the staff room in time for the final conference at 3:30.

Baseball Game.—Early in their stay at S, many candidates, eying the athletic equipment and the open fields, asked eagerly if they would have time for a baseball game before they left. Our answer was usually a good-humored, "Sure, if you think you can get up a team good enough to take on the staff." By the afternoon of the third day of assessment this provocative idea had taken firm root in the minds of several of the candidates, partly because by this time the staff had got the candidates to agree that two cases of beer would be the prize for the winning team and partly because the desire of the candidates to meet the staff on equal grounds had grown as they were being put through the paces of assessment.

And so, after the Athletic Events, the members of the staff who were not serving on staff teams met the students on the playing field. Usually the ten best candidate players made up one team, familiarly known as the "Nylons," and the other team, called the "Ladies' Ready-to-Wear," was made up of the remaining candidates who cared to play (some preferred to umpire or watch or keep score) plus the staff members. With much fanfare, the game got under way with scoreboards and cheering sections ready, and the beer on ice.

As the game progressed, the staff members took every opportunity to show the candidates that the competition was meant to be more frivolous than serious. From time to time, they threatened the candidates with bigger and tougher tests if they played too well. They alternately boasted about how well they could play and complained about their inability to catch pop flies because of too much paper work. They argued about every decision of the candidate umpire against them, but almost always gave in as soon as the candidates joined the dispute. They played their best most of the time (and

it was often necessary in order to make any showing against the candidates),
but they took every opportunity, traditional to baseball, to make it an afternoon of good-natured cheering, fighting, baiting, and clowning.

Some of the candidates caught the spirit of the staff's behavior right away
and joined in the fun immediately. Others took things pretty earnestly for
a while and caught on only slowly. Still others, a small minority, took the
game in dead seriousness, in some cases, perhaps, because that was the only
way they could play ball, in others because they really wanted to beat the
staff. At any rate, the softball game provided the candidates with one more
opportunity to get their minor emotional loads off their chests and give
something of the medicine they had taken. Most of them took great delight
in booing and kidding, every time he dropped a foul tip, the man who had
interviewed them in the basement on the first night. Whenever the men who
had been the "helpers" at Construction came up to bat, they were greeted
by hoots and catcalls and offers from the candidates to "help" them get a
hit, and it was a great day when one of them struck out.

For most of the candidates this was good fun, whether they were playing
to beat the staff, giving back what they had taken for three days, or just relaxing as they watched the game. And then there was the beer, for the win-
ners and the losers.

Interrogation.—In winter or inclement weather an indoor session was
substituted for the baseball game. This meeting was known as Interrogation
and consisted of having each man in turn take his place before the group,
tell his cover story in a minute and a half, and then allow himself to be
subjected to as intense a grilling on the details of his masquerade as his associates could give him. Their aim was to break his story and to demonstrate that he was not the person he claimed to be.

This session was presided over by a member of the staff, and those staff
members not serving on a team made it a policy to sit in on Interrogation
to observe and report to the staff in conference anything of special interest
in the performances of candidates either as defendants or as interrogators.
No ratings were made in this situation, but there was ample opportunity
to observe a man's resourcefulness and poise as he answered questions.
Similiarly the fund of knowledge possessed by a candidate and his skill in
using it in interrogating his associates revealed the extent of his resources
and his ability to bring them to bear upon a novel situation.

With a quick and resourceful group, Interrogation was a lively, extremely
interesting, and at times most rewarding session. With a dull group, of
course, it lagged. At such times the members of the staff had to enter as
active participants into the interrogation in order to carry it along.

After each candidate had been grilled for five minutes, the presiding staff
member called on his associates for a verdict as to whether he was (1) guilty

and should be summarily shot, (2) a suspicious character and therefore to be held for further questioning, or (3) innocent.

The range of performance in Interrogation varied, as one would expect, from that of the painfully shy and diffident young man who could hardly invent a cover story at all, much less defend it, to the confident and imaginative person who gave an account of himself that was rich in detail and carried him all over the world and in no part of which he could be tripped.

Experimental Tests.—The battery of tests employed in the assessment program at S was frequently changed. Before making any alterations, however, it seemed wise to us to have some indication that a test to be added would be appreciably better than the test it was intended to replace. Since the last evening was, in a measure, a marking of time by the candidates, it was possible to use them for experimental purposes without in any way injuring or detracting from our program of assessing them. Accordingly, all candidates were asked to meet in the classroom at 6:30, where for an hour and a half they were given paper-and-pencil tests which we were planning to introduce into the program. This session kept the candidates busy and yielded valuable information for future developments.

Throughout the rest of the evening candidates were busy in further questioning of staff members about the mystery, in working out their group solutions, and in preparing the report of their findings and their conclusions, which they would present to the whole group at ten o'clock.

The Court.—Though the final session at which the solutions of the Murder Mystery were presented was presided over by a judge (played by one of the more humorous members of the staff), it was almost completely controlled by the candidates.

The performance of the teams in presenting their solutions ranged from the most interminably dull recitation of every detail of the case, at one extreme, to a highly diverting, original, and hilarious exhibition of a denouement as fantastic as the murder itself, at the other. Indeed, it frequently happened that the more entertaining solutions made little or no pretense of adhering to the assumed facts. Groups of candidates sometimes dramatized their presentations with considerable skill, and some or all members of the staff were often asked to participate in the presentation of the solution because one of the mythical principals of the murder case had been only lately a senior staff member, the J. W. Weeks whose belongings had been examined by candidates during their first evening at S, and who had suddenly disappeared from the area. To some groups this fact seemed to involve the whole staff in the crime, if not as coprincipals, then at least as material witnesses.

As it was worked out in practice, the Murder Mystery was not simply a bit of "busywork" designed to occupy the candidates while the staff was busy with its deliberations. It served as an exceedingly effective means of releasing the tensions which had been built up during the three strenuous days of testing. The extent to which this function was performed depended upon the leadership of the teams and upon the general social atmosphere created by the interaction of the personalities of the group members. While it may be presumed that all candidates developed a more or less strong wish to put the staff members through some of their own tests and otherwise to turn the tables on them, such procedures were followed by the candidates only in so far as the more aggressive ones were encouraged or discouraged by the leaders and their fellows. In most cases the mood of the group was light, jovial, and relaxed, although an occasional pompous, pedantic, or disgruntled candidate resisted this influence to the end.

The tension-relieving function of the Murder Mystery was best illustrated by those occasions where highly aggressive candidates gave vent to their energies by mauling and otherwise harassing members of the junior staff in their attempts to extract clues, and by putting members of the senior staff into embarrassing positions in the final session. Here, at last, the junior staff members could be repaid for their behavior as helpers in Construction as well as for the harsh interrogation of the Stress Interview.

THE LAST MORNING

Breakfast on the last morning was a gay meal. Humorous incidents of the court proceedings of the night before were recalled with laughter and there was much kidding among candidates and staff. High lights of their experiences in assessment were conjured up by candidates with the comment that they would never forget their stay at S. The affection which they had come to feel for each other was invariably evident, revealed, for example, in their proposals to meet as a group in Washington that evening or sometime after the war.

The tension that had been apparent heretofore was now entirely dispelled. As far as we could see few candidates were really tense on that last morning. To be sure, many of them wanted to know how they had done on the tests, but this, it seemed to us, was not so much because they were worried about the *outcome* of their assessment as it was because they were eager to know the *significance* to them as persons of our findings. Again and again the interviewers would be approached by candidates seeking information about themselves. When told that we had been forced to adopt the policy of not informing candidates of the conclusions we had reached, they would express genuine disappointment. It was regrettable, they protested, that the insights gained by the staff at S should not be made available to them as aids in deciding questions pertinent to their future. We were inclined to agree with them, but we had a service job to do which made it impossible for us to accede to their desires. Among other reasons was the fact that we had to prepare for the next class arriving that afternoon. It would have been simple enough to tell a very superior man that he had done well in everything, but it would not have been so easy, and indeed might have been dangerous, to transmit to a mediocre candidate our impression of his chief weaknesses and powers. Even had there been time, it is doubtful whether we would have instituted this practice. We were too aware of the fallibility of our assessments to want our subjects to be influenced by them in any way. In a less hurried and more thorough postwar assessment program, yes; but not at S.

It was gratifying to have men who had resented being sent to S, and who on arrival had not hesitated to show resentment, end by saying that they had enjoyed the program and felt that they had profited by it. S was a "school" which was designed to teach nothing, yet again and again candidates reported on their last morning that they had learned more about themselves in three days than they had in their whole lives. Certainly S provided men with the opportunity to compare themselves with others and to realize their own effectiveness in a wide range of situations. It would have been strange indeed if many of them had not left S with greater self-knowledge. Candidates seemed to accept their new evaluation of themselves even when this included the recognition that in certain respects they were less able than they had thought. In any event it was characteristic that most of them departed with that lift in spirit which comes from insights newly gained.

There were, of course, those who from first to last were antagonistic to the proceedings at S, and gained nothing from them; but, fortunately, men of this type, as sullen on departure as on arrival, were not common. At first we rather naturally supposed they might be the rule rather than, as it turned out, the exception. Though they did not contribute to our well-being, we owe them a debt for having kept us constantly alert to the necessity of making the program as realistic and as interesting as possible.

After breakfast on this last morning the members of the group were assembled in the living room and given final instructions for their return to Washington: the Army truck which would come for them at nine would take them directly to headquarters, where they would change into their own clothes and then report at once to their respective branches.

The continued cooperation of every man in keeping the secrets of S was requested. The extent to which the success of assessment depended upon men coming to it without previous knowledge was pointed out, and the need for security emphasized. So far as we were able to judge, our graduates kept our secrets very well; and to those of them who may be reading this we again express our thanks.

The director usually closed his remarks in the following vein:

Finally, speaking for the staff, I want to say how very much we have enjoyed you both individually and as a group. You have been a swell bunch with whom to work and we appreciate more than we can say the splendid cooperation you have given us during your stay at S. We have a job to do here. When we first undertook it we expected that it might be rather unpleasant. We could understand why many who would come here as students might dislike our program and even resent being subjected to it. To our surprise that has not been the attitude of the majority, but rather, like you, they have seemed to enjoy themselves here and to have taken everything which we have had to give in the finest spirit and with the best sportsmanship. If we enjoy our work here and are happy in doing it, it is because you have all made it a pleasant task for us. It has been swell working with you and we cannot thank you enough for your cooperation.

By now you know that S is a great place for fantasy. As a matter of fact, we have so many layers of fantasy laid over us that sometimes even we on the staff get a little confused. There is, however, one fantasy that we all take very seriously, and that is the dream that some day when this dirty business is over we can have an alumni day at S with all the classes returning for the best reunion that was ever held anywhere. In anticipation of that day when we shall all meet again there is one final assignment that I have to give you, and that is the task of thinking up tests with which you will test the staff when you return: and that is one test that you won't fail.

It was not uncommon for the farewell remarks of the director to be responded to by a member of the class. Sometimes this man rose spontaneously to speak for his classmates, but more often he had been previously requested by them to express their appreciation of the treatment they had received. The spokesmen were frequently honest in admitting the skepticism and, in many cases, the resentment which they had felt when first informed that they were being sent to the country to be assessed by a group of psychologists and psychiatrists. That experiencing assessment could turn their skepticism and resentment into wholehearted enthusiasm was for members of the staff one of the most satisfying aspects of their work.

After speechmaking was over, there were the more informal and personal farewells to be said all around. At nine the truck arrived. With last-minute threats of "one more test to be given" and shouts of "Good luck," another class of candidates was driven away from S. It was difficult to believe that this was the same group which had arrived four days before.

Chapter V

ASSESSMENT AT S: FORMULATIONS AND RATINGS

In the last chapters we have described the many gears and wheels, axles and cams, making up the complex machine that was S, as well as the principles governing its complex operations. Now let us see it manufacturing its product, the final assessment formulation. To do this we must view the operation from behind the scenes, having so far observed it from the standpoint of the candidates.

THE WORK OF THE STAFF

The picture of assessment in operation would not be complete if the account of the procedures that filled the time of the candidates was not complemented by a description of the activities of the staff. For the members of the staff were more than mere testers and scorers with functions limited to those implied in the description of the tests. They were, as has already been pointed out, a part of the situation itself, components of the differentiated social world with which each candidate had to deal. Also—and this is the function that concerns us here—their clinical judgments were the chief means of arriving at the final conclusions. It was not only that their observations and evaluations provided the major portion of the data to be considered. The data in each case had to be synthesized into a coherent formulation of the personality which could serve as a basis for specific predictions. To suppose that useful evaluations could be reached by an automatic summation of scores on a number of selected aspects of behavior would have been contrary to our basic assumptions; hence the principal activity of the staff consisted of a series of processes the aim of which was to integrate the findings on all single procedures.

The total task may be analyzed for convenience into three component functions: (1) obtaining data (observation and scoring tests); (2) forming a unified conception of the personality (diagnosis); (3) estimating the probable level of future performances (prognosis). While from the start of each three-day period of assessment most of the work of the staff involved all three functions, with passage of time and accumulation of data, diagnosis and prognosis came increasingly to the fore, to be given final formulation in the staff conference. As the following descriptions of procedures will show, the main part of the diagnostic and prognostic work was carried out by the staff functioning as a group.

In order to formalize to some extent the distribution of these functions, the assessors were divided into senior and junior staff on the basis of age, psychological training, and practical experience. Both the giving and the scoring of standardized tests were left to the junior staff, while interviewing was confined to the senior staff's sphere of activity. Both senior and junior staff members participated in observing, in rating, in organizing the findings, and in making the final evaluations. Because of their knowledge of the interview material, however, the members of the more experienced senior staff were better equipped to arrive at a formulation of each personality, and, consequently, to their lot fell the greater share of the responsibility for the final decisions.

The staff was divided into teams usually composed of two seniors and one junior, each team being assigned one subgroup of five to seven candidates. The seniors between them interviewed all the members of their subgroup and conducted most of the situations; the junior member of each team interpreted the bulk of the projective material, and, when necessary, administered certain special individual tests. Otherwise the functions of all team members were the same: individually and then collectively, their aim was to develop a well-founded conception of each personality in the subgroup assigned to them. The composition of the staff teams was varied from time to time, so that in due course everyone had a chance to function on a team with each of the other members of the staff.

The day-by-day activities of the staff as well as those of the candidates were regulated by a strict schedule. With a multitude of events pressed into the short space of a day, with procedures being added and changed periodically, and with the frequent necessity for special tests to be given to individual candidates, the task of scheduling—done each evening for the next day— was exacting and laborious. It was, however, a prerequisite for the smooth running of the program, and the neat individual schedules contributed not a little to the impression that this was a serious, well-regulated enterprise.

The first phase of the staff work consisted largely in acquiring data by observing the candidates in individual and group situations and making independent ratings of each candidate on all the variables involved. For this purpose the six-point scale, as described in Chapter 2, was used. The frame of reference for these ratings, after the first month or two, was the "ghost population" of S, that is, all candidates who had been assessed to date. And in order to counteract the common tendency to confine ratings to one segment of the scale, the staff was instructed to keep in mind a near-normal distribution curve, the frequency of ratings in each category being ideally as follows: Very Inferior (0)—7 per cent; Inferior (1)—18 per cent; Low

Average (2)—25 per cent; High Average (3)—25 per cent; Superior (4)—18 per cent; Very Superior (5)—7 per cent. By combining the two lower and two upper categories, a four-class scale was obtained with 25 per cent of the population theoretically in each class. This distribution, however, was barely approximated in actual practice.

In rating the situations, it was found that finer discriminations were both natural and feasible, and, consequently, the addition of a plus or of a minus to one of the six numbers on the scale became common practice. Since the ratings 0— and 5+ were, in fact, never used, the staff members were operating most of the time with a sixteen-point scale.

The different steps in the scale for each variable were not defined, as they might have been, by listing the forms of behavior illustrative of each category. Consequently, the staff members were not forced to limit themselves to the observation of behavior which could be immediately translated into ratings of variables, but were free to keep their eyes open for any actions which might be indicative of significant individual traits. This freedom, however, had certain disadvantages: it was responsible for certain confusions and inconsistencies. On the one hand, it was desirable to rate each performance of a candidate in its own right, independent of his performance in other situations, and the assessors consciously attempted to do this. On the other hand, as they followed a candidate from situation to situation, familiarized themselves with the scores he had made on other tests, and observed him in informal contacts, their growing understanding of him necessarily influenced their perception and interpretation of the more subtle behavioral and expressive signs, and to that extent also influenced their ratings. Hence the scores in the situations scheduled late in the program were influenced by the cumulative evidence, rather than solely by the performance in the single test. This was the logical outcome of the attempt to arrive at a maximally comprehensive and meaningful personality picture. The goal required that all data on the candidate be available to those whose job it was to study him and that all facts be examined in relation to each other. Consequently, the ratings were not dependable indicators of effectiveness in specific situations.

The ratings in situations were made by each team member independently, although communication between team members during the course of the test was not forbidden; but as soon as the five or more candidates in one subgroup had completed a situation—say, Construction—the team observers met in conference with the sheets bearing their own ratings, one member bringing with him also a blank sheet on which to record final pooled scores. This man usually would act as chairman of the group. Frequently, though not always, the senior or the most dominant staff member assumed the role. It was important who took it, for the personality of the chairman may well have been a significant determinant of the final combined rating.

Ideally this meeting of the team took place immediately after each situational test, though sometimes the press of scheduled appointments forced a postponement of it until later in the day. The purpose of the meeting was to replace the several sets of ratings given to each candidate by one set of ratings which would be recorded as the final evaluation of the various aspects of his performance in the given situation. This set of ratings was to represent the best judgment of the whole team—ideally each member should be willing to subscribe to it. With this aim in view, the disagreements among raters—which we shall see later were not great—were not dealt with by merely averaging the individual scores but rather were resolved by means of discussion. Sometimes disagreements were due to discrepancies in the perceived actions: with several people to be watched simultaneously, each individual observer was bound to miss some significant details. Such disagreements were easily resolved when the observations were recalled and pooled. Differences in interpretation and evaluation of observed behavior presented more serious obstacles, but rarely such as to require resort to a statistical average to get agreement. While it is true that occasionally the consensus achieved was a mere compromise, determined very frequently by factors in the raters' personalities, it is no less true that in many cases the discussions resulted in an interpretation of the candidate's behavior that was better documented, more detailed, and more consistent than the individual interpretations had been, and which was therefore genuinely accepted by all members of the team. In all cases the exchange of opinions served to inform each observer of the criteria of evaluation used by the others and thus contributed to a gradual formation of a frame of reference shared by the whole team. Thus the function of the rating conferences went far beyond that of merely obtaining one set of ratings. Frequently it led to the team's arriving, in a first approximation, at a conception of a candidate's personality, a conception which was to be checked and corrected through further observations.

The bulk of the observations obtained during assessment was assimilated in this way. In only a few of the nonstandardized procedures were the ratings assigned by a single observer (Interview, Post-Stress, OWI, and Manchuria), or obtained by merely averaging the ratings given by two or more observers (Obstacle Course, Debate). The number of rating conferences varied with the number of currently used situational tests, but it never fell below five for each staff team. Thus these conferences served to keep the team members in constant touch with each other during the three-day diagnostic period.

Not all conferences, however, were devoted to the determination of ratings. One procedure, Improvisations, designed to test hypotheses about each personality, called for a different type of group work, both for its preparation and for the evaluation of its results. The candidates first had to be cast in the roles that would be maximally revealing and that could conceivably confirm or disprove definite suppositions about them. This was done in a meeting that took place a few hours before Improvisations was scheduled. Since for Improvisations the class was divided into two sections only, the three or four staff teams were also divided into two groups, each to devise plots for one section. In preparation for this meeting the staff member who was to conduct Improvisations prepared a list of the cover stories invented by the candidates, as well as of their postwar plans, both of which had been written out by the candidates earlier in the day. At the start of the meeting the interviewers and other team members raised questions that they wanted to have answered about each candidate. Some of these questions were quite general (e.g., how skillful were a candidate's social relations), but more frequently they were rather specific, having been formulated on the basis of previous observations in the light of the particular requirements of the projected assignment. The questions might involve the candidate's handling of inferiors or superiors, his tact and resourcefulness, his proneness to guilt feelings, his tendency to blame others, or his reaction to such specific accusations as that of dishonesty or alcoholism, or his attitude toward a particular group, such as Orientals.

After the questions had been defined, the creation of appropriate situations was the task of the assembled staff members, and the nature of the ensuing performances was such as to win for this meeting the nickname of Brainstorms. The problems to be solved were by no means easy: they required a simultaneous consideration of a multiplicity of factors. For each candidate both a suitable situation and a suitable partner had to be found, and the situation had to be such as to provide an opportunity for exposing the crucial dispositions in each of the two participants. In addition, the cover stories of both had to be considered. Not infrequently we would select partners whose personal characteristics and problems were mutually complementary —say, a domineering man whose tact was the point at issue and a meek, unassuming candidate whose ability to stand up for his rights was doubted— only to find that the gap between their professed social roles made it seem almost impossible to bring them together in a plausible situation. For reasons such as these, creative imagination, as well as a knowledge of a wide range of vocational and social situations, was at a premium in Brainstorms. Eventually the seeming impasses would be broken, sometimes through a laborious trial-and-error process, sometimes through a sudden happy idea that led to a perfect solution. As the staff gained experience with Improvisations its members accumulated a repertoire of plots that had proved successful in the past and drew on it freely. Even with this help, however, Brainstorms continued to tax the staff's ingenuity and remained to the end a challenging and highly rewarding task. The largest share of this work fell to the chairman of Improvisations. After the plots had been invented, it was he who wrote out the stage settings in their final form and decided on their sequence and on the exact wording to be used in presenting each situation to the candidates.

Brainstorms was not only a necessary preliminary to Improvisations and a welcome outlet for the creative fantasies of the staff; the necessity to formulate the essential questions to be asked about a candidate forced the interviewers and the situationists to review at this time all material so far obtained, and to formulate problems on points about which they were still unclear or in doubt, as well as on those which might possibly represent sources of potential difficulties. Furthermore, in the course of Brainstorms, the placing of the candidate tentatively in various imaginary situations, with various partners, and the consideration of how he would act in each case, helped to sharpen and conceptualize these problems.

The meeting of the staff that followed immediately after Improvisations provided an opportunity for deciding whether or not these hypotheses had been verified. It was in this highly informal session that the most animated and productive discussions of individual candidates took place. There were no ratings to attend to: an attempt to rate personality variables revealed by the performances in Improvisations was discarded after a brief trial. Since all improvisations were different, the comparison of candidates and traits implied in rating was not feasible; furthermore, it was felt that the mere listening to each plot as it was developed by the "actors," and its subsequent discussion by the group resulted in more insight. In order not to make the performers too self-conscious, the staff members refrained from taking notes, but invariably they left Improvisations with a wealth of impressions which they were eager to exchange. The candidates were discussed one by one, their performances reviewed and evaluated, and conclusions drawn without any formal procedure. The discussions often transcended the immediate occasion, ranging freely over the material previously obtained through other procedures. The team members had a chance to learn what impressions their subjects had made on the other staff members who witnessed their improvisations. This intensive discussion of individual candidates, coming toward the end of the assessment period, and being highly productive of insight, was one of the most important single steps in forming the final opinions of the staff. Not infrequently the preliminary decision to pass or to fail a candidate was informally reached during this session.

The regular meetings of the staff team—such as the rating conferences, Brainstorms, and Post-Improvisation—provided set occasions for group discussions. But exchanges of observations and opinions among the team members were not limited to these occasions. There were many casual contacts and conferences of two or more team members arranged for a special purpose. The interviewer, after having seen a candidate, often told the other team members of the essential findings of the Interview. On other occasions he met with the team member who had interpreted the projective material of his interviewee, and together they went over the conclusions, comparing them with the data obtained from the Interview. Special procedures designed to deal with language handicaps, medical problems, and other particulars also called for discussion, either with team members or with other members of the staff. The person who gave the candidate an individual intelligence test or the Rorschach test, or the physician who obtained a detailed medical history or gave a physical examination imparted his observations and conclusions to the interviewer as well as to the others. Similarly, the results of tests of special skills—the Teaching Test, tests of ability to write propaganda and others—were at least briefly discussed with those who had witnessed or scored them.

All these data were brought together in the last meeting of the staff team which took place on the morning of the third day. The function of this meeting was to sum up the findings of assessment and arrive at a preliminary decision about each candidate which would later be presented to the entire staff in conference. This decision was not always easily reached, nor was it always felt to be satisfactory. At times the material obtained on the candidate did not seem to arrange itself into any meaningful pattern, and the team had the uncomfortable feeling that, although they knew a great deal about the man, they had no real understanding of him. This, however, was a rather infrequent occurrence. Usually the personality picture was fairly clear in the minds of the team members, and they were relatively confident of its accuracy. Yet often there was no equal clarity in their ideas as to how such a person would fit into a job about the requirements of which little was known, and the decision remained a difficult one. Occasionally the team was so much in doubt that its decision was merely tentative, in which case the members would prepare to present to the staff conference the reasons both for and against it, and hope for further clarification.

After all cases had been discussed in this way the work of writing the personality sketches was apportioned. The following is a typical example of the final product.

This competent, energetic, self-confident Sergeant is very well qualified for his assignment by his ability, personality, and background. He is a determined, clear-thinking person who has well-defined values and goals which he pursues with unswerving persistence, fully utilizing his capacity for hard work. In spite of his pronounced tendency toward self-reliance and independence which, combined with his rejection of indiscriminate gregariousness, often leads to bluntness in social relations, he is essentially a person of good will, is frank, sympathetic, sincere, and a good mixer. While his brusqueness and independence may alienate people upon first contact, over a longer period of time the student is likely to win and hold both the respect and the affection of his colleagues. These traits, together with his readiness to take responsibilities for others, to solve problems, and to make decisions, qualify the candidate for a position of leadership higher than one that would be compatible with his rank.

Son of a successful attorney-at-law, the candidate grew up in Oregon and Wisconsin and from an early age developed a great love for outdoor life, becoming proficient in mountain climbing, skiing, riding, and swimming. He was always a good student in school, sociable and active in a variety of extracurricular pursuits. Very close to both parents, and admiring his father's character and achievements, he decided to follow him in the legal profession, and obtained his degree from the University of Missouri in 1941. Expecting to be drafted, he postponed going into practice, and took a job with the U.S. Department of Justice. He enjoyed this work greatly, and in the course of it has acquired some experience in questioning Chinese and Japanese. Inducted into the Army in 1943, he went through basic training and a radio school and has worked as radio instructor for the last two years. In spite of slow promotion, he has adjusted well to this situation, has enjoyed teaching, for which he obtained the highest ratings, and has utilized his free time for extensive reading in the field of law and social science. He wants an overseas assignment because he feels that he should do more for the war effort and feels capable of handling a strenuous and responsible mission. Although the candidate's strong desire to do well makes him nervous and tense in test situations, or in beginning a new type of work, increasing familiarity with the situation quickly dissolves these tensions; the student is well integrated emotionally and has no disturbing conflicts or fears; while he does not seek danger he is willing to take any risks that the assignment might involve.

This candidate was very highly motivated for all of the situations at S. He entered into the assignments enthusiastically and exerted himself to the utmost in order to achieve a successful solution of his group's problems. Possessing a good measure of forcefulness and self-assertiveness, he was usually the first to make any bid for leadership. Only the lack of sufficient ingenuity in field problems prevented him from carrying out this role with distinction. He is adaptable and flexible—attributes which should stand him in good stead in acquiring the leadership techniques and fundamental knowledge necessary to handle his projected assignment effectively.

He has a strong desire to plan and carry out tasks on the basis of his own ideas. As a result, he tends to be somewhat abrupt with others who have different ideas and he is very likely to overlook their point of view in favor of his own. However, he has sufficient insight into himself so that this characteristic rarely becomes so dominant as to interfere markedly with his social relations. Furthermore, his good will, warmth, and sympathetic understanding of others become more obvious as time goes on. He should therefore wear well with any group with which he is associated over a long period of time.

In situations which he regarded as critical tests of his abilities, his tensions expressed themselves in profuse sweating and quivering limbs. He was aware of his uneasiness and discomfiture but controlled himself so well that he never became upset and never permitted his emotionality to interfere with the work at hand.

He is highly recommended for his proposed assignment overseas.

The first part of each sketch was written by the interviewer of the candidate. It was based largely, though not exclusively, on the interview material and contained the essential formulations of the personality structure. Since the reports were designed for the use of the administrative officers, facts and concepts that could convey no clear meaning to the layman were omitted, even though they had been instrumental in arriving at the conclusions presented in the report. The second part of the sketch, which described and evaluated the candidate's behavior at S, was written by one of the situationists. Although this latter account was held on a more concrete level, it still presented ample opportunities for the writer to bring out the significant patterns of behavior which could be expected to repeat themselves in the future. Each situationist wrote on those candidates about whom he had gathered the most material, or into whom he felt he had the greatest insight.

The personality sketch which in the early days of S was limited to one short paragraph, grew in time to considerable dimensions, and came to be considered, by both the staff and the administrative officers, as the most essential part of the S report. While it was expected to follow a certain general outline in all cases, and to cover certain areas, including the subject's life history and his performance at S, this sketch permitted the writer enough freedom to select and organize his material so that the most significant features of each case could be brought out. Of course it had its shortcomings. To the extent to which such a picture was interpretive, it reflected not only the configuration of the candidate's personality but also the writer's preconceptions as to what action patterns are generally significant, or in what areas of life and behavior they are most clearly revealed. This subjective factor was to be checked later by the collective effort of the group in the staff conference.

Through the rest of the third morning and early afternoon the team members were engaged in writing their reports, while staff members who were not on teams completed the administration and scoring of tests. The set of ratings which was most eagerly awaited was that based on the results of the Sociometric. Since the factor of Social Relations was important in our decision, all of us were anxious to discover whether our own estimates of this variable would be confirmed or contradicted by the judgment of the man's colleagues. An additional source of information on this point was the set of personality sketches, written by the candidates about each other, which the interviewers read and rated some time during this third day. Although the understanding of other people revealed in these sketches was measured by the yardstick of our own already formed conceptions of the persons described, the sketches not infrequently contributed pertinent information by reporting behavior that had never been observed by the staff. Occasionally these last-minute additions threw a new light on a candidate's personality and made the staff team change the conclusions it had reached in the morning. This possibility made it necessary for the two team members working on the same report to keep in close touch through the period of writing. Usually the interviewer and the situationist found time to read and criticize each other's reports before the staff conference, and if necessary change them so as to make the joint product maximally consistent and meaningful. The last part of the personality sketch, which stated the preliminary decision as to whether the candidate was fitted for his proposed assignment, was often written by the two in conjunction.

THE STAFF CONFERENCE

The staff conference which began in midafternoon and frequently lasted late into the night was the culmination of the assessment program, and an epitome of the group work of the staff. In this last step of assessment the cases of all candidates were presented, the evaluations criticized, and the dispositions decided on. At this regularly recurring meeting, in the presentation of individual cases and the thorough discussion of all differences of opinion, the staff members gained an intimate knowledge of each other's viewpoints and biases, learned to appreciate each assessor's special talents and to deal with his weaknesses, and were progressively welded into an efficiently functioning working unit.

The keynotes of the conference, which was held under the chairmanship of the director, were informality and dispatch. The presentation of each case was begun by the interviewer, who read first a description of the candidate's proposed assignment and a statement of the qualifications required for it, as formulated by the branch. He then read his part of the personality sketch. The situationist followed by reading his part as well as the recommendations made by the staff team. After that the report was open for discussion. It was up to the whole group now to see that no unwarranted generalizations were permitted to remain and no relevant contradicting observations were neglected. Criticism, freely expressed, was abundant and widely varied. The report might be criticized on such essential points as failure to take account of some significant features of the candidate's behavior or of the requirements of the job, or criticized for lack of integration and consistency, for inclusion of irrelevant or undesirable material, or for such minor matters as grammar and style.

This barrage of comment, however, was only the first step in the work of the group. The purpose of the meeting was to arrive at an optimal characterization and evaluation of the candidate, and unless the report as presented was felt by the group to be completely adequate, it had to be made so through the cooperative effort of the group. While in the majority of cases the report was accepted with minor changes only, some problematic

The Construction Situation

The Stress Situation

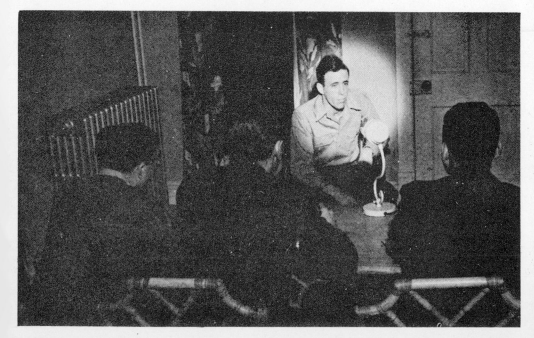

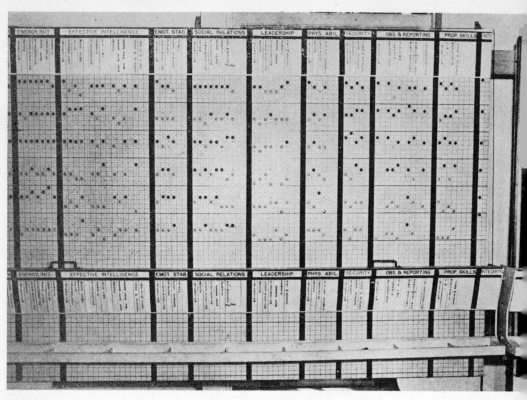

The Rating Board

Staff Conference at S

cases were reviewed and reworked in great detail. This involved another pooling of observations and interpretations. The team presented the material not explicitly mentioned in the personality sketch, and other members of the staff contributed their own impressions of the candidate obtained in special examinations or in casual contacts. Occasionally when the staff learned that certain pertinent information had not been obtained or was not clear, some staff member was delegated to obtain it from the candidate during the conference itself. At other times reports came to the conference on some striking behavior that had just been displayed by the candidate on the athletic field, or in the investigation of the Murder.

As would be expected, the major problem in the difficult cases was the final decision. Frequently the personality sketch as such presented a convincing picture and brought forth no objections, but the opinions as to how such a person would adapt overseas or fit into his particular assignment would still be uncertain or even strongly divided. In such cases the discussions were continued until a decision was reached that was felt by all, or at least by a large majority, to be satisfactory. The candidate could be either approved or failed for his proposed assignment, but neither approval nor failure was necessarily absolute; he might be failed with an indication that he would be approved for a different type of assignment, or he might be approved for some functions or locations demanded by the assignment but not for others. A compromise solution was the conditional approval, or the so-called "red flag." In this case the candidate was approved provided he successfully completed an OSS school and obtained a favorable report from the instructors therein. This, however, was not a solution for all doubtful cases; it was reserved for those where it could be expected that the sojourn at an OSS school would bring forth more evidence on the particular points —such as the candidate's social relations, or special abilities—that made us doubt his fitness. In making such conditional recommendations the staff drew on the information about the activities and life at the OSS schools acquired by the several staff members who had attended them for that purpose. Whatever the final recommendation, the report was not considered satisfactory if it did not also contain more specific recommendations about the candidate's best possible utilization, or at least provide a basis for such decisions through a clear presentation of his assets and liabilities. If the decision finally reached, or the discussions preceding it, necessitated changes in the original report, the authors had to rewrite it in part; if the changes were extensive, the new version would be read to the staff during the last part of the conference.

With the decision once made, the group proceeded to making the final ratings on the main variables. This task was greatly facilitated by the use of a rating board on which had been previously recorded the scores given to all the candidates in all the procedures they had undergone. This device, which functioned as a running record of the candidate's progress through S and which was consulted constantly by the staff throughout the assessment period, merits a detailed description. The candidates' cover names were arranged alphabetically in the first column, and to the right of each name were eleven large vertical columns representing the eleven chief variables measured: Motivation for Assignment, Energy and Initiative, Effective Intelligence, Emotional Stability, Social Relations, Leadership, Physical Ability, Security, Observing and Reporting, Propaganda Skills, and Integrity. Most of these large columns were made up of several subcolumns, each of which represented a situation or test from which a rating on that chief variable could be obtained. A horizontal row was devoted to each candidate. This, in turn, was divided into six horizontal subrows representing the points on the six-point rating scale, zero being at the bottom and five at the top. As the teams determined the final rating on each variable in each procedure for each candidate, it was recorded on this master chart by sticking a thumbtack into the proper square. Blue thumbtacks were used for ratings below average and red ones for those above average, so that it was possible at a quick glance to estimate roughly the level of achievement of the candidate for each of the major variables. (See picture facing page 213.)

When deciding on the final rating of the variables the conference members turned to the board and consulted the thumbtacks, while one person checked them against a more detailed record of all ratings. (Scores on subtests, as well as pluses and minuses, were omitted on the board.) Whenever the ratings of one variable in various tests were fairly close to each other and there were no obvious reasons for questioning their validity, the final rating could be derived by a quick inspection, by averaging at a glance, as it were. When the outcome of such averaging was doubtful, pluses and minuses in the more detailed record were consulted. A wide spread of ratings or a discrepancy between the ratings and the descriptions contained in the personality sketch called for a discussion of the reasons for this and for a decision as to which data should be given the greater weight. Sometimes a wide variation in ratings resulted from the fact that some of the tests were inappropriate for a candidate of a given background. Or it may have arisen from a language handicap or from variations of motivation from one test to another. Such factors could be evaluated in relation to the candidate's job and could be allowed for in deciding upon the final ratings. In other cases the disparity of ratings seemed to indicate true differences between variables or between various components of a single variable. A man's theoretical intelligence, say, could be high, but his mechanical or social intelligence low. Occasionally a candidate's war motivation was found to be high, but his motivation for his specific assignment low, or vice versa. Such differences were recorded on the rating sheet (see page 215) by crossing out those components of the variable (the subvariable listed under the general variable) which were

Secret

STATION S REPORT

Name —————— S-61 —————— Date 8/20/44

MOTIVATION: energy, zest, effort, initiative, war morale, interest in assignment.
Not Measured: Very Inferior   Inferior   Low Average   High Average   (Superior)   Very Superior

PRACTICAL INTELLIGENCE: speed & accuracy of judgment, resourcefulness in solving problems.
Not Measured: Very Inferior   Inferior   Low Average   (High Average)   Superior   Very Superior

EMOTIONAL STABILITY: emotional control & maturity, absence of neurotic symptoms.
Not Measured: Very Inferior   Inferior   (Low Average)   High Average   Superior   Very Superior

SOCIAL RELATIONS: social awareness, goodwill, teamwork, tact, absence of annoying traits.
Not Measured: Very Inferior   Inferior   Low Average   (High Average)   Superior   Very Superior

LEADERSHIP: social initiative, organizing ability, ability to evoke cooperation.
Not Measured: Very Inferior   Inferior   Low Average   (High Average)   Superior   Very Superior

PHYSICAL ABILITY: agility, daring, ruggedness, stamina.
Not Measured: Very Inferior   Inferior   Low Average   (High Average)   Superior   Very Superior

OBSERVATION & REPORTING: ability to search, question, observe & recall, infer, report.
Not Measured: Very Inferior   Inferior   Low Average   High Average   (Superior)   Very Superior

PROPAGANDA SKILLS: ability to affect others through talk, words or diagrams.
Not Measured: Very Inferior   Inferior   Low Average   High Average   (Superior)   Very Superior

More dependable in writing than in speaking

MAINTAINING COVER: caution, ability to remain inconspicuous, shift, mislead, keep a secret.
Not Measured: Very Inferior   Inferior   Low Average   High Average   Superior   (Very Superior)

——— (underlining) means "The candidate is especially high or good in this characteristic."
✕ (crossing out) means "The candidate is especially low or poor in this characteristic."

present to a lesser degree, and/or underlining those which were present to a greater extent.

Even when no striking disparities were found in the separate ratings of a variable, the derivation of the final rating departed from a mere averaging of all ratings because of the differential weighting of the data. This weighting was necessary, first because we did not ascribe equal value to all tests of a variable, and, second, because some tests had a greater pertinence for a given job than did others. In certain traits, notably Emotional Stability, the opinion of the interviewer was weighted more heavily than the ratings given in situations. In Social Relations, on the other hand, the actual behavior at S was considered better evidence than indirect facts obtained in the Interview. The Obstacle Course was considered to be by far the most revealing test of Physical Ability, and unless there was great disparity between performance on this course and in other situations, the rating of the former was considered final. When the candidate's job required definite abilities and skills, such as theoretical thinking, skill in analyzing intelligence material, or in writing propaganda, we tended to give greater weight to the tests that directly involved such capacities than to other items of the battery.

Such weighting and manipulating of scores was not done lightly. After all, a good many man-hours of a trained staff had gone into the making of each average figure. Each constituent rating was conscientiously corrected for the inevitable artificiality of the conditions under which it was made. Only by viewing the ratings in the light of everything else that was known about the individual could such allowances be made. There were two major sources of corrective facts: the psychiatric interview and the cross-fire of critical judgments made by the assembled staff members who, recalling this, that, and the other episode, tried to reconcile apparent discrepancies. Sometimes, following such an interchange, the rating stood and the written report was amended accordingly. Sometimes, if there was a convincing hypothesis as to why the ratings were probably in error, the written report was accepted and the ratings were changed. Much more often, neither needed substantial modification.

In short, the staff at S was faced with the problem of making a recommendation based upon an over-all picture of an individual who must function not just as leader, or just as mechanic, or just as propagandist, but also as a man. Hence all necessary pains were taken to arrive at an evaluation which had psychological self-consistency in spite of apparent contradictions, and which conformed to all the facts as accurately as the staff could understand them.

Such a procedure may seem not only to commit the halo fallacy, but actually to glory in it. If by "halo" is meant the acceptance of the interconsistency of observed behaviors in the light of all that is known about the individual, the staff at S gladly subscribed to the "fallacy"; and if by avoidance of "halo" is meant the insistence upon the equal validity of each independent observation, the staff at S would feel that the avoidance of "halo fallacy" is itself a fallacy.

Another departure from strict averaging was made in an effort to compensate for the fact that in any such procedure which entails combining scores the final resultants tend to regress toward the mean. A consequence of this is that the extreme high and low grades are not used so often as demanded by the theoretical curve mentioned above. To correct for this tendency the group adopted conventions to force the final grade into the extreme categories whenever possible. For example, if all raters gave a 4 or 4+ the final grade would be pushed to 5— or 5. Similarly, agreement on 1's would result in a final grade of 0+ or 0.

After the final ratings of the first ten variables had been decided on, the interviewer commented briefly upon the score he had given the candidate on Integrity. This was necessarily a rather impressionistic estimate based almost entirely upon material obtained in the Interview and consequently was rarely contested by others, for lack of relevant information. After that each staff member independently rated the candidate on his fitness for his assignment, writing the figure on a slip of paper. Then each man announced his decision and the final job-fitness rating was derived by averaging. If anyone made a stand in defense of a different rating, another discussion followed, terminating either in agreement or in a vote. In similar fashion an over-all rating was arrived at, representing an estimate of the total potentialities of the candidates for meeting the challenges of life—an exceedingly vague and difficult concept to define.

The rest of the procedure consisted in filling out various printed forms for the candidate which, together with the personality sketch and the ratings, made up the S report. In the last months of assessment this involved checking one of the following possible decisions: Not Recommended, Doubtful, Recommended with Qualifications, Recommended, Highly Recommended. Although a job-fitness rating as low as 1 did not necessarily preclude a candidate from being considered suitable, scarcely anyone was recommended with a score below 2. The job-fitness rating of 4 or 5 meant high recommendation. A similar scale (not recommended to highly recommended) was used to indicate our estimate of the candidate's fitness for work (i) at a rear base, (ii) at an advanced base, and (iii) at the front or behind the enemy lines; of his fitness for (i) higher, (ii) middle, and (iii) lower level of authority and responsibility; and of his fitness for different types of assignments, such as administrator, intelligence officer, operational agent, and so forth. These ratings, in conjunction with the personality sketch, were an attempt on our part to assist in an adequate placement of the candidate, in case it should be necessary, as it often was, to change his assignment. Because all pertinent data had been thoroughly discussed before, seldom were there difficulties or disagreements in filling out these forms. When they were completed, the reports were taken to the secretaries, who typed them, after which they were carefully proofread and checked by members of the junior staff for errors and inconsistencies.

This step-by-step description of the conference proceedings can give only an inadequate idea of the vigor and vitality which often marked these meetings. Formality was absent, free expression reigned, yet the often heated discussions never became truly violent or bitter, in spite of the great personal involvement of the participants. Behind the uninhibited arguments was an attitude of mutual appreciation which facilitated acceptance of criticism and enabled everyone to join in the frequent outbursts of hilarity, even he, if not especially he, who was the butt of a joke. The sustained enthusiasm was due in large part to the staff's great interest in the candidates and their destinies. The staff members who had observed a given man most closely, particularly the author of the personality sketch, not infrequently developed a strong sympathy (though occasionally an antipathy) for their subjects and became to some extent, however fleetingly, identified with them. It was a commonly recognized phenomenon, and a subject of some amusement, that the interviewer frequently became the spokesman of "his" candidate, defending the more favorable interpretation of his behavior and trying to secure higher scores for him. This tendency was usually corrected by the counteracting weight of the rest of the staff, most of whom were well aware of this bias, both in others and in themselves. The appearance at S of candidates outstanding in achievement, ability, and personality—of whom we had many—contributed greatly to the zest of the staff conferences. The sketches of their characters were the peaks of the meeting, and at times it took a great deal of both serious and humorous mutual warning about the operation of partiality to restrain our enthusiasm and to keep the evaluation of the outstanding candidates within the limits of justifiable praise. The borderline cases and those presenting subtle and intricate problems were especially challenging and very apt to be productive of stimulating discussions and new insights.

It may be accepted as evidence of the effectiveness of our mode of collective action that such a relatively large number of persons as met in staff conference succeeded in attaining agreement through discussion. There was a decided sentiment against arriving at crucial decisions by a mechanical counting of votes, and this device was used only as the last resource. A necessary condition for the effectiveness of this method of discussion was the chairman's democratic mode of leadership. The director of S, acting as chairman, encouraged the free expression of opinion by giving earnest consideration to all points made. While he often took a definite stand himself, he was at all times genuinely intent on making the best judgment of the group instrumental in each single decision. Occasionally the discussion got out of hand, and intervention was required to bring the disputants back to the topic and to a satisfactory conclusion; but, in accomplishing this, the chairman was supported by the unanimous realization that many critical decisions had to be made within a limited period of time.

After the staff conference was over, the director of S read and signed all typed reports. These were delivered early next morning at headquarters in

Washington, but since they might not reach the administrative officer who would act on them until after the candidates had reported back, the director had to call each branch representative on the telephone to notify him which of his men had not been recommended for overseas duty, so that the branch officer would know what to say to each man when he met him. This was the director's most painful task: to explain on the telephone the reasons for rejecting a candidate who, in most instances, had been carefully picked and skillfully recruited, who, not seldom, had left an important position and perhaps traveled a thousand miles in response to the urgent call of the OSS, and who might even be a lifelong friend of the administrative officer. On this day between classes the director frequently had occasion to discuss with administrative officers problem and borderline cases, making clear to them the staff's reasons for passing or failing candidates. In turn, the director usually passed on to the staff the branches' reactions to its decisions, and this information served to keep the staff in close touch with the viewpoints and attitudes of the administrative officers.

The picture we have given of the operations of the staff may strike the reader as being too glowing and idealized. In truth, it presents our staff work at its best, as it was carried out after the program had been stabilized, during the periods when the pressures and disturbances that beset assessment were at a minimum. Such times were sufficiently long and frequent that the experience of being a participant in well-organized, stimulating work carried out with good will and zest became for most members of the staff the outstanding feature of the season spent as S. This high level of vigorous and harmonious functioning could not be maintained at all times. The main factors militating against it were insufficiency of staff, shortage of time, and overload of work. The almost constant unavailability of suitably trained men for the staff often led to an undermanning of teams. At such times the interviewers had to handle more cases than they could thoroughly work out, and were sometimes prevented from attending some of the situational tests. Occasionally, the usual expertness of the schedule makers failed, and a staff member would be bewildered to find himself assigned to two different places simultaneously. The undermanning of teams also affected the quality and quantity of observations. This was particularly true when the number of candidates to be observed in the different situations was larger than usual. It was our experience that five persons working in a group could be easily kept under surveillance, but that it was hard to take in all the activities of a group of seven. The shortage of time resulting from a crowded schedule was particularly damaging to the unscheduled team meetings; the rating conferences were sandwiched in between procedures, and frequently, instead of taking place soon after the situation, they had to be postponed till late in the evening. At such times the team members might find themselves unable to recall their observations of the early morning, and too sleepy to be interested in discussion. Under the combined pressure of lack of time and of fatigue, the discussions would be reduced to a minimum and an averaging of ratings would be substituted for agreement. When a large number of reports had to be written, the meeting of the team on the last day was cut short, or even reduced to a discussion between the interviewer and the situationist who was to write the report. After the two parts of the report were written there was often no time to compare them, so that their integration had to be achieved in or after the staff conference. Some of the reports were even written during the conference, the writers dividing their attention between scribbling and listening. The principle of continuing the staff discussions of difficult cases until clarification was reached could not always be adhered to, because of the limited time. As a result, the director, on reading the typewritten report, might have to consult with its author to decide on further changes.

Reasons other than lack of time and pressure of work were occasionally responsible for departures from the ideal. Forces inherent in social relations generally—mutual likes and dislikes, bids for dominance or prestige, tendencies to yield too readily to group pressure—were not without effect on our proceedings. Thus not all individual prejudices were corrected. On the whole, however, the disruptive influences were at a minimum. In the emotionally positive climate of S they were for the most part freely expressed and easily overcome. The variety of the program and the experimental spirit that pervaded it permitted each staff member to attach himself to some procedure that best corresponded to his interests and abilities and to attain special proficiency in it. Some were noted for their skillful and sensitive handling of Improvisations, evoking maximum spontaneity of the "actors" as well as productive discussions of their performances by the audience. Others were known for the spirited manner in which they conducted the Debate. Still others for their ability to get the most information out of the projective material, or for interviewing skill, or for being able to put their formulations of personality development into the context of a wider sociological background. We had our specialists in standardized paper-and-pencil tests and in statistical techniques, our "idea men" and organizers of research; the Stress Interview was a one-man show. The satisfaction that each man derived from the work itself and from the recognition that his specialized contribution was appreciated by the others went a long way toward maintaining high motivation and toward helping everyone to maintain his poise in the face of the inevitable series of frustrations. The presence on the staff of some persons who attracted the esteem and affection of all acted as another unifying factor, one that greatly enhanced the enjoyment of teamwork. The staff work was more than a mere necessary division of labor, and more than a means of safeguarding conclusions against sources of error inherent in clinical methods. At its best it represented actual collective thinking and collective problem solving which resulted in more valid and adequate decisions than could have been achieved by any one individual.

REFLECTIONS ON PROCEEDINGS

S as a Standardized Society.—S was a society like a ship's crew organized by a temporary necessity which separated them from the rest of the world. It was more than a place where tests and situations were administered. It was where the candidates lived, ate, slept, competed, and played games together. They took each other's measure and assumed their parts in the social intercourse. Some quickly rose to the top and were at once acknowledged as outstanding; some fell to the bottom, and others vacillated, trying to find their rightful place in the scheme of things. A few quit, the problem of adaption being entirely insoluble for them.

Moreover, the adjustment of the individual to this society affected his performance in the various tests, and his performance, of course, affected his adjustment. This was as it should be. Living, doing, behaving, thinking, are not mutually exclusive. As a consequence, the evaluations of the staff combined facts learned from both formal test and informal living. Frequently the most significant data were the uncontrolled observations of casual deportment before and after one of the carefully standardized tests.

What is more, not only did this society at S permit the continuous observation of the adjustment and performance of the subject but it also provided the fullest possible control over the setting of the test administration. Rarely if ever before had the setting been kept so constant, not only during the test but before and after as well.

Perhaps more important than the constancy of superficial conditions of a test, like place and time, was the elimination of formal differences among candidates, by withholding their true names and dressing them all alike in fatigues. This matter was crucial for evaluating the interrelationship of a subject and his colleagues. The effect of name and dress on social relationships and on submission-dominance patterns is obvious, and even the most careful and conscientious observer may be prejudiced, if only unconsciously, by outward appearance and family derivation. And although such factors may well be considered in making final evaluations, it is well that at least such easily changed accouterments be held constant when measuring the personality, especially since the subject may be required to function where "what he is" rather than "who he is" will be vital. By assigning cover-names and cover-alls, S produced a uniform anonymity which shielded psychological judgments from interference by irrelevant and misleading factors. So far as possible the endeavor at S was to see the person whole and to see him real. If he achieved a desirable niche in the society of S he did so on his own merit. If he carried distinction, it was not the distinction bought at

Brooks Brothers or bestowed by virtue of his grandfather's shrewd speculations in railroad stock.

It was similarly desirable that the candidates invent fictional past histories as background for their interpersonal communications. Thus all started on the same level at S, for they could not lean on the prop of former achievements, true or fancied. They could not boast of a high status if they had it, and any status they mentioned was known to be false. The philosopher who said he was a ditchdigger was no more believed than the ditchdigger who said he was a philosopher. And it did not matter; for this was a society where achievement was more impressive than pretension and intrinsic effectiveness more telling than presumption. Each person had to demonstrate his worth; he could not rely on his investitures. He could not produce a large bank roll to offset his superficiality, nor use the pose of "creative artist" to excuse his narcism. He could not silence his fellows by listing the books he had written or by fingering his Phi Beta Kappa key. He came naked. So far as past history and achievement were concerned, all men met on the same terms. The actual case of the general and the corporal who, ignorant of each other's rank, lived as convivial bunkmates was no exception. S was the truly classless society.

Numerous duties and obligations had to be fulfilled—appointments to be kept and tasks to be performed—but there were also opportunities for informal social intercourse. There were kindnesses to do and favors to request. There were opportunities for personal initiative and group cooperation. And always, as in everyday life, there were the barb of competition and the understanding that the achievement and reputation of each were being measured and recorded.

The structures of the societies constituted by the successive classes at S exhibited certain uniformities. As in any group of more than a few members, specific affiliations of two or three persons began to develop soon after arrival. Several factors encouraged this tendency. The sleeping quarters consisted of three rooms, and it was easier to become acquainted with roommates than with others. Then, too, the men sitting together at each of the several supper tables on the first evening were apt to strike up an acquaintanceship and join each other at subsequent meals. The major groupings, however, were the class as a whole and the three subgroups of six, who worked together in the various situational tests. The candidate's loyalty to the whole group was casual, like the soldier's to his company, which competes with other distant companies. But it was quite direct and warm to his subgroup, like the soldier's affiliation to his own squad within the company.

The first interpersonal duties and obligations of the candidate at S were to his subgroup and here also he first competed overtly for status and recognition. The subgroups were composed with an eye toward homogeneity of membership with the widest possible opportunity for personal interaction. They were designed so that the success of each candidate depended, so far as he knew, on the cooperation and effectiveness of every other member of the team. It was here that the sharpest likes and dislikes were formed. It was here that respect and recognition were gained and lost. The effective and the ineffective, the aggressive and the submissive, the leader and the follower were quickly perceived. The "good Joe," the "queer duck," the "lone wolf," the "teamworker" were readily distinguished. The general assumption was that each candidate took his place in the subgroup at S much as he would do in his office or in his field team overseas.

There was, however, another milieu operating, namely, that of the whole group. Here the interaction was not dependent so much on the candidate's accomplishment and efficiency in the doing of specific tasks as on his overall effectiveness and impressiveness under informal circumstances, although there was, of course, some carry-over from one to the other. The difference between the opinion of the subgroup and that of the whole group was very much like the difference of impression formed in the more or less enforced collaboration of the office or platoon and that formed by meeting the same person in a larger population, say, in a country club or in a company dayroom. Interaction is present in both places but on a different plane of intimacy. In both places peculiarities, but different ones, are apparent, likes and dislikes are formed, in-groups and out-groups produced; but these are based in the larger group on social interrelations rather than, as in the smaller group, on working interrelations. Needless to say, in the usual course of things and especially in the requirements of the OSS, the two are equally important for the true evaluation of a candidate.

It was significant and frequently enormously helpful in understanding individuals to know that the person who was most rejected by his subgroup was sometimes also the person who was most accepted by the entire group (excluding, of course, the members of his own subgroup), and that the most respected member of the subgroup was sometimes just a "dud" to the rest of the community.

In making his adaptation and contribution to these various planes of the society at S, the candidate revealed facets of his personality not otherwise observable. At least as much could frequently be inferred about a man from the place to which he was allocated by his fellows as could be gathered from anything he said about himself to the interviewer or did in the formal testing periods. The methods of observation, the role of the staff in this society, and the procedure for obtaining the candidates' judgments of each other are described elsewhere. For a clear understanding of S, however, these three points should be kept in mind: (1) S was a continuous proceeding, with the situations and tests merely incidental to the total process. The informal sociality was as important as the formal measurement, the baseball game as significant as Belongings. (2) No test score or average of test scores was considered as a final judgment. The ratings were merely memoranda to be viewed in the light of the total impress of the subject upon the society and the staff. (3) No test or theory was permitted to hinder the task of assessing each personality as a "single behaving organism in a society."

One example will illustrate the procedure. Charley came to S in a group of eighteen candidates of similar age. His performance on the written tests was outstanding: he scored top grades in Intelligence, Vocabulary, Mechanical Comprehension. He was knowledgeable and well informed. He was willing to help in the subgroup, and although he exerted no leadership, he tried to be useful and friendly. Yet he was not recommended by S for acceptance by the organization. Although the individual scores averaged "satisfactory," Charley, the person, did not. Although he knew all about the writings on sociology, he knew nothing about how to live socially; although he knew the book, he did not know the practice. He was not Charley to his colleagues, but "poor Charley" or "poor old Charley," or "Charley-horse." He was, in the society that obtained at S, a butt and a laughingstock. In spite of certain test scores, he was the class "dunce." He could never be an acceptable member of a team; he could never live congenially in barracks.

In this case validation was almost immediate, for several of his college mates were acquaintances of a staff member. They were unanimous in reporting that Charley was at the top of the class in marks and at the bottom in everything else. "He was," they said, "a kind of superintellectual joke." So far as assessment was concerned, the so-called informal section of the process had contributed more than the formal section. And so it should be, for the activity of adults is rarely in the schoolroom, and their effectiveness hardly ever apparent outside their intercourse with others. After a given minimum of intelligence, there are few jobs that do not depend more on general personality effectiveness in society than on sheer intellectual power in a cell. In wartime and certainly in the OSS, the job that could be done by a superintelligent hermit was rare as compared to the job that could be done by a sociocentric person of moderate intelligence.

Interrelationships of Candidates and Staff.—No facet of the program at S was more essential to the success of assessment than the interaction among the candidates and between them and the staff. The candidates were observed largely against the framework of the society established by the active participation of all habitants of S.

It was a fundamental principle of testing and of assessment at S that the subject be observed when he was trying to do his best, even though some of the tests were designed to catch him at his worst. A standard condition without which assessment is impossible is that all candidates be motivated to do their best and to show themselves in a favorable light. Otherwise it is like measuring the height of people when they are seated or the speed of greyhounds without the rabbit. If living at S was the basic test of the assessment program, it was important that the candidate be motivated to live as well as he knew how. For example, although it might not be especially reprehensible for a man to become drunk at a party in his own home, it was usually counted against him to give in to temptation and become drunk at S. But it was important that intoxication at S should not be the manifestation of a candidate's indifference or antagonism to assessment. It should be a true measure of his inability to control himself, despite his desire to do so. Similarly, lack of intelligence or poor social relations should be measures of the candidate when he exerts himself to do his best, and not be products of his lethargy or resentment.

Thus the society at S had two functions: first, to provide the framework within which various dispositions and abilities could be observed; second, without which the first would have been impossible, to create a friendly atmosphere in which resentments could be resolved and the most favorable relationships between assessors and assessees could be developed.

Contemplating in retrospect the society that was S, one can realize the importance of the tacit working principles that guided and shaped the assessment community. They are rules to be remembered in any future assessment.

1) The prevailing atmosphere should be one of *Gemütlichkeit*, of informal but well-ordered friendliness. Rigid and directed social and athletic programs are likely to prove tedious, but a staff member should always be available for "shooting the breeze," for taking part in a game of badminton, horseshoes, bridge, or even charades. Of course, the usual clubroom paraphernalia should be available as well as the icebox for the "midnight snack." The pervading social climate, except during formal testing periods should be that of a group of congenial associates enjoying an enforced stay with hospitable but not effusive hosts, the staff.

2) Within the framework set by the physical characteristics of the area, the structure of the staff, and the restrictions necessary for the formal testing, each candidate should be given the widest scope for living and self-expression. To evaluate him best he should be given liberty; even more, he should be encouraged to stretch himself in his assessment environment as he would normally.

3) Resentments necessarily engendered in candidates by the character of such tests as Stress and Construction should be dissipated. The process of "decompression," although part of the diagnostic procedure, should be a regular adjunct to any test involving personal humiliation. Frustration in one test should not carry over to affect performance in another. The hypersensitive

individual will evidence himself most clearly if all except him are relieved by the decompression. With accumulating resentment, the hostility toward the single test is diverted to all tests and more especially to the staff, a condition under which the advantageous interaction of staff and candidate is impossible.

4) There should be a clear dichotomy between the method of observation adopted in the formal tests and that practiced during periods of recreation. In the former, the staff member is an overt nonparticipant observer; in the latter, he is a covert participant observer. During moments of leisure, spontaneous sociability is primary, observation secondary. If diagnostic data are forthcoming they will be noted, but if the subject suspects that he is being "sized-up" or "pumped" under the subterfuge of informal conversation, he may withdraw permanently. If the interaction is genuine, the observation will be genuine too. And of course the staff should never intrude on the privacy of the candidate except during the Interview, and should not, except under test conditions, attempt to trip him up on his cover story or similar matters. The greatest compliment that can be paid to a staff's informal observation is that it is not apparent.

Of course, there are no set ways to act in applying these principles successfully. Much depends on the light and shade of interpersonal adjustments within the staff and their reflection in the candidates. It was striking to note how sensitively the classes reacted to moods of the staff. When "things were right," an atmosphere was created which eliminated strain; the widest latitude was given to individual initiative; both candidates and staff worked together for a single purpose—the best evaluation of every man. Under these conditions, the motivation of the candidates to appear at their best, yet to be perfectly frank about their deficiencies, was astonishing. No task was too arduous, no question too intimate. Perhaps most amazing and gratifying was the open appreciation expressed by the candidates for the efforts of the staff.

No rigid adherence to rules can produce a result of this sort, for the latter is the outcome of such intangibles as morale, spirit, *esprit de corps*. One truism worth mentioning is that if the candidates see the staff working hard at a job it takes seriously, they will do likewise. At S, more often than not, so it seemed to us, the required intangibles were operative. Everyone knew it when things were right and knew it when they were wrong.

Friendliness and trust can often be disturbed by a minor incident. For instance, by accident it so happened with one class that at the first supper all the candidates found themselves seated at tables separate from the members of the staff. The remark was clearly heard, "Ah, separate tables— separate food too, I suppose." The next day when the members of the staff took their usual places among the candidates, the question, spoken and unspoken, was, "Slumming, are we, this morning?" And this attitude of separateness and discrimination carried over into the assessment contacts too. Assessment can be easily resented: no one likes to be judged. This accident, however, was the exception. Usually, the candidates who were prepared to scoff at the long-haired psychologists found themselves playing ball, discussing foreign affairs, or swapping yarns over a beer with ordinary human beings. The most frequent comments were, "We came out feeling that we were going to be tested by some professors and discovered instead that we were living with a pretty good bunch of Joes." It is the contention of S that more can be learned of people by living with them as "good Joes" than by testing them as professors.

General Considerations on Situational Testing.—Although every part of the time at S was a free sampling of the candidates' lives, the situational tests were the most carefully structured and observed behavior samples. A wide range of approaches was available, because any circumstance which provokes behavior and gives opportunity for psychological observation is, within the meaning of the term, a situational test. The staff at S experimented with procedures ranging from that of merely leaving several candidates in a room without instructions to that of prescribing rigid rules according to which the men would enact what amounted to the last scene of an unfinished play. It became clear that the first of these was wasteful of time and depended too much on the chance whims of the more restless members of the group, and that the second allowed little leeway for the spontaneous impulses of the participants. The following guiding rules for designing situational tests are based on twenty months of experimentation.

1) Every situational task should have a number of alternate solutions.

2) The accomplishment of a situational task should not require very specialized abilities, because if it does, a large proportion of the candidates will be seriously handicapped and unable to participate on a level with the "experts."

3) Situations should be designed to reveal the kinds of behavior which cannot be registered by mechanical means. As a rule, simple skills and abilities are better measured by rigidly controlled tests; emotional attitudes and social behavior, by more flexible situations.

4) Situations should be constructed which force the candidate to reveal dominant dispositions of his personality. The fruitful problem is one which evokes complex behavior with significant emotional components. A test of skill, of course, may be imbedded in a situational context and two evaluations obtained concurrently—an estimate of the given skill and a judgment as to certain components of personality. For instance, both agility and courage could be estimated at several of the obstacles in the Obstacle Course.

5) The most productive situations are those which involve group inter-

action: each man is called upon to accomplish something with the aid of a few co-workers under conditions which encourage initiative and the display of unique patterns of response. A tug of war, for example, is not a very revealing group situation because it restricts the individual to a narrow norm of action. It is from the friction engendered by competing ambitions within a working group that sparks are struck which illumine the personalities involved.

6) The situational task should be one which requires, for its best solution, the coordination of numerous components of personality. The candidate should be pressed to bring many of his resources to bear on the confronting problem. Testing single aspects of behavior is a questionable procedure, because in real life processes do not occur singly.

7) Modification of the situation to fit the experience and abilities of the candidate may in some instances be advisable. In the Assigned Leadership tests, for example, misleading results will be obtained if tasks are assigned without regard to the individual's talents and training.

8) The candidates should be given an opportunity, either in the course of the task or immediately afterward, to discuss their performance. Much can be gained from the subject's own account of how he would, or of how he did, handle the assigned problem. He is usually capable of giving the most plausible explanation of his own behavior. In making its evaluations of performances in such tests as the Brook and Assigned Leadership, the staff at S was greatly aided by the commentary of the participants. In Improvisations the commentary was an integral part of the proceedings and was therefore still more helpful to the assessors whose task it was to interpret the behavior.

9) The members of the staff should have ample opportunity to confer after the situational task has been completed. This is the time to discuss and synthesize the different interpretations of the observed behavior. We assume that no single examiner is capable of accurately recording and interpreting all the component actions of a complex group proceeding.

These nine guiding rules may be of some use for the immediate future, but they do not, by any means, solve the bulk of the perplexing problems involved in the invention, observation, and interpretation of situational procedures. These situations are still in an early imperfect stage of evolution. Sometimes they "come off" astonishingly well—in those instances, for example, when, at the emotional peak of a tensely developing interaction, the characters of the leading participants are suddenly revealed, as at the climax of a drama, in their true colors. At other times, however, for no apparent reason, nothing very significant transpires.

In evoking emotional components the most successful situation used at Station S was Improvisations. This was the only procedure in which no ratings were attempted, the whole attention of the staff members being directed toward one actor and then the other, in an attempt to interpret the clues to personality structure embodied in words and gestures. One of the most rewarding features of Improvisations was the exchange of views of members of the audience as to how well each participant had handled the other in the given situation. Since both of these were required to explain, if not to defend their actions in the face of such comments, they were likely at this point to become emotionally involved and give some indication of the level of their tolerance of criticism. The insights gained from these miniature incidents were more significant, though assuredly less codifiable, than any other procedure except the Interview.

Chapter VI

ASSESSMENT AT S: ANALYSIS OF VARIABLES

Station S was established as a service center. We had no directive to do research. We were recruited to assess men and women, and those who recruited us expressed their confidence in our ability to fulfill this function. But without exception, we were only too aware of the limits of present knowledge and of the fallibility of our judgments. We would have liked to have had time to plan the program in detail and the opportunity to criticize all that we did. But the war was on; a job had to be done at once, and so with a minimum of theory and all the common sense that we could muster, a program of assessment was set going. This to us was what the Construction situation was to the candidates—a test of frustration tolerance. The branches wanted ratings of certain traits of personality on each recruit —intelligence, emotional stability, social relations, security, and so on— but we wanted an opportunity to discuss the whole problem of traits. After all, we wondered whether there were such things as traits of personality, and if there were, whether the qualities which we had been asked to measure could be classified among them. To have had time to discuss problems of this sort and to come to a group decision on each might have resulted in a much more effective program of assessment.

Then, too, confronted with the unique task of studying a large population of normal and supernormal persons, we would have desired to seize this opportunity for a carefully planned research into problems of the structure, function, and development of personality, to say nothing of research into the technical and methodological problems of assessment.

But the immediate and practical demands of assessment left us no time for the construction of an experimental design. Even the hope that sooner or later the load of assessment would be lightened, or the size of the staff increased to the point where such experimental planning might be done, was never realized. And so, looking back over what we did, we find little to report that can in any sense be regarded as a contribution to a better understanding of personality. Our experience convinced us of the inadequacy if not falsity of much that we had believed in the past about the role of various experimental factors in the development of personality, especially in its abnormal manifestations, but the pressure of work kept us from ever setting up the program of research that might have yielded some of the sorely needed facts pertinent to these issues.

The record of our work must then, perforce, be a description of what we did as a service unit rather than a report of research findings. To be sure, variations both in the over-all program and in individual procedures were frequently introduced, first to improve the quality of assessment, and second, where possible, to suggest the answers to certain theoretical questions. But no claim is made that an analysis of our conceptualizations and measurements of the variables can amount to more than a record of what was done with a few suggestive hints for future research. It is with this warning before him that the reader is invited, if he is still interested, to survey in the pages that follow the psychological and statistical analysis of the variables of personality that were rated in the assessment program at S, and into which we sought, though largely unsystematically, to gain new insights.

THE SEVEN PERIODS OF S

In the rest of this chapter, references will be made to various periods in the life of Station S. These subdivisions of its twenty months' existence were set up afterward purely to facilitate the statistical analysis of the thousands of ratings and scores. The dividing points were chosen to approximate the points at which new procedures were introduced as substitutes for those that seemed least fruitful. All but one of these transitions were minor turning points in the evolution of the program described in Chapters 3 and 4; from June, 1944, to V-J day, no revolutionary changes occurred.

The chronological details of the seven periods are given in Table 1. During most of Period A, the staff saw two classes a week, one from Sunday afternoon to Wednesday morning and the other from Wednesday afternoon to Saturday morning. For six weeks, the assessment load was as high as 80 a week. This large number was handled by picking out five to ten of the obviously satisfactory candidates and returning them to Washington after twenty-four hours. On Tuesdays and Fridays, special classes of six to twelve arrived for a rapid six-hour assessment, these being the forerunners of the one-day classes at Station W. Twenty-five variables were used during Period A, of which at least fifteen were rated for each candidate.

The new schedule of three classes every two weeks was instituted just before Period B began. Another major change was the adoption of the final report sheet with nine variables. The reduction was accomplished mostly by grouping related variables; thus Observation and Reporting was defined to include the grades which had formerly been listed under Observation, Memory, Inference, and Reporting Ability. Also at this time, the practice of having a staff team of three follow the same group of candidates through all tests replaced that of assigning one staff member to observe all candidates on one test. The change enabled each member to obtain a rather comprehensive conception of a few candidates instead of a superficial impression of all of them.

Period C was marked by the abandonment of the time-consuming and barely reliable Flashlight Observation Test, the addition of the OWI Test, and a few minor changes in the variables rated in certain procedures. From

TABLE 1

Subdivisions in the Life of Station S

Period	Class numbers	Dates these classes arrived	Number of candidates assessed
A	1- 44	December 30, 1943—June 2, 1944	962[a]
B	45- 58	June 6, 1944—August 6, 1944	254
C	59- 74	August 10, 1944—October 19, 1944	259
D	75- 91	October 23, 1944—January 15, 1945	257
E	92- 99	January 21, 1945—February 26, 1945	135
F	100-119	March 4, 1945—June 4, 1945	309
G	120-134	June 10, 1945—August 23, 1945	195
		Total..........................	2,371

[a] Includes 230 candidates whose assessment lasted less than a day.

this time on, for example, Social Relations was rated at the Brook. Beginning with Period D, the SIX-2 Test was included in the program, and the interviewer's estimate of the candidate's integrity was recorded for reference and research purposes. While this latter grade was not reported, any suspicions of low integrity were discussed in the report. Period E saw the elimination of the Recruiting Test because this function would not be required in the Far East to the same extent as it had been in Europe.

The Assigned Leadership problems became a regular part of the program with the first class in Period F. Period G was marked by the reclassification of Motivation scores under two variables, Motivation for Assignment, and Energy and Initiative. On the new report form instituted at this time, (a) Propaganda Skills and (b) Observing and Reporting were omitted from the list of variables because these were pertinent to specific assignments only, and because there was a place on the new second sheet for recording estimates of these two aptitudes. Since there was no longer any problem of language handicap among the candidates, the Otis Self-Administering Test of Mental Ability replaced the nonverbal Progressive Matrices and Series Completion Tests. Also, verbal persuasiveness at the Discussion and the Debate was no longer rated as part of Propaganda Skills because it was not relevant to written propaganda in the Far East.

MOTIVATION

From the beginning of the program at S Motivation was defined to include two variables: (1) the candidate's desire to accomplish an assignment in the OSS, and (2) the level of energy and initiative generally displayed by him in pursuit of goals. These two factors, or sets of factors, which may be presumed to be largely independent of each other, were scored on the basis of different types of data. The score on Motivation for Assignment was mostly based on information obtained from the candidate in the Interview, with some additional contributions from Discussion, Debate, and Post-Stress. Energy and Initiative, on the other hand, was rated as a unit largely on the basis of the candidate's performances in group and individual situations. During the first few months (Period A) Motivation and Initiative were treated as distinct variables, but in Period B their separate treatment fell victim to the policy of creating large clusters, and they were combined into one variable under the label "Motivation." It was not until the last few months of assessment (Period G) that they were once again distinguished and assigned separate final scores. In Periods B through F the single rating on Motivation represented a compromise between the average of the Energy and Initiative scores obtained in the various situations and the interviewer's score on Motivation for Assignment, with the latter being given much the greater weight. This disposition to favor the interviewer is well illustrated by the fact that in Period B the final score on Motivation correlated with the interviewer's rating of Motivation .83, whereas the median correlation of the final score on Motivation with all other subscores of this trait was only .44. Because of this marriage of two distinct concepts the statistics involving the final scores on Motivation are relatively unambiguous only for the data of the first and of the last period. For periods in between, the final scores on Motivation represent largely Motivation for Assignment and will be treated as such. It must be remembered, however, that they deviate from the original ratings given by the interviewer to the extent to which they were influenced by the Energy and Initiative factor.

MOTIVATION FOR ASSIGNMENT

Distribution of Scores.—A consideration of the distribution of the final ratings of Motivation for Assignment may help to clarify some of the assumptions underlying the scoring of this variable. The distribution of these ratings for various periods of assessment at S is given in Table 2. Two peculiarities of this set of distributions are apparent at a glance: shifts in distribution between Periods A and C, with stabilization from C on, and the negative skewness of the distribution throughout all periods. This skewness is extreme in Period A, with 58 per cent of the ratings falling in the 4 and 5 categories. The typical distribution of the ratings of this variable is like that of others in having few extreme scores in the lower end of the scale (0, 1);

TABLE 2

Percentage of Ratings in Each Category of the Scale Given on Motivation for Assignment in Each Period of S

Period	N	S Scale					
		0	1	2	3	4	5
A	929	2%	6%	11%	23%	45%	13%
B	258	4	6	14	35	35	6
C	258	2	7	19	42	25	5
D	258	2	6	24	42	21	5
E	135	3	5	20	38	27	7
F	308	0	8	22	44	24	2
G	110	3	7	17	46	20	7
B–G	1,327	2	6	18	39	28	6

but it deviates from all other distributions in showing excessive frequencies of 3 and 4, rather than of 2 and 3. The percentage of highest ratings (scores of 5), while not always reaching the theoretically desirable 7 per cent, is higher than in the distribution of any other variable.

The shift in the distribution between Periods A and C has probably more than one cause. In the beginning we were impressed with the high motivation of our candidates as compared with that of the general population, and consequently gave them high ratings. The fact that in Period B the variable was made to include the Energy and Initiative factor as well as Motivation for Assignment may have had something to do with the changes from Periods A to B. Other changes in the rating procedure instituted at the beginning of Period B, most notably the use of the scoreboard in the conference room, may also have played a role in producing a shift from the extreme toward the middle ratings. On the other hand, the fact that the shift continues beyond the point of introduction of new procedures suggests the possibility that to a certain extent the shift reflects actual changes in the assessed population. In Period A, 58 per cent of the assessed personnel were civilians, as compared to 41 per cent in Periods B and C, 26 per cent in D, and only 14 per cent in Period G. One may assume that with the exception of people recruited for unusually hazardous operations, volunteering from the civilian status was indicative of greater motivation than volunteering from the Army or Navy, since a large proportion of the military personnel expected to be sent overseas anyhow and had little reason to suppose that the OSS was much more desirable than the unit from which they had been transferred. Actually in Periods A and B—but only in these—civilians received a higher percentage of high ratings (4, 5) than did the service men. Furthermore, it appears plausible that among both civilians and Army personnel those who were most eager for an OSS assignment overseas would be among the first to volunteer or among the first, at least, to attract the attention of the organization. One specific factor was the presence in the earlier groups of a large number of *émigrés* who were very articulate in expressing their eagerness to participate in the war against Fascism. This group dropped out toward the end of the European campaign. Then too, with the progressive depletion of man power in the United States, the amount of spontaneous active volunteering seems to have decreased relative to the amount of passive acquiescence in response to recruitment. But whatever the factors involved in the shift of ratings, they either stopped operating after the first twelve hundred candidates had passed through S, or were counterbalanced by other factors. The distribution of ratings from Period C on shows only random fluctuations. As an additional check, in a special study of motivation which included all classes between December 4, 1944, and May 6, 1945, the interviewers' estimates of the strength of the candidate's desire for his assignment, couched in descriptive terms rather than in numerical ratings, show no systematic variation through the period: 55 per cent of the 482 candidates assessed during this period definitely wanted the proposed assignment, and an additional 27 per cent were sincerely enthusiastic about it, willing to make essential sacrifices in order to obtain it. About 15 per cent were neutral, or hesitant though still willing to accept it. Only a negligible percentage definitely did not want the assignment offered to them.

These facts help us to understand the reasons for the skewness of the distribution that persisted throughout. The fact is that in the case of Motivation, although we did compare the candidates with each other, our attempts to distribute our ratings were not very determined and persistent. In the beginning we felt the average motivation of our volunteer population to be high in comparison with that of the total adult population of the country, and scored it as such. In addition, it is quite likely that the semantic factor involved both in the verbal and in the numerical designations of the steps of our rating scale was of particular significance in the case of Motivation. While it seemed reasonable to rate as zero the emotional stability of a person who had suffered a severe breakdown, or the social relations of a person who had managed to antagonize all his colleagues and the staff, it did not seem reasonable to rate as zero, or even as 1, the motivation of a candidate who truly wanted an assignment, even though he was less enthusiastic than the majority. Had our scale started with 1 as the lowest score, or had all steps been designated by letters, our ratings might have been distributed somewhat more normally. However, after having discovered and discussed the skewness of the distribution of ratings we refrained from any attempts to correct it, and for good reasons. High motivation for an assignment was considered a prerequisite for placement by the administrative officers and was used as one criterion of selection in recruitment. In view of the difficulties that we as psychologists had in adhering to the normal curve in our ratings, it seemed futile to try to impress the administrative officers with the fact that a candidate who had been selected from among others because of his special interest in an assignment might obtain a low average score on motivation merely because he was now being compared to a large number of very zestful individuals. Since our whole rating procedure was intended, among other things, to facilitate communication with the branch administrative officers, we acted in accordance with our aims when we permitted the "high" motivation of our candidates to remain high in our ratings.

Types of Motives.—In the rating of the variable Motivation for Assignment various aspects of it had to be taken into consideration. The motivation had to be strong and durable: only sustained motives, well integrated with the person's prevalent needs and attitudes, and not undermined by opposite tendencies, could be relied upon to ensure his persistent effort in the face of dangers, discomforts, frustrations, and boredom. If, as frequently happened, the person selected for a particular job upon arrival in the theater found this job superannuated, he had either to make the best of the totally different work given to him, or to create a job for himself that would be more than a mere makeshift. Strong motivation was necessary to prevent people from turning bitter or cynical under such frustrations. However, strength and persistence of motivation were not enough: its quality had also to be considered. The particular natures of the person's motives were significant; they might make him disregard orders and over-all plans, or break security regulations, or involve him in difficulties with his co-workers or superiors, thus diminishing his usefulness, or even endowing him with a distinct nuisance value. Reports from the field cited instances of people whose qualifications could not be fully used or even used at all, because the nature of their motivation made them security risks, or disruptive influences in their unit, or "problem children" who had to be handled with care. On the other hand, the motivation of some men was of such a nature that it not only ensured their own maximum performance, but was a powerful morale factor which raised the efficiency of the group to which they belonged.

The rating of Motivation for Assignment was left almost entirely in the hands of the interviewer. Some additional information was obtained by another staff member in the course of the Post-Stress Interview, but it was often not particularly clear cut, and was superficial at best. Only in a relatively small percentage of cases did the Post-Stress yield valuable evidence of the candidate's high or low motivation. The ratings of motivation given in this situation correlated .49 (in Period G) with the interviewer's ratings. In case of disagreement they were not given very much consideration: the final ratings of Motivation for Assignment correlated .97 with the interviewer's ratings and only 53 with those given in Post-Stress. Some information on the candidate's war morale as a factor in his motivation was obtained from the sentiments he expressed in Discussion and Debate, but these data appeared significant only in a small proportion of cases.

The interviewers, being left almost the sole judges of the candidate's motivation for assignment, made a point of obtaining as clear and detailed a picture of it as they could. Since this topic was closely related to the candidate's goals in undergoing assessment and was not so personal as to be upsetting, it was frequently used as an opening for the Interview. After asking the candidate how he happened to get in touch with the organization and what he knew about the assignment contemplated for him, it was natural for the interviewer to ask which aspects of the assignment appealed to him and which were less satisfactory, why he had decided to accept it, if he had, and what he stood to gain and to lose by it. Some interviewers pointed out to the candidate that here was an opportunity for him to discuss his misgivings and to weigh once more all pros and cons in order to arrive at a well-founded and satisfying decision. The explicit discussion of the candidate's motives was not the only source from which the interviewer derived pertinent information; the discussion of his past history particularly in relation to work, of his emotional attitudes and opinions, of his postwar plans, often provided clues about the nature of his motivation in general which were helpful in evaluating the specific reasons given by him for wanting his proposed assignment. Within this general frame of procedure the techniques used to elicit information varied from interviewer to interviewer, as did also the frames of reference used in evaluating the strength, reliability, and effectiveness of different motives.

Motivation for Assignment had rather low correlations with other variables, as shown in Table 3. These data are available only for Period G because in earlier periods (B through F) Energy and Initiative was included with it as a composite variable.

Because of the great importance of the problem of motivation it seemed desirable to make a systematic study of the information obtained in the interviews as well as of the interviewers' criteria of evaluation. Therefore for a period of five months (December 4, 1944, to May 6, 1945) a careful record was kept of the reasons given by each candidate for wanting his assignment and of all misgivings that were admitted. It was hoped that in addition to determining the proper criteria of evaluation of the different kinds of motives, the study would also, by tabulating the conscious reasons for voluntary participation in the war effort, contribute to the general problem of "drives toward war."

TABLE 3

Correlations between Motivation for Assignment and Other Variables
(Period G)

Social Relations	.45	Security	.23
Energy and Initiative	.44	Effective Intelligence	.22
Emotional Stability	.43	Physical Ability	.22
Leadership	.36	Observing & Reporting	.18
Propaganda Skills	.35		

The study was conducted by means of a check list which included all motives for wanting an assignment which interviewers remembered as having been given by the candidates who up to that time had passed through S, as well as all misgivings expressed by them. The form also included a list of statements in terms of which the interviewer could indicate the strength of the candidate's desire for the assignment, the nature of his first contact with the organization, and the extent of his orientation about his assignment. The interviewers were asked not to change their usual procedure but merely to check the lists immediately afterward, indicating, on the basis of memory and notes, what motives and misgivings had been elicited during the discussion of the candidate's motivation. They were also at liberty to check motives which were not explicitly formulated by the interviewees, but which could be deduced with a fair amount of certainty from what they had said. If several motives were mentioned by the candidates, the interviewers were asked to double-check one or more motives that appeared to be of primary importance. Multiple motives were admitted in 77 per cent of all cases. The following form was used:

MOTIVATION FOR ASSIGNMENT OVERSEAS

Check List

Student Name_____Class S_____Interviewer_____

Please check the items that fit the candidate's case. Check *all* motives and misgivings that were revealed in the interview, double-checking those that appear to be of primary importance for the student. (Motives listed under D21-31 are not likely to be primary motives.) If the student mentioned a motive that is not listed, check items D32, 33, or E20, respectively, and explain under "Comments."

Any other comments, including characteristic phrases used by the student in describing his motivation, impressions as to the genuineness of the motives given, or guesses at real motives, should be recorded. Try to get the student to name specific motives, not merely state that he wants to participate in the war effort.

A. *GENERAL ATTITUDE:*

1. Does not want to go.
2. No desire but accepts.
3. Neutral attitude (no objections).
4. Ambivalent attitude.
5. Definitely wants assignment.
6. Enthusiastic about going.
7. Ready to make substantial sacrifices.

B. *CONTACT WITH OSS:*

1. Actively approached OSS.
2. Recruited from civilian life.
3. Recruited from one of the services.
4. Ordered to report.

C. *ORIENTATION ABOUT ASSIGNMENT:*

1. Has fairly clear idea of assignment.
2. Has only vague idea of assignment.
3. Hardly any idea of assignment.

D. *REASONS FOR WANTING AN ASSIGNMENT:*

1. To have the job done (get the war over with).
2. Patriotic (do something for my country).
3. Fight for democracy or peace.
4. Fight against Nazism, anti-Semitism.
5. Fight Germany, Japan (hatred of).
6. Personal revenge.
7. Prestige, social recognition (by own children or others).
8. Sense of duty, conscience.
9. To test and prove oneself.
10. Personal development (attain maturity, independence).
11. Participation (in common experience, in significant events of the time).
12. Broadening experiences (travel, etc.).
13. Excitement, adventure.
14. Professional experience, career.
15. Desire for particular type of work (e.g., active assignment, leadership).
16. Desire for work in given country.
17. Financial betterment.
18. Escape from undesirable work.
19. Escape from more dangerous assignment.
20. Escape from personal problems.

Personal qualifications for work:
21. Ability for responsible, independent, organizational work; leadership.
22. Possession of particular skills, knowledge, experience.
23. Knowledge of country, language, natives.
24. Good health, strength.
25. Lack of fear, worries.
26. Freedom from obligations.

Good reputation of OSS:
27. Efficiency.
28. Scope for ability.
29. Less hierarchical organization, discipline.
30. Better class of people.

31. War ends soon.

32. Other personal motives.
33. Other social motives.
34. Other motives related to OSS.

E. *MISGIVINGS ABOUT ASSIGNMENT:*
1. Fear of danger, mutilation, death.
2. Separation from family.
3. Giving up of work, career, security.
4. Giving up of comforts, routine.
5. Obligations—personal and work.
6. Religious, ethical misgivings.
7. Misgivings about war aims and results (lasting peace, etc.).
8. Fear of not being able to "face it."
9. Fear of not being able to do the work (lack of skill, etc.).
10. Misgivings about health.
11. Fear of loss of prestige.
12. Fear of subordinate position.
13. Fear of inadequate leadership.
14. Fear of routine, not worth while, ineffective work.
15. Fear of waiting and idleness.
16. Preference for a different type of work.
17. Preference for a different war theater.
18. Desire to know more about assignment.
19. Lack of confidence in OSS. (Reason?)
20. Other misgivings.

F. *COMMENTS:*

Examination of the check list shows that not all reasons listed were likely to be equivalent with regard to their potential motivating power in seeking an assignment. That those listed under the subheadings Personal Qualifications for Work and Good Reputation of OSS were by their nature subsidiary motives, or complements of other motives, is borne out by the fact that items listed under these headings occurred proportionately less frequently among the estimated main motives than among all motives checked (11 per cent and 27 per cent, respectively).

Apart from this rough division of motives according to whether or not they are likely to function as main motives, they can be grouped in various equally meaningful ways. We shall not attempt any fixed groupings, but in taking up different aspects of the topic shall group the motives in a manner that seems best suited for the discussion of each set of results.

We shall first consider the incidence of different motives in the total group studied. This group consisted of 503 unselected candidates, all men, 43 per cent of them officers, 37 per cent enlisted men, and 20 per cent civilians; 57 per cent were under 30 years of age, 30 per cent between 30 and 40, and 13 per cent over 40. The destination of the overwhelming majority was FETO. All motives elicited from this group are listed in Table 4, in order of frequency of their occurrence; the incidence of motives is given in percentages both of the total number of subjects (representing proportions of candidates naming each motive), and of the total number of motives checked by the whole group. The third column gives the percentage frequency with which the given item was checked as one of the main motives in relation to all other motives that were so checked. The rest of this section consists of a discussion of the data of this table.

The most frequent single avowed motive was the desire for an opportunity to do some particular type of work which, the candidate hoped, the assignment would provide. More than a third of all subjects mentioned this motive; among the main motives checked, its frequency was 16 per cent. This category includes specific wishes, such as the desire of a trained pilot to continue flying, the desire of an anthropologist to collect new material in the field, or the wish of a man who had received specialized training in the Army to apply his knowledge of languages, of intelligence work, or of demolitions. On the other hand, the work desired was often described in a more general way: active outdoor work, or desk work, or interesting, intellectual, stimulating work, and, perhaps most frequently, work that is described as important and worth while and provides opportunities for responsibility, initiative, and leadership, as well as for full utilization of knowledge and abilities. The following statement is representative of many: "In nothing else could I use so much of what I have; the work is interesting and important, and it fits exactly into my civilian and Army background—it is a tie-up all the way through."

TABLE 4

Incidence of Different Motives in 503 Candidates

Motive No.	Motive	Percentage of subjects for whom motive was checked $(N=503)^a$	Percentage of checks given to each motive $(N=2209)$	Percentage of "main motive" checks given to each motive $(N=459)$
15	Particular work	36.4%	8.3%	16.1%
1	Get job done	30.2	6.9	8.9
8	Sense of duty	29.2	6.6	8.7 .
2	Patriotism	27.8	6.3	9.8
22	Possession of skills	27.8^b	6.3^b	5.7^b
12	Broadening experience, travel	22.9	5.2	4.4
18	Escape from unwanted work	22.9	5.2	5.7
13	Excitement, adventure	19.3	4.4	4.1
28	Scope of ability in OSS	18.9^b	4.3^b	0.9^b
11	Participation	18.1	4.1	4.6
14	Professional experience, career	17.3	3.9	4.4
32	Personal motives, miscellaneous	16.7	3.8	3.5
23	Knowledge of country, language	16.7^b	3.8^b	1.5^b
7	Prestige, recognition	14.1	3.2	3.3
16	Work in particular country	12.7	2.9	2.6
24	Good health	12.1^b	2.8^b	0.6^b
3	Fight for democracy	11.3	2.6	2.4
21	Ability for responsible work	10.1^b	2.3^b	1.1^b
4	Fight Nazism	7.9	1.8	2.4
27	Efficiency of OSS	7.9^b	1.8^b	—^{b}
29	Less hierarchy in OSS	7.0^b	1.6^b	0.2^b
25	Lack of fear	7.0^b	1.6^b	0.4^b
9	Test oneself	6.4	1.4	1.5
5	Fight Germany, Japan	6.2	1.4	1.3
10	Personal development	5.8	1.3	1.5
30	Better people in OSS	4.8^b	1.1^b	0.4^b
17	Financial betterment	4.0	0.9	2.0
26	Freedom from obligations	3.6^b	0.8^b	—^{b}
20	Escape from personal problem	3.4	0.8	0.4
19	Escape from more dangerous work	3.2	0.7	0.6
6	Personarl evenge	2.8	0.6	0.2
33	Social motives, miscellaneous	2.0	0.4	0.4
34	Other motives related to OSS	1.8^b	0.5^b	0.2^b
31	War ends soon	1.0^b	0.4^b	—^{b}

[a] The figures in the first column add to more than 100% because the same subjects appear in different categories.

[b] Motives falling in the category of "Subsidiary" (Motives Nos. 21—31 and No. 34)

Depending on the special nature of the activity and on the meaning it has for the person, the desire for a particular kind of work may express widely differing needs in different persons. One can occasionally guess at these needs from the remarks of the candidate as set down by the interviewer. Thus the man who voices an urgent wish "to work at full capacity and do a really good, well-planned job, not the trifling ineffectual sort of thing we did in the Army," expresses needs that differ from those of one who confides that he is after "a not too strenuous job," and probably also from those of one who wants to be given "important work" because he feels he "can do it better than most others." However, such revealing comments are rare in the records, and because of its lack of differentiation the work-motive category remains psychologically somewhat ambiguous. This ambiguity, however, does not invalidate the fact that a large proportion of our candidates were motivated for their assignment by wishes which are integral in their peacetime pursuits and which lack any reference to the war as such. Closely related in content to the motive under discussion (No. 15) are the following: the desire for professional experience and advancement (No. 14) ("If I don't advance in the Army along the line of newspaper work, it will be a strike against me later."); the wish to escape from undesirable work (No. 18); and the subsidiary motives referring to the possession of ability, knowledge, and skill (Nos. 21, 22, 23) and to the efficiency and scope of the OSS (Nos. 27, 28). If one adds the percentages for all these items listed in Table 4, around 36 per cent of all motives given are found to be related to the work aspect of the assignment and the same proportion holds for the main motives. Whatever individual needs—achievement, recognition, or others—were served by the proposed work, except in the rare cases of persons who specifically desire hazardous duty, these needs were not satisfied by any situations specific to the armed struggle and its objectives or by any activities intrinsically connected with it. Since no particular premium is placed on such personal wishes by public opinion in wartime, we have no cause to suspect the veracity of our subjects in giving these reasons for their desire to join the organization.

The motive next most often given was the one (No. 1) that has become familiar to us from the journalistic descriptions of the attitudes of American soldiers toward the war: the wish to have the job done, to get the war over with, frequently with the implied or explicit addition—so that normal life can be resumed, expressed variously as: "Anything I can do to get it over with soon, naturally I want to do it." "Of course I would rather go home, but the job is not done." "We have to get the war over with and come back to normal life again." Unpretentious as these formulations are, they probably represent for our group of volunteers the main channel of expression of socially oriented motivation. For these men the job to be done was felt as a common task, a situation to be cleared up in common, which concerned them as a matter of course, because of their belongingness with others, regardless of whether or not the war had affected them as individuals. Closely related to this most typical sociocentric motive was the less frequently expressed desire for participation in the common experience and common fate (No. 11). This desire was expressed with particular intensity not by men who were secure in their feeling of belongingness, but rather by those who felt isolated and who struggled to bridge the gap between themselves and others; thus in some extreme cases this motive may represent a lack rather than a secure possession of social bonds, but it is still predominantly social in its orientation; it is similar to the occasionally expressed wish to remain with a group of people of which one has become a member (No. 33).

Other sociocentric motives which occurred almost as frequently as the desire "to have the job done" were those of duty and patriotism (Nos. 8, 2). The expressions of the latter varied from a simple mention of the motive ("I guess I am as patriotic as the next guy") and of a wish "to do something for my country" to occasional use of patriotic stereotypes and formulations that invoke the family tradition of serving the state. The explicit formulations seemed to be more typical of immigrants and of missionaries. In some cases patriotic sentiments went hand in hand with more concrete expressions of identification with a group: "As an American I feel great obligations to my country. I hate to see our boys there in China without the information I could give them." In many cases the patriotic motive was almost indistinguishable from the desire to help do the job, the only difference being the more explicit reference to the social organism —country—that is faced with the job.

The motive based on the sense of duty is here considered as a sociocentric one only for the sake of rough grouping, since in this case the participation in a common task or fate serves the purpose of maintaining individual standards of behavior, with personal conscience as their sanction: "I could not live with myself if I would not join." "My conscience does not allow me to stay in this place in safety." Often, however, the duty motive appeared in a milder, less extreme form which permitted an integration with other social motives: "Within the Army a fellow has not done his part if he has not been overseas." "I feel it is my turn now to relieve others."

One conspicuous finding, and one that has been repeatedly made in studies of wartime attitudes, was the rarity of motives based on specific ideology. Only 11 per cent of our subjects mentioned the fight for democracy or peace as one of their goals, as contrasted with the 30 per cent who merely wanted "to do the job," without specifying its ultimate meaning. Among the items checked as main motives, 23 per cent were found in the relatively unspecific categories of "job done," "participation," and "patriotism," and less than 5 per cent in those of "fight for democracy," or "fight against Nazism" (Nos. 3, 4). It is, of course, conceivable that the incidence of ideological motives was higher among earlier groups of candidates assessed for the European campaign. Still less frequent were motives that represented expressions of aggression, without so much ideological foundation, such as hatred of the Germans or of the Japanese (No. 5) and a desire for personal revenge for wrongs or losses suffered (No. 6).

If the percentages listed in Table 4 for the predominantly sociocentric motives discussed above, including duty, ideology, and group aggression are added, it is found that they form 30 per cent of all motives checked, and 38 per cent of the main motives. Thus motives centered around the war as a situation of common concern were no more prominent in the group studied than motives related to individual achievement in work.

The remaining categories cover personal egocentric motives other than those concerned with work. They express various needs of the person which can be satisfied by some aspects of the war situation, but like work motives they have little inherent connection with the nature and purpose of war. The most frequent among them was the desire for travel and for broadening experience in general (No. 12) which was mentioned by 23 per cent of our subjects. The wartime work was seen by them as a welcome opportunity to extend their horizon and to see the world: "There was never a cheaper trip." Closely related to this motive was the almost equally frequent desire for excitement and adventure (No. 13): "There is also a little glamour that goes with secret work; I always loved detective stories." Much less frequent were the motives which explicitly stress the theme of personal development which is at times implied in the wish for broadening experience: the desire to progress in the direction of maturity, manliness, courage, independence or to test and prove one's attainments in these spheres (Nos. 9 and 10). "Such an experience helps one to find oneself." The subsidiary motive referring to a great freedom from regulations in OSS (No. 29) often had similar connotations. All together the motives having to do with gaining enriching experiences listed above formed 12 to 13 per cent of all motives checked, as well as of the main motives.

The motive of prestige, of social recognition to be obtained from an assignment overseas (No. 7), was checked for only 14 per cent of all candidates, and more frequently than in the case of other motives it was checked as merely inferred by the interviewer. From this, as well as from the apologetic remarks frequently accompanying the expression of this motive ("I know it is mainly selfish"), one may suspect that it was present more frequently than admitted. When explicitly formulated, the need for prestige was often expressed in reference to one's family or children, or to one's friends and colleagues. "My family will be proud of me"; "I want to be able to tell my children and grandchildren that I did not sit here during the war"; "My friends are all officers now, scattered all over the world; when they come back they ask you, where have *you* been?" "I spent the last war in this country, while others went abroad; I am ashamed not to have ribbons on my Marine uniform." The desire to join the organization because of the "better class of people" one would meet in it (No. 30) is closely related to the motive of prestige and status.

The desire for financial betterment, for material gains expected from joining the organization (No. 17) was stated, or inferred, in only 4 per cent of all cases. Although this motive may not always have been freely admitted, the impression was that when present, but not mentioned, it was more often a contributing than a determining factor of motivation. There were very few men whose particular and rather exceptional circumstances made them consider the assignment as a way of tiding them over the war, or as a means of solving their financial problems. More often, perhaps, the reputation of the organization as having high priorities and giving people good breaks was one of the inducements to join for the enlisted men: "If you want anything in the FETO—whiskey, steaks—go to the OSS."

While the egocentric motives so far discussed seem on the whole to represent strivings for positively defined personal goals, one small but conspicuous group of motives was characterized by the direction away from some negative state: escape from what was thought to be a more dangerous assignment in the Army (No. 19), or escape from personal problems, such as a difficult marital or vocational situation, or other unsolved conflicts (No. 20). The much more frequent motive of escaping undesirable work (No. 18) can also be put into this category of negative, "egressive" motives, although in some cases the negative formulation seemed to be merely verbal, the freely expressed desire to escape a monotonous unproductive job in the Army being merely a counterpart of the positive motives related to work.

Motives listed under Other Personal Motives (No. 32) consisted largely of specialized personal wishes that do not fit into any of the other categories. They can also be considered as egocentric. All egocentric motives not referring to work, taken together, form 25 per cent of all motives checked, and 22 per cent of the main motives. The 25 per cent for egocentric motives is to be compared with 36 per cent for motives related to work, and 30 per cent for sociocentric motives. The remainder consists of motives, mostly subsidiary, with no clear-cut general connotations, such as desire to work in a particular country, and the possession of qualifications not clearly related to specific goals, such as health, lack of fear, and freedom from obligations.

In summary, the outstanding finding is the extreme infrequency in the group studied of the ideological motives, and the relative infrequency of all motives directly connected with the war and its expected outcome (Nos. 1–5). Only 25 per cent of all motives checked as main motives fall into these categories. Forty-eight per cent of our candidates did not mention any of them, not even as contributing motives. On the other hand, the percentage of those who did not mention any motive related to work is merely 21 per cent. For a group of volunteers whom, by comparison with the total population, we considered to be highly motivated for participation in the war effort, this is a striking result. It would seem that many people in the United States are drawn into modern war mainly because it offers

TABLE 5

Incidence of Main Groups of Motives

	Percentage of all motives checked (N=2209)	Percentage of all "main motives" (N=459)
Work motives	36	36
Sociocentric motives	30	38
Egocentric motives	25	22
Others	9	4

them a chance to do effective work in their own field, using their skills and abilities, seeing immediate results, and advancing along their professional lines, i.e., for reasons that have little to do either with aggression or with any group ideologies.

The purposes and so the composition of the OSS provide a partial explanation of the high frequency of the work motives. The OSS recruited hundreds of trained specialists. Our population of candidates therefore contained a much larger percentage of professional workers than the United States census population, and at the time of our study it was composed largely of military personnel.[1] The candidates had been presumably selected from the more active and ambitious, and the combination of their professional aspirations with the frequent situation of finding themselves in a routine job in the Army may have enhanced their desire for more adequate placement. However, in so far as the disruption and delay in the carrying out of personal plans, often at a period of life crucial for their inception, are typical for the situation of the majority of draftees, our findings are probably fairly representative of the American age group that was called upon to bare the brunt of this war.

The limitations of our data may also have influenced our findings about the incidence of various motives. The interviewer did not, as a rule, systematically inquire after all possible motives; some of them checked, on the average, more motives per candidate than did others. Our method, while it had the advantage of not suggesting answers to the subjects, may well have been responsible for overlooking some of the motives which the

[1] For a detailed description of the assessed population see Appendix A–1, pages 498–501.

candidates may have taken for granted, such as patriotism or the simple desire to "have the job done and over with." Furthermore, the psychological ambiguity of the work motives makes it a likely vehicle of such unexpressed motives, and some of the remarks that were noted indicate that this was sometimes the case. Thus the desire to work at full capacity was occasionally related to a wish to be most useful or to make a worth-while contribution, and these expressions suggest a closer relation to the war situation than was inherent in the work motives as such. It is even conceivable that some of the candidates refrained from mentioning any but individualistic motives out of the feeling that any avowal of patriotism or of loyalty to an institution might be regarded as indicative of sentimentality, stupidity, or hypocrisy. In spite of all these qualifications the data still seem to warrant the conclusion, or at least a fair guess, that very many people volunteered for OSS work primarily because of their interest in a special job, rather than because of their interest in "the job to be done": a finding which reflects the cultural sanctioning of the individualistic sentiments that has been for some time prevalent in the United States.

Evaluation of Motives.—The question that is of importance for assessment is the relative value of the different motives described above for ensuring an optimal performance in an overseas assignment. A decisive answer to this question could be given only on the basis of dependable reports about the motivation on the job and the performance overseas of the candidates whose motives had been adequately ascertained during assessment. Unfortunately, such reports were available for only a small percentage of the subjects of the special study, and, like our appraisal material in general (cf. Chapter IX), they were far from complete and reliable. We can make little use of these appraisal data but can approach the problem only indirectly, by trying to find connections between various types of motivation and various desirable and undesirable characteristics of candidates revealed in assessment and expressed in the ratings of variables. The fields in which such relationships may be expected to be found are emotional stability and social relations, since they represent significant aspects of the dynamisms involved in the formation of the concrete motives of a person. We therefore compared the motives of the candidates who received high scores (4, 5) on the final rating of each of these two variables with the motives of those who received low scores (0, 1). In addition, and by way of a check, we made this comparison also for candidates of high and low intelligence—the general variable which is assumed to be relatively independent of individual dynamics.

As a point of comparison we used the frequency of occurrence of the various single motives included in the check list, as well as of groups of motives of similar nature. These frequencies were computed for each high and low group and expressed in terms of percentage of the total number of motives checked for each group. The significance of the differences was tested by means of the critical ratio.

EMOTIONAL STABILITY.—We shall first compare the groups characterized by high and low Emotional Stability. Table 6 gives for these two groups the incidence of motives classified as described above. There are 92 subjects in the high group and 65 in the low. N refers in this, as in subsequent tables, not to the number of subjects, but to the number of all motives checked for each group.

Motives related to work, taken together, occur with about equal frequency in the high and the low group, and the same is true of several single items of this complex of motives, such as desire for particular work, desire for professional advancement, and desire for assignment based on possession of special skills or knowledge. On the other hand, the wish to escape from undesirable work is four times more frequent in the unstable group, and the desire for assignment justified by possession of ability and leadership is four times more frequent in the stable group. The other differences with regard to single items are not statistically significant, but the stable group tends to value more highly the efficiency of the organization and the scope for initiative it affords the individual, motives closely related to the feeling of having something to offer.

TABLE 6

Incidence of Different Motives in Groups of
High and Low Emotional Stability

	High Emotional Stability (4,5) (N=490)	Low Emotional Stability (0,1) (N=248)	CR
Motives related to work........	34.1%	35.7%	—
Sociocentric motives............	35.4	29.0	1.8
Egocentric motives.............	19.6	30.0	3.0
Other motives.................	10.9	5.3	—

The complex of sociocentric motives differentiates slightly between the two groups in favor of the emotionally stable men. There is no difference between the groups in the most frequent single motive—the wish to "have the job done." There are, however, differences which are significant at the 5 per cent level in the ideological motive to fight for democracy and in the desire for participation, both of which are more frequent in the stable group, as is also the motive of patriotism. The motive of duty, on the other hand, which cannot be considered as a sociocentric motive in the same sense as the others, is more frequent in the unstable group. If this motive is excluded from the sociocentric complex of motives, the critical ratio of the difference between the two groups rises to 2.7.

The motives that discriminate most clearly between the stable and the unstable subjects are the egocentric ones. They are present significantly more frequently in the low group than in the high. Unlike the first two categories, this complex of motives has a greater differentiating power than does any of its single items. The only two of them that yield differences approaching statistical significance are the desire to test and prove oneself and the category Other Personal Motives, both of which are more frequent in the unstable group. To a lesser extent the same is true of the motives of prestige, financial gain, and the wish to escape from danger and from personal problems. Of eleven items making up the egocentric complex of motives, only the desire for adventure and the hope of obtaining a greater freedom from regulations in the OSS have a greater frequency in the stable group.

Although the complexes into which we have arbitrarily divided the motives do differentiate between the groups of subjects of different emotional stability to a certain extent, the fact that some of the single items in two of these complexes are much more diagnostic than the complexes themselves suggests that this classification is not the most pertinent one for emotional stability. In particular the motive of duty shows a direction of discrimination different from the rest of the social motives, and within the other two complexes, motives concerned with the possession of abilities and with desire for adventure also show a different direction of discrimination from those concerned with career, prestige, finances, and escape. In addition, the three subsidiary motives, not included in any category—possession of health, freedom from fear, and freedom from obligations—are more prevalent in the stable group, the differences being statistically significant for the first two items. All of these observations suggest a reclustering of the egocentric motives, including some of the work motives, into (i) the expansive motives, reflecting self-confidence, and into (ii) those that can be interpreted as concerned mainly with security, regardless of whether they stress escape, or striving for self-respect, or striving for status based on prestige and money. Table 7 gives the incidence of the motives thus reclustered in the groups of high and low emotional stability. The only motives from the original complexes that have not been included in this new classification are some of the work motives, the psychological nature of which is not clear: these include the desire for particular work, the wish to use particular skills, or to work in a particular country, as well as the category of Other Personal Motives.[2]

---

[2] The first two of these motives occur with equal frequency in the two groups, while the two motives related to working in a particular country (Nos. 16, 23) are more frequent in the unstable group, as are also Other Personal Motives.

The table shows that motives related to escape, self-respect, and status, taken in their totality, are diagnostic of the group of low emotional stability, whereas motives aiming at activity and new experience, and reflecting a self-confident feeling of ability and well-being are typical for the group of high emotional stability. The subgroups that have the greatest differentiating

TABLE 7

Incidence of Reclassified Motives in Groups of
High and Low Emotional Stability

	High Emotional Stability (4,5) (N=490)	Low Emotional Stability (0,1) (N=248)	CR
Ability motives (Nos. 21, 27, 28).......12.6%		5.6	3.3
Positive self-feeling (Nos. 24, 25, 26).... 7.3		1.2	4.3
Expansive motives (Nos. 10, 12, 13, 29)..12.5		9.6	1.2
All motives expressing self-confidence............32.4%		16.4%	5.2
Escape motives (Nos. 18, 19, 20)....... 2.6%	12.5%		4.5
Status motives (Nos. 7, 14, 17, 30)...... 5.8	11.2		2.4
Self-respect motives (Nos. 8, 9)......... 7.5	12.1		1.9
All motives expressing insecurity.................15.9%		35.8%	5.7
Sociocentric motives (Nos. 1–5, 33)..............28.9		20.1	2.7
Aggressive motives (Nos. 5, 6)................. 2.6		0.8	1.9
All other motives...........................20.1		26.9	

power are those concerned with escape and with the positive self-feeling. This self-confident feeling of the emotionally stable group often results in motives that are relatively unspecific, as compared with the many clearly defined single goals of the emotionally unstable, such as prestige, financial gain, escape from concrete situations, or desire to work in a particular country. As one subject put it: "I don't know myself exactly why [I want the assignment]: perhaps one might call it adventure. It is just that I am young and active and like to see things done." In this connection it is interesting to note that the misgivings sometimes felt by the staff about the emotional stability of people expressing the desire for adventure are not confirmed by our data. The adventure motive proved more typical of the group of high emotional stability than did either of the two related but more "self-conscious" motives: the desire for broadening experience and the desire for personal development. These latter are the only two items among the reclustered motives that show no appreciable difference for the two groups of subjects.

As was mentioned before, the possession of genuine sociocentric motives is characteristic of the group of high emotional stability, although less so than the expression of self-confident attitudes.

In evaluating the significance of these findings one must consider the possible sources of error inherent in the fact that the same person—the interviewer—who checked off the specific motives of the candidate was also the main judge of his emotional stability as indicated by the final score. One might suspect that, according to his own conceptions of emotional stability, or of desirable motivation, he might almost unwittingly be inclined to view one set of data in the light of the other and to adjust them to each other, thus bringing about the relationships discussed above. On closer inspection, however, the possible extent of such adjustments appears negligible. In recording the motives the interviewers usually did no more than check off the items mentioned by the candidate; while they could, by dwelling on the topic of motivation, increase the number of motives named, they usually refrained from asking suggestive questions, and did very little guessing or interpreting, except in a small proportion of cases which were marked as inferences. Therefore the results recorded in the check list may be considered to be relatively independent of any opinions held by the interviewer about the candidate's emotional stability or any other of his characteristics. On the other hand, the interviewer's rating of emotional stability might have been influenced in some cases by the type of the motives revealed by the candidate, as, for instance, by the prevalence of escape motives. It must be remembered, however, that data pertaining to motives were only a small and by no means the crucial part of the evidence on the candidate's emotional stability, since a large amount of material on his past history, his emotional attitudes, and symptoms of maladjustment was at the disposal of the interviewer. Futhermore, except with regard to a few types of motives, such as escape motives, there were no preconceptions among the interviewers as to which motives were indicative of high and which of low emotional stability. For these reasons the ratings of emotional stability and the checks of specific motives are probably not dependent on each other to an appreciable extent. Thus we may assume with a fair degree of certainty that the relationships which were found to exist between them did not result from any technical artifact but reflect inherent dynamic interrelations.

SOCIAL RELATIONS.—Table 8 shows the incidence of the motives in the various categories already described among those candidates who received high and low final scores on Social Relations. There were 61 subjects in the high group and 58 in the low.

The greatest difference between the two groups of subjects was in the incidence of the sociocentric motives which, as might be expected, was higher in the group with high social relations. This difference, although not striking, is greater than the difference that was found to exist between the sociocentric motives of the groups characterized by high and low emotional stability. The greatest differences were found in the items referring to getting the job done, the fight for democracy, patriotism, and participating in the war. The motive of duty occurred with approximately equal frequency in both groups. If this motive is not included in the sociocentric complex, the differentiation of the two groups becomes even more marked. Work motives and egocentric motives are then slightly more frequent in the low group, the difference being most marked in the items referring to career, financial gain, and possession of skills. On the other hand, references to ability, health, and desire for adventure are more frequent in the high group. On the whole, however, the single items do not differentiate the two groups very clearly, nor do such differences as exist suggest any

TABLE 8

Incidence of Different Motives in Groups of
High and Low Social Relations

	High Social Relations (4,5) (N=325)	Low Social Relations (0,1) (N=244)	CR
Motives related to work........ ..	30.9%	38.4%	1.9
Sociocentric motives...........	36.7	26.1	2.7
Egocentric motives............	22.3	27.7	1.5
Other motives................ ..	10.1	7.8	—

principles for a more pertinent clustering of items. Complexes of motives that were found to differentiate between the subjects of high and low emotional stability yield no such clear-cut differences for the subjects with high and low social relations, although the "positive self-feeling" motives were more common in the high group, and the "status" motives in the low one. The incidence of sociocentric motives remains the one clear-cut differentiating characteristic. Since Social Relations was rated largely on the basis of situational tests, with the interviewer being only one of the raters, this relationship is not likely to be a result of any interpretations or biases of the examiners.

EFFECTIVE INTELLIGENCE.—Table 9 contains a comparison of the motives of candidates of high and low intelligence.

The groups of high and low intelligence do not differ at all with regard to the major complexes of motives. This finding would be in line with expectations if our definition of intelligence had been equivalent to the goodness and speed of the functions that operated in responding to an intelligence test, because intelligence so defined is relatively independent of personal dynamics. In the assessment program, however, we were attempting to determine not so much abstract test intelligence as the practical or effective intelligence which shows itself in successful dealings with all aspects of environment, including the social, and which can hardly be conceived of as an entity apart from the other aspects of personal adjustment. One might expect, therefore, that a more detailed examination of the motives of the groups characterized by high and low intelligence would reveal differences similar to those existing between the groups that were

TABLE 9

Incidence of Different Motives in Groups of High and Low Intelligence

	High Intelligence (4,5) (N=497)	Low Intelligence (0,1) (N=230)	CR
Motives related to work........	34.8%	34.4%	—
Sociocentric motives............	32.0	31.8	—
Egocentric motives.............	22.0	22.6	—
Motives related to ability, career, prestige...............	10.4	4.0	3.3
All other motives..............	0.8	7.2	—

high and low in Emotional Stability and in Social Relations. This is actually the case. The escape motives in particular, which provided the best single differentiation between groups varying in Emotional Stability, also differentiated significantly between the groups varying in intelligence, the group of low intelligence mentioning these motives twice as frequently as the group of high intelligence. The motive of duty was also somewhat more frequent in the less intelligent group, whereas motives pertaining to ability were more common among the more intelligent.

There was no difference between the intelligence groups, however, in regard to motives expressing positive self-feeling and expansive desires. The status motives differentiated between the groups in the direction opposite to that obtaining in the groups differing in Emotional Stability and Social Relations: the more intelligent men were more concerned with prestige and professional career (but not with finances) than those of lower intelligence. They were also slightly more involved in their work: if one excludes from the complex of work motives the desire to escape from undesirable work, which was less than half as frequent among the intelligent as among the less intelligent candidates, the work motives show a somewhat higher incidence in the case of the more intelligent group. The examination of single items of this complex reveals an interesting difference between two subsidiary motives. While the mention of the possession of abilities was typical of the intelligent subjects, the reference to particular skills, knowledge, and experience as a motive for wanting the assignment was somewhat more frequent among the less intelligent, although there is no reason to assume that the actual incidence of such qualifications was higher in this group. An analogous difference in the direction in which these two items differentiate between the high and the low groups was found also for groups differing in Social Relations, while for groups of high and low Emotional Stability, the skill motive—unlike the ability motive—failed to differentiate the two groups. This difference between the two motives is the more striking since they are closely related in content and were actually mentioned in the same breath by a number of candidates. Apparently, however, their connotations are not the same. While reference to ability to do responsible work reflects a confidence based on actual accomplishment, a readiness to handle new situations, and a feeling of being able to contribute to a common goal, the reference to possession of specific skills and knowledge seems to indicate a cautious clinging to acquired assets as means of compensating for felt inferiorities and of providing the person with an adequate niche. Thus an overemphasis on the possession of specific qualifications must often be considered as an expression of a person's insecurity and of his feeling of being able to contribute not because of what he is, but because of what he has.

The complex of sociocentric motives, if one excludes from it the motive of duty, occurs slightly more frequently in the more intelligent group, but not significantly so. The motive of participation is the only one that yields a significant difference. The ideological motives are slightly more common in the more intelligent group—the fight against Nazism more so than the protection of democracy—while patriotism is mentioned more frequently by those with lower intelligence.

In summary, the group with high intelligence was marked by motives concerned with ability, professional career, and prestige, as well as by the infrequency of the "escape from work" motive. The combination of the first three motives differentiates this group significantly from that of lower intelligence. For the rest, the intelligent group showed a slight tendency to favor the same motives that were found to be typical of people of high emotional stability and of high social relations.

We now have the data for a tentative answer to the question as to what motives and clusters of motives have a positive or a negative value as indicators of high or low emotional stability, good or bad social relations, high or low intelligence. Motives that are positive on two or on all three of these counts are the sociocentric motives, as well as the motives referring to ability and those expressing a strong positive self-feeling. Motives that are predominantly negative are the egocentric ones, particularly those that express escape wishes, and desire for status. Motives not included in these categories either do not differentiate at all between the high and the low ends of the various scales, or appear positive from one point of view and negative or neutral from another. Thus the desire to test and prove one-self is indicative of low emotional stability, but it is not infrequent among people with high social relations, and does not at all differentiate between varying degrees of intelligence. There is a general tendency, however, for the positive and negative motives to be positive and negative throughout. Whenever an exception to this rule is found it is the relationship to Emotional Stability that should be weighed heaviest, because as our results have shown, the various motives are related to this variable more significantly than to any of the others.

EVALUATION BY INTERVIEWERS.—The question arises whether the interviewers, in rating the candidates' Motivation for Assignment, placed on the various motives the differential values suggested by these findings, or whether they used different criteria of evaluation, each displaying his own personal bias. We can answer this question by comparing the motives of the candidates who were given high ratings on Motivation for Assignment with those who obtained low ratings. Most of the interviewers, on being questioned, agreed that the scores they gave did not refer merely or even mainly to the *strength* of desire for assignment as expressed by the candidate verbally or as demonstrated by his active efforts to obtain an assignment, but rather represented a judgment of the "goodness"—the soundness, effectiveness, and reliability—of his motivation as extended into the future. The ratings, therefore, must have been based largely on the types of motives revealed by the candidates, and consequently must reflect the interviewers' evaluations of these motives. In addition to this objective check, the interviewers were also asked for an explicit formulation of their criteria of evaluation of various motives. Since these opinions could not be obtained from all interviewers, and since they were collected in a rather unsystematic way, months after the completion of the assessment work, they will be used merely to elucidate, when possible, the statistical findings.

Table 10 contains a comparison of the groups rated as high and low in Motivation for Assignment in respect to the incidence of all motives or clusters of motives that were found to differentiate between the extremes of one or more of the three variables discussed above. Because of the skewness of the distribution of the scores on Motivation there are 144 subjects in the high group and only 35 in the low.

All clusters of motives listed discriminate between high and low Motivation in the same direction in which they discriminated between high and low Emotional Stability and high and low Social Relations, but more strikingly so. This indicates that the interviewers' evaluations of the various motives were congruent with the actually existing relationships, as far as we were able to ascertain them on the basis of the data obtained in assessment. There was, however, among the single motives one instance of discrepancy. The desire for work in a particular country appears to have been positively evaluated by the interviewers, probably because it was felt to increase the candidate's interest in his specific assignment: it was checked for none of the subjects whose Motivation was scored as low. However, for some undetermined reason or reasons, this motive was voiced somewhat more frequently by candidates who were rated low in Emotional Stability, Social Relations, and Intelligence than by those placed at the upper end of the scales. Apart from this one specific item, the only bias which is re-

TABLE 10

Incidence of Different Motives in Groups of
High and Low Motivation[a]

	High Motivation (4, 5) (N=770)	Low Motivation (0, 1) (N=108)	CR
Work motives	34.7%	42.5%	1.6
Sociocentric motives	32.0	17.4	3.6
Egocentric motives	21.8	37.8	3.3
Ability motives	10.4	4.6	2.5
Positive self-feeling	7.4	1.8	3.5
Expansive motives	13.4	11.1	—
Escape motives	4.3	14.8	3.0
Status motives	7.1	17.5	2.8
Self-respect (duty) motives	7.6	9.2	—
Ideological motives	5.9	0.9	4.0
Aggressive motives	3.5	0.9	2.3

[a] Since this table includes two different classifications, in some cases one motive may come under two headings.

flected in the interviewers' comments, and partly in the ratings which they gave, is the overvaluation of the ideological motives. Many of the interviewers, while recognizing the infrequency of this kind of motive, still felt that fighting for a cause, when based on a clear insight into the issues at stake, provided the most reliable motivation for war work, and deserved the highest score. They may have been right, but our material, though it places these motives in a positive category, contains no data that could confirm or disprove the high claims made for them. On the negative side there was a general agreement among the raters that escape motives were undesirable, being indicative of maladjustment, and that an exaggerated drive for credit and acclaim was a distinct danger. There was more disagreement on the rest of the egocentric motives. While some interviewers considered the desires for experience, adventure, and advancement as perfectly sound and acceptable, others held them in suspicion and pointed out that if the situation overseas did not come up to expectations in these respects, the candidate's motivation would collapse, unless it were supported by other less individualistic motives. With regard to the motive of duty there was no disagreement among the interviewers, but their evaluation itself was a qualified one. It was felt that the sense of duty provided an adequate motive "up to a point," that is, when it was not extreme and when it was accompanied by an appropriate amount of self-respect based on the man's proved ability to live up to his own standards; if expressed with great intensity by a person who had many unsolved personal conflicts, it was viewed as a sign of neurotic involvement and consequently rated down.

This qualified statement brings up a point which was emphasized by the majority of the interviewers questioned, and which serves to limit the validity of their own generalizations. In considering the value of various motives they felt that hardly any motive could be judged as good or bad in itself, and that each had to be evaluated in terms of its significance for the individual person and its appropriateness to his personality structure. Thus an enthusiastic desire for activity and adventure was felt by some to be appropriate to vigorous young men, but a suspicious sign in older and more experienced candidates. Similarly, it was felt that people of high intelligence and of good educational background should give more evidence of a rational or ideological foundation for their war morale than people without such advantages. Energy and Initiative, persistence, temperament, ambitious ideals, social feeling, group identification, and, most frequently, patterns of emotional attitudes,—these and many other factors were quoted by different interviewers as points to be considered in deciding how the specific motives of an individual candidate should be evaluated.

Care was taken to ascertain not only how deep the desire for an assignment went in a person, but also how wholehearted it was. For this purpose the interviewers tried to elicit all of the candidate's misgivings or counter-motives, and to determine their potential significance in creating an ambitendent attitude toward the assignment.[3] On the other hand, there was the question to consider as to whether different positive motives, when they coexist in one person, mutually strengthen or weaken each other. The interviewers were not questioned systematically as to whether they considered one strong motive as a better source of motivation than a multiplicity of motives, and from the few remarks gathered, it is doubtful whether they had any strong opinions on this subject. However, they checked a larger number of motives for subjects whom they rated high in Motivation than for those whom they

---

[3] The misgivings most frequently recorded by the interviewers were, in order of frequency, those related to separation from the family, fear of physical danger, fear of being given routine, not worth-while work, fear of not being able to do the job, uneasiness about giving up one's work or career, and misgivings about one's health.

rated low with sufficient consistency to make the difference between the mean numbers of motives checked (5.3–3.1) statistically significant beyond the 1 per cent level. This finding may indicate an implicit assumption that different motives can mutually support and strengthen each other. Finally, they thought that the type of assignment and the situations to be encountered had to be considered before the specific motivation of a candidate could be adequately evaluated.

In describing their methods of evaluating motivation, some, though not all, of the interviewers professed to make ample use of the general principles followed in assessment, in attempting to relate motivation to other significant aspects both of the candidate's personality and of the situations in which he was to be placed. To what extent they succeeded in carrying out this program it is hard to judge. By definition, Motivation for Assignment referred not to an enduring pattern of forces but to a relatively segregated system in the sequence of personal strivings; and as such it formed a specific, well-outlined topic of discussion in the interview. If data and time for an integration of this topic into the rest of the personality picture were lacking, one could take the easy way out and base one's rating and description of the candidate's motivation on his own report, taken as a relatively isolated datum. But even a most scrupulous attempt at a contextual evaluation of the revealed motives might fail to bridge a gap that could occur between motivation for *obtaining* the assignment (which was operating at the time of assessment) and motivation in the pursuit of other distal goals that would arise after this proximal goal had been attained.

REPORTS ON PERFORMANCE OVERSEAS.—As was mentioned earlier, we were unable to obtain appraisal data that would permit us to make a real test of our criteria for evaluating motivation. The best procedure would have been to compare reliable reports of each candidate's performance and degree of motivation in the theater with the conception of his motivation obtained during assessment. Such reports, however, are available only for 20 out of the 503 candidates whose motives were systematically checked, and several of these arrived in the theater too late to be able to do the job proposed for them. This group of 20 men were not well distributed in any respect: the lowest job rating was Low Average (2); the range of the overseas appraisals for Motivation was narrow, between 3 and 5. Thus it is impossible to obtain clear-cut results by comparing the incidence in each group of the various types of motives. It may be noted, however, that while none of the 12 persons who were given a high overseas rating (4 or 5) on Motivation had an escape or prestige motive checked at assessment, one or the other of these motives had been checked in 5 out of the 8 men whose Motivation was rated Average in the field.

In considering individual cases, we shall single out 7 persons who were rated high (4 or 5) overseas both on Motivation and on Job Performance. The data for forming a contrasting group are insufficient; none of the men was low in both Motivation and Job Performance, and the reports on the 13 average cases are for the most part incomplete or inconsistent.

Two of the 7 successful men present cases of strong social motivation based on a firm ideological foundation; both had given the necessity to "have the job done" as their main motive, and both related this necessity to patriotism and to the fight against antidemocratic forces. One of the two, in carrying out his specialized technical job, earned general recognition by his conscientious work, his eagerness to help others, and his general friendliness and good nature. The other, a person of expansive temperament, great drive, and idealistic enthusiasms, distinguished himself on dangerous intelligence missions, maintaining high morale over long periods spent under unusually difficult and stressful conditions. A third man, another good leader, described as highly energetic, direct, responsible, and respected by all, had given the desire to do novel and interesting work as his main reason for wanting the assignment, but this was supplemented by the socially oriented motive of participation. No ideological foundation was present in this case, but the strong social orientation reflected in all reports on this man is a characteristic he shares with the first two subjects.

The fourth man presents an exemplary case of sound and sustained motivation based primarily, if not solely, on a rational sense of duty developed in a well-integrated, self-confident personality. A successful technical administrator, this man was drafted for a specialized job. At S he had described his attitude as follows: "I knew that my background was useful and I did not see how I could *not* do it. I'm glad to be doing it. I have felt for some time that I ought to be doing something." There was nothing spectacular about the quality of this man's motivation: because of his unwillingness to leave his business for an indefinite period of time, he even stipulated in advance the duration of his assignment. Yet this limited motivation proved adequate to ensure a steady and generally effective performance. Though a high-class specialist, he willingly did menial jobs when necessary, and his work was praised as painstaking, conscientious, and thorough. He was discreet, tactful, and uniformly friendly in relations with his associates and easily gained their confidence and respect.

The next case requires more interpretation. It is the case of an Army man who during assessment gave as his main motive in volunteering for an operational assignment his conviction that he possessed the requisite skills. Neither this motive, nor the desire for adventure which he professed in addition, seemed to stem from a feeling of self-confidence; the candidate voiced, on the contrary, a number of misgivings about his health, strength, and ability to do the job, commenting that he would not volunteer for any particularly hazardous duty within his assignment, but would not refuse if his superiors felt he could do it. His Emotional Stability was rated as Low Average in assessment. This picture suggests an insecure person whose desire for adventure may have been closely related to a desire to test and prove himself, or to maintain threatened self-respect, attitudes which do not hold much promise of success in an operational assignment. Actually, the candidate never got into the field; while waiting, along with others, for his job to materialize, he volunteered for work as a supply officer. This job he did so conscientiously that he was held up as an example of responsibility personified and won the general approbation of his colleagues, despite the fact that he was not particularly popular as a social creature. This case demonstrates how even motivation stemming largely from insecurity can prove highly effective in certain kinds of situations, especially in situations which are less challenging than those which the person has set himself to meet.

The remaining two cases are those of successful field leaders, both of them described as "authentic heroes," distinguished for bravery. While social motives were not missing from their lists of reasons for wanting an assignment, they were outnumbered by egocentric motives, most, but not all of them, of an expansive, self-confident variety. Although both men were well liked and highly valued as leaders, each presented some problems. One was described as emotionally immature, lacking serious purpose in life. The other was said to be unreliable and uneven in his work, to have no tolerance for routine, and to want recognition first and foremost. He was considered by some of his supervisors as a "problem child" whose ability made him well worth the effort required to manage him successfully. These two cases illustrate admirably both the positive potentialities and the limitations of a predominantly egocentric motivation.

Thus out of seven cases of high motivation that resulted in effective performance, three men showed a strong social orientation, with or without underlying ideology; two were motivated by the sense of duty, or related concerns; and two by predominantly egocentric motives aiming at activity, adventure, and prestige. In most cases, while one motive, or one cluster of motives, seemed to predominate, it was combined with one or more motives of a different nature. Thus even the proponent of militant democracy, who voiced strongly almost all of the social motives listed, was also motivated by the desire to have wide scope for individual ability and action; and the two men oriented to prestige and adventure also mentioned motives like duty and patriotism. This is consistent with the hypothesis that might be tentatively formulated on the basis of our findings: reliable and effective motivation may be the function less of any one particular strong drive than of some pattern of predominantly positive motives well integrated in the personality. The few cases reported here can do no more than exemplify roughly some of these configurations and demonstrate that various patterns

of motives can be equally effective in different situations of overseas wartime service.

ENERGY AND INITIATIVE

The Energy and Initiative aspect of Motivation was perhaps, from the
practical point of view, our least problematic variable. Its rating required
little interpretation and was seldom a subject of discussion or of disagreement among the raters. The reason for this was that the scoring of it was
based primarily on the sheer quantity of the candidate's output, the amount
of his physical and verbal participation in the various situations, especially
the group situations. On the one hand, it was possible for a candidate
merely to stand by and watch the others work, or listen to them talk; on the
other, he could, if he chose, work unremittingly toward the solution of the
problem, be it by executing several physical operations in the field projects,
or by talking frequently and at length in the discussion situations. A person
whose participation was high received a high score on Energy and Initiative,
particularly if he also introduced new ideas, attempted to organize and
direct the work of others, called for speed, and in other ways showed concern and assumed responsibilities for the completion of the project.

The individual situations did not give the subject quite the same opportunities to display these traits, or lack of them, as did group situations.
Being given a task to solve by himself, the subject could not very well remain completely inactive; on the other hand, he had no chance to apply
his energy and initiative to the organization of the efforts of others. For
Period G the final score on Energy and Initiative correlates .41 with the
subscore given on the Obstacle Course, while the coefficients of correlation
between the final score and the subscores given in situations presenting opportunities for leadership range between .51 for Debate and .77 for Assigned
Leadership. The data from the earlier periods also bear out the conclusion
that individual situations contributed markedly less to the final score on
Energy and Initiative than did group situations.

In addition to the amount of work he did, the extent to which a candidate
put himself into situations was also considered in rating his energy: this
was reflected in the physical effort the candidate displayed, in his willingness to take risks and discomforts, in the degree of personal involvement
as he tried to get his convictions across to others in discussions. Situations
that demanded an overcoming of difficulties or involved an element of
frustration (Obstacle Course, Construction) presented a good opportunity
for observing the candidate's perseverance, or lack of it, in the face of obstacles and failures.

The purely verbal situations (Discussion, Debate), and those in which
the exchange of opinions, if at all demanded, were only a means for solving
a physical problem, contributed about equally to the final score of Energy

and initiative. In some individual cases, however, there were great differences between the subject's participation in these two types of situation, differences related to the candidate's interest and competence in different types of work. Some men with academic or literary backgrounds were both inept and inactive in field problems, but came into their own in Discussion and Debate. The reverse was true of those who possessed little information on current issues but had had a great deal of experience in outdoor life or in solving technical problems. Intercorrelations between the scores on Energy and Initiative given in the various situations range, for Period G, between −.09 and .62 with the median at .25. The two lowest correlations are between the Obstacle Course and Debate and the Obstacle Course and Discussion (−.09 and .07, respectively), that is, between a purely "physical" and a purely "verbal" situation. The two highest are between Brook and Assigned Leadership and between Discussion and Debate (.62 and .49, respectively), that is, between situations of the same type, either "physical" or "verbal." However, some correlations between the "verbal" and "non-verbal" situations are also fairly high: thus Assigned Leadership correlates .48 with Debate and .41 with Discussion. The results are similar for the data of earlier periods. On the whole, even though competence in some fields of work favored certain candidates in certain situations, none of the situations used to obtain scores on Energy and Initiative demanded such specialized activity as to preclude participation on the part of any candidate. With a wide range in the kinds of situations used, the chances of penalizing any candidate for lack of competence in a special field were not very great. The full table of intercorrelations may be found in Table 59, page 517.

Table 11 shows the correlations between the final score on Energy and Initiative and the final scores on other variables.

TABLE 11

Correlations between Energy and Initiative and Other Variables
(*Period G*)

Leadership	.71	Social Relations	.37
Effective Intelligence	.56	Propaganda Skills	.37
Emotional Stability	.51	Observing & Reporting	.34
Motivation for Assignment	.44	Security	.23
Physical Ability	.41		

The high correlation with Leadership is understandable when one considers that all acts involving leadership and organizing also contributed to the rating of Energy and Initiative. Although it was possible for a person who limited himself strictly to the role of follower to obtain high ratings on energy by working hard in this role, a leader, by definition, could not be a passive onlooker and would have to display a fair amount of initiative

in order to exercise effective control. In considering the correlation with
Effective Intelligence, it is important to remember that in situational tests
the person who remained inactive forfeited the opportunity to display his
intelligence in words or acts, and was often penalized for it by low ratings.
The correlation with Emotional Stability cannot be explained by such overlapping of the bases of ratings, since in determining the final rating of
Emotional Stability the interviewer's judgment was given the main weight
and since there was only one situation (Construction) that yielded scores
both on Emotional Stability and on Energy and Initiative. One might explain the correlation by assuming that the conflicting tendencies and inhibitions of people of low emotional stability prevented them from acting freely
and vigorously in most situations; on the other hand, we have seen many
candidates whose maladjustments seemed to have resulted in a driving
ambition which led to energetic and persistent action. A sizable correlation
between Motivation for Assignment and Energy and Initiative was to be
expected, since it was necessary to show energy in doing the tests in order
to attain the goal, the desired assignment. The fact that the correlation is
not extremely high, however, perhaps indicates that factors other than
the strength of a momentary, circumscribed goal determine a person's
customary output of energy; these might be a fusion of enduring drives,
such as a desire for achievement and recognition, or pleasure in activity and
an interest in tasks as such, or a physiological factor determining general
level of activity. Although many candidates put forth a deliberate and determined effort because they wanted their assignments, great energy was
not always an indication of such desire. A case in point is that of a candidate who, upon obtaining further information about his proposed assignment, decided not to accept it. Yet he worked extremely hard on all tasks.
He himself laughingly observed that he was almost killing himself trying
to pass the test for a job he did not want.

EFFECTIVE INTELLIGENCE

Some psychologists have defined intelligence, implicitly or explicitly, as
the speed and accuracy of the mental processes involved in responding to a
specified, standard, paper-and-pencil test: the I.Q. is the measure of intelligence. Although this definition has the advantage of being operationally
precise and unequivocal, we must be counted among those who are not in
favor of adopting it, because, in the first place, if "intelligence" is assigned
this very limited meaning, then another term will have to be selected or
invented to denote the *effectiveness of the whole system of mental operations,* and for this it is not likely that any term more suitable than "intelligence" can be found and given currency. In the second place, there are
other kinds of mental ability, not measured by the conventional paper-and-

pencil tests, which seem to be as much involved in so-called "intelligent" operations as are the measured abilities, and are, therefore, equally entitled to be accepted as indications of intelligence.

Although the problem is a terminological one, it cannot rightfully be brushed aside as a "mere" matter of words, because, whether we like it or not, "intelligence" is a highly valued symbol, and its application to one kind of mental ability rather than to another is likely to be determined by a sentiment rather than by factual or logical considerations; and in the second place, the association of "intelligence" with a particular kind of mental ability will solidify the favoring sentiment and the social consequences of this development may be considerable.

Conception of Effective Intelligence.—There is some advantage, we believe, in correlating the term "intelligence" with the effectiveness of any system of mental functions and in designating the nature or purpose of each distinguishable system by an appropriate adjective, such as aesthetic intelligence, social intelligence, scientific intelligence, administrative intelligence, mechanical intelligence, and so forth; and then designating by a suitable term each separable function (mental ability) that is involved in the operation of each system, such as, observational ability, evaluative ability, interpretive ability, memory ability, conceptual ability, imaginative ability, logical ability, predictive ability, planning ability, manipulative ability, and so forth.

Suffice it to say that in the assessment of OSS personnel, our interest was focused on the mental abilities which would be called into play in performing the various roles to which accepted candidates would be assigned. Since there were fifty or more different roles, many kinds of mental ability had to be considered, many more, certainly, than the number involved in responding to a paper-and-pencil test. Thus we were forced to reach for a notion of intelligence which, though not exhaustive, was much more comprehensive than the I.Q. conception, and having once adopted it, we had to abandon the policy of relying wholly on a standard intelligence test as a measure of all that was embraced by it.

Intelligence tests have been remarkably efficient in discriminating persons in the lower ranges of mental capacity (the feeble-minded, imbeciles, and so on) and in predicting, with considerable validity, the scholastic achievement of those with normal minds. As we know, the tests have been developed largely in connection with the concerns and aims of educational institutions (including military schools of all sorts) and, generally speaking, the chief criterion in deciding which of several mental tasks should be included in an intelligence test has been the degree of correlation with school grades mostly based on written examinations and other types of paper work. This is proper in so far as the prime purpose of the test has been to predict scholastic achievement, but it does not encourage us to suppose that this test would be efficient in predicting other forms of attainment. We have no good reason to suppose that scholastic intelligence is highly correlated with aesthetic, social, administrative, military, financial, or mechanical intelligence, or that memorizing ability (an important factor in obtaining good grades at school) is highly correlated with creative ability (imagination, resourcefulness, ingenuity, and the like).

In view of these considerations, the members of the OSS assessment staff agreed, first, that paper-and-pencil tests should constitute only a part of the battery of procedures selected to measure intelligence; and second, that, in order to avoid confusion between the I.Q. and the conception of intelligence which we had adopted, our variable would be called Practical Intelligence (later, Effective Intelligence).

As we shall explain in due course, this matter was not clearly envisaged at the very start of our undertaking. Effective Intelligence was not operationally defined in much detail, and even after a year or more of work, misunderstandings would arise as a result of loose terminology. Occasionally, for example, the writer of a personality sketch would make a statement that was based solely on the scores obtained on two or three paper-and-pencil tests. He would write, "The intelligence of this candidate is inferior according to S standards." In such a case, the branch chief might call for an explanation. "What do you mean by calling X inferior?" he would say. "I have known him for several years and have watched him at work in the office here for five months, and I consider him one of the most intelligent men in this branch."

Since this book is no place for the discussion of fundamental issues, we shall limit ourselves here to a brief account of the conception of Effective Intelligence that was accepted more or less by the OSS assessment staff, and shall make no attempt to demonstrate that this conception closely approximates the most suitable general definition of intelligence.

In defining intelligence there are two basic questions to be answered: (1) To what psychological processes (functions, abilities) can the adjective "intelligent" be fittingly applied? Or, in other words, to what functions should one attend in judging intelligence? (2) What are the most suitable measures of intelligence? That is, in terms of what criteria can a scale of intelligence be defined? As a preliminary step in answering the first question, we would say that any ability which can properly be called mental or intellectual deserves to be included within the sphere of our conception. Hence the first question might be stated in this way: What are the chief kinds of mental processes (functions, abilities)? As a preliminary step in answering the second question, it is necessary, we suggest, to distinguish between (i) efficiency of intelligence (e.g., the speed, economy, precision, effectiveness, with which any mental task is carried out) and (ii) level of intelligence (the degree of difficulty of the accomplished task). At this point it might be well to remind ourselves that each type of mental process can be applied to many different kinds of objects (human, inanimate), and can serve any one of a number of different aims (economic, political, social, aesthetic, or scientific). Since everybody varies in respect to the effectiveness with which his several processes can deal with the different kinds of objects and in respect to the effectiveness with which these processes can serve the different aims, it is necessary to distinguish various classes of objects and various classes of aims.

Mental Abilities.—For the purpose of assessing abilities required by OSS intelligence and operating personnel, it may be convenient to classify them in the following four phases:

A. *Afferent*

1. *Collection of data:* perception, selection of significant facts. The whole range of receptive and recording enterprises from a quick glance to a long and elaborate exploration; watching, listening, and reading; research and experimentation, analysis of findings, judgments of reliability. Also registration of observations: memory, note taking, photography, and so forth.

2. *Diagnosis of the situation:* apperception, interpretation, inference, structuration of the behavioral field, explanation of phenomena in terms of scientific theories, formulations and assessments of personality. Also evaluations of power and merit. The whole range of cognitive processes from a quick insight to a long series of logical inductions; prediction of the uninfluenced course of events, anticipation of possible contingencies.

B. *Efferent*

3. *Conception of plan:* selection of the most strategic goal(s) and improvisation of means thereto; scheduling of projects and subprojects, selection of agencies, designing of instruments. Prediction of the results of action (the outcome of interventions), plans to meet possible contingencies, setting the level of aspiration. Also, communicating plans to others.

4. *Execution of action:* verbal and muscular behavior. The whole range of overt action from a quick response to a life-long undertaking; dealing with things, animals, and people. Managing and administering (leadership) activities, performance of special functions; striving with perseverance until goal is attained.

It is scarcely necessary to point out that there are inseparable gradations and overlaps between each of these phases. The collection of data, for example, is seldom a mechanical accumulation of personal impressions and reported occurrences, but rather a careful selection of facts in terms of several alternative diagnoses of the situation. That is to say, ideas commonly precede and determine perceptions: a man will look for signs which prove or disprove an hypothesis. Also observation and interpretation are very apt to occur together, forming a single indivisible process that results in the immediate retention or rejection of the presented data, depending on whether they are pertinent or not pertinent to a given notion. Discrimination of relevance is thus a function which calls for the interplay of perception (1, collection of data) and formulation (2, diagnosis of the situation). Consequently, in explaining the inadequacy of a man's observations, it may be hard to say whether he is a good observer with an inadequate conceptual scheme (he does not understand enough) or whether his concepts are sufficient but his powers of observation defective.

The above scheme is a convenient one for classifying roles as well as mental abilities. The roles (functions) undertaken by the OSS, for example, can be roughly divided into:

A. *Afferent:* the collection, analysis, interpretation, and reporting of information about significant proceedings in enemy territory.

B. *Efferent:* the planning, teaching, and execution of physical (sabotage) and verbal (propaganda) operations against the enemy.

This mode of classifying roles may be confusing to some readers, since every role necessarily involves all four phases of a total mental arc (observation, diagnosis, planning, action): a secret intelligence agent (afferent role) must decide on a plan of action (exploration, interrogation, and the like) and execute it; and a saboteur (efferent role) must observe and size up the confronting situation before he can act effectively. The two assignments are different, however, in respect to their final goals: no matter how active, physically and verbally, the secret agent may have to be to gain his end, the success of his efforts is measured in terms of the quality and quantity of the information which he obtains; and although verbal action is involved in the communication of his findings, this final efferent phase can be considered secondary to his superordinate afferent role. The success of the saboteur, on the other hand, is measured in terms of the quality and quantity of the damage that is done to enemy installations as a direct result of his efforts. Thus the two roles are complementary: the investigator discovers the location of the strategic targets and the operator strikes them. Presumably the former would be especially fitted, by native talents or training or both, to observe and to interrogate; to remember what he has seen, heard, and read; to analyze, evaluate, and interpret the material obtained, to report his findings and conclusions accurately and succinctly. And the latter, the operator, if functioning on a physical level, should be above average, not only in athletic ability and daring, but in short-range planning ability, resourcefulness, fitness for emergencies, mechanical ability, leadership ability (many of the operators were expected to lead native resistance groups, if not Americans), teaching ability (the instruction of resistance groups in the use of new weapons and explosives was usually included among the functions of a field operator), and sometimes, recruiting ability. When he is functioning on the symbolic level, the operator (propagandist) should presumably be above average in his ability to select strategic goals ("target groups" with points of special psychological vulnerability), to devise novel and ingenious techniques of reaching the target groups, and to influence the target groups by the use of some art (e.g., radio broadcasts, pamphlets, posters).

To list in this way the chief functions of those fulfilling afferent and of those fulfilling efferent roles draws attention to the differences between these roles. Actually, when working behind enemy lines the collector of intelligence and the saboteur used very similar mental abilities: both were in danger; both had to observe and size up new situations quickly and be resourceful in devising ways of meeting them; both had to deal with things, calling for mechanical intelligence, and with people, calling for social intelligence, et cetera. Thus the similarities of functions were often more obvious than the dissimilarities.

Instead of dividing the mental phases into afferent and efferent, we may divide them into peripheral (1, collection of data, and 4, execution of action) and central (2, diagnosis of situation, and 3, conception of plan). This line of cleavage stresses the differences between those who were out in the field restricted to a small region of operations, and the upper-echelon administrators and executives at Washington and at the base in each theater of operations, who received all reports from the field and put them together to make a total picture, and on the basis of this diagnosis decided on long-range goals and subsidiary projects. Presumably those with central, rather than peripheral, functions would have to possess much more than average ability to grasp complicated situations in their totality (e.g., military, political, economic, social), and to select the most strategic targets and objectives, to develop plans for achieving these major aims, to foresee difficulties and devise ways of surmounting them, to select suitable subordinates, to administer efficiently a large organization or branch of activities, to excite loyalty and cooperation, and so forth.

Without going into further details, we submit that this scheme provides a simple means of ordering for our purposes all functions which deserve to be included within the sphere to which the term "intelligence" can properly be applied. In other words, the scheme includes all mental abilities, and, in addition, a few nonmental abilities. We submit that phase 1, collection of data, involves some processes at the sensory boundary of personality, and phase 4, execution of action, involves some processes at the motor boundary, which are so largely peripheral in nature that they had better not be classified among mental processes or abilities. These nonintellectual functions are of two kinds:

1) *Sensory Ability:* chiefly, visual and auditory acuity and discrimination.

2) *Physical Ability:* chiefly, muscular strength, agility, and endurance.

In the OSS, each candidate's sight and hearing and state of health were tested by the Medical Branch, but his athletic skill was tested at Station S and rated as a separate variable, Physical Ability. Aside from these two, sensory ability and muscular ability, everything that is embraced in the above-mentioned scheme should be taken into account in any comprehensive attempt to estimate intelligence.

In the beginning, during the period when the assessment staff's conceptual scheme for personality consisted of a rather large number of components, about thirteen separate variables were used to cover the sphere of intelligence. Classified according to the four functional phases, they are:

A. *Afferent.* 1. *Collection of data*
    i. Observation
    ii. Memory
2. *Diagnosis of the situation*
    iii. Inference (interpretive ability)
    iv. Judgment of People
    v. Test Intelligence (discrimination of verbal and nonverbal forms)
B. *Efferent.* 3. *Conception of plan*
    vi. Planning Ability
    vii. Resourcefulness (ingenuity and originality in solving means-end problems—physical and social)
    viii. Mechanical Comprehension (paper-and-pencil test of the ability to conceive the solution of mechanical difficulties)
    ix. Teaching Ability (ability to explain techniques of action)
4. *Execution of action*
    x. Fitness for Emergencies (ability to react effectively to sudden, unexpected stimuli)
    xi. Leadership (skill in managing people)
    xii. Persuasiveness (ability to affect others with words)
    xiii. Recruiting Ability (involving both judgment of people and persuasiveness)

It may be difficult for the reader to understand why some of these variables are classified as they are. Why, for example, is Teaching Ability subsumed under 3, Conception of plan? It is placed on the efferent side of the arc because, although it included the exposition of facts and interpretations (afferent phase), teaching in the OSS was oriented toward action. Although, on one level, the process of instruction is itself an action, on another it is rather a matter of communicating technical plans of action to those who will put them into effect.

In attempting to classify abilities one soon runs into the problem of the inseparable gradations between categories and the problem of overlap, the mutual involvement of categories, which complicate the task of defining these operationally and devising tests for each. How, for example, shall we define and test mechanical "know-how"? The actual solution of a mechanical or engineering difficulty involves all four phases—observation, estimation of the situation, conception of an efficient plan, and execution of the plan. Under ordinary circumstances only the last phase (the behavioral) is observable. If this succeeds, one knows that the three preceding phases have been successful; but if it fails, there is no telling, without special investigation, which of the four phases was defective. Did the man fail to perceive the rope on the ground and the wrench near by or did he fail to realize the means-end possibilities of these two agencies? Did he fail to estimate correctly the speed of the river's current or was he too weak or clumsy to stand up against it? Was he misguided in calculating that a rope could be thrown over that branch on the other side of the river or was it just awkwardness on his part which caused his attempts to fail? Such questions are often hard to answer. What we were likely to do if we wished to measure mechanical "know-how" was to present the candidate with a fairly clear-cut situation so that observation and diagnosis were relatively simple (within the capacity of everyone) and in this way to eliminate the afferent side of the arc as a distinguishing determinant. Athletic ability and manual dexterity can be eliminated in one or both of two ways: ask the candidate for a plan of action (before directing him to proceed) or make allowances for lack of muscular dexterity or strength based on the results of special tests of these powers.

We do not want to spend any more time on the above list of variables, however, because after four months of experimentation it had not assumed a practically useful form. The first three on the above list, together with several new ones (ability to interrogate, ability to analyze and evaluate data, ability to write concise reports), were absorbed into one variable, termed Observing and Reporting. This embraced almost all of the intellectual abilities on the afferent side of the arc. Leadership retained the status of a separate variable. Recruiting Ability and Teaching Ability were dropped from the regular list because they were applicable only to a minority of the candidates. All the other abilities were absorbed into a new variable, Effective Intelligence.

Effective Intelligence embraced all the functions on the efferent side of the arc. It was taken to denote chiefly the ability to select (within the frame of a designated over-all objective) the most strategic realizable goals and to conceive (select, discover, or invent) the most efficient means for arriving at these goals. Thus we were principally concerned here with functions which fell into the third reaction phase (3, Conception of plan), but which would not ordinarily be exhibited except by way of the fourth phase (4, Execution of action). These two phases are not always highly correlated. A man may think of the best way of doing something, but yet be incapable of accomplishing it himself. An extreme case would be that of a sick old man who worked out the best possible way of climbing Mt. Everest. With us, however, it was not usually feasible or even desirable to attempt a sharp distinction between effective planning and effective performing. The best we could do on the bodily level of activity was to separate out Physical Ability, and more or less assume that the chief remaining determinant of success or failure would be the ability to devise effective means-end solutions of physical problems. (Here we are temporarily disregarding variables belonging to other areas of personality—energy, motivation, emotional stability, and so forth.) On the verbal level of activity, however, no distinction was made between effective planning (e.g., selection of a strategic objective, logical organization of ideas, comprehensiveness of exposition, congruence of concepts and images with facts), and effective performance (e.g., verbal facility, manner of delivery).

Thus our conception of Effective Intelligence shifted the focus from intellection as an afferent function—the conceptualization of one's environment—to intellection as an efferent function—the formulation of plans (e.g., strategic projects, practical techniques). For one period the final rating on Observation and Reporting was taken into account in assigning ratings on Effective Intelligence. Although, by so doing, Effective Intelligence was stretched to contain all four phases of intellectual activity, the practice was discontinued.

Objects of Intelligence.—No mental ability is equally effective in dealing with all kinds of materials. Various innate and acquired factors combine to determine that one man is unusually proficient in music, another in repairing machinery, a third in manipulating numbers and symbols. There seem to be a great many special abilities. Since the OSS staff was not asked to test for any such very specific talents, the matter of their classification need not detain us. For our purposes a very crude classification was sufficient:

1) Ability to deal with things (e.g., physical obstacles, machinery, weapons, radios, gadgets)—mechanical intelligence.
2) Ability to deal with people—social intelligence.
3) Ability to deal with ideas (e.g., concepts, numbers, symbols, abstract formulations, ideologies)—conceptual intelligence.

These have already been casually mentioned in connection with the various mental functions. Mechanical intelligence was tested by one paper-and-pencil test and in several outdoor situations where the candidate was required to find quick solutions for minor "engineering" problems or practical emergencies. One phase of social intelligence was measured by the Judgment of Others Test, another phase by the Discussion and the Debate.

This type of ability, however, was more adequately covered by two separate variables, Social Relations and Leadership, and, to some extent, by Propaganda Skills. Verbal and abstract intelligence were measured by the Vocabulary Test, the Matrix, and later, the Otis, as well as by several group situations (Discussion, Debate, and SIX-2).

Measurément of Effective Intelligence.—The tests and procedures from which ratings on Intelligence were obtained were not, in actual practice, classified according to the categories given above, but, for greater convenience, according to certain technical criteria.

The part of the total battery which was classified "test intelligence" included the Vocabulary Test, the Mechanical Comprehension Test, and at first the Matrix and other nonverbal tests and later the Otis. It was hoped that this combination would yield a measure of the kind of intelligence that is conventionally represented by the I.Q. The excellent Wechsler-Bellevue, an individual test, was administered when there was reason to believe that a low score on the group paper-and-pencil tests was not a valid index of the candidate's intellectual powers. Among the most frequent reasons for this belief were the interference of age (in candidates over fifty) with performance in such speed tests as the Otis and a language handicap impeding progress on the vocabulary tests. Another reason was the occurrence of marked discrepancies between the scores obtained on the different tests of the battery. The Wechsler-Bellevue was also useful in cases where some neurotic or psychotic tendency was suspected.

The chief tests of so-called "verbal intelligence"—judgment, speed, resourcefulness, originality in handling words—were the SIX-2 Test, the Discussion, and the Debate. The first was a written test, the other two were oral.

The part of the battery which was classified as "practical intelligence" was designed to measure each candidate's effectiveness in dealing with simple mechanical or physical tasks in an outdoor setting. The procedures included the Brook and the Assigned Leadership. The latter yielded ratings of intelligence when the candidate acted as a leader and intelligence when he acted as a subordinate.

Finally, there was the Interview, which, as it happened, yielded the most crucial single rating. This represented the interviewer's over-all impression of intelligence based on the candidate's work history, on his past accomplishments, on his present aims and expectations, and on the knowledge and skill manifested by the candidate in analyzing his past experiences, the situations he had encountered, and his motives in joining the OSS. Not only did the interviewer's rating correlate .80 with the final rating of Effective Intelligence, but it rarely varied more than one point from the final rating. The explanation of this finding will be given later.

The scoring of "test intelligence" was done objectively and mechanically and, consequently, presented no problems. It was the lifelike situational tests, especially the leaderless group tests, which gave rise to almost all of our difficulties in rating. To estimate the value of a candidate's contribution to the group's total achievement was hard enough, but to decide how much of his contribution was due to sheer intelligence as distinguished from other variables—energy and initiative, knowledge, long-standing interest in the given task or topic, social ability, leadership experience, emotional stability, and so forth—was in many instances extremely difficult, if not impossible.

One rule which must be observed in estimating any ability—and this applies, of course, to the measurement of "test intelligence"—is that the conditions should be such that the motivation aroused is as high as is necessary to produce the best results. Also, anxiety and other agitating emotions should be absent or governable. If, in one of our group situational tests, for instance, the candidate's motivation was low (he was not interested in the problem) or his emotional stability was low (he was too embarrassed to perform in public), he would let the others do most of the talking and the doing, and thus leave the assessors in doubt as to whether he was stupid or clever. We always made a point of taking into account such possibilities, but, even under the most favorable circumstances, the scores of Intelligence which were given on situational tests probably represented *mental effectiveness under conditions of social stress* rather than mental effectiveness in isolation. Consequently, those who required quiet and privacy to do their best thinking were probably underrated, and those whose mental processes were encouraged by the presence of an audience were probably overrated.

A difficulty of another sort was that of weighting properly evidences of different kinds of mental ability—observational ability, memory ability, and so forth. Faced by the Brook problem, for example, one member of the group would be the first to notice the worn stub of a branch on a tree across the water (suggesting the possibility of throwing over it the noose of a rope), another candidate would propose a practical over-all plan for the division of functions, another would think of a way of tying the rope around the rock, another, without saying a word, would take the hint and show sense and skill in getting his knot firmly placed against a jutting ridge on the rock, and so forth. Should a significant observation be rated as high as an outline of strategy? Should a verbal "know-how" be rated higher than an unarticulated "can-do"? And then, how much should be subtracted from a man's score because of his having made this or that impractical or stupid suggestion? Finally, since we are speaking here of group tests, how much attention should be given to social intelligence? It was not easy, for instance, to decide how to rate the intelligence of a man with an excellent plan who stubbornly persisted in an obviously futile effort to persuade the others of its superior merit and thereby impeded the swift execution of an already adopted, though less efficient plan. It was not possible to embrace all such heterogeneous forms of behavior in one operationally defined rating scale, but something of the sort was established in the mind of each assessor as the result of repeated observations of different groups dealing with the same situation and repeated discussions about how to interpret and rate different kinds of verbal and physical behavior.

The fact that agreement was satisfactory, despite the many difficulties, is indicated by Table 12, which gives the correlation ratio for these raters on two samples, each of which comprised approximately 70 candidates and 200 ratings.

TABLE 12

Correlations among Raters[a]

Situation	η (Correlation ratio)	
	Sample 1[1]	Sample 2[2]
Brook	.71	.69
Discussion	.86	.80
Debate	.82	.85

[a] Each sample is composed of more than 70 men, each with 2 or 3 ratings at each situation.

The figures demonstrate that the assessors whose ratings were included in these computations resolved most of their rating problems in the same manner. This finding, of course, is no proof that they resolved them correctly.

Although we spent a good deal of time trying to estimate Effective Intelligence as a separate attribute, we all knew that our primary aim was to measure the effectiveness of the whole person, and that the determination

TABLE 13

Some Correlations between Ratings on Leadership and Ratings on Effective Intelligence

(*Periods F–G; N=220 to 400*)

Final grades.................................. .63
Brook.. .78
Discussion................................... .79
Assigned Leadership (as leader).............. .79

of which variables were chiefly responsible for each man's successes and which for his failures was a matter of less importance. Furthermore, it was actually impossible to disentangle the different variables, not only because

the processes they represented were mutually dependent components of
more or less unified functional operations, but because the variables overlapped by definition. Leadership, for example, certainly requires effective
intelligence, sometimes of a high order, intelligence in dealing with the
problems which confront the group that is being led, and intelligence in
dealing with the group itself. This relationship is shown by the correlations
in Table 13. Each *r* represents the degree of correlation between the two variables when rated in the same specified situation.

Some of the problems we have been discussing are illustrated by the next
table of correlations (Table 14).

TABLE 14

Some Correlations between Energy and Initiative and Certain Measures of
Effective Intelligence

(*Period G; N=134 except as indicated*)

	r
Energy and Initiative, Final versus Vocabulary Test	.09
Energy and Initiative, Final versus Mechanical Comprehension Test	.10
Energy and Initiative, Final versus Otis Test (*N*=124)	.15
Energy and Initiative, Final versus Effective Intelligence, Final Grade	.53
Energy and Initiative, Brook versus Effective Intelligence, Brook	.68
Energy and Initiative, Discussion versus Effective Intelligence, Discussion	.88

An examination of these figures reveals that the variable Energy and Initiative is not correlated to any appreciable extent with Effective Intelligence
as measured by paper-and-pencil tests, but it is highly correlated with
Effective Intelligence as estimated in two of the situational tests. The chief
reason for this is that the ratings on Energy and Initiative were based, for
the most part, on observations of the degree of zest, activity, and enterprise
exhibited by the candidates during the various situations, some of which
called for physical, some for verbal, actions. If, as explained above, a candidate was relatively inactive in a given situation, whatever intelligence he
possessed was not exhibited and, therefore, his mental ability was likely to
be underrated. Assessors did not ordinarily infer that silence is wisdom.
Contrariwise, if a man manifested a great deal of intelligence in a situation,
an observer was apt to give him a high mark on Energy and Initiative on
the ground that the effectiveness of his thinking was a sure sign of mental
energy, all that was required by the situation. As a rule, it was only when
an individual did or said a good many utterly foolish or stupid things
that the ratings on Intelligence and Energy were at opposite ends of the
scale. Perhaps a cultural factor was operating here, inasmuch as North
Americans are more inclined than people of other nationalities to correlate
activity, physical or verbal, with intelligence. The very high correlation (.88)

between Energy and Intelligence in the Discussion situation, for example, is certainly indicative of an inability on the part of most raters to differentiate sharply between quantity and quality of verbal expression.

The fact that the assessors were estimating the effectiveness of a candidate's whole performance rather than distinguishing the contribution of each separable ability is demonstrated in an even more striking fashion by the following correlations:

Physical Ability, Final versus Effective Intelligence, Final .... .03
Physical Ability, Brook versus Effective Intelligence, Brook .... .47

Here again is evidence that the correlation among variables was much higher when they were scored in a single situation. At first glance, it would seem that at the Brook our ratings for Physical Ability or for Intelligence or for both must have been inaccurate. If the most valid figure is the final rating, then .47 appears spuriously high. Probably it *is* too high, and this because of the impossibility, in most instances, of distinguishing in a field situation between "know-how" and "can-do." Only when a candidate made some excellent suggestions but was awkward and inept in his attempts to cooperate in executing them did the ratings on Effective Intelligence and Physical Ability stand on opposite sides of the mid-line. At the Brook, however, we were testing intelligence in dealing with natural obstacles and, consequently, some correlation with physical ability was to be expected, since most people acquire this as well as other forms of special intelligence by acting, and if they are incapable of acting they are incapable of learning. Exceptions to this generalization are rare but striking. There is Machiavelli, no field marshal, who wrote an excellent treatise on the art of war, and, as another illustration which some Americans may recall, there is that most successful coach of college swimming teams who could not swim himself.

The source of one difficulty in rating intelligence at S was the concentration of OSS candidates in the higher brackets of the normal distribution

TABLE 15

Army Percentiles and S Percentiles Equated with S Grades

	S Scale					
	0	1	2	3	4	5
Estimated Army Percentile	1–40	41–72	73–89	90–95	96–98	99–100
Arbitrary S Percentile	1– 7	8–25	26–50	51–75	76–93	94–100

curve (see Table 49, page 505). Since several Army tests were used at S for short periods, it was possible to make an approximate conversion table to equate Army percentiles to S grades when the latter were distributed according to our arbitrarily selected scheme. (See Table 15.)

The table shows that if the staff members had adhered to the scheme of distribution which was adopted as a rough guide for rating, 7 per cent of the S population would have been given a score of 5 on intelligence, in contrast to 1 per cent of the total Army population, and 7 per cent would have been given a score of 0, in contrast to the 40 per cent who would have been so rated in the Army. The concentration of about 50 per cent of our candidates above the 90th percentile, as measured by Army tests, made it more difficult to discriminate differences in intellectual power among these more intelligent men. Actually only 1.1 per cent of the S population were given the score of 5 (during Periods F and G) and only 2.3 per cent were given the score of 0. Over 70 per cent, instead of 50 per cent, were clustered in the average range (ratings of 2 and 3).

The norms on the paper-and-pencil tests were made to correspond to the S population when distributed according to our arbitrary scheme.

S Scale					
0 Very Inferior	1 Inferior	2 Low Average	3 High Average	4 Superior	5 Very Superior
7%	18%	25%	25%	18%	7%

Since the norms were established by the past population, they lagged behind it. They changed with the population but always *after* it, and sometimes too long after it. If, for example, we received for assessment fifty candidates, most of whom were slated to be writers of propaganda, their scores on Mechanical Comprehension would most likely be in the 0 to 2 range. These scores, being tabulated, would bring down the norms a notch or two, but the writers themselves had, of course, been scored on the higher norms and so their distribution of scores would be skewed. The next group might be comprised chiefly of aviation mechanics, and their scores, aided now by the lowered norms, would be largely in the 4 to 5 range, and as a result there would be more skewness. We cannot say to what extent our population fluctuated in such cycles, but the fact remains that the norms inevitably lagged behind the population for which they were intended. Especially when a new test was used, it is difficult to see how it could have been otherwise with internal norms for populations that shifted.

The most striking thing about the intercorrelations among the various individual measures of Effective Intelligence (Table 60, page 518) is the outstanding agreement between the interviewer's rating and the final grade on Effective Intelligence. This, however, does not dispose us to believe that the average interview can yield a judgment of Effective Intelligence which will correlate .80 with a true measure of it. Surely there was nothing unusual about our interviews nor anything remarkable about the insight of those who conducted them. Something in addition to insights gained in that hour and a half must have been operating to produce so high a correlation. This "something" was due to the fact that the interviewer did not record his rating of the interviewee's Effective Intelligence until the last day. In the meantime he had observed the man in some of the situational tests and had rated his performance in association with other members of his staff team. Under these conditions it was inevitable that his rating of Effective Intelligence would be close to the rating which would be finally agreed to in the staff conference. And, furthermore, almost invariably it was the interviewer's opinion about a candidate that carried greatest weight in the final conference.

Assuming that the final rating is the best measure of each individual's Effective Intelligence, one might conclude, after glancing at our correlations, that the Discussion (or the Debate) is a better index of intelligence than the Wechsler-Bellevue or the Otis. It seems certain, however, that the Debate as given at S, taken alone, is a relatively poor measure of Effective Intelligence, but since it came late in the program, the ratings given then were influenced by much that the candidate had done through the days preceding this situation. Moreover, not everyone was given a rating on Intelligence at the Debate. Frequently only a few, those about whose grades there was less question, were rated. Thus it would be a mistake to infer on the basis of the correlation (.73) that the Debate was a good test of Effective Intelligence. Some of the other tests are open to similar reservations.

Inspection of Table 60, page 518, conforms to the assumption that a few more or less discrete categories of intelligence can be distinguished. Our data may be ordered in this fashion:

1) Physical-Social (Outdoor-Practical) Ability, as measured by the Brook and the two Assigned Leadership tests. Here the tactical skill required was largely mechanical in nature, but it also included the ability to give concise directions. The median intercorrelation of these three tests was .41. None of them correlated as highly as this with any test outside this cluster.

2) Verbal-Social (Speaking) Ability, as measured by Discussion, Debate, Judgment of Others, and Vocabulary. Here the chief requirement was the mobilization of adequate ideas and words. The ability to size up other people was also a factor. The median intercorrelation of these four tests was .52.

3) Verbal-Abstract (Writing) Ability, as measured by the Otis, Vocabulary, and SIX-2. These are all written tests. What is required is the ability to deal with words, and to some extent, with ideas. The median intercorrelation of the three tests is .43. There is some overlap between this and the preceding cluster since the Vocabulary Test enters into both. Also, the median of the correlations with these tests of Judgment of Others, based on written sketches, is .47.

4) Nonverbal Abstract Ability, as measured by Mechanical Comprehension, Nonverbal, and Otis. This cluster is not very homogeneous, due to

the presence of the Otis, which is correlated more highly with the members of the preceding cluster. The Otis is a test of the catch-all sort which is likely to appear in several clusters. The correlations of Mechanical Comprehension with the Nonverbal Battery is .37 and with the Otis .49.

Determination of the Final Rating.—In view of the fact that in 24 per cent of the cases the final rating was not the same as the simple average of all the ratings but was one grade below or above the average, we might examine the data to discover, if possible, some of the factors which determined the shift. One determinant, we would suppose, was the greater validity, in our minds, of some tests as compared to others. By calculating for each test the percentage of ratings which agreed with the final rating, we obtained one measure, not free from ambiguity, of this determinant. The figures show that the interviewer's rating (64 per cent agreement) was the most influential. Next in order were the verbal-social tests, Discussion and Debate (average 54 per cent), followed by the practical outdoor tests (average 51 per cent), the paper-and-pencil tests (average 47 per cent), and Judgment of Others (36 per cent).

Among the other more important factors leading to a final grade that was different from the simple average was the anticipated recommendation. When the staff's decision for a candidate was to be Highly Recommended, the final rating, if changed at all, was likely to be raised; whereas if the decision was to be Not Recommended, the final rating, if changed, was likely to be lowered.

The influence of the interviewer calls for special consideration. Our figures show that when, during the first months of the program, the final grade deviated from the average, the interviewer's grade, in the majority of cases, also deviated from the average and nearly always in the same direction. We conclude from this that it was the interviewer's judgment which determined the shift in most of these instances. In later months his influence was less apparent. It was also found that whenever there was a difference between his rating and the final grade, the former was much more likely to be the higher of the two, which, as we have said earlier, indicates, if we assume that the final rating was our most valid figure, that there was a consistent tendency for each interviewer to overrate the men he interviewed.

But of more significance than this determinant of the final rating of Effective Intelligence, as well as of all other variables, was the frame of reference, or the standard held in mind while making ratings. This is an important problem because if one's frame of reference shifts there will be a corresponding shift in scale values and, therefore, in the distribution of the ratings.

The crucial question is: were we able to maintain unchanged the scale against which we rated the candidates throughout the program at S? Was our frame of reference—the standard we used in rating our candidates—the same in the last period as it was in the first? Here we have one finding which may be pertinent: when the final rating was different from the average rating, the former was much more often *higher* in the first few months of S, and much more often *lower* in the last few months. What is the explanation? Why were we disposed to boost a candidate in the early days and to bring him down toward the end?

Looking back in retrospect upon the men we assessed, those of us who were at S throughout its entire history find ourselves in agreement on the following point: in the early days of S we were tremendously impressed by the quality of the candidates. Certainly there were exceptions, but by and large they seemed to us an uncommonly superior lot. Previously, most of our clinical experience had been with the ordinary run of people, and having derived our standard of the "average man" from them, we were prepared to feel that the OSS candidates were far above this standard. If this is what happened, one can understand why in the early days, when we did something other than accept a simple average of all ratings as the final grade on Effective Intelligence, we moved the rating up rather than down. As we viewed our candidates in the first period at S within the frame of reference of the population we had tested in former days, they looked extremely capable, more capable, we would now guess, than they actually were. If there is any truth in this notion, then it is likely that our early experiences at S with superior candidates (at least superior in relation to our previous standard) gave us a new frame of reference in terms of which we rated subsequent candidates. If, as seems likely, during the last months of S the candidates were observed in relation to the first graduates, they must have suffered by this comparison, the earlier men having by then grown into legendary figures of great prowess.

There is thus reason to believe that the scale for rating candidates changed with time and circumstance. Without a constant anchor, a steady frame of reference, we probably rated candidates too high in the earlier and too low in the later periods. Does this mean that ratings will always be incomparable? At first to some extent, yes. But in so far as this effect can be recognized, corrections can be made for it. Only research into techniques of rating will reveal the ways in which this source of error can be reduced.

EMOTIONAL STABILITY

From first to last, the problem of emotional stability was a central issue in assessment, a vastly important consideration in predicting a candidate's over-all effectiveness in the field. It was the variable of personality most subject to change, and if changed for the worse it could vitiate all the other skills of a candidate. A man with an outstanding knowledge of labor organization in Europe could become valueless to the OSS if his emotional reactions to conditions of living overseas should be such as to interfere seriously with his operating efficiency. Similarly, a man who "went to pieces" while on an operational mission might prevent the success of the project and at the same time jeopardize the lives of his associates. It was not enough to know that a man's motivation was high and his skills were adequate; we had also in the light of our assessment of his emotional stability to estimate what his operating efficiency would be when called upon to work under conditions of frustration and of danger to life and limb.

Coupled with the focal importance of emotional stability in assessment was the necessity of having to evaluate this variable on something less than completely adequate objective test data. In a few cases there was sufficient evidence in a man's history to preclude his being sent overseas, but for a man finally recommended there were never enough objective data to ensure that his emotional stability would remain unimpaired in the face of unpredictable stresses. Given enough time, there was no reason why an adequate staff of psychiatrists and psychologists could not discover the emotional structure which underlay a man's manifest behavior, but in many cases the three-day period of assessment provided little more than a rough understanding of the role and intensity of a man's affective life. The insightful candidate could provide us with highly important data to help round out our estimate of his emotional stability, but many of the candidates had little more than a banal and stereotyped conception of their own emotional dynamics. It was not enough, however, to grasp, as best we could, the emotional make-up of our candidates; we had to predict their probable performance in specific field assignments. This step never failed to challenge us, and though it was a judgment made on the best evidence available, it was never made with complete confidence as to its accuracy.

A difficult task in the assessment of emotional stability was that of estimating the over-all temperamental sturdiness of a man as contrasted with his capacity for adaptation to specific conditions. If a candidate presented a history characterized by resilient and stable adjustment to the major problems of his life, and if the behavior which he manifested at S was consistent with this picture, there was little reason to expect that his adjustment to conditions overseas would be other than sound, especially if his motivation was high. Few candidates, however, presented such a uniform picture, and to send overseas only such sturdy individuals would have limited too severely the number of personnel available for the various OSS missions. Hence the question of specificity of adjustability entered into our considerations. Would the candidate with certain emotional strengths and weaknesses be able to adapt to the particular conditions of a particular job? One immediate difficulty into which we ran in attempting to answer this question was, of course, the somewhat vague knowledge which we possessed of the specific stresses characteristic of the different assignments. Only in the most general terms did we know what a given recruit might encounter. Our realization in the latter part of the program that many candidates would be called upon to carry out assignments other than the ones for which they had been selected and for which we had assessed them served only to complicate our problem.

Essentially our task was to predict the emotional stability of candidates in environments which had little similarity to any of those they had previously known. Prior to the war, few Americans had ever lived completely isolated from their families, among natives who in their behavior expressed some friendliness but often open hostility, cut off from contacts with individuals of the opposite sex of their own age and culture, with marked limitations in food and housing, out of touch with many familiar American recreations and diversions, and under the constant stresses of danger to life and limb. These were the conditions of war, and each man, in his own way, had to adjust to them. Under these circumstances many familiar patterns of adjustment would prove inadequate; many customary modes of living would be impossible. New satisfactions and securities would have to be established.

Accordingly, the genuine satisfactions which a candidate might find in his projected assignment became an important consideration in assessing his emotional stability. The quality and intensity of his motivation provided a preview of what he was seeking, but many times the motivation, as expressed by a candidate, had all of the distortions of untrained subjective analysis. At best the satisfactions which might be achieved in the field would almost certainly be different from those anticipated by a candidate while undergoing assessment. When, however, the expressed motivation was clearly unrealistic there could be little hope that the candidate's emotional stability would be equal to his inevitable disappointments and frustrations.

Few if any of the candidates had a clear and concrete idea of what conditions in the field would be like and little conception of the months of training, the monotonous activity, and the days of waiting which lay ahead of them before their important work would begin. Unless they had had years of Army experience they could easily underestimate the inertia and the irritations they would experience. Once they were in the field, however, there would be experiences and satisfactions which could redeem the months of preparation. How much satisfaction would the candidate be able to derive from submerging himself in a cooperative activity as a member of a group? If he had a unique skill to contribute, what value would it have for him to improve that skill and to use it to best advantage for the aims of his mission? What would be the meaning for him of the close friendships which might be possible in the isolation of working behind enemy lines?

What satisfaction would it bring him to vindicate his self-reliance and his ingenuity in the face of ever-changing obstacles and hazards? These questions, which we tried to answer, suggest some of the possible satisfactions in OSS assignments overseas, and if a candidate could not avail himself of them, there were serious doubts about his continuing emotional stability. If a man's motivation and affective needs could not be satisfied by the actualities in the field, there was reason to consider him a bad risk for overseas work.

Though emotional factors influence the operation of all personality variables, Emotional Stability seemed to us to be most closely related to Motivation and to Social Relations. We conceptualized these as separate variables, but dynamically none of them could ever be considered alone. Motivation is a function of underlying emotional attitudes and needs, and, without stability in the underlying structure, motivation, no matter how high it may be in the moment, will not be of sound quality or of an enduring nature. Conversely, if a man's motivation is sound and realistic, there is reason to believe that his emotional dynamics are relatively stable.

Good social relations, likewise, play a supportive role in the maintenance of high emotional stability. Few if any individuals can live with even minimum contentment without having a degree of acceptance by others. Lack of this approval is often an important direct cause for neurotic disturbances. And in the field situation, with its numerous privations, acceptance by one's fellows becomes highly prized and indeed essential. When a man has little skill in social relations there is an additional burden placed upon his emotional life. Conversely, if he can avail himself of group support, he has good insurance against other possible assaults represented by a stressful environment. Good social relations and the satisfaction they make possible can compensate for other unfilled needs. Indeed, an individual's social relations and his emotional stability are so intimately connected that we have elsewhere raised the question as to whether they are not to be looked upon as two aspects of a more fundamental trait. (See Factor A, Table 54, page 513.) Even when emotional stability was the focus of our concern, it was clear that it could never be properly evaluated without discovering how it was related to social relations and to motivation.

The term "emotional stability" has connotations that may cause the reader to obtain a misleading impression of what it was we sought to conceptualize and rate under this heading. The discussion of the problems which confronted us in our attempts to rate the variable may have served to clarify the meaning we gave to Emotional Stability, but even so a further elaboration of the concept may be helpful and perhaps even necessary. Unfortunately the term suggests something stable and static, placid and even. As a phrase it may, to some, even connote the absence of emotion. Yet it was farthest from our thought that absence of emotion or even emotional flattening is a sound and valuable trait of personality. Almost every situation demands of the normal and healthy person some measure of emotional response, and there are many situations, especially in time of war, which require violent emotional reaction. A high rating on Emotional Stability did not mean, then, the absence of emotion but primarily an appropriateness of emotion in both a qualitative and a quantitative sense. Emotion is dynamic, and, if integrated with action and directed toward appropriate objects, is helpful. It was, then, the integration and direction of emotion by the person which loomed large in our notion of Emotional Stability. There are a number of desirable emotions: for example, enthusiasm, affection for associates, hate of the enemy, and, in some cases, fear, if it leads to prompt coordinated action, all of which might stand a candidate in good stead in his assignment overseas. We looked for these in a man, and if he had them, so much the better. We did not rule them out of our conception of Emotional Stability, but it must be admitted that our focus in this variable was upon a man's ability to manage emotions which might otherwise disrupt his behavior. It is probably fair to say that the core of Emotional Stability as we conceived it was a man's *governance of undesirable emotions.* We looked for emotions that were not directed toward or integrated with actions that would further the success of a man's assignment and so caused conflict which would be incapacitating (e.g., anxiety, phobias), or, if objectified in behavior, would lead to undesirable results (e.g., flight from the enemy, anger against associates, dereliction of duty). Signs of such emotion beyond the control of the subject we took as evidence of emotional instability and accordingly rated the subject low.

Concerning a man's emotional stability there were two questions to be asked: (1) Do undesirable emotions occur frequently and intensely? (2) If such emotions do occur, can they be held in check or canalized in desirable directions? If our answer to the second question was positive, then our rating of Emotional Stability would be raised, but an affirmative answer could be given only for those cases in which there was evidence, usually from the Interview, of superior dynamic structuration (e.g., regnant organization, ego strength) of the personality.

Ultimately, then, our rating of Emotional Stability was an estimate of the extent to which a man's performance in the field would be affected by emotional factors for better or for worse. If a candidate had optimum Emotional Stability, his energies and abilities could be devoted completely to the task at hand without concern on his part as to how he was doing or what others might think of him. He could consider the situation confronting him for what it actually was and would not be distracted by hardships, or frustrations, or the personalities of those around him. Though no one probably ever possessed this degree of imperturbability, it represents the broad conception which guided our final rating of this variable. Our conception might be called an efficiency rating of emotional maturity for the stresses of field work. Within this broad definition was included a man's potentiality for a neuropsychiatric breakdown. No other development could so completely make a man valueless to the organization and indeed a distinct liability to the immediate group in which he worked. In the sense that every man has his breaking point the whole range of our rating scale represented this prediction. But in practice only the lowest third of the scale implied the possibility of a crippling breakdown. For the remainder of the scale the emphasis was on varying degrees of emotional efficiency on the job overseas.

Another consideration which entered into our rating of Emotional Stability—though partly subsumed under the rating of Social Relations—was the effect which a man's affective reactions might have on group morale and the stability of others. One familiar technique for ridding oneself of anxiety, if only temporarily, is that of turning it out in irritability, complaining, and hostility directed toward others. This capacity to "turn outward" his anxiety might in some cases be the crucial factor in an individual's maintaining a moderately good working efficiency. If, however, the extent of a candidate's impairment of group efficiency seemed likely to outweight the contribution which, in other ways, he might conceivably make, it seemed wise not to recommend him for an overseas assignment. The fact that poor social relations of this type are so clearly the result of emotional instability explains why this pattern of adjustment was considered in our rating of Emotional Stability.

A final concern in scoring a candidate's Emotional Stability was the possible presence of psychopathic traits. This factor might seem to match only roughly our concept of Emotional Stability since the psychopath, in the nature of his over-all adjustment, might be stable, in the sense that he would not develop symptoms under the most difficult conditions. And, if his motivation were high, he might be able for a while to perform efficiently. But all things considered, psychopaths could hardly be considered assets to the organization. Their irresponsibility and antisocial tendencies would quickly make them a liability to the group. In most cases they could not be depended upon to make a solid contribution, and they might even jeopardize the lives of others. After all it is the psychopath, par excellence, who lacks governance of emotion and impulse, and this was crucial to our concept of Emotional Stability. When such a deviation in character as psychopathy was uncovered during assessment, the candidate who possessed this particular lack of fitness was rated inferior in Emotional Stability.

During the assessment period there were three major sources of data regarding a candidate's Emotional Stability: the Interview, the situations, and casual observations. The Interview brought together a candidate's projective material, his various inventories, and his personal history form, since all of these were considered concurrently with and interpreted in the light of his life history data and the impressions gained of him during the Interview. The situations which were relevant for the estimation of Emotional Stability were Construction, Stress, and Post-Stress. A supplementary but very important source of data was the incidental observation of candidates in the other situations and in the informal social life at S. By all odds, the opinion of the interviewer concerning a man's emotional stability carried the greatest weight in our deliberations. But each of the three sources of data contributed in a complementary fashion to the judgment represented by our final report and final rating.

The Interview provided the widest range of data both as to developmental history and as to the various levels of affective attitude. It supplied the frame of reference within which a candidate's responses to stressful situations and his informal behavior during assessment were to be understood. Our conception of the dynamic structure of a candidate's personality, as well as our final judgment of his stability, was derived in large measure from the evidence gathered by the interviewer. As compared with the other personality variables, Emotional Stability depended by and large upon the judgment of a single staff member, the interviewer. His was a grave responsibility indeed.

The situational tests were designed to evoke responses to provoking and stressful stimuli. There was no thought that they would supply us with true work samples, nor were the provoking situations closely similar to any that might be anticipated in the field. They were, in a sense, caricatures of field situations. Had the situations in our tests been more conventional and less provoking, the returns from them in the way of personality data would have been diminished considerably. There was no expectation that the emotional response to the provocation would be a direct and unequivocal manifestation of our conception of Emotional Stability. Invariably the behavior in the situations had to be interpreted in the context of the data gathered from all other sources; by itself it might mean a great deal or virtually nothing. Occasionally a candidate would make a creditable and stable response to the stressful situation of a test and yet, in the final judgment of the staff, have poor promise of emotional stability in the field. Conversely, some of the candidates who seemed, on other scores, to possess stable and mature emotionality were genuinely, though perhaps superficially, upset during the provoking situational tests.

The importance of the incidental observations which were made during an assessment period lay mainly in the fact that they provided a wide sampling of manifest behavior in respect to poise, social self-confidence, and apparent social needs. They yielded a picture of the manner in which a candidate handled himself when little more was required of him than that he be a social being. In many cases, a candidate's patterns of social response gave significant clues to his underlying emotional make-up. These informal observations usually provided less for the interviewer working with the candidate than for the other members of the staff, for whom they were especially important. Occasionally, however, a candidate's informal social behavior supplied us with the key which made possible a credible interpretation of the over-all pattern of his personality.

Since the interviewer's judgment so very largely represented the final evaluation of a candidate's Emotional Stability, it is worth while to consider how he came by it. Before embarking on the Interview, he briefed himself for it by a perusal of the candidate's Personal History Form, the projective material, the various inventories, and the Work Conditions Survey. The Personal History Form gave a longitudinal view of the candidate's personality and some information about his education and work experience. The bare outline of the family constellation in which the candidate was reared was often provocative, both of tentative interpretations and of issues to be settled later in the Interview. From the projective material— mainly the Sentence Completion Test and the Projective Questionnaire— a provisional interpretation of overt and covert behavior patterns was made. Any atypical clustering of answers in the inventories raised additional hypotheses and questions. Finally the Work Conditions Survey indicated preferences expressed by the candidate regarding conditions which he thought would make for his best performance in the projected assignment. All of these sources of information yielded a preview of the candidate's personality and though this picture was often changed significantly by subsequent data, the interviewer was prepared by it to make the best use of the interview. With these basic data at hand the interview could quickly become an exploration for the less obvious facets of the candidate's personality.

Necessarily each interviewer had his own methods for establishing rapport, for keeping the interview moving, and for making the transitions from one area of personality to another. One important early consideration was to get a clear picture of the family and the personalities of those who had exerted the first major influence upon the candidate. It was recognized that the character structure nurtured in this early setting represented the basis for future growth. The next important consideration was the direction of development and change which the candidate's personality had taken by virtue of starting school, a changing family constellation, and other major life experiences. Appearance of neurotic symptoms during any of these transitions was suggestive of the degree to which the experiences themselves had not been assimilated, leaving the personality vulnerable to subsequent traumatic experiences. The sheer severity of these crises was less important than the manner in which they had been handled and the new directions which the personality had taken as a result of them. During the formative years each new major experience leads to a reintegration of the personality, either in the direction of further strength and resiliency or in the direction of persistent maladjustive reactions and a narrowing of activities and interests. In the case of many candidates, because of their relative youth, the problem of emancipation from the home merited considerable attention. If this transition had been carried through successfully it was strong indication that previous crises had been handled well. However, beneath this pattern of emancipation it was always valuable to know what the personality was moving away from and what it was moving toward. No matter what transition or major experience was considered, it was important to know what residues of earlier behavior patterns were involved. If there was evidence that an individual tried invariably to utilize an earlier pattern of adjustment for succeeding experiences, his subsequent adjustment was judged likely to be precarious and restricted.

In the ideal Interview the "revisiting" of a candidate's major life experiences provoked a greater variety of feelings than would have appeared had it been limited to a discussion of his current preoccupations. From such discussions of the past one could often estimate how well the early experiences of a candidate had been assimilated. Regardless of the particular topics which might come under discussion, the Interview was an interpersonal experience for the candidate which was likely to evoke attitudes and behavior patterns which also operated in his other relationships. Much of a candidate's typical behavior was here either adumbrated or clearly expressed.

In so far as he was highly motivated, a candidate usually tried to give the best possible picture of himself. It was the interviewer's task, however, to see behind this façade. The candidate's frankness, objectivity about himself, and the ebb and flow of anxiety as he discussed various topics of a personal nature were invaluable clues to his present emotional maturity and stability. His blind spots and his exaggerated feelings, prejudices, or resentments, if they appeared in the Interview, were important signs of how much of a residue of earlier patterns of adjustment still operated in the present personality. Particularly important was the way in which the candidate handled whatever anxiety appeared. Was he defensive, apologetic, submissive, resentful, or hostile toward the interviewer? Did the anxiety seem to radiate, once it had been aroused, over a great variety of topics, or was it limited to specific topics, disappearing when those topics had been discussed? Was his present pattern to turn the anxiety inward with resulting self-recrimination and depressed moods, or did he readily displace it onto his surrounding environment? The answers to questions such as these were high lights of the Interview, the importance of which could hardly be exaggerated.

There was, of course, wide variation in the fruitfulness of the Interview as a source of data. Despite high motivation for an OSS assignment, some candidates covertly challenged the interviewer to find out anything about them. They felt that their past experiences and the intimate aspects of their present personalities had nothing to do with evaluating their fitness for their proposed assignments. Notwithstanding the good intention and the patient effort of an interviewer, suggested leads for discussion often led to noncommittal statements and verbal blind alleys. In these cases the evaluation of emotional stability was more difficult to make and depended in large measure upon the nature of the candidate's manifest behavior in the social life at S, the character of his response to stressful situations in the program, and the presence or absence of severe personality distortions in his projective material. If these additional sources of data suggested a favorable stability, the candidate might be recommended for overseas duty. If, however, this reticence about himself was a consequence of a severely constricted and repressed personality, the likelihood of his maintaining emotional stability in the field was estimated to be low. Such candidates, however, were always difficult to assess, and we never made our ratings of them with any sense of confidence.

Physical symptoms with a possible psychogenesis were considered very seriously in making the Emotional Stability rating. Occasionally a single such symptom, e.g., severe headache, might disqualify a candidate if it was likely to be set off by conditions to be found in the field. If, however, the symptom was seemingly precipitated by something in the candidate's domestic life, e.g., marital unhappiness, it might not by itself preclude his operating efficiently overseas. In any case we deemed it necessary to get some understanding of the origin of symptoms and their unconscious meanings. Any single mild psychosomatic involvement might not be important, but a host of mild complaints almost certainly would be.

The interviewer, because of the greater amount of material available to him, was considered the most reliable person to assess and evaluate the candidate's stability. As a result, the interviewer's ratings of Emotional Stability carried the greatest weight of all ratings of this variable. The correlation of interviewers' ratings of Emotional Stability with the final ratings of the variable ranged between .89 and .94 for the various periods.

The distribution of interviewers' ratings of Emotional Stability for Periods F–G are presented in Table 16. It can be seen that the desideratum of a distribution of 7 per cent of the ratings in the Very Superior and Very Inferior categories, 18 per cent in the Superior and Inferior categories, and 25 per cent in the High Average and Low Average categories was not attained. This failure was largely due to the fact that certain of the ratings acquired specific meanings as assessment progressed. In the last months of the program it had become the practice to assign ratings of 0 to those candidates who had had a psychological breakdown from which they had not as yet fully recovered, and to those who were presently struggling with frank psychoneurotic and psychosomatic disturbances. Ratings of 1 were usually reserved for those unstable candidates who, though less disturbed than those rated 0, presented so great a risk that they could not be recommended for their projected assignments. At the other extreme, ratings of 5 were assigned to those individuals who were so well integrated and so well

TABLE 16

Distribution of Interviewers' Ratings of Emotional Stability in
Terms of Percentage

(Periods F–G; N=442)

S Scale					
0	1	2	3	4	5
2.5	7.2	32.4	36.2	19.0	2.7

adjusted that there was thought to be practically no chance of their breaking down. Since most of the candidates had already been through the screening provided by induction centers and the Army, and since the staff was reluctant to assign Very Superior ratings (since for few candidates could the possibility of breakdown be definitely excluded), it was to be expected that the ratings assigned by the interviewers would cluster in the upper-middle range of the scale.

Among our situational tests, the Construction Test was designed primarily to test the reactions of a candidate to "snafu," to belittling and insulting remarks, and in addition to provide some indication of his ability to manage recalcitrant, irritating, and stupid subordinates. The social atmosphere during Construction was so challenging that before the test was over the candidate was called upon to demonstrate a considerable range of his social and emotional patterns of adjustment.

The ratings of Emotional Stability in Construction correlated .44 $(N=440)$ with final ratings of this variable for Periods F–G. Indeed, if one considers only the magnitude of this correlation, one might well question why the Construction Test was retained in the battery. The truth is that the value and importance of the situational tests in this battery are not readily discernible from the correlations between the ratings of Emotional Stability based on them and the final ratings of this variable. Their contribution was a more qualitative one. The Construction Test, for example, was invaluable in high-lighting certain specific aspects of personality. In one case it might be "snafu" tolerance, in another a sense of humor, in a third, objectivity that would be revealed by the test. But each of these was only an aspect of the total personality. It was unwise and impossible to generalize about an individual's Emotional Stability from any one experimental situation. The final rating on Emotional Stability had to be determined by a multitude of factors, and since only one, or at most, several, of these factors could be observed at any one time in a situational test, it is understandable why the correlation between ratings made in situational tests and final ratings of the same variable was not over .50 for any one of the periods.

The Stress Interview was the second situation in which evidence regarding Emotional Stability was gathered. There were two serious limitations of the Stress Interview as a test of Emotional Stability. On the one hand, the range of possible behavior which might be shown by the candidate in this situation was restricted, being largely confined to the verbal level. The physical expressions of instability were always noted, but often it was difficult to tell how significant they were or how they were to be interpreted. If a candidate became visibly confused or blocked in his speech, it was significant, but this symptom appeared only occasionally. Many times we were hard pressed to agree upon the meaning of behavior observed. Another limitation of the Stress Interview as compared with the Construction Test was that the artificialities of this situation were more obvious and some of the candidates clearly did not take it seriously. If these particular candidates were also fairly resourceful they often made a commendable showing. Yet despite these limitations of the Stress Interview, it served to arouse emotion in many candidates and provided the staff with an opportunity to observe the ways in which candidates handled their anxieties. Although a candidate was attacked less personally in Stress than in Construction, here also he was on the spot so far as maintaining an intelligent and stable performance was concerned. The efficiency of his thinking under these conditions was certainly an aspect of our concept of Emotional Stability.

The correlation between the ratings of Emotional Stability obtained during Stress and the final ratings was of approximately the same magnitude as that obtained for the Construction Test. It was .46 for Periods F–G ($N = 437$).

In the Post-Stress situation which immediately followed Stress, the important questions for the interviewer to answer concerning Emotional Stability were: How intensely had the candidate been aroused? What was his reaction to the test and his opinion of its purposes? What direction did his resentment take? What was his reaction to failure? What mechanisms did he have for assimilating the experience? Another question to be answered in Post-Stress concerned the manner in which a candidate construed this new situation in which he could talk over his experience with a sympathetic staff member. Were his emotions so overflowing that he immediately started talking as though X conditions now prevailed, or did he realize that without permission he must continue to handle himself within the limits of his cover story?

Though Post-Stress had no new provocations for the candidate—unless he were suddenly pulled up short in assuming X conditions—its importance for gauging his Emotional Stability was that it afforded a picture of what went on in him subjectively when emotion was aroused. Here one could get a view of the emotional dynamics of a man when he had not had time to absorb an experience or achieve a sense of distance from it. To this extent it supplemented the Post-Construction Interview and the subject's own analysis of his emotionality in the Interview proper. The ratings of Emotional Stability in Post-Stress correlated with the final ratings of Emotional Stability .36 in Periods F–G ($N = 439$).

The final source of data on Emotional Stability was the constant, informal observation of candidates during their stay at S. Essentially the value of casual contacts with a candidate in the nontest situations lay in their contribution in many undefinable ways to the picture of the man's total personality. Most behavior has some affective tone if the observer is perceptive enough to see it; and in assessment, where the competitive element was strong, the affective coloring of behavior was obvious. A candidate's pattern of social response gave one of the best pictures of the emotional support which he needed from his fellows and of his techniques for achieving it; likewise the degree to which he displaced his anxieties in the way of criticism, irritability, and open hostility was also revealing. Did he need acceptance by others to the extent of being painfully submissive and deferential? Or did he need to dominate others with apparent indifference to their feelings toward him? Each candidate in his unique way possessed a pattern of deference and dominance. The extent to which he was tolerant and forebearing was often a sound indication of a man's emotional maturity. The peculiar value of observing informal interaction of the candidates was that during assessment they did not have the familiar props for maintaining personal security and influence which were present in their normal lives. In this anonymous community, each man, depending upon his genuine self-confidence and his emotional and social resources, established his own social role.

One valuable bit of information which can be subsumed under the rubric of informal observation was a subject's response to alcohol during Improvisations and Debate. Upon occasion some quite unexpected behavior appeared which furnished the basis for a decided change in the rating of a candidate's Emotional Stability. A candidate who through sheer effort had made a creditable showing up to this point in assessment, only to become quite irresponsible and exhibit an ugly truculence while intoxicated, could hardly be considered to possess adequate emotional stability for an overseas assignment.

A relationship that is high-lighted in the table of intercorrelations of ratings of Emotional Stability is the sharp dichotomy between the correlation of the interviewer's ratings and the final ratings of Emotional Stability and the correlation of the final ratings with ratings in the situational tests (Table 61, page 519). These figures express statistically two facts: first, that the interviewer's rating of Emotional Stability was the most important single rating of this trait; second, that the interviewer's rating was based on data largely different from those obtained in the various situations.

If we placed so much reliance upon the ratings of Emotional Stability given by the interviewer one might ask why we devoted so much time and energy to observing candidates in our different situational tests and rating them in these situations. Since we made so little use of these ratings were they worth the time and effort spent in making them? The answer seems to us to be yes, and for four reasons. First, the situations frequently evoked behavior which served to corroborate or to negate a tentative hypothesis which the interviewer had made about a candidate after seeing him in the Interview. Second, upon occasion situations revealed specific liabilities or assets not previously discovered by the interviewer. Situations contributed to our knowledge of our candidates. Third, since the situations were to some degree standardized, they provided the opportunity for a more effective comparison of the behavior of candidates than would have been possible without them. Fourth, the situations provided occasions upon which several staff members observed the behavior of candidates, placing them in a position to question, if not to correct, the biases and prejudices which sometimes crept into the judgment of the interviewers. At S, due largely to our situations, the interviewer was not allowed to speak *ex cathedra*.

The table of intercorrelations of final ratings (Table 58, page 516) reveals that Social Relations correlates with Emotional Stability more highly than any other variable (.54). This finding supports our earlier theoretical statement of the close relationship between these two variables whereby each supports to some degree the other. The relatively high correlation between final ratings of Emotional Stability and those of Leadership (.45) is not surprising, for although one can conceive of emotionally unstable leaders, in general one would expect to find enduring qualities of leadership rather dependent upon a dynamic organization of personality in which desirable emotions would predominate and in which there would be an effective integration and direction of emotion toward appropriate ends. One might expect to find a relatively high correlation between Emotional Stability and Effective Intelligence in so far as one would assume that superior dynamic structuration of personality, one aspect of which is Emotional Stability, would depend in part upon Effective Intelligence (knowing what to do and how to do it, and the like). Actually the correlation of the final ratings of these two variables, .24, suggests that Effective Intelligence did not enter to an important degree into our conception of Emotional Stability, at least as that conception found expression in our rating of the variable. The correlations of Emotional Stability with Physical Ability (.31) and with

Security (.32) are of about the expected order of magnitude. Some measure of physical skill should contribute to emotional stability in so far as it should lessen for a person the number of areas in which frustrations are apt to be experienced. One expression of governance of emotion should be control of one's tongue and of one's egocentric drives; thus the correlation between Emotional Stability and Security. There is no reason to believe that Observation and Reporting as conceptualized by us should be significantly related to Emotional Stability. The correlation of .15 between these two variables is in agreement with expectation. The lowest correlation is that between Emotional Stability and Propaganda Skills (.09). In view of the fact that a large percentage of candidates recruited for work in subversion of morale were artists and writers, this extremely low correlation should come as no surprise. Whether these figures reveal the true relations between the correlated variables or merely reflect stereotypes in our minds is, of course, a question which a matrix of intercorrelations cannot answer.

SOCIAL RELATIONS

The success of any organization depends in large measure upon the ability of its members to function as a harmonious body with the minimum of friction and irritation. It is therefore not surprising that special attention was paid to the social relations of our assessees. While we did not expect to be able to duplicate the stressful conditions prevailing in the theaters of war, nevertheless we hoped that by confronting the candidate with the necessity of adjusting quickly to new people in new situations a fair sample of his habitual social attitudes and actions and his effects on others would be obtained. This, we thought, would provide us with sufficient basis for predicting the candidate's disposition and ability to function as a member of some group overseas.

During Period A one of the twenty-odd traits which were systematically rated was called Getting Along with Others. At the beginning of Period B this variable was given a more precise definition and renamed Social Relations. On the Face Sheet it was described as "social awareness, good will, team work, tact, absence of annoying traits." Except for the subsequent substitution of "discretion" for "social awareness," this definition, designed for the benefit of administrative officers and their chiefs, was never altered. It consists of a list of traits or subtraits which were selected as most conducive to the establishment and maintenance of congenial, trustful, and effective interpersonal relationships within the framework of the OSS. Thus the chief point for decision was not so much the presence or absence of these traits as the probable effect of the candidate on the morale of the unit to which he was likely to be assigned. We would ask ourselves, Is he the kind of man whom others will want as a member of their group?

There is not much difficulty in distinguishing those who get along well with almost everybody and those who get along well with almost nobody, but most people do not fall at one or the other of these two extremes. The average OSS candidate, at any rate, was a man who could fit harmoniously into some groups but not so harmoniously into others. Consequently, in most cases, a knowledge of the personalities composing each OSS unit was a prerequisite for accurate predictions. Only in a few instances, however, did the members of the staff at S have a reasonably congruent conception of the nature of the group in which the candidate had been selected for membership. In the vast majority of cases their conceptions were necessarily vague, and, as a result, they had to decide to what extent each candidate would be acceptable to most people, rather than to some designated group. Another reason for a general, instead of a specific, statement was that most individuals were shifted several times from one group to another during the course of their careers in OSS and no one could predict these shifts in advance. Furthermore, the complexion of each unit changed with changes in its memberships; in the theaters new groups were formed overnight and old ones were broken up. Consequently, almost every member of the OSS had to adjust to a fairly fluid human situation. Moreover, the variable Social Relations included the ability to get along smoothly with members of other OSS units, with the British, the French, and the Chinese, and, not infrequently, with some resistance group in occupied territory. Reports of assessed candidates would be brought back from overseas in which the man had been rated Superior in Social Relations by one group and Inferior by another; but since, as we have said, there was no possible way of foretelling the social dispositions of each candidate's future associates in the field, we were not in a position to make predictions that would cover cases of this sort.

Another difficulty was the estimation of enduring acceptability, as distinguished from initial acceptability. Some people are appealing on first acquaintance and can maintain for three or more days, if necessary, an agreeable social "front," but, as time goes on, their annoying characteristics emerge, one by one, and the feelings of their associates change from positive to negative. In contrast to men of such short-lasting popularity are those who, at first, produce a rather neutral impression, but who, in due course, manifest qualities which inspire affection and respect and end by being widely appreciated. In a three-day program, no matter how suspicious the staff may become of glad-handers and hail-fellows-well-met, it is not always easy to spot the affable man who will eventually get on everybody's nerves and to rate properly the inconspicuous and diffident fellow who will someday be the best-liked man in his outfit. In rating each candidate on Social Relations, the question, 'Will this man wear well?' is always appropriate.

Among the procedures that were used to measure Social Relations at Station S, the Interview was, as always, of first importance. By tactful and indirect questioning of the subject, a considerable amount of information could usually be obtained about how well he had gotten along with others in the past—in school, in business, in the world at large, in the armed services. As the candidate talked, the interviewer would invariably arrive at some impression of his social reactions and the effects he produced, an impression based, if on nothing else, on his attitude and manner in the existing face-to-face situation.

Judicious questioning might elicit that the candidate had left his last three jobs because he could not get along with his superiors or associates; or it might indicate that for the past ten years he had worked successfully at a delicate liaison job. He might be extremely cooperative and friendly during the Interview, or he might be gruff, sullen, and impertinent. It might be determined that he was a dependent individual, wanting, and therefore always going out of his way in seeking, to be accepted by others; or that he was a highly independent self-sufficient person who preferred solitude to sociality.

From the wealth of data obtained in the Interview, it was the task of the interviewer to predict the nature of the candidate's interpersonal relations with those who would be his associates in OSS both in the United States and overseas and then to express that prediction in the form of a rating, as well as to formulate it in words in writing the personality sketch.

That it was the interviewer who formed the clearest impression of a candidate's social relations or that it was he whose opinion carried the greatest weight at the staff conference is suggested by the fact that the interviewer's rating of Social Relations correlated more highly with the final rating of the trait (.69) than did any other rating of it (.39 to .62). It is of course to be remembered that the interview rating on Social Relations was made late in assessment after the interviewer had seen the candidate in various situations, and this grade incorporated the interviewer's total impression of the student.

Ratings of Social Relations were also made in four group situations. Two of them outdoors, Brook and Assigned Leadership, offered an opportunity to observe the candidates cooperating in the solution of physical problems while two of them indoors, Discussion and Debate, made it possible to see how they worked together when confronted with an intellectual problem which required only a verbal solution. Most of the correlations between the ratings of Social Relations given in these situations and the final grades are of approximately the same magnitude (Brook .50; Assigned Leadership .56; Discussion .52; Debate .56), and, interestingly enough, of a higher magnitude than the correlation between ratings in the Construction Test and final ratings (.39). Probably in arriving at the final score on Social Relations less attention was paid to the way the candidate had treated the stooges in Construction than to the way he had reacted to his associates in

the group situations, and this, we think was as it should have been, for
Construction, because of the peculiarity of the stooges' behavior, was less a
test of the candidate's tact and cooperativeness than of his emotional stability and snafu tolerance.

Up until the last period at S, the Judgment of Others Test (the writing
of personality sketches of five candidates) was included in the Social Relations battery. It was incorporated at first because it was thought that the
ability to size up other people is probably correlated positively with the
ability to maintain smooth interpersonal relations. Experience proved that
this was true, but to a much slighter extent than we had expected. In a
great many instances there was a wide gap between knowing and doing in
the realm of social relations. An analysis of our data after Period A revealed
that Judgment of Others correlated lower with the final grade on Social
Relations than any other test of this variable. In Period F, for example,
the correlation was .36. Furthermore, in an inspectional analysis of the
intercorrelations, Judgment of Others stood out as something quite unique.
The decision finally made toward the end of S to drop Judgment of Others
from the battery was based on these two empirical facts.

Relatively early in the program at S a sociometric questionnaire was developed and incorporated in the Social Relations battery. Its primary purpose
was to obtain from all candidates statements of how well they liked each
of their colleagues. This, it would seem, is the real criterion of Social Relations. But, if we could get this information at firsthand from the candidates
themselves, why did we contaminate it with our own judgments? There
are several reasons:

1) We had no reason to believe that every candidate was a sufficiently
good judge of others to say definitely which of his associates were men
with whom he and others could work pleasantly and without friction.

2) There was no gainsaying a candidate's social acceptance or rejection
of certain associates, but it had to be remembered that these reactions were
based on three days of living together and might well be reversed after
longer acquaintanceship.

3) There was always the possibility that candidates were not completely
forthright in answering the questionnaire. They might very understandably
hesitate to express unfavorable opinions about associates to members of an
assessment staff. (The frequency with which critical comments were made,
however, would seem to indicate that this is a very weak objection to relying on the results of the sociometric questionnaire.)

4) The sociometric judgments were made by one group and with certainty held only for this particular group. In making a final decision we
had to bridge the gap between this group and all other groups in which the
candidate was likely to live as a member of the OSS. One might question

whether the reactions to the candidate in outside groups would be as different from the reactions of his associates in his class as we sometimes imagined; or, if there was an appreciable difference, whether this would be larger than the error introduced by our judging his ability to get along with others rather than leaving the decision, in effect, to his present associates. It seemed to us, however, that we on the staff, and especially the interviewer who had gathered the history of the candidate's social relations in many and varied situations of the past, were in a better position than the candidate's associates to generalize from the present (and the past) to future situations.

5) Finally, as psychologists and psychiatrists, we inevitably thought (whether rightly or wrongly, we cannot say) that, by and large, our insights into and judgments of the personality structures of our candidates and of the social relations determined by them were likely to be better than those of most candidates; and so in cases of disagreement we did not find it difficult to rationalize the acceptance of our opinions rather than those of the candidates.

That the ratings of candidates given by their associates differed appreciably from those made by the staff is indicated by a correlation of .26 between the sociometric ratings and the average of ratings given in the various situations by the staff. Perhaps this relatively low agreement is a result of the fact that the candidates rated their associates on the last day of assessment, with the benefit of two and a half days of observation and, especially, after the impressions gained in Improvisations and Debate, while most of the ratings in the situations were made by the staff earlier in the program.

Our figures show, however, that we were not flagrantly partial to our own opinions, although it is clear that we favored them. For example, the correlation between interviewers' ratings and final grades in Social Relations is .69, while the correlations between ratings by associates (positive and negative, respectively) and final grades are .62 and .55. Despite the difference between the situational ratings given by the staff and the sociometric ratings given by the candidates, there seems to have been considerable agreement at the end between staff and students in their estimates of a candidate's Social Relations.

A study of the correspondence between the final rating of a candidate's Social Relations and the recommendation made to his branch concerning his disposition has revealed a number of interesting facts which indicate the important role of this variable in determining the S decision. These facts, based upon an analysis of all cases in Periods B, F, and G, may be briefly summarized as follows:

1) If a candidate received a 5 on Social Relations, he was always recommended, often highly.

2) If a candidate received a 0 on Social Relations, he was almost never recommended for service overseas.

3) If a candidate received a 4 on Social Relations, the chances were about 14 to 1 that he would be recommended, although almost every decision it was possible for us to make was made, at one time or another, for ratings of 4.

4) If a candidate received a 1 on Social Relations, the chances were about 3 to 1 that he would not be recommended. The chances that he would be recommended with qualifications were 1 to 9.

5) A comparison of Period B with Periods F and G shows that a tendency to give greater weight to poor social relations in making our final decisions developed during the later periods. Toward the end of the program it was rare indeed that a person rated 0 or 1 in Social Relations was recomended.

6) Toward the end of assessment, ratings of Social Relations, with almost no exception, bore the following relationship to the final decision:

Rating of Social Relations	Decision
0 and 1	Not recommended
2 and 3	Almost any decision possible
4 and 5	Recommended in some form

A second minor study, unfortunately inconclusive in its findings, but nevertheless suggestive, was made of the relationship between the present Social Relations as rated at S and the character of the early home environments of the candidates. An analysis of the personality sketches of fifty subjects who had received extreme ratings on Social Relations revealed a tendency for high ratings (4 or 5 on this variable) to be associated with a happy, affectionate childhood situation, and low scores (0 or 1) with an unhappy, insecure childhood. This relationship, however, was not sufficiently clear cut to provide a criterion for individual predictions.

The analysis further showed that more than half of the candidates who had received low ratings on Social Relations also had feelings of inferiority, lacked confidence, and tended to be worried, depressed, or dependent. These characteristics were never reported for candidates rated high on Social Relations. The latter, on the contrary, were generally described as confident and secure, or at least, as making progress in overcoming sensitivity and insecurity, phrases never used to describe the emotional adjustment of those who had been marked low on Social Relations.

Although the inadequacy of our data precludes generalizations, our findings suggest an hypothesis to be tested in some future program of assessment where data can be gathered with a view toward answering specific questions. Here we can do no more than report our clinical impression —if not first gained at S at least strongly reinforced by the observations made there—that the social relations of an individual and his emotional stability are mutually dependent. This would apply particularly to situations, such as the war situation, in which men must work together under stress.

This hypothesis is supported by the finding that in Period B, Social Relations correlated with Emotional Stability .43, higher than it correlated with any other variable except Leadership (.61); and in Periods F and G, ratings of Social Relations correlated more highly with ratings of Emotional Stability than with ratings of any other variable (Emotional Stability .54; Leadership .47). This result is due, in part, to the fact that Social Relations and Emotional Stability overlap to some extent by definition. Any manifestation of anger in a social situation, for example, was likely to result in a low mark on both variables.

In a study of candidates rated 0 or 1 on Social Relations, not one was found to have good emotional adjustment or to be making progress toward that state. Although this analysis has several limitations, its findings are at least suggestive. But the most convincing indication of the association between Social Relations and Emotional Stability, as rated at S, appears in Appendix B, (pages 510-515), where a factor analysis of the final ratings of variables is reported. One factor derived from the intercorrelations is heavily weighted with these two variables. This factor might be termed "Adjustability."

Of all the variables, the one which seemed to us to require the greatest amount of time to assess adequately was that of Social Relations. It was in the performance of this task especially that we came to appreciate highly the three-day program at S with its myriad situations, both formal and informal, standardized and free.

LEADERSHIP

During the last two periods of S, the leadership of candidates was rated in seven procedures. Five of these were situational tests, of which three (Brook, Construction, and Assigned Leadership) provided an opportunity to observe behavior in field problems, while two (Discussion and Debate) were designed to reveal qualities of leadership in an indoor situation and in the give-and-take of verbal argument. One of the two remaining procedures permitted each candidate's leadership to be rated by his peers (Rating by Associates) and the other yielded a rating by the member of the staff who had reason to know him best (Interview).

There was nothing novel in our conception of leadership. We thought of it as a man's ability to take the initiative in social situations, to plan and organize action, and in so doing to evoke cooperation.

In the beginning we suspected that the man who most strongly asserted leadership would not always be able to maintain it and that, conversely, a man who had little drive to assume the position of leader might function efficiently in that role when placed there by his colleagues. For this reason, we distinguished, in our early ratings, two kinds of leadership: Leadership Assertion and Leadership Efficiency. Yet at the end of Period A, when the number of variables to be rated on the Face Sheet of our final report was drastically cut, this distinction was given up (in our ratings but not in our thinking or in our observations) and in its place a single variable, Leadership, was substituted.

Actually, throughout period A, ratings of Leadership Assertion and Leadership Efficiency had been highly correlated (.86; $N=200$), not so much, however, because these two forms of behavior could not be distinguished but because the only realistic tests employed at this time were leaderless group situations in which a man's efficiency as a leader could not be seen or rated unless he asserted himself in competition with others. What was needed was a series of group problems in which leadership could be assigned to each candidate in succession. It was unfortunate that this practice was not adopted until late in the history of S.

Throughout, it was our intention to discover operational leadership that was truly effective. We tried not to be deceived by superficial qualities which at first glance look like the real thing—a good appearance, a confident manner, an impressive voice, and so on. Repeatedly it appeared to us that the candidates were much more swayed by such traits than we were and that they were especially influenced by age and graying hair in rating leadership ability. Where such ratings deviated appreciably from those given by the staff, we were forced to wonder to what extent the factors viewed by us as extrinsic to real leadership operations might not in reality be intrinsic to it, since leadership must always be in part determined by the stimulus value of the leader. Rightly or wrongly, we sought to rate the conduct that was shown when active leadership was most needed.

As with other variables, we constantly had in our minds the question of the consistency of the trait of leadership. Is a man's leadership very much the same regardless of the situation in which he is called upon to exert it? Is it reasonable to expect that a man of superior administrative leadership will prove himself equally superior when his leadership is tested in the field? Can the leadership which a man demonstrates in a group discussion of world affairs be taken as a measure of his ability to lead men on an operational mission? It was our inability to answer such questions as these with assurance that led us to introduce a battery of situational tests, and, beyond that, to seek in the Interview some indication not only of the candidate's leadership in the past but also of the consistency and generality with which he had demonstrated this ability.

Our figures show that the median intercorrelation between tests of Leadership, .41 (see Table 63, page 521), is higher than such medians for most of the other variables. Leadership rated in one field situation correlated as highly with the ratings of Leadership given in Discussion and Debate as it did with the rating in another field test. Such a finding suggests that, as against the other variables rated at S, Leadership is a relatively general trait. At the same time, two alternative interpretations of the findings cannot be ignored: (1) that the various situational tests, despite obvious differences, were sufficiently alike to elicit approximately the same behavior from each subject; and (2) that in rating Leadership in the various situations the members of the staff were unduly influenced by an over-all halo effect for each subject.

Of the five situational tests used in the last months at S, three were leaderless group situations. Only in Construction and in Assigned Leadership problems was the role of leader assigned by the staff.

From the very beginning of S, the Construction Test was used for the purpose of eliciting and rating the leadership ability of candidates but it was never a very satisfactory test of this variable, for no matter how much expertness a candidate showed he was doomed to fail because the recalcitrance of the stooges bore no relation to the techniques employed to elicit their cooperation. The behavior of the stooges was designed to frustrate the candidates and to the extent to which it did so the situation became more a test of emotional stability than of leadership. To be sure, leadership, both bad and good, was revealed by candidates in this situation, but there was an obvious tendency on the part of the staff to excuse a poor showing here, especially if other procedures yielded evidence of a different sort. Although Construction provided a sample of behavior which was usually so interesting and revealing that never once was there any consideration of discarding it, nevertheless, it was not one in which ratings were made with confidence, nor were these ratings strongly defended in subsequent staff conferences. The intertest correlation matrix for Leadership shows that the rating in the Construction Test contributed less than any other to the final score.

In order that the final rating of Leadership should not be based solely upon estimates derived from leaderless group situations, several tests in which the responsibility for leadership was fixed were introduced at various times. One of these was a so-called Recruiting Interview in which a candidate interviewed a member of the staff (stooge) to determine his fitness for an assumed intelligence mission. In this situation the stooge observed and rated the Leadership of the candidate in so far as it might be revealed in his ability to organize the interview, elicit information, develop rapport, and inspire confidence in a face-to-face situation. The Recruiting Interview was, at best, only incidentally and rather tenuously a test of Leadership; it suffered from further defects since it did not involve group activity and permitted the variable to be rated by only one staff member.

Another test of Leadership, employed for a time, was a Search Problem in which one man was directed to guide the activities of a group of candidates in tracking down parts of a message which had been hidden in a wood, the partial messages being indicated by converging arrows tacked on trees. This test appeared to be a reasonably satisfactory one. It was soon dropped, however, because of the menace of infected wood ticks, because it was expensive in time, and because proper observation by staff members was hardly possible.

Still a third measure of Leadership was tried for a short while in the early days of S and then dropped because it bore little relationship to the final rating of the variable. The candidate's ability to plan and organize as revealed in a piece of written propaganda that he composed (St. Denis Test) was taken as one measure of Leadership. In retrospect it appears that such "paper planning" is only a small part of leadership, as we conceived it, and that a thoughtful thoroughness in preparing the St. Denis paper probably reflected more of an interest in propaganda than an ability for organization. The rather introverted, slow-speaking, if not slow-thinking, candidates who were dependent upon writing for their most satisfying form of self-expression were very apt to be the ones who received high ratings on "leadership" in this nonsituational, nonsocial test.

Throughout the history of S, the Brook, Discussion, and Debate seemed to be reasonably satisfactory leaderless group situations, possessing the virtues as well as the weaknesses of all such situational tests. They revealed those who had social initiative and some measure of need to govern others. Also the quality of leadership of those who wanted to assert it was exhibited as well as the reactions of others to such leaders. But they offered the staff no opportunity to estimate the potential leadership of all members of the group. Although it seemed likely that the more competent candidates usually maneuvered or were maneuvered into positions of leadership, we could not be sure of this. Nor unless we observed him acting under these conditions, could we be sure whether a man's leadership would suffer or be improved when the responsibility and authority for direction were given him. A willingness and a desire, as well as an ability, to assume leadership in an unstructured situation may characterize a truly superior leader but not a man of lesser endowment. This, at least, was the reasoning that led to the introduction of the Assigned Leadership problems.

There remain two other sources of ratings to be discussed: Ratings by Associates and the Interview. The Sociometric Questionnaire, which was answered by all candidates on the last morning of their stay at S, contained two questions which had specific reference to leadership. The first was: Whom would you recommend as supervisor of a group dealing with problems of planning and organization? In answering this question, candidates were, without doubt, influenced by all the observations they had made of their associates during the period of assessment, but those made the night before in the Debate loomed especially large. The recency of that situation, plus the fact that it was one of two situational tests in which all members of a class were thrown together, inevitably led to an emphasizing of the observations made during it when choosing men for a position of administrative leadership. The second pertinent sociometric question was: If you were a member of a group on a dangerous mission, whom would you prefer to have as your leader? In answering this question, candidates tended to select team members whose performance they had been able to observe in the various situational tests when six men had worked together. There is no doubt, however, that observations of the performance of nonteam members in the Obstacle Course, the second test in which all members of a class were able to observe each other, influenced their selections, since physical ability was generally considered crucial for operations in the field.

The final sociometric rating of each candidate's Leadership was determined by the number of times he was chosen by his classmates for the two kinds of leadership. That candidates were inclined to believe that a man with administrative leadership tended also to possess field leadership is indicated by a small but interesting study of one hundred cases in Periods F and G which revealed a correlation of .71 between selections for the two types of leadership. The same study indicated that members of the staff weighted the two kinds of sociometric selection about equally in arriving at their final rating of Leadership, since rating of associates' fitness for leadership on a dangerous mission correlated .60 and rating of their fitness for leadership in planning and organizing correlated .56 with the final rating of Leadership.

The combined rating of Leadership by associates for Periods F and G correlated .65 with the final rating. Since the median correlation of ratings from all tests with the final rating was .66, it would seem that the judgment of a candidate's associates was neither ignored nor given excessive weight by the staff in determining the final grade.

It was the rating of Leadership given by the interviewer that correlated most highly with the final rating (.79). This cannot, however, be interpreted to mean that the Interview as an interview contributed most to the final rating of the variable. Unfortunately for research, the ratings given by the interviewers were based not solely upon information gathered in the Interview but in part upon impressions gained by observing candidates in many situations. Hence it is not surprising that the interviewers' ratings, often given late in the process of assessment, should match the rating finally agreed upon in the staff conference more nearly than those of other members of the staff. Furthermore, it was the interviewer whose task it was to integrate all ratings for his interviewees in the report which he wrote for each of them. It may be said that the interviewer contributed most both to final ratings and to the final report, but not that the Interview as a separate procedure necessarily did so.

In order to determine, after the fact, what were the characteristics of candidates whom we had rated high in Leadership at the Brook, an analysis was made of a series of performances in this situational test. The study revealed that of the twenty-five men who had received superior ratings of Leadership, only one had received a rating of Intelligence less than high average in the same situation. Four times out of five, the personality sketches of those candidates who had been rated superior in Leadership emphasized energy, zest, effort, or initiative, and never once mentioned a lack of these. On the other hand, the sketches of the twenty-five men who had received the lowest ratings in Leadership contained no reference to these traits. It is clear from these reports that the man who was considered a good leader in the Brook situation almost without exception possessed at least average intelligence, average physical initiative, more than average social initiative, and social relations characterized by tact and good will sufficient not only to avoid friction over differences of opinion but also adequate to enlist in a positive way the efforts of the less enthusiastic members of a team.

A wider scanning of the personality sketches of candidates who had received either high or low ratings on Leadership revealed a number of characteristically associated traits. In the reports on superior leaders frequent mention was made of self-confidence, common sense, originality, assertiveness, cheerfulness, tact, persistence, and a desire to excel. Descriptions of poor leaders referred often to their readiness for anger, conceit, introversion, selfishness, depressive moods, confusion, indecision, excitability, and impulsiveness.

TABLE 17

Correlations between Leadership and Other Variables—Final Ratings
(*Period G; N=133*)

Energy and Initiative	.72	Social Relations	.44
Effective Intelligence	.65	Observing and Reporting	.32
Propaganda Skills	.51	Physical Ability	.21
Emotional Stability	.48	Security	.16
Motivation for Assignment	.44		

An indication of the relations which obtained in Period G between Leadership and the other variables of personality rated at S is to be found in Table 17. It is not surprising to find the strongest relationship between Leadership and Energy and Initiative (.72). The relationship may well have been enhanced by the fact that the majority of situations at S were so structured that if a man were to exercise leadership in them he had to take the initiative.

The relatively high correlation (.65) between Leadership and Intelligence is to be expected, the more so because the intelligence rating was always a measure of a man's practical intelligence, his ability to function effectively in lifelike situations rather than his ability specifically to perform in a superior manner on intelligence tests.

At first glance the correlation (.51) between Leadership and Propaganda Skills may seem strange, but on second thought it is understandable enough. Since two of the situational tests of Leadership (Discussion and Debate) involved influencing others to one's own point of view, a candidate could hardly be expected to be outstanding in leadership unless he possessed somewhat more than average powers of persuasion. Even at the Brook and in Assigned Leadership the effective leader had to convince his colleagues of the superiority of his plans for action. It is not surprising then that Propaganda Skills as well as Effective Intelligence enters significantly into Leadership.

The correlations between Leadership and Emotional Stability (.48), between Leadership and Social Relations (.44), and between Leadership and Motivation for Assignment (.44) suggest that the effective leader did not need to be outstanding in these three other traits, but, on the other hand, that he was not apt to be strikingly deficient in them. And this again fits well with the impression which the staff had gained in its months of observing leaders, good, bad, and indifferent, in the various situational tests.

The fact that leadership correlated only .21 with Physical Ability but .72 with Energy and Initiative suggests that leadership, as conceived and rated by the staff, involved a fair measure of assertive action but not necessarily nor to any important degree physical skill and prowess. In this opinion we may have been in error; perhaps we would more often have hit the bull's-eye in rating Leadership as a predictive measure of performance overseas had we weighted physical ability more heavily. But the fact remains we did not.

The two correlations still to be noted are of about the magnitude to be expected: Leadership with Observing and Reporting (.32), and Leadership with Security (.16).

Most of the procedures which yielded ratings of Leadership also yielded ratings of Intelligence and of Social Relations. This fact suggested that we might profitably ask the question: In the situations in which the three variables were rated, were the ratings of Leadership influenced more by the ratings of Intelligence or by the ratings of Social Relations? To answer this question a series of partial correlations was run of Leadership as rated in the various tests with the final rating, holding constant first Intelligence, then Social Relations, and finally both variables. Table 18 shows clearly that the correspondence between the rating of Leadership in the tests and the final score is lower for every procedure when Effective Intelligence is held constant than when Social Relations is ruled out as an influence. Thus Effective Intelligence is again revealed as an important factor in Leadership.

But this is not to say that any of the paper-and-pencil tests of intelligence employed by us were as good predictors of the final rating of Leadership as were situational tests. The Vocabulary scores correlated .30 with the final rating of Leadership; the Twenty-Minute Otis test correlated only .20. Even had these tests been included in the Leadership battery it is clear that these figures would not have equaled the correlations between situa-

TABLE 18

Partial Correlations of Test Leadership Grades with Final Leadership Grades
(N=290 to 450)

Test	Final Leadership with Test Leadership	Partial r, holding constant the test grade on		
		Effective Intelligence	Social Relations	Intelligence and Social Relations
Interview.......	.79	.72	.74	.68
Brook...........	.73	.53	.66	.45
Discussion.......	.64	.41	.57	.31
Debate..........	.68	.56	.61	.53
Assigned Leadership....	.68	.47[a]	.57	.41

[a] Intelligence as leaders in Assigned Leadership problem.

tional ratings and final ratings of Leadership. Rather, it was Intelligence as rated in the situations that correlated so highly with final ratings of Leadership. The ratings of Intelligence and of Leadership made in the same situation generally correlated in the seventies, actually higher than the correlations between Leadership ratings made in different situations. This finding is further evidence of the close relationship between Leadership and Intelligence as rated at S. It also indicates that Leadership as rated by us was something else than a completely general trait, which is to say that the specific nature of each situational test influenced our ratings appreciably.

In rating Leadership, no less than in rating other variables, the members of the staff sought to approximate the standard distribution of ratings adopted at S, but here again they fell wide of their mark. Distributions of Leadership ratings, by test and by final grade, are characterized by extreme positive skewness. Table 19 shows this to be especially true of Discussion and Debate, where few stood out as leaders or had an opportunity to do so. It is less true of the other situations, where performance of some kind was demanded.

The mean ratings of Leadership were, in general, lower than those of other variables. Why? For one thing, if a man failed to demonstrate leadership, the staff was inclined to rate him down to a degree that was not true when he failed to manifest some other trait. For example, whereas a man's Social Relations would be looked upon as average until shown to be otherwise, failure to show Leadership usually earned a low rating.

It must be remembered that the distribution of ratings shown in Table 19 is for the last two periods of S, when the quality of recruits to be assessed had definitely dropped in comparison with that of the early assessees, and

TABLE 19

Percentage Distributions of Ratings of Leadership in Each Category of the Scale
(Periods F–G; N=268 to 422)

Test	Mean	S Scale					
		0	1	2	3	4	5
Final	1.8	10.9	28.5	35.5	20.4	4.3	0.4
Interview	2.0	9.0	25.0	35.5	23.5	6.3	0.7
Brook	2.0	12.6	21.4	31.0	23.9	9.6	0.5
Construction	1.9	7.7	29.3	35.2	22.0	4.8	0.9
Discussion	1.7	19.6	19.5	33.9	22.3	4.4	0.2
Debate	1.8	16.9	23.1	27.6	25.7	6.3	0.4
Assigned Leadership	2.1	7.8	20.0	33.8	29.2	7.8	1.4
Ratings by Associates	2.5	0.7	21.3	30.6	32.0	9.5	5.9

when, by virtue of this unfavorable comparison of our first and last populations, the ratings of the later candidates were depressed by the unrecognized shift in scale values which had taken place in the minds of the staff members over the months of assessment. Whether a single standard distribution of ratings should be held as a model over any long period of assessment is an interesting theoretical question raised by these considerations, though unfortunately not answered by them.

OBSERVING AND REPORTING

The Observing and Reporting battery was intended to measure some of the special aptitudes and abilities required of those engaged in the gathering, processing, and reporting of intelligence in the field. From the beginning it was understood that Observing and Reporting included five functions, and the different tests that composed the battery were designed to cover these as well as they could be covered in the time available. The five functions were: (1) gathering information (observing, interrogating, discriminating), (2) remembering, (3) evaluating, (4) inferring, and (5) reporting. By necessity, most of the tests involved at least two of these functions, but for purposes of analysis the functions will be considered separately.

Gathering Information.—Three types of ability involved in the gathering of information were measured by several of the tests.

OBSERVING.—Most of the tests in the battery called for the ability to observe accurately the qualities and relations of objects, sometimes in the manner of the military scout, sometimes in the manner of the special investigator or detective. The exercises included a ten-minute search of the brief case of a "suspicious character" (Brief Case Test); the observation of the terrain and the facilities at Station S over a two-day period (Terrain Test); a four-minute examination of a man's belongings laid out in his room (Belongings Test); observation of the action in two three-minute movie sequences (Movie Observation Test); and an eight-minute study of a rough military map (Map Memory Test). Besides the ability to perceive accurately, these tests called for the ability to discriminate the relevant from the irrelevant.

INTERROGATING.—In one test the candidate had to interview an "applicant" for a specialized job and get enough information from him to decide whether or not to hire him (Recruiting Test). In another, the candidate had the opportunity to cross-examine other candidates and try to break down their cover stories (Interrogation Test). The last form of this type of procedure required the candidate to interrogate a "soldier" who had just escaped from a Japanese internment camp in China and to find out all he could about the location of the camp, the treatment of the prisoners, Japanese personnel, incidental intelligence (New Interrogation Test). Success in these exercises called for the ability to follow a directive, to establish rapport, to ask questions that elicit pertinent information, to cover the entire area of requested intelligence, to avoid influencing the answers by mode of questioning. Interrogation required confidence in a face-to-face situation, quick thinking, planning, subtlety of approach, and insight into others.

DISCRIMINATING.—In all the tasks which called for the discrimination of relevant from irrelevant information, some analytical power was required. But, in order to measure this function more directly, a special test was designed in which the candidates were asked to scrutinize the contents of four documents and extract as many separate items as they could find pertinent to a given problem (SIX-2).

Remembering.—All tests in the battery involved memory, because in none of them was the candidate permitted to take notes. But only in the Terrain Test was he expected to remember significant facts for longer than a few minutes. Furthermore, since all the questions were of the true-false or multiple-choice type (except in the Belongings Test, where questions calling for free responses were used), it was recognition rather than recall which was tested. Consequently, it seemed advisable to design a technique which would measure the power of recall, uncomplicated by differences in the ability to observe, and we developed Names and Identifications.

Evaluating.—The evaluation of information is a further refinement of the process of discrimination between relevant and irrelevant material. Besides judging the pertinence of each item to the particular aim, it is necessary to judge its reliability. Therefore, in the SIX-2 Test, when the candidates listed the various scraps of information which they had gleaned from the four documents, they were further required to indicate whether each item was "probably true," "possibly true," or "rumor." The ability to make this evaluation successfully depended upon the candidate's ability to recognize to what extent two different reports of the same thing were confirmatory or contradictory, his ability to estimate the reliability of each source of information, and his ability to judge the value of an item in the context of the entire situation described in the documents.

Inferring.—In some of the tests, the candidates were required to make inferences from their observations. In the Belongings Test, they were asked to infer the characteristics of the man whose things they had examined. In the Terrain Test, in addition to answering the objective questions, they had to write a short account of the history of the estate, based on whatever inferences they could make from what they had perceived. By and large, these and other attempts to test inference ability proved rather unsuccessful. In actual practice they amounted to little more than indirect methods of testing a man's ability to observe, since, in most cases, the inference followed almost automatically from the observation. For example, in the Terrain Test, if the candidate saw the sheep pens in the area, the inference to be drawn was that the owner of the farm once kept sheep. Those who failed to make this inference were not men who lacked the power to infer but men who had not observed the pens or men who had little acquaintance with farms of this sort. Thus this test measured thoroughness of observation, knowledge of farms, and memory of a certain kind.

Reporting.—To a large extent, the effectiveness of an intelligence operator in the field depends on the clarity, completeness, and organization of the reports he sends back to headquarters. His good observations, good memory, careful evaluations, and so forth, can be of no avail if his reports are unintelligible, incomplete, or inaccurate. The SIX-2 Test, which was introduced into the battery near the end of the first year of S, was designed to measure more directly the ability to report. Having studied the documents and having listed the separate items of information, the candidate was required to make a brief written report to headquarters in the form of a radiogram. Here it was a question of the ability to condense a large mass of material into a brief message which covered the topic completely and succinctly, omitted irrelevant details, and was entirely clear. In the New Interrogation Test, introduced in the last half of the second year, the candidate was required to write a report on the basis of his interview with an escaped prisoner of war. This type of report afforded additional estimates of the man's reporting ability, since the discrepancies between what he was able to elicit in the interview and what he reported later could be measured, thereby giving some picture of the man's accuracy, his understanding of the information he had gathered, and his honesty and integrity in reporting.

Since most of the tests in the Observing and Reporting battery were pencil-and-paper tests, objectively scored, it was fairly simple to set up norms for the conversion of raw scores to the standard six-point rating scale. Although efforts were made to keep the conversion tables up to date, the distribution of scores on the different tests shows, in some cases, more deviation from the bell-shaped curve than would ordinarily be expected. Apparently fluctuations in raw scores due to changes in population were greater than anticipated and occurred faster than the conversion tables were revised. As usual, the general tendency was for the frequencies to be excessive in the middle score ranges (ratings of 2 and 3). This is particularly true of the distributions of the final scores in Observing and Reporting, which were arrived at by discussion after averaging the separate ratings.

Evaluation of the Procedures.—During the course of the program, item analyses and revisions based on the results obtained served to improve, as later studies showed, the discriminating power of each test. Reliability coefficients were calculated for each of the tests that remained in the battery at the end of assessment and were susceptible to such treatment. These coefficients were derived by the application of the odd-even reliability technique, using the Pearson r, corrected by the Spearman-Brown formula. The results are presented in Table 20. In general, the level of the coefficients is satisfactory for this type of test.

Examination of the intercorrelational matrix for Periods F–G presented in Table 66, page 523, indicates that the correlations between the subtests of the battery and the final scores in Observing and Reporting are, as one would expect, of a higher order than the correlations between the subtests themselves. The former range from .47 to .67, while the latter range from .13 to .42. Comparison of these data in Table 66 with similar data for Period B shows that correlational values derived for the same pairs of subtests for the different periods of the assessment program are of the same order, varying not more than .07 points, except in the one case of

TABLE 20

Coefficients of Reliability of Tests Remaining in the Observing and and Reporting Battery at the End of Assessment, Based on 100 Cases

Belongings .... .75
Terrain .... .83
Map Memory .... .72
Movie Observation .... .55
Names & Identifications .... .88

the coefficients expressing the correspondence of scores on the Brief Case Test and the Memory Battery (Map Memory Test and Movie Observation Test), .09 for Period B and .30 for Period F. The conclusion that can be drawn from this finding is that the structure of the battery is sufficiently stable, that is, that the degree of correspondence between the different measures employed in the battery does not change appreciably in two separate samples of the data. The relatively low correlation between subtests indicates that, in so far as they are measuring the ability to observe and report, they are measuring different aspects of this ability, which is, of course, one purpose of every battery. Furthermore, the relatively higher correlation between the subtests and the final grade indicates that, in general, the tests are contributing positively to the Observing and Reporting rating. The degree of correlation, however, is not so high as was desired.

It is worth noting that the range of correlations between tests and final rating in Observing and Reporting is smaller than the range of similar correlations in other batteries. One reason for this is that there was a greater tendency for the staff to weight certain tests more heavily in other batteries than any one test in this battery because here there was less subjective conviction about the relative merits of the individual tests. The scores in Observing and Reporting, unlike most of those in the other batteries, were derived almost entirely from objective tests, with the result that when it came to deciding on a final rating at the conference the staff members had nothing to go on except the score on each test and the reputation of the test. Here, in other words, perhaps more often than in dealing with any other battery in the program, the staff relied on the average of the ratings in arriving at the final grade.

The relationship of the final score in Observing and Reporting with final scores in other batteries is generally of a low order. (See Table 58, page 516.) The correlation with Effective Intelligence, however, is rather high (.65), which is as it should be, since all of the tests in this battery are measures of intellectual ability. As explained in the first part of the section on Effective Intelligence, it is convenient, for certain purposes, to divide intelligence into afferent intelligence and efferent intelligence. Afferent intelligence is mostly concerned with accurate observation, discrimination, analysis, memory, inference, diagnosis, conceptualization, and prognosis. Efferent intelligence, on the other hand, though it necessarily includes all of these, is more particularly concerned with planning ability, long- and short-range strategy and tactics, and with using ideas and words in dealing with people and, to a slight degree, with using instruments in dealing with inanimate objects. It is afferent intelligence, especially, which is required of a student at college, of a scientist, and of an intelligence agent; and it is afferent intelligence, chiefly, which is measured by the standard paper-and-pencil tests. Of course, there is a large overlap between these two phases of the total arc of intelligent action. Knowledge of words, for example, is necessary both for understanding written and spoken communication and for influencing others. But there is a significant difference, nevertheless, between the kind of intelligence which is generally shown by a scholar or scientist and that which is commonly manifested by an administrator, politician, or military general. Many of the tests in the Observing and Reporting battery, in fact, are more closely related to the traditional conception of intelligence (as cognition, comprehension, and the like) than are some of the tests included in the Effective Intelligence battery. But we separated the batteries as we did, partly because of the mode of organization of the OSS with its specialized secret intelligence branch, and partly because the relations of the different mental functions were less clear to us at the start of the program.

A close examination of the scores on the different parts of the Observing and Reporting battery made it possible, in some cases, to discriminate different levels of integration, that is, to distinguish the men who could operate best when actively observing and gathering firsthand information in the field from those who were best fitted to analyze, interpret, formulate, and orient toward strategy the data gained by others.

OTHER VARIABLES SYSTEMATICALLY RATED

Besides the variables already discussed in this chapter, three others appeared on the Face Sheet of the S Final Report and, for a year or more, were rated for every subject: Physical Ability, Security and Propaganda Skills. Since these are of less interest generally and were not rated in any of the appraisal procedures that were used to validate our findings, it was decided to omit them from this chapter. The various tests and situations which yielded scores on these three variables have already been described in Chapters III and IV, and we surmise that few readers would derive much benefit from an examination and discussion of our tables of intercorrelations for these variables (see Tables 64, 65, and 67, pages 522 and 524), since these particular methods are not likely to be used in other kinds of assessment and no general principles are derivable from our findings.

Chapter VII

ASSESSMENT AT W, WS, AND F

STATION W

The reasons for which W was originally founded have already been stated in the Preface. As the school became more firmly established, its scope was widened. For a variety of reasons, the branches took advantage of the fact that a shorter assessment period was available, and many candidates for important assignments were routed through the one-day school. However, the majority of those scheduled for operational work in the field continued to be sent to S, where they could be tested in outdoor situations.

The challenge to the W staff, then, was even more stringent than the one at S: in a much briefer period its members had to make a decision in which they felt confidence. But they did have the advantage of prior training at S, and the first W program was first organized as a compressed S experience.

The statements made with respect to the changing character of S apply with equal force to W. New tests and situations were devised; returnees were consulted about their experiences abroad, and regular staff conferences were scheduled to facilitate free exchanges of opinion and refinements of technique. Although the daily program was exceedingly heavy, and the burden of work such that there was no opportunity for relaxation in a ten-hour day six-day week, there was a notable feeling of zeal on the part of the staff. Everyone from the secretary to the chief instructor contributed to the interest and enthusiasm which charged the atmosphere at W. As in the case of S, the events of a typical day at W will give some idea of the feeling which characterized the school.

Since students were not selected for any particular assessment unit, the remarks made in Chapter III with regard to recruitment apply equally well to the candidates who came to W. It was our experience that the briefing given the candidate by the different branch administrative officers in preparation for assessment varied widely. Not only did the individual branches have their own policies in regard to how much they wished to tell each recruit, but the administrative officers within the branch varied in this respect, and efforts to bring about a degree of uniformity were not successful. On the day before he was to report to the assessment school, each candidate was cautioned as to maintaining cover and secrecy, and given a card with his student name and class number, and directions to report to the school:

Name: _____Ben_____

   Class No: ___W-99_____

You will report to ——— — St., N.W., Washington, D.C., ground floor, between 8:15 and 8:30 A.M., Saturday, December 2, 1944. Present this card to the clerk on duty.

In some cases the student was given no more instruction than this, but in most instances he was told that he would be given a series of tests to determine for what assignment he would be best suited, and that he would find the day interesting and profitable as well as strenuous.

From this point on there was a very distinct difference between W and S. Each student reported at W directly and by himself, wearing his customary clothing. Upon arrival, no attempt was made to welcome him or to greet him warmly; in fact, the contrary was true. He entered the office to find a psychiatrist and a member of the junior staff seated at their desks; they looked at him expectantly, and waited for him to make the first move. At the very outset, here was a difficult situation, and assessment had begun by observation of the student's reaction to it. Some were diffident, hesitant, timid, and easily flustered. Others were frankly puzzled but not especially ill at ease. Still others attempted to cover their concern by a cocky, wise-cracking manner. Some were aggressive and sarcastic. Some handed their cards to the psychiatrist immediately; others asked, "Is this the right place?" or "Is this OSS?" and such remarks were always challenged immediately, thus increasing the tension of the situation. Once the candidate submitted his card, the examiner repeated the student name, and introduced himself and his associate. The men were then taken to rooms in the basement where they changed to Army fatigue clothing, while the women went to another room where they removed their coats and hats but did not change from civilian attire. By utilizing several rooms in the basement, some effort was made to prevent the candidates from seeing the differences in rank, but it was impracticable in the short time at W's disposal to make a special point of this. Cover at W played a role that differed somewhat from that in the longer assessment at S. Obvious indiscretion or need to break cover to boast of past achievements, for example, was noted, of course, as revealing highly significant traits of personality. But, with respect to the general matter of security, the emphasis at W was placed more on the security of the organization than on that of the individual. This change to nondescript clothing had some of the effects of removing customary ego supports which the wearing of fatigues had at S. It was striking to note the preservation of

status relations when the candidates knew each other's rank, and to contrast this with the greater freedom when rank was not known. As at S,
this procedure did not always make for more accurate assessment. Since it is
a cold but true fact that rank and status played roles in determining opportunity in OSS, enlisted men often were rated high on their potential who
were bound to be discouraged by their relatively menial assignments. And
officers frequently were rated comparatively low, although they had, and
later demonstrated, ample ability to do a superlative job in the task to which
their rank entitled them. Several such experiences served to remind the staff
sharply that its role was that of assessment and not that of social equalizing.

After changing clothes, the students returned to the office where they
were given their instructions. They were told that it was important to understand these thoroughly, since they would be graded upon their observance
of the directions. The language of the directions was intentionally somewhat vague and ambiguous. Some candidates read the sheet quickly, returned it immediately to the instructor, and went briskly and confidently
to Room 41. Others read and reread the material, stood about awkwardly,
afraid to ask questions, and unable to make any move until prompted.
Whatever the reaction, it was carefully noted by the observers who, after
the students left, collated and recorded the data they had secured.

Instructions

Your attendance at Station W is for the purpose of evaluating your personal
assets and liabilities for an assignment with this organization. Because of the
responsible and confidential nature of the work of OSS, a special attempt is
made to select and place personnel as wisely and as effectively as possible, not
only from the standpoint of the greatest efficiency and effectiveness of the organization, but also from the standpoint of the individual's best interests.

The assessment procedures used at W form a part of this special over-all
personnel program. You will therefore appreciate the importance, both to the
organization and to yourself, of cooperating as wholeheartedly as you can in all
the tasks which you will be asked to carry out. Secondarily, many students have
found that in the course of the various procedures they have been able to learn
some useful facts about themselves, even though it is not practical to give out
the results of individual tests.

You have been given a "student" name. You should use this and only this
during your stay at W. Your "student" name may be your own first name, which
is all right. But at no time today should you reveal, either to a member of the
staff or to a fellow student, what your real last name is. This applies to the
personal interview and to the Personal History Form as well as to all other
situations. In conversation with other students you should also refrain from
talking about your military rank and experience, if any, and the nature of the
work you are doing or expect to do with this organization. In the personal interview and the Personal History Form you are, however, to give all information
requested in this connection, fully and accurately.

In Room 41 start at once to fill out the Personal History Form. It will be necessary to complete this in 60 minutes. Further directions regarding your schedule for the day will be given you after you have completed the form. Please remain in Room 41 until you receive them.

Upon reaching Room 41, the candidates found distributed on work tables pencils and copies of the same Personal History Form as was used at S. In accordance with directions written on the blackboard, each filled out one of these forms.

After one hour, at 9:30 A.M., a member of the junior staff entered the room and directed the candidates to stop work on the form. Those who needed more than the allotted time to complete the task were given an opportunity to do so later in the day, but the schedule for the rest of the morning would be tight and the tempo fast. In the next forty-five minutes they were required to complete the first page of the P-S Experience Blank; the Physical Symptoms Inventory; the Work Conditions Survey; and the Progressive Matrices Test.

Meanwhile, in order to assign the candidates for the Interview, members of the staff reviewed the records of the Arrival Situation and considered the salient points in the Personal History Forms which had been filled out by the subjects. Those who had given a history of definite psycho-neurotic or psychotic episodes or symptoms were always interviewed by the psychiatrists of the staff. For the rest, some effort was made to assign candidates those staff members who had unusual ability to deal with that particular type of personality. At best, this was a rough and not-too-accurate procedure, but it was the general feeling that the practice did have some value.

As soon as the students finished the Progressive Matrices, a member of the senior staff gave the morning security talk:

Good morning, ladies and gentlemen.
When you arrived this morning, you received a page of mimeographed instructions concerning the rules and procedures which you are to follow here today. I want to say a few words by way of emphasizing certain of these rules and to give you some additional information.
First of all there is the matter of individual security. At no time today should you do or say anything that will reveal your own last name. It may be that your student name is the same as your true first name. That is all right. But be careful not to indicate, either to any member of the staff or to a fellow student, what your last name is. It may be that some of you have known each other prior to coming here today. In that case you will probably know each other's last name. If this is true, be just as careful not to use or reveal another's last name as you are about your own. Don't even call anyone you have previously known by his true first name if that name differs from his student name. Use only his or her student name when addressing or referring to a fellow student.

One other point of security. If you are already a member of the OSS, don't discuss your connection or the nature of your work in that organization with any fellow student. Remember that he may not be a member of the organization and that your talking with him about the organization is therefore a breach of security. Likewise, if you are a member of any of the armed services, remember not to discuss your rank or military experience with other students.

I must warn you that your failure to comply with these security rules will be looked upon unfavorably by the staff in assessing you.

Sometime today each of you will have a personal interview lasting about one hour. In that interview the only one of the foregoing security rules which you are expected to observe is the one concerning your last name. In the interview you are at liberty to speak of your military rank and experience and of your connection with and work in OSS if this seems desirable either to you or to the interviewer. In a few minutes, Mr.——— will tell you the time and place at which you will have your interview. He will also give you the name of your interviewer.

At the head of the stairs on the second floor there is a large blackboard. On this blackboard you will find posted the schedule for the entire day. Whenever you are in doubt as to where you should be or what you should be doing, consult this schedule. On or near the blackboard you will also find a clock which you can use to time your comings and goings if you do not have a watch with you. Try to arrive at tests and interviews promptly, but do not arrive at your interview ahead of the time scheduled. If you do you are likely to find the preceding interview has not finished.

I now want to forewarn you about two events this afternoon. About the middle of the afternoon, you will come together for a group discussion. The first part of your task will be to select some problem which you think this country is going to face after the war. It should be a problem which you regard as important, one in which you are interested, and one about which you all have some knowledge. After you have selected your problem, you are to discuss and consider it with a view to arriving at some conclusion or recommendation as to how it should be dealt with. In other words, at the end of the discussion period you should be prepared to submit a program of action on which you, as a group, have reached some agreement. I mention this assignment to you now so that you can be thinking about it in advance and won't come to the discussion as "cold" as you otherwise might be if the assignment were sprung on you without notice.

The other task I want to tell you about is this. At the end of the afternoon, you will be asked to take a test of your ability to size up people after only short contact with them. Therefore, during the day get to know the names of your fellow students, find out something about their backgrounds and interests, and try to develop some feeling for the kind of persons they are. It goes without saying that you are not supposed to use third-degree methods as a means of extracting this information. That might lead to complications if you attempted it. However, you are urged to use any of the more acceptable techniques for getting to know your fellow students and to be able to size them up.

Lunch will be served in Room 21 at about 12:45 P.M. It will probably be announced by the cook shouting, "Let's go back." We have tried to get her to say something more intelligible, but we have better success if we simply tell each class of students in advance what this strange phrase means and let it go at that. A few days ago we failed to forewarn a group of students on this score, with the following result. They had just finished a test on the fourth floor and were all starting downstairs. Just at that moment the cook called out, "Let's go back, everybody go back," whereupon the students dutifully turned around and started back upstairs.

You're going to be kept pretty busy today, but you will have occasional brief breaks when you are free. During these periods we urge you to go to Room 31 in which you will find a ping-pong table, some cards, a checkerboard, and some other small recreational equipment. This is your room and you are encouraged to go to it for visiting, rest, and relaxation whenever you are free.

I am sure it is not necessary to remind you of the special efforts that OSS is making to do a good job on personnel selection and placement. This is important not only from the standpoint of the efficient functioning of the organization but also from the standpoint of your own happiness and effectiveness in the particular job which you may be given in the organization. I am sure, therefore, that you will see the logic of cooperating thoroughly and thoughtfully with all the assessment procedures.

As I have said, your day here is going to be a busy and strenuous one. However, we hope it will also be interesting and perhaps even instructive to you. If at any time you are puzzled about the schedule, the instructions on a test, or anything else, please let us know. However, do not take this as an excuse for being inattentive when instructions are being given. The instructions for all tests have been worked out with considerable care, and if you do not listen closely to them, you may find yourselves rather seriously handicapped in trying to do what is asked of you.

Are there any questions?

Mr.——— will now tell you about your interviews.

Thank you very much.

At 10:30 half the group reported for their clinical interviews, while the others remained behind to take the ACE Test; at 11:30 the groups were reversed.

It should be noted parenthetically that the W standards were quite high (see Appendix A-3, pages 505-509). The Matrix and ACE were used at W in preference to the Otis since they made some distinction between verbal and nonverbal resources, and a majority of the staff felt more secure in their judgments when they had this information available. An individual Bellevue-Wechsler was given to those who obviously performed below capacity on the group tests.

Interview.—The account of the Interview given in Chapter III is a composite of the policies and practices of both the W staff and the S staff.

A buffet luncheon was served at 12:30, the candidates and staff eating together. The place cards at the table were so arranged that no instructor sat with candidates he himself had interviewed. The luncheon situation was often highly illuminating. It was the first moment the subjects found for relaxing after four hours of constant pressure, and some of them took the opportunity to blow off steam. In general, it was the policy to permit the candidates to take the initiative in conversation. Many personality traits could be evaluated by observing the manner in which they attempted to adapt to the social situation. Some were entirely uncommunicative and ill at ease. Others found it difficult to talk of anything other than their experiences of the morning. Some competed constantly for the staff members' attention, snubbing or interrupting their fellows. Some sought reassurance directly; others indirectly by talking of their past achievements, by dominating the group at the table with a continuous display of humor or sarcasm. For the sharp observer there was much to be seen which would be of value at the preliminary staff meeting which occurred at 1:15 after the students went to the Post Exchange Supply Store. At this staff conference, the interviewers brought up salient points about the candidates they had seen, asked others for the impressions gained during luncheon, and discussed any specific problems they wished to consider further. Thus a student might be singled out for extra attention during the afternoon if, for example, the interviewer wished confirmation of his impression that the candidate was quite unable to subordinate his own desires to the aims of a group assignment. In some cases, the man in charge of a situation might even put special pressure on the candidate in question by deliberately appointing another candidate as leader, or by some other device appropriate to the circumstance which was singled out for attention.

The situations were run from 1:30 to 3:30 P.M. Small groups rotated through the Ball and Spiral, the Bridge or, in the case of women, the Filing Test, then they came together for the Group Discussion at 2:45 P.M. Before discussing the specific directions for each task, it is appropriate to consider the functions of the situations at W. Soon after one-day assessment began it became clear that in it situations had less diagnostic power than at S. This defect was due to the fact that the schedule at W was so tight, and the pressure on the candidates so constant, that there was relatively little time for the development of any real group spirit among them. They hardly had time to adjust to one set of conditions before they were rushed to another, and throughout there was a natural tendency to regard the day's task as placing a premium on individual achievement. Further, the group procedures were limited in scope, and it was far more difficult to give them any manifest validity—even at best there was a certain classroom or parlor-game air about them which could be dispelled only with care and effort on the part of the staff. However, this is not to imply that the situations

The Ball and Spiral Situation at W

A Water Situation at WS

The Bridge Construction Situation at H

Lunch in the Compound at H

were regarded as of minor interest. To be sure, it is theoretically possible for the skilled interviewer to find out all he needs to know about a candidate by eliciting complete details about a wide variety of real-life situations in that candidate's experience. But no staff member felt that this could be accomplished in a sixty-minute interview. Accordingly, the situations were looked to for amplification and validation of impressions gained in the interview. And in those cases where the two were at variance with each other, it was incumbent upon the examiner to reinterview the subject to seek an understanding of the traits not hitherto elicited.

Ball and Spiral.—Designed by Dr. John R. P. French at Harvard as a method for studying group structure and attitudes, this task was modified for use at W as a stress situation. The test was given in a room equipped with a blackboard, an electric clock with a timed ringing device, and a two-way mirror through which staff members in an adjoining room could observe the candidates after the completion of the test. The test materials themselves consisted of a ball 4 inches in diameter, and a spiral ramp with a 3-inch tread mounted on a hexagonal platform to which 6 handles were attached. The ramp rose in 4 levels to a 6-inch circular platform, and was divided into 25 numbered segments by radial lines extending from the circular platform at the top to the points at which each of the 6 handles was attached. (See picture facing page 322.)

The directions were as follows:

This is a test both of individual physical coordination and of your ability to work together as a group. The object of the test is this. You are to roll the ball from the bottom of the platform up the ramp to the small platform at the top, by appropriate manipulation of the board. Each of you is to hold one handle by one hand only, but you may change hands at any time. If the ball drops from one level to another, that is an error and you must start over from the bottom. If the ball merely rolls backward along the ramp, it is not counted as an error, and you may reverse its direction by tilting the board. After you get the ball to the top, you are to keep it there and set the board on the floor. Since the floor is not quite level, it is best to bring the ball to rest against the metal rim on the edge of the platform. We will grade your individual performance by assigning each of you as goal that segment of the hexagon immediately to the left of the handle you are holding; if the ball falls off in that area it is scored an error against you. We will grade your performance as a group by the time it takes you to complete the task assigned. To keep you in touch with the score, we will call out each individual error and mark it on the board. To record your progress as a group we will place on this graph the number of the segment at which the ball drops off the ramp, and connect each mark so as to secure a learning curve. You have 15 minutes to complete the test. The bell will ring at 5 minutes, at 10 minutes, and every minute thereafter until the end. The record for a group of 6 is slightly under 4 minutes. Are there any questions? All right, go ahead!

Although it is true that one group did make the record stated above, it is likewise true that not more than 20 groups ever succeeded in completing the task successfully. The test was all the more frustrating because it seemed so simple. When the proper amount of pressure was applied by the staff member, the group could be kept at a very high level of aspiration and tension. It is apparent, of course, that the instructions place premiums on two mutually incompatible goals. In an effort to keep his individual scores low, the candidate would tend to elevate his handle so as to push the ball over to another's segment, and thus sacrifice the group objective. Even those who kept the group objective constantly in mind might sooner or later become irritated if they saw that they were deliberately saddled with the majority of the errors. The possibilities for observing subtle personality qualities were limitless. Did one person naturally take the lead? Did two opposing characters engage in an interpersonal struggle? Did one become more tense as his score built up? Did one become ineffective whenever the pressure was on him? Did one become careless and easily discouraged when the efforts of the group were not soon successful? Did the group hold stubbornly to one procedure in spite of repeated failure? Or did it change its methods too often even though one apparently might lead to success? Did one tend to blame another for his own errors? Was there some unifying spirit which channeled the energies of all toward the common goal? Throughout the test all these situations could be observed and even stimulated by remarks on the part of the examiners, who usually maintained a rather critical attitude.

After time had been called, the examiners left the room, telling the candidates to remain until called for the next test. The observations subsequently made through the one-way screen were often more revealing than the test itself. There was a notable release of tension, and then each subject reacted in accordance with his dominant personality drives. Some persevered in the test, determined not to fail in such a simple task. Others looked sheepishly at their scores. Some built up their feelings of self-assurance by manifesting an air of superiority or disdain. Some vented their frustration and disappointment by expressions of wrath and disgust with all "mind readers"—"What can they learn from this stuff?" Some of the women dropped all other activity to rush to the mirror and powder noses, comb hair, or preen themselves. Some joined the group discussion, while others remained quite aloof. All this information, whatever its nature, was of value to the interviewer. Most often, of course, it merely corroborated what he already knew or strongly suspected, but not infrequently it provided new data for consideration and incorporation into the picture of the total personality.

Bridge.—The Bridge was the only situation at W which gave some direct evidence of the candidates' mechanical skills. Since it was highly artificial, it was only moderately satisfactory. But despite this handicap, it was considered useful in a number of respects, and was used almost consistently during the last six months at W.

The materials for this situation consisted of two raised platforms, 6 feet square, 1 foot high, anchored to the floor 8 feet apart. There were wires, ropes, pulleys, and a number of assorted two-by-four boards which had holes bored in them and pegs which fitted these holes. None of the boards was quite long enough to bridge the gap between the platforms. There were also a pail of water and a large box of paper towels weighing perhaps 20 pounds.

The directions for the test were as follows:

This is a simulated field problem, the best we could devise for a building in downtown Washington. You are to imagine that you are a scouting party being pursued by an enemy force. You have come to a bridge, but find that it has been bombed out. All that remains is this debris and the two platforms that constitute the foundations of the old bridge. These platforms are the distance apart at which you see them, namely 8 feet, but we ask you to imagine that the chasm between them is actually a thousand feet deep instead of being represented by the floor as you see it. Now, we will assume that the problem has begun so we had better all step over to the platform on this side before we fall to a horrible death. Your task is this: the bucket of water on the other side of the chasm represents a water-cooled machine gun. You are to bring it over to this side of the chasm without spilling a drop. The box on this side is supposed to contain some highly secret and valuable radar equipment. You are to transfer it carefully to the other platform in such a manner that it will not be unduly jarred or broken. You may use only the materials you see about you in effecting these transfers. Remember the conditions of the problem. If anything drops into the chasm it is, of course, lost, as would be any man who loses his balance. We have increased the artificiality of the problem to this extent: anything that touches the floor between the platforms is regarded as lost; if it were a real chasm, you could swing down into and over it. And one thing more: make your plans as you would if there were actually a chasm a thousand feet deep; do not do anything that you would not do if that were the case. You will be marked on your speed and efficiency in performing this assignment as a group. When the problem is over, all members are to be standing here on this platform as you are at this moment. You have twenty-five minutes to finish the job. Ready? Begin!

Although there was something of a boy scout flavor about the problem, most candidates went about it vigorously since it was a challenge to what is regarded as one of the more masculine of the arts, namely the building of structures with a minimum of basic material. In this situation we looked for the ability of the students to work together as a group under circumstances involving few of the conflicting elements which obtained in the Ball and Spiral situation. In that case attention had been purposely directed to individual scores; here it was more obvious that participation in group activity was the order of the day. As in all other situations, the potentially valuable observations which might be made were almost infinite. But we were most generally concerned with the following: first, were any of the candidates natural leaders—did the others turn to one of the men for suggestions, or did each of them scatter and attempt to solve the problem by himself? Did the members of the group deliberate and make a plan before they acted? Did they try any number of methods, many of which could easily have been discarded as inoperable before they even started? Was there a struggle for leadership? Who took the lead in finally crossing the chasm (this had to be done) to effect the transfer of equipment? And why did he do it? Was it to show his superiority, or was he really the logical man because of his lighter weight and greater agility? Why did each of the others hold back from the trip? Did they fear failure? Were they afraid that falling into the chasm would constitute a mark against them, and thus increase the possibly bad impression they had made because of a poor score on the Ball and Spiral? All the interpersonal events mentioned for the Ball and Spiral could and did take place here. Did the members of the group look for a plan they thought the instructors wanted them to follow? Some were certain the boards were to be pegged together, and spent the whole period trying to accomplish this impossible task, while others went ahead with an original and highly successful idea without bothering about utilizing the great mass of materials available to them. Data of this nature were collected, and an effort was made to assign numerical marks on the various personality variables which have been listed. However, it is obvious that the chief value of this situation was to raise questions about personality dynamics which required an explanation on the basis of the personality trends already explored. If these could not supply a reasonable explanation, then new information had to be sought, new deductions made.

Filing Test.—Although women could participate in the Bridge Test, it was not particularly well suited to feminine interests or special abilities. It was consequently found desirable to include in the limited battery of performance procedures one test designed expressly for women. For this purpose a simple filing test was developed, the instructions for which follow.

This project is a group enterprise. The problem is to set up a filing system using these materials: filing box, cards, card indices, typewriter, letter file, memos, and pencils.

These memos are to be filed and the cards completely indexed and filled out in the simplest manner possible so that the memos can be pulled according to the writers and the receivers of the memo. Although there are only ten memos to be filed, the system should be set up to accommodate the filing of a large number of memos.

Remember this is a group job and you are working against time. You have a maximum of thirty minutes, but you will be rated according to your speed in completing the project.

Actually the most sensible and, in the long run, economical way of setting up a file of this kind was to file the memos (in the letter file) according to *subject,* with two sets of index cards giving sender and receiver in alphabetical order. It was, therefore, important to watch for the candidates' recognition of this fact and to listen to the discussion which frequently ensued as to whether they should do only what the instructions said or show initiative and imagination along the lines indicated. The test provided a reasonably good opportunity for making observations on Effective Intelligence, Social Relations, Leadership, and Energy and Initiative.

The showing that a candidate made in this situation was naturally influenced to some extent by past experience with filing systems and by the degree of skill which she possessed in the elementary stenographic and clerical skills. This fact was not, however, a serious obstacle to the usefulness of the test, and indeed made it an especially effective instrument for assessing clerical personnel.

A valuable modification of this procedure introduced late in the program was to give the candidates the additional task of assigning each other to as many different civil service levels as there were people taking the test, these to be based on their contributions to the filing problem. These levels were arbitrarily selected by the instructor so as to make it necessary for one or two of the students to take a lower rating than they actually might hold in real life. Relatively few recognized the fact that this was only an imaginary situation; they reacted as though they actually were to be assigned to these hypothetical jobs. Hence the attitudes and behavior in a competitive situation were often clearly delineated. A woman with executive experience, for example, would heatedly insist upon a rating of CAF-7 even though she had made no contribution whatsoever to the filing task. The nature of the arguments used and the manner in which they were advanced were indicative of what might be expected were the candidate accepted by OSS. And this modification of the test was all the more valuable because there was a definite tendency in the organization to recruit able and intelligent women for relatively simple jobs well below their capacity. While this possibility was always pointed out to them in interview, it was frequently most illuminating to note the difference between their intellectual and emotional reactions to the situation as revealed during the filing test.

Group Discussion.—If the schedule had been adhered to, the two subgroups of candidates into which the total class had been divided would have completed the foregoing group procedures at 2:45 P.M. They then assembled in Room 21 and were given these instructions:

This morning you were told that there would be a group discussion this after-noon. At that time you were given some notion as to the nature of this dis-cussion and were told to be thinking about possible problems. Remember that your first task now is to decide upon a problem—some problem which you think this country will face at the end of the war. This can be either an international or a domestic problem, but it should be one that is important, one that interests you, and one that you all know something about.

The second part of your assignment, once you have decided upon a problem, is to discuss and consider it with a view to reaching agreement as to how it should, in your estimation, be dealt with.

You will have only 30 minutes for this project. Precisely at 3:15 one of you should be prepared to make a brief oral report of the group's conclusions and recommendations.

Now let me warn you that many groups fail miserably on this procedure for two reasons: (1) they fail to organize their efforts, and (2) they allow their dis-cussion to degenerate into casual, pointless chatter. Remember that you have a definite objective, namely, to present a good final report, and that you have all too little time.

If any of you wish to make notes, you will find scratch paper here on the mantel. Please go ahead.

In certain respects this was the most significant and productive of all the group procedures. The social situation was left purposely unstructured in order to create maximal opportunity for leadership qualities to come out; and no attempt was made to influence the group in selecting any of a great number of possible topics. Whereas the earlier procedures called upon practical rather than purely intellectual abilities, this situation gave the person possessing mainly the latter types of skill his chance to excel.

Since the whole class was now together and was being observed by most of the staff, the social situation was more complex, and jockeying for pres-tige and the chance to perform impressively was accentuated. The oppor-tunity for the revelation of prejudices and social stereotypes was especially good, and emotional tensions often came out clearly.

Of the twenty or so topics commonly selected, the problem of "Keeping the Peace" and the "Race Problem" were most frequently and heatedly debated.

At the end of the discussion, a few additional minutes were usually al-lowed for "minority reports" and "dissenting opinions," but general dis-cussion was not reopened.

With so large a group, it was difficult if not impossible for any one observer to rate all candidates on all variables. What usually happened was that each senior staff member observed and rated his own two or three interviewees with unusual care and recorded whatever other ratings he felt he could make with reasonable confidence.

Sociometric.—This last procedure was designed to discover what impressions each candidate had made upon the others during the day's activities. As they arrived in Room 41, the candidates were directed to take seats around the outer edges of the three long tables which were arranged to form a U. On sheets of paper provided for the purpose they were then asked to make a rough sketch of this seating arrangement and to write down the name of each member of the group at the place on the sketch corresponding to where that person was sitting. Inasmuch as each candidate wore, in a conspicuous position, a 3″ by 5″ card on which his or her name was printed, it was usually possible for every candidate, by glancing around the tables, to see the names of all other candidates. However, in order to avoid any possible difficulty or embarrassment in this connection, the examiner went around the U calling off the name of each candidate in succession. When the students had completed their seating places, they were then given these instructions:

Earlier in the day it was announced that this afternoon you would be tested on your ability to size up other people on short acquaintance. You were therefore advised to try to get to know something about the background and interests of all your fellow students today and to develop some feeling for the kinds of persons they are. The ability to size up other people is an important asset under any circumstance, but is especially useful in this organization. Today you have been associating with a group of individuals under quite unusual conditions. Save in exceptional instances, you will not previously have known anything whatever about them. Here you have had little or no opportunity to learn "who they are" in the sense of their *past* accomplishments, social status, family connections, etc. All you have to go on is "who they are" in the sense of how they act and what they can do *here and now*. The problem is to see how well you can reconstruct or infer the real personality and character of other people on the basis of this limited kind of information.

In a moment I am going to give each of you a sheet of paper like this one [which examiner displays in his hand]. On the upper half of this page are seven questions for you to answer. For each question write down the name of *one and only one* fellow student. You may give the name of any one student as the answer to more than one question, but you should not, in response to any one question, give the name of more than one student.

In answering these seven questions, consider all the members of the group, regardless of whether you have known them prior to coming here today. However, for the thumb-nail sketch which you are asked to write in the space given on the lower half of the page (and on the reverse side if you need it), you should select someone whom you have not previously known, someone whom you have met for the first time here today. Be sure also that you put your own student name and class number in the places indicated at the top of the sheet.

Now think carefully as you answer the seven questions and as you write your sketch. We are not only interested in how well you can size up other students; we are also interested in the impressions they have made on you. We take the results of this test very seriously; and what you say in it may influence either your own assignment or that of other students.

Incidentally, I should perhaps say that you are not to include staff members in this test, however much you may be tempted to. Please restrict your responses to your fellow students.

There is no time limit on this test, and you may begin work as soon as I give you your paper. If you have any questions, let me know by holding up your hand, but once the test has started there should be no further conversation.

If you feel at all self-conscious about your answers, you may keep them covered with the piece of paper on which you have sketched the seating arrangement. When you have finished fold your paper in the middle, crosswise, and I will collect it.

The seven questions constituting the first part of this test are:

1. With whom would you most enjoy continuing your acquaintance?_____
2. Which member of the group strikes you as the most dogmatic?_____
3. Which member of the group would be most likely to make friends quickly?_____
4. Which person strikes you as the one that people would be most inclined to avoid?_____
5. Which person was most inconspicuous, i.e., least noticeable?_____
6. Which person was most noticeable?_____
7. If you were a member of a work group, which one would you prefer to have as your leader?_____

As might be anticipated, this test, if wrongly administered, can arouse a good deal of resistance and antagonism. In keeping down these adverse reactions, the advance warning about the test and the use of the seating sketch were found particularly helpful. The examiner giving the instructions also encouraged wisecracks and questions as the instructions were given but then firmly discouraged any tendency to comment or carp after the test had actually started. In other words, the aims were (1) to reduce to a minimum the realistic frustrations involved in taking the test, (2) to allow an opportunity for catharsis of such resentment or embarrassment as unavoidably remained, and (3) to block any further expression of aggression or humor which might interfere with the actual taking of the test.

Indoctrination and Farewell.—When all students had finished the Sociometric, a member of the senior staff appeared for the final security talk. This usually proceeded as follows:

You have come to the end of your strenuous day at W. Before you go, I want to thank you on behalf of the staff for the cooperation you have shown today, and to tell you that we've enjoyed having you here. I want to add, too, a word more about the matter of security. This morning we spoke of the importance of individual security, of the care and discretion you should use in concealing your identity. [If some students had broken security it was referred to here.]

There is another aspect of security that I want to mention now. That is the matter of organizational security. I am going to ask your cooperation in not speaking of the procedures of the day here at W to anyone, either inside or outside the organization. We have three reasons for asking this: in the first place, in the light of your own experience, you will appreciate the value in coming fresh to the day, without advance accounts which destroy the novelty; in the second place, we have sometimes found that the student was actually handicapped by the advance warning. The interpretations that are made of the various tests during the day are not, we believe, entirely obvious; and sometimes in the desire to give a friend a break and let him know what he's getting into, some false interpretation is made which puts him at a disadvantage when he comes. In the third place, there is in OSS a special kind of respect for what is "cricket." In this organization, probably more than in any other, it is just taken for granted that we can count on your help in keeping the activities of this day at W in that category.

You may remember that in the instructions this morning you read that "many students have found that in the course of the various procedures they were able to learn some useful facts about themselves." You may have wondered what that meant. We hope that some of you may have been among the number. You may find that in looking back over the day's activities you're now able to put to yourselves some pretty pointed questions. For example, are the motives which are driving you to go overseas clear and strong enough to make you ready to stand pressure or danger or boredom or discomfort or frustration or neglect or any of the hundreds of possible situations that may arise if you go? Most of us are too busy these days to have time to think much about ourselves. Yet during this one day you've been forced to stop and do it. We hope it has been of some value to you, too.

And now again our thanks, and all good luck in the jobs that lie ahead.

Exit Interview.—After the students had completed the sociometric evaluations and the men had changed back to their regular clothing, they were seen in brief exit interviews by the instructors who had worked with them earlier in the day. These interviews gave the students an opportunity to ask questions about their reactions to the tests given during the day, and to discuss any new problems which might have arisen. In some cases, considerable tension could be released at this time. The exit interview was regarded as most helpful in clarifying the purpose of the assessment program. The students were able to offer criticisms and suggestions in an informal atmosphere, and it was believed that this procedure enhanced a favorable attitude toward the whole experience. Further, the change from the student-instructor to the co-worker relationship occasionally brought forth new data concerning the personality of a subject.

The remainder of the period from 4:00 to 5:00 P.M. was spent in a variety of ways. In those instances where it was considered necessary, doubtful cases were reinterviewed either by the original interviewer or by a colleague. The branch administrators could be consulted via telephone for further information concerning the position for which the subject was a candidate —the degree of responsibility with which he might be entrusted, the social and physical requirements he might have to meet, the possibility of his being called upon to do various tasks, alternative positions which might be open to him, and the like. Not infrequently the administrative officer would have some information concerning the student's record which was not noted on the Student Information Sheet which had been sent to W the day before, and his comments might be of great importance. At this time, also, the ratings on the individual personality variables given by the situational observers were collected, averaged, and entered on the temporary record sheet. These were then weighted by the interviewer, and the final ratings for Motivation, Effective Intelligence, Emotional Stability, Social Relations, and Leadership were recorded.

Finally, at 5:00 P.M., the entire staff met in conference. Each candidate was presented briefly, the essential facts of the history were given, the nature of his proposed assignment was explained, and the findings of the day were reviewed. Those on whom there was general agreement were disposed of rapidly, but the problems were thoroughly discussed. In those cases where it was felt that further observation would be necessary before any opinion could be offered, it was recommended that the subject be sent to S for further study. In all other cases the decision was made and the interviewer authorized to write up his report. The form of the report was the same as that used by S, although not all the variables were rated at W because of the shorter period of observation. The interviewers wrote these reports before 10:00 A.M. the following day, turned them in to the chief instructor, who reviewed and signed them, and then submitted them to the appropriate branch. In all cases of rejection or of approval with qualifications the interviewer who had seen the candidate called the branch administrative officer concerned, and discussed with him the reasons for the staff's decision.

STATION WS

In June, 1944, the third OSS assessment unit, WS, was set up in southern California in connection with the newly established West Coast Training Center. Station WS served to expedite the screening of personnel recruited in the West as well as to prevent the occurrence of a serious bottleneck due to overloading at Stations S and W. As predicted, the flow of candidates was intermittent, and, therefore, in this area it was possible to put into effect in some degree the plan of closely observing the behavior of students not only during the four-day screening period but also during their course at the near-by Training Center, the aims being to make doubly certain of their suitability and to evaluate the judgments reached at Station WS.

As a rule, instructors at OSS schools were so fully occupied with their exacting duties—keeping up with developments in their field, assembling materials and teaching aids, preparing projects, lecturing and demonstrating, reading examination papers, administering affairs, and so on—that they had little opportunity to observe their students except during periods of instruction, at which times they were likely to notice and remember only those men who were conspicuously capable or conspicuously incapable of performing the exercises assigned to them. Furthermore, the majority of the instructors were either not interested or not skillful in making impartial judgments of dispositions and abilities in other people. Consequently, it was supposed that not much reliance could be placed on their estimates of personality traits in students, either as predictive of future performances or as standards against which to measure the accuracy of assessment ratings. And so, since it was deemed advisable to continue the process of assessment through the training period, the administration adopted the policy of adding one or two assessors to the staff at the West Coast Training Center. It was also arranged to have meetings of assessors and instructors for the purpose of arriving at some mutually acceptable definitions of trait names (personality variables), so that there would be more justification in the future in using instructors' ratings as measures of the correctness of assessors' ratings. But, because of the instructors' close schedule of obligations and the lack of extra assessors during this period, these two plans—the plan to continue assessment during the training period, and the plan to evaluate ratings made at Station WS—were carried out only to a limited extent.

Station WS was located at the Capistrano Beach Club, Doheny Park, California. The clubhouse with its connecting buildings, standing on the beach within two hundred feet of the ocean, was admirably suited to the requirements of assessment. As at S, there were ample accommodations for the candidates to live and mess with the staff during the period of testing.

There is no necessity of describing the mechanisms of organization: the relations of the assessment unit to other units, the manner in which the candidates were transported from the holding area to the beach club and back again, the disposition of the final assessment reports, and other details. Suffice it to say that the number of assessees in each group, or "class," varied from one to fifteen, most of the groups being composed of about ten men. The testing period was approximately four days.

PROCEDURES

Station WS was the West Coast equivalent of S. The aims and standards set for the two units, the varieties of candidates to be assessed by them, and the types of assignments selected for the candidates were alike. Also, the men selected for the WS staff had had several months' experience at the parent institution and were not inclined to modify in any radical way the basic structure of the program. Thus practices at the two stations were outcomes of a shared policy.

The physical settings at S and WS, however, were markedly dissimilar. Instead of fields and woods, barns and sheds, and, sometimes in the winter, snow and icy winds, there were the Pacific Ocean, a broad white strip of beach, a superb swimming pool, and a beneficent climate that deservedly enjoys its reputation. To conform to these latter conditions new outdoor tasks were improvised and some of the indoor tests current at S had to be changed to some extent. And then, as a further determinant of some of the differences which will be noted, there was the acceptance by both staffs of the policy of repeated experimentation. Constantly readjusted by the ingenuity of different men to dissimilar conditions, the WS scheme of procedures naturally diverged to an increasing, though never great, degree from the forms that were being developed in the East. Finally, in its administrations, analyses, and valuations of tests that were essentially similar, the WS staff differed somewhat from the staff at S.

But, despite the interesting novelties that resulted from the operation of these several factors, the program at WS does not require detailed consideration.

FIRST EVENING

Immediately upon arrival in the late afternoon the candidates were given a welcoming introductory talk to inform them of the rules and purposes of the assessment program. They were then issued fatigue clothing and settled in their quarters in time for chow at five o'clock.

At 6:00 P.M. the evening schedule began with a simple questionnaire form, followed by the Sentence Completion Test, the Rapid Projection Test, and the Thematic Apperception Test.

Sentence Completion Test.—Same as at Station S.

Rapid Projection Test.—This was a group, multiple-choice test of the Thematic Apperception Test variety that was tried out for several months, but since no definite evidence of its efficacy was obtained, no purpose can be served by describing it.

Thematic Apperception Test.—This was presented to the whole group as a written assignment. The directions were as follows:

This is a test of imagination, one form of intelligence. I am going to throw some stereopticon slides on the screen one at a time; and your task will be to make up as dramatic a story as you can for each slide. Tell what has led up to the event shown in the picture, describe what is happening at the moment, what the characters are feeling and thinking, and then give the outcome. You will have ten minutes for each picture, so you will have to write quickly. The average length of stories we have been getting is about a page and a half. I'll tell you when eight minutes are up. Are there any questions? Here is your first picture.

The following pictures (from the Harvard University Press series) were shown:

1. Picture 6BM. A short elderly woman stands with her back turned to a tall young man. The latter is looking downward with a perplexed expression.
2. Picture 12M. A young man is lying on a couch with his eyes closed. Leaning over him is the gaunt form of an elderly man, his hand stretched out above the face of the reclining figure.
3. Picture 18BM. A man is clutched from behind by three hands. The figures of his assailants are invisible.
4. Picture 10. A young woman's (?) head against a man's shoulder.
5. Picture 4. A woman is clutching the shoulders of a man whose face and body are averted as if he were trying to pull away from her. In the background is the figure of a seminude woman.
6. Picture 16. Blank Screen.

The rationale of the TAT is discussed much more comprehensively in the test manual than can be done here. Suffice it to say that it is a projective technique that makes use of the tendency of people to interpret ambiguous human situations in conformity with their own experiences and wants, and the tendency of those who write stories to do likewise.

At first it was felt that the greater the number of pictures the more productive the test, and hence ten pictures comprised the original set as administered at WS. But it was soon discovered that when the number of stories asked for in a single evening was more than six, the candidates would complain of writer's cramps, general weariness, and eyestrain in the dimly lit room. An hour of continuous imagining and writing appeared to be the outside limit. Continuing the test longer than this provoked resentment.

Interpretation is the major obstacle in the inclusion of this test in a brief assessment program, especially where the staff is limited. Each set of TAT stories requires from thirty minutes to an hour merely for a rather quick over-all evaluation. The interpreter must feel his way into the atmosphere of the stories, and even granting talent and experience, this process takes time and concentrated absorption.

No systematic scoring of the responses was attempted, but it was not long before a relatively inexperienced interpreter with sufficient talent could discriminate the stories that were high or low in aggression, passivity, dominance, and so forth, or before he could "feel" the relative dejection or exaltation pervading them. Perhaps more useful for the purpose of a quick personality sketch was the evaluation of each set of stories as a unit. Here it is a matter of asking: What issues, conflicts, or dilemmas are of major concern to the author? With what needs and press, ideas, attitudes, and aspirations does the author seem to be chiefly involved?

The staff member charged with the scoring of these six stories tried nothing more ambitious than writing up these high-low needs and press, summing up the chief situations and plots in the stories, and pointing out the features which were strikingly unique.

The chief value of this test in the program at WS was to provide the interviewer with fruitful hypotheses and promising lines of approach in exploring each candidate's personality.

FIRST DAY

The candidates spent the first three hours of the morning in taking a series of intelligence tests and writing an autobiography. The Discussion came at 11:00 A.M.

Individual and Group Psychometrics.—The customary schedule included two sessions for the group administration of tests belonging to this category. At the first session, held on the morning of the first full day of assessment, the Progressive Matrices, Series Completion, Mechanical Comprehension, and Vocabulary were presented, followed by the Personal History Form. At the second session, on the next day, the Memory for Design and the Memory for Map and Instructions were given. Ultimately it became standard procedure to administer the Wechsler-Bellevue or the Army Wechsler to every candidate individually. Thus because of a smaller flow of assessees at WS, it was possible to measure a little more thoroughly than it was possible at S each candidate's ability to perform the mental operations called for in these tests.

Discussion.—Same as at Station S.

After lunch the candidates were given their medical examination, the Railroad Bridge, the Recruiting Interview, and the Briefcase.

Railroad Bridge.—This was an individual field task which called for observational ability, resourcefulness, and ingenuity.

The problem was to remove a box of "explosives" weighing 300 pounds from a point on one side of an "electrified" barbed wire fence to a railroad bridge on the other side of the fence, without coming into contact with the fence. The candidate was allowed to use such equipment (e.g., wheelbarrow, planks, rollers, block and tackle) as could be found scattered around the area.

The perfect solution involved the removal of the box of explosives away from the fence to the mouth of a culvert near the beach, lowering the box into the culvert, and then pushing the box through the culvert (underneath the fence) to the bridge. The particular difficulty of the problem derived from the fact that the box of ammunition had first to be transported *away* from the bridge in order eventually to get it *to* the bridge.

Recruiting Interview.—Some assignments proposed for OSS candidates called for recruiting ability. This was taken to include the ability to arouse the interest of supposedly qualified persons, to estimate their usefulness, and to persuade them, if judged suitable, to accept membership in a given organization. The Recruiting Interview was designed as an aid in estimating these capacities.

Each candidate was instructed to assume that his job was to recruit personnel for G2 work in Spain. A civilian who had been referred to him by a mutual friend without recommendation was about to apply for a position. After the interview, which would last fifteen minutes, the candidate would be expected to prepare a detailed report of the applicant's qualifications, to rate him on mental ability, tact in dealing with others, dependability, and motivation, and to state whether or not he would hire him and why.

The "applicant" was a staff member, carefully schooled for this test, who acted in accordance with an invented life history and personality pattern. At the conclusion of the interview the applicant rated the candidate on Effective Intelligence (skill in questioning, ability to note inconsistencies, and the significance of information which the candidate had elicited); Social Relations (degree of rapport which the candidate established, his social awareness, tact, and absence of annoying traits); Leadership (planned use of time which the candidate had made, his ability to persuade, and his ability to create confidence); and finally Security (the care with which the candidate guarded not only his personal identity but the nature of the organization and the prospective assignment for which the applicant was being interviewed).

Briefcase.—The Briefcase Test of observing and reporting was similar to the one used in the early months at S but the materials were different: a manila expanding file with some twenty sections containing a variety of papers, pictures, souvenirs, and other odds and ends, thirty in all, pertinent to the identification of the owner of the case, his employer, his home, his acquaintances, places he had visited, and so forth. This situation called for the rapid and acute scrutiny of a number of clues from which certain inferences had to be drawn. In some cases the indications of two or more items had to be connected in order to arrive at the proper conclusion. The test was administered to the candidates individually at intervals of ten minutes. The details of the procedure are sufficiently revealed in the instructions:

In this room you will find a manila filing case which belongs to a person who was formerly visiting this area, and whose identity is unknown to you. You are given the task of examining the contents of this filing case with the purpose of discovering as much information about this unknown person as possible. You are allowed ten minutes in which to make your examination, and during that time you may make whatever notes you feel are necessary. After nine minutes have elapsed, you will be warned that there is but one minute remaining in your examination period, so that at the end of the ten minutes you will have replaced all the material and be ready to leave the room. When you have completed the examination you will be asked to write your conclusions about this unknown person. This account may take any form that you wish, the essential thing being that you give me as much information as possible. After this report has been written you will be given a number of questions concerning this individual, and it may be that you will have answered many of them in your report. However, you will be asked to indicate these answers again. If there are no questions, you may go in.

The schedule for the rest of the afternoon and evening was as follows:
3:30 Committee Report
4:30 Physical Ability
6:00 Propaganda Recognition, followed by Cable Report
7:30 Flashlight and Belongings

Committee Report.—This test was essentially a structured group discussion and differed from the latter in that the candidates were *required* to choose a chairman and an opportunity was afforded to observe their ability to abstract written material and present an oral report of it. Also, since the topic of the discussion was propaganda, it was easier to single out the candidate who was "propaganda wise" than it was in the Discussion.

The candidates were asked to assume that they were members of a committee assigned to advise on the kind of propaganda to be channeled through French Indo-China. They were given a file of information on the region and told that they had fifty-five minutes in which to prepare a list of propaganda suggestions derived from that file. The task required that each man read one of the memoranda and make an oral abstract to the group, and then, that all of them working together, integrate the information and decide on a number of effective lines of action. Leadership, Propaganda Skill, Observing and Reporting, and Social Relations were rated.

Physical Ability.—Physical Ability was tested in five athletic events: swimming under water for distance, swimming for speed any style, broad and high jumps, and the fifty-yard dash. The three track events were performed on a sandy beach which made running and jumping much harder, and increased the importance of sheer strength, relative to agility, as a determinant of success. Other land and water situations were occasionally employed.

Propaganda Recognition.—This test was designed as a measure of a person's ability to evaluate propaganda devices. Part I consisted of twenty pairs of slogans, the candidate being asked to check which one of each pair was likely to be more effective in influencing the general public. Part II consisted of eight pairs of proposed poll questions. In each instance the candidate was told to assume that he was a propagandist interested in convincing others of the wide currency of a certain specified opinion and then, with this aim in mind, to check which one of the pair of questions was likely to draw forth more answers of the sort that he desired. In addition he was asked to give his reasons for each choice.

In devising the slogans for Part I of this test, the following procedure was followed: a list of propaganda techniques was drawn up such as "card-stacking" (e.g., "He has won all his races," instead of "He has won the two races in which he has taken part"); "name-calling" (e.g., "government waste" instead of "government expenditures"); and so forth. Then a number of slogans exemplifying these techniques were selected and paired with plain factual statements. In each case, the propagandistic slogan was tentatively assumed to be the "correct" (more effective) one.

In devising the items for Part II recourse was had to several studies made by the American Institute of Public Opinion (Gallup Poll). In order to shed light on the technique of constructing poll questions, Gallup had sampled cross sections of the population on various matters, using differently phrased questions. He found, in conformity with his prediction, that the wording of the question would sometimes influence the answers obtained. For instance, to the question, "Should the United States increase our Army further, even if it means more taxes?" 88 per cent of the people replied, "Yes." But when the question was changed to, "Should the United States increase our Army further, even if you have to pay more taxes?" only 79 per cent of the people replied, "Yes." Personalizing the payment of taxes, apparently, decreased the number of citizens who favored enlargement of our Army.

Since this test was devised shortly before the closing of Station WS and was administered to only a few candidates, an evaluation of the technique is not possible at present.

Cable Report.—This procedure, like the SIX-2 test at S, was designed to measure a candidate's ability to assemble, analyze, and evaluate the substance of written material and to summarize concisely and correctly the information thus obtained.

The test was given to the group as a written assignment. First the mimeographed sheets (Reports Received at Message Center) were distributed, the candidates being instructed to read them carefully. The following directions were then read:

You are in Bassein, Burma, charged with the responsibility of collecting, collating, and transmitting to the Intelligence Officer of this organization information brought to you in brief written messages from various military observers in Burma. The sheets in front of you represent ten such messages. You are to sift out the information in these messages, determining what is fact and what is rumor, what is essential and what is irrelevant. You are to take for granted that anything stated by the observer as a firsthand report (e.g., "I saw the battleship launched," or "the general passed through here,") is a fact; but that if the information is modified in some form (e.g., "I have heard that . . ." or "It is reported that . . .") it must be considered a rumor, unless there are other confirmatory data.

From the point of view of the Intelligence Officer of this organization, material pertaining to the civil and political affairs of Burma is of equal significance with the strictly military. It need not, of course, be emphasized that the more precise and specific the information is, the greater its value and usefulness. Thus, it is more valuable by far to say that the 12th Division, for example, passed through Bassein than to say only that a division passed. And, of course, rumor may be as valuable as fact for intelligence purposes, but it must be labeled clearly as such.

Your job is to write a radiogram (cablegram) of no more than 40 words transmitting all the essential information contained in these ten messages. You have thirty minutes for this task.

Reports Received at Message Center

—1—

There is fairly authoritative information that all carriers attached to the Third Naval Task Force just arrived at Rangoon were sunk in last action.

—2—

Secret launching of the new super 45,000 ton battleship huge success is report here.

The Fifth Infantry Division based in Siam passed through here. Destination unknown.

—3—

Underground activity in Bassein district satisfactory, but there is dangerous leak of information somewhere along line at Chungking or Calcutta, probably at former. New military establishments, especially quartermaster warehouses and matériel, being brought into Bassein in huge quantities. Concentrated mainly along river front. Do not know for what theater it is intended.

—4—

In whole of Burma, as well as in important Irrawaddy delta area, there remains prewar distrust of Britain, making propaganda piped from India comparatively ineffective, if not actually harmful.

Report current here that four carriers of the Third Naval Task Force sunk.

—5—

There is much talk that the new 45,000 ton battleship capsized when it was launched yesterday.

A news story carrying a Tokyo dateline reports that both carriers of the Third Naval Force are safe in an unmentioned Japanese base. The fleet, said the story, did not sustain losses of any consequence.

—6—

Have had some indication that one of our men in Calcutta or Bombay is unreliable. Chungking man all right. News and instructions piped from China of increasing effectiveness in underground and with population. There is feeling there that fate of Burma allied to that of Chinese. Three infantry divisions formerly based in Siam on move to combat duty. Theater of operations unknown.

Memorial services held in Tokyo yesterday, according to Japanese news broadcast, for those of Third Naval Force lost at sea. The General Staff was present. Losses must have been considerable.

—7—

The Ninth and Seventieth infantry divisions have been ordered out of Siam to an active theater of operations. Guess is that they are on way to China.

—8—

Spoke to a group of sailors at Rangoon. Said that they had been through strangest naval engagement in experience. After two days' battle only losses sustained were both carriers. No destroyers, no cruisers, no tenders. Just the two carriers. Spoke to several sailors who had been aboard the two and rescued. Said both ships were torpedo-bombed. Losses in personnel were considerable; including both commanders. Support on western delta of Irrawaddy. May be Wellington, Bassein, or Myatani.

—9—

Preparations are being made in Manila for receiving three new infantry divisions. It is said troops are en route from China, Siam, and Burma.

—10—

Report that only several destroyers and one light cruiser of the Third Task Force were damaged or sunk, but that both carriers are safe in unmentioned base is front-page story in Rangoon papers. This is to deny widespread rumors that the two carriers attached to the fleet, the Yoshima and Tulagi, had been sunk. Two sailors were court-martialed for telling the story of the recent battle. There is intensive campaign to "button your lip."

I have received unconfirmed information that Gan Boon, Calcutta observer, is on Jap pay roll. Bombay man above suspicion.

The following is a list of the acceptable answers with the raw score for each correct item:

Item	Credit
Calcutta man unreliable	1
Distrust of British high	1
Chinese propaganda effective	1
Third Naval Force in Rangoon	1
Two Carriers lost ⎫ a	½ ⎫
Tulagi, Yoshima ⎭	½ ⎭
Three divisions move from Siam ⎫	½ ⎫
5th, 9th, 70th Divisions on move ⎬ a	½ ⎬
Manila preparing to receive three divisions ⎭	½ ⎭
Bassein new quartermaster base ⎫ a	½ ⎫
For India theater ⎭	½ ⎭

ª The items bracketed were given credit according to the preciseness of the information transmitted. To specify "Tulagi and Yoshima lost" was worth full credit; to say merely "Carriers lost" ½ credit.

The inclusion of erroneous information was penalized rather heavily, one half credit or a full credit being deducted, depending on the gravity of the misinformation. The "17th" Division instead of "70th" (a not uncommon transposition), for example, was penalized ½ credit; to say that the Bombay man was on Jap pay roll cost the writer a full credit. To transmit a fact as a rumor or a rumor as a fact was to lose credit for it. Irrelevant information (such as "memorial services held in Tokyo yesterday") was not scored at all, since the writer had already been penalized by using up some of the 40 words permissible on data which yielded no credits.

That there was a need for a verbal observing and reporting test in the assessment program was undeniable. That such a test might well have taken the form of this one is not unreasonable, but that this was the ideal test was questionable. It was, for one thing, a little too short, the amount of information required to obtain a score of 2 was only slightly more than the amount required to get a score of 1½. Also, the a priori decision as to what was essential and what irrelevant may not hold up under more careful analysis. On the other hand, the test did seem to provide some measure of observing and reporting, since there was a good spread of scores and a positive (.52) correlation between this test and the final over-all rating on this variable. Furthermore, it was noted that those who had had experience in this field of activity did well, almost never being penalized for wrong information, and those who were untutored in collating written information tended to fall below the mean by being penalized rather heavily for transmitting misleading data.

Flashlight.—The Flashlight Test of observing and reporting was similar to one that had been used for some months at Station S, but at WS this test was combined with the Belongings Test, the same materials being utilized in both. The procedure required two sessions.

The candidate was shown into a dark room in which there were thirty-three objects which he had five minutes to examine by the aid of a flashlight. He was told that he would be asked to identify the objects at a later time. On the following morning he reported for the second part of the test. In the meanwhile, the staff member in charge of the test had rearranged the objects in the room and had added a number of items which were very similar but not identical to those present at the time of the first examination. The following instructions were read:

All of the items which were in the room when you made your examination last night are still here. The objects have been moved about and many things have been added. Now you may look around the room and point out the objects which were here last night. I am interested only in the fact that they were present, not in their position, nor am I interested in the objects which were not present.

Belongings.—The Belongings Test for observing and reporting was similar to the one used at S except that the materials were different and at WS it was administered simultaneously with the first part of the Flashlight Test, one assemblage of items forming the basis for both tests.

SECOND DAY

Most of the morning was devoted first to group intelligence tests and then in rotation to individual intelligence tests, the Editorial Test, and the Interview. The intelligence tests have already been described.

Editorial Test.—The form of this test was that of a conversation directed in such a way as to provide some basis for ratings on Observing and Reporting, Social Relations, and Effective Intelligence. An editorial was distributed to the candidates with instructions to read it carefully so that they would be able, on the next day, to give a summary of its contents. (The editorial was a polemic in defense of war.)

When the candidate came to present his summary, the examiner started the conversation by inquiring in an informal manner what he thought of the ideas expressed in the editorial. In the discussion which followed, the candidate was forced to defend his position, the staff member always taking the opposite view.

The data for Observing and Reporting were obtained from the candidate's oral summary of the editorial. Was his memory of the facts precise? Had he selected the major points? Did he present his report clearly and concisely?

In rating Social Relations, the candidate's face-to-face behavior with the examiner was noted. Was the candidate at ease? Did he talk without halting and without embarrassment? Was he too argumentative or too submissive? Did he interrupt frequently?

Effective Intelligence was determined by the student's general handling of the problem. How quickly could he muster arguments? Of what caliber were his ideas? How articulate and accurate was he?

In ending the test, the interviewer brought the conversation back to a more personal plane by saying something in this vein: "Well, this has been very interesting. I wish there were time to continue. How are you enjoying your stay here?" To this question the student frequently responded by launching into an account of his reactions to one or another part of the assessment program.

Interview.—The interviewers at WS carried out this key procedure in much the way it was done at S and W, but they conceived it as being divided into three overlapping phases; the opening phase, the middle phase, and the end phase, and of these three they put more emphasis on the last than did the interviewer at the other assessment areas. In summary, these three phases were as follows: The opening one, by far most crucial, devoted to developing positive transference, a friendly, warm, and confident attitude of the candidate toward the interviewer, with freedom from the usual interpersonal inhibitions. The second, given over to the building up by the interviewer of a concept of the student's personality components. Preliminary hypotheses were continuously abandoned, readjusted, or reinforced, until a coherent dynamic pattern began to be apparent. The third phase began when the interviewer became confident that his concepts were reasonably correct and that they hung together. Then he had two major objectives: to arouse in the candidate recognition of the correctness of his hypotheses; and to restore the candidate's composure with psychotherapeutic reassurances and explanations when indicated. It was not necessary to tell a student whether he had passed or failed, but at least it was desirable that he should be able to understand why he had left a particular impression. It was conceived at WS almost to be the interviewer's obligation to obtain the candidate's permission for him to have the personality impression that he had when the interview was finished. The student was not meant to feel that he had been unjustly evaluated, for there was no other place in the program where such resentment could be removed.

The interviewer's choice of statements, his interpretations, and his inflections were most important in setting the pattern for the staff's reaction to a candidate. Conversely, the interviewer's judgment could be radically influenced by current observations and comments by the staff, and again it was his duty to fit such evidence correctly into a coherent conception. The Interview, then, was not just the hour spent with the candidate. That period provided a certain body of information and an empathic feeling about the candidate, but many casual contacts and conversations with both candidates and staff allowed for an expansion and elaboration of these initial concepts. Only at the close of the assessment period, however, was the Interview considered to be at an end.

The schedule for the afternoon of the second day included, in addition to interviews and individual intelligence tests, the Bridge, the Burma Town, and the Propaganda Leaflet project.

Bridge.—This group task, modeled after the Brook at S, required that a loaded wheelbarrow be moved across a "river." The undertaking called for cooperative activity and provided data for ratings on Effective Intelligence, Leadership, Social Relations, and Motivation.

Burma Town.—A relief map of a Burma town presented the candidates with a novel situation in which their ingenuity, ability to meet unexpected situations, their leadership, and their social relations could be observed.

The members of the group were given the following instructions:

You are to assume that all of you are in an airplane flying over this terrain. You are on your way to a secret mission. None of you knows where you are going except the pilot. You know nothing about the terrain over which you are now flying except that it is some place in Burma. You are all dressed in the uniform of American Army officers of equal rank..

You are flying in this direction [pointing toward the mountains on the relief map]. When the plane reaches a point directly over the town, the plane develops motor trouble. The pilot attempts an emergency landing but crashes into the mountain at this point [indicating the point] and the plane is wrecked and the pilot killed. One of you suffers a broken leg, and the rest get out of the plane uninjured.

You are to assume that you have just stepped out of the crashed plane. What do you do? I want you to plan your procedure as specifically as you can. Decide who is the injured man, what you do first, why you plan as you do, and so forth.

During the ensuing discussion, notes were made on who took the initiative in making suggestions, who had the best suggestions, what frictions arose when contradictory plans were suggested, who was the accepted leader, and the like.

Propaganda Leaflet.—Like the Manchuria Project at S, this test was designed to give a measure of one variable—Propaganda Skills. It did this by pressing the candidate to display whatever ability he had to analyze information about a population which must be influenced, to organize persuasive devices, and to write copy. It was, in short, a propaganda test; but since this was the only extended piece of work—at least four hours in duration—during the assessment period which was left entirely to the candidate's own responsibility so far as the time to be devoted to it was concerned, its value as an indicator of motivation, diligence, and work habits should not be overlooked.

The material for the test consisted of a Report on Bassein and an Assignment Sheet. These were distributed to the members of the group at six o'clock on the third evening (second day) of their stay at WS, with the remark, "This is a rather big job, but you have until six o'clock tomorrow evening to complete it." By this time, all of the group situations and most of the individual tests had been completed. Some of the candidates felt that they had, to use their own words, "taken a beating." And some felt that much of what they had done had been "unreal." They had been asked questions to which they did not know the answers, and they knew the answers to questions they had not been asked; they had played with blocks and built bridges over waterless rivers; they had put mannequins together and pulled Gestalt figures apart.

Against such a background it was not difficult to make the propaganda test real and vital. A staff member, pointing to Bassein on the map of Burma, read the following instructions:

> You have been given the responsibility of organizing, introducing, and carrying through a propaganda campaign in Bassein, Burma. All the information you have is in the attached report. Your long-range purposes are threefold: (i) breed hostility to the Japanese among the natives; (ii) make popular the cause of the Allies; and (iii) reduce the level of morale among the Japanese troops stationed in Bassein.

The candidates were requested to read the assignment sheet by themselves and then to ask any questions that occurred to them. Before leaving, the staff member informed them that they had the entire evening and at least two or three hours of the next day in which to complete the assignment.

THIRD DAY

The third morning began with the Dugout, an outdoor group project (8:00 A.M.). This was followed by another round of interviews and individual intelligence tests.

Dugout.—In addition to eliciting data on Leadership and Effective Intelligence, this task afforded an opportunity to observe Social Relations under conditions of rivalry. The candidates were taken to the beach, divided into two competing groups, and then told that each group was to construct a strategically situated and well-camouflaged dugout capable of holding three men.

The area afforded many different locations for the dugout, each with advantages and disadvantages. The first task was to choose and secure the best location ahead of the rival group. As building materials, for which the groups had to compete, all sorts of debris, boards, and boxes were scattered on the beach.

When the dugouts were completed, each group was asked to criticize the other group's work. During this phase the examiners directed their attention to the following points: Was the candidate more critical of the work of others than of his own? Was his criticism tactfully given? Did he take criticism well? Did he have a sense of humor about it all?

The criteria for Effective Intelligence and Leadership included such matters as choice of location, use made of debris as material, ingenuity of camouflage, efficiency of planning, success of attempts to direct operations, and so forth.

In the afternoon of the third day, the candidates were given some free time in which to complete the Propaganda Leaflet. On the schedule there was the frustrating Coat Hanger situation, and in the evening occurred the Stress and Post-Stress Interviews.

Coat Hanger.—This test provided an opportunity to observe a candidate work under adverse circumstances and to note his reactions to criticism.

The test was administered in a small, boothlike entry (to a locker room), the dimensions of which barely permitted an adult to turn around. Just within reach of the candidate (when he was in the room) were a flat monkey wrench and some boards with their ends chipped so that they would not balance readily on the flat surface of the concrete floor.

The candidate was brought in and told that he had a very simple task to perform. The walls of the room, he would assume, were covered with wet paint which should not, under any circumstances, be smudged. His job was to construct, with the materials available, a stable coat hanger upon which he was then to hang his coat. He had ten minutes for the job.

At the end of the instructions, the examiner conspicuously snapped his stopwatch, and began setting down notations on his scoring pad. In half a minute he announced that "more than a minute and a half are already gone." After the candidate had picked up the three boards and the wrench, and had begun building a wobbly tripod, the staff member said: "Well, that doesn't look too solid or too resourceful, does it?"

The examiner's demeanor would change from a long-suffering to a supercilious attitude, as he became increasingly critical in his remarks, and finally openly derisive. The boards continued to slip, the coat was not hung up, the "paint" became increasingly smudged, and the candidate's state progressively more unhappy. Finally the test was brought to a close.

At the end of the period the staff member explained the purpose of the test. Relieved to hear that they were not "unresourceful" after all, candidates would often be inclined to describe how they would have acted under other circumstances and how, indeed, they had behaved in the past, thus giving firsthand accounts of previous frustrating experiences and their reactions to them.

Stress.—Similar to the procedure at Station S.

Post-Stress.—Also similar to the procedure at S.

The evening ended with the Party.

The Party.—This was ostensibly a period of relaxation for the staff as well as for the candidates and was given on the final evening of the assessment program as an "expression of gratitude" for the candidates' cooperation. It was scheduled following the Stress and Post Stress Interviews, and because the stimulation of these two situations climaxed several strenuous days, a social period complete with hard liquor was gladly accepted by the candidates. The general tone maintained by the staff was one of casualness and conviviality, but the candidates were continuously observed for significant patterns of reaction now that their tongues were loosened by the post-assessment release and the consumption of liquor.

Although the staff endeavored to encourage the participation of the more retiring members of the group, for a few of these the situation appeared to be as stressful as many of the tests had been. Some men, however, who had had little occasion to feel at ease before, suddenly became chief entertainers, if not leaders.

FOURTH MORNING

The candidates were assembled and requested to write a one-page personality sketch of each of their classmates. After finishing these the men were reassembled and given a farewell talk which emphasized security. After lunch, they were returned to the Los Angeles office.

Report.—The schedule at WS, in contrast to that at S, allowed the staff members twenty-four hours in which to write and type their reports on each candidate after the assessment process was concluded.

STATION F

In the fall of 1944, one of the large OSS training stations, Area F, was transformed into a center for the reception and reallocation of personnel returning from the European and Middle East theaters of operation. In reaching a decision as to which of these men were suitable for missions in the Far East, the administrators of the OSS concluded that a few members of the assessment staff might be of some assistance. It was foreseen that a large group of returnees, perhaps a hundred or more, would reach Washington every week or two, and, for several reasons it was agreed that the disposition of every one of them should be settled, if possible, within a few days after his arrival. Therefore, the size of the psychological staff being limited, the time available for the examination of each returnee was very brief, no more than an hour or two per man.

The program adopted at F consisted simply of an interview which was partially based on the responses to two questionnaires that had just been filled out by the candidate.

Although the primary objective of this program was to determine fitness for service in the Orient, it could also be used as one method of estimating the effectiveness of each man in performing his last OSS assignment, and, so, in the case of every returnee who had been previously assessed at S or at W, of validating assessment ratings and recommendations. How this was done is explained in detail in Chapter IX in the section on Reassignment Area Appraisal.

Chapter VIII

ASSESSMENT OVERSEAS

CEYLON, INDIA, AND CHINA

Assessment in the United States had accumulated a large store of experience, and had developed elaborate theories and methods for assessing American personnel. Assessment in the Far East, however, was faced with a host of new problems not encountered before. Further, the demands of the situation, as had been the case in the United States, were such that work had to be started without the advantages of a preliminary survey or a careful evaluation of procedures.

In August, 1944, a small staff was landed by plane in Colombo, dispatched by train through the mountain country of Ceylon to Kandy, deposited in the center of a large tea and rubber plantation, and told to go to work. Thus was assessment introduced to this part of the world, a land of many peoples of contrasting cultures, languages, and habits, and of attitudes strangely different from our own; a part of the world where each of the many racial, religious, and national groups understood little about the others, and distrusted or hated them for reasons that sometimes go back far into the past.

Far Eastern assessment had its headquarters in Ceylon for about eight months; it was uprooted and sent to India, establishing itself on an oasis among paddy fields in the Province of Bengal; then it moved on to the grave-studded hills near Kunming, China; and finally reached Shensi Province to undertake a job in the mountains near Hsian.

With each transplantation came the problems of cultural differences and unfathomable motivations. In Ceylon the predominant cultural influence of the recruits was Burmese and Malayan, in India it shifted to Thai, in Kunming to a mixture of numerous subcultures of China, and in Hsian to the Korean with a tint of the Japanese. With the changes in cultures and nationalities came the changes in languages and dialects. The interpreters who had begun to understand the objectives and techniques of assessment in Ceylon found difficulty in India and would have been unable to carry on in China. With these changes there were accompanying shifts in the required qualifications of the individual candidates. They entered Burma,

Malaya, and Thailand as agents in groups of five or six, and often without the supervision of American personnel. The personality traits required of them were different from those needed in China, where field operations involved highly organized units as large as 180 men under Chinese and American officers.

The many demands, new problems, and unpredictable changes constantly confronting the assessment staff were met philosophically. For, regardless of how unfavorable conditions were at times for making careful evaluations of candidates, it was felt that the tools of assessment were sufficiently flexible to meet almost any situation. Applying them could contribute, to some extent at least, toward raising the standard of the personnel sent into occupied country.

Assessment, as in Washington, was directed primarily toward the estimation of those general qualities of personality judged by the operating branches to be essential for work in the field, rather than toward the measurement of specific abilities. There were exceptions: occasionally, for example, there was an urgent need for radio operators, and tests for code aptitude had to be employed. Circumstances usually required, however, that emphasis be placed upon an over-all personality evaluation. Missions into the field developed in accordance with changes in the military situation, often precluding long-range planning. The agent personnel for these enterprises were taken from a reserve pool where they had been placed after several months of training. As a result, at the time of assessment, information was rarely available on the specific type of work that a candidate would be called on to perform.

The variables considered to be of primary importance by field operators were motivation for the assignment, dependability, and courage. In addition, it was necessary to know something about the recruit's ability to learn (in view of the rigorous period of training that was to follow), his ability to get along with others, his emotional stability, his initiative and practical judgment, and his capacity for leadership.

It was not possible to apply American norms to the behavior of Orientals. Leadership, for example, manifested itself in different ways. In a Javanese group the leader played the role of helping others to accomplish their special duties rather than directing them. In discussion groups there was frequently no debate in the American sense; rather, there was an attempt to overcome differences and ease into an agreement. Among the Karens examined by us, however, leadership had more of the characteristics with which Americans are familiar.

This was in contrast to the Chinese, who almost invariably paid deference to the oldest member of their group. This was true regardless of whether he possessed the necessary experience or had demonstrated outstanding ability. His position would be still further enhanced if he had had more than the average amount of formal education. If in attempting practical group problems he failed to offer a solution, the work would not advance. Activity in progress might stop abruptly if he suggested another approach, the group being willing to accept it without critical evaluation. In discussions there was a reluctance to challenge his opinions.

In the evaluation of leadership sociometric data were not so useful as in the United States. The Chinese recruits, for example, would be apt to base their choices, not upon manifested ability, upon evidences of good judgment or of initiative, or even upon age in spite of the deference paid to it, but rather upon friendship. Living close to the margin for centuries, the Chinese peasants took part in the competition for survival by forming closely knit family units or clans and relying on tested personal loyalty. With those outside this magic circle there was little mutual trust or sympathy.

The estimation of motivation also presented problems. In Ceylon and India most of the natives who accepted assignments with the organization did so because of the pay they were promised. Some were "impressed" into service. Naturally they were not overenthusiastic; they were employed by foreigners, were asked to learn foreign ways, and to risk their lives for a cause which was not intimately related to their personal interests. War morale, as we knew it, did not exist in any theater in the Far East. The Chinese recruits in Kunming were drafted soldiers relatively unaware of the issues for which they were fighting. One recruit hesitated when asked the question, "Whom are the Chinese fighting?" Finally he answered, "The Americans."

Instead of attempting to estimate motivation to fight the Japanese, therefore, the staff asked these questions as to motivation for assignment: Do the recruit's history and his performance during assessment present any reasons for doubting his disposition to carry on in the field? Do his early environment, his work history, his attitudes toward the tasks that were presented to him, his apparent interest and initiative, together with his expressions of willingness to engage in the work, cast doubts on his intentions to execute his mission? Does he catch the spirit of his group, adopt its objectives, and participate to the limit? Or, on the other hand, does he present a history of shady dealings, of irresponsibility, or of egocentric attitudes antagonistic to team cohesion? Has he been sly or tricky in his dealings with the staff, avoided work, ducked out of his assignments? On the basis of all these sources, a judgment was made, not an estimation of motivation *per se,* but rather of those trends and tendencies in his personality, related in part to dependability, that might affect the constancy of his endeavor.

The measurement of courage or daring also revealed interesting deviations from American standards. On the one hand, the Karens consistently demonstrated a high degree of personal valor in test situations. It is a trait which is supported by their cultural expectations. They have been driven into the hill country by the Burmese, an enemy whom they despise, and who in turn regard them as inferior. As a minority group, they have taken a defensive position, avoiding contact with the cities, living instead in small villages in the hills to minimize the dangers of aggressions from their enemy. For purposes of self-defense and hunting in the jungles they have learned the use of weapons. And in the growing boy, who is taught to use them, emphasis is placed upon courage as an attribute of the man. The shy, undemonstrative Karen was a dependable and highly valuable ally in the Burma theater.

In contrast to this group, lack of daring appeared so frequently among the Chinese that it was natural to look for cultural determinants. One factor, mentioned above, is the respect paid to the dignity and wisdom of age rather than to the distinctions of youth—athletic physique and prowess, motility, impulsiveness, adventurousness, flexibility, dash, and speed. Age cannot be successfully challenged by youth. In contrast to the rapidly changing culture of America, where age is associated with outmoded forms of thought and action, Chinese modes of life have a venerable static quality which is best represented by and most congenial to the older members of the population. In China the last years of a man's life are spent on a plateau at the summit of his experience; in America they take a declining course which calls for a renunciation of influence and prestige.

There are other determinants. The Chinese are inclined to compromise differences rather than resort to force. Children, instead of quarreling, take their disputes to an older member of the family for settlement. Emphasis is placed upon harmonious interpersonal relations as an end in itself. Also, of all classes, the scholar, the man of thought and learning, is most highly esteemed, the military class being placed far down on the social scale. In a Chinese family it is usually the least promising of the younger sons who is selected as the one to serve in the Army. He is the black sheep, the boy without scholarly aptitude. The disposition to compromise is found within the Army itself: to defend rather than to take the offensive, to retreat rather than to engage in serious hostilities. These are a few of the reasons, apparently, why physical ability and daring are not so generally esteemed in China as they are in some other cultures.

In view of the complexity of the judgments to be made, a long assessment period was employed when practicable. It required more time to become acquainted with the men, and with a limited staff, more time to secure the necessary number of observations and measurements. A prolonged period was well suited to the program in Ceylon, where assessment itself was imbedded in a preliminary training program; it was well adapted to the program at Camp I in Calcutta, where a work-sample method of assessing special aptitudes was employed on a limited scale; but it was not practicable in Kunming, where 200 recruits were needed immediately, nor in Hsian, where the staff was also under pressure. As a policy, assessment units used all the time that was available.

At no time during the period of assessment in the Far East were men recruited in numbers sufficiently large to permit as high a rejection rate as the staff would have liked. The demands for agent personnel were almost equal to the rate of recruiting, and each man rejected by assessment meant a delay in sending operators into the field. Borderline cases were carefully scrutinized and often passed with qualifications if they seemed suitable for any type of work. This compromise would not have been necessary if the recruiting branch had provided a larger sample. This need for compromise between quality and quantity added to the problems of assessment and increased the probability of error.

A problem that was recognized, but for which no solution was found, was the variation in attitudes toward the Oriental by American personnel and the attendant variation in the treatment he received. During the period of assessment every effort was made to become acquainted with the recruit as an individual. In order to do this, more courtesies and greater considerations were extended to him than Europeans are wont to extend. Besides conforming to the basic assumption that it was due him, this treatment was rewarding in terms of better cooperation. But it was more friendly and sympathetic than the treatment meted out to him by the average American soldier. This difference became an important issue in the field in some instances. The failures of a few native agents on missions were explained by claiming that they had been spoiled during the training period by luxuries and an unduly solicitous attitude. When returned to their native ways of life, as is often necessary under field conditions, they became resentful or defiant. Complete reports are not available on this point, but it is altogether probable that a contributing factor was the scornful, if not abusive, manner of the typical GI.

Security was another problem with which assessment had to deal. There was constant danger that candidates would learn too much about the organization during the period of testing and that those who were rejected and returned to the place of recruitment would carry information with them that should not be spread abroad. This problem was eventually solved in South East Asia Command (SEAC) by establishing the assessment unit in India, thus removing recruits from all possible contact with training and operations conducted in Ceylon. The problem did not exist in China, for there there were so many potential leaks via interpreter, houseboys, and the like that it was useless to take precautions.

Among the ever-present problems was that of the lack of men trained in assessment methods. Something was accomplished by training the American personnel assigned to the unit to serve as assistants, but they, as a rule, were not permanently attached. The interpreters on the staff were also changing constantly, so that during some of the time the senior staff members had the benefit of no observations other than those which they were able to make for themselves.

A small staff restricted the scope of the testing program and complicated the problem of scheduling. During interviews conducted by the senior staff members, for example, many individual and group tests could not be given because for these the presence of an experienced observer is required. Since an interview conducted through an interpreter often lasted from three to five hours, this precedure took up an appreciable slice of the day. The problem was met by having a longer assessment period.

The assessment programs varied from place to place according to the conditions and requirements in the theater. In terms of staff, in Ceylon there were two senior members, eight instructors, and two interpreters; in India, one on the senior staff, three instructors, and two interpreters; in Kunming, four senior staff members and seven junior staff members who were also interpreters; and in Hsian, one on the senior staff, one instructor, and three interpreters. That is only part of the picture, however, for the rate at which recruits were processed varied. In Ceylon approximately 120 men were assessed in eight months; in India 20 men in one month; in Kunming approximately 800 men in thirty days; and in Hsian 40 men in ten days.

The type of assignment for which the men were being trained, as indicated earlier, also varied. In Ceylon, India, and Hsian (China), the men were to operate in occupied country as individuals or in small groups of four to six, while those in Kunming (China) were to be trained to work in combat intelligence units of approximately 180 men.

In spite of these differences in operating conditions and in requirements, the methods employed by assessment throughout the Far East were similiar, varying only in details. An interview, even though very short, was always part of the schedule. Outdoor group tests were invariably included, the problems selected being those best suited to the terrain at hand. Individual tests were also given, the number depending upon the amount of time available. Psychometric tests of one sort or another were likewise considered essential. The unique features of assessment in each of these theaters are described in the sections following.

ASSESSMENT IN CEYLON

Twenty miles from Kandy in the mountains of central Ceylon, assessment set up its first headquarters in the Far East. It was to be known as Camp K. The quarters, high on a hill in the center of a 1,500-acre tea and rubber plantation, commanded a view of rugged tropical country for miles around. Two building units were available for use, close together as the crow would fly across the canyon which separated them, but two miles by a winding road. The larger unit consisted of what had been the Mount School, and was the place where the recruits were housed and where most of the classes and interviews were held. The smaller unit, the Eastern Bungalow, provided quarters and office space for several members of the staff, as well as for a few recruits who had to be kept separate from the others for reasons of security.

There was much to be done here before the assessment unit could be put into smooth operation. After the two staff members from Washington had arrived, there were instructors and interpreters to be found and trained, a schoolhouse in bad need of repair to be put in order, and a program of assessment to be developed which would mesh with the needs of the training and operating branches of the organization. Supplies were scarce, and the OSS was new in the theater, so that the problems of administration were for a while acute. Work began immediately, however, and during the course of the following period these difficulties were ironed out and a program was evolved adapted to the plans for operations in that theater.

Candidates were obtained from many sources. Some were recruited in Calcutta, where the recruiting branch of the organization had its headquarters. These were for the most part Chinese who during the war had filtered into India from Burma, Malaya, and Indo-China. They were selected for their familiarity with those regions. Few of them were native born; rather, they classified themselves as "overseas Chinese." Some recruits were obtained in northern Burma and Assam. The Karens came from these areas. Others were secured by the British, in a sense impressed into service, for they were picked up from junks by submarines cruising along the coasts of Burma and Java, and after interrogation, would be turned over to the Americans. Some were obtained in the United States, and some in Ceylon.

For reasons already indicated, the descriptions of the candidates in terms of personality variables presented problems. Although these variables were used as points of reference, they were not emphasized, and statements about them were qualified. An effort was made, however, to give as full and complete a sketch of the recruit's total personality as possible. Patterns of behavior, basic drives, and anxieties were looked for and evaluated. In view of the fact that the recruits would have to pass a rigorous course in training and the fact that the exact nature of their assignment was unknown, the staff attempted to predict performance at the training camp as well as performance on missions. Not infrequently recommendations were made as to the kind of work for which a candidate was best fitted, as well as the kind of work for which he was least fitted.

The problems of assessing Orientals, with their wide range of cultural backgrounds and language differences, were such as to make the longest practical assessment period advisable. Fortunately time was to be had. A three weeks' program, it was judged, would not impede the schedule of planned operations. But in order to advance the men as rapidly as possible it was decided to give them basic instruction in the courses which they were to take later at the training camp and to assess them while they were engaged in these activities. This plan had certain definite advantages. Assessment could concern itself with specific skills and qualities of personality necessary for the job. It could serve as a probational period of training. Further, by burying assessment in training exercises the staff could operate, as it were, under cover. To all appearances they were instructors, not assessors. Accepting it as a training school, the recruit would be less apt to put on the protective cloak worn by a man who feels that he is under the eye of scientific scrutiny.

The procedures which constituted the final program of assessment in Ceylon can be grouped into three categories: Clinical Interview and Psychometric Tests; Group Situations; and Training Exercises.

Interview.—The Interview was usually conducted through an interpreter with objectives that were essentially the same as those accepted in the United States. It was directed first at obtaining a detailed account of the life history of the recruit, beginning with the first events he could remember. For the interviewer the recurrent question from first to last was: "Is this situation typical of the man's culture or is this a special, fortunate or unfortunate, circumstance to which he was exposed?" The interpreter was often of help here, for he could describe the customary pattern of life at this age in this environment. The incidence of bed wetting, for example, until the age of seven or eight was frequent, but it was found that the parents paid little attention to this habit. People in their community did not use eiderdown mattresses and white sheets and quilts, but slept on straw mats on the floor with a rough blanket, and it made little difference whether bladder control was learned early or late. Such problems call attention to the background of cultural knowledge which is required of assessors, some of which must be obtained during the Interview. This, to some extent, accounts for its much greater length—four or five hours in most cases.

Although attempts at deception were encountered frequently, for example, to conceal desertion from the Chinese Army or to conceal the use of opium, at the end of the Interview it was usually felt that a reasonably accurate history had been obtained. The attitude of these men toward the Interview was generally naïve; questions directed at determining beliefs, habits, and attitudes were answered frankly and often with less embarrassment or self-consciousness than is found in North American culture. The Interview, as in the United States, formed the nucleus about which were fitted the observations of behavior made in other situations.

Psychometric Tests.—Psychometric tests were given soon after the recruits arrived at Camp K. Included in this battery were the Non-Language Tests 2a and 2c from the Adjutant General's Office; the Series Completion, Paper

Form Board, and the Block Design Tests (with Kohs Blocks); the Wechsler Mental Ability Scale, Form B; OSS Memory for Designs; Matrix Test (twenty-minute version); a Figure Analogies Test; and a Word Association Test designed at Camp K. These tests were usually given individually. No standardized directions were adopted; rather, the interpreter gave general instructions until the recruit either understood the task or showed that he was entirely incapable of understanding it. A time limit was set for certain tests in order to differentiate more sharply between recruits.

Although most of these techniques are generally classified as tests of "intelligence," it was obvious that in the case of these recruits other factors were involved. Schooling was one. Often a recruit had not learned such an elementary operation as the use of a pencil, and a fellow recruit would have to write the answers for him. In addition, the attitude toward these tests—keen interest at one extreme and at the other blind submission to the incomprehensible whims of a white man—was partly a function of school experience. Thus in the evaluation of the scores of a particular recruit at Camp K the past history as well as the over-all attitude had to be taken into account.

Memory for Design Test.—This test called for reproducing certain figures exposed for a short time. Its validity was questionable, since many students who did poorly here showed keen powers of observation in outdoor assignments.

Word Association Test.—This required the candidate to speak the first word that came to mind after each of a series of stimulus words. The aim was to provide clues on matters of emotional significance, for example, fear of solitude, tendency to homesickness, and so on. In practice, because of the difficulty in determining the range of normal responses, little weight could be given to the results of this test.

The Sociometric Test.—This was used, as in the past, to obtain information on social relations within a group, to determine who were considered the leaders, who were friends, and who were disliked and why. These were important questions to settle because an outbreak of hostility in the field might threaten the success of an entire mission. A standard series of questions was asked.

Group Discussion.—This was an informal meeting held to discuss postwar problems. It revealed political attitudes, leadership ability on a verbal level, and features of group structure which had not appeared in other situations. Beer served on these occasions augmented the vigor of the arguments.

Group Projects.—Some objective was set for each group of recruits. One class built a relief map, another a part of the rifle range. As a rule the recruits were given the problem and allowed to solve it in their own way. During the undertaking they were observed by a staff member who made notes on intelligence of ideas, attitudes toward the problem, willingness to work, relations between members, leadership, cooperativeness, and so forth.

Code Training Course.—This was started in November, 1944, as soon as the installation of equipment was completed. The recruits were taught first to print the alphabet and then were drilled in the use of the code itself, learning at the same time to send and receive. A series of lessons, graded in difficulty, were automatically sent over the earphone systems, the recruits copying the letters as they heard the sound symbols. Part of each day was spent in communicating with one another. At the end of three weeks of daily instructions aptitude and interest in this type of work were usually indicated.

Use of the Compass.—A knowledge of the use of the compass was basic to mapping and to locating objectives in unfamiliar country. Field problems were started early. After preliminary instruction in reading the instrument, compass runs to various objectives were given. They were graded in difficulty. In conjunction with this course, instruction in camouflage and evasion was included. Attitudes toward the course, persistence, and speed of learning were readily observable.

Close Combat and Weapons.—This was a course that was valuable for the information it yielded on the recruit's general physical condition and coordination. Approximately ten hours were devoted to instruction, and during this time valuable data on social relations were secured; attitudes toward members of the group and willingness to use "dirty" tactics, such as gouging eyes and squeezing testicles, were often significant.

Part of the time was devoted to instruction in the use of the .45 caliber automatic pistol. Here a type of mechanical aptitude was measured. Further, in firing the weapon, anxiety or timidity in some and confidence and interest in others were very evident. These were important things to know about a man before sending him into the field.

Mapping.—In this course the fundamentals of map reading and to some extent sketching and map drawing were taught. The instructor had to start with the most elementary concepts of space representation, but surprising progress was made with training. Since certain features of the course were generally regarded as disagreeable, any tendency toward laziness or inclination to shirk work was quickly revealed here.

Morale Operations.—This course, introduced late in the program, was conducted as a modified seminar and discussion. It was perhaps more frankly an assessment technique than was any other single course. The war attitudes of the students and their sensitivity to social atmosphere were revealed through comments on war pictures and various movies held at the camp. Through a staged interview, where the instructor was questioned by recruits, ability to gather morale intelligence was assessed. Various morale operation techniques were taught through the production of cartoons, leaflets, rumors, and radio speeches.

Observing and Reporting.—Here both instruction and assessment were attempted by presenting recruits with problems of varying complexity. Several types of objects to be observed and reported on were used: a table covered with objects, a human being, an abandoned camp site, a near-by village. The reports could be checked for accuracy, and estimates made of the candidate's ability to search, to communicate ideas, and to infer from observed data. Studies of the significant parts of planes and ships offered further opportunities of testing ability to observe and report, and served to facilitate aircraft identification studies at the training camp.

Review Compass Course.—To complete this course, a knowledge of the compass, of map reading, of sketching, of observing and reporting, of camouflage and evasion was required. Recruits followed a compass course past a Tamil village to a booby-trapped house which they were to search. On the return trip they had to evade "patrols." Observers were posted along the way to note appropriate and inappropriate behavior. Here data were secured on how well candidates had learned the subject matter in the several courses prerequisite for this test. The men had 640 yards of very rugged terrain to traverse at night without lights. Emotional reactions to the dark or to the jungle were occasionally evinced.

Jungle Problem.—This was not introduced until January, 1945, when it was substituted for Group Projects. After being briefed on jungle survival and selecting their equipment for the trip, the recruits proceeded by bamboo rafts to a jungle area. Here, under concealment, they made camp and spent the night, returning to the assessment center on the following morning via a specified route which had been booby-trapped. A critique of their plans and actions was initiated immediately on return. This furnished an opportunity to observe reactions to stress, to fatigue, and to uncomfortable conditions, and how the men concealed themselves and met various practical problems along the way. Instructors accompanied them as observers over the whole course.

Whether or not these situations and these courses actually evoked behavior relevant to the future missions is problematic. In retrospect, the compass, so much stressed at K, was not a good choice, for it was contraband which was dangerous for a native to have in his possession and unnecessary in familiar terrain. Criticism of other training procedures could also be made. The staff felt, nevertheless, that distinct differences in general and special capacities, in energy and morale, in social relations, and in leadership were clearly exhibited over the three-week period.

Preparation of the Final Report.—The assessment process was brought to a focus at a conference where opinions about the recruits were expressed by each member of the staff, assessors and instructors alike. The scores, observations, impressions, and hunches collected from the interview, the psychometric tests, the situational tests, and the instructional exercises were all reported and carefully considered in coming to a decision as to the suitability of the candidate. The report written after the conference consisted first, of a brief chronological résumé of the recruits life history, second, of descriptions and interpretations of his performances at Camp K, and third, of a brief summary followed by the recommendation.

Characteristics of Recruits Assessed at Camp K.—The ninety recruits who were assessed during the first five months differed widely among themselves—in racial origin, in languages spoken, in age, in civilian occupation, in education. They were recruited in various places (ranging from New York City to Calcutta) and in various ways. Twenty-seven were impressed by British forces, 20 were recruited in Calcutta, 14 in Surinam, 11 by a Thai representative in the United States, 7 in Colombo, 4 in New York City, 3 in Burma, 3 through various sources in India, and 1 was recruited from the United States Army in Australia.

Nine different races or nationalities were represented: Chinese (38), Indonesians (18), Thai (12), Burmese (9), Tamils (6), Darnes (3), Malayans (2), Indians (1) and Burmo-Americans (1). The geographic origins of these 90 recruits were even wider and more varied than their national origins.

Of these 90 recruits, most of whom were being assessed for highly specialized OSS activities, 52 had never had any military training, 32 had a bare minimum, and only 6 had had actual combat experience. In most cases his civilian occupation had scarcely prepared the candidate for OSS operations. Eighteen of the 90 were mechanics or truck drivers; 16 were crew members or operators of junks and fishing boats; about 30 had engaged in relatively unskilled labor, such as that of plantation workers, coolies, houseboys, farmhands. There were about 19 "intellectual" workers—teachers, translators, interpreters, and students.

The range in formal education corresponded to the range in occupations.

Eighteen had had no formal education whatsoever. Forty had attended native schools, a number of them reporting that they had "learned nothing" there. Seventeen had attended English-speaking or missionary schools, and 15 had attended college, either native or foreign.[1]

This wide range in origin, training, education, and occupation also reflected itself in the languages spoken, written, and read by the recruits. Thirty-seven spoke English; the rest spoke a variety of other languages, including French, Chinese (eleven different dialects), Thai, Japanese, and Arabic. The problem of communication between the recruits and the assessment staff was an ever-present one; but since most of the recruits were multilingual, only a few interpreters were required.

-Over 55 per cent of the recruits were in the age range between 14 and 29; the average age was 30 years; the youngest recruit was 14, the oldest 53 years. Forty-eight of the recruits were or had been married and 27 of these acknowledged having children.

The chief formal characteristics distinguishing the 29 recuits who were rejected from the 61 recruits who were recommended are hardly worth reporting in detail. The rejected recruit was apt to be older than the successful recruit. The average age of the former was a little over 32, but that of the latter was about 29 years.

National origin was also a differentiating factor between the successful and unsuccessful recruits. Almost half of the rejected ones (48.2 per cent) were Indonesians, this despite the fact that the Indonesians comprised only 20 per cent of the total assessed population. To be more specific, of the 18 Indonesians who were assessed at K, 14 were rejected and only 4 were recommended for further training. On the other hand, all 12 Thai passed the assessment course successfully. It is not possible to say whether this difference was due to a difference in the standard maintained by the several recruiters (the most likely explanation), or to educational differences, or to some general cultural determinant.

Degree of education was another factor. Though 31 per cent of the failing recruits had no education, only 15 per cent of the successful recruits were similarly handicapped. On the other hand, 21 per cent of the successful recruits had had some college training, whereas only 7 per cent of the failing recruits had enjoyed this advantage.

In short, it appears from the data available that the only significant formal differences between the successful and unsuccessful recruits were amount of education, nationality (Indonesian), and, to some extent, age. The other differences seem to have been either negligible or derived from these.

[1] Among the foreign universities and colleges represented were the University of Edinburgh, University of California, California Institute of Technology, University of Pennsylvania, Yale University, Massachusetts Institute of Technology, University of Illinois.

Illustrative Cases of Rejected Recruits.—The reasons for rejection at Camp K were various—low intelligence, lack of dependability, emotional instability, physical deficiency, laziness, cowardice, and so forth. The following abstracted case records describe four typical rejectees:

Case of a recruit who was rejected because of an incompatible or difficult personality:
No. 3   Age: 36   Tamil   Born in Madras, India
Schooling: When 14, graduated from a college in India.
Occupational History: At 16, became an instructor in a girls' school. In 1933, acquired a position in a Training College in Madras. Taught classes in production to civilians and troops for one year. In the spring of 1942 he was ordered to "revert to the Training College" which he regarded as an injustice. After obtaining a leave of absence on medical grounds, he resigned in March, 1943. He then held the position of inspector of food production for the government until he was recruited for OSS in July, 1944.
Summary of K Report: Well educated with excellent command of English, adroit in verbal expression. Quick at understanding but equally quick to make excuses when he made errors or failed in details in practical work. Gave the impression of appearing "superior." He was not liked by others, was obviously pointing toward a teaching position, not toward operations in our organization. Had questionable physical stamina and the poorest coordination of anyone in the group.

It seemed doubtful that his needs and our needs could come together in a smooth and happy solution. On ground of doubtful personality development and incompatibility with our own personnel, it is recommended that a permanent appointment in this organization be avoided.

Case of a recruit who was rejected because of emotional instability:
No. 62   Age: 23   Malay   Born in Singapore
Schooling: In Malaya from 8 to 10. In a university in India from 11 to 18.
Occupational History: Translator for Indian Government.
Summary of K Report: A pleasant, quiet, gentle-mannered, and inactive recruit. Frequently smiles or laughs in conversation, but recently has been more somber and has shown considerable anxiety and even mild depression. Avoids strenuous work for the most part, but could be pushed into it, in which case he might later develop complaints of fatigue or headache, etc. Implied knowledge of mapping, weapons, mathematics, but was quick to evade the issue when challenged to demonstrate his familiarity. Interviews were not revealing. He would "misunderstand" or have "difficulty in explaining" or would repeat previous statements. In some instances he would make flatly misleading statements apparently to cover his inadequacies. His intellectual ability was slightly above average; memory, average; observation, below average.

This recruit had known Captain R since childhood. Was brought into this organization through the Captain's influence. Is extremely dependent upon the Captain, fears that the Captain has dropped him and ascribes his anxiety to that specific concern. Would probably need continuous bolstering by the Captain (or an equivalent person) to keep going, and even then he would be unreliable under physical or psychological stress.

In summary, this recruit's rejection is recommended, because of lack of initiative, lack of physical stamina, and presence of emotional instability.

Case of a recruit who was rejected primarily because of intellectual limitation:
No. 9   Age: 30   Chinese   Born in Malaya
Schooling: Chinese school 2 years.
Occupational History: Clerked in father's store from 9 to 17, then worked at tapping rubber, and as a clerk in a rubber company. Drove trucks on Burma Road for four years, drafted into Chinese Army, deserted, worked in U.S. Army camp in Burma, and in American Air Depot in Burma, as truck driver.
Summary of K Report: Quiet, slow, inconsistent in performance, not rugged, rather silent, can be stubborn. Received low scores in intelligence tests. Showed no special ability to assume leadership or even to plan independently or to act effectively with initiative when thrown on his own. Could work in a group under orders.

Low borderline case.

Case of a recruit who was rejected because of laziness and undisciplined character:
No. 84   Age: 22   Chinese   Born in Malaya
Schooling: Anglo-Chinese school to first standard. Middle school from 7 to 17, passing senior Cambridge exam when 15. Attended college for 3 months in China, and then a college in Malaya.
Occupational History: Teaching English in Malaya for five months. After Pearl Harbor ran out of money in China and did odd jobs—sold liquor, patent medicines, solicited advertisements for Jap-controlled organization. Finally made his way to unoccupied China where he acted as interpreter for Americans in an Infantry Training Center. Later worked as civilian clerk in the office for the U. S. Army in China.
Summary of K Report: In his work at K he tried to avoid work requiring physical effort, showed a neurotic fear of leeches, had egoistic ideas of doing something fine in the war effort, but very doubtful motivation for any war work involving sacrifice. Frequently cooperated rather poorly with others, appearing self-centered, and on a few occasions definitely unreliable. Has a gonorrheal orchitis now under treatment. Has been described here by other instructors as "strictly a loafer," "shuns mental effort," and "a spoiled child." Has a history of self-indulgence and failure to attain ends requiring persistent effort.

Rejection is recommended because of lack of sturdy, disciplined character, unwillingness to make consistent effort, lack of will to attain long-range goals entailing discomfort.

ASSESSMENT IN INDIA

During the first months of 1945, the percentage of rejected candidates rose from 33 per cent, which was well above the ideal figure, to 50 per cent in some classes. This rise was serious because not only did the periodic dismissal of so many men increase security risks, but it testified to a large discrepancy in the conceptions of fitness for OSS operations entertained by the recruiting officers on the one hand and the assessment staff on the other, and so to the wasting of a good deal of precious time and energy. It was either that men of the desired caliber were not to be had anywhere, or that the recruiters were not seeking and selecting the proper types, or that the standards of the assessment staff were too exacting. The problem was solved by moving the assessment unit from Ceylon to India, the intention being to reduce the security risk, since only those men who were judged to be qualified would be sent to Ceylon and so thenceforth there would be only a very few rejected recruits to return to Calcutta with information which might prove valuable to the enemy. Furthermore, by bringing assessment and recruitment into close proximity, differences in viewpoints and standards could be resolved and a more efficient articulation of the two units effected.

In April, 1945, assessment was on the road, leaving Ceylon to take up its work in the little town of Raniganj to the northwest of Calcutta. In the process, unfortunately, the staff was decreased to one senior and one junior member (one more to be obtained if possible), one instructor, and two interpreters. It was possible to get along without the services of more than one instructor since less time would be available for assessing the recruits, and training as a method of providing data for appraisals was to be abandoned. A program of tests conforming to the pattern established at Station S would be designed.

The new site was located 130 miles from Calcutta in the western part of Bengal on the Grand Trunk Road to Delhi. It was in a section of the province that was devoted largely to coal mining during the hot dry season, January to June, and to rice growing during the monsoon season. A large "bungalow," in local terminology, situated on an estate in the midst of paddy farms provided quarters and classrooms. This building had formerly served as the guest house of the Indian landowner of the area. The location was favorable in many respects: there was an adequate supply of water on the property, drawn from a well near the bungalow, and from a tank filled by the rains, which provided muddy water for washing purposes throughout the year. Supplies were readily available in the town of Asanol, 6 miles away. On the property itself were many large trees and the remains of several stone buildings of unrecorded age, all of which offered inviting opportunities for setting up practical outdoor problems.

Circumstances were, in general, favorable for an effective assessment program. The Air Corps was very cooperative; the 305 Air Service Group 6 miles away agreed to provide commissary facilities, the services of their motor pool for maintaining the jeeps and trucks, and hospital facilities. Contact was also established with the Area Engineers, and with materials and personnel provided by them, construction of test equipment was started immediately.

Once a week a new band of recruits was picked up at the recruiting office in Calcutta and brought out to the camp, each group being scheduled to stay twelve days. On arriving, the students were shown to their quarters in the bungalow, and issued GI fatigue uniforms, sneakers, and insect repellent.

Following this they were assembled on the veranda for a short welcoming talk. Through the interpreter, they were told about the purposes of the program, the attitude that they should take toward the Interview and toward the tests, and the rules of the camp. They were advised about health precautions such as the use of insect repellent, sleeping under nets, drinking of boiled water, and so forth. At this time an assignment, to be completed during their spare time, was given: the Individual Projects for which each man was to start planning immediately. This ended the first evening.

The schedule for the next six days, starting at 5:30 in the morning, was devoted primarily to the measurement of code aptitude in conjunction with a preliminary code training course. Failure in code meant failure in assessment since for these candidates a proficiency in this function was a *sine qua non* of suitability. In order to break the monotony of this daily routine, however, and to provide other work during periods when it was too hot for instruction in the code room, some tests were given: Psychometrics, the Pistol Assembly Test, and the Object Observation Test. At the end of this period, with this backlog of training, the extent of code aptitude possessed by the student was apparent. Further, after six days of associating with these men, the staff had become fairly well acquainted with them. The associations during meals, during periods of relaxation in the living room, in the course of outdoor games, all provided opportunities for observation.

In the second week, with the arrival of new students from Calcutta, the men who had finished code training became the "advanced group." Their last six days would be devoted to a variety of undertakings designed to reveal significant traits of character.

Each day, following toast and coffee served at 5:30 A.M., individual tests and group tests were given outdoors. There was the Obstacle Course, the Parachute Jump Test, and the Track Meet. Breakfast was at 8:00. At 9:00 o'clock work began again. An interview was held at this time, lasting until 12:30, and often continuing into the afternoon. While both the interviewer and the interpreter (co-assessor) were thus occupied, only advanced training in code or tests which required a minimum amount of verbal instruction could be scheduled. The program was so arranged, however, that few tests were given without the presence of both the interviewer and the interpreter.

Lunch was served at 1:00, and until the heat of the day had passed, no outdoor tests and a minimum amount of indoor work (other than completing an interview) were required. At 4:00 P.M. the testing program was continued. The hour before dinner was usually devoted to recreation.

Evenings were spent in obtaining sociometric data, in completing the Individual Project, in Group Discussion, or in recreation. The Discussion, encouraged by an ample supply of India's best gin, was usually a productive session.

This schedule continued until the afternoon of the last day, which was set aside for preparations for the trip back. At 10:00 o'clock that night the successful candidates boarded the truck for the drive to Dum Dum Airport, there to take the plane for Ceylon. Those who had failed were returned to the recruiting office in Calcutta.

The various procedures will now be briefly described, beginning with the group situations.

Wall Scaling.—In this test the candidates were brought to the wall of an old building and told that they must build a structure for climbing it which would be adequate for use by a body of men who were following them. They were provided with an axe, jungle knives, and rope, and told they could use anything on the property to aid them in the construction. Timber was available in the woods near by. The disintegrating walls of the building were approximately 16 feet high. The Karens, with their background of experience in the jungle, were particularly quick and agile in solving this problem.

Observation Platform.—This assignment required that the group construct a platform in a tree to serve as a position from which at least three observers could watch the surrounding area. They were told that it should be as high as practicable. The men would usually divide into a ground crew and a tree crew, the former gathering the materials and hoisting them by rope to the latter. The task was provocative of argument because of the decisions which had to be made and because of the differences of opinion which arose as to the best materials to use. Leadership, Social Relations, and Effective Intelligence were the variables most easily estimated in this situation.

Tent Erection.—A large pyramid-type Army tent was given to the men to erect as neatly and as rapidly as possible. The site selected was within clear view of windows in the bungalow, so that the staff, after giving the instructions and retiring, could watch them at work unnoticed. The job was a tough one, for the ground was hard and the tent stakes could not be placed until holes for them had been made with an iron stake driven in with a sledge. Further, erecting one of these tents so that it is square and the side walls are of equal height is a task which requires accurate planning. On a hot day this was not the pleasantest of assignments, and so it proved a good test of motivation and persistence. Done properly, this task took about an hour and a half to complete.

Aerial Erection.—This situation called for the erection of an aerial on an open stretch of ground. Rope, iron stakes, and two lengths of bamboo were provided. The solution involved setting up the two poles in a vertical position, with a line between, and supporting them adequately with stays. Although the solution was easy, the job required planning and teamwork.

Discussion.—As in Washington, the staff took no part in the group discussion except to raise further pertinent problems when the proceedings began to lag. Indian gin was used to release inhibitions. The undertaking was conducted with varying degrees of success, depending upon the intellectual level of the group, the relative ages of its members, the ease with which the candidates understood each other's dialect, and so forth. As described earlier, the presence of an older Chinese was apt to reduce the amount of discussion, the others being inclined to accept his judgment as final. At times, differences in dialects would slow up the progress of the argument, one candidate having to interpret for another. At other times, language would split the group into two parts, each proceeding independently. On occasions, in the excitement, the dialect would shift, let us say, to Mandarin, which no one on the staff understood, and the men would have to be brought back to common ground. In spite of the fact that a good deal of what was said was missed, the discussion was often very productive, yielding data on attitudes, social relations, and so forth.

Sociometric.—In order to obtain even a fraction of the desired information, it was necessary for the co-assessor (interpreter) to take each candidate aside, present the questions verbally, and insist that he commit himself. An Oriental, particularly a Chinese, will generally avoid evaluating the qualities of another man unless he has been acquainted with him for a long time. This reticence is due in part to fear that his statements will be repeated (distrust of the staff member), and in part to the fact that in everyday social intercourse a Chinese does not accept a person as a friend, does not pronounce judgment until the man has stood the test of time. Relationships between them remain on a rather formal level, without many confidences, until the friendship, in the Oriental sense of the word, is established. Once attained, it has then the characteristics of a blood relationship.

About the traits of a mere acquaintance the Chinese is not inclined to speculate. He will say, "But I have not known him long enough"; or "True, but that is only one situation; he may be sociable (courageous, a leader, and so on) in other situations." There is merit in their insistence upon prolonged acquaintanceship, but it reduces the usefulness of the sociometric procedure. In spite of the difficulties, the data that were obtained made it worth the effort.

Besides these group tests there were a number of individual tasks some of which, being similar to those discussed in the preceding pages, do not require comment. Several new ones, however, were introduced because of a greater emphasis placed on certain traits by the field operators in this theater. These will be discussed below.

Psychometric Tests.—These were similar to those used in Ceylon.

Pistol Assembly.—This was a mechanical aptitude and practical intelligence test which was administered in the following way. The recruit was seated before the instructor and told that he would be shown how to reassemble a regulation Army .45 caliber automatic pistol. He was asked to watch closely, for the speed with which he accomplished his job was important. The pistol was then field stripped, assembled, and field stripped again, the instructor indicating certain special features by pointing to them during the demonstration. No language other than the introductory remarks was used. The parts were then turned over to the recruit. Notes were made on his general approach to the problem, the skill and speed displayed.

Object Observation and Memory.—The recruit was allowed three minutes to examine twenty-four objects arranged on a small table. He was tested immediately afterward by being asked to name the objects he remembered.

Observing, Reporting, and Inference.—This test was designed to provide another measure of memory, but, more particularly, to yield information on the individual's ability to make sound inferences from available data. The candidate was taken to an "abandoned camp site" and told to survey the place carefully. After five minutes he reported to the interpreter, who recorded the things he remembered as well as the answers to questions which sampled the quality of his inferences. Data were obtained on the thoroughness, speed, precision, and intelligence shown in exploring the camp.

Code Aptitude.—It was important to obtain a measure of code aptitude which was as nearly valid as that provided by the course of training at

Ceylon. It was decided, therefore, to give what amounted to an introductory course and use this as the testing situation. The equipment and methods of instruction were the same as those employed in Ceylon. As was mentioned earlier, the recruit spent most of the first six days of assessment in the code room, at the end of which period a fairly reliable index of ability and interest had been obtained. In the event of doubt, there were opportunities during the following week for further checks. In addition to this measure of code aptitude, estimations were made of the recruit's mechanical aptitude and his interest in radio equipment, important considerations in view of the problems he was likely to encounter in the field.

Individual Projects.—The students were assigned individual projects at the time the program was outlined to them on the first day. The projects consisted simply of constructing something of their own choosing, the materials for which the staff would provide if they could be obtained. The Karens tended to be specialists in the uses of bamboo—fish traps, bird traps, baskets, hats, and so on; the Chinese, in making things of paper, for example, drawings, ornaments, paper models. Observation of their efforts often yielded significant data on thoroughness, resourcefulness, and initiative. One recruit, a leader among his colleagues, so caught the interest of the others that they spent the greater part of their time on his project rather than on their own. Since there was ample time for each man to make something worth while, failure to do so was often found to be significant.

Four situations were introduced to provide measures of daring in view of the stress placed upon this quality by those in the theater.

Parachute Jump.—In this test the candidate had to climb a vertical ladder to the top of a 35-foot tower. There a parachute jacket was strapped onto him. Over his head was a ½ inch steel cable which extended on an incline toward the ground for a distance of 300 feet. The jacket was attached to a pulley riding on this cable, and when the candidate jumped he would fall free for a few feet until caught up by the lines to the pulley. Then he would coast down the cable until stopped by a pile of rice straw approximately 200 feet away. It was an exceedingly rigorous test which evoked marked emotional responses in all candidates.

Infiltration Course.—This course was constructed in a depression about 25 feet wide and 100 feet long. The starting point at one end was a slit trench built to hold 4 to 6 men. There were several strands of barbed wire stretching across the width of the course, under some of which the candidates had to crawl. Shallow crater holes containing explosives were located at two points along the course. Sandbags were placed around the edge of each hole, also a double strand of barbed wire to prevent entry. One-eighth pound charges of composition explosive were used, covered with dirt to provide falling debris. A machine gun in an immovable position was located on one bank and was fired across the course into the other bank at a level of approximately 8 feet above the ground. The gun was not fired when the student was in the line of fire. Observations were made from the gun emplacement bank.

Each student was instructed to climb out of the slit trench on the signal, and crawl through the course with his head down. He was told that the firing would be 36 inches overhead and that land mines would go off during the course, hence not to enter the double wire enclosures. Danger was stressed and emphasis placed upon the fact that their safety lay in their own hands.

Weapons Firing.—This test was presented to the recruits as a lesson in the use of the carbine and the .45 caliber automatic pistol. The men were observed carefully for evidence of timidity while using the weapons. Though it was an exceedingly easy test, it occasionally yielded significant information.

Demolitions.—This test was also conducted as if it were an introductory lesson. A brief explanation was given of the method of using TNT and plastic, and then under supervision each man prepared a charge and set it off himself. The recruit was observed closely during these operations. Notes were made of his behavior while he worked with the materials, of the amount of nervousness he showed while setting off the charge, and of his behavior as he withdrew from the site after the fuse was lighted. Marked individual differences were apparent in this situation.

Obstacle Course.—Several tests of daring were included in the Obstacle Course, two of which were similar to tests used at Station S. The candidate started the course at the base of a tree. First he climbed this tree; then he crossed to a second tree by way of the walls of an old building, and from there, via parallel ropes, to a large palm. On the palm was a small platform, fifteen feet high, from which he swung by means of a series of seven rings across to another tree. From there he walked on a shaky catwalk to the end, and then down a ramp to the ground. This ended the course.

The swing on the rings was the most rigorous test of the several, and refusals to attempt it were frequent. The course provided, in addition to measures of daring, opportunities for observing agility, physical strength, and, to some extent, endurance.

Track Meet.—This was a competitive situation. It provided further measures of physical agility and endurance. The following events were included:

100-yard dash, 220-yard dash, broad jump, high jump, baseball throw for distance.

In all these tests of physical fitness, the average performance of the recruit was far below that of men in the same age range in the United States. This difference was largely due to lack of experience in the techniques useful in track and field events. But beyond this there was little evidence of general physical fitness such as we were accustomed to see in the States. Although many of these men had been living a fairly vigorous out-door life, their arm and leg muscles were weak, and their endurance as measured in a race, for example, was low. Some of this frailty can be ascribed to years of malnutrition.

Summary.—Twenty-eight days after the arrival of the first class at Camp I Calcutta the last class had departed. The military situation had changed. The campaign in Burma was coming to a close and hence recruiting and assessment in SEAC were to be discontinued. Requirements for assessment in China, however, were pressing, and preparations were started for a move to Kunming to join other members of the assessment staff, who were on their way from Washington.

Generalizations cannot be made from the small sample of candidates tested at Camp I. Suffice it to say that the recruits, in terms of background and race, were very similar to those assessed in Ceylon. That the quality had improved over what it had been during the last two months at Camp K is indicated by the fact that the rejection rate dropped to 25 per cent. The improvement was due, we believe, to the closer liaison that existed between the recruiting and assessment units.

ASSESSMENT IN CHINA

In February, 1945, a cable was received in Washington requesting assessment personnel for a screening program in China. Paratroop commando units, formed from the Chinese Army, were to be trained by OSS and dropped behind the Japanese lines for combat, sabotage, and intelligence operations. They were to be led by Chinese officers with Americans as advisers under a joint Chinese and American strategic plan in connection with a forthcoming invasion of the China coast. Assessment was asked to help select several thousand troops.

Recruiting of assessment personnel for this task started immediately. In the United States, after a two months' search, the services of two qualified Chinese social scientists were obtained. In China, Dr. S. K. Chou, Professor of Psychology at the South-Western Associated University, Kunming, announced his willingness to assist in the program and to recruit graduate students if a need for them developed. Two senior members of the assessment staff in Washington were joined by one senior and one junior member of the Calcutta assessment staff, making a total of four Americans. The two Chinese from America participated in assessment at Station S while awaiting departure, and when in Kunming were part of a staff which finally included six other Chinese: Professor Siegen K. Chou and four well-trained graduate students—Mr. Fan Chun, Mr. Ma Chi-wei, Mr. Tien Ju-kang, and Mr. Tsao Jih-chang. Mr. Ting Tsan came over from Chungking, and somewhat later Miss Chao Wan-ho, an associate of Mr. Ting's at the National Institute of Health, Chungking, also joined us.

There were to be new experiences for assessment in China. Kunming, in southwest China, was a thriving frontierlike town, overgrown several times in size since the loss of coastal China. It was the gateway for supplies coming in over the Burma Road and the main air terminus for air-borne traffic into China. The Stilwell, or Ledo Road, and the fuel pipe line terminated at Kunming. American army units sprawled over the surrounding countryside. Training centers for Chinese troops dotted the side of roads, vying with the Chinese peasants for the land of China. Temples and schoolhouses, rich men's compounds and middle-class homes, and newly constructed buildings housed Chinese and American military units. Amidst this hive of activity, OSS established a training center for China's first parachute jumpers. Large numbers of troops were already in the process of commando training.

The assessment staff was now asked to select men for a replacement pool for the commandos already formed, and more urgently to select men for two "intelligence commandos," men who would not only be good commandos but would also be able to engage in intelligence activities. (It might be pointed out that a "commando" was used to refer to a unit of 135 men, as well as to a single soldier.) For two commandos, approximately 250 men were required; the officers and noncommissioned officers had already been selected. Where could these men be found? Any familiarity with recent Chinese events pointed to the difficulty of getting this number of physically and intellectually fit Chinese enlisted men.

The Chinese armies are somewhat unique in modern military annals. Hampered by ineffective staff work, and ridden with political appointees in high ranks, evolving slowly and showing little evidence of becoming a modern army, they struggled on, sometimes against the Japanese, sometimes merely to exist. Man power was abundant, but of poor quality. There were no adequate records kept of personnel. While a draft law existed, those with influence, power, or wealth, were able to avoid service. It was only the poor and illiterate farm boys who joined the Army, or stayed in after they were forcibly conscripted, for the sake of one bowl of rice a day. Once in the Army their lot was far from enviable. Runaway inflation made their meager salaries seem ludicrous. Medical attention was inadequate; trained doctors and medical supplies were not available in sufficient quantities. Diseases ranging from malaria to scabies were commonplaces. It was from this horde of ragged, dispirited, but long-suffering soldiers that assessment had to select 250 men suitable for intelligence and commando operations.

Official liaison between the American training units and the Chinese Army headquarters was generally satisfactory. The Chinese belonging to the already formed commando units were receiving excellent training in demolitions and combat tactics. Special equipment, extra pay, and the facilities usually accorded American military units had been granted. The men were honored in the district since they were the first in China to receive instructions in parachute jumping. Great fanfare and excitement attended the first jump of the first class trained in Kunming. As the composite American and Chinese officer cadre jumped out of the planes, a brass band played, reviewing generals cheered, and strings of firecrackers popped. Pride in the work increased as national interest became manifest. As assessment was an integral part of the commando program, consideration and cooperation were accorded that might otherwise have been difficult to obtain.

Arriving in Kunming and being informed that several thousand troops were available for recruiting, the assessment staff immediately set out to visit two pools in the hope of finding a quantity of literate men in reasonably good health. But even after modifying our definitions of "literate" and "reasonably good," the yield from these pools, and from two other pools visited the next day, was disappointing. Few of the men had had an education equivalent to that provided by an American primary school, and of those who could read, many were disqualified because of inadequate vision, poor health, or lack of strength. Since none was free from scabies, only those with the severest infestation were disqualified on this count. Nevertheless, at the end of two days 550 men who claimed some ability to read and appeared to be physically sound had been formed into columns and marched to the American training camp.

The site of the assessment was several miles outside of Kunming on a hillside overlooking a great plain of brilliant green paddy fields. There, on the edge of a little village full of children, adjacent to the training grounds of the parachute school, the assessment staff was allotted several areas. Its headquarters were set up in a small country house, which had a garden with an unused dirt tennis court and a swimming pool. On the court several tents were set up to serve as shelters for interviews and written tests; the pool was used for a bridge-building problem. Near by was a spacious temple where other tests could be conducted, and farther up the hill were two parade grounds and a mess hall available to us at certain times. A canyon on the side of one parade ground provided ideal conditions for situational tests and an obstacle course.

The test program may be divided into two parts: Part One was a one-day screening process the purpose of which was to eliminate the illiterate and those of distinctly low intelligence; Part Two consisted of one day of more exacting procedures designed to test energy, motivation, physical ability, leadership, and observational ability among those who had passed Part One.

Part One started in the morning with approximately 120 recruits who had just been selected from a larger number on the basis of a one-minute reading test. This reading test, conducted on the parade ground immediately after the recruits were assembled, was scored as it was given. Those who failed were permanently disqualified; those who passed were lined up, their names recorded, and an identifying numbered card to be attached in plain view to the jacket was issued to each man. After this, one half of the candidates were given a battery of tests to determine educational status, while the other half received paper-and-pencil intelligence tests. In an hour the two groups alternated. This ended the morning session.

The afternoon was devoted to a continuous round of tests, each of which could be administered to a group of 30 men in about forty minutes. In this battery were two outdoor group performance tests, several individual performance tests (the "quickies"), and a perception test. On the basis of the results obtained during the morning and afternoon sessions another elimination of the less suitable men was made.

Part Two began several days later and was applied to all men who had passed the first screening. Again the men were assembled on the parade ground and separated into groups of 30. This procedure was not so simple as one might expect, because the Chinese officers had no method of keeping track of their men. Consequently a portion of the morning period had to be spent in eliminating stray soldiers who had never been tested—as well as those who had been disqualified on Part One but had nevertheless rejoined their successful comrades—and in detecting substitutes who had been hired to assume the names of recruits who had passed Part One but, for one reason or another, had seen fit to quit. These substitutes could be identified by their signatures.

As soon as the bona fide candidates were grouped, a new roster was prepared and a numbered jersey issued to each man. While this was in process, each staff member attempted a quick over-all evaluation of each candidate on the basis of general appearance and reactions to instructions. These procedures followed: (1) Interview conducted by one of the Chinese members of the staff, or by an American assisted by an interpreter; (2) Bridge Building; (3) Obstacle Course; (4) Observation and Memory Battery. These, together with the procedures previously listed, are described in the succeeding section.

The next step in the program was to review the findings and formulate a recommendation. This was accomplished at a staff meeting where each case was discussed, not only in the light of the man's test scores, but also in terms of impressions not susceptible to numerical ratings. The final report prepared by the interviewer was an integrated evaluation of the candidate based on all the information available considered in connection with his future field operations.

Several considerations influenced us to adopt a three-point scale instead of the six-point scale employed in the States. The majority of the staff members were not accustomed to rating traits, particularly in complex social situations. And then, at the start of the program, norms had not been established for this population, and the concept, for example, of a high-average as against a low-average performance was too indefinite to warrant making the distinction. Finally, in working with groups as large as these, the time spent in observing each candidate was too limited to justify fine discriminations. Every rating, therefore, was either Low, Average, or High.

In the following paragraphs, the procedures employed are briefly described. As will be noted, they follow the pattern of those used in America, with modifications required by the necessity of screening large numbers in the shortest possible time.

Sign Reading.—This test was devised to provide a rough measure of degree of literacy. Since it could be administered and scored quickly (one minute per man), it was used in the first rough screening of the recruits as they came from the replacement pool. Literacy sufficient to read a Chinese classic was, of course, too high a standard to require of simple soldiers. Even to demand the ability to read newspapers would have meant the elimination of too large a proportion of the men. Therefore a simple test was devised consisting of a series of key characters, a knowledge of which did not depend so much upon formal education as it did upon an acquaintance with signs which were part of the daily experience of every soldier.

Educational Level Battery.—Since the purpose of the program was to select commandos suitable for intelligence operations, it was decided that the men should demonstrate some ability to count and to write as well as the possession of general information indicative of alertness to their social and physical surroundings. Each of the three tests was administered to groups ranging from 30 to 60 in number.

ARITHMETIC.—This consisted of 25 simple calculations presented on a mimeographed sheet in both Arabic and Chinese characters. The candidates were to write the answers on a separate sheet of paper.

WRITING.—This required the filling in of a mimeographed form consisting of questions about personal history and interests. Space was provided for writing additional information.

GENERAL INFORMATION.—This consisted of 50 statements, on history, geography, politics, and so on, 27 of which were true and 23 false. The statements were read to the recruits, who merely had to indicate *true* or *false* on an answer sheet. Fifteen minutes were allowed.

Abstract Intelligence Battery.—The tests constituting this battery were divided into two parts. Part 1 consisted of the Series Completion Test and the Block Counting Test (Non-Language Test: No. 2a of the Adjutant General's Office), both of which had been employed in Ceylon and India Part 2 consisted of three short individual performance tests (the "quickies"): (a) a set of photographs which had to be arranged in a series according to the age of the subject; (b) a set of pictures which had to be sorted into two groups, males in one, females in the other; and (c) a geometrical form which had to be duplicated with a set of cards cut in different shapes (as in a jigsaw puzzle). One minute was allowed for each solution. The recruit was observed and scored as he worked.

Observation and Memory Battery.—Three tests were used in this battery as indicators of a man's suitability for intelligence work.

DESIGNS.—This measure of the ability to observe and recall accurately was also used to test two hypotheses. "Familiar" Chinese characters and symbols and "unfamiliar" English letters and symbols were drawn on a single sheet of white cardboard. This sheet was exposed for two minutes to a group of candidates who were then instructed to reproduce as many figures as they could recall. A slight imperfection (error or broken line) had been introduced in drawing each figure. The two hypotheses were these: (1) that the candidates would remember more of the familiar than of the unfamiliar figures, and (2) that they would overlook imperfections in the familiar figures more often than they would overlook them in the unfamiliar figures. The results will be discussed later.

SEARCH.—This was similar to the Belongings Test in the program at Station S. The story invented for it was that of a Chinese captain who had been forced by the weather to camp in this place with his troops for the night. On departure he had left some of his possessions behind in the adjoining tent. The candidates, individually or in small groups, inspected the tent and after two minutes returned to the examiner, who asked them:

What have you seen in the tent? Who was the captain who stayed in the tent? Why did he choose to stop in this place?

PERCEPTUAL ACUITY.—This test measured speed and span of perception. Each figure was presented tachistoscopically at 1/10 second by a 35 mm. projector. The figures presented were a row of horizontal dots (from 3 to 7), Arabic digits, simple geometric figures, simple figures with a small gap somewhere in their contour, and so on. The men were required after each exposure to draw the figure seen. This test was designed in Washington and included in the battery chiefly for experimental purposes.

Group Practics Battery.—These tests, three in number, were important for the data they provided on Effective Intelligence, Energy, Motivation, Cooperativeness, Physical Ability, and, to a certain extent, Daring. They corresponded, except in detail, to group field situations as used at other stations.

BRIDGE BUILDING.—This required the construction of a bridge across the 27-foot width of the swimming pool. The recruits, ten at a time, were expected to complete this task in forty-five minutes. They were told to assume that the pool, which was full of water, was a river and therefore it was not possible to walk around it to the other side. Furthermore, the job had to be done without anyone wetting his feet. Two logs, 23 and 9 feet in length, heavy rope, planks, stakes, a sledge, and a pick were the materials provided.

FLAG POLE.—This called for the transportation of a long heavy log across a deep canyon by a group of ten men. The task called for energy and teamwork, and so provided a good opportunity to observe Leadership, Motivation, and Social Relations.

RAVINE.—This involved the construction of a rope bridge across a canyon, two groups working cooperatively, one on each side of the canyon. After the job was finished the examiner called for volunteers to cross the bridge. This was considered to be a measure of daring.

Obstacle Course.—This was constructed in a ravine located next to one of the parade grounds. The obstacles were arranged in a series in such a way as to require the recruit to cross back and forth over the stream as he worked his way up the canyon. The first obstacle was a log resting on the floor of the ravine and leaning at a 30-degree angle against the top of the bank. This had to be climbed to reach a horizontal rope stretching for 40 feet below the crest of the bank. Along this rope, hand over hand, the candidate would then make his way along the almost vertical wall. Here and there he could find some support for his feet. At the end he descended to the bottom via a vertical rope. Next was a 5-foot hurdle in the middle of the stream which he climbed to reach an 8-foot platform on the other side of the bank. From this elevation he jumped back across the stream and then recrossed once more on a horizontal log 10 feet above the water. This brought him to the last obstacle, a pair of parallel ropes suspended between trees 20 feet above the floor of the ravine. He reached these by a rope ladder, and with feet on the lower rope and hands on the upper, he worked his way over to the far side. When he reached the ground the course was completed.

The men were started one at a time at three-minute intervals. This course, easily viewed and scored from the top of the ravine, provided measures of daring, agility, and endurance.

Interview.—Most of the interviews were conducted by two Chinese psychologists and by an American assisted by an interpreter. The interview was necessarily short, from five to fifteen minutes, but it was nevertheless important in view of its being the only face-to-face situation in the program. Frequently it was the deciding factor in settling the fate of recruits whose test scores were on the border line. Special emphasis was placed on the determination of Motivation and Emotional Stability. Ratings were made on all traits, however, and notes were taken on significant features of the man's past history and present attitudes. The method of interrogation, although subject to variations from interviewer to interviewer, was essentially the same as that used at other stations.

General Impression.—This was undertaken as an amusing experiment to see how well the staff could predict the final over-all rating of each recruit on the basis of a few seconds of observation. When the recruits were lined up in the morning preparatory to engaging in the test procedures, each senior staff member rated each recruit as he stood in line. Usually at the moment the judgment was made the recruit was putting on a numbered jersey that had just been issued to him.

The following variables were rated (Low, Average, or High) on the final report form:

Educational Level, based on Sign Reading and Educational Level Battery. If the case was on the border line between two grades, the quality of handwriting, a talent highly esteemed among Chinese, was taken into account.

Effective Intelligence, based on Interview, Abstract Intelligence Battery, Observation and Memory Battery, and Group Practics.

Observation and Memory, based on the battery of three tests—Perceptual Acuity, Design, and Search.

Motivation, Social Relations, and Emotional Stability, three separate variables, each based on the Interview, Group Practics, and Obstacle Course.

Leadership, based on Group Practics.

Physical Ability, based on Obstacle Course and Group Practics.

TABLE 21

Correspondence of the Procedures with the Final Over-All Rating at Kunming

Test	No discrepancy (% of cases)	Discrepancy of 1 category (% of cases)	Discrepancy of 2 categories (% of cases)
Interview......................	71	28	1
Sign Reading..................	64	33	3
Educational Level Battery........	63	35	2
Group Practics Battery	62	35	3
Observation and Memory Battery..	60	37	3
General Impression..............	58	41	1
Abstract Intelligence Battery......	54	43	3
Obstacle Course.................	51	45	4

Since the final over-all rating was arrived at after an examination and discussion of the ratings on the separate procedures, it would be extraordinary if one found anything other than what is indicated in this table, namely, a rather high correlation between the test results and the final estimate of suitability. In the majority of cases the final rating was merely the average of all the other ratings.

The rank order of the different procedures as shown in Table 21 cannot be accepted as definite evidence of their relative merit, since a number of factors, some subjective and some fortuitous, were influential in determining the result. The Interview was clearly first, not only because this was a very revealing procedure, but because past experience had persuaded the staff that considerable reliance could be placed on an interviewer's judgment and also because the staff member who interviewed a candidate usually attained a greater degree of confidence in his ratings than that attained, let us say, by the staff member who observed him on the Obstacle Course. Consequently in the discussion of each case the interviewer was likely to be the one who argued with greatest conviction and was listened to with most respect.

Sign Reading stands high on the list because everyone who received a low rating on this test was automatically disqualified (i.e., received a low over-all rating). Of the seven ratings which appeared on the summary sheet presented to each staff member at the final discussion, four (Abstract Intelligence Battery, Educational Level Battery, Observation and Memory Battery, and Sign Reading) were estimates, direct or indirect, of cognitive functions. Furthermore, the interviewer was very likely to be influenced favorably by evidences of intellectual power. Consequently the average of the seven ratings was more representative of the candidate's intelligence level than it was of his physical energy, motivation, courage, leadership, team spirit, and so forth, which were covered by only two ratings on the summary sheet. This largely accounts for the fact that the Group Practics Battery and the Obstacle Course stand relatively low in the rank order. In this connection another point is perhaps worth mentioning: Chinese generally, and Chinese scholars (e.g., psychologists) especially, are inclined to value the intellect, even within the sphere of military enterprise, more than we Americans do. This helps to explain why the staff members, most of whom were Chinese, were usually more impressed by a high rating on the Educational Level Battery, for example, than by a high rating on the Obstacle Course.

The intercorrelations among the different procedures were relatively high compared to those found when comparable tests have been administered to American groups of similar age. This relationship probably means that some underlying general factor, such as motivational energy, was the chief determinant of excellence on all the tests in which the Chinese recruits engaged. According to this hypothesis the possession of a high degree of motivational energy (ambition) makes a boy more alert, and prompts him to exert himself not only at home, helping on the farm, but also at school; and as a result he will forge ahead of the more complacent majority in most lines of activity. In America, however, specialization begins earlier and is more widespread. A boy finds that he excels in athletics, or at mechanics, or in English composition, and before long we find that most of his energies are being canalized in this direction and in one or two others. Thus at twenty-five he has probably suceeded in developing himself beyond the average in certain abilities, but has fallen behind in others.

The relatively high correlation of General Impressions with final ratings is interesting, particularly since the scores on the former were not taken into account in deciding the latter. Fifty-eight per cent of the average of the staff impressions agreed exactly with the final ratings. The best estimates were made by one of the Chinese psychologists, and the next to the lowest by another. There was no appreciable difference between the averages of the American and the Chinese raters' scores.

In breaking down the scores on Designs into two parts, Chinese designs and American designs, it was found, in conformity with our hypothesis, that familiar Chinese symbols rather than unfamiliar American symbols were recalled better by the Chinese. Of the total number of correct responses, 68 per cent were to Chinese characters or symbols, and 32 per cent were to American. But the hypothesis that familiarity with the symbols would interfere with the observation of slight errors and omissions was not supported by the results. Instead of there being more incorrectly reproduced familiar designs (with the errors in pattern overlooked) there were more incorrectly reproduced unfamiliar designs. The figures were not presented tachistoscopically, however, and it is possible that the recruits, with two minutes to study the patterns, may even have been aided in the recall of the familiar by the special emphasis that these errors and omissions produced. Exposures of short duration might yield results to support the original hypothesis.

Just before the dropping of the first atomic bomb and the subsequent end of hostilities, it was decided that assessment in China should discontinue. Eight hundred men had been processed, 220 of them more intensively than the rest. Although the staff was prepared to assess more groups, suitable recruits were not to be found. Apparently there was nothing left to be done in the Kunming area.

Shortly before our departure, however, one more opportunity to get into action presented itself: the staff was asked by a Chinese general to give a demonstration of its methods by assessing a group of Chinese Army Officers.

Assessment of Chinese Army Officers.—Heretofore assessment had operated under American auspices; now it was to be conducted in a wholly Chinese setting. Among the numerous agreeable discoveries to be made was the fact that convivial tea drinking, poetical wine toasting, and fine feasting were integral parts of the process of setting up a screening program. It was natural to engage in social activities of this hearty sort with considerable enjoyment and gusto, and within a day or two the Americans felt very much at home and in a mood to compromise on any issues that might arise. Although every step called for a sequence of courteous negotiations, in a few days all necessary materials and equipment were assembled, an obstacle course was constructed, and a schedule of procedures was arranged, several of which had to be improvised on the spot. The General, exceedingly cordial at all times, evidenced considerable interest in all our proceedings, and did everything in his power to facilitate preparations.

The group selected for processing consisted of thirty junior grade officers from various units, who had been transferred to main headquarters for a special training program under the General's supervision. Some of the men had engaged in combat in Burma; some had participated in "bandit suppression" expeditions before the Sino-Japanese War. They were all literate; the majority had had a junior high school education, and several were military academy graduates. Their motivation for the program was excellent, the General having exhorted them to cooperate to the limit. He was there to observe them during the whole program.

Four one-story-high school buildings, forming a square compound with a large court in the middle, were put at the disposal of assessment. Situated in the middle of a village about two miles from Kunming and close to the headquarters of the Fifth Chinese Army, the facilities left nothing to be desired. Across the road from the school compound a stream flowing swiftly between steep banks, provided ideal conditions for a bridge-building problem. A half-built house near by was available for an obstacle course. Assessment does not depend upon a definite set of materials or conditions; the program can almost always be adapted in one way or another to local conditions. For instance, if, because of scarcity of materials in China, poles cannot be cut to size but must be borrowed and returned intact, then the problem becomes one of finding a spot that will fit the poles instead of the more usual one of fitting poles to a chosen spot.

There was no need for undue haste; only thirty men had to be assessed. Furthermore, we were not asked to decide the fate of each assessee, to accept or reject him. The program was designed merely to demonstrate our system of assessment to the Chinese General and other interested officers.

The staff remained unchanged except for the loss of two Americans who had left for Hsian, North China. It was augmented by the addition of three more Chinese graduate students and two experienced Chinese psychologists. These new members, three of whom were women, were eager to see assessment in operation.

Three series of tests were scheduled, A, B, and C, each of which lasted half a day. Series A, which took place indoors, consisted in filling out personal history forms and performing a variety of paper-and-pencil tests. Series B included outdoor field situations, individual and group, and an obstacle course. Series C was a sequence of indoor group procedures. The assessees were divided into three subgroups (I, II, and III) of ten men each. While Group I was taking Series A, Group II was engaged in Series B, and so forth. The three groups completed the three series in a day and a half. The interviews took place a few days later, after all tests had been scored and a preliminary sketch of each personality composed. As most of the procedures have already been described, a very brief account of them is all that is required here.

Personal Data Sheet.—This was an abbreviated and slightly modified form of the sheet used at Station S.

Sentence Completion.—Fifty of the phrases used at Station S were translated into Chinese with minor changes. Mimeographed sheets were presented to ten men (one subgroup) at a time.

Modified Thematic Apperception Test.—Ten pictures, carefully selected from Chinese magazines, were divided into two sets, A and B, of five pictures each. While five of the candidates, seated round a table, were occupied with Set A, the other five at another table were busy with Set B. Each candidate was given one of the five pictures placed on his table and told to write a dramatic story in seven minutes for which the picture might be used as an illustration. When time was called, each man was instructed to pass his picture to the man sitting at his right. Thus in thirty-five minutes every candidate had written five stories. After an intervening test of another type, the two sets were exchanged and each man wrote five more stories.

This method of administration proved very successful. The stories, taken in conjunction with the responses to the Sentence Completion, yielded a great deal of pertinent information.

Series Completion and Cube Counting.—These were the same as those used in the assessment of commandos.

Designs.—The same test as that used in commando assessment.

Improvisations.—As at Station S, the assessees belonging to one subgroup were taken in pairs, the members of each pair being told that they must imagine themselves involved in a certain situation (clearly described to them by the examiner) and that they must act as they would in everyday life. In accordance with these instructions, five different episodes (one by each pair) were enacted in front of the staff and the other members of the subgroup, five minutes being allotted to each episode. The situations chosen were close to the experience of these officers; they were not designed to check any special tentative formulation of each assessee's personality. The same five situations were used for all three subgroups.

Speech.—Each man made a three-minute speech before his subgroup on a topic of his own selection. This procedure conformed to the traditional Chinese assumption that a leader must be a good public speaker.

Discussion.—"Relations between the Army and Civilians" was assigned as the topic for an impromptu discussion among the ten members of each subgroup gathered around a table. Since there was a good deal of friction at the time between soldiers and civilians, this topic was both timely and provocative of emotion.

Bridge Building.—Ten men were assigned the task of building a bridge across a 15-foot stream with banks 10 feet high. The problem was basically the same as that presented in commando assessment. This was called "group practics."

Obstacle Course.—A half-built two-story house with rafters exposed, no floors laid, windows open, and roof unfinished served as a frame for the obstacle course. All that was needed was plenty of rope for climbing and swinging. Agility, daring, and strength could be readily estimated by the observers.

Assigned Leadership.—Five outdoor situations, "critical emergencies," were invented, each at a different spot out of sight of the others; and every assessee was given five minutes to show how well he could direct the activities of a squad of four men in solving one of these situations. For this purpose each subgroup was divided into two squads of five men. Squad A started at the site of the first problem; Squad B at the site of the third. From then on the problems were taken in order, at each site a different man being selected to act as leader.

Individual Practics.—Six low stone pylons (supposedly the remains of a blown bridge) placed at irregular intervals on the ground (the bed of an imaginary river) constituted the only supports for a bridge of planks and ropes which had to be constructed from one bank to the other in three minutes.

Sociometric.—The form used at Station S was distributed to all the assessees at the end of the testing period. Since these men were members of a training class which had been living, working, and studying together for several months, everyone had had ample opportunity to observe the behavior of the others and so acquire sufficient basis for judgments of leadership traits and potentialities. Because of our ignorance of the standards that prevailed in the Chinese Army, the findings on this test were heavily weighted when we arrived at our final conclusions.

Interview.—A few days after all the other procedures had been completed and the results analyzed and synthesized, each assessee was given an interview lasting from one and a half to two and a half hours. The advantage of this timing was that the interviewers had a good deal of information at their disposal to guide them to certain critical areas of each man's personality which required further exploration.

The report sheets used in this study were the same as those which had proved useful in commando assessment. There was the same list of variables rated Low, Medium, or High, and a typewritten personality sketch of the assessee (averaging two thirds of a page in length) written by the interviewer. In this final note an opinion was ventured as to the best use that could be made of the officer in question, whether, for example, he was better fitted for combat or for staff work.

Since the war came to an end a few days after the completion of the assessment period, there was no opportunity to evaluate the accuracy of our judgments. We never learned whether any of the assessees eventually engaged in combat against the Communists in the North. In the two weeks devoted to the enterprise we had added to our fund of knowledge as well as to our fund of intensely enjoyed experiences, and the General seemed pleased with what he had seen of the proceedings. This was the height of our expectations. The Chinese members of the staff had been astonishingly quick in grasping our methods and in learning to function effectively in a somewhat complicated schedule of procedures. To them belongs the bulk of the credit for the measure of success that was achieved.

An unfortunate sequel of the assessment process is not without interest. Our friend the General called together his headquarters staff, his training staff, and the thirty men who had been tested and publicly read each assessment report with the man under discussion standing at attention in front of the assembled group. Following each reading, the General lectured or praised the officer, depending on the content of the report, and saw fit to imprison at least one man in a dungeon "to reflect upon his bad moral character," and "rectify himself."

ASSESSMENT IN HSIAN

In response to a request from the Intelligence Branch of OSS a special assessment project in Shensi Province, near the Yellow River Bend, was scheduled. This was to include, first, an evaluation of a group of forty to fifty Koreans who had been in training for several months under the supervision of American and Korean officer personnel. Then on completion of that job, it was planned to select additional numbers from scattered groups of Koreans who had escaped from the Japanese Army. They were located in villages in one of the Chinese-controlled pockets in Central China. According to plan the men selected would enter Korea with radio equipment by any means available for the purpose of reporting upon current Japanese troop movements, local conditions, and so forth. In view of the rigid control exercised by the enemy in Korea, a resourceful, courageous, and intelligent type of man was required for this work.

In July, 1945, an assessment team of one senior and one junior staff member and three interpreters left for Eagle Camp near Hsian. On arrival it was found that the areas surrounding the training camp were under intensive cultivation and offered few facilities for an assessment program. As an alternative, a survey was made of the mountain country which rose abruptly out of the level valley about twenty-five miles from the city. In short order a deserted temple was found in a canyon which could be reached from the valley by a good trail. This site provided excellent facilities. The surrounding area was rugged and wooded and the temple itself was in fair repair. It provided a place to cook and to conduct interviews and written tests, and had, in addition, several rooms with bunks of stone and mud on which to sleep. There were other reasons, besides the camping facilities, for choosing this location. The staff would have the opportunity of living with the men and so of observing them under conditions that would not have been possible at the main camp. Conditions for living were relatively crude and not altogether comfortable. Except for one meal provided by the candidates, the food consisted of K rations, the beds were of stone, illumination at night was by candle, and wood was scarce. Sanitary facilities had to be constructed.

It was arranged to have a truck bring the candidates in the early morning as far as the foot of the hill and return for them on the evening of the second day. The candidates carried the necessary supplies up the hill on their shoulders.

After unpacking personal equipment, stowing supplies, and digging latrines, the candidates were ready to begin. Since the program followed the pattern of those previously discussed, except for a few modifications required by the conditions of this location, a detailed description is not necessary. More than any earlier program, this one was handicapped by a shortage of trained personnel. Although the three interpreters had undergone screening at Station S, they were not familiar with the purposes of the tests they had taken. The presence of the senior staff member was therefore required for the administration and observation of most of the procedures.

The Interviews, therefore, were scheduled during evening hours or at times when the written tests were being held. Interviewing was expedited to some extent by the use of the Personal History Form and the Sentence Completion Test, the replies to both having been translated into English prior to the Interview. The Interview situation was important, particularly in view of the low motivation of these recruits for the type of work for which they were being trained. It was the one situation which would sample their attitudes on this point, and it seems to have been their first opportunity to express their fears.

Of the written exercises, the Personal History Form and the Sentence Completion Test were given first in order to permit the Interviews to start as early as possible. Following these, the Kunming battery of nonlanguage written tests, the Progressive Matrices, and the Pistol Assembly Test were given. Since these candidates had been selected because of having had superior education, performance, particularly on tests of abstract intelligence, was high in terms of norms for the Far East.

Toward the end of the afternoon of the first day preparations for supper were started. This situation was, to all appearances, merely a matter of providing one hot meal for staff and candidates. On the previous day the latter had been given several thousand dollars (Chinese national currency) with which to purchase the necessary ingredients. What they purchased was left to their discretion. As it turned out, the staff was served noodles and chicken with melon for dessert by four successive classes. Each group carried up a wicker basket containing three or four irate chickens, which was placed with other supplies at the feet of Buddha. At suppertime the chickens were dispatched, cleaned, dressed, and immediately thrown into the pot. Barely were they heated when they were being served to us with the noodles. The mixture was savory despite the sinewy meat, for the native seasoning and some accidental additions gave a flavor that was unique.

Facilities and utensils for the preparation of this meal were limited: a mud-brick Chinese stove, a pot for the coffee, and a square GI water carrier for the remainder were all that were provided. This limitation on equipment added both to the problems and to the interest. Although the fare was simple, teamwork and planning were necessary to produce it, and useful data were usually obtained during this hour and a half of eager activity. The informal atmosphere belied the fact that this was a test.

Following dinner, interviews were continued until approximately ten in the evening. At that time the recruits were called together for a group discussion. This session, held by candlelight, was conducted in the usual way, but proved to be more productive than it had been with the Chinese. The difference was probably due to the higher average educational level of the group and to the greater uniformity in age. Further, there were no problems as a result of differences in dialects.

Testing on the second day began after a K ration breakfast. The Interviews were continued, and at the same time the Demolition Test was given. For the latter, as in Calcutta, the men were taken in small groups to a point near the camp. Through the interpreter they were given a brief description of the methods of using TNT. Then under supervision, each man prepared and set off a charge himself. The method of scoring was the same as had been used previously.

A hike farther up the canyon was scheduled late in the morning. K rations were carried for lunch en route. The climb was a rugged one and as such yielded data on the physical condition of the men. In addition, there were points along the way which were particularly well suited for group tests. In a wooded section where the canyon was deep, the Bridge Construction problem was presented, using the same materials and instructions as in Kunming. Later the Cliff Scaling problem was introduced.

Cliff Scaling.—A two-hour climb up the trail from camp brought the candidates to a granite cliff which rose approximately thirty feet from the floor of the canyon. Working from the top, the men were required to devise a safe means for the group to descend to the bottom. They were provided with rope, but were told that it would be necessary to carry it with them after the last man had descended. No one was forced to attempt the descent and there were frequent refusals. When the group had completed the construction, some were unwilling both to descend and to ascend. This test provided additional measures of the same traits as revealed in Bridge Construction, but it yielded in addition another measure of daring.

Weapons Test.—The Weapons Test followed Cliff Scaling at a point on the trail where there was a suitable range. As in Calcutta, it was not given to provide a measure of markmanship, but as an opportunity to observe any indications of timidity in the use of weapons, a mild but, nevertheless, frequently revealing test.

Following this, the group started back to camp. This completed the test program. The men packed their equipment, policed the area, and departed in time to meet the truck in the valley below at five o'clock.

Summary of Results.—As is evident from Table 22, the number of men who were not qualified for agent work was large. In addition to the fact that the standards for qualifications were high, the motivation of most of the men for agent work in Korea was low. Many of the recruits had deserted from the Japanese Army and were reluctant to expose themselves to the danger of recapture. Their lack of drive and resolution had not been communicated to their Korean officers at Eagle Camp. To have admitted their fears would probably have involved the loss of "face."

TABLE 22

Summary of Results of the Hsian Assessment Project

		Reasons for failure		
Passed	Failed	Motivation	Emotional Stability	Effective Intelligence
21	19	10	6	3

But the Interview, which was specifically directed toward the assessment of this disposition, was for them an easily accepted invitation to express their worries. Although in many cases they would not admit anxiety, they often called attention to some physical disability or weakness which they believed would preclude work in the field, despite the fact that these disabilities were not noticeable in the group tests or on the mountain climb, both of which required physical strength and endurance.

On the other hand, motivation in these men was high for work in the

Korean postwar government. There was a general appreciation of the fact that they, as selected personnel of the Korean Independence Army and closely associated with the Korean Provisional Government, would have opportunities in that field at the end of the war. In a large percentage of the cases interest did not extend much beyond this; patriotism, defined as a willingness to sacrifice one's life for one's country, was all but absent.

In seeking an explanation for this, it was observed that low motivation was far more prevalent among college graduates than among noncollege men. Several correlated factors were involved. Those who had been able to afford a college education came from Korean families who had, in general, not fared badly under Japanese rule; several of the recruits had attended universities in Japan. Those who had not been to college, on the other hand, were more frequently from families to whom the Japanese had not found it necessary to make concessions, were members of economic groups which had felt more sharply the discriminations made in favor of Japanese residents in Korea. For them freedom from Japanese domination held definite rewards, and for them the hate engendered by injustice, rather than an intellectual appreciation of the advantages of freedom, was the primary factor determining their willingness to face danger.

Affecting the motivation of the whole group was the fact that none of these men had ever lived in Korea when it was not Japanese-dominated. The freedom to which they were looking forward was a very vague ideal to them. Perhaps in some cases their families, as collaborators, stood to lose by Japan's defeat.

COMMENTS

In surveying the work of assessment in the Far East, it seems evident now that a better job could have been done if the recruiting of candidates had been conducted with greater energy. Failure of recruiters to provide men in excess of the needs of the operating branches, due either to the scarcity of available personnel or to other reasons, very materially increases the problems of assessment. The reason for this is straightforward: if the assessment branch of an organization is forced by the demands of the operating branches to weigh their urgent needs against the risk of passing a doubtful recruit, then the chances for error by assessment are greatly increased. Contrariwise, the chances for error are diminished if all doubtful cases can be rejected.

This problem is a statistical one which has important implications. If we assume that assessment is essentially a complex test, the rules which have been found to hold in using the intelligence tests or special aptitude tests as selection devices should be applicable to the screening process as a whole. The particular rule which is pertinent here is this: in the selection of a given number of men by means of a test possessing a fairly high validity, the *average ability* of those finally selected will *increase* as the size of the sample tested increases. And as a corollary to this: the probability of error in the selection process decreases with an increase in the size of the sample tested. Furthermore, a test of low validity may still be useful if the sample from which selections are made is large. These statistical rules, so pertinent to the recruiting policy of an organization, are too frequently overlooked.

Recruiting for any organization should be as active as is consistent with the resources of the assessment unit, in terms of funds and personnel. Much can be done by an assessment unit to accommodate itself to volume without a great increase in operating costs. For example, coarse screening tests can be administered which will immediately eliminate recruits who do not possess the minimum required ability in some important specific variable. This technique was employed in China, where ability to read was an essential qualification. There the number of men initially brought in from near-by holding areas was well over a thousand. By simply asking those who could read to step forward, the first step in screening was accomplished. This reduced the group to less than half its original size. Then by a one-minute, objectively scored reading test the number of candidates was still further reduced. Only those who remained took part in the more elaborate and expensive personality assessment procedures.

Chapter IX

THE EVALUATION OF ASSESSMENT

From the moment that wartime necessity laid upon the assessment program the responsibility for making many decisive judgments, an objective and disinterested appraisal of their validity became essential. In the short time devoted to each candidate it was hard enough to sketch the broad outlines of a satisfying and meaningful formulation of his personality. Predicting his future behavior under largely unknown circumstances was more challenging. But still more difficult was the task of making an adequate and impartial evaluation of the degree of success of these first two undertakings of assessment. Because OSS urgently needed personnel to carry out its operations, in the early months of the work all energies had to be turned to the pressing requirements of selection; appraisal of the efficiency of the process had to be postponed. When at last it was possible to establish a comprehensive program of validation procedures, the unexpectedly rapid end of the war cut it short. These unfavorable circumstances added tremendously to the difficulty of our basic task: that of establishing satisfactory criteria by which to measure accuracy either of diagnoses of personality or of prognoses of performance in a specific assignment.

These complexities bulked so large that we were unable to overcome them all. Although thousands of man-hours were spent in the evaluation process, the final verdict is a question mark. Nearly all the members of the staff and many of their colleagues in OSS who observed the operation of the program had the strong impression that, by and large, the administration had been furnished with meaningful descriptions of the traits and abilities of the recruits, which were of considerable service in winnowing the wheat from the chaff and in placing the wheat where it belonged. But how valuable is an impression? It was the need for certainty, the compulsion which motivates all scientists, which prompted us to embark on an extensive program to check the ratings and recommendations of assessment. Unhappily the final result was a decrease, rather than an increase, in degree of certainty—a temporarily discomforting, but, in the long run, often productive state of mind.

Our uncertainty stems from the conjunction of three facts: first, that our final over-all correlations between assessment ratings and appraisal ratings are of a low order, a result which proves that errors of considerable magnitude entered into the assessment process, or into the appraisal process, or into both. Second, that the appraisal process was carried out with much less regard to scientific principles than was the assessment process, and so we can hardly avoid the conclusion that a large proportion of the discrepancies between assessment and appraisal is the result of defects in the latter rather than of defects in the former. Third, that an analysis of the circumstances at home and overseas reveals that if assessment had operated perfectly, adhering closely to scientific principles, an appreciable number of predictive "errors" would necessarily and quite properly have been made. Furthermore, that, under the special conditions existing in the OSS, an additional number of predictive "errors" was inevitable, even if the assessment staff had been correct in every one of its judgments. This is a matter which will be discussed in the next chapter. Here it is sufficient to explain that it is our ignorance of the minimal percentage of these inevitable "errors" which makes it impossible for us to calculate the percentage of true errors that resulted from our own deficiencies in technique and clinical judgment.

The negative statistical outcome would probably have deterred us from the huge labor of this book if it had shaken our faith in the general principles underlying the OSS system of assessment and if we had not firmly believed that we had succeeded in distinguishing most of the defects in our implementation of the system. Anyhow, it is clear that the picture presented in this volume is not that of a noble building ready for occupancy, but rather of a mass of rubble with many good blocks of granite and marble out of which a substantial edifice can be erected in the future. This chapter, with its emphasis upon our errors, may prove more useful than any other in the book, especially if the reader pays close attention to the defects in our validation procedures and employs his imagination in thinking of ways to rectify them.

Although the situation which confronted the OSS assessment staff was, in many respects, unique, yet many of the difficulties we encountered are common to all undertakings of this sort. A discussion of our handicaps and mistakes, therefore, should serve to clarify some of the problems of future workers in this field.

HINDRANCES TO THE EVALUATION OF ASSESSMENT

First, there were the difficulties which stemmed from the assessment situation itself. These have been fully described in Chapter I. At this point we have only to take note of the fact that since the job analyses and environment analyses were unavoidably inadequate for assessment purposes, our conceptions of the different roles were extremely vague. Consequently, in assessing each candidate we had nothing specific in mind with which to compare his performances. If we ended by recommending him for his proposed assignment, it was because we thought that he had qualities which would enable him to cope with most situations, as we dimly imagined them, in the designated field of activity—administrative work, gathering intelligence, field operations, and so forth. But, actually, the assessed man who went overseas was not called upon to deal fairly well with a multiplicity of rather general situations, but to deal very well with a limited number of specific situations. In other words, the assessment staffs rated candidates according to their conceptions of a scale of all-round men in a given field of activity, but these men were appraised in the theater according to how effectively they performed a particular role in a particular location. Thus, some of the discrepancies between assessment ratings and appraisal ratings may be attributed to the difference between the two frames of references—*generality* of ability and *specificity* of ability. Other discrepancies may be ascribed to the fact that many candidates were assessed in comparison with necessarily inaccurate conceptions of their roles.

Another factor, mentioned in Chapter I, to which some discrepancies between assessment ratings and appraisal ratings can be attributed was the very frequent occurrence of unpredictable changes in the jobs and in the environments to which men were assigned in the theater. Theoretically, the whole process of validation becomes meaningless under these circumstances: if assessment, in obedience to its directive, had rated each man according to his suitability for a particular assignment, the validity of this rating cannot be determined by comparing it to the rating received for effectiveness in a different assignment. But, as pointed out above, although we held some conception of the assignment in mind while rating each candidate, we knew not only that this conception was defective but that the man was likely to be given a different assignment in the theater; consequently, the notion of an all-round OSS man was probably more influential as a standard for comparison than any precise formulation of job functions. Thus the standard, in most cases, was not specific and yet not entirely general. As we shall see, the correspondence of assessment and appraisal ratings is closer in the case of men who undertook the missions originally proposed for them than it was in the case of men who were given entirely different missions on arriving overseas.

Another source of error, not yet discussed, was differences between the frames of reference employed at assessment and those employed in the theater. At Station S, for example, the variables were rated, not entirely in terms of overt manifestations, but partly in reference to repressed tendencies and to their relations with other variables. We did this despite the fact that it was certain that our conclusions would not jibe with the impressions of many people who knew the candidates only superficially. We knew also that the men would display different facets of their characters to different observers and, as a result, the ratings we obtained from these observers (informants) would not agree with each other; and, if they did not agree with each other, they would not all agree with us. We believed, however, that ratings of the traits based on a dynamic formulation of the whole personality would generally agree more closely with the impressions gained by other observers than these impressions would agree with each other.

Another difficulty involving frame of reference, which affected chiefly the validation of job-fitness predictions, was due to an ambiguity in the thinking of the assessment staff that was never wholly rectified. In giving job-fitness ratings consistency requires that an excellent cook be given as high a rating as an excellent general. But this is difficult to do in a program in which both individuals may appear in the same assessment group, for the over-all superiority of one may so prejudice the staff that they are apt to give him a higher job-fitness rating as well as a higher over-all rating. That this occurred at S is shown by the fact that officers were not only given higher over-all ratings than enlisted men, which is perhaps reasonable, but were also given higher job-fitness ratings, which was probably improper. The comments of laymen who were asked to make ratings of men in the theater clearly showed that they were even more affected by such factors as rank, prestige, and general ability. Thus the differential operation of this determinant lowered the agreement between assessments and appraisals.

Finally, there was another factor worth mentioning which produced a difference between the frame of reference used in assessment and that used in appraisal. The staff at S was probably fairly successful in rating traits uninfluenced by knowledge of the candidate's proposed assignment. It was relatively easy for assessors to make ratings free of this consideration, since all candidates went through similar procedures. The same detachment could not be achieved, of course, in appraisal. Consider two men, both passed by S after having been rated Low Average in Emotional Stability. One was to do administrative work and the other was to take part in field operations. The potential office worker, scheduled for a routine task at headquarters in London, was passed without question with a final job-fitness rating of 3, because he would be in a relatively protected situation and because he had characteristics which made up for his mediocre emotional stability. The operational candidate, faced with a strenuous combat job behind enemy lines in Malaya, was passed reluctantly with a fitness rating of 2, *only* because he had a number of critical compensating abilities. But, when these variables were appraised in the theater, the administrator in London, who had suffered no great strain, was rated High Average in Emotional Stability, whereas the agent in Malaya, who had shown some signs of breakdown under severe stress, was rated Inferior. Thus, in many cases, as a result of the operation of different standards, correlations were poor, even though the assessment ratings may well have been correct.

At S, final ratings were made after sampling the behavior of a subject in a wide variety of situations, all of which had some correspondence with events in life. In the three days, a candidate experienced more frustration, stress, social pressure, tough intellectual work, and physical punishment than he was likely to encounter in a much longer period of routine work. Some of these experiences during assessment were relevant to his proposed assignment and some of them were not, yet a subject's behavior over the entire range of experience was considered when ratings were made on the different variables. If a person reacted inadequately in one or more situations, his job-fitness rating might or might not be affected, depending upon the relevancy of the situation, but one or more of his trait ratings would certainly be affected. Conversely, a man might perform brilliantly in tests having no relation to his proposed assignment and thereby cause his trait ratings to be revised upward while his job-fitness score remained unaffected. Ratings at assessment were made in comparison with a broad frame of reference consisting of the personalities of all candidates who had been through the area.

Judging a candidate against such a broad background, after he had acted in such a variety of situations, yielded considerable understanding of the total personality, but at the same time it resulted in lower correlations with appraisal findings. This difference may be explained by the fact that appraisal raters, generally speaking, were asked to evaluate people who had jobs similar to theirs, and consequently their grades were based on a narrower frame of reference than that employed at S, as well as on less information. For instance, a group of boat crewmen rating other boat crewmen gave intelligence scores varying from 3 to 5. Similar ratings were given by research analysts judging their fellows, but certainly the levels of intelligence included in these two ranges were by no means comparable.

Finally, wartime exigencies prevented the staff from setting up a precisely matched control group either of unassessed or of assessed men whose reports would not be made available to branches for use in deciding on their placement. Thus, the efficiency of the screening could never be appraised under rigid scientific conditions.

From the point of view of validation, one of the defects of the enterprise resulting from the requirements of the practical situation was that only a very few candidates who were not recommended by the assessment staff went overseas. Usually they left the organization. For a satisfactory evaluation of its methods the assessment staff had too great power of decision. Since about 25 per cent of the assessed cases were not recommended, a large number had no opportunity to take part in operations, so that the assessment of their abilities could be checked. The serious aspect of this loss of one quarter of the assessed personnel was that it was the supposedly poorest quarter, those whom we believed would fail. Profitable lessons would have been learned by observing in which cases signs that our assumptions had led us to accept as warnings of impending breakdown or as manifestations of weakness turned out to be invalid. It is likely that a number of commonly accepted old wives' tales of psychology and psychiatry would have been blasted by following these rejected cases and observing individuals with the conventional stigmata of personality deficiency perform well under exacting conditions. Such critical experimentation was out of the question, because sending even a few potential mental cripples into the field for intelligence operations could not have been justified when the paramount goal was winning the war.

To check the accuracy of a prediction of performance level, it is essential to have clear and unambiguous criteria of success and failure. If the job is running a lathe in a large factory, the rate of piece-work production is a satisfactory criterion; if the work calls for social adjustment as well as efficiency, the criteria are more complex, but nevertheless not difficult to define. In OSS, however, assignments included such complex tasks as secret intelligence, sabotage, and propaganda writing. For these no definite objective measures seemed meaningful, since the amount of damage an agent can do to the enemy is largely dependent upon his opportunities, just as the usefulness of the intelligence he reports is largely determined by the place to which he is assigned. Such quantitative measures of efficiency could therefore be accepted to a limited extent only. Since there was little agreement among members of the organization about what constituted success in their respective fields, it was not easy for the assessment staff to define adequate measures. Lacking these, satisfactory appraisals of accomplishment could hardly be achieved.

In the absence of any statement from the administrators of OSS as to how success in overseas missions would be measured, the assessors had to rely on their own judgment in selecting the best criteria against which to validate their methods. We chose what seemed to be the four best types of criteria that were obtainable, although none of these was free from serious shortcomings. Their inadequacy is indicated by the fact that, in measuring job fitness, the four methods showed rather poor agreement, correlating among themselves only from .46 to .59. In respect to the different personality traits, agreement was even worse, the correlations falling between .28 and .50.

Our predicament will, no doubt, recall to the minds of those who worked in other selection units during the war their own difficulties in validating their procedures.

THE FOUR APPRAISAL TECHNIQUES

During the first year of the assessment program, four different approaches to the problem of appraisal were devised. None of these was really satisfactory, each suffering from a number of defects, including some of those mentioned in the preceding section. It was hoped that by making appraisals from a number of different viewpoints a true evaluation of assessment could be made by a sort of triangulation. At least, it was felt unwise to rely exclusively on any single technique when it was possible to carry out a variety.

The four procedures undertaken were called Overseas Staff Appraisal, Theater Commander Appraisal, Reassignment Area Appraisal, and Returnee Appraisal.

Overseas Staff Appraisal.—Two members of the assessment staff obtained appraisals in the ETO, one in the summer of 1944 and one in the winter of 1945. Another former member of the staff sent ratings from the Mediterranean theater in the winter of 1945. In the summer of 1945 appraisals were obtained in China by two staff members, one of whom had previously reported on the performances of assessed personnel in the ETO. Thus reports were received from four different psychological appraisers. These overseas appraisers did not all use identical techniques, but in general the method adopted was as follows:

An appraisal in each case was obtained by interviewing the immediate chief or commanding officer of the individual under consideration, and if possible, several of his associates. After explaining the purposes of the interview and stressing the need for accurate records, the investigator asked: "What has Sergeant Hills been doing since his arrival in the theater?" Then: "Have these jobs been routine tasks requiring nothing but the efficient execution of orders, or have they called for initiative, resourcefulness, and imagination?" Then: "Does he get along well with his associates?" "What effect has he had on the morale of the organization?" And then: "How would you appraise Sergeant Hills' over-all usefulness to the organization —outstanding, average, or unsatisfactory?"

At this point the three categories for rating were defined more precisely:

OUTSTANDING.—All in all he has shown *exceptional* ability in the performance of his duties; he has manifested initiative and resourcefulness; he has cooperated well with others and lifted the morale of his unit.

AVERAGE.—He has been useful to the organization; efficient and cooperative for the most part; a dependable worker, but he has not displayed, or had the opportunity to display, much ingenuity or imagination.

UNSATISFACTORY.—He has not been useful for one reason or another; he has manifested only little ability, or shirked, or disturbed the organization with complaints or outbursts of emotion, or caused friction, or lowered morale.

In obtaining the last series of appraisals (China theater), the middle category was divided into two, High Average and Low Average. This four-category scale proved most satisfactory in getting ratings from in-experienced informants. It was considered that Outstanding corresponded to ratings of 4 and 5 at the assessment center, that High Average corresponded to 3, Low Average to 2, and Unsatisfactory to ratings of 1 and 0.

If the informant's rating did not seem to jibe with his estimate of the individual's performance, or if his rating did not agree with that given by other informants, he was questioned further and asked to give concrete instances to support his judgment. Some informants—branch chiefs, for example—were in a position to characterize 25 or more men, whereas others were able to discuss no more than one. Although for most individuals it was possible to obtain ratings from at least three or four informants, some could be rated by a single person only—for instance, a secretary who had done all her work under the supervision of one officer and was not well known by others.

This overseas interviewing was conducted as informally as possible. The staff investigators went out of their way to develop good relations with their informants, being careful to explain to them that the information was desired for purposes of scientific investigation and the improvement of assessment techniques, and would have no influence on the future of the individuals being discussed. The interviewers desired no one to get the impression that they were acting as "stool pigeons."

Later, two different ratings on the six-point scale were given to each appraisee by the staff investigator: (a) an over-all rating of his total performance in the field, based upon the investigator's observations together with his interpretation of the significance of the individual informants' views of the appraisee's personality; (b) a numerical estimate of the reliability of this rating, taking into consideration how many people had given opinions; how much agreement there was among them; how much opportunity the informants had to know the individual; and how dependable the staff investigator considered the informants to be. Occasionally the staff investigators became well acquainted with the individuals whom they were appraising and saw them working in their assignments. Information so gained was included among the other data upon which the final over-all ratings were based, and such firsthand observations usually had the effect of raising the estimate of reliability.

Theater Commander Appraisal.—In the spring of 1944 the Personnel Board of OSS decided to require that, when any member of the organization returned from an overseas assignment, his immediate superior submit a report including ratings on personality traits as soon as the individual left the theater. The chief purpose of this report was to assist in the decision which had to be made in the case of everyone returning: whether he should be separated from the organization or retained for a further assignment. It also had the secondary purpose of enabling the assessment staff to check on the accuracy of its predictions.

In order to accomplish this latter goal, the staff assisted in developing this form, so that it included, besides basic identification and life-history data, the material shown in Table 23.

TABLE 23

Form for Theater Commander Appraisal

	Superior	Excellent	Very Satis-factory	Satis-factory	Unsatis-factory
MOTIVATION, energy, effort, initiative, interest in assignment..............					
EFFECTIVE INTELLIGENCE, speed and accuracy of judgment, resourcefulness in solving problems........					
STABILITY, emotional control and maturity, absence of nervous symptoms.......					
ABILITY TO WORK WITH OTHERS, teamwork, tact, absence of annoying traits					
LEADERSHIP, organizing ability, ability to win cooperation.............					
PHYSICAL ABILITY, agility, daring, ruggedness, stamina................					

REMARKS:
COMPLETE REASONS FOR RETURN TO U.S.:
RECOMMENDATIONS: (a) Do you recommend his further use in OSS?
                             (b) If so, in what capacity?

For all members of the armed forces in OSS, this report was submitted in addition to the efficiency reports ordinarily placed in military records. An effort was made to make the OSS personnel report more meaningful and complete than these other efficiency reports. To begin with, the OSS form was marked "CONFIDENTIAL" and "SUBJECT MUST NOT SEE THIS." The existence of the report was publicized, and the importance of filling it out carefully was impressed upon commanding officers. In an effort to overcome the leniency error so common in ratings of this type made by inexperienced laymen, extremely laudatory terms were used to head the various columns. SUPERIOR, EXCELLENT, VERY SATISFACTORY, SATISFACTORY, and UNSATISFACTORY were chosen rather than, for example, SUPERIOR, HIGH AVERAGE, LOW AVERAGE, and INFERIOR. Also some clarification of the meaning of the psychological trait names was attempted by putting short definitions after them.

In order to analyze the results from this procedure quantitatively not only were the ratings of the theater commander recorded; his remarks were also read over by members of the assessment staff and given a rating of Low, Medium, or High on the basis of the degree of proficiency in the assignment reflected by them. The staff tried to make 25 per cent of these ratings Low, 25 per cent High, and the rest Medium.

Reassignment Area Appraisal.—The transformation, in the fall of 1944, of Area F from a large training station into a reallocation center provided the psychological staff with an opportunity to carry out another type of appraisal. As we have explained in Chapter VII, the primary function of the staff at F was the reassessment or re-evaluation of personnel who had completed one tour of duty, chiefly in the European or in the Middle East theater of operations, and were being considered for assignments in the Far East.

The F staff was also in a position to assemble data on grievances, to summarize off-the-record criticism of OSS operations, and to detect psychoneurotic disturbances in returning personnel. While carrying out these activities it could also make detailed evaluations of the returnees' personalities and performances overseas, evaluations that could later be compared with the earlier assessment.

The orientation booklet given to men arriving at Area F stated:

The OSS is anxious to learn as much as possible about the war experience of its returnees, the special difficulties, discomforts, and dangers encountered by every man in every theater of operation. It is important for the administrators in Washington to know the mistakes that have been made, to understand why some operations have succeeded and others have failed.

Therefore, every returnee will be scheduled for an interview. . . .

You can help us by speaking frankly of your satisfactions and dissatisfactions during your period of service overseas, your hardships, grievances, and disappointments.

The program at F relied chiefly on the clinical interview in conjunction with questionnaires. When the interviewee reported for his appointment he was asked to fill out an experience and background questionnaire. In this form were check lists dealing with his psychosomatic responses to danger and stress, attitude toward superiors, causes for complaint, state of health, and general outlook at the time of the interview. The second half of the questionnaire asked for information on developmental background, including region of rearing, parents' ages or subject's age at the time of parents' deaths, national background of family, ages of siblings, father's activity during World War I, attitude of family toward World War II, health in childhood, emotional stability in childhood, mental health of family, educational level attained, preferred subjects in school, participation in athletics, positions of leadership held in school or college, and mechanical aptitude.

While the interviewee checked the questionnaire, the interviewer could study the theater report written by the subject's superior officer, which was described above. Assessment reports on the interviewee, however, were not made available. The interview itself, partially structured by a schedule, dealt with three distinct areas: (1) experience in the field, (2) developmental history, and (3) political and social attitudes.

On the basis of his recital of his overseas experience, the interviewee was rated on a number of variables related to his adjustment to the conditions of his assignment. Taking into consideration the amount of stress to which he had been subjected, the interviewer rated, either Low, Medium, or High, the degree to which the following traits were manifested: anxiety, dejection, homesickness, irritability and quarrels, alcoholism, psychosomatic symptoms, and strength of complaints.

A discussion of the developmental background of the man being interviewed was introduced by suggesting to him that, since he had satisfactorily completed a mission, the staff was interested in studying his history in order to attempt to discover how determinants of success may have their origin in behavior and environmental conditions. Then the following topics were covered and the individual was rated on them: family solidarity, relative dominance of parents, amount of respect for parents, parental protectiveness, and childhood attitudes toward difficulties. The interviewer made Low-Medium-High ratings on most of these variables.

The Interview remained sufficiently fluid to permit adequate treatment of special problems arising from the subject's recital of his experiences. Of no set duration, it usually lasted from forty to ninety minutes. If the interviewer were not satisfied with his progress during the initial period, he could arrange for subsequent meetings, or occasionally ask another staff member to review the case. Finally he prepared a short report on the interviewee, rated him on the same personality variables that were used in assessment, and gave an over-all score based on all information he had obtained.

Returnee Appraisal.—Although first devised in the summer of 1944, this technique was not implemented in the assessment program until a year later. It was then applied concentratedly over a period of four months by more than twenty members of the staff, and in this intensive program some degree of information on the performance and personality of a large number of assessed personnel who went overseas was obtained.

Great efforts were expended to make as full use of this method as possible because it was hoped that by getting reports from a number of superior, equal, and subordinate colleagues of each assessee it would be possible to get appraisals free from the particular biases of any given individual, of superior officers, or of members of the assessment staff. The method used was as follows: a member of OSS returning from an assignment overseas would be met by one of the assessment staff, either at Area F or at his office in town. First, his assistance was requested in a scientific project of the assessment staff. Then, when he consented, he was given, with as little explanation as necessary to get his cooperation, a list of names of individuals who had been in his theater, and asked to check the name of each individual whom he knew. This list was composed of the names of all personnel in his theater of operations who had been assessed before going overseas, but the interviewee was not told this until he had finished checking the list. The interviewer then told him the origin of the list and explained that a study was under way to discover, if possible, the effectiveness of assessment. His cooperation was elicited with the assurance that the information which he gave would be treated as confidential, and that whatever he said would have no influence either on his own future or on the future of the individuals under consideration, but would be used only for purposes of studying the validity of the selection program. Since this procedure was adopted largely after the end of the war, many of the people on the list had already left the organization; hence it was only occasionally that informants were unwilling to give candid reports for fear of the effects which might come to anyone on whom they made an adverse report. If the organization had not been disbanding and the informants had not been leaving it, this desire to forestall unpleasant results would undoubtedly have been more important than it was as a factor limiting the usefulness of this appraisal procedure.

The interviewer then read from the list the first name checked, asking his respondent informally what sort of person that individual was. When the interviewee had given as much of a description of the personality as he would without prompting, he was asked how well the man under consideration carried out his assignment overseas. When this had been answered, the interviewer tried to draw out a more rounded character sketch. The comments of the informant were written by the interviewer on a form like the one shown in Table 24.

TABLE 24

Returnee Interview Form

Interviewee_____ Interviewer _____
         (Name and Rank)

Job overseas_____

_____

    (Line left blank to record interviewee's intelligence and reliability after interview)

* * * * * * * * * *

Subject_____   _____
   (Name and Rank)   (How long and how well interviewee knew him)

_____

Job overseas_____

Motivation for Assignment	L M H	Social Relations	L M H
Effective Intelligence	L M H	Leadership	L M H
Emotional Stability	L M H	Job	L M H

COMMENTS:

After these comments had been obtained, the interviewer explained that he would like to have the subject rated on a number of characteristics. The informant was asked to rate the subject on a three-point scale (Low, Medium, High), if possible, and to divide this further into a six-point differentiation when he thought this could be done meaningfully. Low Low he was to designate as 0; High Low as 1; and so on. It was explained that the distribution should fall on the normal curve with 0 and 5 each 7 per cent; 1 and 4 each 18 per cent; and 2 and 3 each 25 per cent. Commonly a diagram of such a curve was shown to the interviewee to help clarify the idea. Further, the interviewee was told that it had been our experience that there was usually a leniency error, so that he should be careful to distribute his ratings into all categories. This point was repeatedly raised throughout the interview, whenever many high ratings had been given, in order to force the rater to make a more normal distribution.

Brief definitions of each of the variables were given to the interviewee, and frequently he added further comments while making his ratings. These comments were also noted down. The interviewer frequently asked the rater to explain one of his decisions and if possible to give illustrative anecdotes. If the informant found he could not rate the individual under consideration on one or more of the variables, he was put under no pressure to do so, but that variable was skipped. For example, one informant might have known a specific individual only socially, and so would be unable to give him a job rating.

In each case, in order to be sure that the person under consideration was properly identified, the informant was asked what position the subject had held overseas. Also he was asked how long and how well he had known the individual he was discussing. All this was noted on the forms by the interviewer, who, at the end of the session, rated the interviewee on his reliability in reporting on this given individual as well as on his apparent intelligence, so that the total reliability of the report could be adequately evaluated later.

This procedure was repeated for each name checked by the informant. Occasionally it would appear that the informant really knew very little about one of the persons whose name he had checked, and if the interviewer were satisfied that this was the case, he passed over that name. Often, though, it was observed that informants used the device of saying they knew little about one person whom they disliked or concerning whom they felt they would have to give an unfavorable report. The interviewer kept constantly on his guard against this possibility, and whenever he suspected it was occurring he made an effort to draw out the informant as fully as possible. Sometimes, if one respondent had checked a large number of names, a fatigue factor entered in. Sometimes, also, there were necessary limitations of time, and under those circumstances the interviewer chose for discussion those individuals concerning whom the informant seemed to have the most information, even though he was aware that in so doing he was destroying the randomness of the choice.

All interview protocol slips so obtained were filed away together under the names of the assessed persons being appraised. In order not to make the appraisal dependent on the possibly one-sided testimony of any one informant, it was decided to establish a minimum criterion below which the individual could not be considered adequately appraised. This criterion was arbitrarily set at the level of three reasonably reliable informants. Moreover, the standard was not considered satisfactorily met unless at least three ratings (or comments which would lead to some idea of a rating) were given on each variable except Leadership. Ratings were much less frequently made on this trait than on the others, because many people had no leadership function overseas.

When enough information was gained about an individual to satisfy this criterion, a conference of one senior and two junior staff members met to decide on final appraisal scores. All the ratings on variables given by informants—High, Medium, or Low, or 5, 4, 3, 2, 1, or 0—as well as the ratings of the informant made by the interviewer, were placed on a blackboard. Then one member of the conference group read all the comments on each protocol slip. Thereupon each member of the conference (conferee) in the light of the comments and the ratings on the blackboard, wrote down his ratings on each variable on the six-point scale. When this had been completed independently, the ratings were read, and if there was agreement they were recorded. When there was disagreement, the conferees tried to see if they could come to agreement by discussion; if they could not, the case was continued in order to get more data.

Not only each of the variables, but also the reliability of each whole appraisal picture was rated, the latter on a scale of Low, Medium, and High. Some cases seemed unequivocal, with little disagreement among all the informants about the individual's personality and performance. These were considered to have high reliability. Other cases were rated Low, either because of disagreement among the informants, or because of some incompatibility in their statements, or because of some deviation in their ratings. Occasionally there was unanimity on all of the variables except one or two, and marked divergence on these. In such cases the final ratings agreed upon in the conference would be put in parentheses, and these ratings were never used in the statistics of appraisal studies. The conferees made an effort to be rigorous even in the cases of low reliability, and many cases which technically met the criterion were discarded because it was thought that a satisfactory picture had not been obtained from the appraisal data.

SHORTCOMINGS OF THE APPRAISAL TECHNIQUES

All of the appraisal methods which we resorted to had faults which seriously diminished their value. This was unavoidable. Some of the faults could be corrected if these techniques were to be used again; others are inherent in the procedures. Some are common to more than one of these methods; others are found in only one. Understanding them all, however, is important as part of the total process of evaluating assessment. First, let us devote some attention to the shortcomings common to more than one of the appraisal techniques and later turn to those specific to each of the methods.

1) An essential limitation of the Overseas Staff Appraisal and the Returnee Appraisal was that when we employed them we were reduced to the democratic but not necessarily correct expedient of accepting as raw data the opinion of any acquaintance or associate of the individual being appraised. Of course it was possible for the staff to give special weight to

the statements of those who seemed best qualified to state the requirements for success in various assignments, but frequently it was difficult to determine whose statements were most insightful, best considered, and based on the most complete background of experience. Hence the procedures often had the obvious disadvantage of giving equal weight to expert and inexpert opinion.

It was obvious, and important in all except the Reassignment Area technique, that informants varied over a wide gamut in ability to judge personality and performance insightfully and objectively. Some were acute and accurate; others were dull and vague. Some praised nearly everyone; others were unduly critical; still others were moderate. As a consequence some reports were much more valuable than others. In the Returnee Appraisal method an effort was made to gauge this difference in usefulness by rating the informants on their intelligence as judges. Also in this procedure and in the Overseas Appraisal, staff interviewers frequently asked for specific illustrative instances of the behavior of persons being appraised to substantiate the informants' opinions, so that overrating or underrating would be revealed. Even with such precautions it was possible to allow only roughly for inequalities among respondents.

2) The Theater Commander Appraisal technique, unlike those mentioned in the last paragraph, relied on the opinions of those who might be assumed to be experts, i.e., immediate superiors in the organizational hierarchy. Such a procedure, however, is likely to give a one-sided picture of a person, for such informants view an individual only from above downward, and as the Returnee Appraisal data showed, frequently disagree entirely with subordinates.

There was danger that in each of the appraisal techniques, but particularly in the Theater Commander and the Reassignment Area procedures, information on which the judgments were based was rendered inaccurate by the desires and sentiments of the informants. *Amour propre* was a potent factor in producing such inaccuracies. In giving ratings, a superior is sometimes swayed by considerations such as a desire to receive credit himself for his subordinates' actions or a wish to make his unit appear better than it really is. Sometimes an uncritical rating is a result of a commander's sincere but provincial belief in the high quality of his own unit. A large number of such high scores turned in by one commander so exasperated his superior in the theater, who reviewed them, that he wrote, "If everyone was so perfect in this unit, why didn't they get more done in the field?"

Prejudice of individual informants, of course, is a significant factor not only in the Theater Commander technique but also in each of the other methods, for each relies on the opinions of one or more respondents. Many of these informants were not motivated strongly to keep their likes and dislikes from influencing their judgments. Many made such comments as: "Yes, George is a very efficient officer, but I don't like him. He's not my sort of guy." The factors observed to operate most often to give rise to prejudiced judgments were these: differences between respondent and the person he discussed in nationality, in civilian or military status, in military rank, in social status, in imaginativeness or practicality, in type of assignment (e.g., operational job or desk job), in attitudes toward order, regularity, and discipline, in temperament, and in drinking habits. When informants described persons of the opposite sex, it was often clear that the personal appeal of the individual under consideration often affected their judgments.

3) In the Overseas and Reassignment Area methods, the attitudes and preconceptions of staff interviewers as well as those of informants were important. In any technique requiring judgments by assessment staff members, there is always danger that their ways of viewing persons, their theoretical assumptions, will influence their interpretations. Thus their final ratings can have spuriously high agreement with the original assessments because job performance and personality traits are seen by them from the assessment viewpoint. Every effort was made by staff interviewers to be objective, but there could be no guarantee that their interpretations were not colored by some such prejudice or that they did not differ from the conclusions which a military man, for instance, might derive from the same data. It must always be recognized that the opinion of the practical military expert on OSS assignments could well be more valid than that of an assessment staff member trained in the comparative seclusion of university halls or hospital wards.

4) The Theater Commander and Returnee methods of appraisal required the associates of the assessed personnel to make ratings on the personality traits in terms of which they had been rated at S or W. Simple definitions of these traits as they were understood by the assessment staff were given to the informants, either by written instructions in the Theater Commander method or by an interviewer in the others. The score or more of interviewers undoubtedly used somewhat different definitions, but nevertheless their divergence was not great enough to be the whole explanation for the disagreement among respondents. It was frequently clear from their comments or illustrative anecdotes that these interviewees did not understand the terms at all as the assessment staff understood them. For instance, it appeared that leadership was equated with intelligence by some officers, and the fact that he was not a leader sometimes was the sole reason given for rating a capable enlisted man as unintelligent. Again emotional stability and social relations were occasionally viewed as going together—if a man were a good drinking companion he was regarded as stable. When it was apparent that differences of conception between various raters existed, an

effort was made to allow for them, but obviously in many cases it was difficult to discover what ideas the raters had about the traits. Certainly "emotional stability" did not, for the lay informants, connote assumptions about psychiatric disease, psychosomatic symptoms, childhood traits, habit control, character defects, and so on, which had been taken into account by the staff at assessment. But what the term did mean to them was often hard to tell.

5) In all four of the appraisal techniques there were marked differences among raters or informants as to how they distributed their ratings over the various steps of the scales. In no case was the curve of distribution comparable to the assessment distribution curves, and in many cases the curves were very greatly different. This fact in itself lowered the correlations between assessment and appraisal findings. The great disparity in the use of the rating scale among five raters employing the Theater Commander technique is shown in Table 25.

TABLE 25

Percentages of Ratings in Each of Five Categories of the Total Theater Commander Appraisal Sample Compared with Similar Percentages for Five Individual Raters

Rater	N^a	— THEATER COMMANDER APPRAISAL SCALE —				
		Superior	Excellent	Very Satisfactory	Satisfactory	Unsatis- factory
Total.....	2,706	26	50	16	6	2
A........	63	2	46	49	3	0
B........	267	90	10	0	0	0
C........	30	61	13	0	13	13
D........	204	80	14	5	1	0
E........	47	11	57	28	2	2

^{a} N = Number of Ratings

It is clear from this table that very slight agreement existed between various raters on what distribution of ratings should obtain. The most common tendency, that of giving predominantly high ratings, is demonstrated in the total distribution of ratings. However, an examination of the distributions of individual raters gives the impression that the chief shortcoming is an inability to discriminate over the whole five-point scale. Rater A, for example, seems to say, "There are two kinds of people in my outfit, whom I will rate 'average' and 'somewhat above average.'" Raters B and D also distinguish essentially only two types, but call them superior individuals and those who fall just short of being superior. Rater C clearly believes that the two types are the superior people and the failures. Mediocrity is ruled out. Rater E appears to have made an effort to discriminate over at least a three-point scale but contends that most of those he rated are considerably above average.

No clear idea was conveyed in the instructions to the raters as to what percentage of personnel overseas should fall into each of the five categories on the scale. Other studies have shown that giving such a predetermined frame of reference is helpful, though only moderately so. It was not feasible to attempt to improve this distribution by the lengthy technique of man-to-man rating in which the rater chooses men in his outfit to represent each of the degrees of a given trait on the scale, then decides how each man he is rating compares to these standard representatives.

Our data indicate that not only inexperienced lay raters skewed the rating scale from a normal distribution and committed the "leniency error" of giving more high scores than low; it seems that staff members made these

TABLE 26

Percentage of Ratings in Each Category of the Scale Given by Each of the Four
Overseas Staff Appraisers

Rater	N	S Scale					
		0	1	2	3	4	5
S Classes							
A	214	0.5	7.5	19.2	45.8	22.9	4.2
B	31	9.7	19.9	25.8	12.9	29.0	3.2
C	100	7.0	8.0	25.0	16.0	35.0	9.0
D	26	7.7	0.0	7.7	53.8	30.8	0.0
Total	371	3.5	8.1	20.5	35.6	27.2	5.1
W Classes[a]							
A	29	3.4	3.4	24.1	41.4	20.7	6.9
D	62	1.6	6.4	11.3	45.2	32.2	3.2
Total	91	2.2	5.4	15.0	45.2	28.0	4.3

[a] Raters B and C appraised no one assessed at W.

errors also, though to a lesser degree, in both Overseas and Reassignment Area appraisals. Table 26, for example, gives distributions of the ratings of the four staff members who appraised overseas.

It looks as if at least two appraisers had given too many high grades. If true, this fact could be explained by supposing that he had taken the reports of his informants too much on their face value and that his grades reflected the "leniency error" usual in layman's ratings. But it is more likely that the skewness of the distribution obtained by these appraisers gives us a truer picture of the personnel situation than a normal distribution of grades would have given us.

Besides the fact that there is little reason to suppose that the efficiency represented by such grades was, in truth, normally distributed, there is the fact that there were numerous units in the OSS no member of which, as far as we could discover, was unsatisfactory in the fulfillment of his duties, and, in such cases, many informants could not bring themselves to give anyone in the group a rating of 1 or 0, even when the appraiser's instructions were clearly and insistently presented to them. Thus the high grades indicate that most members of the OSS could not conform to the arbitrary distribution scale for rating their associates, because this scale did not correspond to the facts as they estimated them. This might be interpreted as evidence of high morale and, indirectly, of the success of the screening process.

In this connection it should be remarked that we imposed on our returnee informants the conception of a normal distribution curve, instructing them to give about 18 per cent of their associates a grade of 1 and about 7 per cent a grade of 0. By so doing we ran the theoretical risk of setting up a rating scale which did not correspond to the assessment scale, and yet later making our statistical computations as if the two scales did correspond. Roughly speaking, if assessment had been completely successful, no man would have deserved a rating of 1 or 0 in the theater, since men of such caliber would have been eliminated in the screening process. As we knew would happen, however, even though we pressed them to use all categories in rating, our returnee informants did not follow the normal distribution closely and the total effect of this manner of proceeding was to compensate to a degree for the leniency error and to give a few men grades of 0 or 1 who probably were not unsatisfactory, but were merely the least effective members of a wholly satisfactory unit.

6) Many evidences of the "halo effect" appeared in all the appraisal techniques, although they were less blatant in the Reassignment Area method, in which staff members determined the scores, than in the others in which laymen were the primary determiners of ratings. If a man being appraised was liked or admired by a respondent, he was very commonly rated high

on all traits without distinction. On the other hand, if he was thought to be low in one trait, or to have done a poor job, he was frequently rated low on all characteristics, although it is unlikely that he could have been so consistently undesirable. Discriminating distribution of trait ratings on a single individual was relatively rare.

7) The accuracy of two appraisal methods especially, the Theater Commander and the Returnee techniques, was diminished by the hasty and careless manner in which some of the ratings were made. Many of the Theater Commander reports were filled out in a haphazard and hurried manner. This could be inferred, for example, from the similarity of ratings given to whole units of men who had obviously performed in the field different sorts of jobs with what must have been different degrees of efficiency. Haste could also be inferred from the absence of remarks on the man's report when it was clear that the commanding officer must have possessed much pertinent information. In a number of instances these reports were filled out, not by the individual's immediate superior, but by some substitute who was scarcely acquainted with the man.

The rating scale was short and there could have been no fatigue effect in rating a few men, but personnel frequently returned home in large groups, and the busy commander would rate them all in one sitting. This necessity sometimes contributed to the slipshod way in which this important job was done.

The interest in the Returnee appraisal indicated by the informants in devoting their energies to this project varied from very little to very great. Those who did it as an obvious chore were released from the necessity of completing it, but even those who did it willingly often glossed over some cases and made snap judgments in an effort to finish rapidly. In the respondents who gave information for more than eight hours, fatigue was unavoidable.

8) In the Theater Commander, Overseas, and Returnee procedures there were wide divergences in closeness of acquaintanceship between the informant and the man being appraised. They may have known each other a short or a long time; in the organization only or before entering it as well; only socially or only in business; casually or as roommates or best friends.

If the respondent knew the individual as a co-worker, he may easily have had a different opinion of his social relations, for example, than someone who knew him only after hours. He may have been a congenial drinking companion and a crabby boss. Each view might have been correct in its own limited area, but it was hard to combine them into one valid over-all rating.

9) The three appraisal methods mentioned in the last paragraph have another fault in common: the relationship in the field between the informant

and the appraisee frequently determined the nature of the report about him. Subordinates and superiors often had entirely different impressions, and in more than one case this was so obvious that it was impossible to arrive at any final conclusion, because the enlisted men had one view of a man while the officers had a distinct and irreconcilably different one. Similarly, when the appraisee and one of the informants were members of the same clique overseas, but another informant was not a member, it was common for markedly different opinions to be expressed. Of course both such views may have a measure of truth in them, but it is not possible to represent the two truths in a single quantitative rating.

10) Interviewees and informants occasionally withheld information because they questioned the purposes of the research, even though assurance was given that the data would be used only for the evaluation of assessment. They thought that anything unfavorable they said about their acquaintances might redound to their own or their associates' disadvantage, and they refused to "stick their necks out." This was particularly marked in the Returnee Appraisal interviews of members of small groups that had had a strong *esprit de corps* abroad and had come back to the United States together.

11) The manner of conducting the Overseas Staff and Returnee appraisals was faulty in that it did not control the factors determining which men were discussed by respondents. Striking characters, good and bad, were reported upon more frequently than less colorful figures, and opinions about such vivid personalities are especially susceptible to the errors of hearsay.

12) To get the information they wished, staff interviewers put questions to the appraisers in the Overseas Staff and Returnee techniques. These psychologists and psychiatrists attempted to ask neutral and nondirective questions, but there can be little doubt that errors repeatedly crept into the data, that ratings were influenced because leading questions were asked of the respondents, that rating categories were given inaccurate definitions, or that certain factors were given undue stress by the staff member.

13) When there was strong disagreement among the informants concerning a specific individual being appraised by either the Overseas Staff or the Returnee method, the staff attempted to discuss the person with enough of his other acquaintances to be able eventually to learn what the preponderant view of him was. Nevertheless it was sometimes impossible to talk to a sufficient number of respondents to be able to develop a synthetic portrait of the man which would explain all reactions to him. In such cases the final ratings had low reliability.

These thirteen sources of error were common to more than one of our appraisal procedures. There were probably others we have not recognized and described. In addition to these were some faults found only in one specific method:

Overseas Staff Appraisal.—1) In the Returnee Appraisal, the interviewers followed with a good deal of uniformity prearranged standard procedures of gaining information; in the Overseas Staff method each appraiser developed his own procedures, since they had not been coordinated before these staff members left the United States. Some of the appraisers, for example, incorporated their own direct observations of performance in the field with facts gleaned from interviewers; one, however, relied wholly on interview data. It is clear that this diversity of approach by the staff members led to dissimilar findings and thus diminished the usefulness of the Overseas Staff Appraisal.

2) It might be thought that the staff appraisers, having been present before they went abroad at the assessment of a number of the appraisees, would have their judgments concerning these persons prejudiced by a natural inclination to seek for confirmation in the theater of the assessment predictions. There was perhaps some element of this, but it was certainly not very great. First, a large proportion of the men appraised were strangers to the appraiser because the latter had not been working at the station at the time assessment occurred. Second, at assessment only the "student" names of the candidates were known, whereas in the theater their real names were used exclusively. Rarely, then, did an appraiser realize that the Captain Jenks who was being rated was Student Bill of Class S-13. Third, all assessment ratings remained in Washington, and it was impossible for the appraiser to remember more than a very few of them by the time he arrived overseas. Finally, though the appraisers tried to be impartial at all times, they were not so much aware that they were seeking confirmation of assessment judgments as they were, occasionally, aware of the reverse. They were attempting to reveal errors, because chiefly through the discovery of errors could the assessment techniques be improved.

3) The principal fault of the Overseas Staff Appraisal is that it was not prosecuted extensively enough. There were not enough appraisers in the field; they did not remain long enough; and they did not get information on enough cases. Besides giving a single over-all rating on performance overseas, the appraisers should have attempted to rate all the personality variables and the job accomplished as well, just as was done at assessment. And perhaps also, the staff members should have tried to base more of their judgments on actual observations of performance on the job, rather than on the reports of others. Of course it would have been impossible to shadow secret agents and saboteurs to see how they discharged their duties, but direct observation of people carrying out many sorts of assignments would have been possible.

Theater Commander Appraisal.—1) Many of the raters were military men accustomed to the accepted procedure in the War and Navy Departments of giving high ratings to anyone who had not failed miserably. Despite the fact that they were told that such methods should not be employed in OSS, these raters seemed to find themselves unable to abandon the usual practice, and nonmilitary raters, realizing this, refused to penalize their own subordinates by using a different procedure.

2) A fault of minor importance in this technique is that the theater commanders were asked to rate the variables on a five-point scale. Hence the scores are not directly comparable to the assessment ratings on a six-point scale. Correlational studies between the two sets of ratings are still possible, however.

Reassignment Area Appraisal.—1) The need for relying on secondary sources also constituted a shortcoming of the appraisal carried out at Area F. The Reassignment Area interviewer may have had a better opportunity to judge the personality of the man being appraised than the staff member in the field, but also there was greater possibility that his impression of the man would color his evaluation of his achievement overseas. While placing chief reliance on the factual information and ratings supplied by the theater commander, the interviewers at the Reassignment Area were forced to depend to some extent on their skill and experience with OSS personnel. It is to be supposed that ineffective men made efforts to disguise their shortcomings; that some mediocre individuals glibly exaggerated their contributions; and even conversely, that highly successful individuals were guilty of understatement. Such distortions of truth commonly diminish the value of brief interviews, and can only partially be compensated for by intuitive interviewers. The task at Area F was made easier by treating the returning member of OSS not as a man on trial, but, rather, as one to whom the interviewer and the organization were indebted because he was qualified to offer constructive criticism and help in other ways to improve the operations and personnel selection of the organization.

Although this approach did much to put the interviewee at ease and prevent him from erecting defenses and barriers, reaction to the Interview was by no means uniform. Attitudes ranged from outright truculence and resentment through polite indifference to eager cooperation and friendliness. Where one person found in the discussion an opportunity for catharsis, another responded to the situation with reserve and demanded that the most innocuous information be treated with utmost confidence. Generally the atmosphere was friendly and informal, but it was clear that the accuracy of the appraisal must have varied widely from one case to another.

2) The over-all rating giving at Area F in some respects differed markedly from assessment or Overseas Staff Appraisal over-all ratings, be-

cause the reallocation program was oriented toward selecting the best men for duty in the Far East. Emphasis was placed upon predicting the success of a man in a new undertaking under radically different environmental conditions, rather than upon the accurate determination of his achievement in his previous assignment. To be sure, past accomplishment was an important datum. It was assumed, naturally, that the general characteristics of the personality would be as important in China as in Africa or France. At the same time it was understood that many members of OSS had been successful in the European and Middle Eastern theaters precisely because of their familiarity with the language and customs, or because their emotional attachment to one of the countries in these regions motivated them highly. Many men who performed well in Europe had little desire for an assignment in China. Others who desired to go to China and the Far East possessed personality characteristics which suggested that their adjustment to Orientals and Oriental customs would be poor. Still others who had made conspicuous successes in previous jobs showed signs of "combat fatigue" which required indefinite assignment in the United States. In a few cases the reverse situation existed, that is, some not suited for European or Middle Eastern jobs appeared to have a combination of traits which would make them successful in the Far East.

As a rating to use in appraising assessment, therefore, the Reassignment Area over-all mark was far from satisfactory, for it was primarily prognostic and only secondarily a judgment of past accomplishment.

Returnee Appraisal.—1) Sometimes several months had elapsed between the time an informant last saw a man and the time he rated him; hence we might surmise that in some cases the informant's memories were less vivid and reliable than they would otherwise have been. It is possible, however, that the judgments of over-all merit were more judicious because of this slight degree of "historical" perspective.

2) The outstanding flaw in the Returnee Appraisal method has already been mentioned. It was that of imposing the normal distribution curve as a frame of reference. If the informants had scrupulously followed the directions given them, 25 per cent of the assessed personnel would have been marked Low (0 or 1), equivalent to Unsatisfactory, even if none of them had been unsatisfactory.

3) There were opportunities for error at the Returnee Appraisal staff rating conference. Frequently the interviewers were not present at the conference and the estimates of the dependability of each informant had to be made without the help of the additional information they possessed. Also, it was often difficult to arrive at a composite figure for the different notations of ratings which were placed on the blackboard—both Low, Medium, High, and 0-5—with some allowance for the leniency error, a large

proportion of all ratings being High. Not knowing who the informants were and not having adequate evidence of their dependability, we had nevertheless to make inferences, realizing that a 2 from one informant might equal a High from another.

4) After the staff conferees made their individual ratings, there were disagreements in some cases. These were not great, as the high coefficients of reliability in Table 27 indicate.

TABLE 27

Reliability of Returnee Appraisal Ratings by Informants and Staff Conferees
(Reliability coefficients—η)

Type of agreement measured	Degree of staff confidence in ratings from protocols		
	Low	Medium	High
Agreement among informants..............	.30	.38	.41
Agreement among staff conferees...........	.68	.78	.92

Table 27 presents the reliabilities (agreements) of the job ratings made by (a) the Returnee Appraisal informants and (b) the staff conferees. It will be seen that the staff conferees agreed well in their ratings, particularly on the group of cases in which they had expressed high confidence in the ratings obtained from the informants. The informants' ratings, however, show only fair agreement and the differences are not great between the coefficients for the groups with the three degrees of confidence.

STATISTICAL ANALYSIS OF APPRAISAL POPULATIONS AND RATINGS

Of the total of 2,748 assessed personnel who went overseas, we obtained some sort of follow-up material on approximately two thirds. Altogether 1,708 persons (or 62 per cent of the total who went abroad) were appraised by the Returnee technique, but the information obtained on 1,197 of these cases did not meet the minimum criteria of acceptability; hence only 511 persons (or 19 per cent of those who went overseas), can be considered to have had satisfactory appraisal by this method. We obtained 468 Theater Commander appraisals (17 per cent of the assessed persons who went abroad); 466 Overseas Staff appraisals (17 per cent); and 411 Reassignment Area appraisals (15 per cent). Of course there were overlaps among these techniques, some individuals being appraised by 2, 3, or even 4 methods. All told, 1,189 persons (43 per cent) received 1,853 acceptable appraisals.

The complete detailed analysis of these appraisal data is not of sufficient interest to justify publication. We shall limit ourselves to a few findings.

Leniency Error.—This error was much more obvious in the Theater Commander appraisals than it was in others. In rating the different variables of personality, theater commanders showed even more leniency than they did in rating job fitness. Their highest ratings were for Motivation, their lowest for Leadership.

Effect of Military Rank on Ratings.—In contrast to most studies of military and semimilitary organizations, appraisals of OSS personnel showed no positive correlation between military rank and ratings. Only on Effective Intelligence and on Leadership were the officers rated distinctly higher than the enlisted men. On Motivation civilians were rated highest.

Length of Overseas Service.—Two of the methods—the Theater Commander and the Reassignment Area techniques—showed that the men who had been overseas longest were likely to receive the highest ratings. The correlation between the general remarks in the Theater Commander technique and length of time overseas was .23 ($N=235$); between the over-all rating in the Reassignment Area method and length of time overseas .19 ($N=411$). Both of these coefficients are significant beyond the 1 per cent level. Perhaps these positive correlations indicate that the first people recruited by OSS were better than those sent overseas later, and indeed it was the impression of the staff that the quality of the assessed personnel gradually fell off as the months of the war progressed and the man-power shortage increased. Another explanation might be that leaders abroad keep with them longest the people they consider best. It is also possible, however, that a fault of the Theater Commander technique is that length of time serving under the superior officer (that is, degree of acquaintance with him) and length of general operational experience are important determinants of the grades. (Since the ratings from this method affected the ratings given at the Reassignment Area, it is understandable that the latter technique would show the same effect.) Whatever the explanation for these slight positive correlations, the operation of this factor is likely to make for less agreement between these two appraisal methods and assessment, because the latter, of course, took no account of how long the individual would be overseas before appraisal.

Adequacy of the Samples.—Our analyses show that the appraised populations do not represent all periods of assessment equally, for there are many more from the earlier S and W classes in each of the samples than from the later classes. This is unfortunate, for it means that the bulk of our data refers to assessees who were subjected to what was probably the least satisfactory assessment.

The figures show that our samples were well distributed in respect to the categories of sex, age, military status, and proposed assignment.

Factors Diminishing Size of Populations Available for Study.—Although respectably large samples of all assessed persons who went abroad were appraised by the different methods, the populations on which it was possible to make appraisal computations were not so large as these. For one thing, it did not seem legitimate in many cases to consider the W and S personnel together, because the two assessments were so different. This one decision served to cut approximately in half the population available for study in any one problem.

Furthermore, for the S population there was no job rating, strictly speaking, until class S-45. Since more than half of the S cases that were appraised fell into classes 1-44, less than 50 per cent of the whole appraised group is available for comparing assessment job decisions with appraisals of overseas performance.

The situation was not precisely the same for the over-all ratings at S, but it is true that a less satisfactory type of over-all rating was given before S–45 than afterward. The earlier rating was made by a single staff member, who read through all of the reports for classes S 1–44 some months after those reports had been written. In the light of these evaluations and the ratings which were made on the variables, often very meager information, he gave over-all ratings of Low, Medium, or High, attempting to put 25 per cent into each of the two extreme categories and 50 per cent into the middle. This was, of course, much less satisfactory than a grade given by agreement of the total staff based on individual ratings which were later pooled, a score which was derived immediately at the end of the discussion of the case at the staff conference rather than months later. Moreover, the definition of the over-all rating used for the first 44 classes was not identical with the definition used later. In Table 28 it may be seen that, although the appraisal populations are relatively large (there being an average of about 1½ types of appraisal for each of 531 W cases and nearly 2 types of appraisal for each of 656 S cases), nonetheless in considering job ratings from S, one of the most important groups of data, there was no sample of more than 100 cases available for study which had been evaluated by any single appraisal technique.

When for purposes of analysis one wishes to hold constant such a variable as the reliability rating of Returnee Appraisal judgments, or when one wishes to investigate a given appraisal method in terms of each of the individual ratings given on the six-point scale, these populations of less than a

TABLE 28

Appraisal Populations

Type of Appraisal	All S	S-45 on (Job ratings available)	All W
Theater Commander..........	237	83	231
Overseas Staff...............	370	88	92
Reassignment Area...........	208	53	203
Returnee...................	290	93	221
Total number of appraisals....	1,105	317	747
Total number of cases appraised	656	202	531

hundred are naturally cut down to much smaller numbers, frequently too small to give reliable results.

It would be extremely valuable for theoretical purposes to compare in detail the various types of appraisal. This can be done most effectively by using cases on whom two or more types of appraisal are available. Table 29 shows the number of overlaps that occurred among the different techniques. It will be seen that never did any two given types of appraisal coincide on more than 258 cases, even when S and W cases were combined.

TABLE 29

Overlaps among Different Techniques of Appraisal

Type of appraisal	Theater Commander		Overseas Staff		Reassignment Area		Returnee	
	S	W	S	W	S	W	S	W
Theater Commander	—	—	112	16	137	121	84	60
Overseas Staff......	112	16	—	—	87	9	124	14
Reassignment Area.	137	121	87	9	—	—	76	44
Returnee..........	84	60	124	14	76	44	—	—

Separating the W and S cases halves the populations, and holding constant other factors quickly reduces populations to very small size.

Intercorrelations among Appraisal Techniques.—The degree of intercorrelation among the four appraisal methods is of interest. We have discussed at length earlier in this chapter the difficulties involved in developing reliable criteria of good and bad performance in the field. The greater the divergences among the criteria embodied in the different appraisal methods, the lower would be the intercorrelations among them. In Table 30 these intercorrelations are shown.

TABLE 30

Intercorrelations among Appraisal Ratings for All Assessed Cases on Which Each Pair of Criteria Was Available

Type of appraisal	Theater Commanders' general comments		Overseas Staff		Reassignment Area		Returnee	
	r	N	r	N	r	N	r	N
Theater Commanders' general comments...	—	—	.59	113	.58	237	.49	117
Overseas Staff.........	.59	113	—	—	.46	96	.50	136
Reassignment Area....	.58	237	.46	96	—	—	.49	109
Returnee.............	.49	117	.50	136	.49	109	—	—

The fact that these coefficients vary between .46 and .59 would indicate that, while there is a small core of agreement among the informants or raters in the various techniques about the qualifications for adequate performance of these jobs, there is also a large number of factors peculiar to each specific technique which lowers the intercorrelations. It is interesting that the range of these correlations is so small, because it shows that no one appraisal method is markedly better than another in respect to common elements. There is, of course, no certainty that the core of agreement among these techniques is in any absolute sense correct—our figures show only that no appraisal procedure revealed this core much better than any other.

The ratings by the different techniques were obtained entirely independently, of course—with one exception: the interviewer who gave the Reassignment Area Appraisal rating in the majority of cases had before him at that time the Theater Commander Report, and he intentionally amalgamated these data with his own findings in arriving at a final grade. It is therefore to be expected theoretically that the agreement between these two types of appraisal would be high. It is, relatively, though there is one other intercorrelation in Table 30 that is slightly higher.

Relationships of Reliability Ratings to Agreement between Assessment and Appraisal.—In an ideal appraisal study, the coefficient of correlation between assessment and appraisal would be unity, if both methods were perfect. The correlation would be diminished to lesser values by imperfections in either assessment or appraisal. If, for instance, the correlation between an appraisal technique and assessment were .5, the assessment might theoretically be entirely valid and the appraisal method so inadequate that the final correlation between the two would be at this level; or contrariwise, the appraisal might be wholly valid and the assessment so poor that the correlation is lowered to .5. It is impossible to tell from a simple correlation which of these situations exists, or whether both assessment and appraisal are imperfect. However, it is reasonable to assume that there are errors in both. If this be true, then doing anything to increase the reliability of appraisal ratings should result in higher correlations between those scores and the assessment data.

In an effort to increase reliability, so-called "reliability" ratings were made of the decisions derived from two types of appraisal, the Overseas Staff and the Returnee. The term "reliability" applied in this way is misleading, because these scores do not measure statistical reliability, but rather represent clinical estimates of how confident we were that the rating given was the "correct" one. If a judgment was obtained by a staff interviewer from a person who was obviously insightful and able to make shrewd analyses of human personality, his rating was considered more "reliable" or "correct" than the average. Similarly, if there were good agreement among a number of informants about a certain individual, their pooled opinion was also considered more "correct."

In the light of such considerations it was decided to determine whether the correlations between assessment job ratings and appraisal job ratings increased as the "reliability" of the latter increased. But, somewhat to our surprise, correlations both for the Overseas Staff Appraisal and for the Returnee Appraisal demonstrated no such effect. There are several possible explanations. Many of the judgments of "reliability" may have been wrong. An interviewer was likely to give a relatively high mark to a very articulate, clever, analytical informant, regardless of the possibility that his thinking was oriented by a strong personal sentiment or prejudice; and he was likely to give a low mark to a man who was unable to give plausible reasons for his rating even though this rating actually represented an emotionally balanced judgment. Furthermore, our practice was to give each informant one over-all grade on dependability, although probably in many cases, he was judicious in some of his ratings but biased in others. Perhaps actually there was not much difference between the appraisal job ratings in respect to their reliability, and so the scores given by the interviewers and conferees were largely artifacts. Also, the populations involved may have been too small to reveal a statistical difference between "reliable" and "unreliable" ratings.

APPRAISAL FINDINGS

None of our statistical computations demonstrates that our system of assessment was of great value. This negative result suggests that two or three, or all, of the following statements are true: (1) The appraisal procedures were to some extent defective. (2) The assessment procedures were to some extent defective. (3) The staff members were to some extent incompetent, partly because they were inexperienced in making predictions of this kind and partly because their knowledge of the jobs and of the environments overseas was inadequate. (4) An individual's relative effectiveness under such shifting conditions as prevailed for OSS men and women overseas depends more upon chance—the occurrence of improbable and unpredictable situations and events—than it does upon relative ability, degree of motivation, and strength of character. Our data are not of much help in deciding to what degree, if any, each of these statements is correct.

The Order of Magnitude of Correlations between Assessment Ratings and Appraisal Ratings.—In Table 31 are shown the correlations between assessment job ratings and appraisal job ratings. Examination of the figures reveals (1) that all the correlations are positive but of a low order of magnitude; (2) that the method of Overseas Staff Appraisal yielded the highest correlations; and (3) that the W job ratings had higher validity than the S job ratings as measured by the Overseas Staff Appraisal and the Reassignment Area Appraisal.

TABLE 31

Correlations between S and W Assessment Job Ratings and Appraisal Ratings

Type of appraisal	S job rating (Classes S-45 on)		W job rating (All classes)	
	r	N	r	N
Overseas Staff Appraisal	.37[a]	88	.53[a]	83
Returnee Appraisal	.19[a]	93	.21[a]	173
Theater Commander's comments	.23	64	.15	158
Reassignment Area Appraisal	.08	53	.30[a]	178

[a] Cases in which correcting r for restricted sample made a significant difference; r given in each case is the corrected one.

From the start, before the correlations were computed, it was generally agreed that the Overseas Staff Appraisal was our most valid method; and now, having found that the ratings obtained by this technique are more highly correlated with assessment ratings than are those obtained by other methods, we are all too humanly disposed to be still more convinced that this one was the best. Its defects are inherent in every validation procedure which unavoidably and realistically relies on the judgments of the appraisee's associates. The Overseas Staff Appraisal and the Returnee Appraisal are very similar in design. Essentially, both are sociometric techniques in which an interviewer, unacquainted with the appraisee, plays an impartial role by defining terms, requesting evidence, and making sure that each rating is given after some reflection by a man who has sufficient ground for an opinion.

The staff members who collected the overseas appraisals did not foresee at the time they were interviewing their informants how crucial their reports would be in deciding the value of assessment procedures. If they had all fully realized the importance of their function, their reports, without doubt, would have been more complete, more detailed, and more accurate. As a result, correlations with assessment ratings might have ranged between .45 and .60, rather than between .37 and .53, as shown in Table 31. These last figures, as it happens, are probably a little too high, because of an error inherent in the Overseas Staff technique (and to a lesser degree in the Returnee technique). A few men who were rated Medium or Superior at the time the staff member visited the theater later proved unsatisfactory. Thus the effectiveness of some men declined with time. Running contrary to this decline, however, was the trend noted earlier, namely, that ratings were higher, on the average, for men who had served a long time in the theater than they were for those who had served a short time.

The correlations between assessment ratings and the ratings derived from the theater commander's comments are very low, but not lower than would be expected by anyone who is acquainted with the way these reports were filled out *en masse* by harassed administrators. The defects in this technique have already been reviewed.

All the pertinent information which the interviewer at the Reassignment Area had at his disposal was contained in the overseas report. Consequently, most of the defects listed in connection with the Theater Commander technique apply equally well to the Area F technique. The Reassignment job rating differed quite frequently from the rating given on the man's theater record, but, in such cases, either the interviewer had little more than his clinical impression to guide him or he was grading the man according to his suitability for an assignment in China, that is, not strictly according to his past effectiveness in the European or Mediterranean Theaters. Thus there is no good reason to expect the Reassignment procedure to be any better than the Theater Commander procedure.

The number of unsatisfactory cases listed in the reports obtained by the last two methods is spuriously high, because of the fact that all "failures" in the theater were sent home, while the "successes" were retained. Consequently, there were periods during which almost all the returnees who reported at Area F were men who had proved unsatisfactory. Although most of these men had gone overseas before assessment was established, some of them had been recommended at S or at W.

These, then, are some of our rationalizations for the low correlations obtained by three of our appraisal techniques. We are disposed to believe that if the Overseas Staff appraisals and the Returnee appraisals had been properly conducted, and the reports and ratings derived from these two methods had been combined, the median of the coefficients of correlation between the assessment and the appraisal job ratings might have been about .5 (it was .45), perhaps lower than this for S and higher for W. This is assuming that the process of appraisal had been executed, not perfectly to be sure, but as well as was humanly possible under the conditions that existed, and, therefore, that one would have to look elsewhere—at assessment procedures and at occurrences in the theaters of war—to explain why the correlation was not higher.

Percentage of Unsatisfactory Cases.—Another measure of the efficiency of the screening process is the percentage of men passed by assessment who were rated Low (0 or 1), or Unsatisfactory, on their performances overseas. Table 32 gives the relevant figures. The errors exhibited here are much

TABLE 32

Unsatisfactory Cases in Populations of Previous Table

(Those appraised Low who were assessed Medium or High)[a]

Type of appraisal	S job rating (Classes S-45 on)			W job rating (All classes)		
	H[b]	M[b]	% Unsatisfactory	H[b]	M[b]	% Unsatisfactory
Overseas Staff Appraisal..	3	10	14.8	1	4	6.0
Theater Commander's comments................	2	9	13.4	7	17	15.2
Reassignment Area Appraisal................	2	4	11.3	1	7	4.5
Returnee Appraisal.......	4	11	16.1	3	3	3.5

[a] Low for Assessment means 0 or 1. Theater commander's comments and overseas staff ratings were made in terms of Low, Medium, and High; for other two appraisals Low means 0 or 1; Medium means 2 or 3; High means 4 or 5.

[b] H means number assessed High, appraised Low; M means assessed Medium, appraised Low.

more serious than those we have been considering up to now. If a man who is rated Medium (2 or 3) at assessment turns out to be High (4 or 5) overseas, or if another is assessed High and is later appraised Medium, these are technical mistakes which worry the assessment staff, but they do not furrow the brow of any administrator. His wrinkles are deepened by the men assessed High or Medium, who fail to measure up to minimal theater standards and so impede the smooth functioning of his unit. These are his headaches.

It appears from the table that about 11 to 16 per cent of the cases recommended by Station S were judged to be Unsatisfactory in the theater, and about 3 to 15 per cent of the cases passed by W were so graded.

An examination of the findings on the W cases shows that the figure derived from the theater commander's comments disagrees with those obtained by the other methods, which is one reason for believing that it has relatively low validity. There are three other reasons. In most cases it was not the theater commander himself who classified the men as Unsatisfactory, but the members of the assessment staff who interpreted his often brief comments. And, then, in making their categories the staff members held in mind the normal distribution curve, a practice which, as we have pointed out, is not legitimate in this instance. Finally, as mentioned earlier, a disproportionate number of "failures" appear among the theater commanders' reports, because the failures were sent home and the successes retained. Omitting the figure furnished by this method does not change the range of unsatisfactory S cases, but it does change the range of W cases. The latter becomes 3.5 to 6.0 per cent, which is about as low as we might have expected under the conditions that prevailed in the theaters, even if assessment had worked perfectly, presuming that we make the allowances for extraneous error discussed in the first section of the next chapter.

For reasons already given we cannot place great reliance on the figures obtained by the Returnee or by the Reassignment Area methods. The Overseas Staff Appraisal is, without doubt, our most valid method; but since in our various statistical computations we scrupulously limited the S appraisees to those (S-45 on) who had been given job ratings at the assessment staff conference, the number of cases on which our figures are based is small. But if we accept the over-all ratings of the assessees belonging to Classes 1 to 44, which were made several months later (July, 1944) on the basis of a careful examination of the S reports—ratings, personality sketches, and recommendations—instead of 88 we get 359 appraisees in our population. Now, of these 359 men assessed at S, 30 (8.4 per cent) were judged Unsatisfactory by their superiors and peers in the theater. The figure for W is lower, 6.0 per cent. These, we would judge, are the most valid estimates we have, except that the percentage for S is probably a little too low, since a few men (the exact number is unknown) who were judged to be moderately effective at the time of appraisal became unsatisfactory later. Perhaps 10 per cent would come closest to the true mark.

Correlations between Assessment Ratings and Appraisal Ratings in Men Who Were Given the Job for Which Their Fitness Had Been Assessed.—The figures we have examined so far include large numbers of assessees who were given assignments in the theater which were very different from those for which they had been recommended by Station S or Station W. If the assessment staff passed a candidate for the position of radio script writer in London and, after some weeks of successful operating in that area, the man was sent to France to broadcast under shellfire, very close to the front, and under this strain proved unsatisfactory, he was counted as an assessment failure, even though it had been stated in his personality sketch that his emotional stability would not stand up under fire. Indeed, it can be said more generally that every unsatisfactory assessee has been recorded by us as an assessment error, whether the staff should properly be held accountable for it or not. For example, a large number of men failed because they did not have the requisite amount of technical skill; and, although not we but the branch administrative officers and their chiefs were responsible for decisions respecting technical skill, all such cases have been included to swell the total of our failures.

Here we have a few figures to indicate the order of magnitude of the correlations when the assignment announced at assessment and the assignment given in the theater were identical.

TABLE 33

Correlations between Assessment (S and W) and Returnee Appraisal Job Ratings for Individuals Who Had Identical Jobs Overseas, and for All Individuals

| Job rating | Returnee appraisal job rating | | | |
| | Identical job | | All cases | |
	r	N	r	N
S................	.39	31	.19	93
W...............	.29	93	.21	173

Since these computations could be made only for cases appraised by the Returnee method, the coefficients are all low. It is clear, however, that they are appreciably higher for men in which the job overseas was identical with the job for which they were assessed. These figures alone provide sufficient ground for supposing that the average of the coefficients for S and W obtained by the Overseas Staff method (.45) might have been somewhat higher if appraisees given jobs for which they were *not* recommended had been omitted from the population.

Relative Effectiveness of S Assessment and W Assessment.—Figures given in Tables 31 and 33 indicate that the job ratings given after the one-day assessment at Station W were generally more valid than those given after the three-day assessment at Station S. This apparent fact is somewhat surprising. Since almost all the procedures used at W were also used at S, the difference in validity can scarcely be attributed to W's technical superiority, although the members of the W staff may have been more competent, by and large, than the S staff members.

In seeking an explanation of the fact that our statistics do not show that a three-day assessment is definitely more valid than a one-day assessment, we might first take account of some differences between the candidates assessed at W and those assessed at S. Disregarding the large core of similarity in both populations, it may be said that the branch chiefs usually sent to S the candidates who were to be given the hardest or most hazardous assignments and about whose qualifications they felt most uncertain. To Station W were sent the highest echelons of executives whose abilities were better known to the administration or who were too busy or dignified to spend three days solving field problems, debating, and composing propaganda at Station S. Also, almost all the women were assessed at W, most secretaries, and a large number of office workers, as well as many highly trained members of the Research and Analysis Branch. On the basis of these facts it is not possible to say that the candidates who went to W were any easier to assess. The most that can be stated is that the branch administrative officers were generally disposed to send to S the men whose qualifications seemed to them most questionable. Station S was the place for perplexing problems. That differences in the character of the assessed populations of S and of W constitute a primary determinant of the difference in the percentage of unsatisfactory cases is indicated by the figures in Appendix A-2. Among other things, these show that 74.0 per cent of the W cases were selected for a rear base assignment, whereas only 28.7 per cent of the S cases belonged to this category. Of the S cases, 42.7 per cent were chosen to operate behind enemy lines, but only 14.8 per cent of the W cases were picked for such assignments. Thus the personnel assessed at S were destined to encounter a good deal more stress and danger than were the W personnel.

In the next chapter we shall submit an explanation of why the one-day assessment was probably as efficient as the three-day assessment under the conditions that existed. Briefly it is this: nothing is gained by defining the personality of a candidate more precisely than one's definition of his proposed assignment. Since our conceptions of the different jobs were necessarily vague, we could not utilize, as a rule, any more information about a candidate than was obtainable in a one-day assessment. A great deal more could be discovered about him in the longer program at Station S, but these additional specific facts and insights were actually of little assistance in deciding whether he was suitable for a given role, because we were ignorant of the specific requirements of the role.

This might explain why S was no more efficient than W, but it does not explain the fact suggested by our figures, namely, that S was *less* efficient than W. Actually, the difference between the two coefficients of correlation is not statistically significant; but suppose it were, how could one account for it? Why should two additional days of testing, observation, and informal relations render an assessor less capable of judging job fitness with precision? Among several possible answers to this question, we shall single out one for comment.

As we shall soon see, our figures indicate that the S staff was apparently more successful than the W staff in eliminating potential psychoneurotics, which suggests that at S, by means of the longer interview, the projection tests, the stressful situations, more evidence of latent and repressed tendencies was accumulated; this material, though helpful in distinguishing neurotic or psychotic components, may have confused and impeded the process of reaching a clear decision as to each candidate's effectiveness as an instrument of the organization. It is possible that having learned a good deal about a man, the S staff members became disproportionately interested in the dynamics of his personality, in his merits as a total individual, and then were uncertain as to how to apply their findings to the practical problem of selection. Most of our present knowledge about psychodynamics has been acquired by clinical studies in connection with therapy; whereas most of our knowledge of different psychological abilities has come from personnel studies which put aside questions of character structure. Since these two branches of psychology have been developed independently, we are not yet in a position to relate the facts and theories pertinent to one branch with the facts and theories pertinent to the other. This, perhaps, defines to some extent the dilemma of the members of the S staff: they had a good many observations of exhibited dispositions and patterns of personality and a good many observations of different types of effectiveness, but, in the absence of substantial knowledge about the mutual dependence of these two kinds of components, they were more embarrassed than facilitated by their riches.

Whether this is a promising line of reflection or not, it leads us to a strategic field of investigation which we would have passed by if the statistics had indicated that the validity of the S ratings was somewhat better than the validity of the W ratings. The discovery that our figures point to the opposite conclusion, if anywhere, does not bring us to the practical and seemingly logical conclusion that the one-day system is best, and from now on should be used exclusively; but, indeed, to the exact opposite of this, namely, that the three-day system should be adopted whenever possible, in order to discover through research the dynamic relations that commonly prevail between dispositions and forms of character, on the one hand, and different varieties of effectiveness, on the other, and in order to train psychologists to observe the significant clues and make the legitimate inferences. It would be profitable, in the long run, for us to assume that the additional information obtained by stretching the screening process from one to three days had diminished the validity of the final decisions, that this much more knowledge was a dangerous thing. But it would be extremely shortsighted to conclude from this that psychologists should stop seeking for much more knowledge. The three-day assessment is the path to that degree of knowledge which will do good rather than harm.

Correlations between Assessment and Appraisal Ratings of Traits. —As we stated earlier, the overseas staff appraisers failed to obtain ratings on the different variables of personality. As checks of our assessment grades we have only the records from the other systems of appraisal, and since for these the coefficients of correlation on job ratings are all low, there is little reason to expect higher correlations between ratings of traits, since the latter are often harder to estimate than is over-all job effectiveness. The results of our computations are given in Table 34. Examination of these figures reveals (1) that all coefficients, except two, are positive, though most of them are of very low order; (2) that Effective Intelligence is the variable about which there is most agreement; and (3) that, in general, the validity of S ratings is no higher than the validity of W ratings.

Comparing the various coefficients for S and for W, we find certain indications which, though slight and statistically insignificant, are of some interest nevertheless. In all cases the S coefficients are higher on Motivation and Effective Intelligence and lower on Emotional Stability and Leadership. Both stations were equally inefficient, as measured by these very questionable figures, when it came to judging Social Relations.

Now these findings could scarcely have been anticipated. We might have guessed that the ratings on Effective Intelligence at both S and W would, as a rule, be more valid than the ratings on other variables, largely because psychologists have applied themselves for so many years to the study, the definition and measurement, of general mental ability. But, assuming there would be differences in validity between S ratings and W ratings, we would have guessed that the W coefficient might be higher on Effective Intelligence, because the standard tests were administered as well at W as at S, but that the S coefficients would be higher on Emotional Stability, Social Relations, and Leadership, because the three-day country situation at S had been designed primarily to test the strength of precisely these attributes of personality. Although the figures we have here do not provide us with a reliable basis for speculation, certainly they do not indicate that the S staff was more successful in judging these important traits than was the W staff.

If it were true that the S staff was not more successful than the W staff in this part of its undertaking, we would have another reason to pursue

TABLE 34

Correlations between Assessment and Appraisal Ratings of Personality Variables for Various Appraisal Methods

(S figures are for Classes S-45 on; W figures are for all classes)

Variable	Methods of appraisal						Median
	Theater Commander		Reassignment Area		Returnee		
	S	W	S	W	S	W	
Motivation.......	.14	.08	.19	.10	.15	.02	.12
Effective Intelligence..........	.33	.09	.30	.20	.53	.35	.32
Emotional Stability.......	−.14	−.07	.12	.18	.03	.13	.08
Social Relations..	.10	.00	.10	.02	.00	.27	.06
Leadership.......	.11	.20	a	a	.11	.30	.16
Median..........	.11	.08	.16	.14	.11	.27	

a =N insufficient.

the course of speculation suggested in the last section. As one of several hypotheses, for example, we would suggest that the members of the S staff were likely to lower their ratings on Emotional Stability, Social Relations, and Leadership whenever they discovered (in a candidate's personality) memories of childhood traumata and evidences of repressed tendencies commonly associated with neurotic illness. This action would have been reasonable since in the history of psychology such components have been studied almost solely in this connection. Little is known of their incidence and influence in highly effective people. Since many fewer of these latent or suppressed elements are exposed during a one-day assessment, the members of the W staff might have been less confused in the process of arriving at their final decisions. In the absence of substantiating data it would be idle to develop this notion any further.

Evaluation of Certain Test Procedures.—By the method of Returnee Appraisal it was possible to get respectably large populations on which to compare Effective Intelligence ratings with the ratings given at Station S on each of the separate tests of this variable. These correlations are shown

TABLE 35

Correlations between Ratings on Effective Intelligence from Various Procedures at Area S and Returnee Appraisal Ratings on Effective Intelligence

(*Classes S-45 on*)

Effective Intelligence ratings, assessment procedures	Effective Intelligence ratings, Returnee Appraisal	
	r	N
Interview..............................	.44	86
Discussion........................	.44	84
Debate................................	.43	72
Non-Verbal Battery (Matrix Test)........ ...	.30	87
Vocabulary Test........................	.38	87
Mechanical Comprehension Test..........	.11	86
Judgment of Others.....................	.44	84
Final Effective Intelligence...............	.53	87

in Table 35. There is nothing noteworthy in these figures. We note merely that the coefficients for the Interview and the two situational tests are a little higher than the coefficients for the paper-and-pencil tests. As validated by these dubious Returnee ratings, the Mechanical Comprehension Test correlates lowest of any procedures. It is fairly clear that this test measures a notably different skill from the other tests of intelligence—a skill that differs from what respondents in the Returnee Appraisal technique meant by Effective Intelligence. This low correlation agrees well with the finding made at S that this test of mechanical comprehension correlated poorly with the other components of the Effective Intelligence battery. The S final rating on Effective Intelligence correlates a little better with the appraisal rating than does any single test of this variable.

Neuropsychiatric Screening.—A brief study was made of neuropsychiatric breakdowns among OSS personnel as reported in the records of the Medical Branch. This branch was entirely independent of the Assessment Unit.

The total number of persons who served in OSS was never precisely

figured. The best figure available is 20,000, which is probably correct within
10 per cent. Out of this group, which includes the 5,391 personnel assessed
at S and W, there were 52 neuropsychiatric breakdowns according to the
records of the Medical Branch. These 52 include all recorded psychotic and
psychoneurotic disabilities which developed acutely and were sufficiently
severe to cause the individual to be removed from duty. This represents
0.26 per cent of the total OSS population.

Of those personnel who had been assessed at S, numbering 2,372, 2 were
included in this list of the Medical Branch. One of these individuals had
not been passed by S, because his neuropsychiatric condition was recognized.
He was retained in the organization, however, despite the decision of the
S staff. The other person was recommended with great caution, with the
condition that he be watched carefully at training centers and used only if
the doubts which existed in the minds of the assessment staff appeared unjustified to his instructors after they got to know him well. If we consider
this cautious acceptance as an error on the part of the S staff, then 0.04 per
cent of those assessed at S were neuropsychiatric breakdowns, as compared
with 0.26 per cent of the total population. If we do not consider this to be
an error, the percentage for Area S was 0.0.

Of the 3,071 candidates assessed at Area W, 7 developed neuropsychiatric
breakdowns. One of these was not approved by Area W because of emotional instability, but 6 were approved. This is an error of 0.20 per cent,
which, though higher than the S rate, is still lower than the percentage for
the whole OSS population.

Evaluation of a Test Battery for a Specific Purpose.—The assessment
staff was approached by an administrative officer of one of the branches of
OSS with the hope of finding some test or series of tests which could be
used to select for intelligence work candidates whose chief function would
be to observe and report enemy order of battle. The staff responded by
requesting the officer to make two lists of agents who had served in his
branch. One list was to be made up of those distinctly good in observing
and reporting the order of battle, and the other of those who were definitely
bad. It seemed impractical to attempt to distinguish more than two degrees
of this ability, very good and very poor. The list was prepared according to
these directions by officers of the branch. The members of the assessment
staff played no part in the selection.

Twelve good observers and reporters were named, and 16 bad. The
first fact discovered was that all twelve of the good men had been assessed
at S. All had been passed, with the exception of one man, who at the time
of his assessment was being considered for an entirely different mission.
Their Over-all ratings had averaged 3.25 on the six-point scale. Only five
of the poor observers had been assessed at S. One had been assessed at W.

The other ten had not been assessed. All six who had gone to assessment centers had passed. The over-all ratings of the five who attended S averaged 1.9.

The comparison of these two small groups was continued by compiling all the ratings for them in the Effective Intelligence battery and the Observing and Reporting battery, and the average score on the six-point scale for each test was determined for the good observers and for the poor. Table 36

TABLE 36

Mean Ratings on Effective Intelligence and Observing and Reporting Tests for Assessed Groups of Superior and Inferior Observers

	Superior observers		Inferior observers	
	m	N	m	N
I. Effective Intelligence...........	3.9	10	3.0	5
a. Interview....................	3.6	7	3.2	5
b. Vocabulary.................	3.4	5	2.5	4
c. Nonverbal Battery.........	2.6	3	2.5	4
d. Stress Interview............	3.0	3	2.7	3
e. Discussion..................	3.4	5	2.0	4
f. Debate.....................	3.8	5	2.0	3
g. Mechanical Comprehension ..	4.0	5	2.7	4
h. Practical Judgment..........	4.0	1	1.5	2
i. Brook.....................	3.2	6	1.8	5
j. Judgment of Others..........	3.4	5	1.7	3
Mean......................	3.5	55	2.4	42
II. Observing and Reporting.......	3.0	9	2.8	5
a. Interview....................	4.0	2	2.0	1
b. Belongings.................	3.4	8	1.8	5
c. Terrain....................	3.0	7	2.2	5
d. Brief Case.................	3.0	5	2.0	3
e. Memory Battery............	2.3	8	3.4	5
f. Names and Identities........	2.5	6	3.2	5
Mean......................	2.9	45	2.6	29

shows the result. The number of individual tests going to make up each mean score is indicated in the column after each score.

It will be seen that there is a difference between the two groups for every test in this table. In all cases except the two memory tests, the superior observers had higher test scores. The mean for all the test results of the good observers, a total of 100 individual tests, was 3.3. For the poor observers the average was 2.5 in 71 tests. The difference between these two means is significant beyond the 1 per cent level, the probability being less than 2 in 1,000 that these results could have come by chance.

This little study is not in itself very impressive because the size of each group is so small. However, it is as complete a roster as could be obtained of all the men who did this sort of work in this branch, and it was not selected on any basis except the ability to observe and report enemy order of battle.

CLINICAL EVALUATION OF THE ASSESSMENT OF A SMALL SAMPLE OF CASES

The selection of men consists of two tasks, arriving at diagnoses of the personalities of the subjects and making prognoses of their effectiveness in assignments. The basis for both of these judgments by the assessment staff is better revealed in the written reports on the candidates than in the arrays of final grades that were assigned to them. An individual's characteristic patterns of adjustment, his personal motivation and desires, his special liabilities and distinctive assets are poorly represented in numerical ratings. In the Returnee method, for example, the informant's appraisal was presented much more adequately in his comments than in his raw scores. It was therefore decided to supplement our statistical appraisal studies with the less quantitative procedure of comparing the written assessment reports with the comments of the Returnee Appraisal informants. These were more comparable to the original assessment reports than any appraisal data except the Reassignment Area reports, and they had the advantage over the latter of being free from the interpretive distortions contributed by the assessors. It was hoped that this study would yield more than an indication of the relative number of assessment successes and failures, since it would also suggest some of the reasons for failure.

Our analysis was restricted to a rather small number of cases (36), since this was the total number on which the following materials were available: (i) the S report; (ii) the Returnee Appraisal protocols with detailed comments and ratings considered sufficiently complete to warrant a high reliability rating. The cases which met these two requirements were a rather selected population, chiefly because high reliability ratings were assigned to those cases for which the staff had clear-cut pictures, which naturally were obtained most easily for individuals who were either very good or very poor.

Since twenty-four out of the thirty-six cases in this study were in the classes before S-45, they had no job ratings. Such ratings were assigned by a staff member for the purposes of this study after reading the report and the ratings on the variables.

All of the cases presented in this study are S cases. Two thirds of them were assessed before Class S-45, and one third after Class S-45. Therefore, the population for this study, like the total Returnee Appraisal group, cannot be considered representative of the S population. It is too heavily loaded with cases from early classes and also excessively weighted with cases which received a short period of assessment, having four times as high a percentage of these as the total S population.

The procedure of this experiment was as follows:

Two groups of judges, each composed of three staff members, were selected to make the comparisons between the S reports and the Returnee reports. Each judge made his decisions independently of the others on his team. The team members followed these instructions:

Please read the S report and decide if the picture that you have of the candidate from the report is complete or incomplete. If it is inadequate, then write the candidate's name under the heading, "Picture very incomplete." After having made the above decision, read the Returnee reports. The picture that you get of the candidate from these Returnee reports is the criterion against which you are to appraise the S report. Then decide, with reference to the criterion, which of the categories listed below describes the case most adequately.

1) Diagnosis and prognosis both essentially correct.
2) Diagnosis essentially correct, prognosis partially correct.
3) Diagnosis essentially correct, prognosis essentially incorrect.
4) Diagnosis partially correct, prognosis essentially correct.
5) Diagnosis partially correct, prognosis partially correct.
6) Diagnosis partially correct, prognosis essentially incorrect.
7) Diagnosis essentially incorrect, prognosis essentially correct.
8) Diagnosis essentially incorrect, prognosis partially correct.
9) Diagnosis and prognosis both essentially incorrect.

The definitions adopted for the terms used in these directions were as follows:

Diagnosis = the description of the main personality variables.
Prognosis = the evaluation (explicit or implicit) of the factors included with reference to effectiveness in the proposed assignment.
Essentially correct = approximately three quarters of the statements in the S report agree with those of the Returnee report.
Partially correct = approximately half of the items in the S report agree with those of the Returnee report.
Essentially incorrect = less than half of the items in the S report agree with the Returnee report.

Of the thirty-six cases, half were rated by each team of judges. When either two or all three team members agreed upon the category into which a case fell, that decision was considered final. Cases in which three different decisions were made were classified as disagreements. Cases in which inadequate data were available for judgment were classified as incomplete. The results of this procedure are presented in Table 37.

TABLE 37

Cases of Special Study Grouped in Categories of Correctness of Diagnosis and Prognosis

1. Diagnosis and prognosis both essentially correct................... 16
2. Diagnosis essentially correct, prognosis essentially incorrect........ 2
3. Diagnosis essentially correct, prognosis partially correct........... 1
4. Diagnosis partially correct, prognosis essentially incorrect......... 1
5. Diagnosis and prognosis both essentially incorrect............... 2
6. Incomplete... 9
7. Disagreements.. 5

After these classifications had been made, the raters were asked to make some judgment on the incomplete cases, even though the evidence was inadequate. They were requested to base their decisions on the overtones and implications of the records. These nine cases were then placed in whatever category was chosen by two or three members of the team. The five cases on which there were disagreements were also reviewed by two additional staff members acting as referees. After reviewing the data, these two decided which of the three different categories checked for each of the cases described it most adequately, and this was its final classification. The dispositions of the incomplete and disagreement cases made in this second

TABLE 38

Cases of Table 37, Including Distributions into Categories of Incomplete Cases and Those on Which There Were Disagreements

Accuracy of diagnosis and prognosis	Agreements	Incomplete	Disagreements	Total
1. Diagnosis and prognosis both essentially correct..............	16	6	2	24
2. Diagnosis essentially correct, prognosis essentially incorrect...	2	—	3	5
3. Diagnosis essentially correct, prognosis partially correct......	1	—	—	1
4. Diagnosis partially correct, prognosis partially correct.........	—	1	—	1
5. Diagnosis partially correct, prognosis essentially incorrect.......	1	—	—	1
6. Diagnosis and prognosis both essentially incorrect...........	2	2	—	4

step are presented in Table 38, combined with the data presented in Table 37.

From these totals it may be concluded that 66.7 per cent were successes, 11.1 per cent were failures, and 22.2 per cent fell between these two extremes.

The data of Table 37 may be regrouped as in Table 39.

TABLE 39

Cases of Special Study Grouped in Terms of Correctness of Diagnosis and of Prognosis

Diagnosis essentially correct	Diagnosis partially correct	Diagnosis essentially incorrect
30	2	4

Prognosis essentially correct	Prognosis partially correct	Prognosis essentially incorrect
24	2	10

This table indicates that a somewhat better job of diagnosis than of prognosis was done on these cases. This result is understandable in view of the fact that throughout most of its history the assessment staff had no job analyses or real knowledge of field conditions in terms of which effectiveness could be judged.

Having learned these facts we proceeded in an attempt to discover the reasons for our complete and partial failures. We studied all the cases except those in which both diagnosis and prognosis had been considered essentially correct on first examination by the majority of judges. This gave us a group of twenty cases.

The first question we attempted to answer was: What significant aspects of the candidate's personality and behavior were neglected or underemphasized at assessment, and which ones were overemphasized? To find an answer to this question two staff members compared paired S reports and Returnee reports, noting those differences between the two which stood out most clearly, and observing whether they were errors of diagnosis or of prognosis. The results are listed in Table 40.

With the exception of one instance of emotional instability and two instances of low intelligence, all cases of neglect or underemphasis represent errors in diagnosis rather than in prognosis. It should not be understood that the reports contain no references whatever to the traits in question. In several instances the presence of these charactristics is either implicit in the description of the candidate, or is mentioned without emphasis. In almost no case, however, could the extent of the deficiency manifested in the subsequent performance have been guessed from the report. Two of the three exceptions were cases where the candidate's poor effective intelligence was clearly seen by the interviewer at assessment, but not given enough weight in the evaluation of his fitness for assignment.

With very few exceptions (cases of "strong drive" and of "shrewdness"), the characteristics overemphasized were actually typical of the persons to whom they were ascribed. However, either they proved to be less significant for the candidate's success or failure than was anticipated, or they did not operate in the expected direction. Thus the overemphases in our sample of reports represent failures not of diagnosis but of prognosis.

TABLE 40

Aspects of Personality Incorrectly Assessed in Cases of Special Study

Aspect of personality	No. of cases in which aspects were neglected or underemphasized		No. of cases in which aspects were overemphasized	
	In diagnosis	In prognosis	In diagnosis	In prognosis
Emotional instability or immaturity	4	1	—	3
Poor social relations	3	—	—	—
Extraversion, social facility	—	—	—	4
Egocentric motivation	3	—	—	—
Strong motivation	—	—	—	2
Low effective intelligence	1	2	—	—
Effectiveness, shrewdness	—	—	1	2
Low integrity	2	—	—	—
Strong drive	—	—	1	3
Past accomplishments	—	—	—	2
Possession of special skills	—	—	—	1

It may also be concluded from Table 40 that the place of emotional stability in the whole personality configuration is difficult to assess and that the assessment staff tended to overvalue some energetic, extraverted persons, and to disregard egocentricity resulting in bad social relations.

In order to answer the question of what kind of people assessment overvalued and which it undervalued, we compared our 20 S reports with their corresponding appraisals and divided them as follows: definitely undervalued, 3; slightly undervalued, 5; definitely overvalued, 8, slightly overvalued, 4.

Of the three who were *definitely underrated*, one is described in the S report as "intelligent and perceptive," "a man of many superiorities of character and experience, but with considerable feelings of inferiority and a considerable load of anxiety." The report adds, however, that in critical situations this man may be counted upon to manage his anxiety. A detailed report on the second man underrated dwells on his vagueness of purpose and lack of clear-cut attitudes, interpreting them as signs of emotional immaturity. This man would have been failed in assessment were it not for his good performance in tests and situations. In the brief report on the third man, the assessor discusses merely a history of asthma and migraine, decides that they are not indicative of emotional instability, and sums up the candidate as "a man of great ability and thoughtful habit, who is believed to be well adapted to service overseas." All three men later did excellent jobs abroad, earning highest praise for their performances, the first two as operations officers, and the third as an administrator. The S reports on two of these cases are brief (they were judged incomplete) and one of them (the last) is not very illuminating, giving no inkling at all of the able administrator and generous, big-hearted, "colorful extravert" described by his colleagues overseas. Yet, considered in conjunction with the ratings on variables, most of which were above average in all three cases, all three reports are definitely favorable to the candidates. While they do not contain adequate indications of these men's actual excellence, the extent of underrating was by no means extreme.

For all five of the cases that were *slightly underrated* the reports are short (four of them were considered incomplete), but the evaluations, while not detailed, are well balanced and adequate. Four candidates were recommended without reservations. The first, a woman, is described in the following way: "She appears to be very capable, exceedingly conscientious, and emotionally stable. She is believed to be a good prospect." Later she was praised by her colleagues and superiors as most conscientious, hard working, cooperative, and efficient: "No. 1 secretary of her branch." The second candidate is described in the S report as "healthy, well oriented, well spoken. and with a sound, moderately conservative political philosophy." It is said that "he has weathered enough personal experience of a hazardous nature to suggest that he would have psychological stamina under stress." This man made a highly effective security officer: energetic, practical, and competent. Of the third candidate the S report says: "Clean cut and neat, capable of considerable feeling and of exerting effort which appears extremely well controlled, friendly and likable, with a mixture of frank openness and appropriate modesty. . . . Likes the challenge for greater responsibility . . . appears to be a good man for hazardous missions." This man became an adjutant, and was praised for his sense of responsibility, his expert handling of the job, and, above all, his excellent social relations with officers and enlisted men alike. The S report on the fourth candidate contains the following statements: ". . . an unusually penetrating and analytical mind which is bulwarked by a remarkably wide and varied body of knowledge. He has keen critical judgment. He is emotionally stable and fit for overseas duty." This man in a short time became an outstanding political analyst. All of these candidates earned superior, or very superior, job ratings in the field, and, what is more, the directions in which they excelled were consistent with the assessment observations. Thus the S reports, in spite of their largely descriptive nature and their incompleteness, captured the essential assets of each case. The ratings on variables are in all these cases consistent with the written characterizations. The only reasons why these cases can be considered slightly underrated are, first, the fact that the reports do not mention *all* of each candidate's pertinent assets, such as the good social relations of the secretary, the energy and leadership ability of the security officer, or the writing ability of the political analyst, and, second, that the favorable conclusions are often couched in rather cautious language. This is partly accounted for by the fact that two of these four cases were given only short assessments, and consequently were not observed in very many situations.

The last slightly underrated case was that of a physically handicapped person with many additional physical complaints. Doubting his energy, intelligence, and particularly his emotional stability, the report seriously questioned the desirability of sending him overseas "unless he has some special talent which is impossible to duplicate." A low-grade technician, he was sent abroad despite the assessment counsel, and, within limitations of his handicap and his ability, did an adequate, conscientious job (Job rating 3), adjusting well to situations of stress, including bombing. The picture given by associates does not contradict the conclusions reached at S, but indicates that the candidate had methods of handling his emotional conflicts that even made him a social asset ("the office wit—his humor not barbed— directed at himself—raises others' morale.") His co-workers liked him as "just a fellow who did the best with what he had." This case was also one of brief assessment. While the interviewer saw the problems and limitations of this man, he did not in the short time available observe the methods by which he was able to counteract them effectively. Since, even at that, the job he was able to do was merely average, the undervaluation in this case can also be considered as slight.

Altogether, undervaluation, as revealed in these eight cases, does not appear to be a serious shortcoming of assessment.

No generalization seems possible about the *kind* of people that were underestimated. They ranged from a self-sufficient, conscientious, somewhat aloof intellectual to a "colorful extravert." It is conspicuous, however, that in four out of these eight cases, including all three cases of definite undervaluation, the main reason for undervaluation was the suspicion of emotional instability. For the rest, undervaluation seemed to be related neither to any factors in the candidates' personalities nor to assessors' biases, but rather to extraneous factors like the shortness of assessment, and possibly also to the unwillingness of interviewers to commit themselves to extreme formulations. The importance of situational observations is emphasized by at least three cases in which they were apparently more valid than judgments made in the interviews.

The cases of *overvaluation* fall into three fairly distinct syndromes. The first includes four cases of definite overvaluation, among them one of the most dramatic failures of assessment. The common feature of these men, and the main reason for their failures on their jobs, is their purely ego-centric motivation, coupled with ruthlessness and lack of integrity in the pursuit of their goals of profit and pleasure. One of them was court-martialed for looting and stealing, another threatened with court-martial for similar offenses, as well as for neglect of security; the other two are described by their associates as opportunists who cared nothing about their jobs except as means to satisfy their desires for enjoyment or prestige. Other features these four men have in common are energy, extraversion, and the ability to "put on a good show." These latter traits provide a key to the reasons for their overvaluation at S.

Two of the assessment reports on this group are rather brief and remain on a purely descriptive level; one of them was incomplete. Except for characterizing one candidate as "vigorous, outgoing, having a lot of drive" and another as "a very ambitious and capable man," they merely report what the candidates said about themselves and about their past records. Although the wording of these reports is noncommittal (care being taken to earmark the candidates' statements as such), the fact that they end in positive recommendations indicates that to a certain extent the interviewers have taken the candidates' self-descriptions at their face value.

The two other reports on this group are detailed, and they indicate more clearly what characteristics of the candidates outweighed their shortcomings in the minds of the assessors. That the staff members were not unaware of these deficiencies is indicated by such expressions as "a promoter of a somewhat unconventional sort . . . ," "primarily interested in self-maintenance . . . ," "to some extent ruthless . . . ," which occur in one report. The other report speaks of the candidate as "possessing the ideal 'salesman' personality," as "impelled by his competitive drive . . . to build himself up . . . ," and as "very anxious for personal advancement." It also mentions his past breaches of discipline and points out that he may be a poor security risk. In both assessment reports, however, these negative comments are overshadowed by favorable remarks, which in the first case verge on enthusiasm. The candidate is described as "a shrewd and realistic manipulator of social situations," yet friendly and generous; praised for "the unusual objectivity with which he appraises himself" and finally epitomized as a "calm, confident, tolerant but nonetheless determined and persistent [person who] seems almost ideally suited for the work with natives." The report on the second candidate emphasizes his "outgoing, affable, frank, uninhibited, gregarious" nature, his "good humor, alertness, and emotional stability." These descriptions are not wholly incorrect, for the first man demonstrated great courage, and both were thought by some to be good company. However, the first is said to have earned the hatred of all enlisted men, and the general consensus about the second was that he was a "conceited, licentious, obnoxious braggart."

One cannot help feeling that in these cases the staff members fell prey to the candidates' salesmanship and were unduly impressed by their toughness, extraversion, and freedom from inhibitions, interpreting symptoms of psychopathy as evidence of superior emotional stability. With their generally positive orientation, the S reports seem also to have overestimated these men's shrewdness and effectiveness. Three of them, rated high on intelligence or resourcefulness at assessment, are described by their colleagues, in one case as "stupid, flighty, always messing things up"; in the second as "not very bright," "relying on others to do his mental work for him," "being taken for a ride"; and in the third as "unable to see another person's point of view." The primary source for their failures, however, was in the area of motivation rather than intelligence.

The failure of the next group of four cases of equally extreme overvaluation resulted from emotional instability or immaturity, which was not clearly seen or was slighted in assessment. The group consists of one man and three women, the women being by far the graver failures. One of them was returned because she was habitually confused and erratic to the point of being completely ineffectual. Another, under the stress of rocket bombing, became a "nervous wreck" and finally decided to return to America. Both these women are described by associates abroad rather sympathetically as well-meaning and conscientious, even though their extreme emotional instability which reduced their efficiency was obvious. The emotional disturbance of the third woman manifested itself less by inefficiency than by indiscreet and tactless social behavior which continually got her into difficulties. This girl was also eventually returned to the United States before completion of her assignment. The man in this group was described as "sophomoric," given to dramatic poses, unable to take responsibility for any decisions, and generally inviting ridicule. However, the opinions varied considerably about the job he did; averaging the widely disparate scores yields an unsatisfactory rating.

The S reports on these four cases are short, two of them being based on brief assessment. The reports on the three women contain some material that might suggest emotional difficulties. Of the first it is said that "her personality is difficult to evaluate, since there is evidence of good accomplishment in spite of some emotional instability." The second is described as an "unusual character . . . whose cautiousness and reserve make it difficult to gain more than a superficial knowledge of her background." The report on the third mentions her unfavorable childhood and her rather unstable work history. However, only in the first case was a tentative diagnosis of emotional instability made, as a result of which it was recommended that the candidate be observed further before being considered for overseas service. In the other two cases, the emotional instability was not clearly seen.

The assessment of the second woman was influenced in her favor by her "quality of individual integrity" and particularly by the extremely strong motivation which she displayed at S. These characteristics of the candidate, later fully confirmed by her associates, made it possible to interpret the signs of eccentricity and social isolation which appeared at assessment as self-sufficiency and independence, an interpretation which her subsequent performance proved to be entirely faulty. This failure of psychological analysis is partly explained by the candidate's reluctance, or inability, to let the interviewer gain a "more than superficial knowledge of her background" and of her emotional attitudes.

No such reserve was displayed by the third woman, who impressed the interviewer as having "a pleasant, friendly manner" and who gave him the impression of getting along well with others. Yet her assessment represents even a greater failure of psychological analysis, since it seems to accept at face value the candidate's self-flattering generalizations about herself. For example, the report contains such conclusions as that "her job history seems to be more indicative of an interest in new experiences than of instability," and that "in spite of her unhappy childhood she is today a well-integrated, emotionally stable, and mature person." The case resembles those in the first group of overvalued cases, in so far as too high a premium was put on outgoing, socially facile behavior.

The report on the man in this group makes no attempt at psychological analysis and contains a minimum of generalizations. The uneventful past history of this "tall, lithe, well-balanced young American" is reported and the conclusion drawn that he is "not outstanding in leadership ability, but as a member of a team can be counted upon to carry out a mission of average difficulty and danger." No material that might be indicative of emotional disturbance appears in the report.

The four cases of undiagnosed or inadequately diagnosed emotional instability are chiefly failures on the part of the staff to pursue psychological analysis beyond the manifest behavior and the self-descriptions of the subject. Factors that contributed to these failures were, on the one hand, the overvaluations of integrity, of strong motivation, and of facile social relations, and, on the other, the paucity of relevant interview material resulting from inhibitions, reserve, or lack of insight on the part of the candidates.

The remaining four cases represent instances of less serious overvaluation, though three of them did an inferior job. Two of them are rather similar. One man is described, in a rather full report, as a person "with few faults and few exciting qualities," a "nice fellow" who lacks both ambition and mental agility, but whose "great capacity for inoffensiveness" enables him to get along "by being pleasant and conventional." The past history of this man is consistent with this picture, containing some indications of ineffectiveness, but none of complete failure. Of the second man it is said that he "describes himself in terms of almost perfect, but colorless normality," "offers little evidence of emotional play or of creative imagination," and is unable to elaborate his reports of concrete events and accomplishments. Like the first man he was rated Average, or Low Average, on most variables, yet approved without question. Both men were subsequently given administrative jobs as intelligence officers and both failed completely. The failure of the first man was accentuated and made more extreme by an emotional upset caused by the loss of two relatives in the service, but this was not the primary cause of his failure. He was described by his associates as a "charming gentleman" and "as ineffectual as a man can be"; wishing to be helpful, but dull-witted and incapable of doing his job; "harmless but useless." The second man was described in very similar terms as a "kindly, neighborly chap," well-intentioned but stupid and slow, a plodder capable of only the simplest routine work under constant supervision. These pictures are consistent with those given in the S reports. The assessors saw the limitations of these men, but treated them with undue leniency. When the interviewer, writing about the first man, concluded that "he still has enough on the ball . . . to do a job . . . particularly if his talents in social relations are capitalized," he unwittingly proved the truth of his own immediately preceding remark that the student's manner inspires more confidence in him "than is justified by his abilities." These two cases, then, might be considered as failures in prognosis rather than in diagnosis, failures caused partly by overvaluation of good will and of social relations.

Of the remaining two cases, one man is similar to the two preceding ones in that his failure on the job was due primarily to lack of ability for which his good motivation, hard work, and sincerity proved unable to compensate. In contrast to the other two, however, this case cannot be considered one of overvaluation in assessment. The S report not only gives a balanced picture of the candidate's assets and liabilities, a picture which is based on an insightful analysis and which was confirmed by associates in every single detail, but also draws the appropriate conclusion that his proved special skills can be utilized, but that he "should not be used in a job where his intellectual limitations and his difficult social relations would be exposed." However, in an emergency, he was made commanding officer of a station, and later an intelligence officer, and failed completely in both jobs. "His practical intelligence was nil"; "he almost broke his neck giving the GI's what he thought they should have," but did not show "the slightest understanding of people," with the result that he antagonized them and caused considerable disturbance. This case is primarily one of bad placement in the job, a decision contrary to the definite recommendations of the assessment report.

The last member of the overvalued group is a linguist whose superior ability was correctly stressed in the S report and whose personality was briefly but adequately assessed as that of a man of "strong drive and intense interest in his work," "a tense individual who is fairly easily wrought up, yet seems to be able to handle his nervous tensions adequately." What was apparently not sufficiently considered was the negative response such a man, with radical political leanings, would evoke in associates who could share none of his interests and convictions. He was considered a "screwball," obstinate, and generally obnoxious. He got along better, however, with people he taught, and, while condemning him as an officer, the majority of informants admitted he was a good teacher. Since he was considered for work as a language specialist, his assessment, even though it disregarded the factor of social relations, cannot be considered seriously inadequate.

In summary, in this group we overvalued (a) energetic, outgoing, egocentric people of low integrity; (b) people of low emotional stability which was covered up in one way or another, and (c) people of low ability who were well-intentioned and socially pleasant. Of the twelve overvalued candidates, only three may be judged to have done an adequate job, and the usefulness of these three was contested by some informants. Since our sample contains, through selection on the basis of high reliability ratings, an unduly high proportion of the indisputable failures within the Returnee Appraisal group, the degree of overvaluation, as revealed in the study of this group, can in no way be considered representative of the work of assessment. Yet the extent of failure of the majority of overvalued candidates in this group demonstrates the disastrous effect of leniency. If a generalization can be made from this sample, both the extent and the danger of overvaluation in assessment appear to be far greater than of undervaluation.

What does the analysis of improperly valued cases reveal about the preconceptions the S staff held as to what aspects of behavior are important and desirable, and how did these preconceptions affect our diagnosis and evaluation of the candidates? Most of the aspects of personality that were improperly assessed fall within the categories of Emotional Stability, Social Relations, and Motivation, interrelated categories which are highly important for personality diagnosis.

Emotional Stability was always a crucial issue in the minds of the S staff, since one of the primary objects of assessment was to weed out those who might break down under stress. This concern is reflected, in our sample of reports, in a tendency to undervalue the candidates who showed such indications of emotional instability as indecision, anxiety, depressed moods, and psychosomatic symptoms. Indirectly, the same concern is revealed in the overvaluation of vigorous, outgoing, uninhibited people, one reason for overvaluation being that their behavior was interpreted as indicative of good emotional stability. Of the three individuals in this group whose pronounced emotional instability we failed to diagnose and who failed on the job primarily because of this defect, only one was inhibited, eccentric, and withdrawn; the other two were active and outgoing. In the case of the woman who later developed anxiety under bombing, emotional instability was recognized at assessment. All of these findings seem to indicate that, intent as we were upon discovering symptoms of instability, we were more sensitive to anxiety or compulsion neurosis than to hysterical character or psychopathy.

Social Relations, though important in determining our judgment of the candidate, seems to have been of less concern during the period covered by these reports than was Emotional Stability. There are few explicit discussions of poor or questionable social relations in these twenty assessment reports. On the other hand, the characteristics of the candidates that led to effectiveness in social relations seem to have concerned us less as a potential disability than as a potential asset. As such they occasionally outweighed in our eyes the recognized limitations of the candidate, such as lack of effective intelligence, lack of integrity, or low emotional stability, and were responsible for overvaluation. Actually, over a long period of time the social relations of these people, though active and facile enough, proved to be so poor that they led to their rejection by associates and contributed greatly to their failures. The chief flaw in our consideration of social relations seems to have been a failure to differentiate between the mastery of social skills and the possession of genuinely positive attitudes toward others.

In the field of Motivation a very similar situation seemed to prevail. We considered strong drive and high motivation as definite assets, but paid relatively little attention to the direction of drive and to the possible pitfalls of strong motivation. The primary reason for the failure in the field of our most overrated candidates was the fact that their strong drive was primarily egocentric and turned them to pursuits that often were opposed to the interests of the organization.

In considering this evidence of the shortcomings of our diagnosis and prognosis one must keep in mind two pertinent points: first, that these generalizations are based largely on an analysis of our failures in the early period of assessment; and second, that the picture presented in the summary has been overdrawn in order to bring out significant points. Actually, in many of the cases described, the shortcomings were caused less by our preconceptions and biases than by extrinsic circumstances. In many instances the superficiality of our analyses was due to the shortness of the period of assessment, which also made it unfeasible to test adequately the candidate's social relations as they developed after the initial contacts and to obtain his associates' opinions of him. In the later period of assessment, after we had had a chance to clarify our concepts and to develop techniques, many of these faults were corrected. The integrity of each candidate was considered carefully, and the danger presented by poor social relations was weighed no less seriously than that involved in low emotional stability. Although the questions as to what represents really good social relations, or what types of motivation are most desirable for specific assignments, were never conclusively answered, there are good reasons to believe that in the later period of the program we were less in danger of missing the cases of emotional instability in various forms, of condoning the extremes of egocentric motivation, or of being overimpressed by mere facility in the use of social skills. However, the tendencies that came to light in the analysis of the early failures of assessment represent definite and probably not uncommon pitfalls of personality evaluation, and as such they seem to deserve being recorded.

CONCLUSION

In this chapter the task of evaluation as it faced the OSS assessment staff, the means that were devised to accomplish it, and the results obtained, have been reported. We have seen that since evaluation is a matter of comparing appraisals with assessments, the process of appraisal should be as scientific, as well defined in operational terms and as well controlled, as the process of assessment. The precision of an instrument cannot properly be measured by an instrument that is less precise. In establishing the OSS assessment unit, we erred in not making provision from the start for validation studies. No member of the staff then had time to devote to the crucial task of organizing a system of appraisal. When we finally came to it, there was no time for anything but a makeshift. Thus we failed to construct an adequate standard for evaluating our work, and at the end are left speculating in the valley of uncertainty.

The recitation of our difficulties and failures, we hope, will stimulate others to concentrate on the problems of appraisal. This enterprise is more difficult than that of assessment, because the conditions under which appraisees operate are more varied and complex, less susceptible to formulation, and the performances of appraisees are likewise more varied and complex, and only a few segments of them are open to inspection. Substantial achievements pass unheralded and acts of little moment make bubble reputations. An adequate system of appraisal must rest on clearly defined criteria of merit arrived at after an analysis of environments and jobs. The task calls for a thorough study of field conditions.

Since the criteria of appraisal define the standard against which the efficacy of assessment will be measured, they constitute the target of prediction. Therefore, we submit, the system of appraisal should be set up *before* the system of assessment. The implementation of this idea is the concluding topic of the next and last chapter.

Chapter X

CONCLUSIONS AND RECOMMENDATIONS

We approach the end of this story. We have described the unusual features of the task which was assigned to the OSS assessment staff (Chapter I), the technical system which was adopted as the best means of accomplishing the task (Chapters III, IV, V, VII, and VIII), the general principles on which this system was based (Chapter II), and the various results obtained (Chapters VI and IX). In this final chapter we shall recapitulate a few of the points made under the first and last of these headings, discuss the aims that could be furthered by an agency that adopted the OSS system of assessment, and end with a list of specific technical recommendations.

RECAPITULATION

A striking defect in the work reported in this volume is the absence of a reliable estimate of its comparative effectiveness. To date no scientific study has been published, as far as we know, presenting statistical evaluations of predictions of performances in the theaters of war, that could profitably be compared with our data, because the task that confronted each of the wartime selection and placement services was, in many significant respects, unique.

More pertinent to our purpose than the results obtained by other units would be several hundred appraisals of the performances of OSS men who had been sent overseas prior to the introduction of assessment. If these appraisals had been procured we would now be in a position to say whether the percentage of unassessed men rated Low or Unsatisfactory in the field was greater or less than the percentage of assessed men so rated. But, here again, a comparison of the two percentages could scarcely lead to an unequivocal conclusion, because the types of assignment for which men were recruited during the last eight months of 1943 were, for the most part, very different from those for which men were recruited during the first eight months of 1944 when assessment was in operation. That the percentage of failures in any appraised sample was largely dependent upon the distribution of the individuals among the different assignments (or among the different branches of the organization) is illustrated by the results of the first validation study of assessees operating in the ETO. The percentage of unsatisfactory cases was found to be o˙ (zero) in four of the six branches, whereas in one of the two remaining branches this figure was 6 per cent, and in the other 14 per cent. Thus the chances of a man's being considered satisfactory in some assignments were better than they were in others. If, in an attempt to minimize these variations, comparisons had been restricted to assessed and unassessed men fulfilling similar functions, the number of men falling into each job category would have been too small to permit the calculation of differences that were statistically reliable.

Thus there is no tangible proof that the OSS assessment staffs produced effects which more than balanced the expenditure of time and money.

The number of assessed men and women who developed neuropsychiatric symptoms in the theater seems low in view of the unusual pressures, responsibilities, and dangers which stood in the line of duty for so many of them. It is necessary to remember, in this connection, that the OSS personnel included a large number of young women working under stress, many of them in tropical countries, many in London during the Little Blitz and throughout the subsequent six months' battering by V-1 and V-2 rockets, as well as scores of refugees and Hollywood writers and performers deprived of the way of living to which they were accustomed, and numerous specialists, many of them intellectuals whose previous style of life was poor preparation for urgent enterprises in military installations overseas. Furthermore, one must take account of the fact that the OSS had been called upon under wartime necessity to undertake projects for which there were no precedents in American history, and, consequently, there had to be a great deal of spur-of-the-moment improvisation, hasty trial and error, and sudden changing of plans which resulted in boundless confusion. It was a matter of quickly learning by quickly doing, novices leading novices. Hence the OSS was not an organization into which an insecure, dependent, unresourceful, or rigidly methodical individual could easily fit. Taking all these points into consideration, the incidence of neuropsychiatric illness seems gratifyingly low. The incomplete records of the Medical Branch of OSS show that only a small minority of the reported breakdowns were screened men. Thus there is some basis for supposing that the assessment staff, by identifying and rejecting the recruits who manifested neurotic or psychotic tendencies at the time of examination, made a substantial contribution to the efficiency of the organization.

Before attempting to arrive at a final verdict we should consider (1) the question of the inevitable and irreducible percentage of failures; (2) the question of the percentage of failures due to deficiencies in special skills, the determination of which was left to the branch administrative officers and their chiefs; (3) the question of the percentage of failures due to the conditions under which assessment was conducted; and (4) the question of the percentage of failures due to the shortcomings of assessment proper.

A certain percentage of errors is inevitable and irreducible because of the occurrence of improbable circumstances which the psychologist, even if he thinks of them as lying within the realm of possibility, will, quite properly, leave out of his figurings precisely because they are incalculable. With the information that we now have, for example, it would have been possible to foretell that a certain proportion, say 5 per cent, of OSS assessees sent overseas would be exposed to an unusual number, variety, or intensity of psychological strains (pain, danger, isolation behind enemy lines, responsibility, criticism, depreciation, confusion, distasteful assignment, monotonous routine, physical discomfort, and so forth) which would so greatly impair the efficiency of many of these men that they would be rated Unsatisfactory. But it was, of course, not possible to foretell which of the men examined (one out of every twenty) would, in the next year or more, be psychologically assaulted to this extent. The candidates had to be assessed in relation to the usual range of stresses—the stresses to which about 95 per cent of them would probably be exposed—because if they had been assessed in relation to the unusually severe stresses, which only about 5 per cent of them would be called upon to meet, a large proportion of the candidates, who, as it happened, performed their duties satisfactorily, would have been rejected.

If the organization which is being served by assessment is insistent upon the minimum percentage of breaks under stress, not only must the standard of acceptance be raised considerably, but, in order to supply enough men with a sufficient degree of stress tolerance, the number of recruits, most of whom will be rejected, must be greatly increased. Thus the setting of a high standard calls for a much more expensive assessment process, which for some institutions may be desirable, but for the wartime OSS, with its urgent plans and its recruiting difficulties, would have been impractical. It must, therefore, be acknowledged that a certain number of failures are inevitable when operating with a standard which is not unreasonably high, principally because no human being can predict which one of an assemblage of men will be called upon at some future time to tolerate a very improbable amount of strain. There is the case of Guy, for instance, who, before joining our organization, had had more than his share of military service, and, as a member of OSS, played a creditable part in several successful intelligence operations during the sweep of the American forces through France. At the time the Allied Armies were approaching the Rhine, Guy, dressed as a French peasant, was parachuted behind the German lines, but not long afterward was picked up as a suspicious character, taken to the nearest Gestapo headquarters, and subjected to a hideous round of tortures which included the pulling of several teeth. The Germans extracted no truthful information from him, but when the advancing Americans found him, he was suffering from complete amnesia which rendered him unfit for further enterprises. The assessment staff, which included neither major nor minor prophets, had passed him as High Average, which was probably fairly accurate; but, as it happened, he was one of the relatively few men who had to face an unusual ordeal and so ended a not undistinguished career as a neuropsychiatric casualty.

In addition to the possibility of an unusual amount of strain, there is the possibility of the improbable occurrence of a specific strain, a kind of strain which is tolerable to most men but intolerable to a few. All assessees who were recommended for overseas duty had a fairly high level of general strain tolerance, but a good many of them were susceptible to one or two specific kinds of strains. Some, we discovered, could not work very well in subordinate positions; others could function competently only as members of an efficient, harmonious unit—snafu was unbearable to them; some were highly trained specialists who hated to devote much time to matters that were unrelated to their fields of interest; others were civilians who resented deeply some of the special privileges enjoyed by officers and were easily offended by any show of military authority; still others would become apathetic and irresponsible when there was nothing definite for them to do; and so it went. The assessors knew that these and many other kinds of pressures were prevalent in the theaters, but they could not guess which candidates would be confronted by which pressures. The specialist, for example, who was invulnerable to a variety of disturbing conditions and expressed intense interest in his proposed assignment could not reasonably be rejected on the general ground that there was one chance in ten that he would be given another and to-him-unbearable job as soon as he arrived in the theater. The restless extravert who was fit for everything except delay and inactivity could not be screened out merely because there was one chance in twenty that he would be forced to wait for a month or two when he reached Calcutta, and it was thought that if he did have that much time on his hands he would take to drink and women. A man's level of performance was likely to depend, in some measure, on the character of his commanding officer and the character of his teammates, but there was no way of discovering ahead of time who these associates would be. A very hearty assessee, Stub, who was considered a rare "find" because he was intimately acquainted with many influential residents of a strategic occupied zone of coastal China, could not be rejected by assessment on the basis that he was a man of strong personal prejudices with whom some people would find it difficult to work harmoniously. He got on well with most of his associates at Station S and was eager for his proposed assignment, but, as luck would have it, when he arrived in China he was paired with an utterly incompatible person. Their tactical conceptions proved to be irreconcilable and they quarreled so violently that it became apparent that it would be impossible for these two to cooperate effectively in carrying out the hazardous project for which our assessee had been recruited. Since there was no qualified substitute, the plan was abandoned. Stub had gone to China to accomplish one specific thing for which he seemed well fitted, but, as it turned out, to do this he had to adjust to a man whose views of means and ends were diametrically opposed to his. The clash unfitted him for the performance of a job that was so perilous and delicate. He was rated Unsatisfactory in the theater. As a guess, we might say that there was about one chance out of a hundred that an assessee who was rated Medium by assessment would find himself, as Stub did, in one of the few situations which he was incapable of managing successfully.

Another possibility was the occurrence in the future of a severe or protracted illness which would have such deleterious effects upon a man's personality that his level of efficiency would fall far below that which had characterized his performances in the past. A number of men, for example, were seriously incapacitated by suffering successive attacks of malaria. Losing zest for perilous undertakings, they were content to remain at base headquarters, performing routine duties in a perfunctory, apathetic manner, amid an unrelenting flood of gripes and grievances. Some found consolation in hard liquor. One man who had taken an energetic part in several dangerous expeditions came home from the Far East and after a happy reunion with his wife and children, so his friends reported, blew out his brains.

One of several other occurrences which might make assessment predictions inaccurate, but which occurred so infrequently that they had to be neglected, is a catastrophe at home (an "over lapping situation" in Lewin's terminology) which would be disturbing enough to impair a man's emotional poise and motivation and hence his usefulness. For example, one high-ranking OSS officer, while operating abroad, received a letter from a friend of his in America informing him that his wife had run off with the local garageman, leaving no message or address. As a result the officer's morale, which had formerly been high, dropped to zero. The assessment staff could predict that a small percentage of men would have to cope with a profoundly depressing or disquieting event of this sort, but, again, it was not possible to guess which of the assessees would be thus afflicted.

These considerations bring us to the conclusion that *there is a certain inevitable and irreducible percentage of prediction errors ascribable to the fact that when it is a matter of deciding whether to accept or to reject a candidate (saying yes or no), only future events which are known to be probable (in the life of a man engaged in an assignment of this type) should be considered in making the decision, but in a certain proportion of cases, events which are improbable—and hence should not be included in the assessor's calculations—will actually occur.* The irreducible percentage, or base-line figure, will be determined by (1) the difficulty of the assignments; (2) the standard of excellence maintained by the organization; (3) the number of new men needed per month; (4) the number of recruits obtainable; and (5) the suitability of these recruits. As a rough guess, we might say that about 2 or 3 per cent failures were the irreducible base-line figure for the assessment of OSS personnel.

In this discussion of inevitable prediction errors the problem has been much simplified for purposes of exposition. Actually the business is much more complicated. For instance, in deciding the fate of a candidate, assessors do not, in fact, disregard all improbabilities, because many candidates are susceptible to a number of different kinds of strains, and, although the probability that this or that particular strain will occur is small, the probability that at least one of the lot will occur may be appreciable. Furthermore, there is a certain probability that two or three strains will occur together or in succession, and that the assessee may be equal to coping with no more than one.

It should be pointed out that although an assessment staff will not be able to reduce the base-line figure of unsatisfactory cases (a figure which is determined by the conditions imposed by the organization), it might be able to reduce the percentage of prediction errors on its own records by listing in each case the improbable strains which would, if they occurred to a marked degree, seriously affect the man's efficiency.

The second major question is that of the number of men who failed because of some deficiency in specific skill. As explained in Chapter I, it was not possible to recruit an assessment staff, to standardize objective tests, and to acquire or build the equipment necessary for measuring dozens of different aptitudes, such as that for training homing pigeons, for setting Japanese type, for drawing posters that would influence the German people, for piloting an airplane, for running a Diesel engine, for taking moving pictures, for speaking Burmese or one of fifty other languages, and so forth. The assessment staff attempted to estimate about ten general abilities, such as physical ability, instructing ability, and recruiting ability, but it was not in a position to measure skills which were as specific as those listed above. Consequently, it was agreed that each branch administrative officer, aided by his associates, would take the responsibility of deciding whether the candidates recruited for his branch possessed the necessary technical qualifications. The administrative officer's decision was based on the candidate's work history, on information furnished by the man's acquaintances, on data supplied by the Security Branch and by the Personnel Procurement Branch, on the results of interviews, on the candidate's record at the OSS schools which he attended, and on his work in the Washington office before he was sent overseas.

Unfortunately, in obtaining appraisals of unsatisfactory assessees in the theater, we did not attempt the difficult task of determining to what extent a lack of specific skill was, in each case, responsible for failure. Our records show an intricate combination of factors in most instances. A member of an organization who cannot do what is expected of him is immediately confronted by the stress of self-criticism and of criticism, implicit or explicit, from his supervisor and from his co-workers. His self-confidence will diminish, and feelings of inferiority will emerge; he is likely to become hypersensitive and defensive in his social relations, and blame others for his own shortcomings. Emotional stability and motivation will decrease and he may end by spending a large portion of his mental energy inventing excuses to justify his inadequacy. Thus, as soon as the strength of one component—in this case that of specific ability—drops below a certain minimum, other components are similarly affected, and, on examination, it is very difficult to ascertain which factor was primarily responsible for the now-pervasive deterioration. Contrariwise, a man whose talents are exactly suited to the job assigned to him and who, therefore, attains or surpasses the level of social expectation for him, will be continually encouraged by signs of approval and of respect from his associates, and under these conditions, his energy and initiative, motivation, effective intelligence, emotional stability, and social relations are likely to reach their maximum. If these facts had been fully appreciated at the start, and if sufficient time had been available, we would have set ourselves the task of making a much more thorough analytical study of the causes of failure.

In the great majority of unsatisfactory cases, incompetence was given as the chief cause of failure, but it was hard to decide (1) whether the incompetence was due primarily or solely to a lack of innate or acquired talent; or (2), if it was due to a lack of talent, whether it was one of the talents which the assessment staff had undertaken to measure. Sometimes an appraiser would say: "My secretary is a nice girl, extremely obliging and good-natured, but she is a very incompetent typist. She is slow, inaccurate, and extremely weak on spelling. She is more trouble than she is worth." Here the decision was simple, because the measurement of stenographic ability did not fall within the sphere of assessment. In many cases, however, the matter was debatable. Take the German-American, for example, who was sent to London to write propaganda script. Assessment found that he had been very successful as a writer of motion-picture scripts and that his verbal facility was unusual. His administrative officer made certain that he was able to read and write the German language. But in London this assessee's branch chief concluded that he was unsatisfactory on two counts: his scripts were not of the sort that would touch the German people, and he could not write creatively in German, his mastery of the language being limited to the amount required for conventional communications. Here the responsibility for the prediction error seemed to lie partly with assessment and partly with the administrative officer. There were many equally equivocal cases, and today we can do no better than to survey data we have at hand and make the conservative guess that about 1 or 2 per cent of the assessees failed primarily because of deficiency in specific skills. Adding this figure to the 2 or 3 failures per hundred due to the occurrence of improbable events, we get a hypothetical rough total of 3 to 5 per cent failures due to factors outside the sphere of the OSS assessment program.

The third major question is that of the number of inaccurate assessments which were due to the embarrassing conditions under which the screening process had to proceed. Since these conditions have already been sufficiently discussed in previous chapters, they need to be reviewed only briefly. As we have said, the most disconcerting condition was the staff's ignorance of the exact nature of each proposed assignment—the nature of the role and the nature of the environment in which the role would have to be fulfilled. In respect to its assignments, the OSS was, indeed, a very peculiar organization, because it was planning to do things which no American had ever done and, therefore, there was no available firsthand knowledge of the tasks to be accomplished. Certainly the psychologists and psychiatrists on the assessment staff knew no more about the character of these extraordinary employments than they did about the kinds of situations which would confront OSS men in different distant areas of the globe. It was not known in the winter of 1944, for example, that one branch in one overseas theater was so frustrated in its plans by other overlapping and competing agencies, and consequently so disorganized, that only a man with a rather high degree of snafu tolerance could work there effectually. This was the branch in which the figure for unsatisfactory assessees was 14 per cent. After a survey of all our cases of failure, our rough guess is that about two out of every hundred assessees were recommended for jobs in which they performed unsatisfactorily, who would have not been so approved if adequate job analyses and accurate accounts of existing conditions in the various theaters had been available, and also—to include a factor which belongs in this category—if each assessee had been given the job, or one of the jobs, for which he had been recommended by assessment.

The OSS was also rather unique among institutions in respect to the great variety of assignments for which candidates were slated, and the urgency which characterized all its manifold undertakings. As a result, it was necessary to test at one time (during a single one-day or three-day period of assessment) a group of recruits who had been selected for many different kinds of assignments. If it had been possible to assess, first, a body of men all of whom had been picked for projects which involved hazardous physical activity, and then, a number of administrators and executors, and, after that, a group of office workers and stenographers, a concentrated and unified assessment program suitable for each type of job could have been devised, in which case the assessors, in observing each successive group, would have found it less difficult to keep in mind the special qualifications required of every candidate before them. With a differentiated system of this sort, it might have been possible to reduce the frequency of failures, say, by approximately 1 per cent. Thus, according to our hypothetical calculations, which, of course, should not be taken too seriously, a total of 3 per cent failures might be attributable to the embarrassing conditions under which OSS assessment was forced to operate.

The percentage of errors which remain is ascribable to defects in the assessment process per se—limitations of the techniques employed and errors of clinical judgment. Since several chapters have already been devoted to descriptions of our procedures, further comments on this score could only serve to oversatiate the reader. But here, before leaving this topic, it might be helpful to call attention to certain important attributes of personality which cannot be well measured by any known assessment procedures. Some of these are as follows:

Endurance.—Physical endurance is so much a matter of whether a man happens to be in or out of training that a series of exhausting exercises is useful only if all candidates have experienced a month or two of equally hard physical conditioning. To attempt to test intellectual endurance or, what is more important, emotional stamina in a one-day or three-day assessment program is scarcely feasible, and so assessors, knowing that endurance is a very important determinant of success, must attempt to estimate it indirectly.

Long-Term Social Relations.—In a three-day program of assessment, a responsive, enthusiastic, genial, quick-witted, and perhaps humorous fellow is apt to make a favorable impression. His exuberance is inviting and contagious; he is facile in conversation and in debate; he is not embarrassed by having to play a part in the psychodrama; he contributes to the liveliness of every occasion, and, in the end, both candidates and staff are likely to give him a high mark on Social Relations. (The assessors at Station S were no doubt unconsciously disposed to overrate men who enjoyed and entered into the spirit of a program which they had designed and were administering.) Some candidates of this type, however, have a number of annoying traits which they are able to hold in check for a short time, when their need to please is uppermost, but which emerge later when vigilance is relaxed. Also there are some ideas, attitudes, and mannerisms which on first appearance are entertaining but, on repetition, become exceedingly tedious and irritating. That it is difficult to pick out all the candidates who will not "wear well" on long acquaintance is evidenced by the fact that the OSS assessment staff recommended several men with exhibitionistic tendencies which appeared, when modulated at Station S or W, to be generally acceptable, if not appealing, but proved, when vented overseas, to be insufferable.

Contrariwise, there is a tendency to underrate the shy, reserved, and taciturn introvert, because a person of this type is apt to take more than three days to warm up and display his full capacity for social relations and leadership. In a short time it is not possible to test the strength of such substantial qualities as integrity, loyalty, patience, and forebearance.

Imagination.—The intelligent management of situations in the future depends to a considerable extent on imagination—the ability to anticipate numerous possible contingencies and to conceive of a host of alternative forms of effective action. But imagination of this sort, the distinguishing mark of a truly superior man, takes a long time to work itself out, and therefore cannot be measured in a three-day session. It depends on the persistence of concentrated thought as well as on the excitement of unconscious processes which intermittently, and often at the most unexpected moments, enter consciousness to provide the needed idea. For this, a period of incubation is required, longer than is usually available to assessment.

These, then, are some of the as yet unsurmounted limitations of assessment.

Having come to the end of this discussion, it might be helpful to summarize our conclusions by listing the chief reasons, as we see them, for the reported failures.

CHIEF CAUSES OF PREDICTION ERRORS

Unavoidable:
1) Occurrence of improbable strains: inevitable and irreducible base-line factors.
2) Present limitation of assessment procedures: no ways of measuring variables which take months to manifest themselves.

Unavoidable under OSS conditions:
3) Deficiencies of some candidates in specific skills falling outside the sphere of assessment.
4) Staff's ignorance of the exact nature of the assignments: no job analyses, no situation analyses.
5) Wide variety of assignments to be considered in assessing members of each group of candidates.

Avoidable:
6) Errors of judgment, defective techniques.
7) Imperfect modes of appraisal.

We do not know whether our level of attainment was higher or lower than that initially expected of us by the administrators of the OSS; nevertheless, it is interesting in this connection to take a look at the level of attainment accepted by everyone as the highest legitimate aim of the members of the Medical Branch.

The Medical Branch was not asked to predict, in each case, whether within the next two years the candidate would be incapacitated by malignant jaundice, thyroid disease, or a fracture of the leg; and when illnesses and accidents did occur in the field, these were not listed as failures to diagnose lack of immunity to such physical conditions. The study of susceptibility to certain diseases as a function of the physical constitution is in its infancy, and it is still an accepted fact that a physician cannot predict from which illnesses, if any, a man will suffer in the future. Knowing the frequencies of different causes of death in a given population, he can foretell with a fair degree of accuracy what proportion of a given sample of human beings will die of heart disease, of kidney disease, of cancer, and so forth; and knowing the incidence of malaria among American troops in Burma, he can guess what percentage of the men who are sent to operate there will contract this disease if conditions remain unchanged; but he cannot pick out the *individuals,* among those examined, who will finally die of this or that illness, or who, if they should go to Burma, will succumb to malaria. Thus he has no basis for selecting some healthy men and rejecting others. His highest aim is to discover all the *existing* symptoms of disease. On his list of failures will be included the names of all those who had symptoms which he failed to note at the time of examination, but not the names of those who developed symptoms later.

The characteristics of personality (mind-brain structure), of course, differ from those of constitution (somatic structure), and, despite the fact that the former are more complex, more flexible, and more fitful than the latter, it is probably possible to make a greater number of correct long-range prognoses about personality than can be made about constitution. Most physical diseases, for example, develop suddenly without warning, whereas the onset of a neurosis or of a psychosis is very likely to be preceded by months or years of premonitory signs. But, today, it is not known in what particulars or with what amount of accuracy psychologists and psychiatrists are capable of predicting future behavior or levels of accomplishment. Performances dependent on certain functions (e.g., intellectual) exercised under certain conditions (e.g., school and college situations) and measured by certain ratings (e.g., grades on examinations) can be foretold with a reasonable degree of certainty by certain tests (e.g., scholastic aptitude); but when these functions are exercised under other conditions or measured by other indices, or when it is a question of the effectiveness of one of a large number of other dispositions or abilities (e.g., leadership in different fields and at different levels), the degree of validity that a trained psychologist can reasonably be expected to reach with his predictions is not known. And since

ignorance is general on this point, the prevalent tendency among enthusiastic clinical psychologists and among laymen who are favorably disposed to
psychology is to place the level of expectation too high, to ignore the fact
that a certain irreducible (sometimes high) percentage of predictions will
inevitably be incorrect. In view of this tendency toward optimism so characteristic of those who venture into unexplored territory, it might be argued
that assessment psychologists should not, for some time, encourage themselves or others to anticipate that they can do more than identify *existing*
deficiencies and proficiencies. Eventually it will be discovered in what respects and to what degrees and under what conditions they are capable
of predicting future behavioral developments.

So far in this chapter, discussion has been restricted to the population of
failures, the recommended assessees who were rated Unsatisfactory in the
theater or in Washington by returnees from the theater. Although these
failures constitute the most serious errors of prediction, they add up to only
a small fraction of the total. One unanswerable question is this: How many
rejected candidates would have proved satisfactory had they been sent overseas? Since all recruits were assessed in relation to our conception of the
usual degree of stress in this or that theater, and since the stresses actually
encountered by a certain proportion of the men were much lighter than those
encountered by the majority, it is certain that some of the rejected men
would have been equal to their confronting situations. But here again, it
was impossible to foretell who, among a given group of candidates, would
be exposed to heavy strains, and who would be exposed to light.

The majority of the errors, however, consisted of apparent overestimations
or underestimations of recommended men who performed satisfactorily
overseas. These errors were reviewed in Chapter IX. To explain them we
would recite the chief causes of screening errors as listed above. We would
be very dubious, of course, as to the proper relative weight which should
be attributed to each of the different factors.

The statistical evaluation of the ratings made by the OSS assessment staffs
is not the sole, or perhaps even the best, index of the value of the program.
As important as the tasks of screening out unsuitable recruits was that of
writing a personality sketch of each candidate which would aid his branch
chief and administrative officer in understanding him and in assigning to
him duties in line with his talents. Whether this task was well performed
by assessment is a question for the branch administrators to decide; but
it can be reported that whereas in the beginning there was a good deal of
outspoken distrust and skepticism, and some opposition, on the part of
many of the OSS administrators and executives, in the end a large majority
of them gave very favorable estimates of the utility of the program, despite
the fact that assessment, by rejecting some 25 per cent of their recruits and
so annulling an incalculable amount of effort, was acting as a frustrating

interference to the smooth and rapid flow of personnel and, as such, constituted an ideal target for pent-up aggression.

THE PROMISE OF ASSESSMENT

The writers of this book have much evidence to support, and no evidence
to contradict, the assumption that the psychologists and psychiatrists of the
assessment staff are virtually unanimous in their opinion that the OSS
system of examination and diagnosis was better than any with which they
had previously been familiar. Certain parts of the program, to be sure, were
not considered valuable by all of us, but, taken as a whole, the series of
procedures gave the members of the staff a surer sense of "knowing a
man," more confidence in ·their formulations and recommendations than
they had ever enjoyed before under similar circumstances, that is, when
called upon to size up large numbers of men and women in a relatively
short time.

Although the all too human tendency, common to members of a congenial
group, to overvalue their own productions must certainly be included
among the determinants of the staff members' favorable verdict, and
although their conviction that assessees would behave in the field as they
did at assessment was probably greater than was justified, nevertheless it
seems that, in the absence of conclusive scientific proof of the special merits
and defects of the system, the consensus of an experienced and ever-critical
staff is a reasonably good index of the worth of the procedures.

In this section, however, we are not concerned with the question of the
efficacy of our system of assessment under the conditions imposed by the
OSS, but rather with the question of its probable utility in the future; and
here the members of the staff are agreed that it could be developed into an
extraordinary instrument for accomplishing three important purposes simultaneously: (1) the selection of the most suitable persons for important jobs;
(2) the advancement of our understanding of personality; and (3) the
adequate training of clinical psychologists and psychiatrists.

Some men are inclined to the opinion that only those sciences which can
offer unequivocal quantitative proofs of their accomplishments are worthy
of financial or institutional backing. Fortunately for psychology, however,
there are a few who judge otherwise, who take the absence of tangible
evidences of accomplishment as an indication that the science in question
is a young one and, therefore, in need of special support for its development.

The fact that the initial researches, the explorations, and pilot studies of
workers in a young science have not led to any definite or startling results
is no argument against the encouragement of that science. As Pasteur
answered to a questioner who was skeptical of the value of the infant science

of bacteriology, "What good is a baby?" Every science must pass through the stages of infancy, childhood, puberty, and adolescence before it reaches the point of maturity at which even the near-blind can see its worth. Since this is inevitably the case, the more encouragement that is given to an immature science the sooner will it arrive at the desired stage of conceptual and practical effectiveness. Let us take an extreme case and assume, for the sake of argument, that it is true, as some have claimed, that not until after 1900 did medicine pass from the stage of doing man more harm than good to that of doing him more good than harm; and then ask ourselves, what would have been the most enlightened attitude to hold toward medicine a hundred years ago? To abolish it or refuse to support it because it was doing more harm than good? Or to encourage it so that some day it would do more good than harm? Let a man with severe diabetes, pernicious anemia, syphilis, or acute appendicitis answer this question. The point is that the scientific method of observation, tentative interpretation, hypothesis making, and verification is almost certain to succeed *in the long run* whether the objects of concern be animal, vegetable, or mineral. Some sciences have already attained a large measure of success, have proved their usefulness and can pay their way; but there are others which have not yet reached the stage of self-sufficiency and so must turn to public-spirited individuals, to government, to cultural institutions, or to foundations for assistance.

Faced by a diversity of plans for scientific research, decision as to institutional or financial support should, in each case, hang largely on the best obtainable answers to four questions: (1) How important to man's welfare would be the ordered knowledge that is the special goal of the given science? (2) What are the chances that the specific objectives of the proposed research will prove to be strategic in the advance of this science? (3) Are the methods selected for attaining these objectives likely to be successful? (4) Is the available staff of scientists equal to the undertaking?

To us it is self-evident that the science of man stands above all other sciences in the rank order of importance, especially today, at this critical point in the evolution of our species. Never so urgent has been the need for knowledge of the determinants, components, and consequences of social forces and interactions, the need for adequate means of surveying, measuring, interpreting, predicting, and controlling the behavior of men. Today's special urgency is the result of the present perilous gap between man's power to create and to manipulate physical forces *effectively* and his power to create and to manipulate them *wisely,* a gap which is correlated with the wide discrepancy which now exists between the state of perfection of the physical sciences and the state of imperfection of the social sciences. One of the chief aims of our time must be to diminish this discrepancy, because material science has taken on the character of a cancerous growth.

and, if not balanced by the development of a usable social science *operating in the service of humanistic values,* it will surely pass from the state of doing man more good than harm to that of doing him more harm than good, if not of demolishing his most valued institutions.

It is within the broad framework of a great plan to advance the basic social sciences all along the line that the present scheme for a research assessment agency, or institute, should be envisaged.

The essential characteristics of the system of assessment we are advocating are as follows:

1) *Social setting:* The whole program is conducted within a social matrix composed of staff and candidates, which permits frequent informal contacts and, therefore, many opportunities to observe typical modes of response to other human beings.

2) *Multiform procedures:* Many different kinds of techniques are employed, running all the way from standardized tests to uncontrolled situations, special attention being given to the interview, to projective techniques, and to performance tests.

3) *Lifelike tasks:* Assessees are given lifelike tasks in a lifelike environment: the tasks are complicated, requiring for their solution organization of thought at a high integrative level, and some of them must be performed under stress in collaboration with others.

4) *Formulations of personality:* Sufficient data are collected and sufficient time is available to permit conceptualization of the form of some of the chief components of the personality of each assessee, this formulation being used as a frame of reference in making recommendations and predictions.

5) *Staff conference:* Interpretations of the behavior of each assessee are discussed at a final meeting of staff members, and decisions (ratings and recommendations) are reached by consensus.

6) *Tabulation of assessments:* The formulations of personality, the ratings of variables, and the predictions of effectiveness are systematically recorded in a form which will permit statistical treatment and precise comparisons with later appraisals.

7) *Valid appraisal procedures:* Special attention is devoted to the perfection of appraisal techniques, so that reliable measures can be obtained of the validity of each test in the assessment program and of the ratings of each variable.

This brief summary should be sufficient as a reminder of the chief features of the methodology described in this volume. The three major objectives of an agency or institute committed to these principles in peacetime would be as follows:

Selection of the Most Suitable Men for Important Positions.—Since the OSS system of assessment is more expensive and time-consuming than other systems, it cannot be recommended when the task is that of picking several thousand men a year for jobs of minor significance, particularly if the qualifications for these jobs are chiefly technical. But our system of assessment is preferable, we believe, whenever (1) an institution or a combination of institutions must pass on the suitability of about four hundred to one thousand candidates a year; (2) the quality of the selectees is a matter of considerable importance; and (3) the requirements include the ability to work effectively with others, either as leader or as cooperator.

Although one thousand candidates a year are about the upper limit for an assessment staff of twelve men administering a three-and-a-half-day program, there is no limit to the number of candidates who can be properly examined if the institution to be served is willing to increase the number of assessment units. Also, although a one-day assessment is not advisable at this stage in the development of the methodology, it should be noted that one staff, administering a streamlined program of this length, can handle over two thousand candidates a year.

The quality of the selectees is a matter of considerable importance (1) if a good deal of time, talent, and money must be spent in training them (e.g., selectees for Annapolis or West Point), and/or (2) if they will eventually be in a position either to benefit greatly or to injure greatly the cause of the people or of the institution they are serving (e.g., business executives, government officials, educators), and/or (3) if it will be difficult to discover their deficiencies and replace them promptly once they are appointed (e.g., foreign representatives of a government or of a business concern).

Since the system of assessment described in this book includes, or can be adjusted to include, not only all the pertinent standardized tests which are used today by personnel pyschologists but, in addition, numerous other more inclusive procedures not heretofore employed, and since this system also embraces, as an integral part of the whole program, a procedure for evaluation which will reveal the specific errors made and thus lead inevitably to a continuous series of technical improvements, it is bound to become, provided its development is in the hands of properly trained psychologists and psychiatrists, the most effective system of assessment. Therefore, it can be recommended, first of all, on the basis of the practical service it is capable of performing.

In this connection two consequences of the operation of an assessment program of the OSS type are worth mentioning: on the one hand, the science of psychology will be greatly benefited by having to demonstrate the validity of its theories and techniques under the exacting conditions imposed by a purposeful organization; and, on the other hand, the administrators of the organization will be benefited by the gradual acquisition of psychological knowledge pertinent to the treatment of its personnel.

Although we believe that assessment will more than pay for itself as a practical enterprise, in the present stage of its development a fairly large fraction of the staff's energies should be devoted to research, and, therefore, an agency of this sort will probably require some financial support from a nonprofit source.

The OSS system of assessment was designed as a means of selecting and placing special personnel, but it can readily be adjusted to serve other purposes, such as that of diagnosis in connection with the rehabilitation of delinquents or the reconditioning of neuropsychiatric casualties. Many of the procedures, for example, could be used effectively in conjunction with group therapy.

Development of the Science of Man.—The main body of psychology started its career by putting the wrong foot forward and it has been out of step with the march of science much of the time since. Instead of beginning with studies of the whole person adjusting to a natural social environment, it began with studies of a segment of a person responding to a physical stimulus in an unnatural laboratory environment. Consequently, after a century of diligent application, psychologists still lack sufficient ordered knowledge of everyday social behavior. Their attempts to overcome this handicap by adding or associating in some way the psychological processes which have been scientifically investigated in the laboratory have not been notably successful.

One reason for the early false step and subsequent distorted growth of psychology is the fact that human beings are not so compliant as chemicals, plants, and animals in submitting to scientific scrutiny and manipulation, especially if the cool eye of the psychologist is focused upon their central determining inclinations, their feelings, and their motives. Consequently, the easiest course for the first experimental psychologists to follow was to limit the field of inquiry to studies of the unrevealing peripheral processes of perception which are least related to the subject's self-esteem and by so doing give the latter no cause for indignation, noncompliance, or deception.

The first to occupy themselves with systematic observations of the determining components of personality were the medical psychologists and later the psychoanalysts, who were forced to it by the necessity of understanding and so relieving the afflictions of their patients. It was possible for these physicians to invade the secret core of personality, first, because their patients, craving some relief and persuaded that frankness was the price they had to pay for it, were willing, if not eager, to confess many of their inmost thoughts and feelings; and second, because the physicians discovered ways of painlessly seeing through, circumventing, or dissolving the forces protective of self-esteem. Thus great progress was made. The psychoanalysts, however, were necessarily more intent on discovering the determinants of morbid complexes than they were on discovering the determinants of effective health, and, as a result, have today more facts and theories pertinent to abnormal than to normal psychology. Some misconceptions advanced by the psychoanalysts were the almost inevitable results of their practice of observing patients in one situation only—that of the consulting room—of their special preoccupation with fantasies rather than with actions, and of their having to construct a picture of the early social relations of a patient almost entirely from the latter's own impressions, many of them shadowy.

The cultural anthropologists and sociologists, however, have succeeded in correcting some of the twists of psychoanalytic thought by furnishing evidence of the determining influence of different cultural forms, ideological and behavioral. Consequently, the modern psychologist, armed with the critical standards and the technical methods—statistics, rules of test construction, and so forth—acquired at the university, and then trained in the theories and methods of sociology and psychoanalysis, is in a position, for the first time, to advance the science of man directly, by the study of relatively normal men and women in a social context, as well as indirectly, by the study, say, of animal behavior.

Although there are numerous psychologists who are now equipped to undertake such studies, there is, as always, the practical problem of finding the situations in which these can be carried out successfully. Under what conditions will normal adults submit to scientific scrutiny without an impeding degree of resistance and resentment? One answer to this question is that the American people have come to concede to institutions the right to test applicants for membership in almost any way they see fit, and, as experience has shown, most applicants undergo the assessment process without resentment. A few desirable men may perhaps be turned away by an aversion to being tested, but a greater number will be attracted by this challenge to their abilities. In fact, the location of an assessment screen at the entrance of an institution is likely to raise the value of that institution in the minds of the public and of the members who succeed in passing the screen, though not usually, to be sure, in the minds of those who fail to pass. It has been demonstrated, furthermore, that assessment can be made so interesting, enjoyable, and beneficial to the assessees that resistance in the course of the program becomes a negligible factor. Thus an assessment agency constitutes one of the most, if not *the* most, acceptable ways of studying normal adult personalities.

For researches into normal personality, the OSS system of assessment, or something comparable to it, is essential, since most other selection systems do not include investigations of the dynamic components of the total personality and without these, one cannot even hope to understand the character structure of human beings. As the result of a tremendous amount of very careful and thorough work by hundreds of psychologists devoted to test construction and test administration we have today a large number of economical techniques, many of which appear to be reasonably valid. Thus something definitely useful has come out of these expert labors. But it is not possible to say that they have added anything to our knowledge of the components and determinants of personality. To advance our understanding of human nature other methods must be used.

There are scores of strategic questions about the determinants of effective behavior which might eventually be answered by an assessment institute that employed the system outlined in this book. For example, there is the great problem of the consequences of various traumatic occurrences in childhood. According to the psychoanalytic formula, neurotic symptoms are resultants of repressed dynamic complexes engendered by traumatic situations in early life. Many different types of traumatic situations have been described, as well as the dynamisms of ego-defense and of complex-formation, and also the different conditions in later life under which a complex is likely to erupt as a manifest symptom. Although certain links in the chain of causation are still obscure, many now believe that the chief determining processes leading from the series of traumata to the final psychological disorder have been convincingly formulated. One of the striking findings of the OSS assessment staff, however, was the frequency of such traumata and such complexes in the past histories of very effective personalities. In not a few instances, indeed, the staff concluded that the complex was more influentially related to the proficiencies than to the deficiencies of the personality. There is nothing very novel about this observation: it conforms to Adler's notion of ambition overcompensating for an initial narcistic wound. But in many of our cases there was no evidence of an exorbitant craving for superiority: the underlying complex had apparently been integrated into a personality structure that was both balanced and competent. And so, to supplement our present knowledge of pathogenic tendencies it seems that we require a much clearer understanding of the positive, creative, and health-building forces which so often succeed in checking, counteracting, or transforming the complexes of early life in such a way as to produce characters which in certain respects are stronger than they would otherwise have been. The question is, What determinants must be taken into account in predicting whether this or that hurtful occurrence will impede or encourage the development of an effective personality? We have learned a good deal about the defense mechanisms of the ego, but a personality cannot flourish by defense alone. Surely it is the forward-reaching and constructive forces which are chiefly responsible for integrated growth. And so, since these long-overlooked positive forces can be best investigated in normal personalities, an assessment institute would be in a favorable position to make a significant contribution to our knowledge of human development.

But the opportunity to study normal people would not be critically important were it not coupled with the possibility of evaluating predictions of behavior against reliable observations in the future. The opportunity to study a group of individuals in one connection or another is not infrequently afforded, but only too seldom is it possible to verify one's conclusions by conducting follow-up studies of the subjects' subsequent careers. Thus an assessment agency is in a peculiarly advantageous position: the candidates examined are destined, if accepted, to work in the institution for several months or years, and hence the staff will have the opportunity to evaluate hypotheses that are set down at the time of assessment. Since we believe that the practice of making predictions and checking them is the method *par excellence* by which the science of man can be most substantially advanced, we submit that an assessment institute would be in a strategic position to contribute to this advance.

Besides the opportunity (1) to appraise and to improve the techniques of assessment proper and (2) to investigate critical problems of personality development, an assessment unit, by including in its program a few systematically varied situations, would have the opportunity (3) to subject selected hypotheses to the test of controlled experiment. Thus no mode of research would be excluded from its proceedings.

The Training of Clinical Psychologists and Psychiatrists.—During the greater part of its short career clinical psychology has been the handmaiden of psychiatry, the psychologist's role being comparable to that of the laboratory technician in a hospital, limited to the administration of standardized tests with some research on the side if there was time for it. The relationship of psychiatrist to psychologist has been almost invariably that of senior to junior, regardless of age. In some institutions the clinical psychologist has been entrusted with the management of personality problems in children, but seldom has he been requested or—when he was so forward as to propose himself—permitted to take full responsibility for the diagnosis and treatment of adults with psychological disorders.

Up to very recently this definition of the psychologist's duties was appropriate, since he had not been trained to function as an expert at the highest integrative level. For years faculties of psychology had been organized to train students to carry on laboratory experiments, but not to educate them in the observation, interpretation, prediction, and control of human behavior under natural conditions. The professors had never considered it their function to collect and transmit an ordered body of knowledge derived from reliable records of personalities developing in social environments, never considered it their function to teach students the best modes of analyzing and reconstructing total human situations and of intervening when necessary. The content of textbooks and lectures dealing with human activity was largely limited to experimental findings—to precise observations and measurements of different processes (perception, memory, intellection, feeling, muscular movement, and so on) reacting, independently of other processes (as far as this was possible), to mild, discrete, impersonal, physical stimuli in an unnatural laboratory setting. By this restriction of the subject matter to functions which could be studied in single experiments under rigidly controlled conditions, some of the most important determinants of everyday behavior (e.g., personal and institutional attachments which take months or years to develop), as well as several entire areas of human activity (e.g., sex behavior), were excluded from consideration in the curriculum. Animal experimentation, because it was chiefly concerned with the development of organized directional behavior, contributed a good deal more than psychophysics did to an understanding of human reactions; but here again a number of important variables (e.g., need for self-esteem, conscience, long-range expectations based on symbolic education, and the like) were necessarily excluded. Thus, for a number of years, few of the facts and theories of academic psychology were applicable to the everyday affairs of individuals or institutions; and, in consequence, the intellectual instruments which the student acquired gave him no advantage over his scientifically untrained contemporaries in comprehending and in dealing with the daily run of psychological problems, his own or those of others. In fact, his relative isolation from elemental human interactions and dilemmas during his student days, the unreality of the theories that were presented to him, the amount of thought and talk devoted to laboratory apparatus, the lack of training in sizing up situations in which many variables are operating, the value which his instructors placed on the suppression of intuition, all tended to reduce him to a level of competence below that at which he had been functioning before commencing his academic studies.

The addition of abnormal psychology to the curriculum made an appreciable difference; but for some time there was a yawning conceptual gap between the theories taught in the elementary courses and the facts of neurotic illness. Also, the textbooks of abnormal psychology which students were given to read and the lectures which they attended were not, as a rule, productions of men who had had intimate experience with the phenomena they described. They were composed at secondhand; and at the end of the term the able student's knowledge was hardly less than his instructor's. Nevertheless, clinical psychology was soon accepted as a minor specialty, the chief requirements being a working knowledge of statistics and a familiarity with the techniques of test construction and test administration. But here, once more, education fell short of the mark; except for some practice in giving standard tests, the students gained but little experience in dealing with other people in a professional capacity, in conducting interviews, establishing rapport, encouraging free expression, interpreting verbal associations, and so forth. And even if these opportunities to learn by doing had been available, the student would have had no one to guide him, to check his interpretations and his interventions, because the members of his faculty were scarcely more experienced than he was in carrying out such operations. In brief, the holder of a Ph.D. degree in psychology possessed few of the conceptions and trained skills needed for the understanding and counseling of relatively normal people, much less for the diagnosis and treatment of neurotics. Hence his career as a practitioner was restricted at the very start.

During this era the situation in psychology was very different from that which has prevailed in medicine. The hierarchy of a medical faculty has always been, with some exceptions, roughly representative of the order of ability to observe, interpret, predict, and control the course of physical diseases. Today, for example, whenever a hospital interne is doubtful as to the diagnosis or the proper therapy in a given case, he can always consult the resident physician, and after him the visiting physician, and after him the chief of the medical services, not to speak of numerous different specialists. As he goes up the scale of consultants, he usually finds an increasing degree of all-around competence. But a student of psychology enjoyed no such opportunity to learn about human nature from older and more experienced men. Ten to one, the head of his department was less interested in the behavior of men and women and less expert in interpreting it than the average novelist, lawyer, or practical politician. In short, for many years there were no college faculties of psychology acquainted with the facts, theories, and procedures that were essential to the education of a fully responsible, practicing psychologist.

In the early thirties, however, the situation began to change: courses of instruction became more realistic, more relevant to the concerns of responsible people. Learning theory, derived from animal experimentation, was successfully applied to the facts of normal development and of morbid complex formation; some of the findings and hypotheses of psychoanalysis were cautiously introduced into lectures on abnormal phenomena; the potency of cultural forms, of role and status, as described by the sociologists and anthropologists was gradually recognized; a more dynamic conception of personality slowly took shape; new tests were improvised which required for their interpretation a considerable knowledge of character structure and of unconscious processes; promising field theories of determinants were elaborated in conjunction with series of observations of behavior in experimentally controlled, lifelike situations.

One result of these and other advances was that graduate students became progressively more interested in the application of their knowledge to human problems. Many of them found positions as applied psychologists in such fields as personnel selection, guidance and counseling, opinion polling; and by 1941 a large number were prepared to adjust quickly to the varied opportunities for significant service created by the war. In many stations, for example, because of the shortage of Army psychiatrists, the clinical psychologists were given much more responsibility in the management of neuropsychiatric casualties than they had ever had before.

Since V-J day the demand for trained clinical psychologists has not diminished but has increased markedly, and, in response to it, more than thirty universities have set up thoroughgoing training programs in this field.

It is important that the profession of applied psychology should not be too narrowly conceived, that the courses of instruction should prepare a man for a responsible and dignified career, not confine him at the outset to a life of subordinate technical routine. Education for this specialty should be built on a broad foundation of general scientific and special psychological knowledge within a frame of humanistic values. Besides reading, lectures, and discussion, what are needed more than anything are opportunities for the student to observe, interpret, predict, and guide human behavior under the supervision of experienced practitioners. Numerous possibilities of this sort are afforded by clinics and hospitals devoted to the treatment of mental disorders, and it is generally agreed that practical experience in one or two of these institutions is a necessary requirement for a degree in clinical psychology. In addition to this training under the direction of psychiatrists, nothing could be of more value to the student, we submit, than opportunities to investigate the personalities of relatively normal people under the expert supervision of practicing psychologists.

As things stand today, it is not easy to prophesy in what respects the tasks and responsibilities of the clinical psychologist of the future will differ from those of the psychiatrist. Perhaps there will be one basic education for both professions. Certainly the clinical psychologist would be better equipped and more secure if he were familiar with the essentials of pathological physiology and had had some experience dealing with seriously sick patients; and the psychiatrist would be better fitted for his calling if he possessed some of the dynamic conceptions, semantic standards, experimental techniques, statistical skills, and test procedures which are now being taught in courses of psychology. But, in any event, in the coming years the psychologist will probably be dealing with mild transitory disorders, with emotional conflicts and situational difficulties, in relatively normal persons; whereas the psychiatrist will be responsible, as always, for the more severe neuroses and psychoses. The psychologist will be asked to aid in the care of the milder disturbances, not only because there will not be enough psychiatrists to treat all sufferers, but because the psychologist's training will prepare him better than the average psychiatrist is now prepared to understand normal people and their difficulties. The psychiatrist's comprehension of personality is apt to be somewhat warped by the operation of barely applicable concepts derived from studies of the psychoses.

As a means of training graduate students as well as physicians in the use of concepts, testing procedures, and statistics appropriate to the exploration of normal personalities, we cannot conceive of a better system than that provided by an assessment center. By serving six months or a year as a junior assessor, a student could not only acquire most of the technical skills necessary for the practice of his profession, but, by regular attendance at staff conferences and special seminars, would learn a good deal about the process of arriving at interpretive and predictive formulations of personality. No other agency could favor him with better conditions for acquiring from more experienced seniors some of the wisdom that is not to be found in books.

Because of what it could contribute to the development of more capable clinical psychologists and psychiatrists, then, as well as because of what it could contribute to the advancement of knowledge through research, an assessment institute can be strongly recommended to a university or foundation; and it can be recommended to any organization which depends for its success on highly qualified personnel because of the practical service such an institute is capable of rendering.

RECOMMENDATIONS

In addition to the few principles of assessment outlined in Chapter II and the methods described in subsequent chapters, we now have certain procedures to propose which are calculated to remedy some of the defects of the system as employed by us. For greater clarity these recommendations will be presented as definite rules. Their value, though not yet unequivocally proved, seems to us hardly open to question.

Recommendation 1.—*Select a staff of suitable size and competence, diversified in respect to age, sex, social status, temperament, major sentiments, and specific skills, but uniform in respect to a high degree of intellectual and emotional flexibility.* Because of the existing ideational heterogeneity among psychologists and psychiatrists, the nature of the assessment procedures will be largely determined by the special theoretical convictions and talents of whoever is chosen to direct and plan the program, and this choice is likely to be determined by irrelevant or chance factors, since administrators of organizations are rarely, if ever, in a position to judge the relative merits of different systems of assessment. It must be understood that what is set down in this section is conditioned by our preference for the methods which in our experience have proved most effective.

The number and kinds of persons who are required for an assessment unit depend upon the number and kinds of procedures to be administered, and these depend upon the number and kinds of candidates to be assessed and upon the personnel standards of the organization. Leaving the matter of economy aside, it can be said that the effectiveness of the staff (its quality remaining constant) will, up to a certain point, be proportional to its size. When there are many techniques to be administered, and many occurrences to be observed and to be interpreted, the more trained eyes and minds there are the better. It goes without saying that most of the senior members of the staff should be experienced clinicians who have demonstrated their ability to size up personalities. If possible, one or more should have medical training and one or more should be expert clinical statisticians.

Furthermore, it is well to have as members of the staff at least two intelligent and impartial laymen who have themselves successfully engaged in the occupations for which fitness will be tested. An "old hand at the game" has usually acquired a fund of knowledge, much of it unformulated, as to the discernible signs of suitability and unsuitability. This knowledge emerges in the form of intuitive judgments which often serve as useful guides to a staff of psychologists. The psychologists will certainly have much to learn in respect to the professional standards and valuations which prevail, justly or unjustly, in the institution which they are serving, and it will be necessary for them to take frequent counsel with its more experienced members. Since it will be the latter who will eventually pass judgment on the performances of the candidates who are accepted by assessment, the staff should, at the very outset, become familiar with the assumptions and sentiments that are likely to influence these judgments.

Among available clinical psychologists selections will be determined, to some extent, by each man's degree of expertness in administering and interpreting the results of one or more of the techniques which will constitute the program. The day has not yet arrived when it can be taken for granted that every graduate in clinical psychology is sufficiently trained in all the essential operations of his craft. For the next few years, therefore, it will be necessary to inquire in detail as to each man's aptitudes and abilities— whether he is professionally familiar with the Rorschach, whether he is an experienced interviewer, whether he has worked with the psychogalvanometer, and so forth.

Having accepted the principle of multiform situations (see Chapter II), it is logical for us to recommend the selection of assessors of different sexes, ages, temperaments, and social backgrounds. Since the assessor is one of the inevitable components of the situation, one way to modify the latter is to modify the former. Sometimes it is important to know to what extent a candidate differs in his response to older as compared to younger persons, to women as compared to men, to exuberant extraverts as compared to reflective introverts, to middle-class as compared to lower-class persons. But, more important than this consideration, is the widely recognized fact that every psychologist's understanding of others is constrained in some measure by the structure of his own personality and by the necessarily limited range of his experiences and acquaintanceships; consequently, the best way of arriving at a comprehensive conception and fair estimate of a candidate's character is to give due weight to the judgments of different examiners. Sometimes one member of the staff, possibly because of certain dispositions he possesses in common with a certain candidate, is better able than anyone else to explain this man's behavior; but this same staff member may be the one least fitted to pass judgment on the next case that is discussed. Thus a diversity of judges is best when it is a matter of deciding the fate of a diversity of candidates.

Perhaps the most disqualifying attributes for a member of an assessment staff are rigidity of mind and rigidity of feeling. A psychologist who believes that his conceptual scheme, whatever it may be, is the only one that is suitable for formulating personalities, and who finds it difficult to work effectively with any other scheme—such a man or woman is likely to impede the development of a set of concepts adapted to the special requirements of assessment. Rigidity of feeling and of sentiment will make it hard for an assessor to adjust rapidly to the great variety of assessees with whom he will have to deal.

Undesirable as assessors are those men whose judgments of personality are influenced to an appreciable degree by their own religious, political, class, or racial sentiments. It is, of course, extremely important that no candidate be given the slenderest reason to suspect that sentiments of this sort will enter into the decision that determines his acceptance or rejection.

Freedom from conspicuously annoying traits might also be mentioned as a requirement for a member of an assessment staff, since the cause of assessment is not furthered by haphazardly irritating the candidates.

Recommendation 2.—*Before designing the program of assessment procedures, conduct a preparatory study of the jobs and the job holders of the organization.* This study should be considered an essential part of a scientific selection program. Several months devoted to it are almost certain to be a profitable expenditure. If this is not feasible, the three-day assessment system like that at S can hardly be recommended, because if the staff is ignorant of the precise needs and standards of the organization, it will be laboring under so great a handicap that its decisions will not be worth the cost of the undertaking.

The steps which comprise this preparatory study are defined by the following eight subrecommendations:

Recommendation 2.1.—*Make an adequate functional analysis of each of the roles for which candidates are to be assessed as well as an analysis of the environments in which each role must be fulfilled.* The reason for this is obvious: you must know what qualities and abilities are required for a given job, or role, before you can select or improvise suitable tests for these variables.

Most roles comprise a number of separable functions; for example, in the OSS these functions included gaining and evaluating information, interpreting situations and predicting the course of events, writing reports, selecting goals and subgoals, planning cooperative activity and communicating plans, selecting personnel, delegating authority, developing trustful relations with superiors, with equals, and with subordinates inside and outside one's own unit, impressing certain officials, engendering good morale among associates, acquiring equipment and supplies, manipulating and repairing certain tools and weapons, instructing others in the use of such instruments, overcoming physical obstacles, parachuting, piloting an airplane, engaging in combat, maintaining secrecy, speaking and translating a foreign language, and so forth. Each of these activities may be regarded as a more or less distinct function calling for knowledge and competence in the use of certain techniques for attaining a definable result. Every role is composed of a cluster of functions of this sort, some of which are of primary, others of secondary or tertiary importance.

Likewise each environment, physical and social, is susceptible of analysis into a number of different components, the less tolerable components being the more critical: tropical heat and rain, physical discomfort, inadequate diet, absence of equipment, physical danger (bombs, heights, combat), pressure of pace (the necessity of completing much work in a short time), insufficient sleeping time, regimentation, incompetent administration, autocratic leadership, depreciation (lack of promotion, ridicule, neglect, and so on), lack of privileges, lack of privacy, noise and confusion, snafu, uncongenial persons as associates, isolation (possibly in the jungle), natives of foreign countries to be dealt with, and so forth.

Information on these points must be obtained by personal observation and by interviews with job holders.

Recommendation 2.2.—*Obtain from members of the organization a list of the attributes of personality which, in their opinion, contribute to success or failure in the performance of each role.* The desired information can be gained in a series of interviews by asking questions such as these:

Who are the six most effective persons in your unit (branch, office, shop)? What are the strong points of No. 1? Of No. 2? And so forth.

Who are the six least effective persons in your unit? What are the weak points of No. 1? Of No. 2? And so forth.

Who has been discharged from this unit in recent months? Why was No. 1 discharged? No. 2? And so forth.

What are the chief requirements, in your mind, for job A? For job B? And so forth.

Recommendation 2.3.—*After a careful survey, analysis, and classification of the information obtained by these observations and interviews (Recommendations 2.1 and 2.2) make a tentative list of the personality determinants of success or failure in the performance of each role. These determinants will constitute the variables which, if possible, will be measured by the assessment procedures.* Besides the single over-all variable, *Job Fitness,* there should be a number of other more specific variables, because, for one reason, in order to discover the defects in the program and so improve it, it is necessary to predict in what respects a candidate will prove to be suitable or unsuitable, as the case may be, and then later to compare these predictions with the appraisals given by competent observers. A staff of assessors may be correct in a large proportion of its predictions of fitness and yet be wide of the mark in the reasons given for each decision. As a result, it may carry on for a long time with an unjustified confidence in the efficacy of its methods.

Most of the variables of personality which are of importance to assessment can be subsumed under one or more of the following five headings:

i) *Dispositions and capacities necessary to perform the functions which constitute the proposed job.* Ability, or ability to learn, is the basic requirement; but to receive a superior rating a man should also be interested in his work (for its own sake) and/or be highly motivated to do well.

ii) *Emotional reactions to the various physical and social situations the candidate is likely to encounter.* Determinants in this category should be considered in connection with those in the previous one, since every task must be executed within certain settings. A man may be able to write excellent intelligence reports *and* he may enjoy company and be very sociable on occasion, but yet be incapable of doing good work in close proximity to other people. Another man may be very creative in composing propaganda script (under favorable conditions), but he may not be creative while living in London away from his family, exposed to daily attacks of flying bombs, and working under a branch chief who does not appear to appreciate the merit of his ideas. Functional efficiency is sometimes greatly impaired by interpersonal conflicts.

iii) *Physical or mental ailments.* Under the previous heading we would list emotional reactions to environmental situations which occur when the man is in relatively good health. These are normal character components. Here, on the other hand, we are concerned with emotional reactions (together with many other things) which fall outside the limits of mental health. They are signs of a pathological condition, the definition of which falls within the special province of the psychiatrist. His task is not only to reveal all current symptoms of neurosis or psychosis, but to discover any susceptibility to one of these states which may exist. In some cases, consequently, he will be uncertain as to whether a given manifestation should be related to a consistent character component (ii) or be regarded as a precursor of disease (iii).

All types of physical disabilities and psychosomatic illnesses are included in this category.

iv) *Effects of the candidate on his associates.* This must be taken into account because some very talented and otherwise desirable individuals are prone to disturb the smooth functioning of units to which they are assigned. They provoke friction and antagonism, or engender confusion, or distract others from their duties, or act as depressants on the general level of morale. Some of them become "problem children," "headaches" to their branch chiefs. Such people, furthermore, are faced by the difficulty of adjusting to the hostility they have aroused: in *their* environments are more strains on emotional equilibrium. And then, lastly, the extent to which an individual is liked and disliked by others is an important factor entering into numerous judgments that affect his career, judgments which determine his acceptance or rejection by certain units, his promotion in rank, and, in the end, judgments that determine his over-all performance rating, the appraisal against which the accuracy of the assessors' predictions must be measured.

v) *Off-duty activities.* This item is important in extreme cases: at one end of the continuum are those who engage in enough drinking, whoring, or general roistering when they are off duty to get them into trouble or to impair their usefulness, and, at the other end, are those who spend their free time at occupations which, in one way or another, serve to promote the undertaking to which they are committed.

If the assessment staff can obtain adequate descriptions of the different jobs and of the conditions under which they must be executed, the variables which are selected for measurement can be fairly specific. Concrete variables of this type, applicable to the position of a mortar instructor working with guerillas behind enemy lines in China, might run as follows:

a) Knowledge of (or ability to learn) mechanism of mortars.
b) Ability to explain mechanism of mortars.
c) Ability to excite the interest and motivation of others.
d) Ability to evoke cooperation, respect, and loyalty.
e) Motivation for this work; interest in the job.
f) Administrative ability; procurement of supplies;
   management of office routine, reports, paper work.
g) Effect on the morale of associates; ability to get along with all kinds of people: absence of annoying traits.

h) Ability to learn to jump from a plane with a parachute.
i) Tolerance of physical danger: gunfire, bombing.
j) Tolerance of physical discomfort: cold, wet, insufficient diet.
k) Physical stamina, endurance, persistence.
l) Tolerance of strain, hard work, pressure of time, confusion, snafu, frustration.
m) Tolerance of authority, arbitrary commands, imposed tasks.
n) Tolerance of neglect, criticism, depreciation, slow promotion.
o) Freedom from neurotic symptoms.
p) Attitudes toward Chinese.
q) Alcoholism,
   and so forth.

The more specific the variables, the more understandable and useful they will be to men who are untrained in psychology, and the easier it will be to estimate them accurately in the field of operations.

But if sufficient concrete information is not available and if the jobs to be filled are so numerous and varied that a list of variables of this degree of specificity would be unmanageable, then it will be necessary to pick more general variables, such as Energy and Initiative, Effective Intelligence, Emotional Stability, and Leadership, the sort that OSS assessment units were forced to fall back on.

Recommendation 2.4.—*Define, in words that are intelligible to members of the organization, a tentative rating scale for each personality variable on the selected list as well as for the over-all variable, Job Fitness.* If every variable on the list is a distinguishable determinant of effectiveness and if the categories composing the scale for each variable are defined in terms of degrees of facilitating and impeding influence upon effectiveness (in actions of a certain class, in situations of a certain class), the practice of rating variables can be strongly recommended. If, in contrast to this manner of proceeding, the attempt is made to define and measure isolated traits divorced from their interrelations, their connections with specified situations, and their effects upon specified performances, the list of scores obtained will necessarily be highly abstract and often misleading. If, for example, Emotional Stability is defined and rated in isolation, the men assigned to the top category on this variable will, in all likelihood, be those who have manifested the least discernible emotion under various types of stress. Among them one would not find General Patton, nor General Montgomery, nor General MacArthur; one would not find Mr. Churchill, whose passionate eloquence sustained the fortitude of our world in its darkest hour. But if Emotional Stability is defined and measured in relation to effectiveness of performance, then Mr. Churchill might head the list on this variable, since it was precisely the intensity of his emotion, its congruence with each situation, and its coherence with thought and speech, which were chiefly responsible for his unique influence.[1]

Some of the rating errors made by OSS assessment staffs can doubtless be attributed to the fact that these considerations, applicable to all variables of personality, were not always kept in mind. In retrospect, for example, we can recall instances when we assigned top ratings on Effective Intelligence to some candidates because they demonstrated an unusual ability to manipulate concepts, without weighing the possibility that these men were deficient in social and administrative intelligence and that an excessive preoccupation with abstractions might even interfere with the effectiveness of the mental processes appropriate to their functions. Thus, as far as fitness for assignment is concerned, a man may have too much intelligence of an unsuitable sort, just as he may have too little emotion of a suitable sort. In any event, the rating scale for each variable should be so defined and so ordered that the top categories are predictive of successful performance, the bottom of unsuccessful performance.

As to the number of graded categories in the scale, we recommend at least three for distinguishing different degrees of suitability among those who are judged to be acceptable, and at least one for distinguishing the unacceptable recruits. The OSS assessment staffs found a six-point scale very convenient. In making over-all appraisals in the theater, however, with men untrained in psychology acting as judges, it was found that a four-point scale was more practical. The four categories were defined somewhat as follows:

4—Superior, Outstanding. This man has shown exceptional energy and ability in performing one specialized function, or several less specialized functions. He has successfully accomplished a number of difficult tasks requiring initiative and resourcefulness. He has shouldered responsibility and worked unusually well under strain. He commands the respect of his associates. He is considered indispensable.

3—Very Satisfactory, High Average. This man has shown a good deal of energy and competence in the performance of duties, most of which have not called for unusual talent. He has done fairly well at a difficult job, or very well at a relatively easy job. Steady and dependable, he has done more than his share of the work. Perhaps he has been very superior in certain respects, but below average in others. He has cooperated well with his associates and helped to sustain their morale. His commanding officer considers him a very useful member of the unit.

2—Satisfactory, Low Average. This man has done what was expected of him,

[1] These reflections, by the way, suggest that Emotional Congruence might be a better term than Emotional Stability. The latter, like other terms which have come out of pathology, is hardly suitable to describe different degrees of emotional involvement on the positive (supernormal) end of the continuum. There is a large class of people whose performances are mediocre chiefly because of the excessive stability of their emotions: either the appropriate facilitating feelings are deficient or they are rigidly repressed.

but no more. He is moderately able, moderately reliable. He may be superior in some respects and unsatisfactory in others, but on the whole he meets the requirements for his position. Although he has perhaps failed in one or two difficult jobs, he has performed his routine duties in a reasonably satisfactory manner. He has his good days and his bad days. His commanding officer is willing to retain him.

1—Unsatisfactory, Inferior. This man has not done satisfactory work. He is decidedly deficient in one or more respects—motivation, intelligence, emotional stability, social relations, or the special ability that is required of him. Perhaps he did well once but his efficiency has been seriously impaired recently by neurotic symptoms, alcoholism, or some other deteriorating factor. He has a depressing effect on morale and is not respected by his associates. His commanding officer wants to get rid of him (or already has got rid of him).

Since at this point in the enterprise the rating scale will be used to *appraise* present members of the organization rather than to *assess* new candidates, one category of unsuitability is sufficient. Busy administrators, and laymen generally, according to our experience, find it difficult to distinguish more than three degrees of acceptable competence, and so we would recommend starting with a four-point scale similar to the one above, but reworded so as to conform to the conditions prevailing in the given institution.

Recommendation 2.5.—*Devise a satisfactory system for appraising the performance of members of the organization both at this time and later.* The immediate purpose of this recommendation is to discover certain facts necessary to the establishment of a frame of reference for the assessment process. But its more important purpose is to construct at this time a satisfactory system of appraisal which can be used to test the merit of the assessment procedures. This second point deserves special consideration, the assumption being that the task of validation must eventually be undertaken for one, two, or all of the following reasons: (1) to measure the value of assessment as a whole and so decide whether it is worth continuing; (2) to measure the efficacy of each test and on this basis decide which ones should be retained, which improved, and which eliminated, and thus gradually to increase the validity of the judgments; and (3) to verify the scientific hypotheses on which certain predictions have been based.

Since the value of the assessment procedures will be judged by the results of the appraisal procedures, the latter certainly deserve as much critical attention as the former; and the recommendation we are making here is that this critical attention be given at the very outset.

One reason for this suggestion is that experience has shown that clinical psychologists have tended to devote the greater part of their energies to the construction and perfection of testing materials, and to be very scrupulous in calculating reliabilities, but, at the last, to be rather uncritical in accepting whatever validating criteria are readily obtainable; that is to say, the degree of scientific sophistication that has been applied to the assessment process is much greater than has been applied to the appraisal process, despite the fact that the proof of the whole enterprise hangs upon the dependability of the latter. By working out the appraisal procedures at the start we can make certain that this final phase of the undertaking will be carried out as satis- factorily, from a scientific standpoint, as the first.

The second reason for this recommendation is that appraisal is the target of assessment, and it is always well to see your target before taking aim. One should know ahead of time, for example, whether the target will be an objectively determined figure, such as the number of units of work a man completes per day, or a rating of his efficiency given by competent observers. If it is going to be a matter of subjective judgments, one should know what men, or at least what kinds of men, will do the judging, and precisely what rules they will be directed to observe in making their judgments. In some studies, possibly, appraisal will consist of a definite matter of fact, such as the election or nonelection of a man to a certain office, or the grades that a student gets in his four years of college studies. In both these cases, however, it will be noted that, although assessment is directed toward the prediction of a fact, the fact is one that depends to an appreciable extent on the per- sonalities of the men who decide it. Thus numerous psychological deter- minants enter into the final appraisal of a man: not only the beliefs, valuations, and standards of the judges who rate him, but the dispositions of those who have a hand in determining the opportunities he is given, or in deciding his admission to this or that group, and so forth. Consequently, in making predictions, assessors should estimate the impression which will probably be made by the assessee on those with whom he will associate, and to do this the assessors must know something about these associates, their assumptions, sentiments, and tastes.

The point that is being stressed here is that whatever the determinants of appraisal may be, it is important to distinguish them at the start, so that the assessment program can be designed to take account of them. The im- portance of doing this was not appreciated by the OSS staff at the time its procedures were being planned. In assessing a candidate no attempt was made by us to take into account the probable sentiments and prejudices of those who would judge him in the future. Our decisions were not influenced by thoughts such as these: "This fellow is below average in intelligence and he is not conspicuously energetic, but we should give a high mark because he has an exceptional sense of humor, is a convivial drinking companion, and is likely to be overrated by his associates." No, we did not try to hit the operationally defined bull's-eye; the results might have been better if we had. We aimed at the ideal bull's-eye, the appraisal that the candidate might receive from a group of omniscient and utterly impartial judges.

Probably, then, in some instances the assessment was nearer the truth than the appraisal.

Since, usually, the judges of a man's performance do not agree precisely in their estimates, the results of the appraisal process might be more accurately conveyed by a pattern showing the distribution of the ratings, rather than by a single figure representing the average or the majority of the ratings.

Disagreement among appraisers is not always, as we are prone to assume, an indication of errors, of the unreliability of the method, errors which are due, let us say, to differences in the number of facts at the disposal of the judges, or to the play of different prejudices, or to differences in ability to observe behavior and estimate effectiveness; disagreement may represent the precise truth of the matter. For example, the social relations of a person, his effect on others, are rarely uniform. In general his effect on those with whom he feels congenial will be more beneficent than his effect on those whom he dislikes. To test this, one would have to question the people who had been affected in one way or another by the man, including in one's sample both friends and enemies. Certainly there would be disagreement among the ratings on the variable Social Relations, but if this disagreement were accepted as a significant fact and represented by a pattern of judgments, instead of being obliterated by arbitrarily averaging the ratings, the conclusion reached would correspond more closely to the actual state of affairs. The same applies to the variable Leadership. And here we are reminded of a certain major who was rated inferior in Leadership by several irate subordinates but superior by all those of equal or higher rank. The average of these ratings placed him in the middle category on Leadership, a result which corresponded to no man's judgment. Unfortunately, we did not appreciate the advantages of using a pattern of appraisals until our evaluation had been completed.

Since most roles are a composite of numerous different kinds of tasks, and since a man is not likely to perform all of them equally well, it is usually desirable to obtain estimates of his effectiveness in fulfilling each of his major functions. And, since the execution of a function calls for repeated and varied efforts to deal with different environmental situations, estimates of effectiveness should be based, if possible, on the observation of many samples of behavior. A man may be skillful in handling Lt. X, but make no headway with Sgt. Y; he may be adept at repairing a jeep but unable to find his way amid the intricacies of more complicated machinery. Equally relevant are judgments of the total organizational efficiency of a man's day's work, the smoothness of coordination among his several functions and several actions. Finally, an over-all rating of total effectiveness must be obtained, due regard being given to the relative importance of each function in the fulfillment of the given role.

One of the essential parts of any system of appraisal will consist of rules pertaining to the number, distribution, and qualifications of the appraisers. If possible one appraiser should be the appraisee's superintendent or superior officer; at least one should be a co-worker of equal rank, and one a subordinate. In addition to this type of sociometric appraisal, we would strongly recommend the use of special staff appraisers who have had no previous contacts with the appraisees and do not know how the latter were rated at assessment. Being uninvolved emotionally in the work situation, the staff appraisers would be capable of a greater degree of objectivity in estimating effectiveness.

Recommendation 2.6.—*Obtain appraisals of a properly distributed sample of the present members of the organization.* The purpose of this is to test the adequacy of the devised system of appraisal (Recommendation 2.5), to determine whether the jobs and their environments have been properly analyzed (Recommendation 2.1), whether the list of personality variables is sufficiently comprehensive (Recommendation 2.3), whether the rating scale is practical (Recommendation 2.4), and to discover the distribution of each variable (especially of Job Fitness) among the present members of the organization. The sample of appraisees should include several representatives of each type of job.

Qualified appraisers (members of the organization) should be interviewed: they should not be permitted to make their ratings on a sheet of paper without guidance. Only by an interview can one make certain that an appraiser understands each term and the definition of the rating scale, and that he gives the task sufficient consideration. Before making his ratings the appraiser should be asked to give in his own words an account of the personality, the special abilities and disabilities, and the total effectiveness of the appraisee, and after deciding on each rating he should be asked to present concrete illustrations of behavior to support his judgment. The interviewer should feel free to question and urge a change of rating if the evidence is not convincing.

Recommendation 2.7.—*Examine the defects of the appraisal system as revealed in practice (Recommendation 2.6), and correct these by revising, where necessary, the list of variables, the definitions, the rating scales, or other elements.* The revised scheme should be shown to the executives, managers, or personnel officers of the organization and their criticisms solicited. Further adjustments of the scheme can be made at this time if called for.

It may be desirable for statistical purposes to define the graded categories of the rating scale in such a way that the members of the organization will be about equally distributed. For instance, if a scale of three degrees of acceptable job fitness is employed, about 33 per cent of the appraisees should fall into each category. This distribution can be arranged by modifying the criteria for inclusion in the different categories, by lowering or raising standards until each category contains the desired percentage of men. Such a scale would be suitable for rating Job Fitness, but it might not be appropriate for other variables. It might produce an unwarranted distortion of reality, or, for some other reason, prove impractical.

Recommendation 2.8.—*Obtain the figures necessary for a brief numerical statement of the personnel history of the organization over the last four or five years.* These figures, we are assuming, may be extracted from the personnel records of the institution. The data required include (1) the number of applicants (recruits) for jobs per year; (2) the number of men accepted (hired) per year; (3) the number of accepted men who were subsequently dismissed as unsatisfactory and the average duration of their employment; (4) the number of accepted men who left on their own initiative and the average duration of their employment; (5) the number of accepted men who have remained with the organization; (6) the distribution of fitness ratings among this last group (as found by the above-mentioned preliminary appraisal); and so forth. These facts and figures are necessary as a record with which the subsequent personnel history can be compared. Without this information it will never be possible to calculate the practical value of the assessment program.

Recommendation 3.—*Design a program of assessment procedures which will reveal the strength of the selected variables; for assessing these variables set up scales which conform to the rating scales that were defined for the purpose of appraisal.* Most of this book has been devoted to descriptions of assessment procedures; on this topic we have nothing to add here. Although some of the techniques used by the OSS staff will prove useful in the selection of almost all types of personnel, a fair proportion of the procedures which will constitute any given program will have to be especially designed to fit the requirements of the organization to be served.

As to the rating scales, our difficulties have led us to suggest a modification of the frame of reference which we used in assessing OSS personnel. Instead of judging a candidate in relation to the population of all candidates examined heretofore, we recommend that he be judged in relation to the present members of the organization. According to this scheme the scale of degrees of acceptability used in assessment would correspond exactly to the scale of acceptability which was defined after the preliminary appraisal of an adequate sample of the membership. For example, if a four-point appraisal scale, similar to the one described above, is selected, the three top categories of the *assessment* scale should be identical with the three top categories of the *appraisal* scale. Thus the standard for Superior, Outstanding (category

4), will then be a sort of composite portrait of all members of the organization who have been assigned to this class by the appraisers; the same would go for Very Satisfactory, High Average, and for Satisfactory, Low Average. The definitions of each of these three categories should be more specific and operational than those given above, and, once adopted, they should be used without modification for both assessment and appraisal. Thus the two rating scales for acceptability will be identical.

For purposes of appraisal one category of unacceptability is probably sufficient; but for purposes of assessment the number of categories that are used to distinguish those who are below standard will depend on the range of inferiority among the candidates. Under some circumstances one category may be sufficient, but usually it will be advisable to define two or three. It is conceivable, for example, that among a hundred applicants or recruits, none is judged to be suitable for membership in the organization. In this case, no correlation between tests would be possible if no distinctions were made between all these unsuitable men. As far as possible, the degree of difference between each of the categories in which unsuitable men are classified should be equivalent to that between each of the categories in which the suitable men are classified.

All this applies not only to the definition of the categories used in rating over-all Job Fitness, but to the definition of those which constitute the rating scale for each personality variable. Every category on every scale should be defined as specifically as possible in terms of the kinds of observable behavior which facilitate or impede effectiveness of total performance.

At Station S, the staff, in the absence of any better criteria, tried to judge each candidate (in respect to the strength of each variable) against an imaginary normal distribution curve of the candidates who had passed through S up to that time. It was assumed that the percentage of men that fell into each of the categories on the six-point scale would be distributed somewhat as follows: 0 and 5, 7 per cent each; 1 and 4, 18 per cent each; 2 and 3, 25 per cent each. Although this scale was somewhat incongruent, and the assessors never adhered to it very closely, it was useful as a rough standard with which the actual distribution of ratings could be compared from time to time, in order to discover whether the staff was exhibiting a tendency to limit its ratings on this or that variable to a few categories rather than to distribute them over the entire scale. At one stage, for example, it was found that a disproportionate number of 4's and 5's had been given on Motivation, whereas relatively few 5's had been given on Emotional Stability. This knowledge led to some clarification of the half-conscious assumptions which had been guiding our decisions.

But we are now convinced that this is not the proper way to proceed. The standard of comparison for each variable should be the behavior of the members of the organization who have been assigned by qualified appraisers to each of the four categories which constitute the scale for that variable—Unsatisfactory; Satisfactory (Low Average); Very Satisfactory (High Average); Superior (Outstanding). Since the distribution of the ratings is determined to a large extent by the definitions of the categories, if a particular distribution is desired, this, as we have said, can be approximated by modifying the definitions. In any case, the obtained distribution of appraisal ratings may be used as a rough guide for the distribution of assessment ratings, provided that the assessors remember that it is their function to increase, if possible, the number of members in the higher categories (Very Satisfactory and Superior) and thus gradually to change the distribution of ratings that was found before assessment was established. This change may not be possible. If, for example, the caliber of the candidates is low, but the need for personnel is urgent, the organization may even request the assessment staff to pass men who fall in the Unsatisfactory category.

In brief, then, our conclusion is that the nature of the rating scale—the number of categories, the definitions of the categories, and the expected distribution of the ratings—should be first determined on the basis of appraisals of an adequate sample of the existing membership. This initial study will define the categories of acceptability. The number of categories of unacceptability will depend on the spread downward of the variables among rejected candidates. We would recommend that the three top categories of the assessment-appraisal scale be designated by the numbers 6, 5, and 4, that is, 6 to stand for Superior, 5 for Very Satisfactory, and 4 for Satisfactory. This will leave three numbers, 3, 2, and 1, for designating different degrees of unacceptability. We do not recommend continuance of the use of 0 (zero) employed in OSS. Some have suggested that a meaningless progression of letters, like J, K, L, M, N, and O, would be an improvement on numbers, since it would do away with false metric assumptions about the scale. Finally, since the assessors will undoubtedly want to distinguish among themselves more than three degrees of acceptability, we recommend the use of plus (+) and minus (–) to indicate finer distinctions within each of the large categories. In this way the three-point scale of acceptability can be converted into a nine-point scale: 6+, 6, 6–, 5+, 5, and so forth. If the same mode of rating is used to distinguish the different possible degrees of unacceptability, the assessors will have an eighteen-point scale as a frame of reference for their own use. In condensing and communicating their findings to the personnel officers of the institution, however, they should omit the pluses and minuses. We are not certain whether it would be better to use a three-point scale of unacceptability for the rejected candidates in the final report or to have only one category for those who are not considered suitable.

The practice of rating specified variables is one way of doing violence to the reality of human nature, but, if one remembers that the ratings are nothing more than convenient abstract symbols, the disadvantages of using them will be outweighed by the advantages.

Recommendation 4.—*Build a conceptual scheme in terms of which formulations of different personalities can be made.* One of the guiding principles of the OSS system of assessment was that assessors should reach the best possible diagnosis of the personality as a whole before making specific ratings, predictions, and recommendations. This rule, we believe, should be retained, provided it is understood that "personality as a whole," as pointed out in Chapter II, is a very vague notion and that its symbolic representation is still very far from being a realizable goal. We lack the ordered knowledge, the proper modes of analysis and synthesis, the concepts, the instruments of examination, and, in most situations, the time necessary even to approximate the ideal. The "best possible diagnosis of the personality" today would be a coherent conception of a few components of several purposive systems, certain striking integrates or complexes, some outstanding abilities, a number of general attributes, and an indication of the degree of integration, stability, and power of the whole.

But psychologists and psychiatrists are not permanently restricted to partial formulations of this sort. One may predict with some confidence that substantial progress can be made in the coming years if social scientists will collaborate in the construction of an increasingly comprehensive, coherent, and usable theory of personality, the adequacy of which can be judged by its ability to explain the past and predict the future.

As explained in Chapter II, the OSS staff members did not attempt to agree upon one explicit theory of personality. They took pains to define only those personality variables which were clearly relevant to the immediate aims of assessment. When it came to interpreting the behavior of a candidate and formulating his personality, each assessor used whatever conceptions and terms seemed most suitable to him. Usually he expressed himself in non-technical language, using adjectives, metaphors, or trait-names; at other times he used scientific concepts. Some assessors would talk quite often of mood swings, incoherence of thought, paranoid trends; others would stress infantile fixations, basic anxiety, and ego-defense mechanisms; still others would be quick to point to evidence of an inferiority complex, social insecurity, overcompensation, and so forth. But despite a good deal of heterogeneity on the ideational level, the staff members seemed to understand each other well enough, and very few theoretical arguments occurred to impede the progress of the conferences. From this one might conclude that there is a considerable amount of concord today among psychiatrists and psychologists on a common-sense pragmatic level, although, as we all know, seemingly radical disagreements arise as soon as the attempt is made to force into definitive molds the fuzzy-edged, half-conscious notions with which we operate. The problem is how to arrive at a common conceptual scheme which will do justice to all existing sectarian schemes without provoking further civil wars among psychoanalysts and psychologists. This must somehow be accomplished if further progress is to be made on a large scale.

Now experience dictates that in situations marked by intellectual confusion and dissension it is necessary to go back to the observed events and their analysis, and to define in operational terms each concept necessary to the formulation of those events. This is always laborious and often difficult, but in the long run it will save much time by putting an end to much futile discussion. In any event, we would urge an assessment staff to define operationally every concept or variable which it will require in the diagnosis of personalities, and to do this before starting their practical operations. The system of variables will certainly have to be modified as time goes on so as to bring it in ever-closer accord with the observed facts: new abstractions will be added and old ones revised or eliminated. But during any one period the concepts used by the staff members in formulating the personalities of the candidates should be drawn from those which constitute the existing scheme.

Since most of the components of personality are forces which vary in strength, their definitions should include criteria in terms of which different degrees of intensity may be rated.

Having defined the separable components of personality, the next task will be to define the various kinds of relations which may exist among them and show how these different relations can affect the perceptible strength and modes of expression of each force. It is generally agreed, for example, that the expression of a strong drive can be so completely checked by an organization of inhibiting forces that its intensity as measured by the usual behavioral criteria will be very low, and yet the strength of the drive may actually be greater than it was before its frustration by the barrier of inhibition. The manifestations of its increased intensity are to be found not in direct overt actions, but in dreams, fantasies, mental preoccupations, affects, bodily tensions, psychosomatic symptoms, and in numerous overt though indirect forms, such as outbursts of humor. The increased strength of the drive will sometimes be exhibited overtly if the barrier of inhibition is suddenly lifted. The intensity and characteristics of a force can also be modified through its fusion or collaboration with forces of a different nature. Consequently, the original operational definitions of each component of personality taken separately must be supplemented by further definitions which describe its manifestations when integrated in various ways with other components.

As an illustration, let us take the so-called Oedipus complex. This is an affective complex of a boy's personality, formed in early childhood, which combines a sex-love fraction directed toward the mother and a jealousy-hate fraction directed toward the father. This component of personality should first of all be defined in terms of a list of ascertainable facts, disregarding for the moment the operation of other inhibiting or transforming forces. A few of the indices of the father-hatred fraction might run somewhat as follows:

1) When he sees his father or thinks of him, the feelings that arise are usually unpleasant—irritation, resentment, rage, or jealousy, possibly accompanied by anxiety and fear, or by contempt.

2) He avoids the company of his father if possible (he may do this by secluding himself in his own room, or staying away from the house, or leaving home); or

3) Sometimes he seeks his father out in order to ridicule, criticize, or blame him, or to worst him in an argument, or to prove his father's inferiority (in some field of taste or knowledge).

4) He thinks very often of his father, particularly of those features of his character which displease him.

5) He speaks harshly or derisively of his father to others, belittles or accuses him, recounts incidents which exhibit the least appealing features of his father's character.

6) He resents and, as far as possible, resists his father's authority: he refuses to obey his father or does so reluctantly; he is negativistic and defiant.

7) He dreams of killing a man who resembles his father.

And so on.

These are merely a few of the ways in which this component (father-hatred) might show itself if uninfluenced by other components, such as father-respect (which might exist alongside of father-hatred), fear of retaliation, of social disapproval, of public punishment, or fear of conscience (superego punishment, remorse), and so forth. After defining these latter variables in terms of concrete indices, the psychologist should distinguish the different kinds of relations which may exist between these components and the father-hatred component. For example, there may be incessant conflict; or the father-hatred component may be severely repressed by one of the other variables, and the exact opposite (father-respect) may develop in an extreme form; or there may be one or another type of fusion or synthesis of the opposites. Each of these different forms must be operationally defined in terms of concrete facts, subjective or objective.

This topic is too complicated to be pursued here. Suffice it to state our opinion: that the science of man will progress on a wide front as soon as social scientists agree on a convenient scheme of critical personality variables, defined in operational terms. For assessment this is a necessary preliminary to the setting up and verification of hypotheses relative to the influence of various components and structures of personality on the effectiveness of different types of performances.

Recommendation 5.—*Set up an efficient punch-card record system which will permit periodic statistical analyses of assessment findings.* It is advisable to have a research unit of two workers who will devote their entire time to tabulating and intercorrelating assessment ratings and correlating these with appraisal ratings. This should be done at regular intervals so that the staff members can be informed of their errors and of the causes of them as soon as possible. Only by providing in this way a rational basis for corrections can the system of assessment be improved. For the staff, assessment is a learning process, a step-by-step adjustment, by hypothesis, trial, and validation, to the realities of a changing situation.

The process of assessment should be organized according to an experimental design which will allow for analysis of variance and covariance, and factor analysis, these being the preferred methods of dealing statistically with events that are determined by a multiplicity of variables.

Recommendation 6.—*Assess candidates for a long trial period withoui reporting ratings or decisions to the organization.* The purpose of this recommendation is to determine how many of the candidates who are judged by the assessors to be unsuitable will, if given the opportunity, perform their duties satisfactorily. Measures of the efficacy of assessment are ordinarily based on follow-up studies of the accepted candidates. The subsequent careers of the rejectees are not traced. What percentage of these should have been accepted? It is important to know the answer to this question because it might be found that predictions of incompetence have a much higher degree of validity than predictions of different degrees of competence, and, consequently, that the chief value of assessment resides in its power to discriminate the least fit rather than in its power to discriminate among the fit. (In this connection we might recall here that the usual effect of eliminating the men at the lower end of the scale is to reduce the correlations between assessment ratings and appraisal ratings and so convey the impression that predictions are less valid than they truly are.)

This brings us to the end of our story, and to a place where a final over-all view of our work is in order. Although our performance, as it turned out, was below the expectations which we held at the beginning and throughout the course of our assessment activity, we do not believe this to be sufficient cause for discouragement as we look to the future, for the results were not conclusive.

In the first place, our methods of appraisal were not dependable, and it is possible that the results were better than the figures indicate. In the second place, not having been able to find out what percentage of OSS personnel proved unsatisfactory before the establishment of the screening process, we have no standard of comparison. It is possible that assessment succeeded in contributing to the efficiency of the organization by greatly reducing the number of failures.

It is unfortunate that a research unit was not set up at the start. A rotating research unit of four men, two to remain in Washington and two to go immediately to the different theaters of operation, would have provided the assessors with facts essential to the improvement and final success of the program: first, these research men could have obtained accurate detailed analyses of the proposed jobs and of the environments in which they would have to be performed, and thus could have provided the assessors with clear-cut targets; second, they could have obtained appraisals of a representative sample of men who had not been assessed and thus secured a standard to which later appraisals of assessed personnel could have been compared; third, they could have collected reports of the performances of the accepted candidates at the OSS schools in the United States, and later obtained appraisals from their supervisors and associates overseas, and by these means kept the assessors currently informed of the errors of judgment they were making; fourth, the members of the research unit who remained in Washington could have analyzed these errors and discovered which determinants of success or failure were being overlooked or overweighted and which techniques were least dependable, and thus initiated improvements of method and of judgment. Finally, these studies would have led to the development of a satisfactory system of appraisal, and today we would have a sound estimate of the value of assessment.

Most of these procedures were carried out eventually but not thoroughly enough or soon enough to enable us to derive much benefit from them. We were recruited to perform an efficient service, not to conduct investigations. In the light of experience, however, we would emphasize that research is a first essential in a new enterprise such as ours.

It now seems likely that, in the absence of the crucial information which a research unit could have furnished, our major practical accomplishment was confined to the detection of definite signs of motivational, emotional, social, or intellectual aberrations or deficiencies, and that this limited objective was about as well achieved in the one-day program at W as it was in the three-day program at S. The proper conclusion might be that the more comprehensive and refined procedures at S yielded more understanding of the personalities of the candidates than the assessors could make use of in the absence of an equally comprehensive and detailed mass of facts relative to the assignments overseas. If one is asked to select among a large number of posts those which will fit a hole that is about five to eight inches in diameter, it is a waste of time and money to do more than determine which ones fall within these limits. This can be done quickly without measuring the posts. But, if the exact diameter of each hole is stated and a neat fit is desired, then it is more economical to take the time to measure every post with comparable precision.

Despite the somewhat equivocal outcome of the whole enterprise, we believe that by trials and errors we have exposed and found remedies for most of the defects of the system, and have finally arrived at a plan as promising as any that is known to us for advancing the science of man, a plan which contains the necessary instruments for its own modification and perfection.

APPENDICES

APPENDIX A

ASSESSMENT POPULATIONS

The tables appearing in the following appendix are designed to present a description of the chief characteristics of the groups of people who went to S and W. Particularly they show in what aspects these populations were specially selected or at least atypical.

Since this information was collected primarily for the clinical assessment of each individual, rather than for use in a census, certain facts are not available concerning all candidates. Moreover, since wide latitude was allowed each candidate in filling out his Personal History Form, and since various revisions were made in this questionnaire, information was sometimes obtained which was incomplete or could not be fitted into certain rigid categories. Also certain problems arose in coding the data for IBM analysis. Despite these faults, the information collected presents a reasonably accurate picture of the large groups studied at S and W.

Each table shows the total number (N) of cases on which its percentages are based. Several of the N's are within a few cases of the whole sum of assessed individuals; most of the N's represent 80 per cent to 90 per cent samples; and only two N's are below 50 per cent of the total population. The total S population was 2,372 and the total W population was 3,071, including 52 assessed twice, at both areas.

The general population data for the United States employed in the tables to follow were obtained from the published summaries of the Sixteenth or 1940 Census data assembled by the Bureau of the Census.[1]

In making comparisons between these data on the country as a whole and the total available populations of areas S and W, differences existing among the three populations in the percentages of each sex represented have with one exception been disregarded, because these differences were unimportant. If the sexes were compared separately in all but this one case, the resulting findings would differ in no significant way from comparisons of the total populations. The exception to this is the table on income (Table 44). Since the wages of women are so much lower than those of men, the marked differences in the percentages of the sexes in the three populations must be allowed for in comparing these groups.

[1] *Population*, United States Summary, Second Series, *Characteristics of the Population*, and *ibid*, Part 1, Vol. III. *The Labor Force*.

APPENDIX A-1

COMPARISONS BETWEEN THE POPULATIONS OF S AND W AND THE POPULATION OF THE ENTIRE UNITED STATES

There can be no doubt that the assessed groups were far more cosmopolitan than the average American, as their language facility and travel experience indicate. This fact, which was one of the reasons why these candidates were so interesting to study, is obviously true even though the Census Bureau has gathered no comparable data about the total population of the United States. We found, for example, that approximately one out of four candidates spoke a foreign language fluently, and one out of twelve had good command of two or more. Over forty-five different languages were spoken fluently by this polyglot group, and there were more than fifty different combinations of foreign languages recorded in subjects' records, ranging from conventional French and German or Italian and Spanish to such esoteric groupings as Chinese, French, and Spanish; French, Turkish, and Arabic; Korean, Japanese, and Chinese; or Batak, Malay, and Dutch. A candidate said to be the only person in the United States known to have a good command of Cambodian was assessed at S.

Approximately one half of the S and W candidates had been outside the United States before joining OSS. One fifth had traveled in Europe, one twentieth had been in Asia or Africa, and one tenth had visited other countries in this hemisphere. Approximately one eighth of the assessed group had traveled in foreign lands of two or more continents. Although the average time of residence in foreign countries was only a few months, the assessed population contained many foreign born and expatriates, so that over one fifth had spent five years or more abroad.

The assessed population was predominantly a young, male, native-born white group with extraordinary educational attainments. The ages were concentrated between twenty and forty years, and by comparison with the general population fell off sharply after forty-four. W candidates were on the average slightly younger than S candidates, a difference no doubt related to their generally lower job status. The data are presented in Table 41.

Although the group of candidates at W had a fair representation of both sexes, the S group was almost all male, and indeed no woman candidate went to S in the last several months.

Foreign-born individuals were sent to S more often than to W, perhaps because on the average they were more difficult than native Americans to assess, as a result of differences in cultural heritage and language difficulties.

The most striking disparity between the assessed group and the general Ameri-

TABLE 41

Comparison, by Age Distribution, of the Assessed Populations with the Total Population of the United States

Age (in years)	U.S. (18 and over) %	S (N=2,344) %	W (N=3,061) %
18–20	7.9	1.1	1.6
20–24	12.4	19.9	28.6
25–29	11.8	26.9	28.4
30–34	10.9	20.5	20.0
35–39	10.2	13.4	11.2
40–44	9.4	7.9	6.1
45–54	16.5	8.1	3.4
55 and over	20.9	2.2	0.7
Total..........	100.0	100.0	100.0

TABLE 42

Comparison, by Educational Attainment, of the Assessed Populations with the Total Population of the United States

Years of school completed	U.S. %	S (N=2,343) %	W (N=2,997) %
Elementary school or less...	59.5	1.6	2.2
High school:			
1 to 3 years..............	15.0	5.2	3.9
4 years.................	14.1	14.2	19.6
College:			
1 to 3 years..............	5.4	23.5	26.4
4 years or more.........	4.6	55.5	47.9
Not reported..............	1.4	—	—
Total...............	100.0	100.0	100.0
Four years of college, or graduate work:			
Four years of college...................		26.1	27.1
Graduate work without degree..........		10.3	8.5
Master's degree........................		5.3	4.3
Doctor's degree or equivalent...........		13.8	8.0
Total........................		55.5	47.9

can population was in educational attainment. While 59.5 per cent of the general population have had no more than elementary school education, 55.5 per cent of S students and 47.9 per cent of W students had one or more college degrees. Startling statistics are the 13.8 per cent of the S population and 8.0 per cent of the W population with a doctor's degree or its equivalent. Table 42 records the educational data.

In Table 43 the groups that attended S and W are compared with the total census figures of the United States in terms of occupational groups.

Because of the great need for special talents and training in OSS, it is not surprising to find in professional fields a much larger proportion of the assessed group than of the whole American population. Nor is the heavy loading of clerical workers in the W distribution unexpected, since one of the functions of W was the screening of lower-echelon personnel. Because the occupational data are cast into the broad categories of the Census Bureau, an outstanding feature

TABLE 43

Comparison, by Major Occupational Group, of the Assessed Populations with the Total Population of the United States

Major occupational group	U.S. %	S (N=1,967) %	W (N=2,653) %
Professional workers..............	6.5	38.9	27.6
Semiprofessional workers.........	1.0	4.7	5.5
Proprietors, managers, and officials, including farmers..............	19.9	20.2	8.6
Clerical, sales, and kindred workers	16.7	19.2	43.9
Craftsmen, foremen, and kindred workers......................	12.6	5.0	5.0
Operative and kindred workers....	18.3	4.6	3.4
Domestic service workers.........	4.7	0.4	0.1
Service workers except domestic...	7.8	4.9	3.1
Laborers......................	12.5	2.1	2.8
Total......................	100.0	100.0	100.0

of the assessed population is masked, namely, the extreme diversity of its occupational background. At one time or another the S and W staffs saw taxidermists and lawyers, cartographers and trapeze artists, financiers and sound-effects technicians, ivory traders and experts in forgery, model makers and economists, foreign-language typesetters and historians, photographers and leather workers, missionaries and advertising writers.

The relatively high proportion of professional men and women, business executives, proprietors, and high-grade craftsmen explains the high incomes earned by the assessed candidates before they came to OSS. For example, the highest incomes before 1940 of the females seen at S and W were well in excess of women's salaries generally and roughly equivalent to the male income distribution for the U.S. The most striking differences were in the highest income brackets. For instance, 12.3 per cent of the males in the S group and 6.4 per cent of those in the W group had top incomes over $5,000 a year before 1940, but the census listed only 1.4 per cent of the males in the general population as being in this range. The figures presented in Table 44 indicate that the assessed population had definitely been recruited from high-income groups.

TABLE 44

Comparison, by Income,[a] of the Assessed Populations with the Total Population of the United States

Annual income (in dollars)	U.S. Male %	U.S. Female %	S (N=1,533) Male (N=1,463) %	S (N=1,533) Female (N=70) %	W (N=1,794) Male (N=1,200) %	W (N=1,794) Female (N=594) %
No income (student)	b	b	34.9	18.6	28.4	17.7
Other 0–799.........	b	b	4.0	8.6	4.2	7.9
Total 0–799.........	43.0	66.8	38.9	27.2	32.6	25.6
800–1,199...........	17.7	18.7	5.1	17.1	8.1	19.0
1,200–1,599..........	16.3	8.7	10.1	22.8	15.3	20.2
1,600–1,999..........	8.8	3.0	7.2	14.3	10.9	21.6
2,000–2,499..........	6.9	1.6	8.8	7.1	10.7	7.4
2,500–2,999..........	2.7	0.5	6.3	5.7	5.0	3.5
3,000–4,999..........	3.2	0.6	11.3	2.9	11.0	2.4
5,000 and over.......	1.4	0.1	12.3	2.9	6.4	0.3
5,000–9,999..........	b	b	8.1	2.9	4.7	0.3
10,000 and over......	b	b	4.2	0.0	1.7	0.0
Total (excluding first two and last two lines).............	100.0	100.0	100.0	100.0	100.0	100.0

[a] For the assessed populations income is defined as the largest amount received by an individual from his primary job before 1940.

[b] Data not available.

In summary it can be said that the facts presented in this appendix indicate that the candidates who came to assessment had already been highly selected, and, measured by a number of customary standards, were in general of upper socioeconomic status.

APPENDIX A-2

COMPARISONS BETWEEN THE POPULATIONS OF S AND W ON VARIOUS ASPECTS OF THE ASSIGNMENTS PROPOSED FOR THE CANDIDATES

Every branch of OSS was allowed to choose the assessment station to which it sent any given candidate. But, as a rule, the branch officers followed the directive issued at the time that Station W was established. Station W was set up to relieve Station S of three classes of candidates: (i) those who would be subjected to little stress overseas; (ii) those lower-echelon personnel whose work involved limited responsibility; and (iii) those few who, because of the press of circumstances, could not spare three days for assessment. To some extent, W also handled the overflow which could not be fitted into the S schedule. That the policies set down were largely carried out is reflected in the tables below.

TABLE 45

Proposed Position in Field at Time of Assessment[a]

Position	S (N=876) %	W (N=2,691) %
Rear base..........................	28.7	74.0
Advanced base....................	7.3	5.7
Front, or behind enemy lines......	42.7	14.8
United States....................	6.2	2.3
Undecided.......................	1.7	0.3
"Not behind enemy lines"........	13.4	2.9
Total......................	100.0	100.0

[a] These data should be interpreted with caution because they were derived from fragmentary descriptions of proposed jobs which frequently did not make the locale clear.

Table 45 shows that three out of every four W subjects were scheduled for assignment at rear bases, whereas half of the S students were proposed for duty at advanced bases or behind enemy lines.

Closely related to this difference in proposed position is the fact demonstrated in Table 46 that nine out of ten S cases were in the military service, whereas nearly one in three W students was a civilian, many of these women, who were not sent near the front.

TABLE 46

Service Status at Time of Assessment

Status	S (N=1,654) %	W (N=2,263) %
Officer......	51.0	28.4
Enlisted man...................	40.7	40.3
Civilian.......................	8.3	31.3
Total.....................	100.0	100.0

S handled two executives or officers of the middle echelon for every one seen at W, while W assessed almost twice as many candidates for lower-echelon positions. These facts, presented in Table 47, fit in with the data of Table 46, showing that one out of two S subjects was an officer, while at W the ratio was only one out of four.

Analyses of the representations of the various branches of the organization at S and W must be made with the realization that each branch was free to send

TABLE 47

Proposed Echelon at Time of Assessment[a]

Branch	S (N=2,037) %	W (N=2,625) %
Higher: senior executive, high command.....................	2.8	4.6
Middle: junior administrator, subordinate command.............	60.1	29.8
Lower: office worker, member of group.......................	36.3	65.3
Undecided.....................	0.8	0.3
Total.....................	100.0	100.0

[a] These data should be interpreted with caution because they were derived from fragmentary descriptions of proposed jobs which frequently required the assessment staff to guess in which echelon they would fall. Moreover, the staff was not always clear as to the distinctions between the echelons and hence there were undoubtedly inconsistencies in their judgments.

its candidates to whichever school it wished, and sometimes made the choice for various reasons of expediency. Also it must be realized that many sorts of training were provided in each branch. However, certain generalizations can be made from Table 48.

TABLE 48

Branch Affiliation at Time of Assessment

Branch	S (N = 2,342) %	W (N = 3,012) %
Research	2.5	10.6
Intelligence	30.7	22.4
Operations	24.4	14.4
Propaganda	21.2	6.6
Services	1.9	20.0
Other Branches	19.3	26.0
Total	100.0	100.0

It can be concluded from these data that S usually saw those faced with hazardous duty (Operations), those who were recruited for work requiring a wide range of ability and flexibility (Intelligence), and those expected to engage in creative activity (Propaganda). For understandable reasons it was harder for a man to succeed in the branch devoted to propaganda than in any other branch. The W staff, on the other hand, saw fewer such people, but more who were to do research, carry out services, or be administrators at rear bases.

COMPARISONS BETWEEN PERFORMANCE ON STANDARDIZED
TESTS OF S AND W POPULATIONS AND GENERAL NORMS
FOR THE TESTS

At various times a number of standardized tests of intelligence and skills were included in batteries used at S and W. Generally these were restandardized on an assessment population and the raw scores then converted to the assessment six-point scale. The norms for the general population were disregarded as irrelevant for the exceptional groups seen at S and W. It is profitable and instructive, however, to compare the distributions of raw scores of the assessed subjects with the norms for these tests.

The Army General Classification Test (Form 1b), given to all personnel entering the Army, was administered to 125 subjects selected at random from a group of successive classes. A comparison of the scores of this sample with the AGCT theoretical curve of normal distribution, which the grades for the whole Army approximated, enables us to contrast the test intelligence of S candidates with that of the Army. In making the comparison it must be emphasized that the S sample was composed of approximately 90 per cent service personnel, most of

TABLE 49

Comparison of the Theoretical Distribution of Standard Scores on the Army General Classification Test with the Actual Distribution of a Random Sample of the Population Assessed at S

Standard score on AGCT	Army %	S (N=125) %
140-159	2	30
120-139	14	50
100-119	34	17
80-99	34	3
60-79	14	0
40-59	2	0
Total....................	100	100

whom had taken the same test or some form of it previously. Even if considerable allowance is made for practice effect, it is, however, still evident that the S average was far above the Army average. The figures are presented in Table 49.

The Atwell-Wells Wide Range Vocabulary Test was administered at S for some months. The words on this test are arranged in order of increasing diffi-

TABLE 50

Comparisons of Distributions of Total Scores on the ACE between a Representative Sample of College Freshmen and the W Population

Raw scores	Men		Women	
	Freshmen (N=2,011) %	W (N=1,588) %	Freshmen (N=6,775) %	W (N=814) %
200	0.0	0.0	0.0	0.0
190–199	0.0	0.2	0.0	0.0
180–189	0.0	1.6	0.1	0.4
170–179	0.5	3.8	0.2	2.1
160–169	0.9	7.4	0.7	6.0
150–159	3.0	10.1	2.0	8.6
140–149	6.4	12.2	4.5	11.2
130–139	11.4	11.4	8.9	13.9
120–129	14.2	13.0	12.1	13.1
110–119	16.6	11.6	14.8	11.4
100–109	15.8	7.8	14.8	10.7
90– 99	12.8	7.2	13.4	7.6
80– 89	7.9	5.0	11.1	5.3
70– 79	4.7	3.3	6.9	3.8
60– 69	2.8	1.9	4.9	2.7
50– 59	1.6	0.9	2.9	2.1
40– 49	0.9	0.9	1.6	0.6
30– 39	0.4	0.9	0.7	0.4
20– 29	0.1	0.4	0.3	0.1
10– 19	0.0	0.3	0.1	0.0
0– 9	0.0	0.1	0.0	0.0
Total..........	100.0	100.0	100.0	100.0
Average raw score....	110.7	124.4	104.1	120.8
Standard deviation of raw score distribution..............	24.7	32.0	26.4	29.7

culty, and the raw scores can be converted to norms for various educational levels. An average adult score may be considered as in the neighborhood of 50, according to the published instructions. The S candidates included a number of foreign born to whom English was a second language. Nevertheless, a sample of 215 S

TABLE 51

Comparisons of Distributions of Scores on the Quantitative Section of the ACE between a Representative Sample of College Freshmen and the W Population

Raw scores	Men		Women	
	Freshmen (N=2,011) %	W (N=1,576) %	Freshmen (N=6,775) %	W (N=814) %
80	0.0	0.0	0.0	0.0
75–79	0.2	0.3	0.1	0.0
70–74	0.9	1.8	0.1	0.2
65–69	2.2	3.3	0.7	1.1
60–64	5.5	6.4	1.6	2.2
55–59	9.3	10.4	4.1	4.8
50–54	15.7	14.9	9.8	11.6
45–49	18.9	16.4	16.3	14.1
40–44	17.3	16.3	18.3	19.8
35–39	12.9	12.7	17.3	18.3
30–34	6.4	7.2	12.0	11.7
25–29	4.7	4.1	7.4	6.8
20–24	3.0	2.6	4.8	4.5
15–19	1.9	1.9	3.7	2.5
10–14	0.8	1.1	2.8	1.8
5 9	0.2	0.5	0.9	0.4
0– 4	0.1	0.1	0.1	0.2
Total..........	100.0	100.0	100.0	100.0
Average raw score....	45.0	45.1	39.2	40.0
Standard deviation of raw score distribution..............	11.8	12.8	11.7	11.6

cases taking the test early in the program had a median score of 86.2 with an interquartile range of 11.6. This means that three out of four of these S students were in the college range in vocabulary as measured by this test.

At W the American Council on Education Psychological Examination (1943 edition) was administered to most of the candidates. Two factors, language

TABLE 52

Comparisons of Distributions of Scores on the Language Section of the ACE between a Representative Sample of College Freshmen and the W Population

Raw scores	Men		Women	
	Freshmen (N=2,011) %	W (N=1,563) %	Freshmen (N=6,775) %	W (N=819) %
120	0.0	0.1	0.0	0.1
115–119	0.0	1.9	0.0	1.5
110–114	0.2	4.7	0.2	5.0
105–109	0.3	6.7	0.5	6.1
100–104	0.6	6.1	1.2	7.2
95– 99	1.9	8.6	2.1	9.6
90– 94	4.0	8.3	3.7	10.1
85– 89	6.2	8.8	5.4	7.5
80– 84	7.4	8.8	7.8	8.3
75– 79	8.8	7.2	9.5	10.3
70– 74	11.0	9.0	10.5	6.6
65– 69	12.1	6.2	10.7	7.1
60– 64	12.9	6.0	10.8	3.7
55– 59	10.4	4.8	9.9	5.3
50– 54	9.2	3.5	9.1	3.7
45– 49	5.4	3.5	6.6	1.5
40– 44	4.2	1.9	5.2	2.7
35– 39	2.4	1.3	3.0	2.0
30– 34	1.6	1.0	1.8	0.6
25– 29	0.8	0.8	0.8	0.4
20– 24	0.4	0.5	0.6	0.6
15– 19	0.1	0.1	0.3	0.0
10– 14	0.1	0.1	0.2	0.1
5– 9	0.0	0.1	0.1	0.0
0– 4	0.0	0.0	0.0	0.0
Total..........	100.0	100.0	100.0	100.0
Average raw score....	66.2	79.2	65.6	81.1
Standard deviation of raw score distribution.............	16.1	23.7	17.3	21.1

ability and skill in handling quantitative material, are explored in this scholastic aptitude test, resulting in a point score. In Tables 50, 51, and 52 the W raw score distributions in terms of percentages are compared with those of a representative sample of college freshmen.[2] It will be observed that while the W groups have higher average scores, their range of variation is greater. The finding is in accord with the wide distribution of the educational attainment of the W group, which included candidates who never reached high school as well as others with doctoral degrees.

It will be noted that the W population was unusually able in the language section of the test, but hardly above the average freshmen on the quantitative section. Because of the large groups involved, the averages are highly reliable and, for the language and total scores, the differences between the means for the two populations are significant far beyond the 1 per cent level of confidence.

[2] The sample of college freshmen is that used in the preliminary report of norms for the 1943 edition of this test.

THE INTERRELATIONSHIPS AMONG THE VARIABLES

Intercorrelations.—The variables on the final rating sheet were originally selected, not to represent independent characteristics, but to embrace the essential qualifications for most OSS work. In view of this condition and the fact that each was a composite of the various aspects listed on the report scale, it is not surprising that these variables showed considerable interdependence. A representative set of their intercorrelations is given in Table 53 below, which is based on a population taken from the last twelve full-length classes at S, a period during which Energy and Initiative was a separate variable on the final rating sheet. Omitted from the group were all men for whom any final grade was missing, the chief influence of this selective principle being to exclude men older than thirty-nine because they were not allowed to run the Obstacle Course and were not rated on Physical Ability.

The first eight variables in Table 53 are those listed on the final form of the report rating sheet. While Observing and Reporting and Propaganda Skills were not reported because they were relevant only to specific assignments, they were routinely rated to help provide a basis for two of the recommendations on the check sheet. The "Over-all" rating was a staff decision recorded for research purposes only and broadly defined as an estimate of the individual's maximum possible contribution (past or future) to the welfare of mankind. Because of its unique nature, it is not included in the calculation of the median intercorrelation.

The median of all values in Table 53 (omitting Over-all) is .33, which indicates some lack of independence among the variables. Aside from those for the rather specific and homogeneous grades on Physical Ability and Security, the medians are all of about the same size. It is noteworthy that these same two exceptions show the lowest correlations with the Over-all rating, which is itself highly related to all the other variables.

The relatively great communality among the variables is due to several influences. One is the fact that all grades were based upon behavior noted during the brief time-span of three days. While the object was to predict the candidate's reactions during the next few years of service in OSS, the basis was an observation period of less than sixty waking hours. Although the interviewer sought to rate on the basis of past history, the data on that history were reported by the candidate during the assessment period and were probably influenced in some slight degree by the candidate's contemporary attitudes such as his desire to get into OSS, his desire to make a favorable impression, his approach to the unique assessment situation. Inevitably in several psychological measurements made at the same time, there is the common effect of extraneous influences technically known as "error" factors because they interfere with the attainment of "true," unbiased measurements. This consideration is even more important in the situation ratings which contributed to the final grades. Of the total of more

TABLE 53

Intercorrelations among Final Variables

(N=*133—All Men in Latest Group of Classes Rated on all Variables*)

	Motivation	Energy & Initiative	Effective Intelligence	Emotional Stability	Social Relations	Leadership	Physical Ability	Security	Observing & Reporting	Propaganda Skills	Over-all
Motivation for Assignment.....	—	.47	.31	.43	.39	.44	.26	.27	.23	.37	.42
Energy & Initiative..	.47	—	.56	.53	.38	.72	.41	.21	.31	.36	.54
Effective Intelligence..	.31	.56	—	.23	.27	.65	.06	.11	.63	.70	.70
Emotional Stability...	.43	.53	.23	—	.62	.48	.34	.37	.22	.21	.47
Social Relations......	.39	.38	.27	.62	—	.44	.38	.33	.32	.28	.57
Leadership...	.44	.72	.65	.48	.44	—	.21	.16	.32	.51	.63
Physical Ability....	.26	.41	.06	.34	.38	.21	—	.13	.07	−.07	.22
Security.....	.27	.21	.11	.37	.33	.16	.13	—	.18	.21	.29
Observing & Reporting........	.23	.31	.63	.22	.32	.32	.07	.18	—	.53	.53
Propaganda Skills.....	.37	.36	.70	.21	.28	.51	−.07	.21	.53	—	.59
Over-all.....	.42	.54	.70	.47	.57	.63	.22	.29	.53	.59	—
Median Intercorrelation	.37	.41	.31	.37	.38	.44	.21	.21	.31	.36	.54

than fifty separate scores entered on the candidate's summary rating sheet, the majority were made in eight situations, so that the same extraneous influences due to any given situation affected several scores, usually in a given direction. For example, if a candidate was restrained at the Brook by a dislike for handling dirty objects, he might receive generally lower ratings than his "true" or final grade warranted. Or a candidate coming out of a Personal History Interview with a number of vivid new self-insights might be preoccupied during the Discussion situation and fail to do his best.

Another general influence upon all of a candidate's grades was the S staff's total reaction to him. Not only did the staff concentrate its attention on the basic question of his suitability for work in OSS, but also, especially in the final staff conference, there was a general tendency to consider him an outstanding fellow, an average GI, or an unfortunate misfit. While the staff members were fully aware of this halo effect and sought to minimize it, they could not abolish it.

Finally it must be remembered that psychological research has almost always found positive relationships among abilities and among socially desirable traits. While a comparison between the degree of these relationships in this study and in others cannot be made without a careful analysis of the relative ranges of the abilities or qualities, the size of these intercorrelations is not unusual as compared with other relevant researches.

Factor Analysis.—In a field like personality, factor analysis is an especially appropriate technique since it is a method for discovering basic factors or elements in a set of measurements. Although the assessment program was not designed to afford data for factor analysis, it represents one of the first attempts to measure abilities and traits in a series of lifelike situations, and for that reason an analysis of its variables may yield suggestive results which would serve as the basis for further investigations.

Using the above intercorrelations, a factor analysis was performed to produce further information on the variables themselves by bringing out recognized and unrecognized central factors running through them. It is immediately obvious that the results are not of general applicability because the data were obtained under the unique conditions of wartime assessment for overseas work in OSS and because some of the variables are peculiar to that situation, e.g., Motivation for Assignment and Propaganda Skills. Furthermore, the data are not well suited for a factor analysis: the number of subjects (133) is not great, the number of original variables is only eleven, and each variable is itself a composite of several scores with only moderate degrees of interrelationship. Bearing these considerations in mind, we can examine Table 54, which shows the obtained factors and their loadings. The heaviest loadings are italicized.[1]

Factor A has been labeled Adjustment because it embraces not only emotional adjustment as measured by Emotional Stability but also social adjustment or Social Relations. It might also be called Adaptability because it has loadings on Social Relations and Security, both of which require a modification of one's behavior to conform with external requirements. The finding of a factor common to both Emotional Stability and Social Relations is not surprising because the latter can be conceived as highly dependent on the former. Although the inclusion of Security may be less expected, it is consistent with the nature of the three variables. Security involved the ability to assume a role more or less at variance with one's true identity and the ability to control one's behavior sufficiently to avoid revealing certain information regardless of the intensity of one's desire to

[1] The technical reader who is interested in the centroid matrix and the transformation matrix will find them in Tables 56 and 57.

impress or convince another. Good Social Relations also require a control over inappropriate asocial impulses and an ability to fit one's self into the group even at the risk of losing part of one's individuality. Emotional Stability is in part emotional control and in part maturity, which includes the capacity for looking at one's self objectively. There are therefore common elements in the three variables. It is noteworthy that the next highest weight is on Motivation for Assignment. While this specific variable is not well represented in any factor, its highest loading is on Factor A. Perhaps high war morale and a desire to serve in a

TABLE 54

Factors and Factor Loadings

(Italicized values are for variables on which factors have high loadings)

Factors	A Adjustment	B Effective Intelligence	C Physical Energy	D Authoritative Assertion
Motivation for Assignment....	.26	—.03	.16	.20
Energy & Initiative..........	.00	.00	*.53*	*.42*
Effective Intelligence.........	—.18	*.55*	.14	.24
Emotional Stability......	*.46*	—.09	.11	.04
Social Relations.	*.40*	.14	.02	—.15
Leadership......	.03	.14	*.35*	*.39*
Physical Ability..	.05	—.10	*.42*	—.04
Security.........	*.42*	—.02	—.15	—.06
Observing & Reporting........	.02	*.52*	—.08	—.07
Propaganda Skills	.09	*.42*	—.13	.21
Over-all.........	.14	*.43*	.06	.05

special war organization represent a type of adjustment to wartime conditions and social pressures in the United States.

The second factor is definitely Effective Intelligence, which has loadings on the variable of the same name and on the two specific aptitudes for intelligence and propaganda work. Most striking is its sizable contribution to the Over-all rating, which has negligible weights on the other factors. Apparently the rating on this general variable was determined primarily by the candidate's ability.

The third factor has been labeled Physical Energy because it has high loadings on Energy and Initiative and on Physical Ability. The latter variable has no other significant loadings. While Factor C also has a loading on Leadership, it appears to be determined principally by the other two, and this particular loading seems to be based on the energy necessary to maintain leadership, especially in the leaderless situations of assessment.

The fourth factor, tentatively called Authoritative Assertion, has loadings on only two variables, Energy and Initiative and Leadership. (While both are also weighted with Factor C, the two factors have a negligible intercorrelation.) The first variable contributes the initiative to the assertion. The authoritative aspect is derived from the small loading on Effective Intelligence, while the other small loading, on Propaganda Skills, reflects the ability (and perhaps the desire) to influence the behavior of others.

Most of the intercorrelations among the various factors are fairly sizable, as shown by Table 55. The Adjustment factor is highly correlated with the Physical Energy factor, possibly because physical energy assists the process of adjustment but also (and more likely) because a satisfactory adjustment allows potential energy to be utilized for other purposes because it is not drained off by unsolved problems of adjustment. The correlation between the Adjustment and Effective Intelligence factors may be attributed in part to the fact that Intelligence aids in personal and social adjustment and, conversely, adjustment permits the effective exploitation of capacities. The correlations between the Effective Intelligence fac-

TABLE 55

Intercorrelations of Factors

	A Adjustment	B Effective Intelligence	C Physical Energy	D Authori- tative Assertion
A. Adjustment...................	—	.58	.70	.06
B. Effective Intelligence..........	.58	—	.37	.48
C. Physical Energy..............	.70	.37	—	.09
D. Authoritative Assertion.......	.06	.48	.09	—

tor and the Energy and Assertion factors may be related to the use of several leaderless situations where the candidate with ability could readily show initiative and assert leadership.

The extent of these intercorrelations is slightly greater than those for the eleven variables and reflects the same influences toward a "halo effect."

For those readers who are interested in the details of the factor analysis of the final variables, the following tables are presented.

TABLE 56

Centroid Matrix

	I	II	III	IV
Motivation for Assignment....	.589	.171	−.051	.108
Energy & Initiative..........	.755	.099	−.437	.046
Effective Intelligence.........	.710	−.550	−.141	−.054
Emotional Stability..........	.652	.424	.123	.063
Social Relations.............	.665	.288	.275	−.090
Leadership..................	.765	−.095	−.297	.090
Physical Ability.............	.351	.451	−.185	−.194
Security....................	.380	.216	.288	.095
Observing & Reporting.......	.574	−.349	.190	−.137
Propaganda Skills............	.634	−.478	.103	.124
Over-all Rating..............	.822	−.194	.102	−.074

TABLE 57

Transformation Matrix

	A	B	C	D
I	.249	.284	.205	.178
II	.431	−.630	.260	−.131
III	.596	.265	−.849	−.594
IV	.630	−.672	−.411	.774

APPENDIX C

INTERCORRELATIONAL MATRICES

TABLE 58

Intercorrelations of Final Ratings[a]

(*Periods F-G;* N=*397 to 443*)

Variable	Effective Intelligence	Emotional Stability	Social Relations	Leadership	Physical Ability	Security	Observing & Reporting	Propaganda Skills
Effective Intelligence.........	—	.24	.31	.63	.03	.32	.65	.66
Emotional Stability..........	.24	—	.54	.45	.31	.32	.15	.09
Social Relations.............	.31	.54	—	.47	.31	.32	.27	.29
Leadership..................	.63	.45	.47	—	.23	.26	.40	.48
Physical Ability.............	.03	.31	.31	.23	—	.06	.10	—.14
Security....................	.32	.32	.32	.26	.06	—	.26	.30
Observing & Reporting......	.65	.15	.27	.40	.10	.26	—	.57
Propaganda Skills...........	.66	.09	.29	.48	—.14	.30	.57	—
Median correlation with other variables.................	.32	.31	.31	.45	.10	.30	.27	.30

Median of all correlations between these variables is .31.

[a] Motivation for Assignment and Energy and Initiative are omitted because they were combined in Period F and separated in Period G. For intercorrelations between these two variables and others in Period G only, see Table 3, page 238, and Table 11, page 263.

TABLE 59

Intercorrelations of Energy and Initiative Ratings

(*Period G;* N=74 *to* 147)

Test	Final Energy & Initiative grade	Interview	Brook	Construction	Assigned Leadership	Obstacle	Discussion	Debate
Final Energy & Initiative grade......................	—	.78	.67	.56	.77	.41	.55	.54
Interview....................	.78	—	.60	.43	.69	.31	.46	.50
Brook......................	.67	.60	—	.36	.62	.37	.25	.19
Construction................	.56	.43	.36	—	.38	.19	.19	.32
Assigned Leadership.........	.77	.69	.62	.38	—	.25	.41	.48
Obstacle....................	.41	.31	.37	.19	.25	—	.07	−.09
Discussion..................	.55	.46	.25	.19	.41	.07	—	.49
Debate.....................	.54	.50	.19	.32	.48	−.09	.49	—
Median correlation with other tests.....................	.56[a]	.44	.36	.34	.43	.22	.33	.40

Median of all correlations between tests is .37.

[a] Median correlation with final grade.

TABLE 60

Intercorrelations of Effective Intelligence Ratings

(Periods F-G; N=77 to 443ᵃ)

Test	Final Effective Intelligence grade	Interview	Vocabulary	Nonverbal (Period F only)	Otis (Period G only)	SIX-2	Discussion	Debate	Mechanical Comprehension	Brook	Assigned Leadership: Leader	Assigned Leadership: Sub-ordinate	Judgment of Others
Final Effective Intelligence grade	—	.80	.63	.53	.61	.50	.67	.73	.40	.39	.48	.55	.54
Interview	.80	—	.55	.44	.46	.37	.64	.66	.26	.34	.36	.44	.47
Vocabulary	.63	.55	—	.34	.55	.41	.51	.54	.19	.07	.16	.22	.48
Nonverbal (Period F only)	.53	.44	.34	—	—	.38	.23	.29	.37	.07	.10	.16	.25
Otis (Period G only)	.61	.46	.55	—	—	.43	.26	.37	.49	.24	.12	.13	.47
SIX-2	.50	.37	.41	.38	.43	—	.27	.29	.24	.04	.02	.12	.32
Discussion	.67	.64	.51	.23	.26	.27	—	.57	.08	.26	.29	.40	.40
Debate	.73	.66	.54	.29	.37	.29	.57	—	.04	.10	.30	.29	.52
Mechanical Comprehension	.40	.26	.19	.37	.49	.24	.08	.04	—	.19	.17	.21	.14
Brook	.39	.34	.07	.07	.24	.04	.26	.10	.19	—	.32	.41	.03
Assigned (Leader)	.48	.36	.16	.10	.12	.02	.29	.30	.17	.32	—	.59	.22
Leadership (Subordinate)	.55	.44	.22	.16	.13	.12	.40	.29	.21	.41	.59	—	.18
Judgment of Others	.54	.47	.48	.25	.47	.32	.40	.52	.14	.03	.22	.18	—
Median correlation with other tests	.54ᵇ	.44	.41	.27	.40	.29	.29	.30	.19	.19	.22	.22	.32

Median of all correlations between tests is .29.

ᵃ The minimum N for correlations based on Periods F and G together is 246.

ᵇ Median correlation with final grade.

TABLE 61

Intercorrelations of Emotional Stability Ratings

(Periods F–G; N=430 to 442)

Test	Final Emotional Stability grade	Interview	Construc-tion	Stress	Post-Stress
Final Emotional Stability grade........	—	.90	.44	.46	.36
Interview.............	.90	—	.39	.31	.28
Construction..........	.44	.39	—	.36	.15
Stress.................	.46	.31	.36	—	.25
Post-Stress.............	.36	.28	.15	.25	—
Median correlation with other tests..........	.45[a]	.31	.36	.31	.25

Median of all correlations between tests is .30.
[a] Median correlation with final grade.

TABLE 62

Intercorrelations of Social Relations Ratings

(Periods F–G; N=173 to 443)

Test	Final Social Relations grade	Interview	Brook	Construction	Discussion	Debate	Assigned Leadership	Ratings by Associates Pos.	Neg.
Final Social Relations grade...............	—	.69	.50	.39	.52	.56	.56	.62	.55
Interview..............	.69	—	.43	.37	.48	.49	.51	.42	.31
Brook................	.50	.43	—	.36	.33	.31	.50	.29	.13
Construction..........	.39	.37	.36	—	.29	.21	.30	.17	.06
Discussion............	.52	.48	.33	.29	—	.40	.40	.26	.17
Debate...............	.56	.49	.31	.21	.40	—	.33	.30	.30
Assigned Leadership....	.56	.51	.50	.30	.40	.33	—	.30	.08
Ratings by {Pos.	.62	.42	.29	.17	.26	.30	.30	—	.49
Associates..... {Neg.	.55	.31	.13	.06	.17	.30	.08	.49	—
Median correlation with other tests..........	.56[a]	.43	.33	.29	.33	.31	.33	.30	.17

Median of all correlations between tests is .30.
[a] Median correlation with final grade.

TABLE 63

Intercorrelations of Leadership Ratings

(Periods F–G; N=223 to 442)

Test	Final Leadership grade	Interview	Brook	Construction	Discussion	Debate	Assigned Leadership	Ratings by Associates
Final Leadership grade.......	—	.79	.68	.54	.64	.66	.68	.65
Interview..................	.79	—	.57	.44	.48	.47	.53	.54
Brook.....................	.68	.57	—	.37	.47	.41	.42	.41
Construction..............	.54	.44	.37	—	.30	.33	.33	.24
Discussion................	.64	.48	.47	.30	—	.56	.37	.41
Debate....................	.66	.47	.41	.33	.56	—	.39	.52
Assigned Leadership........	.68	.53	.42	.33	.37	.39	—	.37
Ratings by Associates.......	.65	.54	.41	.24	.41	.52	.37	—
Median correlation with other tests.....................	.66[a]	.50	.42	.33	.44	.44	.38	.41

Median of all correlations between tests is .41.

[a] Median correlation with final grade.

TABLE 64

Intercorrelations of Physical Ability Ratings

(Periods F–G; N=174 to 320)

Test	Final Physical Ability Grade	Interview	Obstacle Course	Athletic Events	Brook
Final Physical Ability grade...............	—	.65	.94	.66	.58
Interview..............	.65	—	.56	.52	.53
Obstacle Course..........	.94	.56	—	.55	.52
Athletic Events.........	.66	.52	.55	—	.38
Brook................	.58	.53	.52	.38	—
Median correlation with other tests...........	.66[a]	.53	.55	.52	.52

Median of all correlations between tests is .52.
[a] Median correlation with final grade.

TABLE 65

Intercorrelations of Security Ratings

(Periods F–G; N=230 to 440)

Test	Final Security grade	Interview	Stress	Post-Stress	Ratings by Associates
Final Security grade.....	—	.62	.44	.48	.67
Interview..............	.62	—	.29	.15	.38
Stress.................	.44	.29	—	.05	.20
Post-Stress.............	.48	.15	.05	—	.18
Ratings by Associates...	.67	.38	.20	.18	—
Median correlation with other tests...........	.55[a]	.29	.20	.15	.20

Median of all correlations between tests is .19.
[a] Median correlation with final grade.

TABLE 66

Intercorrelations of Observing and Reporting Ratings

(Periods F–G; N=200 to 443)

Test	Final Observing & Reporting grade	Interview	Belongings	SIX-2	Terrain	Memory Battery	Names & Identifications	Brief Case (Period F only)
Final Observing & Reporting grade...	—	.67	.61	.63	.48	.64	.63	.47
Interview...........	.67	—	.42	.37	.24	.33	.42	.26
Belongings..........	.61	.42	—	.33	.23	.34	.31	.24
SIX-2...............	.63	.37	.33	—	.25	.26	.28	.13
Terrain.............	.48	.24	.23	.25	—	.25	.20	.14
Memory Battery	.64	.33	.34	.26	.25	—	.37	.30
Names & Identifications	.63	.42	.31	.28	.20	.37	—	.19
Brief Case (Period F only).............	.47	.26	.24	.13	.14	.30	.19	—
Median correlation with other tests...	.63[a]	.35	.32	.27	.24	.32	.30	.22

Median of all correlations between tests is .26.

[a] Median correlation with final grade.

TABLE 67

Intercorrelations of Propaganda Skills Ratings

(*Period F; N=126 to 292*)

Test	Final Propaganda Skills grade	Interview	OWI	Manchuria	Discussion	Debate
Final Propaganda Skills grade.......	—	.70	.66	.83	.69	.63
Interview.....	.70	—	.40	.61	.75	.58
OWI..........	.66	.40	—	.44	.41	.30
Manchuria....	.83	.61	.44	—	.50	.37
Discussion....	.69	.75	.41	.50	—	.55
Debate........	.63	.58	.30	.37	.55	—
Median correlation with other tests...	.69[a]	.60	.40	.47	.52	.46

Median of all correlations between tests is .47.
[a] Median correlation with final grade.

(*Period G; N=119 to 145*)

Test	Final Propaganda Skills grade	Interview	OWI	Manchuria
Final Propaganda Skills grade.................	—	.69	.66	.84
Interview...............	.69	—	.42	.55
OWI...................	.66	.42	—	.38
Manchuria..............	.84	.55	.38	—

Median of all correlations between tests is .42.

INDEX

528

Index